Writing as Material Practice:
Substance, surface and medium

Edited by
Kathryn E. Piquette and Ruth D. Whitehouse

]u[

ubiquity press
London

Published by
Ubiquity Press Ltd.
Gordon House
29 Gordon Square
London WC1H 0PP
www.ubiquitypress.com

Front Cover Illustrations:
Top row (from left to right): Flouda (Chapter 8): Mavrospelio ring made of gold.
Courtesy Heraklion Archaelogical Museum; Pye (Chapter 16): A Greek and Latin
lexicon (1738). Photograph Nick Balaam; Pye (Chapter 16): A silver decadrachm of
Syracuse (5th century BC). © Trustees of the British Museum. Middle row (from left
to right): Piquette (Chapter 11): A wooden label. Photograph Kathryn E. Piquette,
courtesy Ashmolean Museum; Flouda (Chapter 8): Ceramic conical cup. Courtesy
Heraklion Archaelogical Museum; Salomon (Chapter 2): Wrapped sticks, Peabody
Museum, Harvard. Photograph courtesy of William Conklin. Bottom row (from left
to right): Flouda (Chapter 8): Linear A clay tablet. Courtesy Heraklion Archaelogical
Museum; Johnston (Chapter 10): Inscribed clay ball. Courtesy of Persepolis
Fortification Archive Project, Oriental Institute, University of Chicago; Kidd (Chapter
12): P.Cairo 30961 *recto*. Photograph Ahmed Amin, Egyptian Museum, Cairo.
Back Cover Illustration:
Salomon (Chapter 2): 1590 de Murúa manuscript (de Murúa 2004: 124 verso)

Printed in the UK by Lightning Source Ltd.

ISBN (hardback): 978-1-909188-24-2
ISBN (EPUB): 978-1-909188-25-9
ISBN (PDF): 978-1-909188-26-6
DOI: http://dx.doi.org/10.5334/bai

Suggested citation:
Piquette, K. E. and Whitehouse, R. D. (eds.) 2013 *Writing as Material Practice: Substance,
surface and medium*. London: Ubiquity Press. DOI: http://dx.doi.org/10.5334/bai

To read the online open access version of this
book, either visit http:dx.doi.org/10.5334/bai
or scan this QR code with your mobile device:

Contents

Acknowledgements

This volume grew out of a conference of the same title, held at the Institute of Archaeology, University College London in May 2009. The conference was the winner of the conference competition held each year by the Institute of Archaeology and we are very grateful to the Institute for the grant of £2000 that provided our basic funding. The conference was a very lively, stimulating and enjoyable occasion and we would like to thank all those who gave papers and contributed to discussions. Over the course of three days, papers addressed the theme of writing as material practice from the perspectives of Archaeology, Anthropology, Classics, Communication Arts, Conservation, Design, Digital Humanities, Education, History of the Book, and Information Studies. In addition to several UK institutions, international institutions in Australia, Croatia, Germany, Greece, Ireland, Italy, New Zealand, Norway, and the US were also represented. We are particularly grateful to Jonathan Taylor, British Museum Assistant Keeper of Cuneiform Collections, and Paul Antonio, professional freelance calligrapher, both of whom brought materiality onto the conference floor, with their workshops on cuneiform and Egyptian scripts, respectively. We would also like to thank the conference volunteers (Sarah Doherty, Sarah Foster, Gabriel Moshenska, Massimiliano Pinarello, Daniela Rosenow, and Jenny Wexler) whose help with organising everything, from refreshments to furniture moving and organisation of PowerPoint presentations, made the conference run so smoothly.

The transformation of conference papers into a published volume has proved more complex and taken longer than we had originally planned. We are grateful to all our contributors for the patience and good humour with which they have responded to the delays and our frequent requests for editorial changes and additional information. We would like to thank Brian Hole, Tim Wakeford and Paige MacKay at Ubiquity Press for their help and co-operation in bringing the volume to successful fruition. Having taken on publication of the book at a late stage, they also took on our editorial commitment to publish within the timeframe for the REF (Research Excellence Framework) currently dominating research in UK universities, that is the end of the calendar year 2013. We greatly appreciate their understanding and assistance in meeting this goal. Support during the later phases of volume preparation was also provided by the Excellence Cluster TOPOI in association with the Freie Universität Berlin.

Finally, we would like to thank our respective partners, Andrew Gardner and John Wilkins, for their patience and tolerance — and occasional technical assistance — during the long gestation of this project.

Kathryn E. Piquette, Ruth D. Whitehouse
25 November 2013

Contributors

John Bennet is Professor of Aegean Archaeology in the Department of Archaeology at the University of Sheffield. His research interests include early scripts and administrative systems, the integration of textual and archaeological data, and the late prehistoric complex societies of the Aegean (Crete and mainland Greece), where he has also carried out fieldwork. He has published on Aegean administration and scripts as well as co-editing, with John Baines and Stephen Houston, a more general collection of papers on scripts: *The Disappearance of Writing Systems: Perspectives on literacy and communication* (2008). He is currently working on *A Short History of the Minoans*.

Craig Cessford is a Senior Project Officer with the Cambridge Archaeological Unit, part of the Division of Archaeology of the University of Cambridge, where he specialises in medieval and later urban archaeology and has directed excavations at the Grand Arcade and Old Divinity School sites. He has worked in both academic and developer-funded archaeology for over 20 years and has published over 100 book chapters and journal articles including *Between Broad Street and the Great Ouse: Waterfront archaeology in Ely* (2006), several chapters in the Çatalhöyük monograph series and papers in *American Antiquity, Antiquity, Archaeological Journal, International Journal of Historical Archaeology, Journal of Field Archaeology*, and *Oxford Journal of Archaeology*.

Sarah Finlayson is a PhD student in the Department of Archaeology, University of Sheffield. She is currently writing up her doctoral thesis, *A Comparative Study of the Archaeology of Writing in the Bronze Age Aegean*. Her research interests lie in the broad landscape of writing practices in the Bronze Age Aegean; unpicking the complex and changing relationships between script-based writing, seal use and other marking practices such as potmarks and mason's marks, and in understanding what motivates both their continuity and change. Forthcoming papers include a discussion of how best to define writing in this period, and an overview of where writing was produced or consumed and its significance.

Georgia Flouda is a Curator at the Heraklion Archaeological Museum, where she is involved in the redisplay of the Minoan Collection. She has a PhD from the University of Athens and specialises in Aegean prehistory and Classical archaeology with a focus on Aegean scripts. Her interests centre on the cognitive aspects of Aegean writing systems, theoretical approaches to

funerary practice, museum exhibits design, and interconnecting museum narratives with traditional field research and archaeological material studies. She co-edited *Archaeology and Heinrich
Schliemann a Century After His Death: Assessments and prospects: Myth – History – Science* (2012).
Recently affiliated with Princeton University, where she held a Stanley J. Seeger Visiting Research
Fellowship in Hellenic Studies, she is working on the publication of the material from the Minoan
settlement and Tholos Tomb A at Apesokari / Crete, and on the politics of excavation of this site
during World War II.

Sarah E. Jackson is Assistant Professor in the Department of Anthropology at the University of
Cincinnati. She holds a PhD in Anthropology (Archaeology) from Harvard University (2005). She
is an anthropological archaeologist, with a focus on Classic Maya culture; her research interests
include indigenous systems of governance, hierarchy, and the construction of difference, materiality, and the intersections of texts and the material record. She is the author of *Politics of the Maya
Court: Hierarchy and change in the Late Classic Period* (2013). She co-directs an archaeological
field project at the site of Say Kah, Belize.

Alan Johnston is Emeritus Reader in Classical Archaeology in the Institute of Archaeology,
University College London and Research Fellow of the Institute of Classical Studies, University
of London. He works in particular on Greek epigraphy and ceramics and is currently involved
with projects regarding material from Naukratis and amphora stamps in the British Museum, and
Greek graffiti from Croatian sites. His publications include *Trademarks on Greek Vases* (1979) and
Corpus Vasorum Antiquorum, Ireland 1 (2000). He is a Fellow of the Society of Antiquaries and
currently Chairman of the Publications Subcommittee of the British School at Athens.

Stephen Kidd is an Assistant Professor at Brown University. He studies Greek literature with
interests in comedy, the concept of education (*paideia*), Hellenistic Egypt, and the comparison of
ancient literatures beyond those of Greece and Rome. He has published articles in *Bulletin of the
American Society of Papyrologists* ('Dreams in Bilingual Ptolemaic Papyri'), *Classical Quarterly,
Transactions of the American Philological Association,* and has a book forthcoming (*Nonsense and
Meaning in Ancient Greek Comedy*).

Roger Matthews is Professor of Near Eastern Archaeology at the University of Reading, previously at the Institute of Archaeology, University College London. He has directed archaeological
research in Iraq, Iran, Syria, and Turkey, with a focus on prehistoric and early historic issues. He
has published on early texts and use of cylinder seals in Early Dynastic Mesopotamia, in particular
in his book *Cities, Seals and Writing* (1993). He is currently researching the origins of sedentary
farming in the Zagros Mountains of western Iran and eastern Iraq.

Elisa Perego is the 2013–2014 Ralegh Radford Rome Fellow at the British School at Rome and an
Honorary Research Associate at the Institute of Archaeology, University College London, where
she was awarded her doctorate in 2012. Elisa's main research interests include Mediterranean
archaeology, archaeological theory, the development of social complexity in late prehistory, and
social marginality. Her current research projects explore the construction of inequality and social
exclusion in Bronze Age and Iron Age Italy. Her publications include the edited volume *Food and
Drink in Archaeology 3* (2012) as well as several articles on alcohol consumption, ritual, personhood, and gender in late prehistoric and early Roman northern Italy.

Kathryn E. Piquette is a Marie Curie COFUND Fellow at the Dahlem Research School,
Freie Universität Berlin. Working within the Excellence Cluster TOPOI – The Formation and

Transformation of Space and Knowledge in Ancient Civilizations – her research revolves around early Egyptian and Near Eastern script and image, with emphasis on material practice and its impact on symbolic meaning. As a specialist in Reflectance Transformation Imaging, she is using this computational photographic method to investigate artefact surfaces for evidence of graphical production and consumption. She also carries out fieldwork in West Aswan, Egypt. Her recent publications include the co-edited volume *Narratives of Egypt and the Ancient Near East: Literary and linguistic approaches* (2011). She is a founding member of Digital Classicist Berlin and Honorary Research Associate at the Institute of Archaeology, University College London.

Elizabeth Pye recently retired as Professor of Archaeological and Museum Conservation, at the Institute of Archaeology, University College London where she taught both theoretical and practical aspects of heritage conservation. Her current research focuses on practical and conceptual effects of physical access to museum objects. She is author of *Caring for the Past: Issues in conservation for archaeology and museums* (2001), and editor of *The Power of Touch: Handling objects in museum and heritage contexts* (2007).

Frank Salomon is the John V. Murra Professor Emeritus of Anthropology at the University of Wisconsin-Madison. An ethnographer and ethnohistorian of the Andes, he is the author of *Native Lords of Quito in the Age of the Incas* (1986), *The Huarochirí Manuscript: A testament of ancient and colonial Andean religion* (1991), *Los Yumbos, Niguas, y Tsátchila o "Colorados" durante la colonia española* (1997), the *Cambridge History of the Native Peoples of the Americas — South America* (1999), *The Cord Keepers* (2004), *La revisita de 1588: Huarochirí veinte años antes de "Dioses y hombres"* (2010), and *The Lettered Mountain* (with Mercedes Niño-Murcia, 2011). A past president of the American Society for Ethnohistory, he has held NSF, Guggenheim, SAR, and NSF fellowships. His current researches concern the survival of the *khipu* (Andean knotted-cord script) into modernity.

Rachael Thyrza Sparks is Lecturer and Keeper of Collections at the Institute of Archaeology, University College London. She began her education at the University of Sydney, combining her undergraduate and postgraduate studies with regular fieldtrips to Jordan. On completion of her doctorate in 1999, she became Curator of the Petrie Palestinian Collection at the Institute of Archaeology, UCL. From 2003 she held a research position at the Pitt Rivers Museum, working on the project *Recovering the Material and Visual Cultures of the Southern Sudan: A museological resource,* before returning to UCL in 2005. Her publications include *Stone Vessels in the Levant* (2007) and, jointly authored and edited, *A Future for the Past: Petrie's Palestinian collection* (2007). She currently teaches an undergraduate course on *Texts in Archaeology*, as well as lecturing on various aspects of Near Eastern archaeology, artefact studies, and museology.

Helena Tomas is an Assistant Professor in Aegean Archaeology and Mycenaean Epigraphy and, since 2011, Head of the Department of Archaeology, University of Zagreb. She obtained a DPhil from the University of Oxford for her thesis, which was published as *Understanding the Transition from Linear A to Linear B Script* (2003). Her research interests include Aegean Bronze Ages scripts and administration and correlations between the Aegean, the Balkan Peninsula, and Central Europe during the Bronze Age. She works with the Kabri Archaeological Project in Israel, excavating a Canaanite site that includes a Bronze Age palace with Aegean-style paintings.

Ruth D. Whitehouse is Emeritus Professor of Prehistoric Archaeology at the Institute of Archaeology, University College London. Her research interests throughout her career have focussed on the prehistory of Italy and the West Mediterranean, concentrating on social archaeology and specifically on ritual and religion. Another major research interest is gender archaeology. Her publications include *Underground Religion: Cult and culture in prehistoric Italy* (1992) and edited volumes *Gender and Italian Archaeology* (1998), and (co-edited) *Archaeology and Women* (2007). In the last 10 years she has also pursued research into the early writing systems of Italy, with a focus on both the social context and the materiality of writing. She is a founding member of the Accordia Research Institute, devoted to the study of ancient Italy, and a general editor of its publications. Since 2007 she has been General Series Editor of the publications of the Institute of Archaeology, UCL.

Helène Whittaker is Professor of Classical Archaeology and Ancient History at the University of Gothenburg. Her research mainly revolves around the Greek Bronze Age, with a particular focus on religion and social organisation. The edited volume *The Aegean Bronze Age in Relation to the Wider European Context* (2008) was concerned with investigating the different interpretative frameworks employed by archaeologists working on the Aegean Bronze Age and the European Bronze Age. She has also published within various areas of Greek and Roman history, philosophy, religion, and literature. Her latest book is *Religion and Society in the Greek Middle Bronze Age* (forthcoming in 2014).

Abstracts

Chapter 1. Introduction: Developing an approach to writing as material practice
Kathryn E. Piquette and Ruth D. Whitehouse

In this chapter we introduce the topic of the materiality of writing and the approaches and methods needed to study writing from a material perspective. Within this interpretive theme analysis concentrates not on the linguistic and semantic meanings of 'texts' but on their physicality and how this relates to creators and users. We also introduce the individual chapters of the book, which cover a chronological span from *c.*3200 BCE to the present day and a geographical range from the Americas to the Near East and Europe. We end with a brief survey of research on writing as material practice and set out the role that we hope the present volume will play in developing this exciting new research theme.

Chapter 2. The Twisting Paths of Recall: Khipu (Andean cord notation) as artifact
Frank Salomon

Khipu, the cord- and knot-based Andean information medium, had a one-century heyday (15th century – 1532 CE) as the administrative script of the Inka empire. Before and after this period, however, the cord medium underwent a varied evolution, including the development of material attributes different from Inka norms. In this chapter, I review innovative recent work on the material-meaningful nexus in Inka khipu, and then suggest how other studies — both archaeological and ethnographic — further clarify our notions of khipus' 'inscribed object-world'.

The best-understood property of Inka khipus is the use of knots to register numbers and calculations in decimal registry. However, knotted arithmetic falls far short of explaining all the physical attributes of khipus, such as many-stranded and multicolored cords of varied structure, attached tufts and bulbs, and knotting arrays that defy the decimal structure.

Archaeologically, elaborate khipus are known to have predated the Inka format by at least a half-millennium. Such pre-Inka khipu were less knotted than Inka ones, but more colorful and perhaps more aesthetically driven. Khipus also continued to be made well into the 20th century CE, and have been ethnographically studied. Studies of khipu in communities that used cords for herding or as media for internal administration also point to properties other above and beyond knotability. Foci of the present essay include the fact that this eminently flexible medium exists in different physical states during its use cycle; that its composition by physically discrete parts lends it to use as a simulation device as opposed to text-fixing device; that its physical mode of articulating parts tends toward diagrammatic representation of data hierarchies, rather than sentential syntax; and that the act of 'reading' was physically distributed among cord-handlers, calculators, and interpreters, implying that there was no such actor as the unitary reader. Without denying that there were established practices for verbalizing khipu content, I suggest that Tufte's notion of "data graphic" may be more faithful to khipu practice than models premised on 'writing proper'.

Chapter 3. Writing as Material Technology: Orientation within landscapes of the Classic Maya world
Sarah E. Jackson

This chapter considers how writing may be understood as a material technology. In this way, we can understand text as not only having an effect or impact because of its *content*, but also because of its *material form* and the ways that form is perceived and used. Textual objects — a phrase that emphasizes the simultaneously material and textual nature of the artifacts I discuss — accomplish certain types of work that draw upon both the content and the material nature of the text. By considering texts in an artifactual light, I argue that texts do important work in organizing the material world. Furthermore, the specific material forms that texts take impact the ways in which such work is carried out, and the ways in which their meanings are perceived and visually consumed. I explore these ideas in the context of three Maya text objects, all inscribed with Classic Maya writing: a stone monument, a painted ceramic vessel, and a set of incised bone needles; in each case, I suggest that an orientational technology is at work. That is, the perception and use of these text objects serve to locate people in culturally defined landscapes, and in particular, within socio-political landscapes that include both experiential and imagined aspects. The experience of these texts allowed ancient viewers to situate themselves along a series of axes, not all of which are obvious or visible through other modes of material analysis. In both modern and ancient instances, orientational technologies involve accessing content that shapes human actions in the world, and that is experienced in specific ways representative of particular, shared worldviews. The text objects that I examine encode perspectives that located Maya individuals in relative positions through expressions of the shape and nature of the realms in which they lived, including dimensions of territoriality, conceptions of temporality, and constructions of personal and institutional difference. Significantly, the text objects examined are not reified in their material state, but change both in form and in place and manner of use, yielding surprisingly dynamic characteristics.

Chapter 4. Writing (and Reading) as Material Practice: The world of cuneiform culture as an arena for investigation
Roger Matthews

The ancient Near East was home to the world's earliest written texts, from 3200 BCE, and the tradition of writing on clay endured for more than 3000 years, lasting from the Late Chalcolithic until the end of the Iron Age of Mesopotamia and neighbouring regions. A great many languages, generally unrelated to each other, were written in the so-called 'cuneiform culture'. Cuneiform texts form an integral part of the socio-political and material culture of multiple societies of the ancient Near East, including early states, cities, and the world's first empires, but hitherto their study has focussed on philological and historical issues. A new wave of research addresses the materiality of cuneiform texts, and I review and elaborate on that research here. In this consideration of current approaches to the materiality of text in the ancient Near East, I explore several significant issues relating to the materiality of writing in the cuneiform tradition. Key questions are: what was the extent of literacy (writing and / or reading) in the ancient Near East; who were the intended audiences for cuneiform texts of varying types; what is the significance of variation in the physical media of texts; and, how representative are surviving corpora of ancient writing systems? In reviewing these questions, I aim to demonstrate that the extremely rich assemblages of cuneiform documents, often in the form of archives, constitute a major resource for ongoing and future exploration.

Chapter 5. Re-writing the Script: Decoding the textual experience in the Bronze Age Levant (c.2000–1150 BCE)
Rachael Thyrza Sparks

Writing in its many forms was an important part of the political, economic and cultural landscape of the Levant during the 2nd millennium BCE. Diverse scripts were used to record both local and foreign languages, and included Egyptian formal and cursive hieroglyphs, hieratic, cuneiform, alphabetic cuneiform, Proto-Canaanite, Hittite hieroglyphs, and linear Aegean scripts. While the corpus is not large, it is significant and hints at the range of writing practices and knowledge available.

This chapter reviews the evidence for Middle and Late Bronze Age writing from a primarily archaeological perspective, showing how a study of object function, materiality and contexts of use can inform on broader questions of textual availability, awareness, and execution. Texts played a variety of roles within the communities they served. Texts could act as educational tools; to exert political authority, impress, and intimidate; to enhance objects used in funerary or ritual settings, and to mark personal ownership. Across these roles, we can also evaluate more broadly how writing technique, material, and script converge, and what the choices that were being made in this respect can tell us about how writing was being organised and managed.

This leads to the conclusion that, despite strong script diversity in the region, most forms of script appear to have been used in discrete environments with little overlap between them. Many uses were confined to a professional setting, with scribes operating within local and imposed administrative networks as representatives of the status quo. Beyond this, writing was generally restricted to elite consumers and so had limited impact on society as a whole. The exception lay in more visible forms of writing, such as publically erected stelae, and in special classes of object such as amulets and amuletic objects, such as the scarab, which could be privately owned by a wider group of people. Accessibility, however, did not necessarily equate with understanding, and for the majority, the significance of a text may well have lain in its visual and material qualities and associations rather than in the actual words recorded.

Ultimately it was the more personal and unofficial applications of writing that proved to be the most robust, and it was these that survived to bridge the gap between the end of the Late Bronze Age and the emergence of a whole new set of polities and writing practices in the Iron II period.

Chapter 6. The Function and Meaning of Writing in the Prehistoric Aegean: Some reflections on the social and symbolic significance of writing from a material perspective
Helène Whittaker

In this chapter I discuss the materiality of writing in the Bronze Age Aegean, with a particular focus on evidence from Crete. It is from here that the earliest forms of writing in the Aegean derive, dating to before the end of the 3rd millennium BCE. In the period of the first palaces there seem to have been two systems of writing in use: Linear A and the so-called Cretan Hieroglyphic Script. The development of these scripts coincides more or less with the construction of the first palaces at Knossos, Malia, and Phaistos, and it is probable that the early use of writing on Crete was closely associated with the emergence of centralised administration at the transition from the Early Bronze Age to the Middle Bronze Age. In the first part of the chapter I review the different types of support (clay, stone, metal, bone) that are known from archaeological excavation or for which there is indirect evidence (wood, papyrus, leather). I consider their particular material qualities in relation to the act of writing as well as to the types of documents for which they were used and the contexts in which they were produced and put to use. In the second part of the chapter I discuss Aegean writing in terms of its social and symbolic meanings. It is possible that the ability to record information in a visible and tangible form may have been seen as a form of esoteric power. Early examples of writing occur on seals, which would have been objects of prestige and perhaps authority, as well as on clay tablets. Writing on stone and metal artefacts has been found in cultic contexts, which suggests that writing may have been associated with religious meaning as well as having been a way of enhancing objects made of valuable materials.

Chapter 7. Form Follows Function: Writing and its supports in the Aegean Bronze Age
Sarah Finlayson

The phrase 'form follows function', originally conceived as an aesthetic principle, has been applied to fields as disparate as architecture and software engineering. I use it here as a starting point from which to unpick the complex and changing relationship between writing and its supports during the Aegean Bronze Age, with the basic hypothesis that the shape, and to a lesser extent, material, of objects that bear writing change according to the purpose to which they, object + writing, are put.

I examine the evidence at two levels. Firstly, the use of writing supports in each of the three main Aegean scripts, Cretan Hieroglyphic, Linear A. and Linear B, is reviewed. Cretan Hieroglyphic and Linear A are both in use on Crete during the First and early Second Palace Periods, although largely in different areas, offering the possibility of comparing contemporary approaches to the creation and use of different objects on which to write what seem to be (given that both scripts are undeciphered) broadly similar subject matters. Cretan Hieroglyphic ceases to be used later in the Second Palace Period, and Linear A use spreads — likewise, Linear B replaces Linear A in the Third Palace Period; these two transitions allow us to look at how practice changes through time, but also, potentially, at the deliberate refinement of writing supports as certain forms are carried from old to new script, new shapes are introduced, and others go out of use.

While keeping these longer term patterns in mind, I then focus on Linear A; its diverse range of writing supports offers the potential of building up a more detailed picture of how and where different kinds of writing-bearing object are used within a particular chronological period. Writing appears on objects we classify as administrative, such as clay tablets, but also, intriguingly, on what seem to be non-administrative items like metal pins or stone 'libation tables', giving the impression of a loose and flexible attitude to what can be written upon. Key questions to consider include to what extent this diversity of shape is 'organised'? Does the shape of the writing support add meaning to the usually brief inscription, or vice versa? And, is it possible that people interacting with writing might have visibility of only one kind of support — what would this mean for their conception of writing, and our definitions of literacy?

To conclude, I return to the longer view, and my original hypothesis, to consider whether form really does follow function with Aegean Bronze Age writing, and whether the changes that occur result from writing-users refining the system, or the system refining the users.

Chapter 8. Materiality of Minoan Writing: Modes of display and perception
Georgia Flouda

In traditional narratives of Minoan archaeology, the visual display of writing is usually overlooked. This chapter seeks to outline a framework for exploring the modes of display and the perception of Minoan writing by focussing on artefact categories bearing Cretan Hieroglyphic and Linear A inscriptions. Since both scripts are still undeciphered, they lend themselves to a study of their attestations as signs in the Peircean sense. Attention is therefore redirected from the written form of the specific inscriptions, the 'signifier' or 'representamen', to the physical aspects of their material supports and to the symbolic messages projected by them. Semiotic relationships that are grounded in the material properties and the performative capacities of the artefacts themselves are examined, in order to detect aspects of artefactual meaning that may not be immediately obvious from a conventional perspective. Parameters like material, size, shape, and other functional aspects of Minoan inscribed artefacts are analysed. Special emphasis is also placed on artefacts that possibly served as symbolic devices, mainly inscribed sealstones and their impressions on clay. The combination of script with images that may have constituted a visual code, and its potential for assessing literacy, is explored in the case of the Archanes Script and Cretan Hieroglyphic sealstones. Clay, metal, and stone objects carrying Linear A inscriptions of a non-administrative character are also systematically considered. The different ways scale, directionality, alignment, and the small scale of writing have informed the creation of these inscribed objects constitute one of the main questions posed. How small size could have affected the use of some inscribed objects in display events and rituals that included performance is also explored.

In order to address the modes of perception of Minoan writing, the analysis relies on examining how the graphic symbols of the two scripts are arranged in the 'graphic space', namely the area where text is positioned and read. In this framework, directionality, alignment, and scale of the Hieroglyphic and Linear A signs are treated as indexes. Finally, the study focusses on the ways in which these parameters may have affected the experience of the inscribed artefacts by social actors, as well as the role of these objects in practices of remembrance.

Chapter 9. Saving on Clay: The Linear B practice of cutting tablets
Helena Tomas

The practice of cutting clay tablets is evident in both Minoan Linear A and Mycenaean Linear B administration. Tablets were most probably cut after having been inscribed, when the residue of clay with no text was removed, either to be reused for producing further tablets, or to minimise space needed for their storage. This habit is especially apparent in the earliest deposit of Linear B tablets — the Room of the Chariot Tablets — where nearly 20% of all tablets were cut. It is precisely these tablets that will be discussed in this chapter.

Most of the cut tablets from the Room of the Chariot Tablets are of elongated shape. Some were cut on the sides immediately before the first sign or immediately after the last one. This may reflect the practice of saving clay whenever possible. The tablets generally give an impression of economy: their entire surface is usually inscribed without leaving any unused space; when a tablet was larger than needed, the unneeded parts seem to have been excised and reused.

Another explanation has been proposed for the cutting of these tablets: the practice of dividing a set of information into separate records. Although cut and separated in the past, scholars recently joined some of these tablets proving that these small documents initially belonged to one larger tablet. The name introduced to describe this kind of a document is a *simili*-join. As for the purpose of *simili*-joins, it has been previously suggested that larger tablets were divided into smaller units for the purpose of rearranging the information, and this is a possibility that is further explored in this paper.

Apart from the actual cutting, another feature may be an indication of the practice of *simili*-joins. A certain number of elongated tablets from the Room of the Chariot tablets have vertical lines incised across them. It seems that their function was to divide certain sections of a tablet. Perhaps these lines were incised to indicate where to cut the tablet, as suggested by Jan Driessen. By following this line of thought, it will be proposed that records of this type were probably written with the anticipated need for rearranging of the data, meaning that the *simili*-joins may have been planned in advance — hence the practice of marking tablets with vertical lines for cutting. These lines must have been incised when the tablet was still moist, i.e. either while inscribing the text, or not much longer afterwards. If so, the question is: why did such tablets remain undivided?

Chapter 10. Straight, Crooked and Joined-up Writing: An early Mediterranean view
Alan Johnston

The role of different surfaces in the development of writing styles in the earlier periods of literacy in the Mediterranean world has rarely been discussed. I examine some aspects with particular reference to writers of Greek and Etruscan. The study is of course impeded by the limited nature of the evidence preserved for us, but we can make some estimates of the character of lost materials, most notably skin and papyrus, from a few secondary sources, largely from Greek literature.

A major factor with respect to the influence of the medium (whether the surface or the tool) is the extent at any given period of tendencies towards 'cursivity'; the concept is discussed briefly and some sporadic examples are noted of the usage of 'flowing' letters in the material that is preserved in the period down to *c*.400 BCE. However, a contrary development is seen in the more formal texts on stone appearing from the later 6th century in the '*stoichedon*' style of patterned 'four-square lettering'. The appearance of such, mainly official, texts on stone or bronze may have reined in any incipient moves to casual, 'joined up', writing. This is suggested by the few glimmers of Greek texts on papyrus that survive from the period before *c*.350 BCE (and the sole Etruscan one after that date), where the lettering remains in 'capitals'.

With respect to overall tendencies within the broad geographical area, not many individual polities have yielded sufficient material for solid judgements to be made; local usages can be occasionally isolated, but the general pace of change to the cursive writing that indeed eventually emerges is slow between the 7th to 4th centuries; some comparanda can be seen in other areas of material culture where ease of manufacture and utility are somewhat haltingly developed.

In the course of the chapter I draw on examples from inscribed ceramics to papyrus, mummy bindings and rock-cut graffiti and other stone inscriptions to illustrate both local phenomena and more general tendencies pertaining to individual types of surfaces and writing instruments. Virtually all emerge from the basic form of alphabet developed in some areas of the Greek-speaking world in the period *c*.850–775 BCE from a Semitic model; the initial re-working of the signs that were borrowed at that time can be seen to be grounded in the current decorative style of the period, the so-called Geometric style, which appears in more or less 'rigid' versions throughout the area. In the background there will remain the topic of the relationship of writer to reader, and the extent to which the former may have had the latter's interests in mind; a general trend away from the use of interpuncts is an indication that such interests were not of any deep-seated nature.

Chapter 11. "It Is Written"?: Making, remaking and unmaking early 'writing' in the lower Nile Valley
Kathryn E. Piquette

Conventional analysis and interpretation of inscriptions and associated images often focus on their status as finished objects, with less attention being devoted to image 'life histories', particularly the creative processes involved in physical expression. The aim of this chapter is to explore the unfolding of written culture across time–space in relation to particular material media and the implications of their transformations for the role of inscribed objects. For its basis, this inquiry grapples with evidence from the lower Nile Valley during the Late Predynastic–Early Dynastic periods (*c.*3300 / 3100–2800 / 2770 BCE), including perforated bone, ivory and wooden plaques or 'labels', stone vessels, and funerary stelae from cemetery contexts, with particular focus on the Upper Egyptian site of Abydos. Tool and other marks on these objects provide detailed insight into sequences of technical action involved in the writing process. However, I move beyond a general consideration of the writing act to focus on different degrees of un-making and partial making, as well as episodes of adjustment, addition, and possible re-making. Whole compositions and parts thereof are obliterated through vigorous scratching or scraping away while some are scored or crossed out. Yet other images are tidily removed. Additions may be made after initial inscription using different or similar writing tools and techniques. In at least one case, the drafting phase appears complete while the subsequent carving remains unfinished. Drawing on the notion of *chaîne opératoire* and practice theory, including structuration, I examine these secondary and other transformations and consider their implications for maker intention and choice, and object function and meaning. In contrast to notions of writing as enduring and transcendent, embodied in terms such as 'record' or 'source', a material practice approach prompts consideration of the ways in which writing and related symbolic modes may be unstable. Based on the form, content and modes of expression, as well as spatial and temporal distribution, Egypt's earliest script was clearly bound up with the development of the Egyptian state, playing an important role in high status funerary practice. However, despite the centralisation and increasing standardisation of scribal and artistic activities, the ways in which the writing 'system' was practised on more local and individual levels could be variable and contingent.

Chapter 12. Written Greek but Drawn Egyptian: Script changes in a bilingual dream papyrus
Stephen Kidd

This chapter explores the conceptual background behind shifting from writing Greek to Demotic in a 3rd century BCE Greco-Egyptian bilingual letter. In this letter, a man writes to his friend about a recent dream. He is writing in Greek, but in order to describe his dream accurately, he says, he must write the dream itself in Egyptian. He writes in Greek, "it seemed like a good idea to tell you about the dream, so that you may know the way which the gods know you. I have written below in Egyptian, so that you may accurately understand". After saying his Greek farewell he begins writing in a Demotic hand: "I saw myself in a dream in the following way: I am standing at the doorway of the sanctuary. A priest is sitting there, and many people are standing beside him. The priest spoke to the people who were standing there…".

What is the reason for this code-shift? Could it be that the letter-writer's Greek was not proficient enough to describe the dream? As was noted long ago, this cannot be the case, since one would then expect that the letter-writer would not have written his addressee a Greek letter in the first place. Although one might suggest linguistic or cultural reasons for the code-shift, I look to the scripts themselves and how they were written for clues. I argue that the two scripts (not just the two languages) inform the letter-writer's decision to choose and elevate Demotic as the proper vehicle for recounting his dream. The argument is made in three parts: first, there is an examination of the different ways that these two languages were physically written; second, a description of the process of writing an alphabetic (Greek) versus a logographic (Demotic) script; and third, a conjecture of the subjective experience of the alphabetic-logographic shift through comparative evidence (English and Chinese).

Chapter 13. The Other Writing: Iconic literacy and Situla art in pre-Roman Veneto (Italy)
Elisa Perego

This chapter explores the relation between the metalworking tradition of 'Situla Art' and alphabetic writing in the Veneto region, north-east Italy, between *c.*650–275 BCE. By taking further the approach of Italian scholar Luca Zaghetto, who suggested interpreting the iconographic motifs of Situla Art as a real language, I adopt and expand upon the concept of iconic literacy to elucidate the elaboration and fruition of both this sophisticated decorative technique and 'traditional' literacy in a phase of tumultuous socio-political development for Iron Age Veneto. Notably, the aim of this study is neither to demonstrate that situla art was structurally equivalent to alphabetic writing nor to identify general similarities in the logic of iconic and verbal literacy. Rather, by drawing on different strands of research that propose (a) breaking down the dichotomy between verbal and non-verbal modes of communication and (b) focussing on the value of literacy as a power-laden, historically-situated social practice, my analysis investigates the development of situla art and 'traditional' writing in Iron Age Veneto by tackling the socio-cultural milieu(s) in which they developed. As both Venetic situla art and writing appear to have initially spread in various elite contexts as a consequence of deep cultural contact with Etruria and other neighbouring populations, I explore their role in promoting the status of high-ranking individuals at different ceremonies, by advertising both their wealth and access to exotic ideas and materials. In particular, I discuss how situla art products and inscribed objects became variously part of a 'package' of selected ideologies, rituals, forms of display, and eating and drinking habits — often imported from outside Veneto — that came to draw a line between the elites and marginal social groups unable to access these resources. While analysing how the adoption and re-elaboration of these different ritual techniques and consumption practices shaped the Venetic elite lifestyle and communicative system, I also draw attention to some specific differences in the ritual use of situla art and writing, despite their potential connection to the same social sphere.

Chapter 14. 'Tombstones' in the North Italian Iron Age: Careless writers or athletic readers?
Ruth D. Whitehouse

Several different types of inscribed stone monument of the North Italian Iron Age are interpreted as funerary markers and so could be described as 'tombstones'. In the traditional classification of these monuments, the primary criterion used is the language of the inscription — Etruscan or Venetic — and the monuments assigned to the two different language groups are almost never discussed together. A second criterion is the typology of the monuments, variously described as *stelae, cippi* or *ciottoloni*. What is never included in the classification process, and is rarely discussed at all, is the arrangement of the writing on the surface of the stone and its relationship to the iconography, where present.

The present chapter examines the tombstones from a different perspective, which places the form and arrangement of the writing at the centre of the analysis. The monuments in question exhibit widely varying arrangements of text, including horizontal or vertical lines on flat surfaces, horizontal lines around the circumference of cylindrical monuments, straight lines around the sides of figured panels, and a few unique elaborate arrangements. The arrangement of the writing on inscriptions with multiple lines of text also varies: some are written as sitting on separate baselines, so that the letters are all the same way up, while others are inscribed as on a continuous baseline, so that the letters of the second line are upside down in relation to those on the first. These different ways of organising the text have implications for the way people engaged with the monuments, both those who produced the inscriptions (traditionally labelled 'writers') and those who interacted with them subsequently (traditionally 'readers'). The analysis considers the bodily movements involved in reading the inscriptions, the character of the original experience of visiting the cemeteries, and the implications for understanding the nature of 'reading' in Iron Age North Italy.

Chapter 15. Different Times, Different Materials and Different Purposes: Writing on objects at the Grand Arcade site in Cambridge
Craig Cessford

During the 18th–20th centuries writing is extremely common on objects made from a wide range of materials that are recovered archaeologically. This evidence is particularly susceptible to nuanced interpretation, as it often forms part of short term deliberate depositional events linked to specific households and consisting of large numbers of items. The nature of the evidence also means that a biographical approach to both individual items and groups of objects can be fruitfully applied. Despite this, such finds have attracted relatively little attention, principally because they are conceived of as part of an unproblematic 'familiar past'. By looking in detail at six assemblages of material spanning the late 18th to early 20th century recovered during recent excavations at the Grand Arcade site in Cambridge, England, this chapter focusses on how the different materials, sizes, forms, and functions of different types of artefacts affect how writing was employed upon them, as well as why writing does not occur on certain types of artefacts. What was the function of the various types of writing and who was the intended audience? To what extent is some of the writing primarily tactile rather than visual? To what extent was some of the writing meant to be read at all, as some of it was effectively hidden? It also explores the relationship between writing on materials that survive archaeologically and the dominant form of writing on paper that has usually perished. It emerges that much of the writing relates to regulation, although there is also evidence for resistance, as well as a repeated a link to children, and commercial and institutional branding. As writing on objects becomes more common between the late 18th and early 20th centuries and a text-saturated culture develops, the individual texts in later assemblages are often less visible than in earlier groups and are frequently apparently not intended to be read by the consumers of the objects themselves.

Chapter 16. Writing Conservation: The impact of text on conservation decisions and practice
Elizabeth Pye

The purpose of conservation is to investigate and preserve objects, and the information they hold, and to make them available for study and enjoyment now and in the future. Illustrated with several examples, this chapter explores the way in which conservation approaches objects which carry written text. Objects can be seen as documents waiting to be read, and much of the embodied information remains latent until elucidated during conservation. The thinking and practice of conservation are governed by a number of concepts and principles including the need to establish the significance of an object and its future use; treatments should not affect the identity of an object and should change the object as little as possible, both materially and conceptually, while securing a satisfactory conservation result. The identity of an object is seen as the sum of the values assigned to it. Values may be material or conceptual: so the material form of writing may also carry meaning, as in early printing, or in handwriting. The conservator is faced with a dilemma if an object demonstrates several values because it may be necessary to prioritise one value over another. In practice, because of its evidential value, the presence (or assumed presence) of any form of writing will almost always take priority over other factors when making conservation decisions, even if this affects other evidence. Conservation cleaning may risk loss of material of an object such as the corrosion layers on a coin, in order to reveal the materiality of text, and here permanent material change is accepted if it results in exposure of the text. The recent development of digital imaging has introduced the concept and practice of 'digital preservation' which provides the possibility of virtual investigation and virtual restoration of text, thus obviating material change. Other modern techniques such as computerised tomography have shown potential for the detection of text by virtual unrolling or flattening of distorted documents. However, the 'real thing' still has considerable power and will continue to need material care. Furthermore, digital imaging introduces another dilemma as the hardware and software involved in producing the images which document and disclose textual materialities will themselves require conservation.

Introduction: Developing an approach to writing as material practice

Kathryn E. Piquette and Ruth D. Whitehouse

Freie Universität Berlin and University College London

Scope and Impetus

This book grapples with the issue of writing and related graphical modes as forms of material culture. The diverse case studies are unified and underpinned by the notion that writing is fundamentally material — that it is preceded by and constituted through the material practices of human practitioners. From this vantage point, understandings of things that are written must therefore go beyond study of textual meanings and take account of the material worlds in which writing is inextricably embedded. In aligning along this common theme, analytical and interpretive priority is given, not to the linguistic and semantic meanings of graphical marks, but to their physicality and the ways in which this relates to creators and users. Covering a temporal span of some 5000 years, from *c.*3200 BCE to the present day, and ranging in spatial context from the Americas to the Near East, the papers bring a variety of perspectives which contribute to both specific and broader questions of writing, its meaning and significance. As such, these case studies also contribute to an emerging discourse (below) on 'writing' and 'materiality'. They also contribute to the development of contextualising paradigms equipped to cope with the complexities of graphical cultures in relation to the people who created and attributed meaning to them through a diverse array of individual and wider social practices.

While an increasing emphasis on materiality has characterised many fields of archaeological research over the last 20 years, studies of writing have lagged behind in this respect. The main reason is a long established and difficult-to-shift disciplinary division between archaeology and philology, in which the philologists — often brought in by archaeologists as technical experts whose interpretations are hard to challenge — have had the upper hand. This has led to an

---

How to cite this book chapter:

Piquette, K. E. and Whitehouse, R. D. 2013. Introduction: Developing an approach to writing as material practice. In: Piquette, K. E. and Whitehouse, R. D. (eds.) *Writing as Material Practice: Substance, surface and medium.* Pp. 1-13. London: Ubiquity Press. DOI: http://dx.doi.org/10.5334/bai.a

emphasis on the *content* of inscriptions and other writing, concentrating on languages, scripts and the semantic meanings of texts. These studies not only neglect materiality, which is our focus here, but they also tend to neglect *context* (both the specific archaeological context of the artefact, and the broader cultural and historical context into which written surfaces fit). Studies of content, context and materiality are all necessary for a holistic study of writing and many of the papers in this volume, while concentrating on material aspects of writing, do also deal with the meaning of the texts being studied and the contexts of their production and use.

Our concern with the question of writing artefactuality was prompted by methodological problems arising out of our own research on ancient writing (e.g. Piquette 2007; 2008; 2013; forthcoming; Whitehouse 2008; 2012). Our interest in exploring writing materialities cross-culturally is also inspired by the work of several scholars who also challenge the traditional disciplinary division between archaeology and philology (e.g. Moreland 2001; 2006; cf. Bottéro 1992; 2000). "Text-aided archaeology" (Hawkes 1954; see also Little 1992) and discussions of text *and* archaeology come closer to providing integrated understandings of the written pasts but nevertheless embody a paradigm where text is a largely immaterial source *about* the past. Moreland and others have highlighted the methodological drawbacks of de-materialising treatments of written objects, and while a gradual 'material turn' is underway in some areas (Andrén 1998; Gardner 2003: especially 2, 6; Matthews 2003: 56–64), an emphatic disciplinary-wide shift to a more holistic and inclusive framework has yet to be realised — whether from philological or archaeological points of departure. We therefore sought to contribute momentum to this shift by convening a conference of the same title in 2009 and assembling this edited volume of many of the papers delivered at that meeting. We feel this represents an important step towards focussing and stimulating a more sustained engagement with this theme, within archaeological discourse, textual studies, and hopefully beyond. Before outlining the contents of the volume we would like to briefly discuss the three key terms which bind the papers together, namely 'writing', 'material', and 'practice'.

Writing

Contributors to this volume address the subject of 'writing' in a broad sense, including written-text and signs taken to represent units of language as well as marking systems that are less clearly related to spoken language, although the former dominate. Ontologically writing is treated as both a process and an outcome; authors distinguish the act of writing from the result of that action to explore how aspects of production and consumption actively constitute written meanings. The notion of meaning as unfolding in particular times and places, as part of a socially-situated *chaîne opératoire*, challenges the conventional epistemological role often assigned to writing as a source *about* the past (Moreland 2006: 137–138, 143). Papers thus focus on writing as an integral part of cultural practice and demonstrate that this data type not only augments archaeological reconstruction of the past, but can fruitfully be studied as material culture and as an *active* constituent of the past — just as it continues to be so profoundly in the present (below).

Materials: Writing as artefact

Essential to achieving the paradigmatic shift whereby writing is understood as wholly embedded in, and a dynamic constituent of social worlds, is the theorisation of the 'material' in written culture. Linked to this is the relationship of material to past embodied writers, readers and others involved in the production and consumption of written objects. A conceptual framework that we found useful in developing the volume (and conference) theme is expressed in the second part of the volume title: substance, surface and medium.[1]

These are the components of a tri-partite model for material properties developed by American Psychologist James Gibson in his book *The Ecological Approach to Visual Perception* (1979: especially chapter 6). His framework is not explicitly directed to writing, but it nevertheless provides a useful guide for examining the significance of the marks of writing in relation to the material surfaces on which they occur — and importantly — their multisensory perception by humans in different environmental conditions (see also Ingold 2007).

Taking as example the inscription of a lead curse tablet from the Roman site of Uley, in Gloucestershire, England (**Figure 1**): its particular material substance of lead, the semi-smoothness of the hammered metal surface punctuated by impressions *cum* incisions as formed by pressing and dragging a stylus into and across its surface, and the environmental medium of, for example, lamp or candlelight, come together to provide certain 'affordances' or opportunities for visual perception and other sensory and bodily interactions. Whether viewing, touching, carving, incising, applying ink and so on, writing acts are directly informed by material properties. Of course, they are also mediated to varying extents by cultural knowledge (e.g. tacit, explicit) for a given mark-making system — conventions of script production and meaning to both creator and intended / unintended audiences. The material results of specific actions — the subtractive and additive marks or other types of surface transformations encountered on a range of artefacts and surfaces — deserve documentation, study and explanation alongside palaeographical, philological, linguistic, and historical analyses. The case studies in this volume highlight the kinds of additional insight gained by investigating substance, surface and medium (albeit variously defined), and their implications for the content meaning of writing. Moreover, this focus on material properties encourages clearer articulation and reflexive consideration of the distinction between graphical evidence as a source *about* the past, and how an object was also *constitutive* of that past (Moreland 2001; 2006).

Writing played an active and meaningful role in the construction of past social lives, the material constitutive nature of which is raised emphatically by Gibson's triad. It also makes imperative setting materials in relation to human perception. Perception of material surfaces is thus an embodied process which unfolds in time and space; practice is implicated at its very core. Given that material substances and their surfaces can only be put to use as writing spaces through bodily action, and can only be identified as writing through sensory perception, it is clear that the concepts of practice must be central to a material approach to written evidence.

The term 'material' is conceptualised in variable ways in the volume's chapters, but overall it refers to the stuff on which writing appears, and for additive techniques that which physically constitutes written marks. The term 'materiality' can be unhelpful if it is simply used as a substitute for 'material' (see Ingold 2007). However, we suggest it can be useful for distinguishing between a necessarily passive notion of 'material' (substance) that precedes analysis and interpretation, and a more active concept involving material as incorporated subsequently into a narrative of socially situated marking practices. 'Materiality' can thus refer in a general way to the material aspects of artefacts, while also, and importantly, prompting their situation in relation to mutually-informing sets of practices. This enables material to be described as more than a mere 'support' for writing. It becomes active in the construction of meanings, from the preliminary work of manufacturing artefact 'blanks' on which marks are made, and the techniques of surface transformation which give rise to written marks, to the ways in which these physical objects were incorporated into subsequent activities, from reading / viewing (where intended) and display, to discard, deposition or loss. In addition to seeing writing as meaningful through the materiality of its expression, the papers in this volume also advocate study of the way the written is bound up in individual and group interactions and perceived cultural norms, and how these are reproduced or renegotiated.

a

b

Figure 1: a) Incised lead tablet bearing a curse written in the Roman Imperial period. From the Uley Shrines, West Hill, Gloucestershire (Woodward and Leach 1993: 118, No. 1). WH77.1180, British Museum; b) Detail derives from Reflectance Transformation Imaging (RTI) visualisation using the 'specular enhancement' rendering mode to clarify ductus and surface transformations made by the writer's stylus and other surface morphology. Photograph and RTI detail Kathryn E. Piquette, Courtesy Roger Tomlin and Trustees of the British Museum.

Practice: Text as process and outcome

Practice is another conceptual theme which underpins the studies in this volume. Theoretical approaches to practice (e.g. Bourdieu 1977; Foucault 1979; Giddens 1979; 1984) have been brought to bear on the study of archaeological data for more than three decades (e.g. David and Kramer 2001; Dobres 2000). A dominant concern among these studies has been with technology and charting innovation, change, and continuity. Particular emphasis has been placed on agency, identity, and the body, but in keeping with traditional disciplinary divisions, writing has been largely omitted from this discourse. The recognition engendered by a material practice perspective — that the act of writing and its material products are fundamentally technological — makes it incumbent upon archaeologists to study the marks of inscription in the same way that lithic, ceramic or other types of data are examined.

Similar to analyses of these archaeological data types (Schlanger 1996; Tite 2008), it follows that explanatory frameworks developed for studies of mark-making should also incorporate theories of practice. Etienne Wenger's concept of "communities of practice", with its emphasis on learning, and participation and reification (1998: 58–62), offers ways for exploring writing on the levels of both individual and collective practice. Practices are reified, or not, depending on accumulations of individual participation. Reification in everyday life may remain abstract in its manifestation, such as the practice of taking a tea break at an appointed time or shaking hands upon meeting, but reification also shapes experience and meaning in more materially enduring ways. The computer and printing technologies used to produce this volume constitute the nature of writing and reify a particular view of it materially, in contrast to many of the writing practices addressed in the contributions themselves. The concept of "communities of practice" draws on Anthony Giddens' notion of "structuration" — the negotiation of the relationship between individual agency and social structures through situated practice. This concept of agency as constituted by, and constituting of, social structure ensures a framework for understanding practice that is neither over-individualising nor over-generalising (cf. Gardner 2004: 2–4 with e.g. Barrett 2001: 149; Hodder 2000: 25).

While a concept of agency that is set in relation to social structure can be fruitful for explaining how individuals choose to act and participate (or not) in writing cultures (see Piquette 2013), archaeological theory is also well-equipped to provide new explanatory frameworks for addressing writing in the context of bodily practice. One direction in which engagement with material practice leads us is a concern for the senses, through which human beings experience the material world. The broader spectrum of human sensory experience of past materialities has been investigated within archaeology since the early 1990s and has become more prominent in recent years (Fahlander and Kjellström 2010; Skeates 2010), albeit with limited concern for past writing. The emergence of Visual Cultural Studies during the late 1980s as its own discipline, and the field of Image Studies as well (Mitchell 2002: 178), represents an important move to treat imagery and its materiality from a more multisensory perspective (Jay 2002: 88; despite the visual bias implied in its name), but here too writing has been sidelined. Perhaps some insight into why certain barriers persist for work across some disciplinary boundaries is required. Marquard Smith (2008: 1–2) makes an interesting observation with regard to publication in his discipline, Visual Cultural Studies, which parallels our experience in bringing this volume to press. It is commonplace to encounter numerous books with 'visual' and 'culture' in the title in university libraries, bookshops or online booksellers, but where they are shelved or how they are otherwise categorised ranges widely. From Art History, Aesthetics and Anthropology to Critical Theory or Sociology, no one is quite sure where to put visual culture or where to find it. The present volume seemed to present a similar classificatory conundrum (and thus marketing difficulties according to one publisher we approached). The ontological challenge presented by the notion of writing as object, and an object that is embedded within the full spectrum of human sensory experience, presents an interesting paradox. If one pauses to survey one's surroundings, graphical culture of all sorts is clearly embedded in the material world. In the present day we cope easily with the interweaving of writing and associated image types in day-to-day life. Whether we are checking text messages on a phone, flicking through a magazine, licking a stamp, struggling to unfurl a newspaper on a crowded bus, or reading this very text as part of a paper-based or e-book, it is easy to see how these material contexts and sensory experiences beyond the visual are important to writing-related practices and meanings. Yet, as long as we fail to develop an epistemological infrastructure which supports investigation of these complexities, we cannot develop an understanding of the wider networks which constituted past written meaning or properly evaluate its cultural significance. Likewise, archaeological thought on decision-making processes, choice and intentionality also stands to contribute to research on the selection of writing materials, and the choices past people made for how to write, read, view or otherwise engage with written surfaces.

However we understand material practice in general, in any given case study we need to ask both *who* were the practitioners and *how* they practised. Here we come up against another set of problematic terms — literacy, reading and writing — on which there is a substantial literature. In the more linguistically oriented studies devoted to the subject of literacy there is a strong emphasis on 'reading' and 'writing,' understood very much in present day terms (see Collins and Blot 2003 for an overview). Archaeologists and ancient historians have devoted much time to discussion of the extent of literacy in any given society (by which they usually mean the number of people who could read and write, rather than what is indicated by these terms; see, for instance, Harris's seminal work *Ancient Literacy* (Harris 1989) and the responses of a number of other scholars (Beard et al. 1991). However, the kind of approach adopted in this volume requires the reconsideration of definitions of both 'writer' and 'reader' and also to consider a wider range of practitioners than can be encompassed in these terms, for instance the people who made the artefacts, who may well have been different from the people who wrote on them.

When thinking about 'writers' we need to be explicit about whether we mean the people who wielded the pen, stylus, brush or chisel, or those who composed the message. These may have been the same people, but equally may not have been, especially where materials were used that required complex technologies and specialist artisans. We also need to consider the role of people commissioning an inscription who might not themselves have been able to write or read. For instance, the production of a bronze tablet to be put up in a public place, as known from the Roman world, might involve four different types of maker: a member of the political or religious establishment to commission the work, a literate bureaucrat to compose the text, a bronzesmith to fashion the tablet, and probably a different bronze worker to chisel the letters. Of these people, only the bureaucrat had to be literate, in the sense of understanding the sense of the text. The person who produced the actual writing (whom one might think reasonable to label the 'writer') might have been copying a prototype and have had little understanding of what the text meant. Maureen Carroll (2009: 47) mentions a splendid example of this, the Roman stone funerary inscription from Annaba that reads *hic iacet corpus pueri nominandi* (here lies the body of the boy . . . insert name): the letter cutter had failed to notice that he was meant to insert a specific name!

'Readers' are equally difficult to define. We might identify fully literate (in the modern sense) readers, who could understand texts completely; we might also consider those who could perhaps read a little, but could not decipher a text in detail. There would be others who could not read at all but who 'consumed' writing through oral performance by others. Or those who did not even do this but who viewed the texts and knew they were important in some way. And who were the readers of hidden inscriptions (those on the inside of sealed tombs or even built into the construction itself)? If the intended viewers were dead people or supernatural beings, in what sense were they 'readers'?

Outline of the Book

Having formulated the theme and methodological framework for the conference in late 2008 / early 2009, we were astounded by the scale and range of the responses we received to the call for papers — a testament to the interest and need to bridge the gap between philologically and archaeologically oriented studies of writing. Twenty-five papers in total were presented at the annual conference of the Institute of Archaeology, University College London, held in May 2009. These were delivered by staff and graduate students from a range of museums and universities across the UK and from around the world, including the US, Europe and Australia.

A selection of these papers appear in this volume, exploring writing practices from the ancient past to more recent contexts, although there is a particular concentration on writing from the ancient Mediterranean region, and the Aegean in particular. This concentration reflects the responses to the original conference invitation and subsequent choices by both contributors and editors; interest in the materiality of writing is more developed in some fields than others. The diversity and asymmetry of temporal contexts and cultural areas represented may seem unconventional compared with conferences or publications for the traditional subject areas of textual or material cultural studies. Nevertheless, when mapping out a new research landscape differential engagement is to be expected — as methodological intersections between writing and material culture are identified and explored and new configurations which encourage fuller theorisation and sustained critical discourse are developed. Under these circumstances, which can be defined as a phase of ongoing epistemological reassessment, we feel that breadth should precede depth.

Fifteen[2] case studies set writing and related symbolic modes in relation to material practice including writing production, consumption and related performance and sensory experience. These studies critically explore traditional definitions and treatments of 'writing' to develop new perspectives and approaches that offer more holistic understandings of this evidence type. The volume also includes this Introduction and an Epilogue.

In spite of our emphasis on new perspectives and approaches, we have nevertheless organised the chapters in a somewhat conventional manner, generally following a geographical ordering with exceptions to allow for the treatment of subject matter according to chronological sequence. Starting with South and Meso-America, case studies shift to the Near Eastern heartland of writing and then return westwards to the Mediterranean, and on to Great Britain. We end with a methodological paper relating to the conservation of writing. This collection is not necessarily intended to be read in order, but rather dipped into at points of relevance, concern, and curiosity — hopefully prompting the reader to engage with less familiar evidence, and provoking consideration of analytical methods and interpretive frameworks that might be fruitfully adopted, adapted, or otherwise used to broaden the reader's perspective.

Indeed, over the decades, explorations of the various facets of 'written' objects make clear that the question of what constitutes 'writing' in a given society must remain an open one if it is to be understood in the terms of its users, and need not be confined to notation systems that are related directly to spoken language. In his study of the *khipus* in Andean society, **Frank Salomon** looks at the functional implications of recording with fibre. He argues that *khipus* functioned not as fixed texts but as operational devices or simulators — visual models rather than verbal transcriptions. Whether this counts as writing is less important than recognising "graphical excellence" (Tufte 1983: 182) in one of its less familiar forms.

Sarah Jackson places similar emphasis on the importance of a context sensitive approach. Mayan image and text intersect and intertwine in profound ways and it is difficult if not ill-advised to attempt to separate them. In practice, writing may not be distinct from other symbolic modes, or may encompass multiple symbolic functions. Too rigid a definition may preclude identification of significant and meaningful relationships, hence the importance of taking account of this evidence type in terms of situated practice. Jackson interprets her examples of Mayan writing as an "orientational technology" that serves to locate people in culturally defined landscapes, especially socio-political landscapes that include both experiential and imagined aspects.

Roger Matthews discusses the earliest, and one of the longest-lasting, traditions of writing: the "cuneiform culture" of the ancient Near East. Initially developed as a system of writing on clay tablets and used mainly for accounting purposes, cuneiform also appears on many other media and was used for many different languages and a great variety of purposes. He shows how new research focussing on the materiality of cuneiform texts is addressing questions about the role(s) of writing in different Near Eastern societies.

Rachael Sparks considers how during the 2nd millennium BCE the southern Levant became the meeting point for a number of different writing traditions, involving different languages and scripts, but also different materials, tools, and practices, as well as different contexts of use. She shows how this mixture of influences and practices allowed an unusual fluidity and experimentation with writing that led to the local development of alphabetic scripts.

Helène Whittaker investigates material practices associated with all the scripts of the Aegean Middle and Late Bronze Ages — Hieroglyphic, Linear A and Linear B (c.2000–1200 BCE) in the context of palace bureaucracies. While concentrating on the materials employed and the techniques used for writing, in addition to script and language, she also demonstrates the relationships between context, text-content and the forms of material expression employed in constructing wider social meaning.

Sarah Finlayson also examines the three main writing systems of the Bronze Age Aegean in terms of the relationships between writing and its material supports. She adopts the basic hypothesis that the shape of objects which bear writing derives from the use to which they, object + writing, are put and the shape changes as this purpose changes. Focussing particularly on Linear A, which appears on a diverse range of writing supports, she assesses whether the different materials and objects relate in an organised way to the different uses they were put to, e.g. clay tablets to administrative purposes and 'libation tables' to ritual use.

Georgia Flouda focusses on Minoan writing (therefore excluding Linear B) and considers how different forms of expression worked, examining features such as material, shape, mode and direction of writing, as well as archaeological context. She demonstrates different trajectories for Hieroglyphic (seals, tablets, and other types) and Linear A respectively. She draws heavily on semiotic theory especially the work of Peirce, suggesting, for instance, that the isolated 'pictographic' signs first appearing on the seals were understood as semasiographic codes.

Helena Tomas also considers Aegean Bronze Age writing, but concentrates on one specific phenomenon: the practice of cutting clay tablets (with a special emphasis on Linear B). A detailed study of the location of the cuts and the way they were carried out suggests two different motivations. Whereas the page-shaped tablets were probably cut in order to remove unnecessary clay (probably to keep tablet size to a minimum), elongated tablets may have been cut for the purpose of rearranging the information (for instance, a reclassification according to the origin of the people registered).

With particular emphasis on Greek-speaking and -writing areas, **Alan Johnston** examines the influence of different surfaces and the use of brush, pen and chisel on the appearance of text in the early centuries (c.800 to 300 BCE) of alphabetic writing. In addition to writerly issues, aids for the reader such as the boustrophedon system and use of interpuncts are also considered for the tensions they exhibit between aesthetic concerns and practicality.

Whereas writing is often understood to be a system developed by elite members of society to consolidate authority, and fix social meanings and relationships, **Kathryn Piquette** explores late 4th and early 3rd millennium BCE evidence from Egypt which reveals the dynamic unfolding and reformulation of early writing and related imagery. Focussing on funerary labels of bone, ivory and wood, stone vessels and a stele, Piquette considers the implications of practices of un-making, re-making, and incompletion.

Stephen Kidd considers a single document, a 3rd-century BCE Greco-Egyptian letter inscribed on papyrus: a bilingual letter, written in Greek and Demotic. The second language is used specifically to detail a dream which the author, Ptolemaios, claims has to be described in Egyptian. The change of language also involved a change in script, associated with very different material practices. So the shift was informed not only by the languages as they were processed in the author's brain, but also by the scripts themselves as they were experienced in the motions of his hands, the movement of his eyes, and the material objects he used to interact with these scripts.

Elisa Perego considers 'Situla Art', an elaborate figurative decorative style found mainly on bronze objects during the 7th to 3rd centuries BCE around the head of the Adriatic Sea. She adopts the concept of iconic literacy — the skill of producing and interpreting images — to study situla art and compare it to traditional textual literacy, which develops at approximately the same time in parts of the region. She argues that both inscribed objects and the products of situla art were employed to negotiate and promote the social role of high-ranking individuals. However, because true writing and situla art rarely occur on the same objects, she suggests that they were seen as *alternative* systems of communication, and that situla art, which was not restricted to the users of a single spoken language, could be understood over a wider geographical area.

Ruth Whitehouse's chapter is also based on evidence from the north Italian Iron Age and looks specifically at tomb markers of different types and inscribed in two different languages, Etruscan and Venetic. In contrast to traditional studies concerned with languages and scripts, she concentrates on the different physical arrangements of the inscriptions on the stones and what these meant in terms of bodily movements and sensory engagements on the part of both the makers ('writers') and consumers ('readers') of the texts.

We then turn to **Craig Cessford** who examines 18th- and 19th-century writing from the Grand Arcade site in Cambridge, England. He focusses on the ways in which material type, size, form and function of different kinds of artefact affect how writing was deployed. Cessford also considers why writing occurs incompletely or not at all on certain object types, highlighting a general yet critical issue for investigators of written culture — of accounting for absence alongside presence, and visibility as well as invisibility.

Elizabeth Pye draws our attention to the impact of the presence of writing, or the potential to reveal writing, on objects for decisions relating to conservation procedures and perceived values of objects. The common practice of prioritising the revealing of writing may lead to adverse effects on the preservation of the writing supports — a problem that may be alleviated by modern techniques of digital imaging. However, digital imaging produces its own problems, as computer hardware and software themselves require conservation.

Finally, **John Bennet** brings the book to a close with an overview of writing and its ancient material expressions as covered in the chapters in this volume, while also reflecting on changing materialities and practices associated with modern emerging writing technologies.

Writing as Material Practice: Previous and recent research

Since the inception of the conference in early 2008, its convening in mid-2009, and in the course of editing this volume, we have learnt of work on material aspects of writing relating, both ancient and modern, which were unfamiliar to us and which we would have been unlikely to discover through usual bibliographic search mechanisms. Nonetheless, at the time of writing, no book-length work exists that takes the materiality of writing as its central theme, nor is there one that draws together a wide range of examples from different cultural contexts. This does not mean that there is no interest in the subject — far from it — but research has been intermittent and dispersed. Traditionally writing has been almost exclusively the realm of philologists, linguists, historians and literary specialists who have been concerned primarily with issues of language and the meaning (in the sense of translation) of texts. Such work is vital, but as recent research is demonstrating, attentiveness to the relationship between scribal practice, materials and tools, and textual meanings is also essential (e.g. Taylor 2011). Other areas of textual studies such as book history and religious studies are increasingly recognising that writing is not a transparent medium of language which needs materiality only at its place of application or illustration, but that "... writing's very materiality influences the range of interpretive responses and receptions of the text" (Frantz 1998; see also O'Hara et al. 2002).

Within archaeology, 'writing' and other forms of 'visual culture'[3] have remained peripheral to discussions of material culture and past human experience. Reconstructed material worlds are populated with pots, lithics and other implements, items of adornment and an array of other objects, but inscriptions, writings, documents, texts, manuscripts, and so on feature all too rarely. Similarly, charting change and continuity in the technologies of past societies represents a core area of archaeological research, and here too the technological aspects of writing production and use as material artefact only make brief appearances, if at all (e.g. Schiffer and Skibo 1987). That technological features and relationships are significant for understanding script appearance, meaning and function has long been recognised within papyrology (e.g. Tait and Leach 2000). The mechanics of writing, from tool use and material selection, as well as posture and the bodily movement of the scribe at work are important for understanding writing technologies. Writers may produce their materials and tools themselves, or acquire them from others (Palaima 1985: 102; 1988: 27; Quirke 2011: 280; Sjöquist and Åström 1991: 7, 20, 29–30; Taylor 2011: 7–12, 21–23). The importance of materiality and technology is also recognised within cuneiform studies. Jonathon Taylor (2011) has recently presented a survey of material aspects of cuneiform clay tablets. While sign morphology may be the primary vehicle of meaning expression, it can also be bound up with other material aspects, such as types of clay, their preparation and use as tablet cores or the sheets of finer clay wrapped around them, overall tablet shape, surface formatting, stylus shape and the techniques of incision or impression. Fuller consideration of writing materials and technologies are crucial to a holistic account of textual and related meanings, from dating to charting processes of change and continuity (Quirke 2011: 280), knowledge transfer and skills acquisition and processes of professionalisation, to aspects of writer or copyist social identity and relationships (e.g. Janssen 1987) within scribal and wider communities of practice. It is within this unfolding discourse that this volume aims to contribute momentum.

Concluding Remarks

This collection of papers explicitly addresses the roles of materials and materiality in the contexts of production and consumption of writing, as well as problems of scholarly documentation of writing and the incorporation of its material aspects. By uniting diverse researchers around the common theme of writing as material practice, it is clear that regardless of temporal, geographical or cultural context, investigation of graphical culture for its material qualities constitutes a rich and fruitful area of inquiry. We hope that this volume provides an invaluable resource for those seeking to develop their own research in this area, and for all with an interest in the phenomenon of 'writing' in its broadest sense.

Notes

[1] Contributors to this volume use these terms slightly different ways.

² In assembling these chapters from authors using both American and British spellings, we have decided to let each author follow either convention, while maintaining consistency within each chapter.

³ This term is used here with an awareness of the importance of other forms of sensory perception.

References

Andrén, A. 1998. *Between Artefacts and Texts: Historical archaeology in global perspective.* New York: Plenum Press. DOI: http://dx.doi.org/10.1007/978-1-4757-9409-0

Barrett, J. C. 2001. Agency, the Duality of Structure, and the Problem of the Archaeological Record. In Hodder, I. (ed.), *Archaeological Theory Today.* Cambridge: Polity Press, 141–164.

Beard, M., Bowman, A. K., Corbier, M., Cornell, T., Franklin Jr., J. L., Hanson, A., Hopkins, K. and Horsfall, N. (eds) 1991. *Literacy in the Roman World* (Journal of Roman Archaeology Supplementary Series 3). Ann Arbor, MI: Department of Classical Studies, University of Michigan.

Bottéro, J. 1992. *Mesopotamia: Writing, reasoning and the gods.* Chicago: University of Chicago Press.

Bottéro, J. 2000. Religion and Reasoning in Mesopotamia. In Bottéro, J., Herrenschmidt, C. and Vernant J. P. (eds), *Ancestor of the West: Writing, reasoning and religion in Mesopotamia, Elam and Greece.* Chicago: University of Chicago Press, 3–66.

Bourdieu, P. 1977. *Outline of a Theory of Practice* (translated by Richard Nice) (Cambridge Studies in Social and Cultural Anthropology 16). Cambridge University Press. DOI: http://dx.doi.org/10.1017/CBO9780511812507

Carroll, M. 2009. 'Vox tua nempe mea est': Dialogues with the dead in Roman funerary commemoration. *Accordia Research Papers* 11(2007–2008): 37–76.

Collins, J. and Blot, R. K. 2003. *Literacy and Literacies: Texts, power, and identity* (Studies in the Social and Cultural Foundations of Language 22). Cambridge: Cambridge University Press. DOI: http://dx.doi.org/10.1017/CBO9780511486661

David, N. and Kramer, C. 2001. *Ethnoarchaeology in Action.* Cambridge: Cambridge University Press.

Dobres, M. A. 2000. *Technology and Social Agency: Outlining a practice theory for archaeology.* Maiden, MA: Blackwell Publishers.

Fahlander, F. and Kjellström, A. (eds) 2010. *Making Sense of Things: Archaeologies of sensory perception* (Stockholm Studies in Archaeology 53). Stockholm: Postdoctoral Archaeological Group Publications.

Foucault, M. 1979. *Discipline and Punish: The birth of the prison.* Harmondsworth: Peregrine Books.

Frantz, N. P. 1998. Material Culture, Understanding, and Meaning: Writing and picturing. *Journal of the American Academy of Religion* 66(4): 791–816. DOI: http://dx.doi.org/10.1093/jaarel/66.4.791

Gardner, A. 2003. Seeking a Material Turn: The artefactuality of the Roman empire. In Carr, G., Swift, E. and Weekes, J. (eds), *TRAC 2002: Proceedings of the 12ᵗʰ Annual Theoretical Roman Archaeology Conference, Canterbury 2002*, 1–13. Oxford: Oxbow.

Gardner, A. 2004. Introduction: Social agency, power, and being human. In Gardner, A. (ed.), *Agency Uncovered: Archaeological perspectives on social agency, power, and being human.* London: UCL Press, 1–15.

Gibson, J. J. 1979. *The Ecological Approach to Visual Perception.* Boston, MA: Houghton Mifflin.

Giddens, A. 1979. *Central Problems in Social Theory.* London: Macmillan.

Giddens, A. 1984. *The Constitution of Society: Outline of the theory of structuration.* Berkeley: University of California Press.

Harris, W. V. 1989. *Ancient Literacy.* Cambridge, MA: Harvard University Press.

Hawkes, C. 1954. Archaeology Theory and Method: Some suggestions from the Old World. *American Anthropologist* 56(2): 155–168. DOI: http://dx.doi.org/10.1525/aa.1954.56.2.02a00020

Hodder, I. 2000. Agency and Individuals in Long-Term Processes. In Dobres, M.-A. and Robb, J. E. (eds), *Agency in Archaeology*. London: Routledge, 21–23.

Ingold, T. 2007. Materials Against Materiality. *Archaeological Dialogues* 14(1): 1–16. DOI: http://dx.doi.org/10.1017/S1380203807002127

Janssen, J. J. 1987. On Style in Egyptian Handwriting. *Journal of Egyptian Archaeology* 73: 161–167. DOI: http://dx.doi.org/10.2307/3821527

Jay, M. 2002. That Visual Turn: The advent of visual culture. *Journal of Visual Culture* 1(1): 87–92. DOI: http://dx.doi.org/10.1177/147041290200100108

Little, B. J. (ed.) 1992. *Text-Aided Archaeology*. Boca Raton, FL: CRC Press.

Matthews, R. 2003. *The Archaeology of Mesopotamia: Theories and approaches*. London: Routledge.

Mitchell, W. J. T. 2002. Showing Seeing: A critique of visual culture. *Journal of Visual Culture* 1(2): 165–181. DOI: http://dx.doi.org/10.1177/147041290200100202

Moreland, J. 2001. *Archaeology and Text*. London: Duckworth.

Moreland, J. 2006. Archaeology and Texts: Subservience or enlightenment. *Annual Review of Anthropology* 35: 135–151. DOI: http://dx.doi.org/10.1146/annurev.anthro.35.081705.123132

O'Hara, K. P., Taylor, A., Newman, W. and Sellen, A. J. 2002. Understanding the Materiality of Writing from Multiple Sources. *International Journal of Human-Computer Studies* 56(3): 269–305. DOI: http://dx.doi.org/10.1006/ijhc.2001.0525

Palaima, T. G. 1985. Appendix. In Åström, P. and Sjöquist, K.-E. (eds), *Pylos: Palmprints and palmleaves* (Studies in Mediterranean Archaeology, Pocket book no. 31). Göteburg: Paul Åströms Förlag, 99–107.

Palaima, T. G. 1988. *The Scribes of Pylos* (Incunabula Graeca 87). Rome: Edizioni dell'Ateneo.

Piquette, K. E. 2007. *Writing, 'Art' and Society: A contextual archaeology of the inscribed labels of Late Predynastic–Early Dynastic Egypt*. Unpublished PhD dissertation, University College London.

Piquette, K. E. 2008. Re-materialising Script and Image. In Gashe, V. and Finch, J. (eds), *Current Research in Egyptology 2008: Proceedings of the ninth annual symposium, which took place at the KNH Centre for Biomedical Egyptology, University of Manchester, January 2008*. Bolton: Rutherford Press Limited, 89–107.

Piquette, K. E. forthcoming. Scribal Practice and an Early Dynastic Stone Vessel Inscriptions: Material and aesthetic implications. In Dodson, A., Johnston, J. J. and Monkhouse, W. (eds), *A Good Scribe and an Exceedingly Wise Man: Studies in honour of W. J. Tait*. London: Golden House.

Piquette, K. E. 2013. Structuration and the Graphical in Early Dynastic Culture. In Dann, R. J. and Exell, K. (eds), *Egypt: Ancient histories, modern archaeologies*. Amherst, NY: Cambria Press, 51–99.

Quirke, S. 2011. Agendas for Digital Palaeography in an Archaeological Context: Egypt 1800 BC. In Fischer, F. Fritze, C, and Vogeler, G. (eds), *Kodikologie und Paläographie im digitalen Zeitalter 2 - Codicology and Palaeography in the Digital Age 2* (Schriften des Instituts für Dokumentologie und Editorik 3). Norderstedt: Books on Demand (BoD), 279–294. http://kups.ub.uni-koeln.de/id/eprint/4354 [accessed 18 October 2013]

Schiffer, M. B. and Skibo, J. M. 1987. Theory and Experiment in the Study of Technological Change. *Current Anthropology* 28(5): 595–622. DOI: http://dx.doi.org/10.1086/203601

Schlanger, N. 1996. Understanding Levallois: Lithic technology and cognitive archaeology. *Cambridge Archaeological Journal* 6(2): 231–254. DOI: http://dx.doi.org/10.1017/S0959774300001724

Sjöquist, K.-E. and Åström, P. 1991. *Knossos: Keepers and kneaders* (Studies in Mediterranean Archaeology, Pocket book no. 82). Gothenburg: Paul Åströms Förlag.

Skeates, R. 2010. *An Archaeology of the Senses: Prehistoric Malta*. Oxford: Oxford University Press.

Smith, M. 2008. *Visual Culture Studies*. Los Angeles: Sage.

Tait, J. and Leach, B. 2000. Papyrus. In Shaw, I. and Nicholson, P. (eds), Ancient Egyptian Materials and Technology. Cambridge: Cambridge University Press, 227–253.

Taylor, J. 2011. Tablets as Artefacts, Scribes as Artisans. In Radner, K. and Robson, E. (eds), *Oxford Handbook of Cuneiform Culture*. Oxford: Oxford University Press, 5–31. DOI: http://dx.doi.org/10.1093/oxfordhb/9780199557301.013.0001

Tite, M. S. 2008. Ceramic Production, Provenance and Use — A review. *Archaeometry* 50(2): 216–231. DOI: http://dx.doi.org/10.1111/j.1475-4754.2008.00391.x

Tufte, E. 1983 *The Visual Display of Quantitative Information*. Cheshire, CT: Graphics Press.

Wenger, E. 1998. *Communities of Practice: Learning, meaning, and identity*. Cambridge: Cambridge University Press. DOI: http://dx.doi.org/10.1017/CBO9780511803932

Whitehouse, R. D. 2008. *The Materiality of Writing: Case studies from first millennium BC Italy*. McDonald Lecture. 19 November 2008; unpublished.

Whitehouse, R. D. 2012. Epilogue: Agency and writing. In Englehardt, J. (ed.), *Agency in Ancient Writing*. Boulder, CO: University Press of Colorado.

Woodward, A. and Leach, P. with contributions by Bayley, J. 1993. *The Uley Shrines: Excavation of a ritual complex on West Hill, Uley, Gloucestershire, 1977–9* (Archaeological report [English Heritage] 17). London: English Heritage in association with British Museum Press.

The Twisting Paths of Recall: Khipu (Andean cord notation) as artifact

Frank Salomon

University of Wisconsin-Madison

The most complex system of writing (using the word in a broad sense) that Andean peoples possessed before the Spanish invasion of 1532 was the cord- and knot-based medium called *khipu* (Quechua) or *quipu* (Spanish). The material makeup of khipu is a story of variation over time, with some longue durée continuities. Khipu had a brief, spectacularly productive heyday as the official medium of the Inka state (established some time during the 15th century CE until 1532 CE). The great majority of all the 600-odd more or less complete khipus held in museums and accessible private collections are catalogued as imperial Inka artifacts, but new radiocarbon results show that some date from the Spanish colony (Cherkinsky and Urton, forthcoming). The Ethnologisches Museum in Berlin and the American Museum of Natural History in New York have the largest collections. Online offerings suggest that an unknown number of them (some fake) are in other hands. Inka khipus were largely standardized in format and material content (**Figure 1**).

But Inkas are not the only principals in this story. The cord medium underwent a long, varied evolution both before and after khipus' brief Inka florescence. Both pre- and post-Inka khipus differed widely from Inka ones in physical substance and form. This chapter consists of a historical and a functional section. In the first half I discuss material attributes of Inka, pre-Inka, and post-Inka khipus, respectively, with emphasis on change. By contrast, in the second half of this chapter I emphasize material continuity: material traits that make a khipu a khipu, and how they affect culture as lived through inscription. For the spatial distribution of the evidence discussed, see the map in **Figure 2**.

Recent Research Historical Variation in Khipu

Material Support of Meaning in the Inka Canon

Inka-era khipus' physical characteristics as substrate for meaning have been the object of intense study since the 1920s, largely by archaeologists hosted in museums. Inka khipus are

How to cite this book chapter:
Salomon, F. 2013. The Twisting Paths of Recall: Khipu (Andean cord notation) as artifact. In: Piquette, K. E. and Whitehouse, R. D. (eds.) *Writing as Material Practice: Substance, surface and medium*. Pp. 15-43. London: Ubiquity Press. DOI: http://dx.doi.org/10.5334/bai.b

Figure 1: Khipu demonstrates repeating colour sequence. 64-19-1-1-6-2 of the Musée de l'Homme (now in Musée du Quai Branly).

overwhelmingly made of cotton, but a few camelid wool examples survive (Conklin 2002: 61). The predominance of cotton may just be an artifact of better preservation on the cotton-using desert coast. Early colonial sources with Inka informants usually mention camelid wool as the common medium. Basic Inka khipu structure (**Figure 3**) consists of a main cord to which knottable pendant cords were fixed by half-hitches. Pendants are frequently grouped in sets of n cords, with spaces between them. Often, a group contains a repeating sequence of colors. But the alternative — colors occurring in bands — is also common. In this author's opinion the two patterns reflect complementary genera, such as planning / execution. Pendant fiber is usually of natural color (Peruvian cotton being of varied hue in the white-to-dark brown range), but dyed colors (particularly blue) occur. At least three separate techniques were used to create bi-colored or multicolored pendants: a 'barber pole' pattern of spirals, a mottled pattern, and a type in which a single cord changes color along its course.

Especially in main cords, plying may be complex. Occasionally a bright-colored thread is 'run through' as supplementary ply, acting to 'underline' a cord. Pendants may carry subsidiary pendants as in **Figure 4**, and subsidiaries in turn may carry sub-subsidiaries, etc. Registries may be several hierarchical layers deep. Knots were normally of only three types (**Figure 5**). It is now over 80 years since Leland Locke (1923; 1928) discovered how the three types were deployed in decimal arrays, encoding arithmetical relationships. The pioneering khipu experts Marcia and Robert Ascher argue that about 80% of khipu are numerical. A pendant normally bears a single number expressed in base-10 positional notation (**Figure 6**). Sometimes special pendants called top cords contain summations over pendants.

Locke's work, however, left out of account almost all properties *except* knots. A surge of research beginning in 1990 has striven to change this situation. The point of departure was Ascher and Ascher's massive 1981 study of museum khipus (republished 1997: 57). The Aschers emphasized

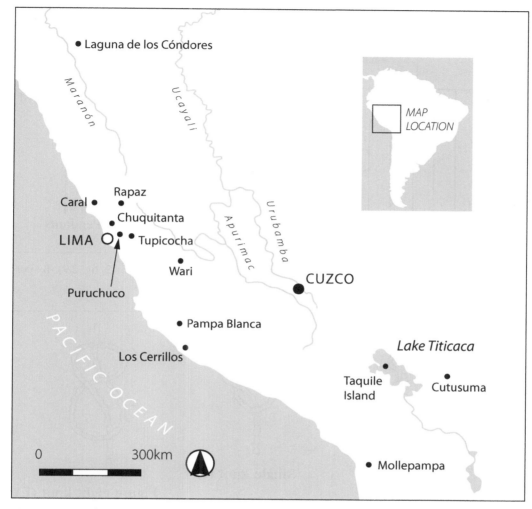

Figure 2: Map showing main locations mentioned in the text.

"Inca insistence" on "spatial arrangements [that] use formal repetition and recombination of basic elements": in other words, that the combinations of knots signaling numbers are only parts of larger combinatorial structures.

The textile archaeologist William Conklin concentrates on the material basis of such structures. He has revisited khipu structure with a maximalist hypothesis, cognate to Urton's model (2003) about how many features might bear coded meaning. Beyond knotting, he also considers colors, color combinations, S / Z (rightward versus leftward), plying, S / Z knotting, and 'obverse / reverse' (also called 'recto / verso') placement of pendants' attachment loops. The maximalist approaches of Conklin and Urton have greatly increased the number of potentially recognizable patternings, and with it the quantity of information khipus could plausibly be supposed to hold. Estimating six data-bearing variables (of which one is a knotted number up to 10,000), and calculating the number of possible data-states they allow, Conklin calculated that "each…secondary cord [i.e. pendant] could theoretically hold…8 million differing combinations or states" (Conklin 2002: 81). Where the line between 'emically' meaningful variation and variation in sub-meaningful material support lies, remains a fundamental question.

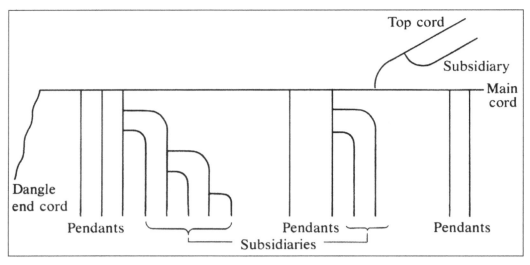

Figure 3: Basic khipu terminology and structure (Ascher and Ascher 1997: 12, fig. 2.7). By permission of Marcia Ascher and Robert Ascher.

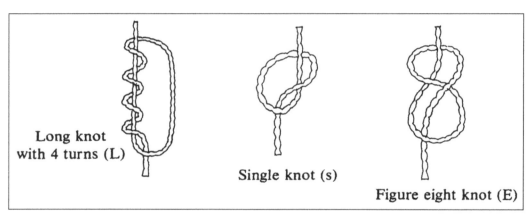

Figure 4: Three common knots used in Inka khipus: Left: Inka long knot of value four, used in units place; center, simple (s) knot; right, figure-eight (E) knot (Ascher and Ascher 1997: 29, fig. 2.11). By permission of Marcia Ascher and Robert Ascher.

In the course of a vast continuing study which has almost tripled the number of Inka khipus under study at the time of the Aschers' book (1997 [1981]), Gary Urton formulated a more precise model of the relation between cord structures and encoded meanings. He holds that inherently dualistic processes of spinning and plying (over / under, left / right) are congenial analogues for Native South American cultures' pervasive cultural binarism (Urton 2003: 149–151). Andean societies prefer dual models for many sorts of organization: 'high' and 'low' moieties, left / right bank settlements, senior / junior lineages, dry/wet semesters, mountainside / valleyside lands, male / female cults. Such binarisms are not simple symmetries but have an element of markedness / unmarkedness in the linguistic sense. I have previously characterized such pairings as "symmetrical in form, complementary in function, and unequal in rank" (Salomon 2004: 192). Andean anthropologists generally agree that the pairing of many things and roles reflects a general cultural template. From Inka to modern times whole khipus have been made in sets of two (**Figure 7**, see also **Figure 20**).

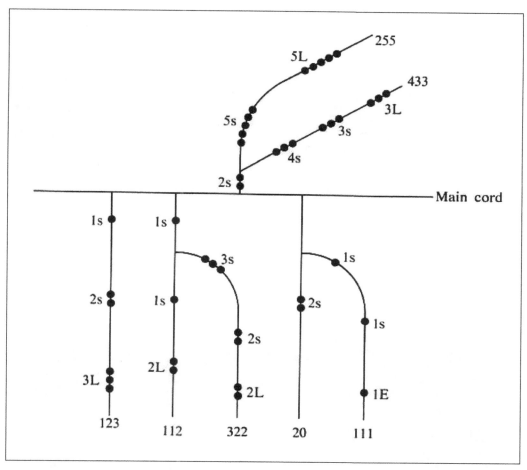

Figure 5: A khipu with arithmetical values. The topcord sums the values of pendants, and the topcord's subsidiary those of the pendants' subsidiaries (Ascher and Ascher 1997: 31, fig. 2.14). By permission of Marcia Ascher and Robert Ascher.

For Urton, a sequence of seven binary manufacturing operations, of which knotting is only the last, produces cords. Each step involves a choice between dual alternatives, e.g. cotton versus wool fiber (with wool as marked) or S / Z (rightward versus leftward) final plying (with Z as marked). The seven, in sequence, are 1) choice of fiber; 2) choice of colors considered as choice between two locally conceived spectra; 3) S / Z final plying; 4) recto / verso pendant attachment; 5) S / Z knotting; 6) 'number class' (a variable constructed upon an Andean model of complete / incomplete numbers); 7) decimal / non-decimal 'information type' (Urton 2003: 120). Thus, he holds, any given pendant constitutes a 'seven-bit' data aggregate.

Inka khipu code, he therefore argues, is made of such data-chunks materially incarnated in fiber, much as ASCII computer code is made of eight-bit groups of 0s and 1s materialized as bands of magnetized / demagnetized surface. Meaningfulness is not knotted onto a blank cord; the sum of all the cord's attributes determines its meaning. The inventory of possible seven-bit cords is, however, not in itself a code. Rather it makes up an array of related physical forms which become a code when meanings are assigned to each. Meaning may have been assigned in variable ways.

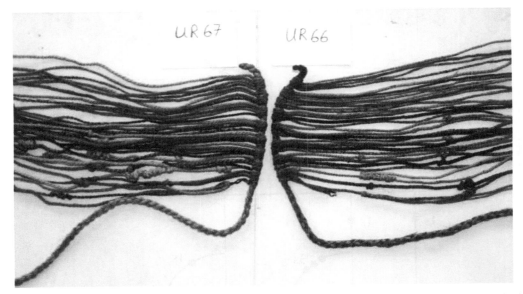

Figure 6: Paired khipu from Puruchuco: these two Inka-era specimens (UR 66–67) were rolled together, and bear similar color patterning. Photograph courtesy of Gary Urton.

Figure 7: Khipus of Wari affiliation, several centuries earlier than Inka examples, bear information in the form of colored thread lashed around pendant cords. American Museum of Natural History T-223. Photograph courtesy of Carmen Arellano.

Much as eight-bit bundles of 0s and 1s can be programmed to stand for alphabetic characters, but equally well for colors or sounds, a cord might well be coded to stand for a word (and thus become a logogram); but it might equally well be coded to a nonverbal entity.

Figure 8: Wrapped sticks from funerary context at the Paracas site of Cerrillos. Photograph courtesy of Jeffrey Splitstoser.

Thus Urton's model is more a model about *how* cords can mean, than about *what* they mean. On those terms, it has proven productive. Urton has shown that previously unstudied physical variables do in some specimens obey non-random patterns which all but certainly were made to convey a meaning. For example in one case (Urton 2003: 87), the maker of a khipu divided it into four quadrants, two of which use Z-knots and the other two S-knots. Was this a 'meta' feature, like punctuation, which shows a user how to voice or interpret the data? Or was it a direct classification of the referents into four subsets, forming pairs among themselves, within the dataset? We do not know. But the maximalist hypothesis about how many Inka khipu features are significant, i.e. contribute to sign value, is now known to yield patterned Inka complexities above and beyond arithmetical patterns.

Before the Inka Canon: Wrapping and knotting for the dead and the living

Up to this point I have commented only on canonical Inka-type khipus. But it has become evident that, like many of the culture traits which the Inkas falsely claimed as their own inventions, khipu had a long and varied pre-Inka history. In this matter, too, William Conklin has made a decisive contribution. In 1982 he showed that about 700 years before the Inka conquests began, khipus had already reached an elaborate — but very different — physical format (see **Figure 7**). One corpus consists of eight fragmentary khipus found with a Wari culture mummy at Pampa Blanca on the south coast of Peru. The burial is dated about 700 CE on ceramic criteria. Similar specimens have less clear context.

Wari, an expansive culture associated with a southern Peruvian state of possibly imperial makeup, was one of two cultures that characterize the period of far-flung cultural sharing called the Middle Horizon. Conklin identified three material peculiarities: first, "the shanks of the pendant cords are wrapped with patterned multicolored thread" (Conklin 1982: 268); second, knotting is less salient and varied: the only knots are multiple overhand knots; third, final plying is uniformly Z. Two more unprovenanced khipus, each small enough to fit in one hand but richly crafted, belong to the same type. Their thread lashings are bright-colored and complexly patterned with color bars and Xs. Both subsidiaries and knots, in contrast, are much less frequent than in Inka examples. Conklin describes a final, large and remarkable thread-wrapped khipu with 100 pendants in groups of five, and 10 different types of subsidiaries hanging from them. Conklin (1982: 277) suggests that the numerical system is base five.

Long before the Inkas, then, Middle Horizon khipu seem to have had a different material constitution. It corresponded to an exalted use, as we know from their treasure-grade craftspersonship. One equally luxurious specimen seems transitional between the Middle Horizon and Inka khipus (Pereyra 1997). The Inkas held Middle Horizon remains in reverence as 'prototypes' (*dechados*; Betanzos 1987 [1551]: 11–13) of their world, and may have viewed thread-wrapping as a sign of archaic glory. If they associated wrapping with remote antiquity they were not mistaken, for this practice appears in textiles of a cultural horizon very much older than even the Middle Horizon: that is, the Chavín or Early Horizon, about 1000 BCE.

There is another Andean medium that emphasizes wrapping. Thread-wrapping of sticks had a two-millennium life alongside thread-wrapping of khipus. Jeffrey Splitstoser has studied four-color Chavín-influenced wrapped sticks from the Paracas site of Cerrillos (Conklin and Splitstoser 2009; see **Figure 8**). They accompanied a female burial dating to about 200 BCE. Imagery of birds carrying such sticks ranges from Chavín through Middle Horizon chronology. Numerous wrapped sticks of immediately pre-Inka, Inka, or immediately post-Inka times are preserved in museums (see **Figure 9**). Herrmann and Meyer (1993) have published astonishing images of late prehispanic mummies holding wrapped sticks (see **Figure 10**).

What do wrapped sticks have to do with mummies? Miguel Cabello Valboa, a chronicler who had access to local native informants (Núñez-Carvallo 2008: 92), among them the half-Inka Jesuit Blas Valera, states that the last prehispanic Inka sovereign, when he felt death approaching, "made his testament as was the custom…putting lines [*rayas*] with different colors on a stick, from which they knew his last and final will, and which was given in care to a khipu master" (Cabello Valboa 1951 [1586]: 393).

It seems, therefore, that a very ancient, elaborate thread-wrapping medium belonged to funerary culture, perhaps holding directives for the permanent ritual treatment of the ancestor. Middle Horizon khipu may have been born when another, knot-based medium was combined with it. The origin of the knotting medium is unknown. Ruth Shady et al. (2000) identifies a knotted object from Caral on the Pacific coast as a khipu at least 3000 years old (Mann 2005: 1008), but other archaeologists have yet to confirm the identification. On less controversial grounds Shady et al. (2000) also show a knotted specimen *c.*650–750 CE from Lima, roughly contemporary with Conklin's (1982) thread-wrapped type.

After the Inka Canon: The khipu – paper interface and its modern successors

Contrary to what one reads in classics of grammatology, khipus had a vigorous continuing history in the colonial era (Salomon 2008). Khipu use up to about 1600 CE has been well researched, most comprehensively by Pärssinen and Kiviharju (2004), and also by historians such as Sempat Assadourian (2002), de la Puente Luna and Curátola (2008), and Loza (1998).

Figure 9: Wrapped sticks of late prehispanic and / or colonial dates in the collection of the Peabody Museum, Harvard. Photograph courtesy of William Conklin.

The transition from early, unstable, improvised colonial governance to the bureaucratic regime associated with Viceroy Toledo (1569–1581) also brought a transition in the information technology of empire. As a small ethnic minority in a multilingual empire thousands of kilometers long and inhabited by millions, Spaniards were at first dependent on khipu-based information flows to set up their colonial state. Spaniards from the 1530s through the 1550s relied upon khipu masters for accounting of native tribute and labor. In the 1560s they came to systematically integrate cord records with the production of new administrative papers. There arose a system of articulation between the khipu art and what the Uruguayan humanist Angel Rama (1996 [1984]) called "the lettered city" of Hapsburgian scribes and notaries. Well before 1569 Spanish courts and tribute administrators were accustomed to accepting khipu-based information as evidence in lawsuits and tribute proceedings (even though the Council of the Indies never authorized this). After 1569, in the age when *reducción* (forced resettlement) and the new political establishment of 'Indian *cabildos*' (village councils) came to counterweight the power of prehispanically-derived local dynasties, colonial governance did much more than passively take note of khipus. Spanish functionaries actively required villages to make and present administrative khipus. Lawyers, scribes, and notaries created a specific protocol governing the interface between intra-indigenous and imperial information conduits (Burns 2004).[1]

Although C14 dates of museum khipus sometimes overlap the conquest era, no museum collection has been radiocarbon dated exclusively to the colonial era. We do not yet know what material traits may correspond specifically to the colonial cord – paper interface. Urton (2001) has persuasively interpreted one specimen found in context of a post-hispanic mummy as an account of

Figure 10: Mummy from Chuquitanta with wrapped sticks. Photograph courtesy of Berndt Herrmann.

colonial tributes of the 1560s; in material makeup it resembles Inka work, with peculiarities that are more likely regional than chronological.

Early in the 17th century Spanish judges stopped admitting khipu masters to official functions. Increasingly, the khipu art apparently lodged in folk-legal proceedings off the colonial ledger. In the course of three colonial centuries, khipu shifted from being the Andean politico-administrative medium *par excellence*, to being very local, intracommunal records created in a sphere of cultural privacy.

After independence (various dates of the 1820s in different republics), creole states recognized no specifically 'Indian' authorities as such. Now no pan-Andean khipu user community existed. Khipus were shown to outsiders mostly in the course of administering private latifundist estates. Max Uhle in 1897 published the first full description of an 'ethnographic khipu', a herder's log of animals from Cutusuma, Bolivia. Several other 20th-century reports describe herding khipus (Nuñez del Prado 1990 [1950]; Prochaska 1988; Soto Flores 1990 [1950–1951]), one from as far afield as Ecuador (Holm 1968).

Such ethnographically known khipus are the best understood ones, because in these encounters researchers were able to discuss individual khipus with their makers and users. In 2002 I interviewed several families near the northern and western shores of lake Titicaca, some Quechuaphone

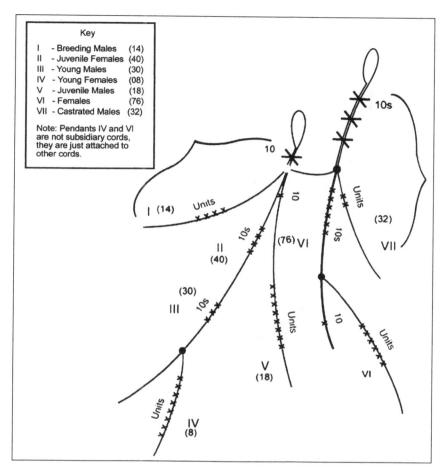

Figure 11: A herder's khipu from modern Peru, studied by Carol Mackey in the late 1960s (in Quilter and Urton 2002: 334). It analyzes a herd of llamas by reproductive status.

and others Aymarophone, about recent memories of the khipu art. Their elders could still simulate khipus made to track household properties: private herds, harvests, debts, and pending obligations. They described household khipus as small khipus which would usually be pegged to a wall, either inside the house for privacy or outside, under the eaves, for daytime convenience. All 'ethnographic' khipus are of wool.

What stands out in such 'ethnographic' khipus is their nonstandard physical makeup. Carol Mackey's important but still incompletely published 1970 study of 24 modern specimens, some of whose owners were still competent in the art, uncovered "great variability in morphology and in numeral notation" (Mackey 2002: 324), including one major class without a main cord to suspend pendants (see **Figure 11**), and another with a main cord. In the former, a data-bearing cord is bent in a 'U' and lashed to form a two-tailed armature for attaching smaller cords. Besides morphology, another general problem of khipu design is at its most visible in modern 'ethnographic' khipus: iconicity. Some 'herders' khipus' include small non-cord objects in knots. Prochaska (1983) reports that Taquile Island khipus included wood bits taken as iconic of individual animals and their condition. A few Inka specimens have tuft inclusions, as do all Rapaz specimens (see concluding section). Whether inclusions should be understood under the rubric of index, icon, or logogram remains an important issue.

Figure 12: In Tupicocha, Peru, 1995, Celso Alberco assumed the presidency of his *ayllu* (a net-work of families) by donning its khipu. Author's photograph.

Not all the modern forms of khipu, however, derive from the private sphere. Modern khipus of governance do exist, at village rather than state level. In the early 19th century, decades of weak republican administration (Thomson 2002: 269–280) gave communities in some provinces a chance to invigorate local Andean institutions of government. Some chose to prolong the use of khipu in self-administration. In a few cases, these have survived as patrimony of peasant com-munities, or their components, the segmentary corporate lineages called *ayllus*. Like herders' khi-pus, they show wide divergences in structure, as one might expect in situations of local cultural privacy. All originate in high-altitude villages (over 3000 m above sea level), and all are of wool.

A few such 'patrimonial khipus' have been studied in material detail. The most fully published patrimonial case is that of Tupicocha, in Huarochirí, Peru. Tupicocha owns 10 historical khipus (Salomon 2004; **Figure 12**) and one recently made simulacrum to replace a lost one. From 1994 to the 2009 writing of this chapter, no-one claimed competence in reading khipus. The village holds them in reverence, and uses them as regalia in the annual 'town meeting' at which authori-ties render accounts for money and works. The actual records are now made on paper, but the *quipocamayos* or *caytus* are presented as their former and forever-valid prototypes.

Tupicochan khipus are of medium size. In overall design they closely resemble the canonical Inka type (**Figure 13**). They show little if any of the 'reduction' or 'defectiveness' characteristic of

Figure 13: A khipu belonging to *ayllu* Segunda Satafasca of Tupicocha. The overall design matches canonical Inka design. Author's photograph.

moribund scripts. Made wholly or almost wholly of camelid wool, they bear richly ornamented end knobs and dorsal markers. They were obviously made to be treasured, and are spoken of as treasures: "They are our Magna Carta" is how one elder put it. The heterogeneous artifice of pendants suggests they are the work of many hands. Tupicochan khipus match in detail the khipus drawn by the "Indian chronicler" Felipe Guaman Poma de Ayala toward 1615.

Rapaz, another central-Peruvian high altitude village, owns the first set of patrimonial khipus ever to catch the eye of a researcher (Ruíz Estrada 1982). The khipu patrimony of Rapaz is the only known case where khipus endure in the original architectural complex of ritual, governance, and storage they were made to serve (**Figures 14–15**). Moreover, these buildings still house the ongoing work of traditional ceremony and production management, for whose sake khipus are held sacred. The collection consists of 263 discrete cord objects. It is not, as repeatedly misreported, a single "giant khipu" — except in the sense that the ensemble as a whole, with its separate parts, formed in local theory a single register.

The Rapaz patrimonial khipus could hardly be farther from Tupicochan khipus in material makeup (Salomon et al. 2006). Whereas Inka specimens have a single main cord from which multiple knot-bearing pendants are suspended, all the Rapaz khipus share a unilinear design in which all apparent signs are attached directly to a single, sometimes very long cord of camelid or (less often) sheep wool. Some exceed 15 m, but it remains to be seen how much of the length is due to mending. The unilinear Rapaz design is more suggestive of seriated emblems (such as a Siouan winter count, that is, a chronicle composed of emblems for memorable events, or a Panamanian Kuna pictographic manuscript) than of data arrayed on the dual (horizontal / vertical) axes of Inka design. Rapaz emblems, unlike signs on blank hide or paper, rest upon a linear substrate that is complex in its own right. Both S and Z final plying of main cords are common. Main cords range very widely in design, from monochromes to eight-ply specimens with elaborate multiple plying. Almost all their colors are natural fiber hues, but in a few cases plies of

Figure 14: Kaha Wayi, the house of ritual and traditional governance in Rapaz. It houses a large collection of vernacular khipus. Author's photograph.

Figure 15: In 2004, Toribio Gallardo shows Rapaz's khipu collection. Author's photograph.

Figure 16: Some Rapaz khipus bear textile figurines. Author's photograph.

died wool extend through mostly-natural cords. Dye colors are greenish-blue or mustard yellow. The features attached to the main cord are not pendants in the Inka sense. Only one pendant-like structure in the whole collection is attached with the conventional Inka half-hitch. Rather, attached signs are typically knotted onto the main cord. Common attached signs can consist of either a short piece of tied-on cord, or a short tie-on holding some small object. Most such cords are knotted onto the whole main cord overhand, while some run between plies of the main cord. The objects they bear at their distal ends are tufts of wool in various natural colors, tags of raw-hide, tags of hide with wool still on it, pompoms (frequently bicolored), and, in 10 cases, figurines (**Figure 16**).

One other patrimonial corpus has been described. Nelson Pimentel (2005), working in south-western Bolivia, has written about what might be called patrimonial 'memory khipus'. Their originals have been lost. Elders who informed Pimentel replicated with modern yarn four khipus of apparently communal scope. These cords appear to have served as accounts of sacrifices (*challay*), genealogy, harvests and herds. In some of them, design at the coarsest level resembles the Inca canon. Smaller features may also be relevant to Inka traits: for example, one occasionally finds an Inka pendant tied around an adjacent similar one, a structure here explained as meaning that the former cord annuls the latter (Pimentel 2005: 29). Pimentel's cords also include structures and conventions potentially relevant to Inka format but not recognized in Urton's scheme: length of pendants, thickness of pendants, internodal distance, and minor but significant variations of shade within one color (e.g. violet for 'rebellion' as against purple for 'war', Pimentel 2005: 143). Salomon found related attributions of meaning to these academically unrecognized variables in Tupicocha. And finally, there are structures unknown in Inka khipus, such as cord interlacing (taken as a sign of actions in concert).

The Functional Implications of Recording with Fiber

Up to this point I have only supplied a factual base about the changing materiality of khipus. But were there material constants that affect the properties of the medium as a whole? And how consequential are they for expression and meaning? How did the specificity of cord influence ways to share meaning visually?

Relatively Light Requirements for Tools and Special Inputs

Inka testimonies claimed khipu as a monopoly of the imperial bureaucracy. But it is hard to see how the medium could have been monopolized, once one notices that all the materials and manufacturing skills — dyeing, spinning, knotting, ornamenting — are present in the routine of plebeian agropastoral households everywhere from southern Colombia to central Chile. Except for certain dyeing equipment, all the necessary gear was and is home-made and portable. Conklin (2002: 61) notes that one's own hands and toes suffice as a frame to make even complex cord. I have seen modern villagers make khipu-quality cords in minutes using no tools but the ubiquitous drop spindle.

Materially, then, khipu had a demotic potential. Moreover, Inka administration itself relied on widespread khipu competence available throughout rural society, and not on a restricted clique of experts. Martín de Murúa (1946 [1590]: 124) noted that local ethnic groups had their own khipu resources apart from Inka officialdom, and that officials depended on them for detailed records. From the 1560s through the 1590s trials often show local lords of non-Inka origin adducing khipu evidence as work of their own *khipukamayuqkuna* (khipu masters). Basic numerical khipu knowledge was widespread among *campesino* herders (male and female) up to approximately the 1960s. This demotic development underlay the medium's ability to convincingly represent Tupicocha as a totality to its own members: cords did not contain information reserved or manipulated by outsiders, but instead information transparent only to insiders.

Movable Parts

Against the grain of khipu literature, I argue that khipus functioned as operational devices or simulators, and not as fixed texts. The physical attributes of khipus, especially those in Inka or Inka-like format, suggest mobility and not fixity as the default (for other examples of physical adjustment cf. Piquette, this volume). Hernando Pizarro (1920 [1533]: 175) said that Inka accountants updated accounts by adding and removing knots. The first scholar to show that ancient khipus actually have changeable — and changed — parts was Carlos Radicati di Primeglio, in his book on "the Inka system of accounting" (1979(?): 97–102). He later summed this up:

> A quipu with knots removed from its cords and re-knotted is, strictly speaking, a palimpsest, which can be reconstructed... It is amazing with what facility one can remake the knots, based on the traces which they leave marked on the cords. Unknotting is usually found on isolated cords, but sometimes also on a whole section. (Radicati di Primeglio 1990 [1987]: 91)

Figure 17: An Inka-era khipu with all its knots removed. Photograph courtesy of Gary Urton.

By "traces" Radicati was alluding chiefly to cuts, kinks and / or color discontinuities visible where a knot was removed. One known specimen has been completely un-knotted (**Figure 17**). When the "Indian chronicler" Felipe Guaman Poma de Ayala drew khipus, he drew all but one of them knotless.

And indeed many feature of the canonical khipu seem designed for ease in making alterations. If the default is operability — that is, if the working assumption of the makers was that khipus would change — then an operational khipu would have technical features allowing easy movement, removal, and attachment of elements. This is borne out in several ways. First, the standard attachment of pendants, the half-hitch, is the optimal one to allow either removing and reattaching a pendant individually, or repositioning it by sliding, without disturbing the rest of the structure. Some Tupicochan specimens show stretches of bare main cord while other specimens have jammed main cords. These seem to be carrying more pendants than they were designed for, so cords were likely added as time went by. Second, if a *quipocamayo* served as an operational device it is likely to show heterogeneity of manufacture. Tupicochan pendants in a single band do vary in texture, tightness, diameter and degree of wear. Third, if the hallmark of an operational device is movability of sign-bearing parts, those parts which are not to be moved, or to be moved jointly if at all, should bear signs or mechanical devices that impede mobility. Several such devices are in evidence, the firmest one being the binding of a group of pendants to each other with stitches right through their attachment loops.

Lightness, Portability

It has often been noticed that khipu are a portable medium *par excellence*. They weigh little, and can be easily compressed, flexed or rolled. They are not fragile. They are well suited to a society in which logistics over extreme mountain terrain was and remains a problem. The Inka state created a human Pony Express of relay runners (*ch'aski*) who carried khipus; Guaman Poma (**Figure 18**) drew a *ch'aski* of the Inka post tearing past with a khipu labeled "letter" in his hand. The Inka empire, with its intricately standardized systems of intervention and control over local polities, can hardly be imagined without the means to move large bodies of data in standard formats over distances. It would be no exaggeration to call coding of information on textile fiber a core infrastructure of Andean social organization.

Flexibility Yielding Variable Physical State

Flexibility is also a central property, affecting storage, reference and display.

The Coiled Storage State

From Inka times to the present (**Figure 19**) khipus have been stored in a spiral position: the users extend the main cord horizontally with pendants hanging free, then wind it from the knob-end to the tail end, so that the main cord forms a spiral cone with knob-end protruding. The dangling tail end then serves to bind the pendants into a flexible, cylindrical fascicle which can be bundled with minimum tangling.

Flexible-storage design served to ease retrieval. The end knob probably identified khipus. In the surviving Tupicocha suite, each *ayllu* had paired display khipus with elaborate, distinctive knobs resembling their respective mates. Some Inka khipu also have end knobs (**Figure 20**). Having found the right khipu in storage state, a khipu user would then study the spiral-cone storage view of the main cord, using it as a table of contents, before unwinding it. Since pendants are usually clustered and color-coded, it would be easy to find the relevant cluster and string. Since khipu pendants can number over a thousand, this would be a non-trivial advantage. 'Markers' (usually colorful tufts) lashed onto main cords also served as 'bookmarks' pointing out important loci.

The Overknotted Display State

In Tupicocha, khipus are moved from storage to the annual 'town meeting' or *huayrona* in a special arrangement used at no other time. The coiled storage setup is lifted from either end, and twisted so that the whole fascicle of pendants is changed into one thick cable (10 cm or more in diameter). The handlers then wrestle the cabled khipu into a single immense knot (**Figure 21**). The owning *ayllu* parades it in state, displayed on a cushion, en route to the meeting. It acts as a visual image symbolizing all the data (knot) which will be resolved (unknotted) at the assembly. At the end of the meeting, the khipu is not re-cabled but rather carried to its home unbound, signaling the resolution of data. This practice is unknown in archaeological evidence. It appears to be a colonial or postcolonial practice derived from the inherent physical potentials of the medium.

The Suspended 'Reading' State

Surviving colonial images of khipus in use, like the numerous lawsuits registering work of khipu accountants, sometimes indicate that consultation of khipus was done by at least two people jointly as holder(s) and reader(s). An immense specimen from Mollepampa, Chile, required two people just to suspend it (Museo Chileno de Arte Precolombino 2003: 20). In Tupicocha, upon unwinding, the pendants are 'combed' by finger for clear positioning. To judge by the use of fingers in de Murúa's 1590 rendering (**Figure 22**) this might be an ancient practice.

Figure 18: Felipe Guaman Poma de Ayala drew this Inka postal runner with a khipu labeled "letter" (1980 [1615]: 178).

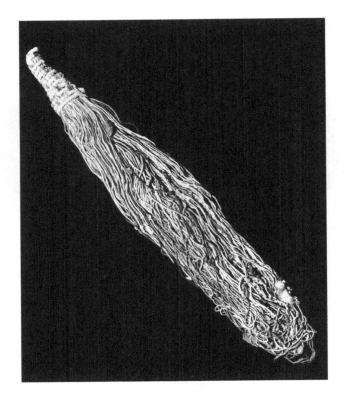

Figure 19: Inka khipu bound in fascicle for storage. Photograph courtesy of William Conklin.

Figure 20: Khipu(s) 41-2-6993 of the American Museum of Natural History are apparently marked as a pair by common attachment to a single end knob. Author's photograph.

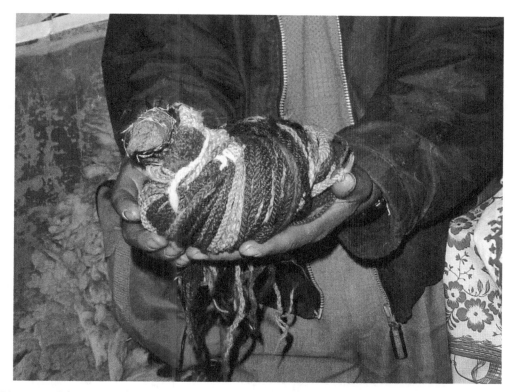

Figure 21: The Tupicochan practice of twisting an entire khipu into a single huge knot. Author's photograph.

A very few archaeological khipus have wooden frames which, instead of coiling, serve to hold the pendants in constant 'open' array for 'reading'. One example (Ascher and Ascher 1997: 97–101) consists of a pair of framed khipus with matching mathematical frameworks (Tupicochan khipus were also paired). The array is quite complex. By threading the main cord in and out of holes in the frame, the makers created "subcharts…physically back-to-back". Perhaps this technique was suited for benchmark or summary khipus requiring frequent reference, comparable to a book-stand for bound texts that need to lie open.

The Draped Ceremonial State

In Tupicocha, but not in archaeological contexts, the khipu is draped upon the body of the person who will incarnate its authority during the coming year. This, too, is a four-handed job. The out-going *ayllu* president lifts it and drapes it from the right shoulder to the left hip of the incoming president, then ties it "like a presidential sash" (as in **Figure 12**). This act climaxes and dissolves the 'town meeting', marking the moment when all past business is considered resolved and a new polit-ical cycle initiated. Although it is wordless act, draping is considered an embodied oath of office.

Draping appears to be another emergent colonial or postcolonial practice derived from the inherent physical potentials of the medium. All these khipu states functioned *between* at least two persons. Tupicochans were surprised by my attempts at solitary khipu use, as I spread khipus out horizontally on a table. They considered it indecorous to prostrate the khipu flat and to use it without social support. All signs point toward the conclusion that khipu use was considered an inherently cooperative activity.

Figure 22: The 1590 de Murúa manuscript illustrates cooperative reading and finger-sorting of cords (de Murúa 2004: 124 verso).

Expandability Through Nested and Conjoinable Design

From something hanging, one can hang something else. To something tied, one can tie something else. Khipu design uses these two physical facts to enable (in principle) the indefinite formal extension and proliferation of any given data frame. To put the same thing another way, canonical Inka khipu design and some vernacular versions are recursive, like the syntax of natural languages: into a relative clause one may insert another relative clause, etc.

Nestedness

With few exceptions (markers and other metasigns) any given cord structure may be part of a larger cord structure of the same design, or may conversely bear subordinate members of like

Figure 23: At Laguna de los Cóndores, some Inka-era khipus found with enshrined mummies were tied to each other. Photograph courtesy of Gary Urton.

design. A pendant bears subsidiaries but subsidiaries bear sub-subsidiaries. Subsidiary structures up to 12 levels deep have been found. Even a whole khipu, i.e. main cord plus pendants, may be a part of a larger khipu. Conklin observed that already in Middle Horizon khipus, "string groups… are virtually little quipus in themselves, containing up to three more hierarchies of dependency" (Conklin 1982: 277). Urton found more pervasive examples of this principle in the khipus from Laguna de los Cóndores. Two examples are visible in the lower left part of **Figure 23**. He calls the small sub-khipus slung from the main cord 'loop pendants' (Urton 2007: 25). One main cord held 24 loop pendants, each related to a corresponding but separate first-order pendant.

Nestedness pervades fiber structures. Nestedness greatly interested Inka designers, even to the point of designing tunics whose surface consisted of emblems (*tukapu*) of other whole tunics. Nested structures are congenially congruent to many hierarchies in which small structures combine to make large ones of the same form: for example, *ayllus*, or decimal brackets in Inka administration.

Conjointness

There is another way for a khipu to form a part of a larger khipu: instead of nesting, main cords are attached directly to each other (**Figure 23**). In practice it is hard to tell which junctures imply horizontal combination of two corpora, and which ones imply hierarchical subordination, but horizontal combinations certainly exist. In one case, they are joined to make a ring of main cords (**Figure 24**). Conjointness is congruent to relations among peer units, like allied polities, neighboring villages, or sibling-*ayllus*. It is important to notice that such relations do not necessarily imply equality or interchangeability, because peer segments are often seriated; in Andean ritual they stand in relations of ritual precedence, which imply rank among fellows.

Figure 24: The Peabody Museum at Harvard holds a ring-shaped set of five conjoined khipus. Photograph courtesy of the Peabody Museum.

Urton has studied numerical and categorical relations among khipus of less and more aggregated nature within a single Inka-era khipu archive, developing from the phenomenon of nesting a model of khipu 'intertextuality'. Numerical patterns in lower-level detailed khipus were extracted and summarized in more aggregated high-level ones. This practice in effect extends the phenomena of nestedness and conjointness upward and outward, regardless of whether the parts are physically tied together.

Articulation with Auxiliary Media

Formal relations within khipu could readily be transcribed into other secondary media to speed up manipulation. Transcripts of colonial trials involving khipus mention that khipu testimony was not necessarily rendered directly from cords to verbal forms, but often through an auxiliary medium, of which the usual one was small stones arranged and manipulated on the ground. Apparently this procedure enabled experts to answer by reorganizing and perhaps recalculating partial khipu contents, as one might do today with a spreadsheet, schedule chart, or wiring diagram. Manipulation through an accessory medium could be a complex enough process to require a court recess (de la Puente and Curátola 2008). We also know that Andean peoples possessed abacus-like aids in the form of counting-boards called *yupana* which held counting tokens in ordered cells (Wassén 1990 [1931]).

Inclusions and 'Semiotic Heterogeneity'

Tying one thing onto another does not necessarily imply tying on more of the same kind of thing (as in the nested structures discussed above). Khipu makers also sometimes tied on non-cord items such as tufts of wool, small sticks, rawhide tags, or even figurines. These might seem extraneous to cord media as such. But Galen Brokaw points out that mixing signs from several codes with separable reference systems is normal in many scripts: "Most complex media have a certain degree of semiotic heterogeneity. Alphabetic script is based on the principle of phonemic representation, but it also incorporates non-phonemic conventions such as Arabic numerals, punctuation marks, and spaces between words" (Brokaw 2010: 21). Extending the alphabetic example, one could point out that the mixed codes in heterogeneous sign-sets not only refer to different things (speech sounds, speech rhythms and intonations, and quantities) but also refer in different ways (letters being phonographic, numerals semasiographic and word spaces iconic). On khipus, sticks taken as likenesses of animals introduce iconic reference, while wool itself may be an indexical one.

Normal as 'semiotic heterogeneity' is, cord physicality seems a particularly open invitation to it, since cord is *par excellence* the means of binding varied objects together. This kind of heterogeneity seems most typical of post-Inka khipus. It reaches an extreme in Rapaz's seriated-emblem khipus.

Linearity

Whatever else cords may be, they are linear right down to their atomic level (raw fiber). Tim Ingold could have made them a key case in his book *Lines*, on the way cultures construe linearity (Ingold 2007).

Khipu students have long wondered whether cord lines might not have served iconically to represent paths in spatial relationships. It is an Andeanist commonplace to comment that the *ceque* pattern of ritual lines radiating out from the Inka sacred city of Cuzco, with shrines forming nodes along them, looks like a giant khipu laid onto the landscape.

Inca-linked informants often said cords supported narratives: dynastic history and genealogy, laws, *chansons de geste* and ritual protocols. The Aschers (1982: 75) pointed out that a narrative, considered as a sequence of stylized or generic speech events (strophe, episode, etc.) could be matched to the linear, segmented, discrete format of khipu. A cord series knotted with indicators of certain types of events and values for them would suffice to structure, for example, a dynastic chronicle — though not the necessarily phonological representation of specific words in it. Catherine Julien (2000: 11–13, 226–228) and Brokaw (2003) argue that Inka dynastic histories rendered from, or written by, Andean experts bear specific formal structures carried over from khipus. Far from the Andean orbit, Wassmann (1991 [1982]) provides a detailed ethnography of how a Sepik River group in Papua-New Guinea practices an elaborate sequence of ritual oratory based on a cord device.

Abercrombie (1998) has gone the farthest in asking us to see khipu cords as predominantly 'pathways'. He regards cords as iconic maps or guides representing passages through space and

/ or time ('chronotopographs'), or even trains of thought moving through a purely mental space such as hierarchy.

Three-Dimensionality

It has been noted (Cummins 1994) that, in part and in whole, khipus inherently are solids rather than pure lines. This allows tactile legibility, at least theoretically. One colonial source asserts that a blind man made and read an immense khipu as an aid to Catholic confession (Harrison 2002: 281). Experienced spinners can indeed recognize many structures by touch, but the central importance of color makes the idea of tactile legibility less plausible.

Concluding Suggestions

Physical properties of khipus do not by themselves bear centrally on the question of whether khipu *could* have encoded linguistic sound-segments and thereby entered the sacred circle of 'true writings'. Khipu materiality does, however, suggest that the medium was exceptionally strong in representing relations other than linguistic ones. The technology has an inherent bent toward emphasizing discrete category, hierarchy, number and grouping. One cannot create a canonical khipu without implications about some of these. It also seems to have been inherently strong for usage as an operational simulating device. Khipu would be as good for representing ongoing updates or rearrangements of information as it is for permanent fixation.

Khipus' physicality compels us to pay special attention to category and number, the same variables Damerow (1999) identified as the core of meaning in Proto-Cuneiform. A canonical khipu has some resemblance to the rationing tables, rich in both semasiograms and numerals, which Damerow deciphered. However the term 'proto' misleads one into thinking that inscription built up from noun-number inscription has an inherently low functional horizon. Perhaps the khipu art represented 'proto' inscription carried onward toward elaborateness in its own terms, rather than redirected to phonographic representation via the rebus mutation. One way to combine the now well-developed mathematical study of khipus with newer findings about color, mirror-symmetry variations, and hierarchical structure would be to think of khipus as a script which is inherently a diagram.

The philosopher Nelson Goodman, in studying the properties of different semiotic toolkits, invented a special usage of the word *model* which seems to capture very well the peculiar relation between matter and meaning in khipus. "Models...in effect diagrams...in more than two dimensions, and with working parts; or in other words, diagrams are flat and static models. Like other diagrams, models may be digital or analog or mixed" (Goodman 1976 [1968]: 172–173). One can think of Andean societies, especially but not only Inka-era ones, as engaged in constructing themselves by storing, updating, and exchanging visual models rather than verbal transcriptions. Whether or not that is 'writing' does not need to be fought about immediately. What does matter is learning to recognize "graphical excellence" (Tufte 1983: 182) in its less familiar forms.

Note

[1] Another khipu – alphabetic interface seems to have been invented on the ecclesiastical side: the hybrid khipu – alphabetic objects known as 'khipu boards'. Two drawings which may show khipu boards in the catechesis of women come from the remote north coast *c.*1789 (Martínez Compañón 1985 [*c.* 1779-1789]: 53–54). In 1852 the scientific traveler Mariano Rivero observed that "in some parishes of Indians, the khipu were attached to a panel with a register of

the inhabitants on which were noted "their absences on the days when Christian doctrine is taught" (Sempat Assadourian 2002: 136). Toward 1923, Julio C. Tello and Próspero Miranda observed one in use at Casta, near the northern edge of Huarochirí Province. Its function was to govern participation in the village's canal-cleaning collective labor days and associated rites honoring the divine owners of water. As late as 1968 another specimen of 19th-century origin was discovered, in disuse, at the church of Mangas in central Peru (Robles Mendoza 1990 [1982]: 9).

References

Abercrombie, T. A. 1998. *Pathways of Memory and Power: Ethnography and history among an Andean people*. Madison: University of Wisconsin Press.

Ascher, M. and Ascher, R. 1997 [1981]. *Code of the Quipu: A study of media, mathematics, and culture*. New York: Dover Publications.

Betanzos, J. de 1987 [1551]. *Suma y narración de los incas* (edited by María del Carmen Martín Rubio). Madrid: Atlas.

Brokaw, G. 2003. The Poetics of Khipu Historiography. *Latin American Research Review* 38(3): 111–147. DOI: http://dx.doi.org/10.1353/lar.2003.0029

Brokaw, G. 2010. *A History of the Khipu*. New York: Cambridge University Press.

Burns, K. 2004. *Making Indigenous Archives: The Quilcay Camayoc of colonial Cuzco*. Paper given at conference "Archives and Empires", University of Notre Dame, April 3–5, 2004.

Cabello Valboa, M. 1951 [1586]. *Miscelánea antártica*. Lima: Universidad Nacional Mayor de San Marcos.

Cherkinsky, A. and Urton, G. forthcoming. Radiocarbon Chronology of Andean khipus. *Open Journal of Archaeometry*.

Conklin, W. J. 1982. The Information System of the Middle Horizon Quipus. *Annals of the New York Academy of Sciences* 385: 261–281. DOI: http://dx.doi.org/10.1111/j.1749-6632.1982.tb34269.x

Conklin, W. J. 2002. A Khipu Information String Theory. In Quilter, J. and Urton, G. (eds), *Narrative Threads: Accounting and recounting in Andean khipu*. Austin, TX: University of Texas Press, 53–86.

Conklin, W. J. and Splitstoser, J. 2009. *Andean Stick Wrapping: A review of its 2000 year history*. Paper given at the 2007 Annual Meeting of the Institute of Andean Studies, Berkeley.

Cummins, T. 1994. Representation in the Sixteenth Century and the Colonial Image. In Boone, E., and Mignolo, W. (eds), *Writing Without Words*. Durham, NC: Duke University Press, 188–219.

Damerow, P. 1999. *The Origins of Writing as a Problem of Historical Epistemology*. Berlin: Max Planck-Institut für Wissenschaftsgeschichte. Preprint 114.

de la Puente Luna, J. C. and Curátola, M. 2008. *Nudos, piedras, y maíz: Los quipus coloniales de la provincia de Lucanas (1581)*. Paper given at VII Congreso Internacional de Etnohistoria, Lima, 5 August 2008.

de Murúa, M. 2004 [1590(?)]. *Códice Murúa: historia y genealogía de los reyes incas del Perú del padre mercenario Fray Martín de Murúa: códice Galvin*. Madrid: Testimonio Compañía Editorial.

de Murúa, M. 1946 [1590]. *Historia del origen y genealogía real de los reyes Incas del Perú*. Madrid: Biblioteca Missionalia Hispánica, Instituto Santo Toribio de Mogrovejo, y Consejo Superior de Investigaciones Científicas.

Guaman Poma de Ayala, F. 1980 [1615]. *Nueva corónica y buen gobierno del Perú* (edited by John V. Murra and Rolena Adorno, with translations by Jorge L. Urioste). 3 volumes. México DF: Siglo XXI.

Goodman, N. 1976 [1968]. *Languages of Art: An approach to a theory of symbols* (2ⁿᵈ edition). Indianapolis: Hackett Publishing.

Harrison, R. 2002. Pérez Bocanegra's *Ritual Formulario*. In Quilter, J. and Urton, G. (eds), *Narrative Threads: Accounting and recounting in Andean khipu*. Austin, TX: University of Texas Press, 260–290.

Herrmann, B. and Meyer, R. 1993. *Südamerikanische Mumien aus vorspanischer Zeit: Eine radiologische Untersuchung*. Berlin: Staatliche Museen zu Berlin–Preussischer Kulturbesitz.

Holm, O. 1968. Quipu o sapan: un recurso mnemónico en el campo ecuatoriano. *Cuadernos de Historia y Arqueología* (Guayaquil) 18:(34/35): 85–90.

Ingold, T. 2007. *Lines: A Brief History*. London and New York: Routledge.

Julien, C. 2000. *Reading Inca History*. Iowa City: University of Iowa Press.

Locke, L. 1923. *The Ancient Quipu, or Peruvian Knot Record*. New York: American Museum of Natural History.

Locke, L. 1928. *Supplementary Notes on the Quipus in the American Museum of Natural History*. (Anthropological Papers of the American Museum of Natural History 30). New York: American Museum of Natural History, 30–73.

Loza, C. B. 1998. Du bon usage des quipus face à l'administration coloniale espagnole (1500–1600). *Population* 1–2: 139–159. DOI: http://dx.doi.org/10.2307/1534240

Mackey, C. 2002. The Continuing Khipu Tradition: Principle and practice. In Quilter, J. and Urton, G. (eds), *Narrative Threads: Accounting and recounting in Andean khipu*. Austin, TX: University of Texas Press, 320–348.

Mann, C. 2005. Unraveling Khipu's Secrets. *Science* 309(5737): 1008–1009.

Martínez Compañón, B. J. 1985 [c.1779–1789]. *Trujillo del Perú, Volume 2*. Madrid: Instituto de Cooperación Iberoamericana.

Museo Chileno de Arte Precolombino 2003. *Quipu: Contar anudando en el impoerio inka*. Santiago: Museo Chileno de Arte Precolombino and Harvard University.

Núñez-Carvallo, S. 2008. Cabello Valboa, Miguel (c.1530–1606). In Pillsbury, J. (ed.), *Guide to Documentary Sources for Andean Studies, Volume 2*. Norman: University of Oklahoma Press, 91–94.

Nuñez del Prado, O. 1990 [1950]. El kipu moderno. In Mackey, C., Pereyra, H., Radicati, C., Rodríguez, H. and Valverde, O. (eds), *Quipu y yupana: Colección de escritos*. Lima: CONCYTEC, 165–182.

Pärssinen, M. and Kiviharju, J. (eds) 2004. *Textos andinos: Tomo I: Corpus de textos* (Serie Hispano-Americano 6). Madrid: Instituto Iberoamericano de Finlandia.

Pereyra, H. 1997. Los quipus con cuerdas entorchadas. In Varón Gabai, R. and Flores Espinoza, J. (eds), *Arqueología, antropología e historia en los Andes: Homenaje a María Rostworowski*. Lima: Instituto de Estudios Peruanos, 187–198.

Pimentel, H. N. 2005. *Amarrando colores: La producción del sentido en khipus aymaras*. La Paz: CEPA, Latinas Editores.

Pizarro, H. 1920 [1533]. *A los Señores Oydores de la Audiencia Real de Su Magestad*. In Urteaga, H. H. (ed.), *Informaciones sobre el antiguo Perú: Colección de Libros y Documentos Referentes a la Historia del Perú, Volume 3* (2ⁿᵈ series). Lima: Sanmartí, 16–180.

Prochaska, R. 1983. *Ethnography and Enculturation of Weaving on Taquile Island, Peru*. Unpublished MA dissertation, University of California at Los Angeles.

Radicati di Primeglio, C. 1979(?). *El sistema contable de los Incas: yupana y quipu*. Lima: Libreria Studium.

Radicati di Primeglio, C. 1990 [1987]. Hacia una tipificación de los quipus. In Mackey, C., Pereyra, H., Radicati, C., Rodríguez, H. and Valverde, O. (eds), *Quipu y yupana: Colección de escritos*. Lima: CONCYTEC, 89–95.

Rama, A. 1996 [1984]. *The Lettered City* (translated by John Charles Chasteen). Durham, NC: Duke University Press.

Robles Mendoza, R. 1990 [1982]. El kipu alfabético de Mangas. In Mackey, C., Pereyra, H., Radicati, C., Rodríguez, H. and Valverde, O. (eds), *Quipu y yupana: Colleción de escritos*. Lima: CONCYTEC, 195–202.

Ruíz Estrada, A. 1982. *Los quipus de Rapaz*. Huacho, Peru: Centro de Investigación de Ciencia y Tecnología de Huacho.

Salomon, F. 2004. *The Cord Keepers: Khipu and cultural life in a Peruvian village*. Durham, NC: Duke University Press. DOI: http://dx.doi.org/10.1215/9780822386179

Salomon, F. 2008. Late Khipu Use. In Baines, J., Bennet, J. and Houston, S. D. (eds), *The Disappearance of Writing Systems: Perspectives on literacy and communication*. London: Equinox, 285–310.

Salomon, F., Brezine, C. and Falcón Huayta, V. 2006. Los khipus de Rapaz en casa: Un complejo administrativo-ritual centroperuano. *Revista Andina* 43: 59–92.

Sempat Assadourian, C. 2002. String Registries: Native accounting and memory according to the Colonial sources. In Quilter, J. and Urton, G. (eds), *Narrative Threads: Accounting and recounting in Andean khipu*. Austin, TX: University of Texas Press, 119–150.

Shady, R., Narváez, J. and López S. 2000. La antigüedad del uso del *quipu* como escritura: Las evidencias de la huaca San Marcos. *Boletín del Museo de Arqueología y Antropología* (Lima) 3(10): 2–23.

Soto Flores, F. 1990 [1950–1951]. Los kipus modernos de la localidad de Laramarca. In Mackey, C., Pereyra, H., Radicati, C., Rodríguez, H. and Valverde, O. (eds), *Quipu y yupana: Colección de escritos*. Lima: CONCYTEC, 183–190.

Tello, J. and Miranda P. 1923. Wallallo: Ceremonias gentílicas realizadas en la región cisandina del Perú central. *Inca: Revista Trimestral de Estudios Antropológicos* 1(2): 475–549.

Thomson, S. 2002. *We Alone Will Rule: Native Andean politics in the age of insurgency*. Madison: University of Wisconsin Press.

Tufte, E. 1983 *The Visual Display of Quantitative Information*. Cheshire, CT: Graphics Press.

Urton, G. 2001. A Calendrical and Demographic Tomb Text from Northern Peru. *Latin American Antiquity* 12(2): 127–147. DOI: http://dx.doi.org/10.2307/972052

Urton, G. 2003. *Signs of the Inka Khipu: Binary coding in the Andean knotted-string records*. Austin: University of Texas Press.

Urton, G. 2007. *Los khipus de la Laguna de los Cóndores*. Lima: Nuevas Imágenes, S. A.

Wassén, H. 1990 [1931]. El antiguo abaco peruano según el manuscrito de Guaman Poma. In Mackey, C., Pereyra, H., Radicati, C., Rodríguez, H. and Valverde, O. (eds), *Quipu y yupana: Colección de escritos*. Lima: CONCYTEC, 205–218.

Wassmann, J. 1991 [1982]. *The Song to the Flying Fox: The public and esoteric knowledge of the important men of Kandingei about totemic songs, names, and knotted cords (Middle Sepik, Papua New Guinea)* (translated by D. Stephenson) (Apwitihire: Studies in Papua New Guinean Music, 2). Boroko, Papua New Guinea: Cultural Studies Division, the National Research Institute.

Writing as Material Technology: Orientation within landscapes of the Classic Maya world

Sarah E. Jackson

University of Cincinnati

Introduction

Writing as Material Technology

Our shared charge in this volume is to consider writing as material practice. In this way, we endeavor to shift our perspectives on texts from the transparent view that allows us to look past pages, monuments, and objects straight to the content or meaning of recorded signs, and instead to think about the embodied and material nature of writing, and the connection of texts to the material world. These material musings, and the reframing of text to include its physical nature and existence in an experiential world, led me to reflect on how writing may be understood as a material technology. I draw inspiration from Walter Ong (1982) in particular, who frames the emergence of writing in this light. In this way, we can understand text as not only having an effect or impact because of its *content* (an insult causing a war, an acknowledgement confirming affiliation), but also because of its *material form* and the ways that form is perceived and used (akin to stone tools changing the possibilities for cutting or processing, the wheel impacting experiences of distance and connection). Textual objects — a phrase I use to keep in the forefront of our minds the simultaneously material and textual nature of the artifacts I discuss — accomplish certain types of work that draw upon both the content and the material nature of the text. By considering texts in an artifactual light, I argue that texts do important work in organizing the material world. Furthermore, the specific material forms that texts take impact the ways in which such work is carried out.

I explore these ideas in the context of Classic Maya writing. For the Maya text objects I examine — a stone monument, a painted ceramic vessel, and a set of incised bone needles,

How to cite this book chapter:

Jackson, S. E. 2013. Writing as Material Technology: Orientation within landscapes of the Classic Maya world. In: Piquette, K. E. and Whitehouse, R. D. (eds.) *Writing as Material Practice: Substance, surface and medium.* Pp. 45-63. London: Ubiquity Press. DOI: http://dx.doi.org/10.5334/bai.c

all adorned with Maya hieroglyphic writing — I suggest that an orientational technology is at work. That is, the perception and use of these text objects serve to locate people in culturally defined landscapes, and in particular, within socio-political landscapes that include both experiential and imagined aspects. The experience of these texts allowed ancient viewers to situate themselves along a series of axes, not all of which are obvious or visible through other modes of material analysis. Particularly important are the juxtaposed perspectives of the immediately accessible aspects of a polity (spatial, temporal and political), and the more abstract ideas of what lay beyond.

As an orientational technology, these text objects are quite different from modern technologies that serve to give us our bearings upon visiting a Maya archaeological site: a topographic map, a compass, a GPS unit, and, of course, a wristwatch. And yet, in both modern and ancient instances, orientational technologies involve accessing content that shapes human actions in the world, and that is experienced in specific ways representative of particular, shared worldviews. As we read a site name or elevation on a worn and floppy paper map, or time from numerals on a metal object that we wear, we participate — consciously or not — in shared understandings of relative positioning in the universe. The text objects that I examine encode perspectives that located Maya individuals in relative positions through expressions of the shape and nature of the realms in which they lived, including dimensions of territoriality, conceptions of temporality, and constructions of personal and institutional difference.

A Few Thoughts on Technology and Landscapes

I mentioned above that Ong's work (1982) provided inspiration for considering writing as a type of technology. For him, technology is marked, at least in part, through "the use of tools and other equipment" (Ong 1982: 80–81). This is a fairly limited definition, though he notes that the transformational power of technology is not only as an "exterior aide", but also as yielding "interior transformations of consciousness" (Ong 1982: 81). Following in the footsteps of Ingold (2000: 294–299), I extend Ong's premise and embed those tools within active processes and particular types of knowledge, emphasizing both the material extensions of human selves that carry out work (in this case, both the tools that create texts, and subsequently the texts themselves) and the cultural knowledge necessary for these technologies to be created and put into action. For the purposes of this chaper, I do not introduce the concept of technology as an opposition to art, a dichotomy that implies a division between execution and conception (Ingold 2000: 295), and which may not accurately describe relationships between rulers and artisans, often conceived as attached specialists in Maya contexts (Inomata 2001). Rather, by using the term 'technology', I shift our interpretation of Maya text objects from an aesthetic interpretation or historical reading, to an appreciation of the constructive cultural work being carried out through textual implements.

As I explore the idea that Maya text objects may be considered as a type of efficacious technology serving to orient viewers and readers, I refer to the idea of landscape. I describe in this chapter a variety of culturally constructed landscapes (spatial, temporal, political, and gendered). While the natural landscape and environment are critical elements to examine in understanding ancient societies, the work that the text objects I consider are doing is focused on mediated and experiential surroundings: how people would have perceived their place in the world, on multiple planes, based on both actual experience and imagined extension. As human constructs, the landscapes I consider are unstable and constantly transformed, and require maintenance in order to retain their contours, or to change in response to shifting circumstances. I argue that text objects provide a particularly powerful communicative avenue for carrying out this work.

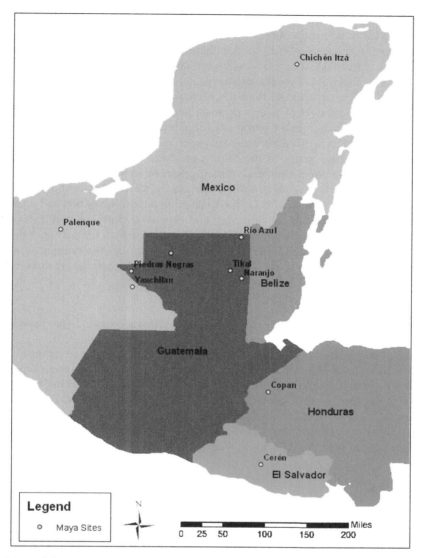

Figure 1: Map of the Maya area, including sites mentioned in the chapter. Map by Dayna Reale. Reproduced with permission.

A Brief Background on the Maya

Before exploring these ideas through three case studies, I first provide some background for those less familiar with Maya contexts. The texts I discuss in the following examples were created by Maya scribes in Central America (**Figure 1**) during the Classic period (*c.*AD 250–850). The world of the Classic Maya was characterized by a fragmented political landscape of independent city-states each ruled by a *k'uhul ajaw* (holy lord), whose authority was based on both political and religious stature. The Classic-era apogee of Maya culture was a period of trade, social and political interaction between sites, ongoing development of the governing apparatus, as well as conflict between competing polities.

The sophistication of the Maya world is marked in part by their elaborate writing system, one that allows us to learn the names of some of that era's key players, and to establish a tightly controlled chronology for the histories of these polities. Some of the extant texts that epigraphers examine today are carved on stone monuments, both upright stelae that were exhibited in public places, as well as architectural elements such as panels, lintels, and benches that would have been located in more restricted spaces. Additionally, hieroglyphic texts are found on portable objects such as painted ceramic vessels, as well as personal items such as carved bone and shell objects. The challenges of preservation in a tropical environment mean that more perishable substances that likely were vehicles for writing, such as bark paper, rarely survive.

The complex logosyllabic script of the Maya constituted a limited resource — legible to a restricted segment of the population, and written primarily by trained scribes, many of whom were also members of the royal court. In Maya contexts, however, literacy should not be seen as a binary issue (Houston and Stuart 1992). The frequent juxtaposition of text and image led to an interpretive interplay between the written word and expressive depictions. In the examples that follow, the texts and images on Maya artifacts interact with the material nature of the objects to become powerful communicative devices, accomplishing work by conveying meaning, but also through orienting and situating those who interacted with these text objects in both literal and metaphorical landscapes.

Orientation through Text Objects in the Classic Maya World: Three case studies

My interest in viewing texts in their material form, and as connected to material practice, is two-fold. I consider both how the content of texts shapes the landscape of lived experience, and also how the material format that these texts take impacts the consumption of their messages. As I introduce the orientational aspects of the following three examples, I will focus first on how they act as markers within various landscapes, with reference both to textual content and form. In the subsequent section, I will explicitly consider the communicative channels at work, and how the material form of each object works to transform each text into a particular type of tool.

Piedras Negras Panel 3: Framing locations in immediate and distant spaces

In considering the roles that text objects played in shaping and controlling Classic Maya landscapes, let us look first at Piedras Negras Panel 3 (**Figures 2–3**), a carved stone monument from the site of Piedras Negras, located on the banks of the Usumacinta River in the department of Petén, Guatemala; this monument has garnered the attention of multiple scholars over the years (including Houston and Stuart 2001; Marcus 1976; O'Neil 2005; 2012; Proskouriakoff 1963). Its perceived power in ancient times is indicated by the purposeful defacement of the figures within its frame. As I lead us into the space of the royal court that is represented on Panel 3, it will become clear that this elite and circumscribed socio-political space — as depicted on the monument — served to orient its high-status members and also individuals beyond its borders within several immediate and distant landscapes.

Panel 3 is not a large object, measuring approximately 60 × 120 cm, and yet stands out from other monuments in the Maya corpus for its notably naturalistic and lively depiction of the ruler of Piedras Negras and other members of his courtly coterie. In contrast to the kinds of formal and stoic portraits often found on standing stelae, this scene of the k'uhul ajaw of this polity and his court serves as a reminder of the variety of individuals beyond the apical ruler who were included in the inner social and political gatherings of the city, as well as the lively nature of such human

Figure 2: Piedras Negras Panel 3. Photograph by Megan O'Neil, courtesy of Megan O'Neil and the Museo Nacional de Arqueología y Etnología de Guatemala, and the Minesterio de Cultura y Deportes, Dirección General de Patrimonio Cultural y Natural.

Figure 3: Drawing of Piedras Negras Panel 3 (from Schele and Friedel 1990: 304). Drawing by Linda Schele, © David Schele, courtesy Foundation for the Advancement of Mesoamerican Studies, Inc., www.famsi.org.

exchanges. The monument was associated with Structure O-13 at Piedras Negras, and may have been mounted on its stairway, though its original location is uncertain (**Figure 4**).

I suggest that several experiential landscapes are represented on this monument — spatial, temporal, and political. These orientational axes help situate viewers within immediate contexts, but also suggest imagined contexts that were not immediately accessible to them. In this way, Panel 3

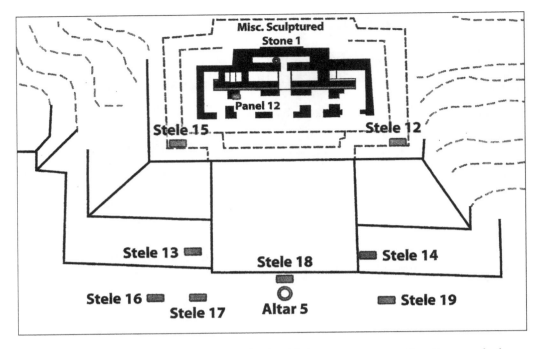

Figure 4: Plan of Piedras Negras Structure O-13, with known monument locations marked; precise original location of Panel 3 is unknown (from O'Neil 2012: 141). Image by Megan O'Neil and Kevin Cain (INSIGHT). Reproduced with permission.

does not just describe or depict particular moments or events, or even a historical series of such events, but rather creates a multi-dimensional space in which individuals are placed, and then made aware of alternate locales beyond their immediate placement.

In investigating the types of orientation involved in the visual consumption of this monument, I begin with the spatial aspects of the sociopolitical world — the most concrete and physically real of the landscapes I suggest. Visually engaging with Panel 3 involves entering, or peering into, the throne room of Ruler 4. Within this indoor architectural space, Ruler 4 is centrally located. In front of him are two seated lines of courtiers, most labeled with names and/or titles, arranged on either side of a drinking cup of chocolate. The scene is framed and bounded by architectural elements — a step, walls (composed partially of text), a rolled-up curtain. Our position as viewer is on the edge of this space. Whether derived from visual conventions indicating hierarchical relationships or from textual descriptions of the names and titles of these exalted individuals, the ancient viewer perceives a defined central space of his or her city. Furthermore, the location of this monument in or on the impressive pyramidal Structure O-13 would have situated the viewer of the text object within the grand and open architectural space of the East Group Plaza. Panel 3 was spatially fixed and the viewer would have had to move him- or herself into a clearly articulated space of authority and governance in order to view it. The viewer, depending on his or her identity within the evoked hierarchy, might identify with the characters and context pictured, or might be estranged from the scene and the communicative devices through which the information is conveyed. In either scenario, the consumption of this text involved relative positioning of the self, both in relation to this object as it is viewed, and in connection with the people and events depicted in image and text.

Panel 3 does more than provide a lively image of a central space of governance at Piedras Negras. Rather, the space of the royal court — a central religious-political axis at each site — is thrown into relief by the presence of visitors from the neighboring site (and independent polity) of Yaxchilan. Houston and Stuart have identified the individuals standing to the left of the throne as a group of individuals visiting from Yaxchilan; the textual captions label one of them as an *ajaw*, or lord (Houston and Stuart 2001: 72). Their presence in an iconic depiction of centrality and status within Piedras Negras's kingdom serves several purposes. The presence and identification of these others locates Piedras Negras, its leaders and its inhabitants, on a larger stage. The authority projected by the *k'uhul ajaw*, and the hierarchy enacted by the bodies differentially arranged within this space, are thrown into relief by the reminder of alternate hierarchies in other spaces — and, here, by the movement of these foreign bodies into the Piedras Negras court. For ancient viewers who were not were not themselves acquainted with a wider world beyond their home city, this depiction places them, as local viewers, in the center of a much more broadly drawn plane.

In addition to this local and distant spatial orientation, Panel 3 works to orient the viewer in a temporal framework, though the effect may actually be one of disorientation, or lack of a fixed place. The Maya's extensive use of calendrical references in their texts — such as the Long Count and Calendar Round that begin the Panel 3 inscription, specifying a precise date — yielded a specific and temporally-grounded sense of location, the distinctive type of situating described by Ong (1982: 96) in relation to societies that keep track of time.

While the nature of Maya calendrical recording allowed for precise identification of particular dates, Piedras Negras Panel 3 has remained puzzling to scholars over the years due to certain ambiguities in the temporal references within the text. The text engages with two different eras of Piedras Negras's history — the reign of Ruler 4 (including both his accession and later death), and then the commemoration of Ruler 4's burial place by Ruler 7 (Houston and Stuart 2001: 69). If this is indeed Ruler 4 pictured in the image, then his carefully delineated court — complete with names and titles — is reconstructed some 20 years after the fact. While this possible temporal disjunction represents an interpretive issue for modern interlocutors, it may have carried other meanings for contemporary Maya individuals. The ambiguity of reference or event may have been purposeful, evoking multiple eras simultaneously and reminding the viewers of the ongoing relevance and even presence of the past in the form of ancestors and cyclical time (Carlsen 1997: 47–70; McAnany 1995). Panel 3 also implicitly refers to future events through the inclusion of a child among the ruler's family members standing to the right of the throne. This young boy is named a *ch'ok yokib ajaw* — a young Piedras Negras lord (Houston and Stuart 2001: 72), which may label him as an heir to the throne. In this image, he literally waits in the wings. Nonetheless, his presence and the text that labels him serve as reminders of future generations and future occupants of the throne. Maya individuals who were temporally oriented within specific moments in time were also explicitly reminded of their connections to the past and the future, eras that in the thinking of the Maya were not linearly separated, but rather cyclically overlapping.

Finally, Panel 3 orients individuals within a political landscape, at both micro and macro scales. Artistic conventions such as a vertical hierarchy and direction of gazes help to order the group of people depicted into a legible and ordered hierarchy (Houston 1998; Houston et al. 2006; Jackson 2009). The careful labeling of names and titles of the various individuals gathered here makes relative position and affiliation explicit, organization that is replicated through relative arrangement of bodies. In visual, if not textual, rhetoric, the viewer of this scene becomes implicated as well, joining the imagined unnamed masses that would have witnessed such a scene through the frame of the doorway, standing outside in the plaza.

Like the different scales of spatial organization, larger political orientations are manifest in this monument as well. Larger-scale political maneuverings are revealed through knowledge of broader political history of this era. While the presence of the visitors from Yaxchilan on this monument might suggest a cordial diplomatic exchange, the textual references to the reason for their presence are vague. When correlated with the textual history (or, rather, lack thereof) at Yaxchilan, we find a perplexing disjunction between Piedras Negras's claim to have welcomed a lordly delegation, and Yaxchilan's textual silence during this period — an era known as the inter-regnum at the site, when no ruler was acknowledged (Martin and Grube 2000: 127). While we can only speculate on the true circumstances that led to this textual mismatch, the authors of Piedras Negras's history clearly are asserting something at odds with Yaxchilan's own official history. Here, the reader in Piedras Negras is placed not only within a larger spatial sphere, but also within a political network that likely exceeds his or her own personal experiences, reinforcing the power differentials between sites, and naming their hometown — Piedras Negras — not only as a central space, but as an arbiter of political history.

Using the frame of technology to describe the work that Maya text objects are doing, Piedras Negras Panel 3 works to orient the viewer within multiple realms. Significantly, in each, there are references both to immediately experienced settings, and to ones that are not directly accessible, and thus require evocation or imagination in order to make them part of an inner cartography. Of the three examples considered in this chapter, this panel is the one immobile monument, and thus the one instance in which the viewer revolves around its fixed location (cf. Whitehouse, this volume). Engagement with this text object must necessarily always happen in the same architectural setting, though perceptional qualities of light, weather, and accompanying viewers would have varied, perhaps yielding different readings in these different situational contexts.

Río Azul Cacao Pot: Containing individual and group identities

The second object I consider, as we continue the exercise of reframing texts within their material forms and exploring the consequences of this interpretive move, is a striking ceramic vessel from the site of Río Azul in northeastern Guatemala (**Figure 5**; Adams 1999; Macri 2005; Stuart 1988). This pot — Vessel 15 — is, like many ceramic vessels, intended as a container. In this case, both the hieroglyphic text on the outside of the container (Stuart 1988) and testing for theobromine and caffeine (Hall et al. 1990) reveal the ancient contents of this pot: chocolate. For the ancient Maya, drinking chocolate was a special substance, perfumed and flavored with various additives (Stuart 1988). The bubbling froth on top of a cup of chocolate represented the vitality — even life force — believed to be contained within this special drink (Marcus and Flannery 1994: 58). In the case of Vessel 15 from Río Azul, this lidded vessel, complete with screw top and handle, was more likely used for the preparation of this drink. It was recovered from Tomb 19, one of Río Azul's elaborate painted tombs, located under Temple Structure C-1 (Adams 1999: 96–97), and dated to the Early Classic period (likely in the second half of the 5th century AD [Stuart 1988: 153]).

The text on the outside, as interpreted by Stuart (1988: 154–156), and Macri (2005) is fairly simple in content, describing the contents of the container as *kakaw* (cacao, or chocolate), and the owner of the vessel as "an advisor to a prince" (Adams 1999: 97). This type of formulaic text, labeling contents and ownership, is typical on Maya ceramic vessels, often following a pattern referred to as the "Primary Standard Sequence" (Coe 1973). This explicit labeling serves to reify the experiential and necessarily dynamic nature of personal identity, and the actions that underscore such an identity. While a Classic Maya lord reclining on a jaguar-skin pillow on a sunny afternoon, savoring his cup of chocolate, may not need to have his name or titles and drink of choice textually identified (is it not obvious to himself and his attendants who he is, what he is doing, and the social meanings of his privileged access to certain foodstuffs?), this labeling allows such actions and meanings to be made permanent. For painted vessels on which chocolate drinking cups and consumption are actually pictured, this continual re-enactment or reproduction (Giddens 1979) is strikingly explicit. In the case of the Río Azul vessel, its likely use as a tool of preparation or storage, without figural iconographic reinforcement of the act of consumption, directly bridges the functional form of the pot (a closed, lidded container) with the evocation of identity and privilege indicated through the textual label. The vessel becomes a container of multiple substances: the

Figure 5: Río Azul Vessel 15. Photograph by George F. Mobley / National Geographic Creative. Reproduced with permission, and with the generous support of the Charles Phelps Taft Research Center, University of Cincinnati.

chocolate itself, the associated privilege of access to this special substance (not to mention the ability to commission and display text), and the identity of the individual who drinks such chocolate and owns such a special container. In considering the frame of orientational technologies, this text object serves to identify and orient in relation to a particular, individual person.

Such special vessels do more than mark individual identities through text and usage, however. As LeCount has convincingly argued, consumption and feasting play key roles as modes of social competition and competitive display in Maya contexts (2001). Within ceremonial feasting contexts, chocolate was a charged and marked substance, and the associated paraphernalia for serving (and, presumably, preparation) acted as "political currency" (LeCount 2001: 935–936). In this way, the Río Azul vessel — and other analogous pots — become contextualized within larger spheres in two ways. First, such special ceramics were used in public moments of display and interaction, critical to integration within particular polities, and between elites from competing Maya polities. The marked substances, including chocolate, that were consumed on such occasions become a medium of social exchange and their containers the literal and metaphorical vessels for such substances and the resulting relationships.

Second, the idea of these vessels containing not just individual identities, but connective relationships is represented by LeCount's (2001: 936) characterization of such vases as currency, referring to the frequent gifting of elaborately painted vessels between high-ranking individuals across polity lines — perhaps a memento of a notable feast, and visit. The ability of these text objects to move contrasts sharply with the previous example of Piedras Negras Panel 3, which was profoundly rooted to place within the Piedras Negras polity, even as it referenced other sites. While we do not have evidence that Vessel 15 traveled during its lifetime, its portable size and medium mean that it (and other similar pots) could have appeared in a variety of places and social settings, thus becoming a player itself within the elite social landscape of this era. As we imagine such vessels moving between sites, a contrastive landscape of difference is enacted through style: artists' hands and local conventions of depiction of both text and image are visually accessible, and the form of the text would have communicated the outlines of boundaries crossed as artifacts circulated in the Classic-era world (Jackson 2009: 76–77). The orientation occurring through this vessel is not only individual, but also relates to broader and more complex social landscapes, evoking relationships with individuals both present and absent.

I have just mentioned the forms of texts and images as notable to an ancient viewer, who may have been able to detect differences between styles associated with different polities or regions. We imagine texts on vessels like the Río Azul example being powerful to this Classic period viewer — if we conjure him or her as a literate individual — both for the information conveyed and for the appreciation of the skill and power involved with creating (on the part of the scribe) and commissioning (on the part of the owner) such a textual statement. Indeed, hieroglyphic texts were a perquisite of the elite, displayed and — in the case of the ruler — bestowed as aspects of the construction of distinct elite identities marked by access to "high culture" (Baines and Yoffee 1998: 235). This value placed on possession of text is made more complex by the presence of numerous Classic-era painted ceramic vessels — directly analogous in form to the precious serving vessels described above — decorated not with content-filled hieroglyphic texts, but with meaningless pseudoglyphs, representing nothing more than a visual gestalt of a textual record (Calvin 2006). We might assume that these are the ceramic "knock-offs" of would-be Maya elites, but the presence of such vessels even in high-status tombs (Calvin 2006: 249) indicates that evocation of text was — at least at times — as technologically effective as the actual text itself. In our discussion of the work that text objects are doing, the presence of these pseudoglyphs reminds us starkly that texts are accomplishing things quite apart from their specific content.

I have argued in the discussion of the Río Azul pot for particular, quite specific, landscapes of privilege and of political affiliation that are recorded, evoked, and solidified through text objects, with reference to both the ceramic vessels involved as well as the information — especially labeling of owner, rank, and contents — recorded thereon. However, as the existence of apparently content-empty pseudoglyphs illustrates, other messages are in fact encoded through text that have no connection to specifically expressed and recorded narratives. These are accepted as efficacious, despite this lack of content. Here, the material records of 'writing' accomplish work that has become ritualized, if you will, and evokes shared (and when moving beyond a single polity, conceptual) landscapes of high culture, specialized knowledge, and limited resources in a Classic period version of an imagined community (Anderson 1983).

Naranjo Weaving Bones: Implements of production and change

In considering the Río Azul vessel, I observed that the text was fairly short and simple — an indication of the Maya's predilection for name-tagging — but that the text object nonetheless was able to accomplish significant work in defining and reinforcing individual, local identities, as well as broader group identities, and relationships between individuals located at greater distances. This type of labeling is common (Houston and Taube 1987; Houston et al. 1989): as seen above, we are likely to learn something about an emic categorization of the object type (e.g. Houston et al. 1989), as well as the name and possible affiliations of the owner of the object. Analogous types of formulaic sequences appear on multiple types of artifacts, not just painted ceramic vessels; a perspective that takes in both the textual information and the associated material form transforms

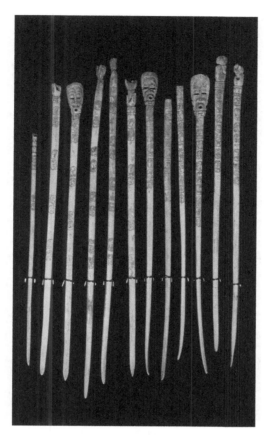

Figure 6: Naranjo weaving bones. Photograph by Chelsea Dacus. Reproduced with permission.

these brief texts into much richer cultural expressions. To underscore the role that the material aspect of these texts plays in interpretation of the actual writing, let us look now at a set of artifacts that are name tagged, but which in comparison to the previous example do quite different work, as conceived both literally and metaphorically.

These objects are a set of 24 whole weaving bones, 13 of which are inscribed with glyphs, as well as 15 fragments of weaving bones, reported to have been recovered from a woman's tomb at the site of Naranjo, a lowland Maya site in Petén, Guatemala, not far from the Belizean border (Dacus 2005; Houston and Stuart 2001; **Figures 6–8**). Measuring 15 to 25 cm in length (Dacus 2005: 32), many of these seem to have actually been used for weaving, given the polish visible on their surfaces (Dacus 2005: 33–34). The bones are diverse in decoration, with a combination of plain and text-inscribed surfaces, and a variety of decorative elements topping them. Those that are inscribed showcase brief texts that specify that the inscribed objects are the needles (*u puuhtz'*) or bone needles (*u puuhtz' b'aak*) of a woman described with various combinations and spellings of her personal names and appellatives, identifying her as a woman of elite standing (Dacus 2005: 15, 58–78). These bone tools are notable both for being valued possessions of this person, and productive tools that were used to carry out particular activities, namely weaving and the production of textiles.

A few words on the significance of weaving in Maya contexts are in order. While in most cases, perishable textiles do not survive in the archaeological record of the tropical lowlands, both the rich iconographic record of Classic period sources and the ongoing importance of an elaborate

Figure 7: Naranjo weaving bones, continued. Photograph by Chelsea Dacus. Reproduced with permission.

textile tradition among modern Maya groups inform our understanding of this craft activity. Ethnographic research on weaving by Prechtel and Carlsen (1988), coupled with broader understandings of the Classic-era significance of specialized craft production (Inomata 2001; Reents-Budet 1998), allows us to see the making of cloth as far more than a quotidian or even artistic endeavor. Craft activities in ancient Maya contexts have a supernatural overlay, in which the creation of objects is set up as parallel to, or evocative of, godly types of creation (Inomata 2001: 331–332). In the case of weaving, this traditionally feminine activity replicates aspects of giving birth (Prechtel and Carlsen 1988), underscoring the ultimate productive power of female members of society (Halperin 2008; Hendon 2006).

For the woman who was buried with these weaving bones, these text objects marked her in several ways. As was discussed above in considering the Río Azul vessel, similarly tagged, they provide her with a specific identity — including names, titles and association with a specific polity, thereby marking salient aspects of her self and sphere. Additionally, for these objects, gender roles and ideas about gendered behaviors transform them into signs within another orientational landscape. While much commentary on relative gender roles in Classic Maya contexts consists of a marked/unmarked dichotomy in which the interpretation of extensive textual attention devoted to male subjects is contrasted with the frequent absence of female interlocutors, there are a few instances that allow us to discuss ancient female actors on their own terms. Some of these are striking instances in which women — contrary to apparent tradition — took control of leadership themselves (including at Naranjo [Martin and Grube 2000: 74–75]). In the case of the needles, the concurrence of the remains of this elite woman with tools that reveal one of the activities she carried out provides evidence for an outlet for female productive power through particular creative or constructive practices that were apparently defining activities for her, in real or symbolic terms.

The example of these weaving bones is also critical to consider in the argument developed in this chapter — in which writing acts as a material technology — because they are the only one of the three case studies that literally qualifies as a tool, and connects directly to a particular, concrete type of technology (that of textile production). In this instance, the bone tools in this set (with or without textual inscriptions) are key aspects of a productive process. According to Dacus, based on their size, shape and curvature, these implements were likely used as weaving pins or picks in conjunction with a backstrap loom (Dacus 2005: 16, 37–38). These functional objects facilitated the creation of fabric of the type that would have been worn as a *huipil* (an embroidered blouse), or presented in folded stacks as tribute offerings as seen on vessel paintings. Elite women weaving in courtly contexts would have produced and reproduced particular designs in their cloth (one can think here of modern Maya villages that traditionally have associated particular designs with specific locales), as well as the knowledge needed to carry out these complex activities. A weaving bone decorated with hieroglyphs moving between strands of thread, a profoundly portable, and movable object, does not literally yield a different design than a plain implement. It does, however, weave the restriction of knowledge associated with text into the communicative designs of a woman's fabrics. This distinction would be visible as she created the textiles, or if her tools were viewed at moments when they were not in use. The landscape within which this woman was oriented was one of gender-determined outlets, and one of alternate routes to power — including the creation of additional, parallel modes of communication in textiles. Her text objects were quite literally the tools that enacted these placements for her.

These weaving bones are distinctive from the previous two examples in their status as a related set, allowing us to compare objects that are not just similar or analogous from different places or times, but objects that would have been used together and were understood to belong together. I draw attention here to the varied states of decoration of these bones: some with elaborate carving and hieroglyphic texts, others with only one mode of decoration, others still with a single curving line, and some that are completely plain. Dacus does not argue for different functions for the majority of these tools, suggesting that they might have been basically interchangeable, or representing a few complementary functions (Dacus 2005: 17). What do we make of the presence of texts on some of these implements and not on others — and yet, the grouping of the whole set together? The contrast seems to me to be a more extreme version of the pseudoglyph example above, in which general forms of glyphs may evoke the same or similar effect as real texts themselves (see also Sparks, this volume). Could we say the same of the differing communicative channels of a carved finial element, a single line, or even a blank needle — that in an environment of special, elite production the impact that a text produces can also be produced through blank space? This is an extreme suggestion. And yet, I wonder about the juxtaposition of elaborately carved stelae in Maya public plazas with other sites that exhibit erect stelae that are completely blank, though the form clearly indicates the genre of monument that is intended. These plain monuments may have been plastered and painted in ancient times. Or, perhaps there are instances in which invisible text, or absent text (or even imagined text) is able to do some of the work that realized texts can do (cf. Cessford, this volume). Dacus proposes a life history for these bone objects in which texts were added at different times, as indicated by different levels of wear on the bones and glyphs (Dacus 2005: 34–35), which similarly suggests that non-textual objects (especially in groups or sets within textual contexts) may not be entirely 'blank', but rather incipient in their textuality. I am offering some fairly wild speculations, but these thoughts are a reminder that despite the apparent solidity of texts, and materialized texts, they are not as stable or unchanging as we might think (see also

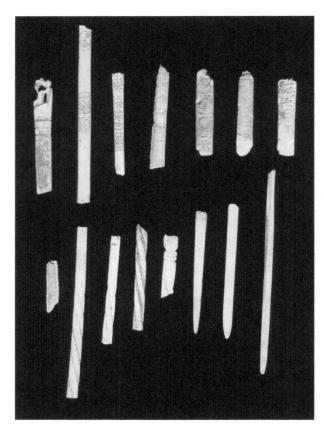

Figure 8: Naranjo weaving bone fragments. Photograph by Chelsea Dacus. Reproduced with permission.

Piquette, this volume). As we consider their technological efficacy, we must take into account the ways in which they change, and readings or experiences of them change.

Finally, as we remember to consider the shifting life story of text objects, it is important to note that a few of the needles included within this collection were broken fragments (**Figure 8**), including some that feature fragments of texts (Dacus 2005: 87–96). We confront here the ultimate materiality of these texts — that they may be destroyed, broken or decommissioned in their physical forms. As a tool for making textiles, a broken weaving needle is no longer efficacious. As a text, a partial statement is a less than completely clear communicative channel. And yet, the inclusion of these objects in this assemblage suggests that the power and meaning of this technology is not completely drained despite this alteration of physical form.

The weaving bones are literally technological: they yield a special type of product, a textile, which is in itself a communicative channel. Their status as text objects makes multidimensional the ways in which they make and remake identities, both connected with individuals (a particular elite woman at the site of Naranjo), and in conjunction with culturally held ideas of gender roles, providing an additional landscape of orientation. We are also reminded that the instability and change that I have commented on in conjunction with constructed landscapes similarly characterize these technologies themselves: they are not stable or static, and the changes within them also impact how they are used and consumed by humans.

Material Channels of Communication

Interaction of Multiple Communicative Channels

In the discussion above of the three case studies, I have considered these text objects through their roles in ordering a variety of landscapes, while also considering how ancient viewers would have interacted with their material forms. In thinking and writing about these objects I have, at times, had to remind myself that our collective focus is on text (not image) and materiality: image and text intersect and intertwine in profound ways on Maya objects, and it is difficult and problematic to attempt to separate them.

The implications of this are several. These objects have powerful voices because there are multiple interpretive modes through which they can be engaged. Literacy is not a black and white proposition for ancient Maya individuals (Houston and Stuart 1992), and one can imagine different levels or types of understanding that would have guided readings of these text objects at varying depths. I argue that the wide range of possibility in reception of these texts makes them powerful as technological agents, and efficient in accomplishing their orientational work — though, presumably, with differing results depending on the viewer's knowledge and interpretation.

I also want to point out that in the preceding discussion, I have often referred to the content of the texts, despite our interest in this volume in moving beyond a transparent reading, and engaging with material practices connected to such text. I have attempted to combine an understanding of the material forms of these text objects with commentary on the content; in the subsection that follows, I will look more closely at how the form of each object impacts the way the text is consumed, and thus how the work of the text object is accomplished. Nonetheless, in thinking about juxtapositions of text and materiality, the examinations above have underlined how analysis of contextualized content, in fact, returns us to material practice, in the form of orientations that shape ancient individuals' sense of self and place — and, by extension, resulting action — within the spheres that they inhabited. As these text objects were encountered and interpreted, they acted to provide direction and instruction to the viewers, through both form and content.

Material Forms of Text Objects

In thinking about Piedras Negras Panel 3, Río Azul Vessel 15, and the Naranjo weaving bones, I acknowledged the different forms of each, and imagined something of how each text object would have been interacted with. What is the impact of the different material forms of these text objects on the work that they accomplish in providing orientation in a number of planes? What is significant about the physical form that they take, and the way that this form is experienced by the viewer?

At Piedras Negras, the ancient viewer would have stood in front of Structure O-13, on the edge of an open, paved plaza, having traveled to this place to see this object, or encountered it by chance while walking through the city. The Río Azul pot was passed from hand to hand, tilted for pouring, set down on the floor, picked up again and filled with fragrant liquid. It was displayed and moved. At Naranjo, the weaving bones were put to use in a loom, and then folded up, perhaps, in a cloth pouch for safekeeping. They were touched and moved, possibly shared with a fellow crafter, and occasionally broken.

As we consider these texts as technology, we must picture how they are put into play and used. By imagining an ancient viewer, we are invited to consider how the text is consumed or internalized. Each of these objects accomplishes their work, and allows for engagement or interaction with itself, through the interface of its material form.

In the case of Panel 3, the form that this text object takes is — clearly — a carved stone wall monument. But, I would argue, thematically this text object operates as a *frame*. Visually, we perceive a social and architectural space (which the text itself helps to bound). The types of local and distant orientation discussed for this monument — spatial, temporal, political — are conveyed through things understood to be within this frame, or to exist beyond its borders.

Analyzing the form of Vessel 15 from Río Azul reveals that, not at all surprisingly, it is (and acts as) a *container*. It holds literal and metaphorical substances that may be consumed or replenished within this volumetric space, and which allow for the storage and movement of these substances to other places and for other people. As a container, this vessel is handled and handed on: it moves between social spaces on individual and group scales.

Finally, the weaving bones are *implements*. They carry out work in direct and indirect ways, and are personal and connective when used for their primary function. As they move in and out of sight, they pass through important substances (textiles), and enter into a recursive process of creating further communicative avenues. Their changing nature is a reminder of the dynamism associated with tools and text objects, as well as their products.

These may seem like less than revolutionary characterizations of these text objects — I am merely placing them into broader descriptive categories. And yet, each of these thematic characterizations says something about how the text and message are transformed by the particular form in, or on, which they are expressed. These descriptors similarly suggest how these texts are interacted with and the modes through which they are interpreted. As we think about these material forms carrying out the orientational work I have described throughout this paper, it becomes clear that the material nature of the text objects themselves provides the avenue through which this expression and maintenance of cultural landscapes is carried out.

Effectiveness Through the Real and the Imaginary

In considering the cultural landscapes that are created and maintained through texts and written technology, I have emphasized that some of these are real and tangible, while others are abstract, distant, or even imaginary to the viewer. Thus, these objects operate on, and locate individuals within, far wider spheres than immediate experience would yield. As we consider the ways that the material forms of these text objects make them particularly effective in their work, we must also notice the effectiveness of these objects in terms of how they combine or juxtapose the real and the imagined.

Throughout, the interest here has been in remaining in touch with the materiality of these objects — these are artifacts, things, that could be (and still can be) touched. In this sense, there is no 'realness problem' with these objects. They were physically present in the ancient world, and remain physically available today. And yet, these objects are static and unanimated: a frozen stone scene of a court, a pot, a collection of carved pieces of bone. For them to carry out their work most effectively, they are used, interacted with, made part of social practices. Intriguingly, some of the very same characteristics I have highlighted in terms of the material natures of these objects are ones that in a very different field, that of literary studies, have been argued to provide authors with powerful ways to lift objects from the page and allow the reader to vividly animate textual descriptions (Scarry 1999). According to Scarry, the presence of a frame (beyond which bodies move, enter, and exit), a tilting motion (of a vessel poured and righted again), and the action of repeated appearance and disappearance (of a bone weaving implement) all are key characteristics of the vivacity of image in literary and cognitive contexts (Scarry 1999: 100–157). In our case, these objects are not imagined, and do not need to be lifted from a two-dimensional page. However, it may be that their physical properties render them especially nimble for being put into motion in the mind, or recalled later when not present or not in active use. By the nature of their material forms, and the ways that these forms are used in practice, these text objects hold particular promise for vivacity and duration in the effects of their work.

Conclusions

Through the discussion and exploration of these three objects, I have argued for text objects acting as a type of material technology, carrying out orientational work in a variety of cultural and experiential landscapes for the people who viewed and used them. Texts are thus intertwined with the material world through the impacts they have on individuals' practices (especially in relation to how they operate in sociopolitical planes, as determined by their relative location and identity), and through the ways in which their material form channels certain types of interactions and interpretations.

Far from being reified in their material form (a common contrast drawn between oral and literate traditions, Ong 1982: 90), we see that the text objects discussed here are changeable in both their material forms and contexts (McGann 1991: 182–186; van Peer 1997). As artifacts, these objects have life histories (Holtorf 2002) and can change in their form and in their place and manner of use. As text objects, the written record becomes implicated with these changes, and may be seen as dynamic, transforming and transformative.

Changeability of these text objects is also important to consider as we imagine their reception among ancient viewers, who would have varied widely in their knowledge, background, and identity. Not all viewers would have perceived all of the orientational directions I have suggested above. Nonetheless, these text objects encode information that potentially provides locational instructions in a material form that is particularly effective due to their combining of multiple communicative channels, and the distinctively evocative and vividly imaginable characteristics of the objects themselves. Understanding these texts in their material forms, and embedding their important content within the physical format that transmitted them, highlights the experience and actions of textual consumption, and allows us to better understand content and form in a synthesized fashion.

Returning to the opening premise of orientational technologies, the carved stone panel, ceramic vessel, and incised weaving bones discussed here all act as markers in experiential landscapes through the ways in which they were used and perceived, and through the work that their textual components do. They are shifting, in form and in perception, a quality that corresponds with the constructed and reconstructed (and thus transforming) nature of cultural landscapes. And, when their material forms are not immediately present or accessible, these text objects may be powerfully evoked, continuing orientational work and uniting both the experiential and imagined aspects of ancient sociopolitical landscapes.

References

Adams, R. E. W. 1999. *Río Azul: An ancient Maya city*. Norman: University of Oklahoma Press.

Anderson, B. 1983. *Imagined Communities: Reflections on the origin and spread of nationalism*. London: Verso.

Baines, J. and Yoffee, N. 1998. Order, Legitimacy, and Wealth in Ancient Egypt and Mesopotamia. In Feinman, G. M. and Marcus, J. (eds), *Archaic States*. Santa Fe: School of American Research Press, 199–260.

Calvin, I. E. 2006. *Between Text and Image: An analysis of pseudo-glyphs on Late Classic Maya pottery from Guatemala*. Unpublished PhD dissertation, University of Colorado.

Carlsen, R. S. 1997. *The War for the Heart and Soul of a Highland Maya Town*. Austin, TX: University of Texas Press.

Coe, M. D. 1973. *The Maya Scribe and His World*. New York: Grolier Club.

Dacus, C. 2005. *Weaving the Past: An examination of bones buried with an elite Maya woman*. Unpublished MA dissertation, Southern Methodist University.

Giddens, A. 1979. *Central Problems in Social Theory: Action, structure, and contradiction in social analysis*. Berkeley: University of California Press.

Hall, G. D., Tarka Jr., S. M., Hurst, W. J., Stuart, D. and Adams, R. E. W. 1990. Cacao Residues in Ancient Maya Vessels from Río Azul, Guatemala. *American Antiquity* 55(1): 138–143. DOI: http://dx.doi.org/10.2307/281499

Halperin, C. T. 2008. Classic Maya Textile Production: Insights from Motul de San José, Peten, Guatemala. *Ancient Mesoamerica* 19(1): 111–125. DOI: http://dx.doi.org/10.1017/S0956536108000230

Hendon, J. A. 2006. Textile Production as Craft in Mesoamerica: Time, labor, and knowledge. *Journal of Social Archaeology* 6(3): 354–378. DOI: http://dx.doi.org/10.1177/1469605306067841

Holtorf, C. 2002. Notes on the Life History of a Pot Sherd. *Journal of Material Culture* 7(1): 49–71. DOI: http://dx.doi.org/10.1177/1359183502007001305

Houston, S. D. 1998. Classic Maya Depictions of the Built Environment. In Houston, S. D. (ed.), *Function and Meaning in Classic Maya Architecture*. Washington, DC: Dumbarton Oaks, 333–372.

Houston, S. and Stuart, D. 1992. On Maya Hieroglyphic Literacy. *Current Anthropology* 33(5): 589–593. DOI: http://dx.doi.org/10.1086/204117

Houston, S. and Stuart, D. 2001. Peopling the Classic Maya Court. In Inomata, T. and Houston, S. (eds), *Royal Courts of the Ancient Maya, Volume 1: Theory, comparison, and synthesis*. Boulder: Westview Press, 54–83.

Houston, S. and Taube, K. 1987. "Name-tagging" in Classic Mayan Script: Implications for native classifications of ceramics and jade ornament. *Mexicon* 9(2): 38–41.

Houston, S. D., Stuart, D. and Taube, K. A. 1989. Folk Classification of Classic Maya Pottery. *American Anthropologist* 91(3): 720–726. DOI: http://dx.doi.org/10.1525/aa.1989.91.3.02a00130

Houston, S. D., Stuart, D. and Taube, K. A. 2006. *The Memory of Bones: Body, being, and experience among the Classic Maya*. Austin, TX: University of Texas Press.

Ingold, T. 2000. *The Perception of the Environment: Essays on livelihood, dwelling and skill*. London: Routledge.

Inomata, T. 2001. Power and Ideology of Artistic Creation: Elite craft specialists in Classic Maya society. *Current Anthropology* 42(3): 321–349. DOI: http://dx.doi.org/10.1086/320475

Jackson, S. E. 2009. Imagining Courtly Communities: An exploration of Classic Maya experiences of status and identity through painted ceramic vessels. *Ancient Mesoamerica* 20(1): 71–85. DOI: http://dx.doi.org/10.1017/S0956536109000066

LeCount, L. J. 2001. Like Water for Chocolate: Feasting and political ritual among the Late Classic Maya at Xunantunich, Belize. *American Anthropologist* 103(4): 935–953. DOI: http://dx.doi.org/10.1525/aa.2001.103.4.935

Macri, M. 2005. Nahua Loan Words from the Early Classic Period: Words for cacao preparation on a Río Azul ceramic vessel. *Ancient Mesoamerica* 16(2): 321–326. DOI: http://dx.doi.org/10.1017/S0956536105050200

Marcus, J. 1976. *Emblem and State in the Classic Maya Lowlands: An epigraphic approach to territorial organization*. Washington, DC: Dumbarton Oaks.

Marcus, J. and Flannery, K. V. 1994. Ancient Zapotec Ritual and Religion: An application of the direct historical approach. In Renfrew, C. and Zubrow, E. B. W. (eds), *The Ancient Mind: Elements of cognitive archaeology*. Cambridge: Cambridge University Press, 55–74. DOI: http://dx.doi.org/10.1017/CBO9780511598388.008

Martin, S. and Grube, N. 2000. *Chronicle of the Maya Kings and Queens: Deciphering the dynasties of the ancient Maya*. London: Thames and Hudson.

McAnany, P. A. 1995. *Living with the Ancestors: Kinship and kingship in ancient Maya society*. Austin, TX: University of Texas Press.

McGann, J. J. 1991. *The Textual Condition*. Princeton, NJ: Princeton University Press.

O'Neil, M. 2005. *Making Visible History: Engaging ancient Maya sculpture*. Unpublished PhD dissertation, Yale University.

O'Neil, M. 2012. *Engaging Ancient Maya Sculpture at Piedras Negras, Guatemala*. Norman: University of Oklahoma Press.

Ong, W. J. 1982. *Orality and Literacy: The technologizing of the word*. London: Routledge.

Prechtel, M. and Carlsen, R. S. 1988. Weaving and Cosmos among the Tzutujil Maya of Guatemala. *Res* 15: 123–132.

Proskouriakoff, T. 1963. Historical Data in the Inscriptions of Yaxchilan, Part 1. *Estudios de Cultural Maya* 3: 147–167.

Reents-Budet, D. 1998. Elite Maya Pottery and Artisans as Social Indicators. In Costin, C. L. and Wright, R. P. (eds), *Craft and Social Identity*. Arlington, VA: American Anthropological Association, 71–89.

Schele, L. and Freidel, D. A. 1990. *A Forest of Kings: The untold story of the ancient Maya*. New York: Morrow.

Scarry, E. 1999. *Dreaming by the Book*. New York: Farrar, Straus and Giroux.

Stuart, D. 1988. The Río Azul Cacao Pot: Epigraphic observations on the function of a Maya ceramic vessel. *Antiquity* 62: 153–157.

van Peer, W. 1997. Mutilated Signs: Notes toward a literary paleography. *Poetics Today* 18(1): 33–57. DOI: http://dx.doi.org/10.2307/1773232

Writing (and Reading) as Material Practice: The world of cuneiform culture as an arena for investigation

Roger Matthews
University of Reading

Let me read the tablets in the presence of the king, my lord, and let me put down on them whatever is agreeable to the king; whatever is not acceptable to the king, I shall remove from them. The tablets I am speaking about are worth preserving until far-off days. (7th century BC cuneiform inscription on clay tablet from Nineveh, capital of the Neo-Assyrian empire, see Frame and George 2005: 278).

In an age where 'the death of the book' is heralded almost daily (Ehrenreich 2011 poetically situates the debates), and where new modes of expression and consumption of the written word are freely elaborated, we are perhaps especially sensitised to the materiality of the writings, and the readings, that inhabit our world. In this chapter, following a brief review of current research, I consider some key questions in the materiality of writing, drawing on case-studies from the world of "cuneiform culture" that dominated the ancient Near East for more than 3000 years from its beginnings around 3200 BC (Radner and Robson 2011).

Current Research into the Materiality of Ancient Near Eastern Texts

Following a long and occasionally fraught relationship between archaeologists and historians of the ancient Near East (Liverani 1999; Matthews 2003; Zimansky 2005), the topic of textual materiality is increasingly considered in studies by Near Eastern epigraphists and archaeologists working together to achieve shared aims. It has long been appreciated that the shape and format of clay tablets bearing cuneiform script is frequently related to the content of those texts (e.g.

How to cite this book chapter:
Matthews, R. 2013. Writing (and Reading) as Material Practice: The world of cuneiform culture as an arena for investigation. In: Piquette, K. E. and Whitehouse, R. D. (eds.) *Writing as Material Practice: Substance, surface and medium.* Pp. 65-74. London: Ubiquity Press. DOI: http://dx.doi.org/10.5334/bai.d

Radner 1995) but such associations, and many others, are now being explored in more rigorous detail and with new scientific methods.

In his recent book, Dominique Charpin (2010: 25–42) has articulated a manifesto for what he terms a "diplomatics of Mesopotamian documents", whereby attention of the historian expands beyond the purely textual content of cuneiform documents to a concern with physical form, including materiality (of tablet and stylus), the palaeography of written signs, the layout of texts, and the use of seals on texts (see also van de Mieroop 1999). In the broader context, the historian must also consider issues of how specific texts, or groups of texts, came to be written in the first place and how they came to be preserved within archives, or otherwise, for ultimate discovery in the archaeological record. A model of fruitful collaboration between epigraphy and archaeology is the study by Italian scholars of Ur III texts (late 3rd millennium BC) from southern Iraq currently housed in the British Museum (D'Agostino et al. 2004). Their study combines conventional epigraphy with analytical approaches to a range of material attributes including formal typology of tablet shape and size, location and type of fingerprints, and the varying uses of seals on texts. Most innovative is their application of archaeometric methods (Inductively Coupled Plasma — Optical Emission Spectroscopy and Inductively Coupled Plasma — Mass Spectrometry) in order to characterise the clays employed in tablet manufacture. While so far limited in its interpretive scope, their pilot study starts to map out the contours of a future landscape of investigation, offering approaches and methods which may have applicability across and beyond the world of cuneiform culture.

Two larger-scale developments encourage the belief that holistic, integrated approaches to the materiality of texts from the ancient Near East, and beyond, are becoming established in the academic arena, as advocated throughout the 2009 Writing as Material Practice conference (see Piquette and Whitehouse, this volume). Firstly, in April 2010 at the 7th International Congress on the Archaeology of the Ancient Near East (7ICAANE) in London a one-day workshop, organised by Jon Taylor of the British Museum, was devoted to the topic of 'Composition and Manufacture of Clay Tablets'. Papers covered a range of material topics including plant and shell inclusions within clay tablets as potential indicators of provenance and local environment, the recycling of tablets, the possible detection of increasing salinity in the Mesopotamian environment through analysis of diatoms, phytoliths and shells contained within clay tablets, and applications of portable X-Ray Fluorescence (pXRF) to clay tablets. Subsequent publications by Taylor and colleagues confirm the strong trajectory of this area of research (Cartwright and Taylor 2011; Taylor 2011). Secondly, at Heidelberg University a generously-funded Collaborative Research Centre has been established by the German Research Foundation in order to investigate 'Material Text Cultures: Materiality and presence of the scriptural in non-typographic societies', with the commendable ambition to apply a range of scientific and humanities approaches to the study of textual materiality from many societies of the ancient world, including Egypt and Mesopotamia. Here, indeed, a new 'textual anthropology' is taking shape (for information on the new centre see: http://www.materiale-textkulturen.de).

Who Wrote the Text in Question and Why?

All texts have authors and all texts have reasons for being written and for being read. In considering this question of who wrote the text in question and why, we encounter issues such as the spread and extent of the ability to write and read within specific societies, the role, social status, and training of scribes, and the situation of written texts at the intersection of a range of social components with potentially differing angles of engagement with specific texts. The extent and spread of writing within ancient Near Eastern societies was highly variable through time and space (**Figure 1**). At its origins in the late 4th millennium BC world of Uruk Mesopotamia, writing

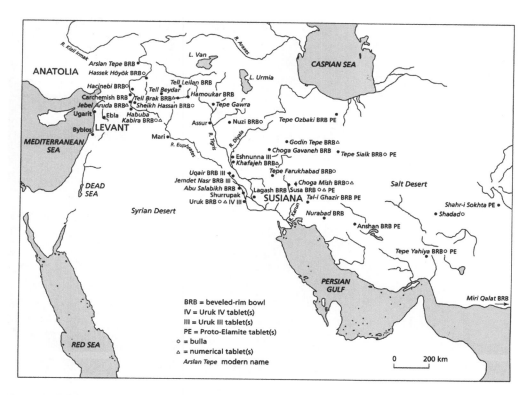

Figure 1: Map of the proto-cuneiform world (after van de Mieroop 2004: 36, map 2.2).

was an instrument of centralised control developed in order to facilitate temple administration of labour and agricultural production (Algaze 2008; Englund 1998; Liverani 2006). The world's earliest writing, in the so-called proto-cuneiform tradition, was produced exclusively by and for bureaucrats working on behalf of large centralised institutions at the very origins of the state. Echoes of this role for writing are attested in outposts of Uruk control along major trade routes reaching out from Mesopotamia, as for example at Godin Tepe in central-west Iran where a small collection of clay tablets, some with seal impressions, indicate the presence of a cadre of Uruk, or Uruk-influenced, bureaucrats exercising their newly developed administrative technology in order to control local agricultural activity and production (Matthews 2013). The quantities and range of commodities attested in the Godin Tepe texts, such as small quantities of domestic animals and dairy produce, are so limited that one wonders whether their administration through written texts was not so much a bureaucratic necessity as a means of demonstrating the power of those who could write over those who could not. As Algaze points out (2008: 138), from its earliest manifestation the written text appears to align with Lévi-Strauss' dictum that "the primary function of writing, as a means of communication, is to facilitate the enslavement of other human beings" (1964: 292).

In later times cuneiform culture expanded to incorporate a broader remit of social and economic engagement (**Figure 2**). Writing, increasingly regularised in its execution and with a much-reduced sign repertoire, was used both in a wider array of roles — for letters, contracts, lists, treaties, prayers and annals — and also to express a diverse wealth of largely unrelated languages, including Sumerian, Akkadian (Assyrian and Babylonian), Hurrian, Hittite, Elamite, Ugaritic, and others distributed across the ancient Near East (Zimansky 2005). The extent of the ability to write and read needs investigation in each individual case through time and space. Charpin (2010:

a

b

Figure 2: A sample of the variety of shapes and sizes of cuneiform texts on clay (after Taylor 2011: 9–10, figs 2A and 2). a) (Top) Archaic: administrative (BM 128826); Early Dynastic: administrative (BM 15829, BM 29996, BM 102081); Old Akkadian: administrative (BM 86281, BM 86289, BM 86332); Ur III: administrative (BM 24964), cone (BM 19528). (Middle) Ur III: administrative (BM 19525, BM 104650, BM 13059, BM 19176, BM 26972, BM 26950, BM 110116). (Bottom) Old Babylonian: administrative (BM 16825), letter (BM 23145), administrative (BM 87373), scholarly (UET 6/3 64, on loan to the British Museum; Old Assyrian: administrative (BM 120548). © Trustees of the British Museum; b) (Top) Nuzi: administrative (BM 17616, BM 26280); Amarna letters (British Museum, ME 29883, ME 29785); Middle Babylonian: administrative (BM 17689, BM 17673, BM 17626). (Left) Neo-Assyrian prism (BM 91032), scholarly (British Museum, K 750), letter (British Museum, K 469), administrative (British Museum, K309a), scholarly (British Museum, K 159, K 195, K 4375, K 2811). (Right) Neo-Late Babylonian: barrel (BM 91142, BM 30690), administrative (BM 29589), scholarly (BM 92693), administrative (BM 30912, BM 30690), scholarly (BM 38104, BM 34580). © Trustees of the British Museum.

7–24) has questioned the conventional assumption that reading and writing in Mesopotamia were solely "the business of specialists", arguing that differing levels of competence in writing, and reading, the cuneiform script are attested by texts from a range of archaeological contexts. In the early 2nd millennium BC there is good evidence that Assyrian merchants were capable of writing and reading by themselves, without input from specialist scribes, employing a limited syllabary of fewer than 70 signs (Charpin 2010: 19). Lion (2011) has stressed that in the same period in Assyria and Babylonia significant numbers of women as well as men could read and write.

Veldhuis (2011) has explored the versatility inherent in the cuneiform writing system, which enabled several types and degrees of literacy to co-exist. Not everyone had to be a top-level scholar, with years of expert training behind them, in order to participate in the cuneiform system. Veldhuis identifies three broad categories of cuneiform literacy – functional, technical, and scholarly. Functional literacy could be attained by a wide range of citizens of the Mesopotamian city-states, in particular during the huge expansion of the uses of writing during the early 2nd millennium BC, the Old Babylonian period, while technical literacy relates to expertise in specialist areas of cuneiform practice, such as divination and mathematical texts. The most accomplished scribes can be described as 'scholarly literate', defined by Veldhuis as exhibiting "the pride of the scribes in their craft, emphasizing and even increasing complexity and demonstrating the joy of discovering rare and unusual features of the system" (Veldhuis 2011: 74). It would make an interesting exercise to track the shifting proportions of these three types of literacy through the 3000-year history of the cuneiform world and to consider their variability in the light of changing political and social regimes.

A related issue concerns societies which choose not to write. In a rare study of this question Lamberg-Karlovsky (2003) surveys through time the interaction of literate societies with non-literate societies across the ancient Near East, detecting only one example (the short-lived Proto-Elamite phenomenon) of a non-literate society adopting the practice of writing through contact with a literate society. His interpretation is that indigenous societies deliberately rejected writing because of its association with forms of externally-imposed control and with specific religious and social contexts that were alien, indeed hostile and exploitative, to non-literate societies.

How were textual traditions maintained and sustained through time and space? The transmission and control of written knowledge in the ancient Near East was materialised through two intersecting networks, forming a chrono-spatial framework. A horizontal network in space involved largely elite and merchant elements of states and empires, operating across the geographic span of specific states by means of movement of letters, contracts, and archives as well as of the writing skills and capabilities, in the form of scribes, (the website Knowledge and Power in the Neo-Assyrian Empire provides excellent coverage of these and related issues: http://oracc.museum. upenn.edu/saao/knpp/). But there was also a network of vertical transmission, and indeed control, of knowledge through time which was sustained and enriched by the very materiality of cuneiform culture, through not just decades or centuries but over millennia.

Archives of clay tablets appear from the very start of the cuneiform tradition and last until its end (Pedersén 1998). They served as a major means of the vertical transmission of knowledge through the curation of archives and libraries within the context of palaces and temples in imperial core cities, as attested at Nineveh and many other cities. Assurbanipal's 7th-century BC library of c.28,000 clay tablets (plus an unknown number of wooden texts that have not survived) constitutes vivid evidence that the king could take a personal and learned interest in the reception, definition, and transmission of knowledge through time (Frame and George 2005). At a deeper level, we can also see a role for the materiality of texts in the persistence of templates of social power, of cultic belief and practice, of knowledge control and transmission through the entire epoch of cuneiform culture.

Why do people stop writing texts? While much study has been invested in the origins of scripts and writing traditions, less attention has been devoted to what has been called "script obsolescence" (Houston et al. 2003; for numerous case-studies of the rise and demise of languages and their texts see also Baines et al. 2008; Ostler 2005). The only answer can be that people stop writing, at all or in specific ways, when the social context of their writing disappears or is transformed beyond sustainability. An illustrative example is the steady disappearance of skills in Arabic calligraphy in contemporary Lebanon, and elsewhere in the Islamic world, due to the rise of computer-generated calligraphy. Here a technological shift, embedded in social change, is transforming classical calligraphy into "a visual art rather than a useful tool" (http://www.alarabiya.net/articles/2011/07/30/160088.html).

Who Was Meant to See or Read the Text?

With the question of who was meant to see or read a given text, we are concerned with issues such as audience and accessibility of texts. The earliest proto-cuneiform texts were not designed to be read outside the administrative sphere, and so to the historian today they can be laconic and obtuse in their content. Even their language (or languages?) is unreachable through the distribution of incised signs, some 900 of them, that early scribes marked on the soft clay tablets with their styli. Their most approachable component is the array of numerical systems employed to count and account for quantities of people, animals, and products as they made their way through the bureaucratic world (Chrisomalis 2010 provides a brilliant comparative study of the world's systems of numerical notation, including those of ancient Mesopotamia).

How were cuneiform texts read? Charpin (2010: 20–22) proposes that in almost every case a cuneiform text would be read aloud either by a literate reader to him / herself or by a scribe to a non-literate listener, such as an official or royal recipient. Additionally, Charpin cites rare evidence that scribes might silently read texts to themselves as a means of rapidly checking their content. When we sit today in the British Museum study room and see the distinguished cuneiform scholars silently working their way through trays of broken clay tablets, perhaps we should encourage them occasionally to voice their readings aloud so that we might share in the aurality of the text and thereby gain an idea of how an ancient reader / listener might have encountered the written word (for a bold attempt at spoken Akkadian, by Irving Finkel of the British Museum, see http://www.bbc.co.uk/news/world-middle-east-13733615).

What Was the Physical Medium and Context of the Text?

The analysis of clays used to make tablets in the cuneiform tradition is in the early stages of development (Taylor 2011). Most significant has been the work of Yuval Goren and colleagues in applying mineralogical and chemical analyses to corpora of clay tablets in order to explore issues of provenance and movement of inscribed clay tablets (Goren et al. 2004). The basic premise of their work is that "Even within an assemblage of documents composed by the same individual, each tablet should be treated as a unique artefact, created under very special and distinctive circumstances" (Goren et al. 2004: 316). As mentioned above, methods have built upon earlier uses of Neutron Activation Analysis, applying Inductively Coupled Plasma analyses combined with systematic study of micropalaeontology and micropalaeobotany in order to characterise inclusions within clay matrices (Cartwright and Taylor 2011). In a pioneering and exhaustive study by Goren et al. of around 300 clay tablets found at el-Amarna in Egypt, dated to the mid-14th century BC, these approaches have been integrated with geological and historical studies in the generation of truly significant interpretations relating to the selection of clays for tablet manufacture, the deliberate addition of inclusions to the clay, the processes of firing of tablets to ensure durability, and a host of insights into the historical specifics of cuneiform communication between city-states of several regions of the ancient Near East in the international age of the Late Bronze Age.

The most promising recent development has been the application of a new generation of portable X-Ray Fluorescence (pXRF) analysers to clay tablets from the Near Eastern past, as conducted by Goren et al. (2011) on tablets from the Hittite capital Hattusa and other sites. Increasingly sensitive capabilities of pXRF, coupled with the ability to characterise clay elements through non-invasive, non-destructive means, have opened a new chapter in archaeometric investigation of clay tablets and clay sealings. As touched on previously, the full implications of the new technology have yet to be articulated and realised but there is hope that access can increasingly be had to multiple museum collections of tablets and sealings in systematic programmes of analysis and interpretation. Such programmes will need to comprise integrated strategies involving archaeologists, historians, geologists and materials scientists.

The materiality of each text has a specific and contingent trajectory. The display of Neo-Assyrian texts, cut into stone slabs, within their palatial contexts has been an especially fruitful arena for integrated epigraphical and archaeological investigation, centring on the physicality of text. To the forefront has been the work of John Russell (1999) whose meticulous study of the location of stone inscriptions within Neo-Assyrian palaces begins with a vivid description of the materiality of text in Assurnasirpal II's 9th century BC palace at Nimrud:

> "Once upon a time, a long time ago, anyone fortunate — or unfortunate — enough to enter the palace of 'the king of the world, king of Assyria', would have been surrounded by texts. In the first great Neo-Assyrian palace, the palace of Assurnasirpal II at Kalhu (Nimrud), texts were everywhere. The bull and lion colossi in the major doorways carried texts. The pavement slabs in those doorways, and in every other doorway, carried texts. Every floor slab in every paved room carried a text. And each one of the hundreds of wall slabs, sculptured and plain, carried a text" (Russell 1999: 1).

Russell (1999) interprets the role of texts within the architectural scheme of Neo-Assyrian palaces at several levels, including the materialisation of a desire to mark royal ownership of the newly-built palace, the decorative transformation of "dull structural fittings into active royal monuments", the affirmation of a royal aura to the palatial monument, and above all the agency of texts as "visual icons of kingship" (Russell 1999: 230).

How Representative are Surviving Texts of the Corpus of Their Place and Period?

Scholars of the ancient Near East are fortunate in that the subjects of our study wrote on clay. We already have hundreds of thousands of cuneiform-script clay tablets in our museums, and there are certainly many times that number still to be excavated — hopefully only through modern legal archaeological investigation. The recent looting and destruction of entire ancient cities in southern Iraq (Stone and Farchakh Bajjaly 2008) has without doubt led to serious disruption to the evidential base of cuneiform culture, in particular as regards its all-important archaeological context, but we have no way of measuring the full extent of that disruption. Nevertheless, it is important that we consider how representative is our so-far recovered collection of cuneiform texts. A thoughtful comment on this topic is provided by Aage Westenholz (2002):

> "I reckon that of all the texts that were produced, 99 per cent were destroyed, most of it quite soon — the clay of the tablets was recycled. Of the 1 per cent that survived and is still buried in the ground, about 1 per cent has been recovered in excavations; and of that, about one-half has been made available to scholarship in often less-than-adequate publications. A sample of one in 20,000, quite unevenly distributed by random chance!" (Westenholz 2002: 23–24).

It is worth noting that ancient Near Eastern scribes also wrote on materials other than clay tablets and stone monuments, especially towards the end of the cuneiform period. Writing-boards, papyri and parchments are attested by occasional archaeological evidence, such as waxed boards from Nimrud (Wiseman 1955) and the Ulu Burun ship-wreck (Payton 1991; see also Whittaker, this volume), and by depictions on Assyrian reliefs. The Great Temple at Hattusa, capital of the Hittite empire of Anatolia, employed in the 13th century BC no fewer than 52 scribes, 33 of whom were noted as writing on wooden boards not on clay tablets (Bryce 2002: 60). This scribal proportion suggests that as much as 60% of the Hittite written record may have been recorded on wood. Needless to say, none of those wooden tablets have yet been found in the archaeological record while so far more than 30,000 clay tablet fragments have been recovered from Hattusa and other Hittite sites (Collins 2007: 141). There are also rare instances of cuneiform script cut into metal plaques such as the famous bronze treaty of Tudhaliya IV from the Sphinx Gate at Hattusa (Otten 1988).

We can make a final point about the durability and materiality of cuneiform culture. The transmission of knowledge from the ancient Near East to scholars today is largely direct and physical, without intermediaries, unlike most extended texts from the Classical world which reach us in the form of the modern printed page (or digital screen) having been copied and often altered over centuries of transmission through a variety of media. Today we can hold in our hands the very first exemplars of writing from the city of Uruk, impressed on the soft clay some 5200 years ago. We can feel the weight and shape of the tablet, even smell its clay, very much as the ancient scribe did. Our encounter with cuneiform culture through the shape and texture of its surviving clay tablets keeps us firmly attached to its ancient materiality, preserved indeed from far-off days.

I conclude by briefly considering some issues of broader relevance relating to the materiality of writing. One main area of study addressed in several papers at the conference (see Piquette and Whitehouse, this volume) relates to the sources of raw materials and the processes of manufacture of the supports used for writing (primarily clay tablets in the case of cuneiform writing); these studies are relevant to assessing who the writers and readers might have been, as well as who else might have been involved in the creation and consumption of the finished artefacts. The combination of traditional epigraphic studies (concerned with the content of texts) with the study of both the materiality of the inscribed artefacts and their archaeological contexts offers the greatest interpretative possibilities.

The relationship of materiality to the contexts of storage and display is also important: in the cuneiform world there is a strong contrast between the clay tablets, the majority of which come from archive contexts and were probably intended for use by those who could read them, and inscriptions on stone which were mostly situated in public or semi-public places and were meant to be seen and to impress a wide range of people including those, probably the majority, who could not actually read them, as in the Neo-Assyrian palaces described above. The materiality of writing on stone set up in public places is clearly related to the exercise and display of power by elites.

Another important aspect of the materiality of writing supports, as well as that created through the application of materials to surfaces, relates to their likelihood of preservation and survival both in ancient times and down to the present day. Taking of account of what types of writing or related cultural context may not be represented archaeologically is equally important for understanding the various roles it played in past lives. The development of holistic, integrated approaches to the materiality of cuneiform texts is well underway, as I aim to have illustrated here. The application and continued development of methods which integrate material perspectives alongside general archaeological and philological methods are vital for fuller understandings of written culture.

References

Algaze, G. 2008. *Ancient Mesopotamia at the Dawn of Civilization*. Chicago: University of Chicago Press. DOI: http://dx.doi.org/10.7208/chicago/9780226013787.001.0001

Baines, J., Bennet, J. and Houston, S. D. 2008. *The Disappearance of Writing Systems: Perspectives on literacy and communication*. London: Equinox.

Bryce, T. 2002. *Life and Society in the Hittite World*. Oxford: Oxford University Press.

Cartwright, C. and Taylor J. 2011. Investigating Technological and Environmental Evidence from Plant Remains and Molluscs in Cuneiform Tablets. *British Museum Technical Research Bulletin* 5: 67–72

Charpin, D. 2010. *Writing, Law, and Kingship in Old Babylonian Mesopotamia*. Chicago: University of Chicago Press. DOI: http://dx.doi.org/10.7208/chicago/9780226101590.001.0001

Chrisomalis, S. 2010. *Numerical Notation: A comparative history*. Cambridge: Cambridge University Press. DOI: http://dx.doi.org/10.1017/CBO9780511676062

Collins, B. J. 2007. *The Hittites and Their World*. Atlanta: Society of Biblical Literature.

D'Agostino, F., Pomponio, F. and Laurito, R. 2004. *Neo-Sumerian Texts from Ur in the British Museum*. Messina: Grafica Cristal.

Ehrenreich, B. 2011. The Death of the Book. *Los Angeles Review of Books*. 18 April. http://lareviewofbooks.org/essay/the-death-of-the-book [accessed 7 November 2013]

Englund, R. K. 1998. Texts from the Late Uruk Period. In Bauer, J., Englund, R. K. and Krebernik, M. (eds), *Mesopotamien: Späturuk-Zeit und Frühdynastische Zeit* (Orbis Biblicus et Orientalis 160/1). Freiburg: University of Freiburg, 13–233.

Frame, G. and George, A. R. 2005. The Royal Libraries of Nineveh: New evidence for king Ashurbanipal's tablet collecting. *Iraq* 67: 265–284.

Goren, Y., Finkelstein, I. and Na'aman, N. 2004. *Inscribed in Clay: Provenance study of the Amarna Letters and other ancient Near Eastern texts*. Tel Aviv: Tel Aviv University.

Goren, Y., Mommsen, H. and Klinger, J. 2011. Non-Destructive Provenance Study of Cuneiform Tablets Using Portable X-Ray Fluorescence (pXRF). *Journal of Archaeological Science* 38(3): 684–696. DOI: http://dx.doi.org/10.1016/j.jas.2010.10.020

Houston, S., Baines, J. and Cooper, J. 2003. Last Writing: Script obsolescence in Egypt, Mesopotamia, and Mesoamerica. *Comparative Studies in Society and History* 45: 430–479. DOI: http://dx.doi.org/10.1017/S0010417503000227

Lamberg-Karlovsky, C. C. 2003. To Write or Not to Write. In Potts, T., Roaf, M. and Stein, D. (eds), *Culture through Objects: Ancient Near Eastern studies in honour of P. R. S. Moorey*. Oxford: Griffith Institute, 59–75.

Lévi-Strauss, C. 1964. *Tristes Tropiques*. New York: Atheneum.

Lion, B. 2011. Literacy and Gender. In Radner, K. and Robson, E. (eds), *The Oxford Handbook of Cuneiform Culture*. Oxford: Oxford University Press, 90–112. DOI: http://dx.doi.org/10.1093/oxfordhb/9780199557301.013.0005

Liverani, M. 1999. History and Archaeology in the Ancient Near East: 150 years of a difficult relationship. In Kühne, H., Bernbeck, R. and Bartl, K. (eds), *Fluchtpunkt Uruk: Archäologische Einheit aus Methodischer Viefalt. Schriften für Hans Jörg Nissen*. Rahden: Verlag Marie Leidorf, 1–11.

Liverani, M. 2006. *Uruk: The First City*. London: Equinox.

Matthews, R. 2003. *The Archaeology of Mesopotamia: Theories and approaches*. London: Routledge.

Matthews, R. 2013. The Power of Writing: Administrative activity at Godin Tepe, central Zagros, in the later 4th millennium BC. In Petrie, C. A. (ed.), *Ancient Iran and Its Neighbours*. Oxford: Oxbow Books, 327–341.

Ostler, N. 2005. *Empires of the Word: A language history of the world*. London: Harper Collins.

Otten, H. 1988. *Die Bronzetafel aus Boğazköy: ein Staatsvertrag Tuthalijas IV*. Wiesbaden: Harrassowitz.

Payton, R. 1991. The Ulu Burun Writing-Board Set. *Anatolian Studies* 41: 99–106. DOI: http://dx.doi.org/10.2307/3642932

Pedersén, O. 1998. *Archives and Libraries in the Ancient Near East, 1500–300 BC*. Bethesda: CDL Press.

Radner, K. 1995. The Relation Between Format and Content of Neo-Assyrian Texts. In Mattila, R. (ed.), *Nineveh 612 BC: The glory and fall of the Assyrian Empire*. Helsinki: University of Helsinki Press, 63–77.

Radner, K. and Robson, E. (eds) 2011. *The Oxford Handbook of Cuneiform Culture*. Oxford: Oxford University Press. DOI: http://dx.doi.org/10.1093/oxfordhb/9780199557301.001.0001

Russell, J. 1999. *The Writing on the Wall: Studies in the architectural context of Late Assyrian palace inscriptions*. Winona Lake: Eisenbrauns.

Stone, P. G. and Farchakh Bajjaly, J. 2008. *The Destruction of Cultural Heritage in Iraq*. Woodbridge: Boydell and Brewer.

Taylor, J. 2011. Tablets as Artefacts, Scribes as Artisans. In Radner, K. and Robson, E. (eds), *The Oxford Handbook of Cuneiform Culture*. Oxford: Oxford University Press, 5–31. DOI: http://dx.doi.org/10.1093/oxfordhb/9780199557301.013.0001

van de Mieroop, M. 1999. *Cuneiform Texts and the Writing of History*. London: Routledge.

van de Mieroop, M. 2004. *A History of the Ancient Near East ca. 3000–323 BC*. Oxford: Blackwell Publishing.

Veldhuis, N. 2011. Levels of Literacy. In Radner, K. and Robson, E. (eds), *The Oxford Handbook of Cuneiform Culture*. Oxford: Oxford University Press, 68–89. DOI: http://dx.doi.org/10.1093/oxfordhb/9780199557301.013.0004

Westenholz, A. 2002. The Sumerian City-State. In Hansen, M. H. (ed.), *A Comparative Study of Six City-State Cultures*. Copenhagen: C. A. Reitzels, 23–42.

Wiseman, D. J. 1955. Assyrian Writing-Boards. *Iraq* 17: 3–13.

Zimansky, P. 2005. Archaeology and Texts in the Ancient Near East. In Pollock, S. and Bernbeck, R. (eds), *Archaeologies of the Middle East: Critical perspectives*. Oxford: Blackwell, 308–326.

Re-writing the Script: Decoding the textual experience in the Bronze Age Levant (*c.*2000–1150 BC)

Rachael Thyrza Sparks

University College London

Introduction

A review of the types of writing found in the Southern Levant during the Middle and Late Bronze Ages underlines one fact: textual evidence is much rarer in this region than contemporary Egypt, Syria-Lebanon or Mesopotamia. There is a dearth of significant deposits of clay tablet archives or sealings, and the organic materials on which so much ancient writing was probably carried out, such as wood, leather and imported papyrus are only rarely preserved. Even within the materials that have survived, there are further problems with chronology and context, as many examples are poorly provenanced, making it difficult to pinpoint exactly when various developments in palaeography or technique took place. The fact that these data are both statistically insignificant and heavily biased towards certain types of materials makes it something of a challenge to establish how and when different types of script were introduced into the area and the ways in which they were subsequently used, and there is the constant risk that we may have to 'rewrite' our understanding of these processes as fresh evidence comes to hand. Most studies that have been done on writing in the region have been quite specialised, focusing on particular scripts and tending to concentrate on aspects of language rather than the way in which writing is created and used. In particular, the material aspects of this technology have rarely been addressed. This has served to obscure its overall range and diversity.

There are currently around 61 cuneiform texts attributable to the Bronze Age (recording Sumerian, Akkadian, and West Semitic languages; Horowitz et al. 2006), three in alphabetic cuneiform, some 17 Proto-Canaanite examples (Sass 1988; Hamilton 2006; 2010), six in Hittite hieroglyphic (Singer 1977; 1993; 2003) and two probable examples of Aegean scripts (this figure

How to cite this book chapter:
Sparks, R. T. 2013. Re-writing the Script: Decoding the textual experience in the Bronze Age Levant (*c.*2000–1150 BC). In: Piquette, K. E. and Whitehouse, R. D. (eds.) *Writing as Material Practice: Substance, surface and medium.* Pp. 75-104. London: Ubiquity Press. DOI: http://dx.doi.org/10.5334/bai.e

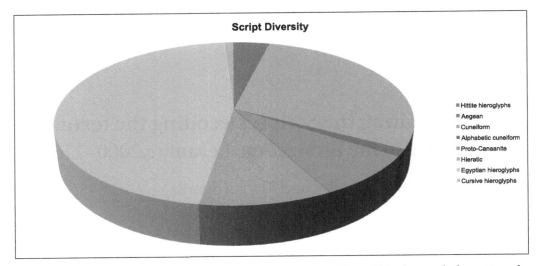

Figure 1: Script diversity in the Southern Levant *c.*2000–1150 BC. This data excludes pot marks and hieroglyphic-shaped amulets, as it is debatable whether these functioned as writing rather than as symbols or markers. It also excludes hieroglyphic and pseudo-hieroglyphic scarab and seal inscriptions, because the quantity of objects involved would be overwhelming and obscure other patterns in the material.

excludes pot-marks based on the known Cypro-Minoan syllabary, as their identification as writing can be questioned: Cross and Stager 2006; Dothan 1979: 12, fig. 15). Hieratic is represented by at least 21 objects. However the most common group of texts are in Egyptian hieroglyphic; at least 118 examples are known, across a wide range of object types, and the figure explodes into the thousands if one includes the texts moulded or incised onto personal scarabs. Two examples of the less common cursive form of hieroglyphic complete the known repertoire of script forms. No single catalogue of either hieratic or hieroglyphic texts from the region has ever been published, but various studies have dealt with differing aspects of both (Eggler and Keel 2006; Goldwasser 1984; Keel 1997; Maeir et al. 2004; Mumford 1998; Porter and Moss 1952; Sweeney 2004). A summary of script and language diversity may be found in **Figures 1–2**.

While the linguistic demands of each speciality make a focus on individual scripts understandable, it is worth revisiting the phenomenon of writing in the region in a more holistic fashion, considering what archaeology can contribute to current debate through a study of the materiality of script use, and how this relates to the needs of different individuals and communities. This perspective raises new questions, including what types of materials and objects are used to carry writing, how script size, shape, location and so on inform use and meaning, where such inscribed objects are found, and what these material features and archaeological contexts can tell us about *who* is using them.

In Middle Bronze Age Canaan, the evidence for use of script is both limited, and mixed in nature. Cuneiform is poorly represented by discoveries of clay tablets at sites such as Hazor and Shechem, clay liver models and appearances on a ceramic jug, and on stone and clay cylinder seals of this period (Horowitz et al. 2006: 46, 65–80, 83–85, 88–91, 95, 121–123). The technique of execution depends on the material being utilised; signs are generally impressed on clay and incised into stone. An exception is a ceramic jug from Hazor, where a cult symbol was drawn in the clay before firing and an Akkadian personal name scratched into the surface afterwards (Horowitz et al. 2006: 65–66). The former points to an intent to use the vessel for cult purposes at the point of production, while the latter points to additional customisation at some later stage.

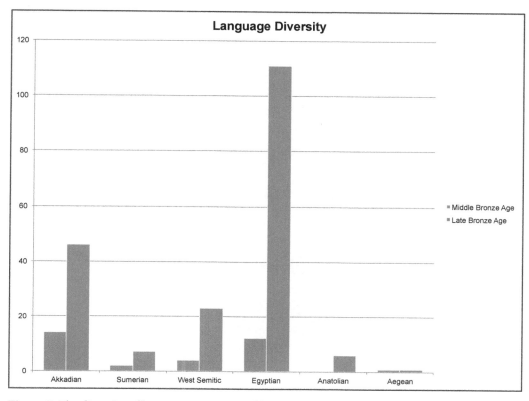

Figure 2: The diversity of languages represented by Bronze Age texts found in the Southern Levant.

Proto-Canaanite appears sporadically, incised and impressed onto ceramic vessels before firing and cut into the surface of a bronze dagger (Sass 1988: figs 140, 143, 271), and there is a single Minoan graffito on a sherd from Tel Haror (Oren et al. 1996). Egyptian hieroglyphic texts of this period are best represented on scarabs and are usually carved into the surface; there are also a few clay bullae, a carnelian bead and a faience cylinder seal (Giveon 1985: 108, no. 138; Keel 1997: 116, cat. 39; Petrie 1930: pl. 10, no. 111; Ussishkin 2004: fig. 23.40.2). Inscribed stone statuary produced at this time would appear to have been looted from Egypt and brought to Canaan at a later date (Weinstein 1975). Cursive hieroglyphs or hieratic script do not yet appear to have been introduced to the region.

During the Late Bronze Age the frequency and range of both scripts and language increases, as does the variety of objects on which text appears. When Canaan was conquered and incorporated into the Egyptian empire, a process formalised with the introduction of Egyptian administrative control during the reign of Tuthmes III (1479–1429 BC), the result was both to reinforce already existing markets for use of writing and to create a whole series of new audiences. Particularly important with regard to the latter was the need to provide efficient communication between Egypt and her new vassals. The language and script of international diplomacy, Akkadian cuneiform, already in use between Near Eastern governments, was now pressed into use for communication with Egypt as well, by means of the traditional clay tablet (Goren et al. 2004; Millard 1999: 317–318, figs 1–2; Moran 1992).

At the same time, changes in the way the region was managed led to the establishment of Egyptian-run garrisons and administrative centres at key locations, such as Gaza, Deir el-Balah and Beth Shan. Their roles included providing logistical support for the empire, provisioning troops and

Figure 3: Ceramic storage jar with impressed stamps bearing cartouches containing the names of Tuthmes III and Hatshepsut in Egyptian hieroglyphic. UCL Institute of Archaeology Collections EXIII.112e/21.

other Egyptians stationed there or moving through on official business, controlling local security, and organising local corvée labour from Canaanite settlements. Managed by Egyptians, we suspect these centres made use of Egyptian hieratic to support many of these activities, although only a few texts inked onto ceramic vessels and sherds have survived. Vessels were also the primary surface material for hieratic votive and religious texts, predominantly added to the surface in ink or paint after firing. Hieroglyphs appear to be used in a wider range of settings. Stamps bearing cartouches were impressed onto storage jars before firing, from the co-regency of Hatshepsut and Tuthmes III onwards, probably to mark the property of royal estates (Higginbotham 2000: 254; **Figure 3**); they were carved into the surface of stone architectural elements, statuary and stele, incised into elite ivory objects such as musical clappers, pen cases and furniture inlays, or metal signet rings, and included in the glazed designs of faience vessels and votive objects, while the popularity of scarabs continued. This was a market driven by a combination of Egyptian imperial policy, increasing numbers of Egyptians working in the region, and a desire to emulate Egyptian visual styles amongst Canaanite elites. The sum total of these varied spheres of use would have been that Egyptian writing was much more visible to the local population than ever before.

In addition to these developments, the alphabetic Proto-Canaanite script continued to be used sporadically amongst local elites, most probably recording a local West Semitic language, although the shortness of most inscriptions makes clear identification difficult. It is applied to a range of personal items, including a gold signet ring, and ceramic bowls, jugs, a lidded pyxis and spouted cup (Hamilton 2010; Sass 1988: 101, figs 143–147, 156–160, 163–167, 178–184, 268–270; **Figure 4**). Inscriptions were painted or incised both before and after firing with all this implies for the agency behind the text. The signs are often cursive in character using either technique, but

Figure 4: Ceramic spouted cup (spout now missing) from Tell el-'Ajjul Tomb 1109, with painted Proto-Canaanite ownership inscription reading: 'this (belongs) to *Yrṣ*', (the) Can[aan]ite' (Hamilton 2010: 107). UCL Institute of Archaeology Collections EXIII.115/1.

occasionally when incised are rendered in a more linear fashion. They appear in tombs, temples and as domestic refuse, pointing to a wide range of contextual settings. Tablets written in Proto-Canaanite have not been found. This script appears to have been used in a less formal and managed way than either cuneiform, Egyptian hieroglyphic or hieratic.

Additional foreign scripts make a sporadic appearance. A clay bulla with an impressed royal Hittite seal was found at Aphek, where it had been discarded in a building thought to be used by a local administrator (Goren et al. 2006); the remaining Hittite texts are inscribed into either metal or stone and served as personal seals and signet rings (see below), perhaps representing sporadic diplomatic activity. Finally, there is a limestone bowl with a capacity inscription cut into the exterior upper walls in a script that is possibly Linear A (Finkelberg et al. 2004).

The following discussion will attempt to review the evidence for Bronze Age writing, in all its material forms, according to the role it may have played within local communities. This involves dividing the evidence into a number of categories: uses for administration and information management, communication, education, diplomacy and politics, to support religious beliefs (funerary, votive and protective) and to mark ownership. These categories are a useful tool, although it should be noted that official and private uses may have sometimes overlapped and at times be difficult to categorise. This study has been deliberately limited to the distribution of texts in the Southern Levant (modern Israel, Palestinian Authority and Jordan), as quite different circumstances may have been operating on cities further north, such as Byblos, with its particular links to Egypt, or Ugarit, a trading entrepôt with an unusually cosmopolitan nature due to its physical location on the interface between the Near Eastern and Mediterranean spheres. Core data used in charts and tables has been drawn from material that can be dated to the Middle and Late Bronze

Middle Bronze I	2000–1750 BC
Middle Bronze II	1750–1650 BC
Middle Bronze III	1650–1550 BC
Late Bronze I	1550–1400 BC
Late Bronze II	1400–1150 BC
Iron Age	1150–520 BC

Table 1: Chronological chart of the Southern Levant.

Ages only. It excludes material whose identification or chronology is uncertain, and texts comprising a single sign, which may have functioned as identification marks or symbols rather than writing. Scarabs and scaraboids were also excluded from statistical comparisons, as the data set was too large to be included; a smaller case study of some aspects of this material has however been incorporated. A chronological chart of the periods covered by this chapter may be found in **Table 1**, and a map showing sites under discussion in **Figure 5**.

Administrative Uses of Writing

Writing was needed to support local Canaanite government and the later imposed superstructure of Egyptian government. Both would have similar requirements, including account keeping to manage personnel and supplies, to maintain and legitimate communications and record legal matters. It seems likely that the language and script used to record these activities would have differed depending on the authority behind them.

Surviving texts suggest that Akkadian cuneiform was the writing used to manage local government, with 13 tablets recording lists of goods or personnel, 19 letters, and three legal texts ranging across Middle and Late Bronze Age contexts (Horowitz et al. 2006). Only a single administrative text has been found that utilises West Semitic language and alphabetic cuneiform script: a legal tablet from Taanach, dating to the early 12th century BC. The execution of the text is unusual on a number of grounds, including the way the letters are shaped, the direction the text is to be read, and the lack of word dividers, which may reflect a weakening of scribal tradition and the appearance of a less professional class of scribe at this time (Horowitz et al. 2006: Taanach 15). This rare example aside, what is noticeable in this assemblage is the standardisation in the way 'official' texts are being rendered, with no variation in material use or object form that we can see. Official writing is very much tied to the stylus and tablet paradigm, limiting the physical contexts of its use.

In Egypt itself hieratic is the traditional script used for administrative purposes, and this practice appears to have been imported to the Southern Levant during Egypt's Late Bronze Age occupation of the region. However, remarkably few physical examples of these sorts of texts have survived, making us suspect that records were often made on perishable materials, such as papyrus or wooden writing boards, also mirroring scribal practice back in Egypt, which have left little trace in the archaeological record bar the occasional imprint on the back of clay bullae (e.g. Dothan 2008: 65; Mumford 1998: 1614 and n. 390). There are, however, hints at more casual uses of writing. A broken sherd at Tell Sera' was used as a surface for a legal text, added in ink (Goldwasser 1984: pl. 7.2), and another inscription was inked onto the shoulder of a storage jar at the Egyptian garrison site of Beth Shan as a form of quality control (Wimmer 2007: 688–689, pl. 77.2). These examples hint at a greater flexibility in how this technology was applied.

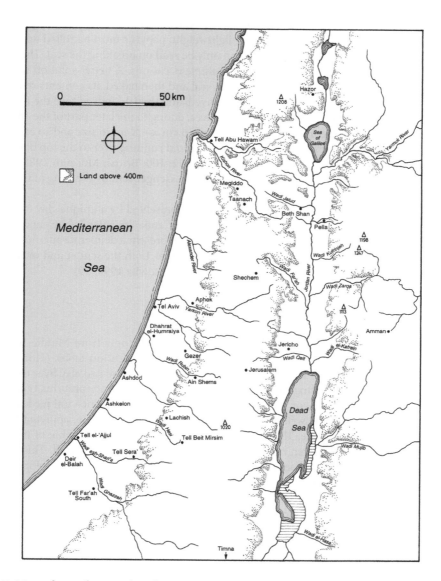

Figure 5: Map of sites discussed in the text.

Travellers between Egypt and the Levant were often used as couriers for official correspondence, as described on the recto of Papyrus Anastasi III, where letters are seen passing through a border post en-route to Egyptian officials and the Prince of Tyre (Higginbotham 2000: 48–49). It would appear that writing was used not only to give a message of authority and provide future accountability, but also to identify and legitimate the couriers themselves. Textual references point to the use of 'passports': government documents granting the bearer permission to travel through Egyptian territory without hindrance or charge, and offering proof of the official nature of their activities. Such a document, described as 'rescripts from Amon-Re', is referred to in the Report of Wenamun, an Egyptian literary text describing a journey into the Levant and thought to have been composed in the 21st dynasty; however, the physical appearance of this authorisation is never specified (Simpson 2003: 117).

One can nevertheless hypothesise that letters of passage would need to be both portable and secure against unauthorised tampering. While lightweight, papyrus must be rolled up and sealed with a clay bulla to secure its contents, which can only be read on breaking the seal. This would be of little use if the passport had to be shown on multiple occasions. A better solution would be to use a clay tablet, as once impressed with an official seal and then baked, its contents remain fixed. A few actual examples of these passports have survived, and they do indeed take the form of clay tablets. They were found in the Tell el-Amarna archives, dating to the later part of the 18th dynasty. One such is EA 30, a small sub-rectangular tablet, only 6 cm × 4.8 cm in size and so easily held in one hand, with its Akkadian text impressed on one side and running over to the top of the reverse where it was impressed with a cylinder seal (Moran 1992: 100; British Museum 1988.10-13.64). The contents of this tablet tell us that it accompanied a messenger sent by the King of the Mitanni, in Syria, to the Egyptian court.

A more 'unofficial' mode of communication may be represented by a unique clay cylinder seal from Beth Shan, inscribed with a letter addressed to the Canaanite ruler Lab'aya and written in Akkadian cuneiform. It has been suggested that this may represent a deliberate attempt at secrecy, by choosing a shape that could masquerade as a personal seal; both the sender and recipient were known to have been involved in anti-Egyptian activities (Horowitz 1997: 99).

Writing and Education

The earliest traces of writing being used as an educational tool come from Middle Bronze Age Hazor, where a clay prism was found bearing cuneiform multiplication tables (Horowitz et al. 2006: 78–80, Hazor 9). Another specific form of text is represented by two clay liver models with cuneiform inscriptions instructing the student on how to 'read' and interpret this type of object (Horowitz et al. 2006: 66–68, Hazor 2–3; **Figure 6**). These models represent a unique learning tool in many ways, as they combine written instructions with a visual template, applying the text to physical three-dimensional space. The meaning is made clear by the positioning of the text over the appropriate feature of the liver, not by any description within the text itself. This distinctive approach can be linked to the purpose of the text, which is not an exercise in developing writing technique or learning vocabulary, but in the art of divination.

From the Late Bronze Age come a handful of lexical tablets. These include two prisms found at Aphek; these are made out of local clay and provide lists of terms in Sumerian, Akkadian, and a West Semitic language (Goren et al. 2006: 162–164; Horowitz et al. 2006: 29–32, Aphek 1 and 3). Similar lists are known from tablets at Ashkelon and Hazor (Horowitz et al. 2006: 42–43, Ashkelon 1, 73–74, Hazor 6). Analysis has shown that many of these tablets were made out of locally sourced clay, pointing to local scribal activity (Goren et al. 2004; 2006). This is supported by idiosyncratic usages of Akkadian that suggest scribes were trained regionally and independently of other writing traditions (Gianto 1999: 127).

What makes these objects physically suited to educational purposes? Both prisms and tablets were designed to offer multiple surfaces for writing, with the scribe manually turning the object over as each surface was complete. The experience would be similar for those reading the text, aided by the comparatively small size and lightweight character of the objects themselves. The small size and density of cuneiform signs meant that reading, in particular, had to allow for flexibility in handling — moving the object itself to take advantage of light and shadow, and differing personal focal lengths.

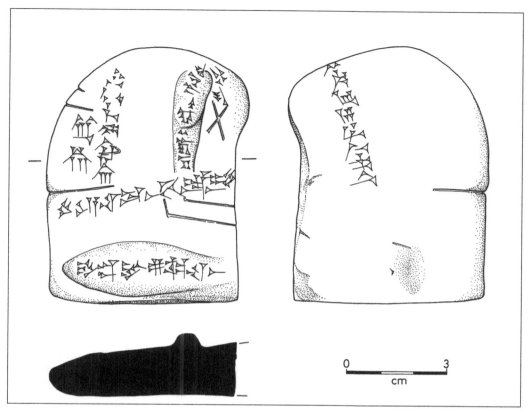

Figure 6: Clay liver model fragment from Hazor with impressed cuneiform inscription (after Landsberger and Tadmor 1964, and Horowitz et al. 2006: 209).

Writing as Propaganda

Bronze Age writing was still a restricted technology, usually associated with power and authority. It is not surprising then that it also had political applications. Stelae commemorating Egyptian victories and marking the extent of political control would have been a public statement of both achievement and intent; a similar effect would have been achieved through the erection of royal statuary. Examples of both these phenomena have appeared at a handful of locations in the southern Levant, most notably at Beth Shan, Tell el-Oreimeh, Ashdod, at-Turra and Tell es-Shihab (James and McGovern 1993: 249–250; Schulman 1993; Weinstein 1981: 20). Both classes of object most frequently appear in basalt, a challenging material with a Mohs hardness of six, that could be locally sourced in flows running from Eastern Galilee into the Hauran (Sparks 2007: fig. 59). At Beth Shan, this material was common not only for monumental texts but also for uninscribed vessels and tools, prompting the suggestion that the town housed its own basalt workshops (Sparks 2007: 164). However the style of carving and the use of linguistically acceptable texts points to the Levantine monuments being produced by craftspeople who were fully trained within the Egyptian system. Their choice of this material over other locally available and softer stones such as limestone may therefore have been more than a matter of accessibility; it may also have held cultural and ideological overtones. Basalt has a hardness comparable to that of granite, a material more often used for royal statuary and stelae in Egypt itself. This may have made it an acceptable substitute, containing similar potential to impress, a potential also achieved through the use of monumental scale. Its durability may also have been a metaphor for the durability of pharaonic control in the region. Such monuments were intended to last (cf. Piquette, this volume).

In both cases, the strongly Egyptian style of execution would make their ideological meaning readily identifiable even to the non-literate. It seems likely that this sort of monument would have been erected in visible, public places, such as marketplaces, near gateways and in temple precincts. It is also likely that they would be subject to processes of curation and be kept in the public eye for extensive periods of time. This has an obvious impact on the archaeology of this type of artefact, as many such texts will be found in deposits that date well beyond their original period of manufacture, making assessment of the way they were originally presented problematic. This appears to have been the case for stelae of Sety I and Ramses II, presumably erected during the reigns of their respective pharaohs, but recovered from a much later deposit in Beth Shan Lower Level V where they appear to have been erected on plinths in an area west of the northern temple (James 1966: 34–38). Over time, however, the value of such monuments was reduced as the rulers and officials that commissioned them ceased to be important, often leading to damage and reuse in far less prestigious surroundings (e.g. as door sills and sockets, Albright 1952: 24; Albright and Rowe 1928: 281).

Another potentially political use of writing was to mark presentation objects and diplomatic gifts. Gift exchange was an important part of creating and maintaining power relationships between elites across the Near East, as reflected in the Amarna letters and other correspondence between royal courts. While these letters do not actually tell us about whether gifted objects were inscribed, numerous high quality, prestige items bearing writing have been found that could reflect this type of event. The use of Egyptian royal names on luxury stone vessels may have been one example of this phenomenon (Sparks 2003), and a limited distribution of this type of artefact to strategically important cities and centres of power would support the idea that they were being directed at allies and courts where the Egyptians sought influence, rather than at controlled, vassal states. Only one stone vessel with a royal name has been found in the southern Levant, a calcite jar fragment at Gezer with the cartouche of Ramses II (Sparks 2003: fig. 3.4d). Its context, an LBII cistern, does not really explain how it came to be there, but one would suspect it began its career as a gift from the Egyptian court. Other types of objects with royal names are more common in the region, such as ivory objects including a pommel, pen case and semi-circular plaque (Feldman 2009: 180; Higginbotham 2000: 247; Macalister 1912, volume 2: figs 388, 456; Macalister 1912, volume 3: pl. 209, no. 97). Many of these are elite items that could have been presentation gifts. The contexts of others suggest they are more likely to have been votive offerings, perhaps being made on behalf of the king or invoking the royal cult (e.g. **Figure 7a**; Franken 1992: figs 3–9.5, pl. 4b; Rothenberg 1988: Egyptian catalogue nos 19, 26–28, 30, 41–47, 50, 83a, 96, 102–103, 180, 193, 195, 222).

The distribution of the special class of commemorative scarab issued throughout the reign of Amenhotep III could be considered another expression of textual name-dropping, although here we may see the recipients being Egyptians in positions of power both at home and abroad, as well as foreign elites. Examples have been found at Beth Shan, Beth Shemesh, Gezer, Lachish, Jaffa, and Qla'et Twal in Jordan (see **Figure 7b**; Blankenberg-Van Delden 1969). Unlike commemorative stelae or statuary, these were intensely personal objects, carved from steatite in the form of a scarab beetle, with a detailed inscription on the underside of the base recording in several registers a number of significant events in the pharaoh's reign. They could be held in the hand, but unlike other types of scarab, are significantly larger and almost cover the palm. They are both weightier, and more impressive. To a Levantine audience familiar only with small ring-mounted scarab amulets, the difference would have been remarkable. These were also objects to be possessed, rather than just displayed, as the dense text becomes visible only once the user has picked the object up.

Commemorative scarabs also stand out on a stylistic level. Scarab texts found in the region often feature strong visual symmetry, with flanking pairs of signs framing important elements

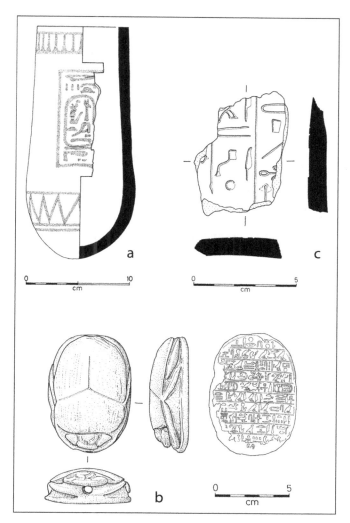

Figure 7: Objects with Egyptian hieroglyphic inscriptions. a) Faience vessel with cartouches of Tausret from Deir 'Alla (after Franken 1992: figs 3–9.5); b) Commemorative scarab of Amenhotep III from Beth Shan (after Goldwasser 2002: 192); c) Calcite canopic jar fragment from Tell el-'Ajjul. UCL Institute of Archaeology EXIII.117/1.

such as cartouches, or using hieroglyphs as filler motifs to frame figurative designs. In the case of the commemorative scarab, the surface area of the flat base is much greater, and consequently less constrained by the oval form of the object. The result is a much more formal and traditional layout for the texts, which are neatly arranged in a series of horizontal registers. The execution is also more careful and precise than usually seen. Both these features add to the prestige of the object, and underline its source in an Egyptian royal workshop.

The comparative scarcity of commemorative scarabs would also have increased their desirability. It is hardly surprising then that some commemorative scarabs seem to have been retained as heirlooms and curated for as much as several hundred years (Goldwasser 2002: 191; Jeffreys 2003: 206–207; Sweeney 2003: 58). These scarabs have been seen as a way of issuing royal bulletins, and reminding foreign rulers of Egyptian power and influence (Goldwasser 2002: 193; Sweeney 2003: 58). In each case, the text is an important element in the function and meaning of the object; while an Egyptian official might be expected to be able to understand the text, one might assume that the delivery of the gift to a Levantine ruler was accompanied by a formal 'reading'. After the event, the distinctive Egyptian character of the hieroglyphs and shape, magnified tenfold as appropriate for a royal recipient, would serve as a visual reminder of the purpose of the gift, whether or not the owner could revisit its specific contents. It seems likely that what was ultimately remembered generations later was the formal relationship represented by the gift, rather than the more transitory bulletin inscribed on its base.

Funerary Writing

Egypt was home to a well developed industry that provided funerary goods on which writing was an important part of the function of the object, including the Book of the Dead, heart scarabs, shabtis and funerary stelae. Access to script for funerary purposes was desirable, but nonetheless dependent on economic circumstances and so while inscriptions are common in wealthy burials, the poor often had to go without. In contrast, writing does not appear to be a usual part of funerary customs in the Southern Levant, irrespective of status. When inscribed goods do appear in burials, they appear as oddities, rather than the norm, and are usually on objects that were also used in life such as amuletic scarabs, finger rings, daggers and vessels, rather than being specifically funerary in character (e.g. Magrill et al. 2004: fig. 24.12; Sass 1988: figs 140–141, 166–167, 268–279).

The exception to this rule may occur where we see Egyptians being buried in the region, as it might be expected that Egyptians living abroad would bring with them their own attitudes to what was suitable as provision for death. In such cases, even though there may be a cultural predisposition to certain funerary texts and services, the ability of the family of the deceased to provide these may not be entirely dependent on wealth. Funerary goods, including suitable texts, are a by-product of support industries. In Egypt, these industries were well developed and there was probably a great deal of competition between suppliers to keep prices at an acceptable level. In the Southern Levant, only certain goods and services may have been locally available, and in particular, the services of suitably trained scribes may have been difficult to obtain. If scribes were in limited supply, and those that were available were chiefly employed by the Egyptian administration, private commissions may have been both expensive and difficult to secure. This may have been equally true of some of the necessary raw materials, such as papyrus. The consequence may have been that only the most wealthy of Egyptians working abroad would have been able to obtain suitable funerary inscriptions for their families, unless they had already arranged for the necessary items to be brought over from Egypt.

It is therefore not surprising that Egyptian funerary texts are extremely scarce in the Southern Levant. An exceptional example is a coffin from Tomb 570 at Lachish. This was crudely painted with a scene depicting the Egyptian goddesses Isis and Nephthys and a hieroglyphic inscription from the Book of the Dead, which it has been argued was executed by a poorly trained scribe (Tufnell 1958: 132). Higginbotham has suggested that this coffin was created by someone not conversant with the proper forms, in imitation of Egyptian funerary practice (Higginbotham 2000: 244). However there is little enough evidence that Egyptian funerary texts were available in the region to serve as the inspiration for this sort of imitation. A more likely explanation is that it was executed by an Egyptian scribe who was not used to this type of commission but was nonetheless aware of the source text.

Another class of funerary text known from the region appears on stone stelae. One example was found reused in the lining of an Egyptian pit burial at Deir el-Balah, but was thought to have originally been set up as a marker over a more expensive grave (Dothan 2008: 155; Mumford 1998: 1663, 1657; Ventura 1987: 105, 115). Ventura (1987: 113–114) has suggested that such markers may have been a substitute for Egyptian cult chapels and the focus of ritual activity. The fact that the lower portion of the object was left undecorated supports the idea that it was designed to be set into the ground in this way, while the choice of stone is entirely appropriate for something that was intended to have continued effectiveness over and beyond the mere event of the burial. Three similar stelae, now in the Israel Museum, have no reliable provenance but are thought to have been looted from the same site (Ventura 1987). All these texts refer to Osiris and give the name of the deceased. Other stelae with Egyptian funerary inscriptions have been discovered in Jerusalem (Barkay 1996: figs 5–6), and Hazor (Goldwasser 1989: 344–345); an uninscribed fragment from a funerary stele has also been found at Beth Shan (Ward 1966: C4, 171). The majority of these stelae were probably made from local materials, suggesting a meas- ure of expediency, but in at least one case the stone was said to be imported Nubian sandstone (Goldwasser 1989: 344).

A well executed funerary inscription was also discovered in the 1500 house at Beth Shan, com- prising fragments of a stone lintel for The Commander of Troops, Ramses Weser-Khepesh (James 1966: fig. 93.1, 4). This was part of the structure of the building, which was decorated with a number of inscriptions on door posts and lintels, and is thought to have been the residence of the highest ranking Egyptian at the site. Funerary inscriptions of this type are said to have been placed in private houses at a number of sites in Egypt (Ward 1966: 161, 168) and so reflect a space for the living with commemorative aspects, rather than a space for the dead. This sort of architecture would have made a substantial impression on the non-Egyptian residents of the site, whose own dwellings were constructed with simpler mudbrick superstructures. This elaborate stone archi- tecture and the investment of resources it represented sent a message of power and control. The inscriptions would probably have been placed at visible points such as major entranceways to capitalise on their impact. Although comparable grandeur was present in contemporary temples and palaces at nearby sites such as Pella and Hazor, there does not appear to have been a local tradition of incorporating visible writing into the design in this way, so this feature in particular would stand out. Such buildings would also have had an impact on Egyptian personnel. The sight of Egyptian architecture decorated with Egyptian script would have provided a familiar and com- forting environment for those stationed in otherwise alien surroundings.

Another object on which we might expect to see funerary texts is the Egyptian shabti, a type of mummiform figurine that became common in Egyptian funerary assemblages of the New Kingdom. The inscription on a shabti has a very specific role, as it gives the object the power to function as a substitute worker for the deceased in the afterlife, freeing them from manual labour. To this end, shabti texts were usually personalised, with the name of the owner and a formulaic spell. In some cases, a space was left blank for the name to be filled in at or after the time of purchase (Stewart 1995: 47). This seems like a very practical solution to the unpredictability of death, allowing stock to be built up which could presumably be taken and customised elsewhere if required. Despite their popularity in Egypt, and despite the fact that numerous Egyptian person- nel were stationed in the Levant and presumably must have sometimes died there, only a handful of clay and faience shabtis have been found in burials across the region, at Timna, Deir el Balah, Tell el-'Ajjul, Arsuf and Beth Shan, (Dothan 2008: 148; Oren 1973: figs 45.24, 47b.26–28, 49.22–24, 50.13, 76.9; Rothenberg 1988: fig. 28.2). Within this group only the single shabti found at Timna had been inscribed. How should we interpret the absence of such inscriptions? Is this simply coincidence — after all, uninscribed shabtis are sometimes found in Egyptian tombs of the period (e.g. Gurob Tomb 20; Petrie 1890: 38)? Or does this reflect either a deliberate adaptation of usual Egyptian practice, or unusual circumstances relating to local production of this type of object? Several possible scenarios can be proposed to explain this phenomenon.

- A personalised or inscribed shabti is something confined to wealthier individuals, and the kinds of people represented in the tombs discovered to date did not fall into this category.

- It was too difficult, or expensive, to import inscribed shabtis from Egypt. Time may also have been a factor, as mummification was not practised on any of the burials found in association with shabtis in the Levant. Consequently, the body would have begun to decay before funerary equipment could be ordered and sent from Egypt.
- While the personnel servicing the funerary industries at each site included craftspeople who could make shabti bodies, they did not include support staff with scribal training who could create the necessary hieroglyphic inscriptions.
- The idea of the shabti has been accepted but the accompanying texts were deliberately dispensed with.

Each scenario has its own implications with regard to the identity and cultural affiliations of those working and being buried in the Southern Levant. Whatever the circumstances were, although they lack inscriptions the shabti forms are themselves accurately portrayed, which would argue against production by craftspeople who were unfamiliar with this type of object. Similarly there is no attempt to create a 'pseudo' inscription, which might be the case if either craftsperson or client wanted to reproduce the look of a shabti without having accurate knowledge of how it should actually appear.

Egyptian funerary equipment is also represented by rare fragments of canopic jars at Gezer and Tell el-'Ajjul (Macalister 1912, volume 3: pl. 210, no. 64; Petrie 1933: pl. 16, no. 48, pl. 17; Rockefeller Museum 35.4260). Such jars were used to contain the internal organs of the deceased, carefully removed from the body and preserved. Each jar was guarded by a particular deity, with formulaic texts invoking their protection. They are embodiments of not only Egyptian attitudes to death, but also the mechanics of preparing the body for burial, and can therefore be a strong indicator of Egyptian cultural practice. The Tell el-'Ajjul example comprised a single calcite sherd from the body of the jar, inscribed with a typical funerary formula of the New Kingdom and found in topsoil (UCL Institute of Archaeology EXIII.117/1; Stephen Quirke pers. comm. 2000; **Figure 7c**). The text was cut into the surface at the time of manufacture, and is an integral part of the overall design; the time and level of skill involved in hollowing the vessel out from a solid block of stone point to some investment of resources, and hence some value for the piece. It is possible that it was brought to the Levant as potential furnishing for an Egyptian-style burial; if so, it does not appear to have been used in this way as it was not found in a mortuary context. Alternatively, it may have been looted from a burial in Egypt and exported as recycled material for manufacturing beads and other small objects (Phillips 1992). In this scenario, the value of the object would lie not in the cultural meaning of the finished object, transformed by its shape and the power of script, but in the physical attractiveness and scarcity of the material from which it was made, and the fact that the thickness and only slight curvature of the vessel's walls would make it suitable for reworking for a new market.

Votive Writing

Short inscriptions can be notoriously difficult to interpret, and in cases where the archaeological context is unclear, it may not be possible to determine whether an ownership inscription was intended to add prestige to personal property or to mark a votive offering. The scarcity of certain scripts during this period might point to the latter scenario as being more plausible. This might apply to the alphabetic cuneiform inscriptions incised on a bronze knife at Nahal Tabor (Horowitz et al. 2006: Tabor 1, 152, 163–166), and clay axe head from Beth Shemesh (Horowitz et al. 2006: Beth Shemesh 1, 157–160). The latter was made in a mould and then impressed with a stylus while the clay was still moist. It was found in a domestic context, and although the text is an incomplete abecedary, it is unlikely to represent a training piece. Not only does it appear on an unusual object

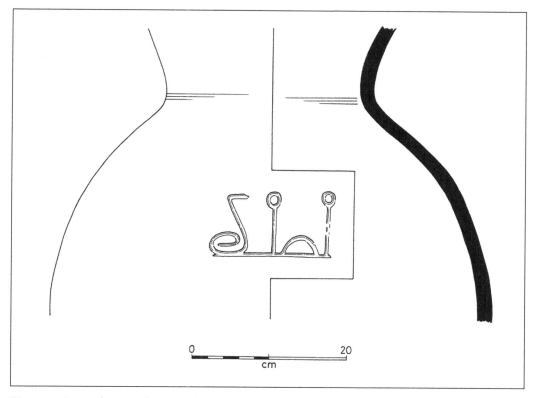

Figure 8: Jar with incised cursive hieroglyphs from Beth Shan VII (after James and McGovern 1993: fig. 11.4).

(symbolic, rather than functional, as indicated by the unusual choice of material for this form), but the text itself has to be read by rotating the object — an unhelpful characteristic if the purpose had been to educate.

A clearer use of script to mark dedications is seen on a clay model bread offering from Beth Shan level VI, stamped with the hieroglyphic phrase *imny.t,* or 'daily offering' (Higginbotham 2000: 225, although for an alternative interpretation, see Brandl 2009: 662–663; James 1966: fig. 105.9–10, 12). Other examples include a ceramic jar from the level VII temple at Beth Shan, bearing the word 'ka' in painted cursive hieroglyphs (**Figure 8**; James and McGovern 1993: 181, fig. 11.4), a jug with painted Proto-Canaanite dedicatory inscription to 'my lady Elat' found in the Fosse Temple at Lachish (Tufnell et al. 1940: 47–54), a cuneiform Akkadian dedication cut into a stone vessel from a ritual context at Hazor (Horrowitz et al. 2006: 85–86, Hazor 13), and a ceramic jug from the same site with a symbol representing the god Addu, incised before the vessel was fired, and a personal name, Isme-Addul, scratched in cuneiform into the surface afterwards (Horowitz et al. 2006: 65–66, Hazor 1). Official ritual activity may be represented by a fragmentary execration text in hieratic found on a ceramic storage jar fragment in a temple courtyard at Beth Shan, which has been interpreted as protection of the site against evil forces (Higginbotham 2000: 45–46; James and McGovern 1993: 181, fig. 15.6). This was painted onto the surface after firing.

Within this group, objects such as the clay axehead, model bread offering, and Addu and Elat jugs appear to have been made specifically as votive offerings. For some, the form is exceptional or specialised in function, while for others the nature of the inscription or decoration adds meaning to the shape. However the other objects and vessels could have been produced with other

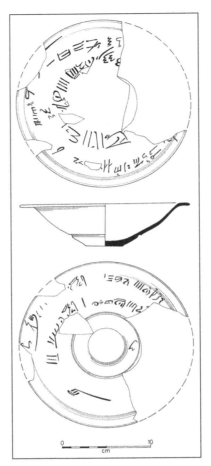

Figure 9: Bowl with painted hieratic inscription from Lachish (after Sweeney 2004: fig. 24.2).

purposes in mind, as their inscriptions were all created subsequent to manufacture of the form. It is only by the addition of the texts that they are tailored for ritual use, a potential that is realised when the actual act of dedication takes place. Their archaeological contexts show that this was achieved in the majority of cases.

An important class of object that should also be considered under this category of ritual activity is represented by a series of ceramic bowls, and possibly two jars, bearing hieratic inscriptions added after firing in ink (**Figure 9**; Goldwasser 1984; 1991; Goldwasser and Wimmer 1999). These inscriptions have been found at Lachish, Tel Haror, Tell Far'ah South, Tell Sera', and Deir el Balah, and initially provide something of a dilemma in terms of how the text should be interpreted. On the one hand, their content seems quite administrative in nature, recording specific dates and quantities of grain (in some cases, very *large* quantities); they are usually viewed in the context of produce being delivered from Canaanite vassals to Egyptian authorities as part of their tax burden. Yet it seems wrong to view the bowls themselves as a form of 'documentation' (Goldwasser and Wimmer 1999: 41) because the way in which the texts are applied to the vessels themselves is anything but administrative.

Many of our surviving examples are fragmentary, but from the more complete bowls we can see that inscriptions were placed on the exterior and sometimes on the interior as well, in one to two horizontal registers following the curvature of the walls. Opinion is divided as to whether the text read from inside to outside, or vice versa (Sweeney 2004: 1607), but they do appear to have been read together. Yet how easy is it to read this sort of inscription? To understand the text, you need to turn the bowl around in your hands and tilt it to different angles, to compensate for the curvature both inside and outside. On the exterior, there is the additional problem on this example of the everted rim making it hard to read the top line, unless you hold the bowl rather unnaturally. Then, if you put anything *in* the bowl — surely the point *of* a bowl? — you cannot read the interior inscriptions at all.

As an administrative record, this makes little sense, being hard to read and not remotely suited to either storage or retrieval. Wimmer's early idea that the bowls served as 'receipts' for taxation, should therefore be discounted (Wimmer 1990: 1090; cf. Higginbotham 2000: 63). Of course, as recognised by Goldwasser, while these bowls seem to record an administrative event, they represent in themselves not a bureaucratic object, but a religious one (Goldwasser 1984: 85; Goldwasser and Wimmer 1999: 41). This is because the recipient of the grain taxes they record were temple authorities, and as such the two roles overlapped. As votive objects, the text makes much more sense in relation to the object, as its aim is not to be 'read' by the living, but to give meaning to an event, and be 'read' by the gods. An ordinary bowl, by virtue of the added inscription, and being then made part of a ritual act whereby goods are being 'offered' to the temple, becomes representative of a much larger process, namely the subjugation of Canaan to Egypt and the provision of resources to Egyptian temple estates, such as the temple of Amun in PaCanaan (Higginbotham 2000: 56–59).

In Egypt, bowls are sometimes the bearers of votive inscriptions, but with some differences; there, the texts tend to relate to much smaller food offerings and the vessels themselves are often model forms (Goldwasser 1984: 85). There are however some exceptions. Occasional examples are known of hieratic letters being written on offering bowls and then being left in tombs as a way of communicating with the dead, often asking them to intervene in family problems (e.g. Petrie Museum of Egyptian Archaeology, UC 16163), while execration texts are also sometimes written on bowls before being ritually broken. The tradition of bowl inscriptions back in Egypt clearly favoured the use of hieratic. Was this choice of script for the Canaanite tax bowls a continuation of this tradition, or did it reflect some local factor, such as the circumstances under which the texts were written (perhaps reflecting a lack of time to draft formal hieroglyphs), or the types of scribes available (administrative rather than religious)?

In Canaan, uninscribed bowls appear to have a particular role as votive offerings in the temples of Lachish and may have been locally produced specifically for that purpose (Goldwasser 1984: 85; Tufnell et al. 1940: 81; a similar abundance of bowls was noticed in the governor's residence of Tell Sera', Oren 1972: 169). It may be hypothesised that the inscribed examples had a related role, but one that related more specifically to the Egyptian deities who were the recipients of these grain levies. The bowl form would be suited to a dry, rather than a liquid offering, and may well have contained a sample of the produce it represented, while the actual goods (in one case, at least 2000 sacks) would probably have bypassed the temple sanctuary and been delivered directly to one of its storerooms or warehouses (Goldwasser 1984: 80). The actual practice of combining tax inscription with offering bowl may therefore represent a hybrid response combining existing local custom, the use of votive offering bowls, with an Egyptian formula and script.

Writing as Protection

Some uses of writing are designed to be very personal, and into this class fall a number of inscribed objects that would usually be worn close to the body, including scarabs, cylinder seals, beads, pendants, and finger rings. These could serve a dual function of adornment and protection, and so were generally suited to roles both in life and death.

Scarabs and Scaraboids

Scarabs and scaraboids were a popular personal possession in the southern Levant. A narrow perforation was bored through the centre, which allowed them to be mounted and worn in a variety of ways. They could be threaded onto a string and worn around the neck or wrist, traces of which rarely survive in the archaeological record other than by the position of the scarab on the body in tombs. Scarabs could also be mounted onto a narrow pin, which fitted into the flattened and perforated ends of a metal finger ring. The pin fitted loosely, allowing the scarab to be swivelled on its setting so it could be worn with the inscribed base flat against the skin for comfort, but rotated if the owner wished to look at the inscription or use it as a seal.

This most Egyptian of objects was adopted and then adapted by Canaanite craftspeople, who set up their own workshops during the Middle Bronze Age, perhaps under the influence of Canaanite communities in the Egyptian Delta and Byblos (Ben-Tor 1998: 162; Goldwasser 2006: 122). Their popularity quickly spread, so that by the MBIIB scarabs were considered an important part of the funerary assemblage; at Jericho, for example, they appear in nearly 70% of all Middle Bronze Age tombs. Most people now agree that their primary function in these contexts was as a protective amulet (Ben-Tor 1998: 162). A variant on the inscribed scarab is an all-in-one faience ring, a form that appears in Egypt during the early 18th dynasty, and somewhat later in the Levant (Higginbotham 2000: 245). These typically comprise either a royal name or a religious inscription; less commonly they might feature a single amuletic sign, such as an *udjet*, which represented the eye of Horus (e.g. James and McGovern 1993: fig. 74.1). They are therefore less diverse in design and content than contemporary scarabs, although their function is assumed to be similar. However, their design is always visible, worn openly on the hand, whereas scarabs were mounted with the inscribed surface hidden against the skin.

While some of these objects were imported directly from Egypt, and represent canonical use of writing for their form, this was not always the case with locally produced scarabs. The way in which hieroglyphic writing was adapted within Canaanite workshops suggests that the signs were not being read as texts *per se,* with the appearance of pseudo-hieroglyphs and errors in the shape of various signs, as well as combinations of signs that make no linguistic sense (Ben-Tor 1998: 158). However the limited repertoire that is borrowed and repeated as decorative elements, often arranged into symmetrical patterns, may point to the borrowed signs having particular significance to Canaanite markets. As a pictorial script, this sort of transference is entirely plausible (Goldwasser 2006: 121). Either way, the popularity of scarabs and scaraboids meant that many Canaanites were able to come into close personal contact with Egyptian hieroglyphs and to develop a familiarity with the general appearance of the script, without necessarily developing any literary skills. They were accessible, in a way that some votive texts, funerary stelae or lintels over the doorways of Egyptian administrative buildings may not have been.

I sampled a series of scarab assemblages from sites across the region in order to examine this phenomenon and test how important hieroglyphs were as an element in this class of object. These were chosen on the basis of the availability of comprehensive scarab data for each site, and to represent possible regional variation based on geographic location; to avoid contaminating the results, purchased scarabs and those found in post-LB contexts were excluded. This resulted in a dataset of 1205 scarabs from Tell el-'Ajjul, 401 scarabs from Jericho, 71 from Pella and 430 from Lachish. The scarabs from each of these sites were analysed according to the role played by hieroglyphic signs in scarab decoration. The aim was not to distinguish between good or 'readable' inscriptions and the more decorative or symbolic uses of hieroglyphs, but to determine how important script elements were to the overall design, and hence function, of scarabs in the Southern Levant. The more prominent this element, the more visible, and hence accessible it becomes to Canaanite populations on the most personal of levels.

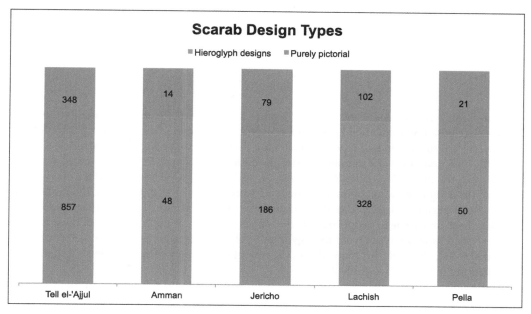

Figure 10: A comparison of scarabs with purely pictorial designs and those incorporating hieroglyphic signs from selected South Levantine sites.

The assemblage was categorised into scarabs based purely on figurative imagery (humans, deities, animals) or geometric designs (scrolls, twists, concentric circles), and those which incorporated hieroglyphs, either as the sole decoration or as filler motifs surrounding figurative or geometric scenes. This enabled a comparison of scarabs with and without script, which demonstrated an interesting phenomenon: irrespective of location, in all the sites studied script-based scarabs made up between two thirds and three quarters of the total scarab assemblage (**Figure 10**). This shows that to local consumers text was somehow seen as an important part of what a scarab was and how it functioned. Most Canaanites, it would seem, *wanted* their scarabs to have hieroglyphs. This may well relate to the idea that writing has power, and is therefore particularly suitable for objects that have protective or magical functions; in such a case, not being able to read such writing only adds to its value and mystique. The fact that the writing was Egyptian, and therefore foreign and exotic, may have only served to increase its potency; while of course by the time of the Late Bronze Age there were other associations to be made, namely with a country and culture that had become the dominant political and military power of the region.

Another class of object where we might expect to see a similar use of writing is the cylinder seal, which was frequently used as an amuletic or votive item, and which could be worn in a ring, as a necklace, or suspended from a toggle pin. However here we see that text, or elements of text, were very much the exception rather than the rule, and where they do appear, there is a stronger association with semi-precious materials such as jasper, lapis lazuli and hematite than less prestigious materials such as faience, although the latter does occur. Those that carry cuneiform inscriptions are mostly concerned with seal ownership (Horowitz et al. 2006: 39, 47, 95–97, 105–107, 149); however the rare examples with Egyptian script are more eclectic. An example from Tell Far'ah South offers a combination of signs more usually seen on the Canaanite *anra* scarab series, so-called after its use of a particular subset of hieroglyphs, and which presumably carried the same local significance, although they do not make any sense as an Egyptian text (Parker 1949: 10, no. 17; Richards 2001: 11–12). Another seal from Jericho is more of a cultural mix, incorporating two *ankhs* into an otherwise very Near Eastern scene (Teissier 1996: 115, cat. 242), and one from Tell Beit Mirsim goes so far as to use both hieroglyphs and what may be stylised cuneiform signs together (Teissier 1996: 110, cat. 226).

Amulets

The Late Bronze II period sees the introduction of a small group of amuletic pendants, the shape of which are based on individual Egyptian hieroglyphs (**Figure 11**). These made up some 14% of McGovern's corpus of pendant types for the region (to which can be added James and McGovern 1993: fig. 75.5, making 117 examples), and eight basic types appear to be represented — corresponding to the *ankh, djed, heh, tit, udjet, hst, ib,* and *nefer* signs (McGovern 1985: class V, 58). Many of these signs are also common to the local scarab series — with the *ankh, djed, udjet,* and *nefer* being especially popular. Like the scarabs these are very personal objects that would probably have been accessible to people outside the official administration. A number of these amulets are prescribed funerary types from the Egyptian Book of the Dead (e.g. Andrews 1994: *tit* 44, *ib* 72, and *djed* 83), although this is not always the type of context in which they appear to have been deposited in the Levant (see **Table 2**).

These amulets appear to have a comparatively limited distribution, having been found at Beth Shan, Megiddo, Tell Abu Hawam, Dhahrat el-Humraiya, Lachish, and Tell el-ʿAjjul. There was a particular clustering of examples at Beth Shan, where they may actually represent a rather limited number of individual collar necklaces (McGovern 1985: 63, 128); there is also evidence that many of these may have originated in Egyptian-run faience workshops at the site (James and McGovern 1993: 162). Those signs with a naturally vertical orientation may have a single suspension loop at the top, and so could have been worn as pendants. Others in this class have loops at both top and

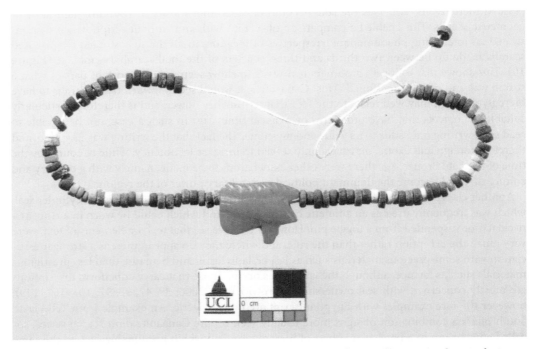

Figure 11: Faience bead necklace with carnelian *udjet* amulet, from Tell Fara Tomb 949, dating to the Late Bronze Age IIB. UCL Institute of Archaeology Collections EVI.23/16.

Amulet form	Tomb	Temple	Other	Totals
Nefer	30	6	0	**36**
Udjet	6	4	3	**13**
Djed	1	22	2	**25**
Hst	0	12	0	**12**
Tit	0	16	1	**17**
Ib	0	2	0	**2**
Heh	0	7	0	**7**
Ankh	0	1	4	**5**
Totals	**37**	**70**	**10**	**117**

Table 2: The comparative frequency of Egyptian hieroglyph-shaped amulets according to context type (based on data from McGovern 1985: 125–259, and James and McGovern 1993).

bottom, and were probably strung as elements in a more complex, perhaps even multi-stranded piece of jewellery. The exception appears to be the *udjet* amulet, or 'Eye of Horus', which has a naturally horizontal orientation and is perforated through its length in order to maintain this. While these objects could have been used as everyday amulets by either Egyptians or Canaanites, the fact that the majority of examples are known from temple contexts has suggested that they were probably used as votive offerings or to dress cult statues (James and McGovern 1993: 128–129). It seems likely that many people using these amulets would not be able to 'read' the script these signs were taken from; yet the way the design maintains some sense of orientation shows that this was considered an aspect worth preserving. It is equally likely that there was an accepted meaning for each type, and that they were told this significance when purchasing the items. It is less clear whether the owners and depositors of these objects were Egyptian or Canaanite, and it is worth remembering that amulets in the shape of hieroglyphic signs may have been assigned a different set of meanings, depending on the cultural background of the user.

Marking Ownership

Ownership inscriptions have been briefly touched on above in relation to cylinder seals and votive offerings; the cup with Proto-Canaanite inscription in **Figure 4** is an example of a text marking ownership being deposited in a funerary setting. There is, however, an additional variant found in the region, namely the personalised signet ring. These may have functioned as seals or simply as markers of identity, but are to be distinguished from the amuletic rings discussed earlier both in function and method of manufacture, being made for specific individuals, from more prestigious material, and being shaped by hand rather than being mass produced from moulds for unknown consumers. Three unusual examples have been found in the southern Levant in which the script used was Hittite hieroglyphs. The first of these is a bronze signet ring, found in a male burial at Tel Nami in association with bronze pomegranate-headed 'sceptres' and incense burners. The ring is incised with a male name, possibly *us/sa* and according to Singer (1993: 190) the form of both ring and name point to a Syrian owner who had adopted the use of Hittite script.

Two similar finger rings, this time in silver, were also discovered by Petrie at Tell Far'ah South (UCL Institute of Archaeology EVI.64/8–9; Singer 2003). These were inscribed with the names of

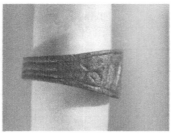

Figure 12: Silver finger ring with incised Hittite inscription, bearing the personal name *Ana*. UCL
Institute of Archaeology Collections EVI.64/8.

their presumed owners, a man called *Zazuwa* and a woman called *Ana* (**Figure 12**). Both were
found in the same deposit, Area EF level 386, which also contained four faience, two glass, two
steatite and one limestone scarab, silver, gold and bronze earrings, faience vessel fragments and
some 295 beads, pendants and amulets, made out of glass, faience, and diorite, carnelian and other
stones. Many of these items have an Egyptian or Egyptianising character (MacDonald et al. 1932:
pls 73.58–70, 78; most of them are now in the University College London, Institute of Archaeology
Collections). The structure they came from was part of a series of rooms built near the former
gateway of the site. There is nothing in the architecture or pottery of this locus to suggest that it
was functioning as a cultic space, and so the most likely explanation for the deposit was that it was
a domestic or commercial cache of jewellery, with the rings being included for their intrinsic or
exotic value. Unfortunately Petrie did not publish any comments on the specific findspot, and it is
therefore not clear if they were found in occupation debris or had been secreted away.

How did these small objects bearing the script of the Hittite empire find their way to the southern Levant? As personalised items it seems likely that their owners originally carried them there,
but it is not at all certain that they still belonged to those owners when they finally entered the
archaeological record. It also seems likely that the texts they bore would have been unintelligible
to almost everyone in the region. The same could be said of a Hittite steatite button seal found at
Megiddo (Singer 1988–1989: 106), or a hematite cylinder seal from Beth Shan which may carry
Hittite hieroglyphs (James and McGovern 1993: 231, no. 2). However, like Egyptian hieroglyphs,
the script used is intrinsically decorative and these objects may have been valued by non-Hittites
simply for their exotic 'foreign' design; their materials may also have held appeal for their recycling
value. Small, portable, personal objects such as these contrast with the more direct and official
Hittite activity suggested by the Hittite royal bulla found at Aphek, which a recent study unexpect-
edly demonstrated to have been made from a local source of clay (Goren et al. 2006: 166–167).
However ultimately these few examples only serve to underscore the fact that Hittite material
culture has left very little imprint on the region, suggesting that this particular variety of cross-
cultural encounter was rare.

Correlations of Technique, Material and Script

In many contexts of use, there would appear to be some correlation between the properties of
different materials and the way in which writing was applied to them; however craft and scribal
training, cultural preference in tool use and expediency may also have been factors in the choice of
writing technique (**Figures 13–14**). The traditional and most common application of cuneiform
and alphabetic cuneiform scripts, whatever the language, was to impress it into moist clay using
a stylus capable of producing wedge-shaped marks (e.g. **Figure 6**). As such, it had to be added
during the manufacture of an object. In many cases, the object was created solely as a surface for

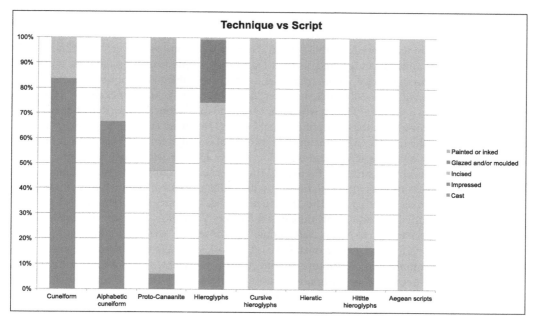

Figure 13: This chart shows the different ways in which texts can be added to objects, and how these techniques relate to script choice.

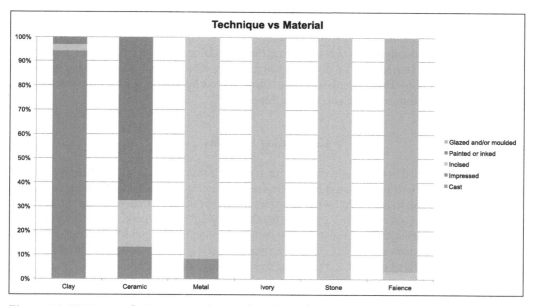

Figure 14: Writing technique can relate to the physical properties of the surface being written upon. This chart shows how technique and material relate to one another across the range of Bronze Age South Levantine texts.

the writing and so was inseparable from it. Yet cuneiform and alphabetic cuneiform were also applied to stone surfaces and to ceramics after the clay had hardened or been fired. The technique then became one of incision. In the case of cylinder seal and stone vessel inscriptions the signs were carefully cut to imitate the characteristic wedge-shape of the impressed version, even though different tools were in use and the material does not naturally lend itself to this kind of effect, suggesting that the script itself carried with it certain visual expectations, whatever the medium. Only occasionally is this convention ignored, as seen on a bronze knife from Nahal Tabor, where the alphabetic cuneiform signs have a more triangular head, comparable to inscriptions on metal artefacts at Ugarit (Horowitz et al. 2006: 163, n. 3; Yon 2006, 171, cat. 63). Another example is the post-firing inscription on a jug from Hazor, where the writer has abandoned the wedge-shaped letters of their Akkadian cuneiform for a simplified, linear effect (Horowitz et al. 2006: 65–66, Hazor 1).

In other scripts, the links between material, writing tool and sign form appear to be more consistent. Hieratic was a cursive script, and is predominantly applied using what is assumed to be a reed pen and ink on ceramic surfaces (**Figure 9**). There is a single example of a hieratic inscription being added to a ceramic vessel before firing, by dragging a pointed tool or stylus through the moist clay (Maeir et al. 2004: fig. 6). The difference may well be one of context, with the majority of texts being added by individuals outside the pottery workshop. This may in turn reflect a stronger degree of separation between craftspeople and those with scribal training. In the case of hieroglyphs, however, the two groups must have often worked closely together in the production of objects such as monumental sculpture, architectural components, scarabs and stone vessels, where the primary method of inscription was through different techniques of cutting (e.g. **Figure 7b–c**), or faience vessels, where the scribe had to work with moulds and glazes (**Figure 7a**). On other occasions, the texts could have been supplied to workshops ready made, as when cartouche stamps were used to impress ceramic vessels prior to firing (**Figure 3**). Finally, Proto-Canaanite scribes, like those using other cursive or pictorial scripts, tend to draw their signs freehand rather than applying jabbed impressions. A pointed tool is either dragged through clay before a vessel is fired, or cuts into the surface afterwards, or paint or ink is applied, most probably using a brush (**Figure 4**). In only one case was an inscription impressed, and then this seems to have been done using a carved stamp, similar to Egyptian practice (Sass 1988: fig. 271). The one writing technique that finds favour across all scripts in the region is that of incision, as it can be applied across a wide range of different materials and be done anywhere, using tools that need not be specific to the scribe. Its use may show the desire to modify existing objects by adding texts at a later date, and a need for flexible settings in which this may be done.

Concluding Remarks

The categories outlined in this chapter and summarised in **Table 3** are designed to help explore the implications of how writing was used in the Bronze Age Levant, and should be seen as suggestive rather than definitive. In actual fact writing often functioned in more than one context, and thus an ownership inscription could be seen as a way of identifying the donor of an object when it was used as a votive offering, or an amulet that protected a person in life could be taken to the grave to extend that protection into death. Similarly inscribed artefacts can belong to multiple owners, with consequent shifts of context and meaning over the life of the object.

One striking fact about the data is how many sites have produced examples of multiple scripts in a range of materials and techniques, in some cases even when the actual sample size is very small. This appears to be a phenomenon of the Late Bronze Age, with the most cosmopolitan cities on the Canaanite map in this respect being Beth Shan and Lachish. Both shared the full range of Egyptian scripts (hieroglyphs, cursive hieroglyphs and hieratic) and the presence of cuneiform and Proto-Canaanite (while no cuneiform has been discovered at Lachish itself, this site is known to be the source of some of the Amarna correspondence, Goren et al. 2004: 289; Millard 1999: 318, fig. 2). Lachish was also the home of a rare example of an Aegean script, thought to be related to Linear A, cut into the shoulder of a vessel made of local limestone (Finkelberg et al. 2004: 1631).

	Adminis-trative	Education	Propa-ganda	Funerary	Votive	Protective	Owner-ship
Cuneiform	X	X			X		
Alphabetic cuneiform	X				X		X
Proto-Canaanite	?				X		X
Egyptian hieroglyphs	X		X	X	X	X	
Hieratic	X				X	X	
Cursive hieroglyphs					X		
Hittite hieroglyphs	X						X
Aegean	X				X		?

Table 3: The relationship between script and its context of use, as determined by evaluating the object type and function, alongside the content of the text itself.

Despite the diversity of scripts available at many sites, it is difficult to determine whether individual scribes were conversant in writing multiple languages. One way to demonstrate this would be through the presence of single objects with multiple scripts. Actual examples of this sort of practice are very rare. There is a clay stopper from Megiddo, stamped on its upper face with an Egyptian hieroglyphic seal (most probably a scarab), and impressed on the sides in cuneiform, giving an Egyptian personal name and a Sumerian unit of capacity (Horowitz et al. 2006: 107–108, Megiddo 5). This might point to an Egyptian scribe with cuneiform training, a scenario that makes sense for a region which represents an interface between the two writing technologies. However, it should be pointed out that the hieroglyphic element of the object was produced by a seal, and so is not actual proof that the scribe in this case was able to render both hieroglyphs and cuneiform, or indeed, even read the former. Another example cited earlier was a cylinder seal with both cuneiform and hieroglyphic elements in the design (Teissier 1996: 110, cat. 226). In this case, there is even less proof of a craftsperson familiar with both languages, as the use of script as a decorative element has very different implications compared with script intended to be read, and the inaccurate rendering of many of the signs points to a lack of understanding of their meaning.

In actual fact most forms of script appear to have been used in discrete environments. Cuneiform, for example, was primarily an administrative script that was adopted for diplomatic communication, and otherwise used only within what appears to be a very small and largely closed community of professional scribes (Gianto 1999: 127). This probably explains the strong formality in the way the script tends to have been executed, irrespective of the surface material involved. Hieratic appears to have been used primarily in sites in the South Sharon plain and Negev; the bulk of examples have a votive or ritual use, with one possible legal text and an inspection marking (Goldwasser 1984: pl. 7.2; Wimmer 2007), and all appear to have functioned within the context of the Egyptian administration of the region. These sorts of texts would have been used in settings which made them inaccessible to the majority of the population, so it is not surprising that they had so little impact on Canaanite material culture and practices in general.

One possible exception to this trend may be seen with Egyptian hieroglyphs. These have the strongest visibility of all scripts, largely due to their use on a range of personal jewellery and amulets, and the spread of some elements of this script into contemporary decorative art. These personal uses of writing parallel the more official or governmental ones, and set the scene for transformations of meaning and use of the type that we do not see occurring elsewhere. Signs that were adopted into Canaanite repertoires in scarab and other workshops do not appear to have been transferred along with mechanisms that would allow new users to be trained in the 'correct way' of using them. Indeed, the pictorial nature of the signs left users free to assign new meanings, and use them in ways that the originators of the script had never intended (Goldwasser 2006: 126, 131, 134, 151). As such, these signs lost their ability to record Egyptian speech and language. Goldwasser concludes that it was the informal context in which these signs were now being used, and this very lack of formal scribal training that paved the way for the evolution of new applications of script and the invention of the alphabet (Goldwasser 2006: 152–153). Interestingly, while the meanings of individual signs were being renegotiated, the objects on which these signs appeared did not seem to undergo the same level of transformation, and so the overall design of the scarab amulet retained strong links with its Egyptian counterparts.

The Iron I period, 1150–1000 BC, saw a gradual falling away of the visibility and use of all the scripts previously found in the Southern Levant. However it was the cuneiform and hieroglyph/ hieratic traditions that appear to have suffered the most, as the urban administrative systems that supported technical training fell into disarray and the international networks that provided much of the rationale for their use dissolved. Many major centres were abandoned or went into decline, with urban populations moving into smaller village communities, while the Egyptians eventually closed down their Levantine strongholds altogether. The Report of Wenamun, discussed earlier and thought to be set in this period, points to the continued existence of writing in Lebanon where there appears to have been stronger cultural and urban continuity at this time. But elsewhere in Canaan, archaeological evidence for the use of cuneiform, Egyptian hieroglyphs and hieratic, suggests that these scripts became increasingly irrelevant to activities within Canaan itself. In contrast, the Proto-Canaanite alphabets that had been apparently peripheral to core activities became more valued in the newly reconfigured geopolitical landscape of the Iron Age Levant. This may be because they were less formally tied to official purposes and scriptoria, traditionally being used in a more private context to mark personal property and offerings. The use of a greatly simplified sign list that was visually less complicated and more memorable than cuneiform may also have helped its spread amongst the wider community and made it less vulnerable to social and economic change. Ultimately it was this accessibility that led to transformed varieties of this writing such as Phoenician and Hebrew becoming an important tool for use by the emerging new polities in the region.

Acknowledgements

The author would like to thank Graham Reed for providing the illustrations in **Figures 5–9**, and the Institute of Archaeology, University College London, for permission to publish objects in **Figures 3–4**, **7c**, **11** and **12**.

References

Albright, W. F. 1952. The Smaller Beth-Shan Stele of Sethos I (1309–1290 BC). *Bulletin of the American Schools of Oriental Research* 125: 24–32.

Albright, W. F. and Rowe, A. 1928. A Royal Stele of the New Empire from Galilee. *Journal of Egyptian Archaeology* 14(3/4): 281–287.

Andrews, C. 1994. *Amulets of Ancient Egypt*. London: British Museum Press.

Barkay, G. 1996. Late Bronze Age Temple in Jerusalem? *Israel Exploration Journal* 46(1–2): 23–43.

Ben-Tor, D. 1998. The Relations Between Egypt and Palestine During the Middle Kingdom as Reflected by Contemporary Canaanite Scarabs. In Eyre, C. J. (ed.), *Proceedings of the Seventh International Congress of Egyptologists*. Leuven: Peeters, 147–163.

Blankenberg-Van Delden, C. 1969. *The Large Commemorative Scarabs of Amenhotep III*. Leiden: E. J. Brill.

Brandl, B. 2009. Scarabs, Seals, Sealings and Seal Impressions. In Panitz-Cohen, N. and Mazar, A. (eds), *Excavations at Tel Beth-Shean 1989–1996, Volume 3*. Jerusalem: Israel Exploration Society, 636–684.

Cross, F. M. and Stager, L. E. 2006. Cypro-Minoan Inscriptions Found in Ashkelon. *Israel Exploration Journal* 56(2): 129–159.

Dothan, T. 1979. *Excavations at the Cemetery of Deir el-Balah* (Qedem 12). Jerusalem: Hebrew University of Jerusalem.

Dothan, T. 2008. *Deir el-Balah: Uncovering an Egyptian outpost in Canaan from the time of the Exodus*. Jerusalem: Israel Museum.

Eggler, J. and Keel, O. 2006. *Corpus der Siegel-Amulette aus Jordanien: von Neolithikum bis zur Perserzeit*. Freiburg: Academic Press.

Feldman, M. H. 2009. Hoarded Treasures: The Megiddo ivories and the end of the Bronze Age. *Levant* 41(2): 175–194. DOI: http://dx.doi.org.libproxy.ucl.ac.uk/10.1179/0075891 09X12484491671130

Finkelberg, M., Uchitel, A. and Ussishkin, D. 2004. The Linear A Inscription (LACH ZA 1). In Ussishkin, D. (ed.), *Renewed Archaeological Excavations at Lachish (1973–1994), Volume 3*. Tel Aviv: Tel Aviv University, 1629–1638.

Franken, H. J. 1992. *Excavations at Tell Deir 'Alla: The Late Bronze Age sanctuary*. Leuven: Peeters.

Gianto, A. 1999. Amarna Akkadian as a Contact Language. In van Lergerghe, K. and Voet, G. (eds), *Languages and Cultures in Contact: At the crossroads of civilizations in the Syro-Mesopotamian realm*. Leuven: Peeters, 123–132.

Giveon, R. 1985. *Egyptian Scarabs from Western Asia from the Collections of the British Museum*. Göttingen: Vandenhoeck and Ruprecht.

Goldwasser, O. 1984. Hieratic Inscriptions from Tel Sera' in Southern Canaan. *Tel Aviv* 11(1): 77–93.

Goldwasser, O. 1989. Some Egyptian Finds from Hazor: Scarabs, scarab impressions and a stele fragment. In Ben-Tor, A. (ed.), *Hazor III–IV: An account of the third and fourth seasons of excavations, 1957–58, Text*. Jerusalem: Israel Exploration Society, 339–345.

Goldwasser, O. 1991. An Egyptian Scribe from Lachish and the Hieratic Tradition of the Hebrew Kingdoms. *Tel Aviv* 18(2): 248–253.

Goldwasser, O. 2002. A 'Kirgipa' Commemorative Scarab of Amenhotep III from Beit Shean. *Ägypten und Levante* 12: 191–193.

Goldwasser, O. 2006. Canaanites Reading Hieroglyphs: Horus is Hathor? — The invention of the alphabet in Sinai. *Ägypten und Levante* 16: 121–160.

Goldwasser, O. and Wimmer, S. 1999. Hieratic Fragments from Tell El-Far'ah (South). *Bulletin of the American Schools of Oriental Research* 313: 39–42.

Goren, Y., Finkelstein, I. and Na'aman, N. 2004. *Inscribed in Clay: Provenance study of the Amarna tablets and other ancient Near Eastern texts*. Tel Aviv: Emery and Claire Yass Publications in Archaeology.

Goren, Y., Na'aman, N., Mommsen, H. and Finkelstein, I. 2006. Provenance Study and Re-evaluation of the Cuneiform Documents from the Egyptian Residency at Tel Aphek. *Ägypten und Levante* 16: 161–171.

Hamilton, G. J. 2006. *The Origins of the West Semitic Alphabet in Egyptian Scripts*. Washington: Catholic Biblical Association of America.

Hamilton, G. J. 2010. The Early Alphabetic Inscription Painted on a Spouted Cup from Tell el-'Ajjul. *Maarav* 17(2): 103–148.

Higginbotham, C. R. 2000. *Egyptianization and Elite Emulation in Ramesside Palestine: Governance and accommodation on the imperial periphery*. Leiden: E. J. Brill.

Horowitz, W. 1997. The Amarna Age Inscribed Clay Cylinder from Beth-Shean. *Biblical Archaeologist* 60(2): 97–100. DOI: http://dx.doi.org/10.2307/3210598

Horowitz, W., Oshima, T. and Sanders, S. 2006. *Cuneiform in Canaan: Cuneiform sources from the land of Israel in ancient times*. Jerusalem: Israel Exploration Society.

James, F. 1966. *The Iron Age at Beth Shan: A study of levels VI–IV*. Philadelphia: The University Museum, University of Pennsylvania.

James, F. and McGovern, P. E. 1993. *The Late Bronze Egyptian Garrison at Beth Shan: A study of levels VII and VIII*. Philadelphia: The University Museum, University of Pennsylvania.

Jeffreys, D. 2003. All in the Family? Heirlooms in Ancient Egypt. In Tait, J. (ed.), *'Never Had the Like Occurred': Egypt's view of its past*. London: UCL Press, 197–211.

Keel, O. 1997. *Corpus der Stempelsiegel-Amulette aus Palästina/Israel. Von den Anfängen bis zur Perserzeit. Katalog Band I: von Tell Abu Farag bis 'Atlit*. Freiberg: Universitätsverlag Freiburg Schweiz.

Landsberger, B. and Tadmor, H. 1964. Fragments of Clay Liver Models from Hazor. *Israel Exploration Journal* 14(4): 201–218.

Macalister, R. A. S. 1912. *The Excavation of Gezer, Volumes 1–3*. London: Palestine Exploration Fund.

MacDonald, E., Starkey, J. and Lankester Harding, G. 1932. *Beth Pelet II: Prehistoric Fara*. London: British School of Archaeology in Egypt.

Maeir, A. M., Martin, M. and Wimmer, S. J. 2004. An Incised Hieratic Inscription from Tell es-Safi, Israel. *Ägypten und Levant* 14: 125–134.

Magrill, P., Jasnow, R. and Kyle McCarter Jr., P. 2004. A Newly Discovered Egyptian Inscription. In Ussishkin; D. (ed.), *Renewed Archaeological Excavations at Lachish (1973–1994), Volume 3*. Tel Aviv: Tel Aviv University, 1618–1625.

McGovern, P. E. 1985. *Late Bronze Palestinian Pendants: Innovation in a cosmopolitan age*. Sheffield: American Schools of Oriental Research.

Millard, A. 1999. The Knowledge of Writing in Late Bronze Age Palestine. In van Lergerghe, K. and Voet, G. (eds), *Languages and Cultures in Contact: At the crossroads of civilizations in the Syro-Mesopotamian realm*. Leuven: Peeters, 317–326.

Moran, W. L. 1992. *The Amarna Letters*. Baltimore: John Hopkins University Press.

Mumford, G. D. 1998. *International Relations Between Egypt, Sinai, and Syria-Palestine During the Late Bronze Age to Early Persian Period (Dynasties 18–26: c.1550–525 B.C.): A spatial and temporal analysis of the distribution and proportions of Egyptian(izing) artefacts and pottery in Sinai and Selected Sites in Syria-Palestine*. Unpublished PhD dissertation, University of Michigan.

Oren, E. D. 1972. Tel Sera' (Tell esh-Shari'a). *Israel Exploration Journal* 22: 167–169.

Oren, E. D. 1973. *The Northern Cemetery at Beth Shan*. Leiden: E. J. Brill.

Oren, E. D. Olivier, J. P., Goren, Y., Betancourt, P., Myer, G. H. and Yellin, J. 1996. A Minoan Graffito from Tel Haror (Negev, Israel). *Cretan Studies* 5: 91–117.

Parker, B. 1949. Cylinder Seals from Palestine. *Iraq* 11: 1–43.

Petrie, W. M. F. 1890. *Kahun, Gurob and Hawara*. London: Kegan Paul.

Petrie, W. M. F. 1930. *Beth Pelet I*. London: British School of Archaeology in Egypt.

Petrie, W. M. F. 1933. *Ancient Gaza III*. London: British School of Archaeology in Egypt.

Petrie Museum of Egyptology. On-line Catalogue. http://www.petrie.ucl.ac.uk/index2.html [accessed on 19 May 2010].

Phillips, J. 1992. Tomb-robbers and their Booty in Ancient Egypt. In Orel, S. E. (ed.), *Death and Taxes in the Ancient Near East*. Lewiston/Queenston/Lampeter: Edwin Mellen Press, 157–192.

Porter, B. and Moss, R. L. B. 1952. *Topographical Bibliography of Ancient Egyptian Hieroglyphic Texts, Reliefs and Paintings VII: Nubia, the deserts, and outside Egypt*. Oxford: Clarendon Press.

Richards, F. 2001. *The Anra Scarab: An archaeological and historical approach* (BAR International Series 919). Oxford: Archeopress.

Rothenberg, B. 1988. *The Egyptian Mining Temple at Timna*. London: Institute of Archaeology, University College London.

Sass, B. 1988. *The Genesis of the Alphabet and Its Development in the Second Millennium B.C.* Wiesbaden: Harrassowitz.

Schulman, A. R. 1993. A Ramesside Queen from Ashdod. *'Atiqot* 23: 111–114.

Simpson, W. K. 2003. *The Literature of Ancient Egypt: An anthology of stories, instructions, stelae, autobiographies and poetry*. New Haven: Yale University Press.

Singer, I. 1977. A Hittite Hieroglyphic Seal Impression from Tel Aphek. *Tel Aviv* 4(3–4): 178–190. DOI: http://dx.doi.org.libproxy.ucl.ac.uk/10.1179/033443577788497696

Singer, I. 1988–1989. The Political Status of Megiddo VIIA. *Tel Aviv* 15–16(1): 101–112.

Singer, I. 1993. A Hittite Signet Ring from Tel Nami. In Rainey, A. F. (ed.), *Kinattutu sa darati: Raphael Kutscher memorial volume*. Tel Aviv: Institute of Archaeology.

Singer, I. 2003. Two Hittite Ring Seals from Tell el-Far'ah (South). *Eretz-Israel* 27: 133–134, 287*.

Sparks, R. T. 2003. Egyptian Stone Vessels and the Politics of Exchange (2617–1070 BC). In Matthews, R. and Roemer, C. (eds), *Ancient Perspectives on Egypt*. London: UCL Press, 39–56.

Sparks, R. T. 2007. *Stone Vessels in the Levant*. Leeds: Maney Publishing.

Stewart, H. M. 1995. *Egyptian Shabtis*. Princes Risborough: Shire Publications.

Sweeney, D. 2003. A Lion-Hunt Scarab and Other Egyptian Objects from the Late Bronze Fortress at Jaffa. *Tel Aviv* 30(1): 54–65.

Sweeney, D. 2004. The Hieratic Inscriptions. In Ussishkin, D. (ed.), *The Renewed Archaeological Excavations at Lachish (1973–1994), Volume 3* (Monographs of the Sonia and Marco Nadler Institute of Archaeology, Tel Aviv University 22). Tel Aviv: Emery and Claire Yass Publications in Archaeology, 1601–1617.

Teissier, B. 1996. *Egyptian Iconography on Syro-Palestinian Cylinder Seals of the Middle Bronze Age* (Orbis Biblicus et Orientalis 11). Göttingen: Vandenhoeck and Ruprecht.

Tufnell, O. 1958. *Lachish IV: The Bronze Age*. London: Oxford University Press.

Tufnell, O., Inge, C. H. and Harding, G. L. 1940. *Lachish II: The Fosse Temple*. London: Oxford University Press.

Ussishkin, D. 2004. *Renewed Archaeological Excavations at Lachish (1973–1994), Volume 3*. Tel Aviv: Tel Aviv University.

Ventura, R. 1987. Four Egyptian Funerary Stelae from Deir el-Balah. *Israel Exploration Journal* 37: 105–115.

Ward, W. A. 1966. The Egyptian Inscriptions of Level VI. In James, F. (ed.), *The Iron Age at Beth Shan: A study of levels VI–IV*. Philadelphia: The University Museum, University of Pennsylvania, 161–179.

Weinstein, J. M. 1975. Egyptian Relations with Palestine in the Middle Kingdom. *Bulletin of the American Schools of Oriental Research* 217: 1–16.

Weinstein, J. M. 1981. The Egyptian Empire in Palestine: A reassessment. *Bulletin of the American Schools of Oriental Research* 241: 1–27.

Wimmer, S. J. 1990. Egyptian Temples in Canaan and Sinai. In Israelit-Groll, S. (ed.), *Studies in Egyptology presented to Miriam Lichtheim, Volume 2*. Jerusalem: Magnes Press, Hebrew University, 1065–1106.

Wimmer, S. J. 2007. A Hieratic Sign. In Mazar, A. and Mullins, R. (eds), *Excavations at Tel Beth-Shean 1989–1996, Volume 2: The Middle and Late Bronze Age strata in Area R*. Jerusalem: Israel Antiquities Authority, 688–689.

Yon, M. 2006. *The City of Ugarit at Tell Ras Shamra*. Winona Lake: Eisenbrauns.

The Function and Meaning of Writing in the Prehistoric Aegean: Some reflections on the social and symbolic significance of writing from a material perspective

Helène Whittaker

University of Gothenburg

My primary purpose in this chapter is to assess the function and meaning of writing in the prehistoric Aegean by focusing on the material practices of writing. During the Middle and Late Bronze Ages (*c.*2000–1200 BC) an uncertain number of scripts was in use on Crete. In the pre-Mycenaean period, the two most important are known as Linear A and Minoan or Cretan Hieroglyphic (**Figures 1–2**; see also Flouda, this volume). Although the two writing systems do not seem to have been used for exactly the same purposes, as they occur on different types of documents, they were both associated with the palatial administration. Linear A is in its earliest form found at the Palace at Phaistos in south-central Crete, while Minoan Hieroglyphic was associated with the palaces at Knossos, Malia, and Petras in the north and northeast (see also Flouda, Finalyson and Tomas, all this volume). Both scripts are syllabic. After the destruction of the first palaces (*c.*1700 BC), Cretan Hieroglyphic seems to go out of use and is replaced by Linear A for reasons that are still unclear (cf. Finalyson, this volume).

As the two forms of writing can be geographically differentiated in the early palatial period, it is a plausible assumption that they represent different languages, but in view of the fact that neither script has been deciphered this cannot be verified (cf. Olivier 1986: 387; Schoep 1999: 265; 2007; see Younger and Rehak 2008: 176 for the view that there was only one Cretan language). It has, however, been suggested that Linear A and Cretan Hieroglyphic have a common origin in an earlier prepalatial script, known as the 'Archanes script' (**Figure 3**). This early form of writing takes its name after Archanes in central Crete, where a number of seals inscribed with this script were found in burials (Schoep 1999: 266–267; 2006: 45–46, n. 73). If it is the case that both Linear A and Cretan Hieroglyphic have the same origin, the later development of two different

How to cite this book chapter:
Whittaker, H. 2013. The Function and Meaning of Writing in the Prehistoric Aegean: Some reflections on the social and symbolic significance of writing from a material perspective. In: Piquette, K. E. and Whitehouse, R. D. (eds.) *Writing as Material Practice: Substance, surface and medium.* Pp. 105-121. London: Ubiquity Press. DOI: http://dx.doi.org/10.5334/bai.f

Figure 1: Green jasper seal with signs in the Minoan Hieroglyphic script, side A, from Crete, *c.*1700–1550 BC. Length: 1.1 cm; Width: 0.5 cm; Thickness: 0.5 cm. GR 1934.11-20.1 AN34822001. © Trustees of the British Museum.

Figure 2: Bronze double axe inscribed with Linear A, said to be from the Lasíthi Plateau, Crete, *c.*1700–1450 BC. Length: 18.5 cm. GR 1954.10-20.1. © Trustees of the British Museum.

forms of writing associated with the palatial administration in different parts of the island is perhaps to be seen in terms of the deliberate construction of separate regional identities, in which language may or may not have been a factor.

In the Late Bronze Age a new script known as Linear B was invented and became the only script in use on both Crete and the Greek mainland (**Figure 4a–b**; see Tomas, this volume). Linear B was developed from Linear A in order to write Greek and was closely associated with the Mycenaean

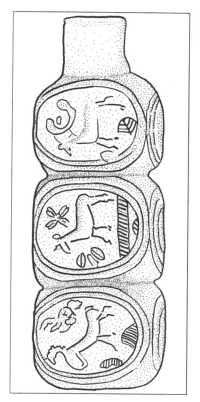

Figure 3: Bone seal with inscribed faces from Archanes *c.*2000 BC. Length: 4.0 cm. Drawing by Sven von Hofsten (after Sakellarakis and Sapouna-Sakellaraki 1991: fig. 79).

Figure 4: Linear B tablets found at Knossos, 1450–1400 BC. a) GR 1910.4-23.2; b) Length: 16.0 cm; Width: 4.0 cm; Thickness: 2.0 cm. GR 1910.4-23.1. © Trustees of the British Museum.

palace administration. In contrast to Linear A and Cretan Hieroglyphic, Linear B has been deciphered and the documents on which it occurs can be read with a high degree of certainty. Exactly when Linear B was invented is an open question, but it may have been much earlier than the date of the first documents that have been preserved. Whether Linear B was first used on Crete or on the Mainland is also an open question.

A thin clay disc known as the Phaistos Disc represents another possible but controversial example of writing. It was found with a fragment of a Linear A tablet and dates to the Middle Bronze Age. A number of signs, some of them repeated, are arranged in a spiral on both sides of the disc. A few are vaguely comparable to signs of the Cretan hieroglyphic script, but on the whole they bear no conclusive resemblance to either Linear A or Cretan Hieroglyphic. If the signs constitute writing it is in an otherwise unattested form. As a writing support the disc is also unique in its circular shape and in contrast to the clay tablets used in the palatial administrative systems it had been deliberately baked. Strictly speaking, a form of writing that is attested solely on a single artefact should not be really classified as an example of a functional writing system. I have elsewhere suggested that the inscription on the Phaistos Disc could be an example of pseudo-writing (Whittaker 2005; cf. Flouda, this volume).

In the Aegean writing occurs on a number of different types of material supports, made of clay, bone, stone or metal. The use of these varies with time and place. The range of materials used as supports is much more extensive for Crete than for the Greek mainland. Clay tablets represent the largest group of preserved texts. Their use was associated with the palatial administration on both Crete and the mainland and spans the Middle and Late Bronze Ages. Their first occurrence is associated with the establishment of the Minoan palace system c.2000 BC. The latest tablets date to the destruction of the Mycenaean palaces c.1200 BC. Clay was a material that was readily available, as good sources are found on both Crete and the Greek mainland. Clay tablets are objects that have been fashioned solely for the purpose of being written on, and their shape and size would have been determined by the specifics of this use, by the system of storage, or by the needs of the scribes. They were used for all three of the major scripts, and the shape of the tablet correlates with the type of writing found on them. Cretan Hieroglyphic is generally found on two-sided or four-sided bars, while Linear A and Linear B are found on page-shaped tablets; the ones used for Linear A are generally smaller than the ones used for Linear B. Linear B is also found on tablets which are much wider than they are long (often called leaf-shaped or palm leaf-shaped). The tablets sometimes have writing on more than one side; the four-sided bars are generally inscribed on all sides. All types of tablets were made in the same way. After being fashioned from the wet clay, they were air-dried until they had hardened to the consistency of leather and were ready to be written on. Some kind of stylus with a sharp point was used for writing. It has been claimed that the function of several thin rods made of bone and in one case of bronze found at Tiryns was for writing Linear B (Cultraro 2006: 24). Otherwise, styli have not been recognised in the archaeological record, which may be an indication that they were commonly made of wood and thus less likely to survive. This is perhaps indicated by the fact that some inscriptions include the impressions of a stylus that had been roughly made and in some cases had a split end (Hallager 1996: 29). Chadwick (1976: 18) suggests that a thorn fastened to some kind of holder could have been used for the very fine writing found on some tablets.

When a scribe had finished recording information on a tablet it was left to dry completely before being placed in a basket or a wooden container and archived. It was possible to reuse a tablet which had already been inscribed and dried by moistening it so that the surface could be flattened and whatever had been written on it erased. When it had dried sufficiently, the tablet could then be re-inscribed. Many Linear A tablets are in fact palimpsests, indicating that the palace bureaucracies had some kind of recycling scheme in place (Schoep 2002: 79). The use of clay tablets can be seen as providing material weight and durability to the information recorded on them. It is, however, possible that for certain types of texts in the palace bureaucracies, clay may have been chosen as a support because its material properties afforded impermanency as much as permanency (see also Piquette, this volume). In light of evidence for re-use, the information recorded on clay tablets, in all or most cases, may have been of an ephemeral nature. Nevertheless, since all Aegean tablets were unbaked, their survival as archaeological artefacts was dependent on them being exposed to fire in some other way. The majority that have been preserved as legible documents have been found in the destruction layers of the palaces, which they do not in most cases antedate by long periods of time.

Other types of clay objects that may carry script are the so-called roundels, various types of sealings, and ceramic vessels used for storage or transport. Roundels are thick clay disks with seal impressions, which have usually been inscribed with signs in Linear A on one or both faces (see also Finalyson, this volume). Their function is uncertain, but almost all have been found in archival contexts; one suggestion is that they were receipts given in return for the delivery of goods from the palaces (Hallager 1996: 116–120). Their use is restricted to the period of the new palaces on Crete (c.1700 – c.1450 BC). All three scripts can occur on sealings. However, while a stylus was always used to write Linear A and B on all types of clay documents, Cretan Hieroglyphic could also be written with seals, which were pressed into the clay in order to produce a meaningful text. Like the tablets, roundels and sealings have only been preserved if they have been accidently burnt. All three scripts can also be found either inscribed or painted on different types of ceramic vases. Texts in Linear B were normally painted on the pots before they were fired. Inscriptions on pots were meaningful in the sense that they were intended to provide information about place or time of fabrication, ownership or function. Potsherds, often referred to with the Greek word *ostraka*, were commonly used for informal writing in the historical Greek period (Thomas 1992: 57, 83 compares them to our scrap paper). This does not seem to have been the case in the Bronze Age. As far as I know, the only example from the prehistoric Aegean is an ostrakon from Akrotiri on Thera in the Cyclades, which has some kind of calculation in Linear A scratched on it (Michailidou 1992–1993).

Stone

On Crete writing is found on stone artefacts of various types. The Archanes script is found on three seals made of steatite (Godart 1999; Olivier and Godart 1996: #201, #203, #251; Schoep 2006: 45). This is a stone that is widely used on Crete as it is fairly soft and therefore easy to work. Two other seals with the Archanes script are made of marble and agate; as these stones are harder to work they may be later in date (Olivier and Godart 1996: #205, #292). Soft stones such as steatite or serpentine were used to make the earliest seals with inscriptions in Cretan Hieroglyphic. When the introduction of the horizontal bow-lathe in the 17th century BC made it possible to inscribe harder stones, red carnelian or green jasper also occur (Rehak and Younger 2001: 403). Serpentine and steatite were locally available on Crete, and there are a few sources of marble (Warren 1969: 134–135, 138–141). Green jasper (also known as *antico verde*) was imported from the Greek mainland, while agate and carnelian may have come from Egypt. Most of the seals inscribed with Cretan Hieroglyphic have three or four faces, of which one or two carry writing. Seals were used to impress clay and the fact that the earliest writing on Crete is found on seals implies the use of clay sealings and possibly other types of documents made from clay from the time that writing was invented on Crete.

Inscriptions in Linear A are found on a number of stone vessels that have been classified as libation or offering tables (Schoep 1994; Warren 1969: 62–68; **Figure 5**). These offering tables belong to a fairly well-defined type; they are usually square in shape and have a round bowl in the centre. They are made of serpentine, steatite or limestone. The inscription is sometimes on the wide flat rim surrounding the bowl, but in some cases it is found on the sides of the table. A sharp,

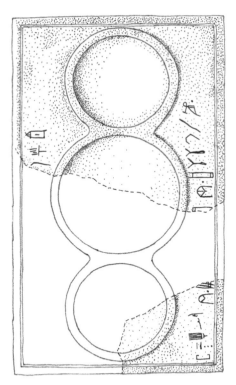

Figure 5: Steatite offering table with Linear A from the Psychro Cave *c.*1600 BC. Length: *c.*20 cm. Drawing by Sven von Hofsten (after Bendall 2013: fig. 256–257).

pointed implement was used to scratch the inscriptions onto the surface of the stone. The stone vases with inscriptions in Linear A date to the period of the new palaces. They have most often been found in cultic contexts, but some examples have been found in domestic contexts (Schoep 1994: 11). This practice of inscribing stone contrasts in material, purpose and context with the use of (recycled) clay in the administrative system of the palaces, surfaces fashioned expressly to carry writing.

On the Greek mainland writing is found on stone only very rarely. A fragment of schist with two Linear A signs was found at Ayios Stephanos in Lakonia (Janko 1982). It probably dates to the early Mycenaean period. The nature of the object is obscure, but it may be a weight. Two Linear A inscriptions on grave markers dating to the beginning of the Late Bronze Age have been illustrated by Evangelia Protonotariou-Deilaki (1990: fig. 28). One comes from Argos, the other from Grave Circle A at Mycenae.

Although perhaps not 'writing' strictly speaking, mention can also be made of the so-called mason's marks which first appear at the beginning of the Middle Minoan period. These are signs that have been inscribed on stone building blocks, which would have been mostly, but not always, invisible after the building had been completed. Mason's marks include the depiction of stars, double axes, branches and tridents, and they can be compared to signs in the Archanes Script, Cretan Hieroglyphic and Linear A. They have also in a few isolated cases been found on the Greek mainland. At Peristeria in Messenia two mason's marks of Minoan type, a double axe and a branch, had been cut into the facade of Tholos 1, a monumental burial structure, while three, one trident and two branches, have been identified on stone blocks at Mycenae; a double axe occurs on a building block on a wall below the palace at Pylos (Hood 1984: 36; 1987).

Metal

Writing is also found on metal artefacts. Linear A inscriptions have been found on at least six double axes made of bronze from various parts of Crete (Fri 2007: 68–71). The inscriptions had been made on finished axes. They are all functional axes and several of them show clear evidence of use. A bronze cauldron from Grave IV of Grave Circle A at Mycenae, which has what seems to be a single Linear A sign inscribed near the handle, represents, with the schist fragment and the grave markers mentioned above, one of the very few examples of Cretan writing found on the Greek mainland (Karo 1930–1933: no. 576; Palaima 2003*a*). Linear A inscriptions occur on three miniature replicas of double axes made of gold, which have been found at Archalochori in central Crete (Marinatos 1935). A large double axe made of bronze was also found in this deposit. It carries an incised inscription, arranged in three vertical columns, in the middle on one of its faces. The signs on the Archalochori Axe are idiosyncratic, and like the Phaistos Disc this may be an example of pseudo-writing (Whittaker 2005). A gold ring and four pins made of gold or silver also have texts in Linear A (Alexiou and Brice 1972; 1976; CMS II.3:38; Godart and Olivier 1982: KNZf13, KR(?) Zf1, PLZf1, KNZf31; Olivier et al. 1981; Platon and Pini 1984: 38). Crete is poor in metals and the copper and tin needed for bronze, as well as gold and silver, must have been imported. Gold and silver, and perhaps also bronze, represent rare and valuable materials (Watrous 2001: 165; Rehak and Younger 2001: 415). However, the range of metal objects on which writing is found on Crete suggests that writing may have been in more common use on materials which do not survive well than the actual archaeological evidence would indicate.

Bone

The evidence for the use of bone as a support for writing is limited to a few seals. With one exception the seals found at Archanes are made of bone (Olivier and Godart 1996: #202, #252, #315; Sakellarakis and Sapouna-Sakellaraki 1997: 326–330). The six seals with script from Archanes were found in Burial Building 3, Burial Building 6, and Burial Building 7, which date to the Middle Minoan IA period (*c.*2000–1900 BC). The largest has the form of three superimposed cubes, giving 14 sealing surfaces, of which two bore writing (**Figure 3**).

Other Materials

All preserved examples of Aegean writing are on clay tablets or other administrative documents that have been recovered from destruction layers of buildings destroyed by fire, or on small-scale objects made of durable materials whose survival was dependent on archaeological chance. It is clear that various kinds of perishable materials, such as leather, wood or papyrus, could have been, and almost certainly were, used to write on. The nature of the scripts themselves provides one indication that this was the case. The signs of Linear A and B are quite complex and consist of curved as well as straight lines. They are therefore more suited to writing or painting with ink on papyrus or pottery than to being inscribed in semi-dried clay (Chadwick 1976: 27; Palaima 2003*b*: 171). This suggests that some form of 'paper' support was used from an early period. It is possible that the development of Linear A from the Archanes script, which, as far as we know, could only be written by pressing seals into clay, should be seen in relation to the availability of imported papyrus or the acquisition of a technology for turning animal skins into a suitable writing surface. Since contacts between Crete and Egypt go back to the Early Bronze Age, it is not unlikely that papyrus was imported and used as a writing material also on Crete. A type of sealing known as the single-hole hanging nodule consists of a triangular lump of clay which had been

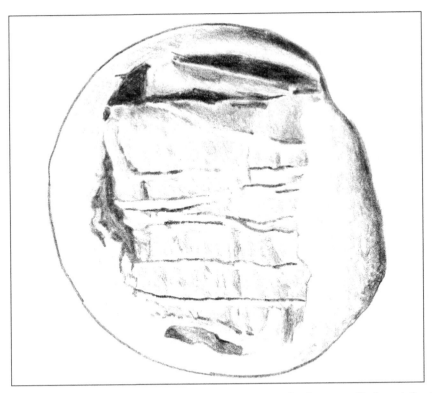

Figure 6: Flat-based nodule. Diameter: 2.1 × 2.75 cm. Drawing by Sven von Hofsten (after Hallager 1996: fig. 55).

formed around a knot at one end of a string. Hallager has argued that nodules of this type were attached to the string used to fasten papyrus documents (Hallager 1996: 198–199). However, the only things that are known for certain about the function of the single-hole hanging nodules is that they were attached to string and that they must have been used for some specific purpose in the Minoan palatial administration. The majority of them were inscribed in Linear A, usually only with a single sign, which may have indicated the category to which whatever they were attached to belonged.

A type of sealing known as flat-based nodules has more certainly been regarded as evidence for lost types of texts. These are lumps of clay with one or more seal impressions; in some examples impressions on the base of the nodules show that they had been attached to pieces of very thin leather which had been tightly folded and tied with thin string (**Figure 6**). This has led to the suggestion that leather or even parchment was in common use for writing (Hallager 1996: 135–158; Weingarten 1983: 38–42; see also Chadwick 1976: 27–28; Krzyszkowska 2005: 156; Schoep 2006: 56, n. 2; Shelmerdine 2008: 12; Younger and Rehak 2008: 175). It is in fact hard to imagine what other than written documents the folded and sealed pieces of leather could have been.

Like papyrus, leather and parchment, wood has few chances of survival in the Greek soil. Evidence from later periods of Greek antiquity and from contemporary Egypt and the Near East shows that wood could be used quite extensively for different type of supports for writing. Wooden boards covered with stucco and textile, which could be written on in ink, were used in Egypt from the Old Kingdom onwards (Cribiore 1996: 65). For all we know, similar wooden boards could have been in common use on Crete. Numerous inscriptions on stone survive from Greece in the historical period, testifying to the use of writing in official contexts and public display. However, textual evidence indicates that large whitened wooden boards were also used for public notices in Athens (Thomas 1992: 83). None of these survives, but as pointed out by Rosalind Thomas, wooden boards rather than stone might in fact have been the main medium for official inscriptions. There is no reason why wooden boards could not have been used in the Bronze Age as well for a similar purpose. The possibility that monumental public inscriptions existed in the Bronze Age Aegean cannot be completely ruled out, despite the total absence of evidence. It can, however, be considered certain that stone was not used, as in that case one would have expected some fragments at least, if not entire texts, to have survived.

Writing-boards

Chance survivals can on rare occasions provide a glimpse of lost types of text-objects. Fragments of a wooden writing-board were found in a 14th-century BC shipwreck off the south coast of Turkey near Ulu Burun (Bass et al. 1989: 10–11; Payton 1991). It is of a type which, as is now clear, was in use from the Bronze Age to the Medieval period (see Brown 1994 on Medieval writing-boards). The Ulu Burun writing-board consists of two rectangular pieces of wood, the insides of which, apart from a border along the edges, had been hollowed out to allow them to be filled with wax. The two boards were joined by ivory hinges on one of the long sides and when closed could be fastened with string or leather thongs. Although the wax has not been preserved, it was probably coloured as seems to have been the case generally with ancient and medieval writing-boards (cf. Brown 1994: 7; Clanchy 1979: 91; Lalou 1992: 234; Small 1997: 146). Adding colour to the wax would have had a decorative function, but it would also have made the inscribed characters easier to read. Black was the most common colour, but red, yellow or green could also occur. An 8th-century BC wooden writing-board from Nimrud in Mesopotamia was found with some of its wax preserved. Analysis showed that it consisted of 25% orpiment, which would have given it a brilliant yellow colour (Mallowan 1954: 98–99). Orpiment, which was in common use as a pigment in Antiquity, was in fact found in an amphora on the Ulu Burun wreck (Bass 1986: 278–279; Bass et al. 1989: 10–11). The remains of two other wooden writing-boards from the Ulu Burun wreck have also been identified (Shear 1998: 187). Since the contents of the ship included goods and artefacts from different parts of the eastern Mediterranean, it is impossible to determine their provenance; they could be Syrian, Egyptian, Cypriote or Mycenaean (cf. Symington 1991: 112). There is ample textual evidence for the perhaps widespread use of wooden writing-boards in the Near East from the time of Ur III (Symington 1991: 111; MacGinnis 2002). As stressed by Nicholas Postgate, Wang Tao and Toby Wilkinson, the Ulu Burun writing-boards should be regarded as representatives of what may have been a large and important class of Bronze Age objects (Postgate et al. 1995: 478; cf. MacGinnis 2002: 227).

Information on the specific uses of Near Eastern writing-boards relies on evidence from texts which sometimes mention the type of document on which specific information was recorded. The fact that no evidence of this type exists for the Aegean cannot be taken to preclude the idea that wooden writing-boards might have been used in similar ways. If wooden writing-boards were used in the Aegean in the Bronze Age, it is possible that they were used for different types of texts than those found on clay tablets. Since wooden writing-boards are lighter and stronger and therefore less cumbersome than clay tablets, it is possible to imagine that they were used for transporting information from one place to another. A wooden writing-board can be worn about the person (hanging from the belt vel sim.), and would therefore be suitable for quickly noting down information in passing, which could then later be transferred to a clay tablet or a papyrus document (cf. Brown 1994: 9; Clanchy 1979: 91–92 for this use of wooden writing-boards in the Medieval period). The wax surface used to write on could be easily wiped clean and reused. Wooden writing-boards may also have been used for writing of a more permanent character. In the Near East they were in some periods extensively used along with clay tablets for accounts and inventories of a permanent nature (MacGinnis 2002; Symington 1991: 118–123).

Hinges from wooden writing-boards made of ivory or bronze (or fragments thereof) should be fairly easy to recognise in the archaeological record, but no certain examples from Minoan Crete or the Greek mainland have been published. Ione Mylonas Shear has suggested that seven bronze hinges with traces of burnt wood found with Linear B tablets at Knossos and twelve bronze hinges found with Linear A tablets in the Archive Room of the palace of Zakro might represent the remains of wooden writing-boards (Shear 1998; cf. Perna 2007). Seven bronze hinges were found along with clay tablets and sealings in the Archive Complex of the Palace at Pylos (Palaima 2003b: 181; Shear 1998). One of the hinges from Pylos preserved traces of carbonised wood. In both cases, the hinges have been identified as the remains of wooden boxes, used for storing clay tablets (Platon 1971: 151). However, as argued by Shear, it would seem more likely that they represent the remains of writing-boards as their size corresponds to that of the ivory hinges from the Ulu Burun writing-board. Hinges of the type used on the writing-board from the Ulu Burun wreck could have been made from wood just as well as from ivory. The hinging system on the Ulu Burun writing-board is quite elaborate, as well as being made of a prestigious material. It would therefore seem reasonable to assume that wooden writing-boards may have more commonly been hinged or tied together with string or leather cords. Massimo Perna's objection that the fact that large numbers of bronze, bone or ivory hinges have not been found in archival contexts (or elsewhere) could be an indication that wooden writing-boards were not in common use in the Aegean area may therefore not be valid (Perna 2007: 226). Clay sealings may document the use of wooden writing-boards on Crete. In this regard, particular mention can be made of the balls of clay with seal impressions called two-hole hanging nodules which were used to fasten the two ends of a string together. They are believed to have been used to seal and / or label moveable commodities, although exactly what is uncertain (Hallager 1996: 36–37, 159–199; Krzyszkowska 2005: 21). Clay lumps called crescents with inscriptions in Cretan Hieroglyphic were also formed around string and are assumed to have sealed containers of some kind such as bags or boxes (Schoep 2004: 287). Alternatively, it would seem possible to suggest that the function of these types of sealings was to seal the string which tied the two parts of a wooden writing-board together. It may be relevant in this connection that the two-hole hanging nodules have been found with other archival documents. Some of the clay crescents are inscribed with signs that can be identified with logograms signifying wine, grain and olives (Schoep 2004: 287). If they were used to seal wooden writing-boards, it would seem to imply that these were used for archival purposes.

Social and Symbolic Implications

Because clay tablets found in archival contexts constitute by far the largest group of artefacts carrying script, most interest in Aegean Bronze Age writing has concentrated on its use as a bureaucratic tool. The invention of writing on Crete towards the end of the 2nd millennium BC has been regarded as a result of or even necessitated by the transition from small-scale to the more complex palatial societies. The fact that writing first occurs on seals rather than on other types of objects can be seen as first and foremost a consequence of developments in the administrative system but it can be proposed that the use and display of writing was also intertwined with social and symbolic meanings. In the rest of the chapter I shall try to evaluate the non-utilitarian functions of writing in the Bronze Age Aegean.

As stated above, the earliest form of writing is the Archanes script which is found on seals made of bone or stone. The invention of the Archanes script predates the establishment of the palaces and centralised administration. Only about 10 signs in all are represented in the Archanes script, and it might therefore be questioned whether it can reasonably be regarded as writing in a strict sense of the word. It could be argued that the signs represent rather some form of complex iconography and had a more decorative function (cf. Krzyszkowska 2005: 70–71; Shear 1998). However, in addition to the fact that several of the signs occur more than once, similarity with signs in Linear A would seem to indicate that they represent the sounds of words and that the inscriptions record meaningful text (cf. Schoep 2006: n. 74). Most seals with the Archanes script were found at Archanes in central Crete, but some have been found elsewhere and it is possible that the earliest form of Aegean writing may have been more widespread than is indicated by the available evidence.

That seals were used sphragistically for administrative purposes in Prepalatial Crete seems certain. Even though clay sealings which can be dated to this period are not many, the fact that they do exist can be regarded as incontrovertible evidence that seals were actually used to seal something and were not or not exclusively used for personal adornment or as amulets (Krzyszkowska 2005: 77–78; Pini 1990: 34–37; Schoep 1999). There is therefore no reason to doubt that the seals with early writing were also used for sealing purposes. The fact that Minoan writing first occurs on seals can plausibly be seen as an extension or elaboration of the administrative system that was already in existence. There is a continuity of use into the Palatial period in that seals inscribed with Cretan Hieroglyphic occur after the Archanes script has been superseded.

In addition to their administrative use, it is likely that seals functioned as badges of authority and were important status symbols from the Prepalatial period onwards. In the Palatial period this is most clearly indicated by the use of colourful, valuable and imported materials. The fact that seals are often perforated probably indicates that they were intended to be worn visibly as ornaments. In the Prepalatial period, when bone and mostly soft and locally available stone types were used, an association with the expression of individual prestige is, as proposed by Alexios Karytinos, perhaps indicated by the many different and in some cases elaborate shapes of the seals (Karytinos 1998: 79; cf. Krzyszkowska 2005: 21; Schoep 2006: 50). In the Prepalatial period Archanes seems to have been an important and wealthy centre (Sakellarakis and Sapouna-Sakellaraki 1991). The evidence comes primarily from the cemetery at Phourni, where several monumental burial structures were uncovered. The earliest dates to the middle of the 3rd millennium BC. These burials undoubtedly represent the emergence of an increasingly hierarchical society, and the grave goods attest to the wealth, far-flung connections, and prestige of those buried there. It would seem not implausible that writing was first invented at Archanes. The finds in Burial Building 6, where four of the seals with writing were found, were particularly rich and included jewellery, amulets made of bone, ivory, and gold, seals made of ivory and steatite in a variety of shapes and with different types of scenes, both figural and geometric, an Egyptian faience scarab, clay figurines, bronze tools, stone vases and many clay vessels (Sakellarakis and Sapouna-Sakellaraki 1991: 98–104; 1997: 202–205). It is certainly significant that in its earliest occurrence Aegean Bronze Age writing is found associated with prestige items in rich burials which attest to the wealth and social standing of their owners (cf. Karytinos 1998; Schoep 2006: 46–47). This can furthermore be seen in the context of the social importance of funerary ritual to the display of power and status in this period (Branigan 1970: 130–138; Murphy 1998: 36–39).

Also noteworthy is an apparent link between the earliest writing on Crete and religious expression. The signs in the Archanes script include representations of a double axe, a jug, a bucranium, a branch, a sistrum, objects that almost certainly had religious connotations (Nikolaidou 1999; Sakellarakis and Sapouna-Sakellaraki 1997: 351–356). It would seem significant that the earliest form of Aegean writing was based on signs which were imbued with religious meaning. Some of these signs also continue into the later Cretan writing systems. The signs found on some of the seals have been compared to the inscriptions in Linear A on stone vessels from cultic contexts. This could indicate that the inscriptions in Archanes script record religious texts (Sakellarakis and

Sapouna-Sakellaraki 1997: 329; Schoep 1999: 266, 273, n. 4). If that is the case, it is possible that the text was intended to enhance the function of the seal by providing additional religious protection when it was used to seal something. It is also possible that the seals with inscriptions were used mainly or exclusively for religious purposes. The seals themselves may furthermore have functioned as a sign of religious status or authority of some kind, and may have served to identify the owners as high-standing religious functionaries.

There has been some debate concerning the reasons for the invention or initial use of writing, whether a utilitarian or a symbolic function should be seen as primary (see e.g. Cornell 1991; Postgate et al. 1995; Stoddart and Whitely 1988; Thomas 1992). When it comes to Crete in the Bronze Age, it can be suggested that the distinction between a utilitarian function, on the one hand, and a ritual or ceremonial function, on the other, represents a false dichotomy. Religious ideology was most likely an integral part of the economy and the administrative system in the Prepalatial as well as in the Palatial periods, and there may not have existed any meaningful distinction between religious significance and administrative sphragistic use. It is arguable that the ideological and religious meanings associated with early Minoan script as seen at Archanes were part of the background against which the development of Cretan Hieroglyphic and Linear A and the uses of writing in the palatial administration should be seen.

The clay tablets with Linear A and Cretan Hieroglyphic represent an administrative development that can be associated with the establishment of palatial rule on Crete. The largest number of tablets has been found in palatial archives. However, a number of tablets with Linear A come from other contexts on Crete and in a few cases also from outside the island, testifying to the relatively widespread currency of this script. How, when, and if the information recorded on the clay tablets, which were kept in the palace archives, was later consulted is difficult to reconstruct. Despite the fact that clay tablets were clearly meant to be preserved for some length of time, it is often assumed that they represent temporary records, and that the information on them was later transferred to more permanent archival documents, for which papyrus or some other material which has not been preserved would have been used (Hallager 1996: 32; Olivier 1986: 386–387; Schoep 2006: 55). The fact that many of the Linear A tablets have been recycled is seen as evidence for the view that the clay tablets were temporary records (Schoep 2002: 79). Although clay as a material was readily available, the production of tablets of a standard type can be considered a fairly elaborate process that must have involved a number of people in the palace administration, including scribes who had specialist skills and may have worked full-time. From that perspective it is hard to understand why clay tablets would have been chosen as a medium for temporary documents.

It can, however, be suggested that whatever their function in the administrative processing of information the clay documents were also symbolic objects which played a role in expressing the power of the ruling elite. The possession of information is an effective instrument of political power, and this would have been clearly expressed through the bulky materiality of the clay tablets, regardless of whether they were ever consulted at a later date. It is also possible that the act of recording the goods that came into the palaces on clay tablets may in itself have been intended most of all to impress visitors with the control of the palatial elites over resources, labour and people. The ability to use a common material such as clay to transform speech into material form may also have been seen as a reflection of divine power. The fact that in many instances the information which is written down is minimal could suggest that the contents of the text were in some sense of secondary importance. The palace archives may not then have been intended as repositories of information that could be consulted by officials when necessary, but more as a display of the *capability* of the palace administration to collect and store information. If that was the case, it would not have been necessary to preserve the information on the tablets for long periods and they could be reused as needed.

The inscribed stone offering tables which have been found in cultic contexts constitute clear evidence for an association between writing and ritual (see also Flouda, this volume). Several of the inscriptions consist of the same recurring sign groups, usually transcribed as A-SA-SA-RA. It would seem likely that this represents a dedicatory formula. The purpose of the inscription, which is found only on very few of the stone vessels found in sanctuaries, may have been to increase the value of the object and to provide a permanent record of the wealth and piety of the dedicator (Schoep 1994: 20; 2006: 57; Whittaker 2005: 30). The display of writing could in that case be said to have functioned as a means of commemoration and authentication. The fact that these inscriptions occur on objects that are made of a durable material further suggests that the permanence given to the act of dedication by being recorded in writing and the indestructible nature of the material of which the objects are made were believed to reinforce each other.

It can be argued that the fact that writing occurs on double axes made of metal reflect the same idea. A few double axes made of bronze have been incised with one or two signs in Linear A (**Figure 2**). Although it is clear in some cases that they had been used as tools, it is possible that the inscription marks them as votive offerings that had been deposited in a sanctuary. Unfortunately, their find contexts are generally uninformative and several have no known provenance. The double axes made of gold that were found at Archalochori, on the other hand, were miniatures made of thin foil and could not have had any practical function. They can be classified as votive replicas. It may be relevant in this connection that in addition to durability and immutability, gold as a material is characterised by its bright and glowing colour. Evidence from different cultural contexts show that the quality of luminosity is universally or near-universally perceived to be associated with the materialisation of the supernatural (Keates 2002; Parisinou 2005). It is arguable that the use of gold for votive objects was intended to express an association with divinity, which was reinforced by the inscriptions. Along these lines, it could be proposed that examples of writing on gold and silver jewellery, which were presumably worn by members of the elite, were intended to demonstrate not only social status but also religious authority.

As discussed above, the question of whether wood was used as a support for writing in the Aegean Bronze Age continues to remain open, as there is no decisive archaeological or textual evidence from the Bronze Age Aegean itself. It is therefore not easy to speculate about possible social or symbolic meanings. In the *Iliad* there is, however, a single mention of a writing tablet, which may be of relevance in this connection. In the passage in question, king Proitos of Argos is described as sending the prince Bellerophon, whom he wishes to get rid of, to his kinsman in Lydia with a letter asking that the bearer be killed (*Iliad* VI.168–169). The letter is described as being written on a double tablet which could be folded together. It is not stated explicitly that it was made of wood, but had it been thought of as made of some other material this would no doubt have been included in the description. Accordingly, it can be assumed that the poem's audience was meant to imagine a wooden writing-board. While the *Iliad* was not composed and written down before the 8th century, Greek epic poetry has its roots in the Bronze Age. It is therefore possible that the occurrence of a writing-board as a crucial element of this story reflects the material culture of the Bronze Age. The recovery of several writing-boards from the Ulu Burun wreck raises considerably the odds in favour of the possibility that the story of Bellerophon reflects the use of wooden writing-boards in the Mycenaean period for communication over geographical distance (cf. Shear 1998: 189).

The more or less complete wooden writing-board from the Ulu Burun wreck was found in a pithos, which also contained the substantial remains of pomegranates, probably indicating that the jar had been filled with the fruit, several ballast stones, a bronze chisel and a bronze razor (Bass et al. 1989: 10–11). This has been taken to indicate that it contained information concerned the ship's cargo (Perna 2007: 226). However, the Ulu Burun writing-board was clearly an object of some value and on that account it seems unlikely that it and the two other writing-boards of which fragments were found in the wreck had been used for keeping track of the merchandise (Payton 1991: 106). It could be speculated that they rather represent diplomatic correspondence (cf. MacGinnis 2002: 221; Symington 1991: 119–120 on the use of writing-boards for letters in the Near East in the Bronze Age). If that was the case, the boards themselves may have played a role in elite gift exchange. Although perhaps not outstandingly valuable objects, the wooden writing-boards from the Ulu Burun wreck would have been striking artefacts with their ivory hinges and brightly coloured writing surfaces. As modern top level gift exchange demonstrates, the gifts themselves need not always be characterised by expense or exclusivity (e.g. President Obama's gift of an iPod to Queen Elizabeth II, see also Sparks' discussion of gift exchange, this volume). In the *Iliad*, the fact that King Proitos writes his message on a writing-board rather than on a rolled or folded and sealed piece of papyrus is possibly a reflection of the use of writing-boards as gifts between rulers in the Mycenaean period (cf. Shear 1998; see also Crielaard 1995: 213–124).

Concluding Remarks

In the Aegean writing is found on a fairly wide range of materials and in this chapter I have attempted to provide a concise overview of the various forms of writing and materials, as well as of other types of supports that have not been preserved, but may have existed. It is evident that beyond its primary function as a medium for storing and conveying information in a stable form, writing was in many contexts associated with various social and symbolic meanings, relating to power, status and religious expression. These meanings were associated with the nature of the writing itself and the materials used as supports, and with the contexts in which writing occurred. There was thus an interdependence between text types and the materials that the artefacts on which they are found are made of. This is well illustrated by the occurrence of writing on objects made of materials, such as stone or gold, which have been found in ritual contexts. The fact that the durability of these materials was reinforced by an inscription which gave permanence to the act of dedication enhanced the meaning of the artefacts as votive offerings. Conversely, the use of clay tablets, which were cumbersome, but which could also be easily erased and reused, in the palatial administrative systems suggests that permanence of information was of less concern than the need to let people see that a record was being made. In the Aegean case focusing on the physical aspects of writing in relation to the types of material supports rather than on the decipherment and understanding of texts can provide additional insight concerning the social role of writing in societies in which literacy would have been very limited.

References

Alexiou, S. and W. C. Brice 1972. A Silver Pin from Mavro Spelio with an Inscription in Linear A: Her. Mus. 540. *Kadmos* 11(2): 113–124. DOI: http://dx.doi.org/10.1515/kadm.1972.11.2.113

Alexiou, S. and W. C. Brice 1976. A Silver Pin from Platanos with an Inscription in Linear A: Her. Mus. 498. *Kadmos* 15(1): 18–27. DOI: http://dx.doi.org/10.1515/kadm.1976.15.1.18

Bass, G. F. 1986. A Bronze Age Shipwreck at Ulu Burun (Kaş): 1984 campaign. *American Journal of Archaeology* 90(3): 269–296. DOI: http://dx.doi.org/10.2307/505687

Bass, G. F., Pulak, C., Collon, D. and Weinstein, J. 1989. The Bronze Age Shipwreck at Ulu Burun: 1986 Campaign. *American Journal of Archaeology* 93(1): 1–29. DOI: http://dx.doi.org/10.2307/505396

Bendall, L. 2013. The Aegean Bronze Age Scripts. In Galanakis, Y. (ed.), *The Aegean World. A guide to the Cycladic, Minoan and Mycenaean antiquities in the Ashmolean Museum.* Oxford: Archeopress, 133–152.

Branigan, K. 1970. *The Tombs of Mesara: A Study of funerary architecture and ritual in Southern Crete, 2800–1700 B.C.* London: Gerald Duckworth.

Brown, M. P. 1994. The Role of the Wax Tablet in Medieval Literacy: A recent find from York. *The British Library Journal* 20: 1–16.

Chadwick, J. 1976. *The Mycenaean World.* Cambridge: Cambridge University Press.

Clanchy, M. T. 1979. *From Memory to Written Record: England 1066–1307.* London: Edward Arnold.

Cornell, T. 1991. The Tyranny of the Evidence: A discussion of the possible uses of literacy in Etruria and Latium in the Archaic Age. In *Literacy in the Roman World* (Journal of Roman Archaeology Supplementary Series 1). Ann Arbor: Journal of Roman Archaeology, 7–33.

Cribiore, R. 1996. *Writing, Teachers, and Students in Graeco–Roman Egypt.* Atlanta: Scholars Press.

Crielaard, J. P. 1995. Homer, History and Archaeology: Some remarks on the date of the Homeric world. In Crielaard, J. P. (ed.), *Homeric Questions: Essays in philology, ancient history and archaeology, including the papers of a conference organized by the Netherlands Institute at Athens (15 May 1993).* Amsterdam: J. C. Gieben, 201–288.

Cultraro, M. 2006. *I Micenei: Archeologia, stori, società dei Greci prima di Omero.* Rome: Carocci editore.

Fri, M. L. 2007. *The Double Axe in Minoan Crete: A functional analysis of production and use.* Unpublished PhD dissertation, Stockholm University.

Godart, L. 1999. L'écriture d'Arkhanès: Hiéroglyphique ou Linéaire A? In Betancourt, P. P., Karageorghis, V., Laffineur, R. and Niemeier, W.–D. (eds), *Meletemata: Studies in Aegean Archaeology Presented to Malcolm H. Wiener as He Enters his 65th Year.* Liège: Université de Liège, 299–302.

Godart, L. and Olivier, J.–P. 1982. *Receuil des Inscriptions en Linéaire A* (Études crètoises 21). Paris: École française d'Athènes.

Hallager, E. 1996. *The Minoan Roundel and Other Sealed Documents in the Neopalatial Linear A Administration. Volume 1* (Aegaeum 14). Liège: Université de Liège, Histoire de l'art et archéologie de la Grèce antique.

Hood, S. 1984. A Minoan Empire in the Aegean in the 16th and 15th Centuries B.C. In Hägg, R. and Marinatos, N. (eds), *The Minoan Thalssocracy, Myth and Reality: Proceedings of the Third International Symposium at the Swedish Institute in Athens, 31 May–5 June, 1982.* Stockholm: Swedish Institute in Athens, 33–37.

Hood, S. 1987. Mason's Marks in the Palaces. In Hägg, R. and Marinatos, N. (eds), *The Function of the Minoan Palaces: Proceedings of the Fourth International Symposium of the Swedish Institute in Athens, 10–16 June, 1984.* Stockholm: Swedish Institute in Athens, 205–212.

Janko, R. 1982. A Stone Object Inscribed in Linear A from Ayios Stephanos, Laconia. *Kadmos* 21: 97–100.

Karo, G. 1930–1933. *Die Schachtgräber von Mykenai.* Munich: F. Bruckmann.

Karytinos, A. 1998. Sealstones in Cemeteries: A display of social status. In Branigan, K. (ed.), *Cemetery and Society in the Aegean Bronze Age.* Sheffield: Sheffield Academic Press, 78–86.

Keates, S. 2002. The Flashing Blade: Copper, colour and luminosity in North Italian Copper Age society. In Jones, A. and MacGregor, G. (eds), *Colouring the Past: The significance of colour in archaeological research.* Oxford: Berg, 109–125.

Krzyszkowska, O. 2005. *Aegean Seals: An introduction*. London: Institute of Classical Studies.

Lalou, É. 1992. Inventaire des tablettes médiévales et présentation générale. In Lalou, É. (ed.), *Les tablettes à écrire de l'Antiquité à l'époque modern*. Turnhout: Brepols, 233–288.

MacGinnis, J. 2002. The Use of Writing Boards in the Neo-Babylonian Temple Administration at Sippar. *Irak* 64: 217–236. DOI: http://dx.doi.org/10.2307/4200524

Mallowan, M. E. L. 1954. The Excavations at Nimrud (Kalḫu), 1953. *Iraq* 16(1): 59–114. DOI: http://dx.doi.org/10.2307/4199583

Marinatos, S. 1935. Ἀνασκαφαὶ ἐν Κρήτῃ. *Praktika* 196–220.

Michailidou, A. 1992-1993. 'Ostrakon' with Linear A Script from Akrotiri (Thera): A non-bureaucratic activity? *Minos* 27–28: 7–24.

Murphy, J. 1998. Ideologies, Rites and Rituals: A view of prepalatial Tholoi. In Branigan, K. (ed.), *Cemetery and Society in the Aegean Bronze Age*. Sheffield: Sheffield University Press, 27–40.

Nikolaidou, M. 1999. Formulaic Uses of Religious Imagery in Protopalatial Crete. In Betancourt, P. P., Karageorghis, V., Laffineur, R. and Niemeier, W.-D. (eds), *Meletemata: Studies in Aegean Archaeology Presented to Malcolm H. Wiener as He Enters his 65th Year*. Liège: Université de Liège, 555–559.

Olivier, J.-P. 1986. Cretan Writing in the Second Millennium B. C. *World Archaeology* 17(3): 377–389. DOI: http://dx.doi.org/10.1080/00438243.1986.9979977

Olivier, J.-P. and Godart, L. (eds) 1996. *Corpus Hieroglyphicarum Inscriptionum Cretae*. Paris: De Boccard.

Olivier, J.-P., Godart, L. and Laffineur, R. 1981. Un épingle minoenne en or avec inscription en Linéaire A. *Bulletin de correspondance hellénique* 105: 3–25.

Palaima, T. G. 2003a. The Inscribed Bronze 'Kessel' from Shaft Grave IV and Cretan Heirlooms of the Bronze Artist Names 'Aigeus' *vel sim.* in the Mycenaean Palatial Period. In Duhoux, Y. (ed.), *Briciaka: A tribute to W. C. Brice*. Amsterdam: Adolf M. Hakkert, 187–201.

Palaima, T. 2003b. 'Archives' and 'Scribes' and Information Hierarchy in Mycenaean Greek Linear B Records. In Brosius, M. (ed.), *Ancient Archives and Archival Traditions: Concepts of record-keeping in the ancient world*. Oxford: Oxford University Press, 153–194.

Parisinou, E. 2005. Brightness Personified: Light and divine image in ancient Greece. In Stafford, E. and Herrin, J. (eds), *Personification in the Greek World: From antiquity to Byzantium*. London: Centre for Hellenic Studies, King's College London, 29–43.

Payton, R. 1991. The Ulu Burun Writing-Board Set. *Anatolian Studies* 41: 99–106. DOI: http://dx.doi.org/10.2307/3642932

Perna, M. 2007. Homer and the "Folded Wooden Tablets". In Morris, S. P. and Laffineur, R. (eds), *Epos: Reconsidering Greek epic and Aegean Bronze Age archaeology. Proceedings of the 11th International Aegean Conference / 11e Rencontre égéenne internationale Los Angeles, UCLA – The J. Paul Getty Villa, 20–23 April 2006*. Liège and Austin, TX: Université de Liège and University of Texas at Austin, 225–231.

Pini, I. 1990. The Hieroglyphic Deposit and the Temple Repositories at Knossos. In Palaima, T. G. (ed.), *Aegean Seals, Sealings and Administration: Proceedings of the NEH-Dickson Conference of the Program in Aegean Scripts and Prehistory of the Department of Classics, University of Texas at Austin, January 11–13, 1989*. Liège: Université de Liège, 33–51.

Platon, N. 1971. *Zakros: The discovery of a lost palace of ancient Crete*. New York: Charles Scribner's Sons.

Platon, N. and Pini, I. 1984. *Die Siegel der Neupalastzeit (Corpus der minoieschen und mykenischen Siegel II.3)*. Berlin: G. Mann.

Postgate, N., Wang, T. and Wilkinson, T. 1995. The Evidence for Early Writing: Utilitarian or ceremonial? *Antiquity* 69: 459–480.

Protonotariou-Deilaki, E. 1990. Burial Customs and Funerary Rites in the Prehistoric Argolid. In Hägg, R. and Nordquist, G. (eds), *Celebrations of Death and Divinity in the Bronze Age Argolid*. Stockholm: Swedish Institute in Athens, 69–83.

Rehak, P. and Younger, J. 2001. Neopalatial: Final Palatial, and Postpalatial Crete. In Cullen, T. (ed), *Aegean Prehistory: A review* (American Journal of Archaeology Supplement 1). Boston: Archaeological Institute of America, 383–465.

Sakellarakis, J. A. and Sapouna-Sakellaraki, E. 1997. *Archanes: Minoan Crete in a new light, 2 volumes*. Athens: Ammos Publications.

Sakellarakis, J. A. and Sapouna-Sakellaraki, E. 1991. Ἀρχάνες. Athens: Ekdotike Athenon.

Schoep, I. 1994. Ritual, Politics and Script on Minoan Crete. *Aegean Archaeology* 1: 7–25.

Schoep, I. 1999. The Origins of Writing and Administration on Crete. *Oxford Journal of Archaeology* 18(3): 265–276. DOI: http://dx.doi.org/10.1111/1468-0092.00083

Schoep, I. 2002. *The Administration of Neopalatial Crete: A critical assessment of the Linear A tablets and their role in the administrative process* (Minos Suplementos 17). Salamanca: Ediciones Universidad de Salamanca.

Schoep, I. 2004. The Socio-Economic Context of Seal Use and Administration at Knossos. In Cadogan, G., Hatzaki, E. and Vasilakis, A. (eds), *Knossos: Palace, City, State*. London: British School at Athens, 283–293.

Schoep, I. 2006. Looking Beyond the First Palaces: Elites and the agency of power in EM III–MM II Crete. *American Journal of Archaeology* 110(1): 37–64. DOI: http://dx.doi.org/10.3764/aja.110.1.37

Schoep, I. 2007. The Social and Political Context of Linear A Writing on Crete. In Lomas, K., Whitehouse, R. D. and Wilkins, J. B. (eds), *Literacy and the State in the Ancient Mediterranean*. London: Accordia Research Institute, 53–62.

Shear, I. M. 1998. Bellerophon Tablets from the Mycenaean World? A tale of seven bronze hinges. *Journal of Hellenic Studies* 118: 187–189. DOI: http://dx.doi.org/10.2307/632241

Shelmerdine, C. W. 2008. Background, Sources, and Methods. In Shelmerdine, C. (ed.), *The Cambridge Companion to the Aegean Bronze Age*. Cambridge: Cambridge University Press, 1–18. DOI: http://dx.doi.org/10.1017/CCOL9780521814447.001

Small, J. P. 1997. *Wax Tablets of the Mind: Cognitive studies of memory and literacy in Classical antiquity*. London and New York: Routledge. DOI: http://dx.doi.org/10.4324/9780203441602

Stoddart, S. and Whitley, J. 1988. The Social Context of Literacy in Archaic Greece and Etruria. *Antiquity* 62: 761–772.

Symington, D. 1991. Late Bronze Age Writing-Boards and Their Uses: Textual evidence from Anatolia and Syria. *Anatolian Studies* 41: 111–123. DOI: http://dx.doi.org/10.2307/3642934

Thomas, R. 1992. *Literacy and Orality in Ancient Greece*. Cambridge: Cambridge University Press. DOI: http://dx.doi.org/10.1017/CBO9780511620331

Warren, P. 1969. *Minoan Stone Vases*. Cambridge: Cambridge University Press.

Watrous, L. V. 2001. Crete from Earliest Prehistory through the Protopalatial Period. In Cullen, T. (ed.), *Aegean Prehistory: A review* (American Journal of Archaeology Supplement 1). Boston: Archaeological Institute of America, 157–223.

Weingarten, J. 1983. *The Zakro Master and his Place in Prehistory*. Göteborg: Paul Åströms förlag.

Whittaker, H. 2005. Social and Symbolic Aspects of Minoan Writing. *European Journal of Archaeology* 8(1): 29–41. DOI: http://dx.doi.org/10.1177/1461957105058207

Younger, J. C. and Rehak, P. 2008. Minoan Culture: Religion, burial customs, and administration. In Shelmerdine, C. (ed.), *The Cambridge Companion to the Aegean Bronze Age*. Cambridge: Cambridge University Press, 165–185. DOI: http://dx.doi.org/10.1017/CCOL9780521814447.008

Form Follows Function: Writing and its supports in the Aegean Bronze Age

Sarah Finlayson

University of Sheffield

Introduction: From office blocks to office stationery

The architect Louis Sullivan coined the phrase "form ever follows function" in an essay laying out the aesthetic laws for designing a new and exciting phenomenon of the late 19th century, the office block; his fundamental principle was that "the shape, form, outward expression, design…of the tall office building should in the very nature of things follow the functions of the building, and that where the function does not change, the form is not to change" (Sullivan 1896: 408). I use it here as a starting point from which to unpick the complex and changing relationships between writing and its material supports during the Aegean Bronze Age, with the basic hypothesis that the shape of objects which bear writing, the Bronze Age 'office stationery' so to speak, derives from the use to which they, object + writing, are put and the shape changes as this purpose changes.

Following an overview of the datasets included in this study, I review the use of writing supports for each of the three main Aegean scripts, Cretan Hieroglyphic (**Figure 1a–f**), Linear A (**Figure 2a–g**) and Linear B (**Figure 3a–d**), before focussing on Linear A practice to consider how the form and function of different kinds of writing-bearing object interrelate within a particular chronological period. As will become clear, a long time period is covered here, at least 500 years or so, but at points the evidence is embarrassingly meagre and inevitably there are large gaps in our understanding of how, when and where writing is being used. For all these reasons, it is appropriate to keep the following discussion rather general and tentative.

What is written, where?

Before presenting the data, I should acknowledge its arbitrary nature. I pass over the 'Archanes Script' (but see Flouda, this volume, Whittaker, this volume) and broader prepalatial seal use,

How to cite this book chapter:
Finlayson, S. 2013. Form Follows Function: Writing and its supports in the Aegean Bronze Age. In: Piquette, K. E. and Whitehouse, R. D. (eds.) *Writing as Material Practice: Substance, surface and medium.* Pp. 123-142. London: Ubiquity Press. DOI: http://dx.doi.org/10.5334/bai.g

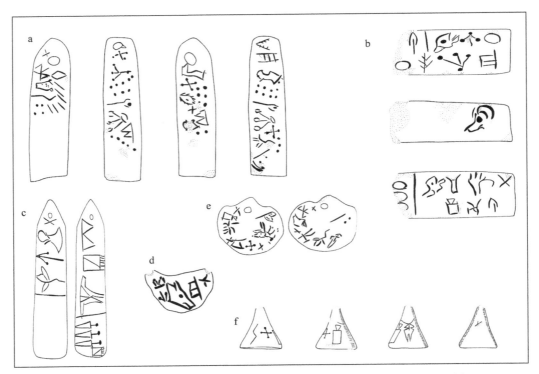

Figure 1: Key Cretan Hieroglyphic document shapes (not to scale). a) Four-sided bar, Knossos Hh (04) 03 (Olivier and Godart 1996: 111); b) Tablet, Malia Palace MA/P Hi 02: front, side and back faces shown (Olivier and Godart 1996: 174); c) Label, Malia Quartier Mu MA/M Hf (04) 01 (Olivier and Godart 1996: 140); d) Crescent, Knossos Ha (04) 01: face gamma shown, with CH inscription (Olivier and Godart 1996: 78); e) Medallion, Knossos He (04) 06 (Olivier and Godart 1996: 92); f) Cone, Malia Quartier Mu MA/M Hd (02) (Olivier and Godart 1996: 126).

which could well represent the beginnings of writing and administration on Crete (Schoep 1999*a*: 268). Making sense of seal use throughout the Bronze Age is rather tricky; at times, it could arguably be considered a form of writing, particularly those seals bearing Cretan Hieroglyphic (hereafter CH) signs, while at others, seal use is better viewed as writing's "quasi-complementary, quasi-supplementary and quasi-independent partner" (Palaima 1990: 83). While my focus is on those material supports which bear writing, it is necessary, as will become clear, to include in the discussion those sealing shapes which do not. I leave to the side more marginal, less well-understood, writing practices such as potters' and masons' marks.

The CH corpus comprises around 200 clay documents, 136 seals and 16 miscellaneous items (incised and painted pots, and an incised stone block, e.g. **Figure 1**). These are distributed widely across central and north-eastern Crete (**Figure 4** shows the key sites mentioned throughout), with seal impressions and a prism-shaped stamp seal found on Samothrace and Kythera respectively (Lebessi et al. 1995: 63; Olivier and Godart 1996: 20–21, 22; Tsipopoulou and Hallager 1996: 165). The four key deposits are: Quartier Mu, Malia (an elite residential complex); the *Dépôt Hiéroglyphique*, Palace of Malia; the Hieroglyphic Deposit, Knossos; and Petras (all palatial buildings). The clay documents comprise crescents (all terms are defined below), noduli, flat-based sealings, cones, medallions, labels, three- and four-sided bars, and tablets (Olivier and Godart 1996: 10–11; Younger 1996–1997: 396). There are also substantial numbers of direct object sealings, which show seal impressions but no incised writing (Krzyszkowska 2005: 99). One should

Figure 2: Key Linear A document shapes (not to scale). a) Different shapes and layouts of LA tablets: all deal with commodity AB 30, figs, ideogram marked with rectangle (Schoep 2002*a*: 95); b) Four-sided bar, oblong tablet and three-sided bar: inscribed face and end profile shown (Schoep 2002*a*: 17); c) Roundel: arrows indicate seal impression (Hallager 1996: 23); d) Two-hole hanging nodule (Hallager 1996: 23); e) Noduli: arrows indicate seal impression (Hallager 1996: 23); f) Flat-based nodules: arrows indicate seal impression (Hallager 1996: 23); g) Single-hole hanging nodules: arrows indicate seal impression (Hallager 1996: 23).

Figure 3: Key Linear B document shapes (not to scale). a) 'Palm-leaf tablet', Pylos Aa 98; b) Page-shaped tablet, Pylos Cn 4; c) Label, Pylos Wa 114; d) Gable-shaped hanging nodule, Pylos Wr 1328: lines indicate string holes (Pini 1997: pl. 25) (Figures 3a–c after Bennet et al. 1955: 14, 1 and 15, respectively). © 1955 Princeton University Press, 1983 renewed PUP. Reprinted by permission of Princeton University Press.

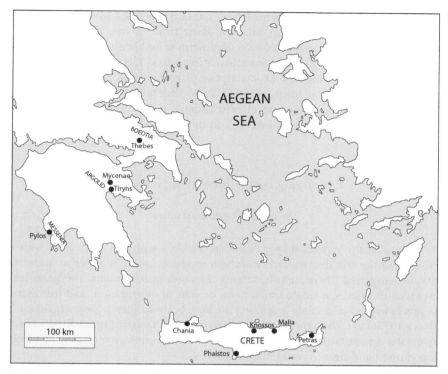

Figure 4: Map showing key sites referred to in text. Base map courtesy of John Bennet.

note that, throughout the Bronze Age, while seals come in a huge range of shapes and materials, impressions are almost always made by stamping the seal on the clay, not rolling it. CH is used in the First Palace Period, Middle Minoan II, at Quartier Mu and Petras, and into the early Second Palace Period, Middle Minoan III, at Knossos and Malia Palaces (Olivier and Godart 1996: 27–28; Schoep 2001*a*: 157–158).

There are around 1370 Linear A (LA) clay documents (Schoep 2002*a*: 38; e.g. **Figure 2**). There are some 300 tablets, together with a few three- or four-sided bars, and a single 'label' comprised of a flat, oblong piece of clay, pierced at its pointed end (Hallager 1996: 33, 37; Schoep 2002*a*: 16, 20–21). The sealings can be classified as noduli, flat-based nodules, roundels, and single-hole and two-hole hanging nodules (Hallager 1996: 35–37). Direct object sealings are restricted to the First Palace Period (Krzyszkowska 2005: 155). LA is also incised, engraved or painted on a range of other supports, including stone vessels, gold and silver pins and a ring, walls, pots and a terracotta figurine; these objects are found in religious and domestic contexts, and their distribution is mainly concentrated in central Crete (Schoep 2002*a*: 13–14). LA is used during the First Palace Period at Phaistos; this use proliferates during the Second Palace Period, Middle Minoan III to Late Minoan IB, when it is widely distributed across Crete and on Thera, Melos and Kea (Karnava 2008: 418; Schoep 2002*a*: 17–19, 21).

There are over 5000 inscribed clay documents in the Linear B (LB) corpus (e.g. **Figure 3**), the most numerous of which are tablets. The only LB sealing type which can bear an inscription is the gable-shaped hanging nodule, and there is also a very small number of clay 'labels' (Krzyszkowska 2005: 280). Sealing types without inscriptions are irregular hanging nodules, combination sealings, direct object sealings, stoppers and noduli (Krzyszkowska 2005: 280). The principal deposits are the palatial sites of Knossos and Chania on Crete, and Mycenae, Thebes, Tiryns and Pylos in mainland Greece; the Room of the Chariot Tablets, Knossos, is probably the earliest use of LB, in Late Minoan IIIA1, with the documents from Chania, Thebes and Mycenae dating from Late Minoan / Helladic IIIA2–late into IIIB1–late, and those from Tiryns, Midea and Pylos coming from Late Helladic IIIB / C (Driessen 2008: 76; Shelmerdine and Bennet 2008: 292).

There are also nearly 180 examples of Inscribed Stirrup Jars (ISJs), a type of large coarse-ware storage or transport jar on which an LB inscription is painted before firing, dated to roughly Late Minoan / Helladic IIIB (van Alfen 2008: 235, 238). They are found at several mainland sites, although ceramic analysis indicates that most originated from the Chania region in Western Crete (van Alfen 2008: 235). Finally, LB written on non-administrative objects is extremely rare (Palaima 1987a: 502).

Classifying Form / Identifying Function

The Linear B Administration

Turning now to what the various shapes of document 'do', I will start at the end, with LB, as its large database and the fact that we can read the inscriptions make it easier to understand how documents are being used. There are two variants of recording documents. The 'palm-leaf' tablets (**Figure 3a**) record, usually, a single transaction, or unit of information, and this dictates their shape; the text is written in a single line along the long horizontal axis (Bennet 2008: 17; Ventris and Chadwick 1973: 111). The large, rectangular page-shaped tablets (**Figure 3b**) are ideally suited to holding greater amounts of data, and their sophisticated linear formatting enables information to be well organised and clear to read (Palaima 1990: 97).

The labels (**Figure 3c**), some of which resemble elongated nodules but with LB inscriptions only and no seal impressions, are possibly an adaptation of the nodule form (Krzyszkowska 2005: 280). Some show the impression of wickerwork on their reverse, and this, together with analysis of their findspots, where known, and their inscriptions suggests they could be labels for boxes of tablets, with the text providing an 'abstract' for the box contents (Chadwick 1958: 4).

Of the sealed documents, the most numerous, and obscure, are the irregular hanging nodules; these are clay sealings of no fixed shape, formed around string, most often found broken along their long axis, i.e. along the line of the string (Hallager 2005: 255–256). Impressions of the string holes often show imprints of two cords, twisted together within the sealing, suggesting these nodules are actually sealing, in the sense of physically securing, the objects to which they are attached (Krzyszkowska 2005: 281). These sealings are carelessly made and fastened on their strings (indicating they are not meant to travel far), and then broken and discarded, both factors suggesting that they, and the information they carry, were intended to have a short life-span (Hallager 2005: 256–258; see also Shelmerdine's discussion following Hallager 2005). Hallager's (2005: 258) interpretation of the sealings as attached to items stored within the palaces, with the seal impression identifying the individual responsible either for the delivery or the storage, is plausible. That these sealings are deliberately broken, whereas other types are not, seems significant, and one wonders whether that is, in a sense, their purpose, and also the reason why they are kept, at least briefly, prior to discard; their breakage could indicate a change in status of the goods (move from storage into use, for example), or the end of an individual's responsibility for them.

Easier to understand are the gable-shaped hanging nodules (**Figure 3d**). These sealings are carefully shaped around a knotted string, and carry a seal impression on one face (Krzyszkowska 2005: 280). The majority are uninscribed (only 22 out of the 164 sealings from Pylos carry an inscription), but on those examples with incised text, an ideogram is usually written over the seal impression, and additional sign-groups can appear on the other faces (Palaima 2003: 174; Krzyszkowska 2005: 280). Analysis of the cache of 60 nodules from Thebes, 56 of which have inscriptions, has enabled a convincing reconstruction of their use. The gable shape of the nodules results from the way the clay is held between the fingers while impressing the seal and writing the inscription (Piteros et al. 1990: 113). This shape, together with its suspension cord, give a small, solid, virtually indestructible and very portable document (Piteros et al. 1990: 183). In this instance, form does not strictly follow function, but rather the two aspects are intertwined in a more complex way. A key part of these documents' function is their portability, and this governs their very small size, which in turn means only the most important information is recorded, namely the seal impression, the ideogram which identifies the goods, and, rarely, a small amount of additional data, such as anthroponyms, toponyms, transactional terms (Piteros et al. 1990: 177). The formula 'personal name (here represented by the seal impression) + object + toponym / second personal name' is equivalent to that recorded on the 'palm-leaf' tablets. Numerals are rare, because that information is supplied by the object itself. It is suggested that each nodule accompanies a single item, mostly livestock in the Theban examples, from the hinterland into the palatial centre, with the nodule acting as a primary document, recording the most crucial information about its object, the sex of the animal, for example, and also certifying or authenticating, by the seal impression, who is responsible for it (probably in the sense of 'owing' the item to the palace; Piteros et al. 1990: 183–184).

Analysis of scribal hands at Pylos indicates that some nodules there are written by palace tablet-writers, and while the scribes could travel out of the palace, Flouda suggests that these nodules are written and sealed within the palace (Flouda 2000: 236). Rather than enabling data to travel, as with the Theban nodules, these examples would have the dual function of labelling the goods to which they are attached, with the information supplied in the text, and acting as 'certificates', with the seal impression authenticating their receipt (Flouda 2000: 237).

It is important to note, however, that, except at Thebes, there are considerably fewer inscribed than uninscribed nodules. Sealings of this type would therefore seem to be primarily recording instruments within transactions that do not require the use of writing (Palaima 2003: 174), although this is not incompatible with their being primary documents as described above.

Combination sealings (nodules which hang from a cord and are pressed against the object sealed), direct object sealings, and stoppers (lumps of clay plugging the neck of stirrup jars, some of which have seal impressions), operate at "a slight degree higher than the merely practical action of closing", securing an object physically, but also authenticating it, and identifying a responsible party by means of the seal impression (Palaima 1987b: 257). Applying the clay directly to the object creates a close physical association between the seal impression and the artefact it references (Knappett 2008a: 150), which is not seen with the two kinds of hanging nodules.

So few noduli survive that it is difficult to understand how they functioned (Krzyszkowska 2005: 284). I discuss this form below as they are significantly more common in LA administration.

In the case of the final LB document shape, the ISJs, the function of the writing support is clear; they are jars for the transport and / or storage of olive oil, unguent or perhaps wine (van Alfen 2008: 235). The function of the inscriptions, which take the form 'personal name + toponym + personal name in the genitive', has been debated, but van Alfen's proposal that they are acting in the same way as the inscriptions on the gable-shaped hanging nodules, recording the fulfilment of an individual's obligation to supply oil to a 'collector' (a representative of the palatial administration), is convincing (van Alfen 1996–1997: 253–254; 2008: 238). The fact that no nodules dealing with raw oil are known suggests the jars themselves are being used instead (van Alfen 1996–1997: 273).

There are far fewer inscribed than uninscribed stirrup jars, and it is not clear why this should be, although the same is true of the gable-shaped nodules; one marked jar could label the entire batch, or some production could be taking place without written records (van Alfen 1996–1997: 272–273). It is clear that the inscriptions function early on in the production process, when the jars are sent from the oil producers to their superiors (van Alfen 2008: 238). However, the fact that the inscriptions are painted on before the jars are fired and filled suggests that the data to be recorded are known, or prepared, earlier. Once the jars move into the next stage, the inscriptions lose their intended primary meaning; unlike the nodules, which are discarded, the ISJs could be reused, and it is possible that the inscriptions then become decorative; hoards of 70 ISJs at Thebes and 40 at Tiryns may indicate vessels collected specifically for the prestige or novelty value of their inscriptions (van Alfen 2008: 239). While the ISJs are not meant to serve as archival documents, unlike tablets (van Alfen 2008: 235), their inscriptions objectify them, turning artefact into textual document (Knappett 2008a: 152).

Since the bulk of LB is incised with a stylus on soft clay, it is interesting to note the effect painting with a brush on a pot has on the palaeography of signs; they can be painted much larger, often giving a distorted, elongated appearance, as on jar TH Z 839, or in a freer way with additional elements included that would otherwise be hard to reproduce on the significantly smaller tablets (van Alfen 2008: 237). Nevertheless, the placement of most inscriptions on the shoulder, between the jars' handles, suggests they are intended to be viewed easily, even if the jars are tightly packed together on the floor (van Alfen 1996–1997: 255).

Pulling this together, one can propose a hierarchy of document forms that reflects the upward flow of information through the palatial administration. Using the documents at Pylos as an example (following Palaima 2003: 182–184), on the primary level are the nodules, or other 'labelling' sealings, that relate to delivery of materials, such as nodule PY Wr 1328 shown in **Figure 3d** (it has a seal impression on face a [top illustration], and the text on faces b and c [middle and bottom illustrations] reads *shafts for infantry spears*, with the quantity provided by the pieces of wood themselves); these data are transferred onto 'palm-leaf' tablets as quantities of different items, but without further information, for example, PY Va 1324 (line 1, *shafts for spears 30*, line 2, *shafts for spears 20: axle-sized pieces of wood 2*). The tablet-writers then compile this information onto page-shaped tablets, adding additional details, such as assignments of materials to personnel, as on PY An 1282 (line 1, *for chariots MEN [an ideogram] 18, for wheels MEN 18*, line 2, *for flint points MEN 13: for halters MEN 5*, line 3, *for shafts MEN 36*). At the highest administrative level, a single tablet from the Archives Complex, PY Vn 10, summarises the overall transaction on a regional scale (line 1, *thus contribute the woodcutters*, line 2, *to the wheel-assembly workshop saplings 50*, line 3, *and axle-sized pieces of wood 50*, line 4, *and so many the territorial organisation of Lousos, axle-sized pieces of wood*, line 5, *100 and so many saplings 100*). This chain of documents is probably not the only way that administration is done, and, in fact, Palaima (2000: 237) suggests certain textual features on some inventory tablets at Pylos (erasures, data grouping, layout, and arrangement) point to them being written up from information dictated to the scribe rather than being compiled from a review of nodules.

Whether there is a level of administration above the page-shaped tablets, or indeed the recording of non-administrative subjects, on perishable materials, has been much debated but not resolved. Four of the sealings from the Room of the Chariot Tablets, in Third Palace Period Knossos, have been classified as flat-based nodules, but they differ from the earlier LA versions (for which, see below). The imprints on their undersides suggest they sealed pieces of leather, folded length-wise and bound once in the middle with leather or gut (Krzyszkowska 2005: 217–218). This form then disappears from use, and there is no further direct evidence to suggest the use of other writing materials in LB administration. On the contrary, several factors, both contextual and administrative, suggest that the clay documents are the most important administrative medium; both the transferring and summarising of information between records, and the care taken to prepare and correct the tablets suggest they are the highest level of recording and not "mere impermanent records", operating within an administrative cycle of about a year (Bennet 2001: 27–28, 29; Killen 2008: 162).

It is possible that wooden writing-boards, such as the set found on the Ulu Burun wreck (Payton 1991: 99–103), are used, perhaps to accompany moving goods (Perna 2007: 229), although the evidence, seven hinges each from Pylos and Knossos, is meagre; the hinges could have come from small boxes, although this is thought less likely (Mylonas Shear 1998: 188–189). But the reusable nature of writing tablets, where writing can be repeatedly made and erased on the wax, suggests they should in fact be regarded as an impermanent record (John Bennet, pers. comm. 1 October 2009; see also Whittaker, this volume; cf. Piquette, this volume).

Steele uses the example of a land-dispute between the priestess *Eritha* and the *damos*, summarised on Pylos tablets PY Ep 297 and 704, to argue that 'bilateral' documentation (which records and provides legal evidence of a transaction between individuals or groups) does not exist for this period. The tablets do not record either party having any written or sealed documents to back up their claims, but instead they give spoken statements, "*Eritha* the priestess has and claims to have an *etoinon* for the god, but the *damos* says she has an *onaton* of *ktoinai kekemenai*" (PY Ep 704.5–6; Steele 2008: 35, 43–44). That is, it is not that we have lost the laws, contracts, sales documents and so on, assumed to have been recorded on perishable materials (Olivier 1986: 387), but that these data are never written down, instead transacted orally and maintained by memory.

Linear A Document Forms and Functions

In LA administration, the principal recording shape is again the tablet (**Figure 2a**); in the First Palace Period, both oblong and page-shaped, but by the end of the Second Palace Period, only the page-shaped version is used (Schoep 2002a: 16). Two-, three- and four-sided bars (**Figure 2b**) are also found incised with LA in the mixed CH and LA deposits at Knossos and Malia in the early Second Palace Period (Schoep 2002a: 16–17). Although the LA tablets' purpose is to record quantities of data, they are smaller than the LB versions, and their formatting and contents (principally agricultural produce, as far as we can tell) suggest they do not have exactly the same administrative role as in LB (Schoep 2002a: 189, 192). In comparison with the LB tablets, LA tablets lack standardisation, and are more difficult to read; they are frequently written on both sides, contain multiple sets of entries, and have entries running from one line to the next (Schoep 2002a: 72).

When compared with the typological restriction of LB sealings, the variety of sealed document types in LA (**Figure 2c–g**) is quite overwhelming. Schoep (2002a: 193) suggests differentiating between 'active' sealings, which play a role in the transmission of goods, and 'passive' ones, which are auxiliary documents, attached to or sealing the actual written documents and not functioning independently, and that this division reflects different administrative functions. Roundels, and perhaps noduli, are 'active', independent mini-documents, whereas single-hole nodules, flat-based nodules, and perhaps two-hole hanging nodules, are 'passive', attached to documents or goods (Schoep 2002a: 193).

Roundels (**Figure 2c**) are clay disks with one or more seal impressions around their rim, and usually with a LA inscription on one or both faces, but with no trace of having been hung from or pressed against another object (Hallager 1996: 82). The number of seal impressions on the rim probably specifies the quantity of the commodity recorded in the inscription (livestock, agricultural produce, cloth, vessels and so on), with each impression representing one unit (Hallager 1996: 100–101, 113). Analysis of impressions and inscriptions suggests that at least two people made a roundel, one wielding the seal and another, the stylus (Hallager 1996: 112). These two factors have led to the interpretation of these documents as receipts, created and held by the central administration to record goods disbursed; the seal user would be the recipient, certifying with his or her impression the quantity of goods received (Hallager 1996: 116). Significantly, the physical limitations of these documents necessarily restrict the size of transactions, with 15 units being the largest amount attested (Palaima 1990: 92).

Noduli (**Figure 2e**), disk- or dome-shaped lumps of clay with a seal impression but no perforation, imprints of objects, or other visible means of fastening ("sealings that do not seal" [Weingarten 1986: 4]) are a very long-lasting document form, found from the early First Palace through to the Late Bronze Age, but they are particularly common in Second Palace Period LA administration, with around 130 examples known (Krzyszkowska 2005: 161; Weingarten 1990*a*: 17). Only eight have LA inscriptions or countermarks over the seal impression (Hallager 1996: 127). As they are clearly not attached to anything, noduli are independent documents, and their primary purpose seems to be to carry a seal impression, that is to authenticate or certify something. By analogy with Old Babylonian practice, Weingarten (1986: 18) suggests they are originally dockets, receipts for work done, with the seal impression being made by the overseer to authorise 'payment'; as the form becomes more widespread in the Second Palace Period, they become more like tokens, to be exchanged for goods or services, or as *laissez-passer*, with the seal impression identifying the carrier as legitimate (Weingarten 1990*a*: 19–20).

Moving on to the 'passive' sealed documents, single-hole hanging nodules (**Figure 2g**) are roughly triangular clay sealings, formed around a knot at the end of a piece of string or cord (Hallager 1996: 160–161). They have a seal impression on one face, and a single incised LA sign, or very rarely another seal impression, on one of the other faces (Hallager 1996: 161). There are five sub-categories of single-hole nodule, differentiated by shape and position of seal impression or inscription (pendant, pyramid, cone, dome / gable and pear, see **Figure 2g**) with pendant being by far the most common (Hallager 1996: 162–163). About 13 signs or ligatures are found on these nodules, but it is very difficult to discern their meaning; the restricted range might suggest they are acting as arbitrary symbols, along the lines of 'A', 'B', 'C', rather than as syllabograms (Krzyszkowska 2005: 160). These nodules hang from something, although there is no evidence for what (Krzyszkowska 2005: 160). Hallager has proposed a use similar to that observed in contemporary Egypt, where nodules were hung from rolls of papyrus as identification labels, with their cord threaded through holes in the lower part of the scroll to enable it to be unrolled and read without breaking the cord or sealed nodule (Hallager 1996: 198–199).

Two-hole hanging nodules (**Figure 2d**) are also lumps of clay, usually triangular, formed around a knot in a cord, but they differ from the single-hole variety in that the cord runs horizontally through the nodule and out each end (Krzyszkowska 2005: 160), suggesting they hang horizontally with the string running left and right (Hallager 1996: 160). One surface carries a seal impression, while the other two may be empty, have other seal impressions or, on four of the 74 nodules of this type, a single sign inscription (Hallager 1996: 161, 234). As the knot or twist in the cord is to prevent the nodule from slipping, rather than to tie two pieces together, and the nodules hang freely, a function as tags or labels seems likely (Krzyszkowska 2005: 160).

Flat-based nodules (**Figure 2f**) really represent two documents; they are clay sealings, with a seal impression and, very rarely, an inscription, applied around a folded piece of parchment bound with thread (both parchment and thread survive only as impressions in the underside of the sealing, Hallager 1996: 136). Care is taken to keep the nodule firmly on the parchment by winding the thread into the clay (Krzyszkowska 2005: 156). There are two sub-types, standing, which are taller than they are broad, and recumbent, which are broader than tall, and each kind can have varying numbers of seal impressions (Hallager 1996: 136–137). The function of the flat-based nodules is clear: they very carefully secure the integrity (and secrecy?) of folded parchment, with the seal impression authenticating the whole. The function of the folded parchment is less clear; the assumption is that these are written documents, perhaps concerning subjects not recorded on clay, such as legal matters like loans, sales or contracts, or diplomatic correspondence (Schoep 2002*a*: 195). However, analysis of the impressions indicates the documents would be very small when unfolded, rarely exceeding 6 × 6 cm, so the messages would have to be brief (Krzyszkowska 2005: 156).

Most flat-based nodules are made of clay local to the site where they are found, indicating they are produced and stored locally (Hallager 1996: 158), but others travelled, between Crete and Thera, or within Crete (Krzyszkowska 2005: 158). It is not clear whether the nodules are still intact and sealing their parchment at the time of their deposition; some examples seem intact, while others are clearly fragmentary, but if the message is unopened, does it imply that it had just arrived, or awaits despatch? Or were the parchment documents sealed on site for storage (Krzyszkowska 2005: 173, n. 52)?

Direct object sealings, lumps of clay stuck onto objects like jars, wooden or wicker containers, or over the pegs that closed chests or doors, and then impressed with a seal, are very common in the First Palace Period, occurring in all the major sealing deposits, and as part of both LA and CH administrations (Krzyszkowska 2005: 99). It is unfortunately not possible to distinguish between sealings from pegs closing doors (indicating control of storerooms) and those sealing chests (control of movable property; Krzyszkowska 2005: 28), but the general function of these sealings is to identify, by the seal impression, the individual responsible for the object or its security. These sealings almost entirely cease to be used in the Second Palace Period; singletons have been found at Phaistos, Knossos, Ayia Triadha and Chania, but the peg sealings from chests and doors, which particularly characterise the earlier Phaistos deposit, seem to fall out of use (Krzyszkowska 2005: 155).

Trying to recreate the system of information processing from this array of document forms is difficult. Part of the problem is that the conjectured upper layer of parchment or papyrus summary documents (to which the single-hole hanging nodules might be attached) is lost, but we are also unable to identify the primary documents from which the tablets are drawn up. Their format and content suggest they are compiled from both a primary source and some kind of more detailed reference document, which provides the information lacking from the terse tablets, but none of the extant sealing shapes contain the right kind of data (Schoep 2002a: 194–195). It is possible tablets are compiled from documents on perishable materials, or perhaps more likely, from other tablets, but information cannot be tracked through different tablets as it can with some LB examples (Schoep 2002a: 196).

Schoep reconstructs three stages of information processing: gathering, processing and storage, and suggests several possible parallel hierarchies of document shapes working through these stages; for example, information gathered on primary tablets or noduli could be copied onto other tablets for processing, before being transferred onto perishable materials, sealed by a single-hole hanging nodule, for storage: alternatively, roundels or noduli could be the primary documents, with information processed on different roundels as an intermediate stage, before storage on 'final document' roundels or perishable materials (Schoep 2002a: 197, fig. 4.4).

It seems likely that the tablets form a more or less autonomous body of information, separate from that contained on the 'active' sealed documents and the flat-based nodules; rather than the sealings and tablets forming consecutive stages in a hierarchy of document forms, they are instead complementary or parallel, reflecting different administrative concerns, types of transactions or spheres of control (Schoep 2002a: 197).

Cretan Hieroglyphic Administration

Analysing the CH corpus is the most challenging given our inability to read the script and compounded by the very small number of documents (**Figure 1a–f**); there are, for example, only two cones (**Figure 1f**), and one should ask whether we can say anything meaningful about such a tiny sample. There is also the complication of the use of seals carrying CH signs as part of their design. These are impressed on administrative documents alongside non-hieroglyphic seals, but what they 'say' (names or titles are perhaps more plausible than economic data) and how they differ from seals with decorative or pictorial motifs is unknown (Krzyszkowska 2005: 97).

There are only four tablets written in CH (**Figure 1b**), but they, and the bars, carry more text than the other document forms, and it is possible to identify what look like headings, commodities and numerals; it seems reasonable to suggest, by analogy with the LA and LB tablets, that they are recording quantities of more complex data (Hallager 1996: 31; Younger 1996–1997: 386).

The bars (**Figure 1a**) are usually rectangular, inscribed on all four sides, and sometimes pierced with a hole at one end (Hallager 1996: 33). That the bars could be suspended suggests they might be used as labels attached to objects for transport or storage, but the information on them seems to be much like that on the tablets, and, in fact, the unpierced examples are perhaps best understood as variants of the standard tablet format (Hallager 1996: 33). Olivier (1994–1995: 268–269) offers an intriguing alternative explanation, that the bars are not attached by cords to any object, but instead hang together on some sort of horizontal rod to enable them to be sorted and stored, or taken down when additional data are inscribed on them; he envisions the bars operating like the LB 'palm-leaf' tablets, for compiling basic data.

Labels (**Figure 1c**) are yet more rectangular pieces of clay, pointed at one end and pierced for suspension, with inscriptions on one or both sides (Hallager 1996: 33). They can record single sign-groups, or string two or more together, but rarely have ideograms or numerals, although the inevitable exception records the surprisingly high number 7000 (Hallager 1996: 33; Younger 1996–1997: 387). There are few labels, making it difficult to define their function, beyond that they hang from something (Hallager 1996: 33). The lack of ideograms could suggest that the object to which the label is attached supplies this information.

Also pierced for hanging are the medallions (**Figure 1e**), which are lentoid-shaped clay disks. Most have a sign-group on one face and an ideogram, or short inscription plus numerals on the other (Hallager 1996: 33–34). The information recorded seems to be numbered quantities of something, so the medallions could be attached to objects as another sort of label; the examples from Quartier Mu do not carry numerals, so presumably this information is supplied by the objects themselves (Hallager 1996: 34). The layout of the medallions, with text on one face and ideograms + numeral on the other, seems significant, although it is hard to say of what; certainly, if they are suspended, it would be very easy to flip the medallions around on their cord to read or display one side or the other.

The crescents (**Figure 1d**) are different in that they bear a seal impression as well as incised text, although the written message, whether incised or impressed with a CH seal, seems to predominate (Hallager 1996: 34). They are three- or four-faced crescent shaped lumps of clay, formed around a knotted cord, and impressed with one or more seals on one face, and with inscriptions on the others (Krzyszkowska 2005: 101). The knot in the cord stops the clay from slipping, rather than tying two ends together, suggesting that the crescent does not actually secure anything, although it could hang from an object (Krzyszkowska 2005: 101). The inscriptions contain a wide variety of sign-groups and ideograms, among which can be identified grain, olives and wine, but no numerals. It seems reasonable to suggest, by analogy with the LB gable-shaped hanging nodules, that crescents are attached to travelling commodities as primary authenticating documents, with the objects themselves supplying the quantity information (Schoep 2001b: 91).

Direct object sealings, noduli and flat-based nodules have the same forms as their LA counterparts, so it seems reasonable to assume they have similar functions. The flat-based nodules, found in the Hieroglyphic Deposit at Knossos, show impressions of parchment on their undersides, but whether there is an upper level of recording on perishable materials, as suggested for LA, is very difficult to say; only one example of a single-hole hanging nodule with a CH inscription has been found (Younger 1996–1997: 386).

A very tentative administrative process can be reconstructed as follows. Commodities could arrive at a central place labelled with crescents, medallions, labels and bars, or be provided with labels on receipt, or information concerning the delivery might be recorded on cones (Younger 1996–1997: 385–386). Higher level data could then be compiled from these labelling documents onto bars or tablets (Younger 1996–1997: 386). Contextual information from Quartier Mu, which is the only site to provide evidence for CH documents in use, adds weight to this basic hierarchy of documents: tablets, medallions, direct object sealings, crescents and noduli were all found in magazines or storage areas, and some additional medallions came from the Workshop, suggesting that these are working documents, associated with commodities delivered, stored or disbursed to personnel (Poursat 1990: 28–29).

Focussing in on Linear A

Returning now to LA administration, it seems that a link exists between the architectural context of deposits and their composition and function (Schoep 2002b: 25). Although few documents have been found in primary contexts, it is nevertheless possible to identify three commonly occurring groupings (Schoep 1995: 57). "Full combination deposits" always contain single-hole hanging nodules, alongside tablets and other sealings; as the single-hole nodules are postulated to hang from the highest-level records, on perishable materials, these deposits may be 'archives' (Schoep 1995: 61). This seems to be supported by their location, in central buildings (including Malia Palace, Zakros House A, and the 'villa' at Ayia Triada), usually on an upper floor in residential quarters, clearly separated from storage or work areas, and by their association with valuable objects (Schoep 1995: 61, table 3, 62). 'Single type deposits' consist of direct object sealings, tablets or noduli, and most seem to be in the location in which they functioned; the direct object sealings are found in magazines suitable for bulk storage, as at Monastiraki, while tablet or noduli deposits can also occur in smaller-scale storage rooms, for example, Houses I, Chania or FG, Gournia (Schoep 1995: 62–63). "Limited combination deposits" fall somewhere in between; deposits from the 'villa' at Ayia Triada and Zakros Palace contain tablets and sealed documents, in workshop or storage areas, while other deposits contain only sealings, such as the flat-based nodules and roundels from Phaistos (Schoep 1995: 63). One of the Ayia Triada deposits, tablet HT 24 and 45 uninscribed noduli, found in an area used for storage, points towards these being active, working (and possibly linked) documents. All noduli are nearly identical and impressed with the same seal, their uniformity indicating they had been prepared on the spot for distribution, and as the tablet records 47 units of something, it is tantalising to suppose the noduli are 'receipts', prepared in advance of the tablet's expected delivery (Krzyszkowska 2005: 162; Schoep 1995: 63).

The distribution of documents within settlements has been taken to indicate three levels of administration, central, decentralised and private; significantly, roundels and single- and two-hole hanging nodules are not found in private administrative contexts, suggesting their use is a prerogative of central administration (Schoep 1996: 80). The absence of single-hole nodules could suggest that 'archives' on perishable materials are not kept in private houses (Schoep 1996: 80).

This prompts the question of how visible each document form would be? Tablets and noduli are the most widespread documents, occurring on their own, in private buildings as well as those connected with the central administration (Schoep 1996: 79), so are potentially more visible than documents kept in central building 'archives', which are stored, together with precious objects, upstairs in residential quarters (Schoep 1995: 62). However, all of these are, broadly speaking, 'elite' contexts, the central buildings as the seats of some sort of regional power, and the private dwellings marked out by their architectural elaboration and spatial organisation (Schoep 1996: 78–79). As such, it is likely that access to the documents within these buildings is in general restricted to those living or working there, and, as Michailidou suggests, "ordinary people presumably did not come into contact with the typical 'document' of a tablet" (Michailidou 2000–2001: 8).

There are two possible exceptions to this, however: the roundel and the 'active' nodulus (that is, when it is being used, prior to archiving). According to Weingarten's (1990a: 19-20) reconstruction, noduli are mobile and transferable documents, being carried by travellers as a form of identification, or to exchange for goods and services, or acting as dockets to claim 'payment' for work done. Thus, they would be visible to a wide range of people, including some, such as labourers or those offering lodgings, who are unlikely to be creators of documents themselves; significantly, they use seal impressions rather than script to convey the necessary information. While some roundels, receipts held by the central administration for goods it issues, are created by a seal-user and scribe who are both employed within the administration, others are not (Hallager 1996: 115), suggesting that the seal-user came into the central building from outside. While Hallager (1996: 120) interprets the number of seal impressions on the roundel as a device to protect the individual from fraud on the part of the administrator, an alternative interpretation is that it enables a potentially illiterate seal-user to confirm the quantity of goods received. It does seem likely, then, that 'ordinary people', in the course of interacting with the central administration or local elites, would use roundels and noduli rather than other document forms, and moreover, that these two are geared towards use by those who cannot necessarily write, or read much beyond the limited range of ideograms used. Having said that, if the seal-user is impressing a roundel to verify receipt of a certain quantity of goods, this would require some numerical literacy.

Interestingly, given our tendency to focus on administrative documents, it is also possible that some non-administrative inscribed objects might have equal, potentially greater, visibility to the general population. The Inscribed Stone Vessels (ISVs), which have an inscription carved on the top face or sides, are probably the most visible to a wide sector of society, being found amongst the offerings at open-air peak sanctuaries, as well as in domestic contexts (Schoep 1994: 11). There are far fewer ISVs than non-inscribed examples — 4% of the stone vessels in the peak sanctuary of Iouktas have inscriptions (Karetsou et al. 1985: 102) — but they are found mixed together with other votive objects, so are presumably involved in the same rituals (Schoep 1994: 19). Inscriptions occur on crudely carved, simple stone vessels as well as better-made ones, and although a few examples from Iouktas may have been made specifically to be inscribed, on most the inscription is dependent on the shape of the vessel (Schoep 1994: 19, n. 113). The two inscribed hair or dress-pins from tholos tombs at Mavro Spelio and Platanos, on the other hand, may have been shaped deliberately to provide a surface suitable for engraving (Alexiou and Brice 1976: 20; see also Flouda, this volume).

Unlike the text on the administrative documents, which are 'interrupted' by ideograms and numerals, most non-administrative inscriptions are continuous and written to be aesthetically pleasing, but their function is uncertain beyond what they contribute to the intrinsic meaning of the object, either in the context of elite conspicuous consumption, and / or ritual activity (Michailidou 2000–2001: 18; Schoep 2002a: 14, 17). This could be another example, as with the ISJs above, of adding writing to make an artefact into a textual document (Knappett 2008a: 152), in the case of the inscribed pins or ring, a text perhaps to be 'read' with the fingers as you put the object on, or, if the support is the significant component, of giving an otherwise ephemeral prayer or dedication a solid and permanent form.

The extent to which these patterns of administration map onto political organisation is uncertain. The appearance of matching impressions from a small number of metal signet rings on flat-based nodules at Thera in Late Minoan IA and various Cretan sites in Late Minoan IB has been taken as evidence that Knossos is the paramount centre at this time, issuing official documents to subordinate centres, sealed by precious-metal seals engraved with propagandistic imagery (Hallager 1996: 207–209; Krzyszkowska 2005: 189–191). Several of the assumptions underpinning this can be questioned though: that high-quality gold rings could only be made at Knossos, for example, or that the iconography is exclusively Knossian, and these documents and their sealings are perhaps better regarded as evidence for a particular sort of communication between elite groups within and beyond Crete (Krzyszkowska 2005: 189–191).

The lack of standardisation visible in LA use, with different shapes and formats of document type, suggests, rather, that local administrators are acting independently, and this could reasonably be a reflection of regional centres managing their own affairs, whilst communicating interregionally using the flat-based nodules (Schoep 1999b: 220). Political or ideological control does not always imply economic or administrative control, of course, but if a single centre is controlling most of Crete at this point, its power is insufficiently centralised to influence local administration procedures (Schoep 1999b: 220).

In reviewing the evidence for LA use in the Second Palace Period, one gets an impression of a widespread use of writing on several media, and for several purposes, with either the writing support being manipulated to add meaning to the text (as with the clay administrative documents) or the other way around (as might be the case with some of the non-administrative objects). Although examples of writing are relatively widespread in the landscape, this need not necessarily equate to widespread literacy, not least because it seems likely that writing is principally an elite activity, and furthermore, that restricted contexts of use possibly mean that ordinary, non-writing, people might well interact with only a single kind, or a small range, of documents, creating a sort of sub-category of literacy, where understanding part of a text's meaning derives largely from the form of its support and context of use.

Discussion

The two basic components of Bronze Age administration are seals and script (Hallager 1996: 31), and a distinction can be made between recording documents, whose primary function is to accommodate writing, and sealed documents, which authenticate something by their seal impression (Schoep 2002a: 9). This functional division is reflected in the document forms, most clearly seen in the CH, LA and LB tablets, and CH bars, which are recording documents, shaped to carry quantities of written data. The sealed documents are more complex: the variety of shapes suggests that the form itself identifies a role in addition to that of authenticating (Schoep 2002a: 9). Where text appears on hanging sealings, the frequent absence of numerals, and occasionally ideograms, suggests these data are derived from the items to which the sealings are attached, creating, in effect, a larger document composed of object + sealing.

Clearly, for some of the sealed document forms, the loss of whatever they were associated with means our understanding of their use cannot, without speculation, extend much beyond inferring that they hung from or were affixed to something. Generally, the taphonomy of writing in the Aegean is problematic, as we depend on it being applied to materials that are preserved archaeologically; in the case of clay documents that were not deliberately fired, this means accidental preservation in a wider burnt context (Bennet 2008: 6). There is then an inevitable risk that, in an effort to make up for the gaps in the evidence, particularly with CH and LA where we cannot read the texts, we rely too heavily on aspects like differences in form, which might be a reflection of our own 'etic' analyses rather than of different ancient practices (Bennet 2005: 269). "*Classer, c'est interpréter*" (Godart and Olivier 1979: xxiv) is a crucial principle for understanding a large and complex database at the macro scale, but runs the risk of misrepresenting, at the micro scale, differences in form that result from regional peculiarities of use, or are a function of the way different individuals form and seal or inscribe each shape, as seems likely, for example, for some of the variation amongst LA single-hole hanging nodules (Krzyszkowska 2005: 159–160). Because the LB documents are relatively well understood, the temptation is, of course, to project their usage back onto those LA and CH documents with similar forms. This is one aspect of a broader tendency to retroject our models of the social, political and economic structures of the Mycenaean palaces onto the First and Second Palace Periods, which has rightly been challenged (Cherry 1984: 33; Schoep 2006: 38).

While these points must be borne in mind, it is nevertheless reasonable to suggest that the observable changes in document forms point to alterations in the methods of data gathering, processing and storing (Palaima 1984: 305). I would pick out two as particularly significant. The first is the bundle of changes in sealing practices between the First and Second Palace periods (i.e. between CH / limited LA use, and widespread LA use): direct object sealing is abandoned, suggesting, on the one hand, that the security of storerooms and their contents is managed differently, in a less physical way (Weingarten 1990b: 107–108), and, on the other, that direct control of commodities, by means of attaching sealings to them, is replaced by more indirect methods of controlling commodity information with hanging nodules and tablets (Knappett 2001: 86, n. 26). Furthermore, writing, with one exception, no longer appears on seals themselves, but from this point on is incised or painted rather than formed by stamping (Bennet 2008: 9–10).

Secondly, the transition to LB sees a dramatic reduction in the number of different sealed documents, and an increase in the number and use of recording documents, with the development of 'palm-leaf' tablets and labels for baskets (Palaima 1984: 305). The hierarchy of document forms suggests a more systematic approach to recording fuller and more specialised kinds of information than before, while at the same time the loss of the roundel, a document form key to LA administration, could point to a distancing from those to whom the administration issues goods (Bennet 2008: 18; Palaima 1984: 305).

What drives these changes is difficult to evaluate, not least because we assume that changes in sealing systems are necessarily tied to changes in writing systems (and possibly language; Bennet 2005: 270). Palaima's suggestion that LA replaces CH because the latter script is inadequate to record increasingly complex economic activities (1990: 94) is a case in point, and this sort of utilitarian motivation underestimates the potential for writing to be used for ideological reasons. The transition from CH to LA, and from LA to LB, can arguably be seen as part of a deliberate construction of new identities, through the manipulation of knowledge resources or material culture, by elite groups, seeking to differentiate themselves from their predecessors, or exclude others from participating in political or economic life (Bennet 2008: 20; Schoep 2007: 59). Knappett's observation that, in seeking to look through artefacts to see "the people behind them", and their motivations or choices, there is a tendency for the objects themselves to be reduced to mere ciphers or emblems of human activity (Knappett 2008b: 122), is also pertinent here. He suggests that more attention be paid to the agency of artefacts, to the possibility that things can "take on a life of their own, entangling humans and pushing them along new, previously unrecognised paths" (Knappett 2008b: 122); while ascribing agency to objects is problematic (Morphy 2009: 6), Knappett is nevertheless right to stress the complexity of the relationship between artefacts and their users.

Finally, what does seem significant is a conceptual shift between CH / LA and LB administrations: the reduction of document shapes in LB suggests that writing now predominates over both the physical aspects of document forms (Schoep 1996–1997: 403), and the image, with signs superscribed over seal impressions, while in LA practice impressions are generally kept clear (Palaima 1990: 96). Furthermore, CH is "messy" (Younger and Rehak 2008: 174), and LA tablets generally poorly organised, unstandardised, and sometimes too large or small for their text (Schoep 2002a: 73), suggesting that the text and its support are considered to be separate entities, yet both contributing information to the overall message. In contrast, the LB tablets, with their neat, standardised layouts, and text which usually fits the tablet well, seem to be conceived of as a unit, with text and support integrated into a coherent and well-defined document. Form may ever follow function, but these changes bespeak a fundamentally different view on the part of those creating and consuming writing in the Bronze Age Aegean of how writing and its support ought to interact.

Acknowledgements

The editors and John Bennet provided helpful comments and corrections to a draft of this chapter. The errors remain my responsibility. I thank Dr Olivier and Professor Godart, Dr Schoep, Dr Hallager, Princeton University Press and Prof. Pini for their permissions to include images here.

References

Alexiou, S. and Brice, W. C. 1976. A Silver Pin from Platanos with an Inscription in Linear A: Her. Mus. 498. *Kadmos* 15(1): 18–27. DOI: http://dx.doi.org/10.1515/kadm.1976.15.1.18

Bennet, J. 2001. Agency and Bureaucracy: Thoughts on the nature and extent of administration in Bronze Age Pylos. In Voutsaki, S. and Killen, J. (eds), *Economy and politics in the Mycenaean Palace States: Proceedings of a conference held on 1–3 July 1999 in the Faculty of Classics, Cambridge* (Supplementary volume 27). Cambridge: Cambridge Philological Society, 25–37.

Bennet, J. 2005. Response to Erik Hallager. In D'Agata, A. L. and Moody, J. with Williams, E. (eds), *Ariadne's threads: Connections between Crete and the Greek mainland in Late Minoan III (LM IIIA2 to LM IIIC). Proceedings of the International Workshop held at Athens, Scuola Archeologica Italiana, 5–6 April 2003* (Tripodes 3). Athens: Scuola Archeologica Italiana di Atene, 267–272.

Bennet, J. 2008. Now You See It; Now You Don't! The disappearance of the Linear A script on Crete. In Baines, J., Bennet, J. and Houston, S. (eds), *The Disappearance of Writing Systems: Perspectives on literacy and communication*. London: Equinox, 1–30.

Bennett, E. L. Jr. 1955. *The Pylos Tablets. Texts of the inscriptions found 1939–1954*. Princeton: Princeton University Press.

Chadwick, J. 1958. The Mycenaean Filing System. *Bulletin of the Institute of Classical Studies* 5(1): 1–5. DOI: http://dx.doi.org/10.1111/j.2041-5370.1958.tb00606.x

Cherry, J. F. 1984. The Emergence of the State in the Prehistoric Aegean. *Proceedings of the Cambridge Philological Society* 30: 18–48. DOI: http://dx.doi.org/10.1017/S0068673500004600

Driessen, J. 2008. Chronology of the Linear B Texts. In Duhoux, Y. and Morpurgo Davies, A. (eds), *A Companion to Linear B: Mycenaean Greek texts and their world. Volume 1*. Leuven: Peeters, 69–80.

Flouda, G. S. 2000. Inscribed Pylian Nodules: Their use in the administration of the storerooms of the Pylian palace. *Studi Micenei ed Egeo-Anatolici* 42(2): 213–245.

Godart, L. and Olivier, J.-P. 1979. *Recueil des inscriptions en linéaire A. Volume 2: Nodules, scellés et rondelles édités avant 1970* (Études Crétioses 21.2). Paris: Paul Geuthner.

Hallager, E. 1996. *The Minoan Roundel and Other Sealed Documents in the Neopalatial Linear A Administration. Volume I* (Aegaeum 14). Liège: Université de Liège, Histoire de l'art et archéologie de la Grèce antique.

Hallager, E. 2005. The Uniformity in Seal Use and Sealing Practice During the LH/LM III Period. In D'Agata, A. L. and Moody, J. with Williams, E. (eds), *Ariadne's Threads: Connections between Crete and the Greek mainland in Late Minoan III (LM IIIA2 to LM IIIC). Proceedings of the International Workshop held at Athens, Scuola Archeologica Italiana, 5–6 April 2003* (Tripodes 3). Athens: Scuola Archeologica Italiana di Atene, 243–266.

Karetsou, A., Godart, L. and Olivier, J.-P. 1985. Inscriptions en Lineaire A du Sanctuaire de Sommet Minoen du Mont Iouktas. *Kadmos* 24: 89–147.

Karnava, A. 2008. Written and Stamped Records in the Late Bronze Age Cyclades: The sea journeys of an administration. In Brodie, N. J., Doole, J., Gavalas, G. and Renfrew, C. (eds), *Horizon: A colloquium on the prehistory of the Cyclades*. Cambridge: McDonald Institute for Archaeological Research, 417–426.

Killen, J. T. 2008. Mycenaean Economy. In Duhoux, Y. and Morpurgo Davies, A. (eds), *A Companion to Linear B: Mycenaean Greek texts and their world. Volume 1.* Leuven: Peeters, 159–200.

Knappett, C. 2001. Overseen or Overlooked? Ceramic production in a Mycenaean palatial system. In Voutsaki, S. and Killen, J. (eds), *Economy and Politics in the Mycenaean Palace States: Proceedings of a conference held on 1–3 July 1999 in the Faculty of Classics, Cambridge* (Supplementary volume 27). Cambridge: Cambridge Philological Society, 80–95.

Knappett, C. 2008*a*. The Neglected Networks of Material Agency: Artefacts, pictures and texts. In Knappett, C. and Malafouris, L. (eds), *Material agency: Towards a non-anthropocentric approach.* New York: Springer Science and Business Media, 139–156.

Knappett, C. 2008*b*. The Material Culture. In Shelmerdine, C. W. (ed.), *The Cambridge Companion to the Aegean Bronze Age.* Cambridge: Cambridge University Press, 121–139. DOI: http://dx.doi.org/10.1017/CCOL9780521814447.006

Krzyszkowska, O. 2005. *Aegean Seals: An introduction* (Bulletin of the Institute of Classical Studies Supplement 85). London: Institute of Classical Studies, School of Advanced Study, University of London.

Lebessi, A., Muhly, P. and Olivier, J.-P. 1995. An Inscription in the Hieroglyphic Script from the Syme Sanctuary, Crete (SY Hf 01). *Kadmos* 34(1): 63–77. DOI: http://dx.doi.org/10.1515/kadm.1995.34.1.63

Michailidou, A. 2000–2001. Indications of Literacy in Bronze Age Thera. *Minos* 35–36: 7–30.

Morphy, H. 2009. Art as a Mode of Action: Some problems with Gell's *Art and Agency. Journal of Material Culture* 14(1): 5–27. DOI: http://dx.doi.org/10.1177/1359183508100006

Mylonas Shear, I. 1998. Bellerophon Tablets from the Mycenaean world? A tale of seven bronze hinges. *Journal of Hellenic Studies* 118: 187–189. DOI: http://dx.doi.org/10.2307/632241

Olivier, J.-P. 1986. Cretan Writing in the Second Millennium B.C. *World Archaeology* 17(3): 377–389. DOI: http://dx.doi.org/10.1080/00438243.1986.9979977

Olivier, J.-P. 1994–1995. Un Simili-Raccord dans les Barres en Hiéroglyphique de Knossos. *Minos* 29–30: 257–269.

Olivier, J.-P. and Godart, L. 1996. *Corpus Hieroglyphicarum Inscriptionum Cretae* (Études Crétioses 31). Paris: École Française d'Athènes and École Française de Rome.

Palaima, T. G. 1984. Preliminary Comparative Textual Evidence for Palatial Control of Economic Activity in Minoan and Mycenaean Crete. In Hägg, R. and Marinatos, N. (eds), *The Function of the Minoan Palaces: Proceedings of the Fourth International Symposium at the Swedish Institute in Athens, 10–16 June, 1984.* Stockholm: Svenska Institutet i Athen, 301–305.

Palaima, T. G. 1987*a*. Comments on Mycenaean Literacy. In Killen, J. T., Melena, J. L. and Olivier, J.-P. (eds), *Studies in Mycenaean and Classical Greek Presented to John Chadwick* (Supplement 20–22). Salamanca: Ediciones Universidad de Salamanca, 499–510.

Palaima, T. G. 1987*b*. Mycenaean Seals and Sealings in their Economic and Administrative Contexts. In Ilievski, P. Hr. and Crepajac, L. (eds), *Tractata Mycenaea: Proceedings of the Eighth International Colloquium on Mycenaean Studies, held in Ohrid, 15–20 September 1985.* Skopje: Macedonian Academy of Sciences and Arts, 249–266.

Palaima, T. G. 1990. Origin, Development, Transition and Transformation: The purposes and techniques of administration in Minoan and Mycenaean society. In Palaima, T. G. (ed.), *Aegean Seals, Sealings and Administration: Proceedings of the NEH-Dickson Conference of the Program in Aegean Scripts and Prehistory of the Department of Classics, University of Texas at Austin, January 11–13, 1989* (Aegaeum 5). Liège: Université de Liège, Histoire de l'art et archéologie de la Grèce antique, 83–99.

Palaima, T. G. 2000. The Pylos Ta Series: From Michael Ventris to the new millennium. *Bulletin of the Institute of Classical Studies* 44: 236–237.

Palaima, T. G. 2003. 'Archives' and 'Scribes' and Information Hierarchy in Mycenaean Greek Linear B Records. In Brosius, M. (ed.), *Ancient Archives and Archival Traditions: Concepts of record-keeping in the ancient world*. Oxford: Oxford University Press, 153–194.

Payton, R. 1991. The Ulu Burun Writing-Board Set. *Anatolian Studies* 41: 99–106. DOI: http://dx.doi.org/10.2307/3642932

Perna, M. 2007. Homer and the "Folded Wooden Tablets". In Morris, S. P. and Laffineur, R. (eds), *EPOS: Reconsidering Greek epic and Aegean Bronze Age archaeology* (Aegaeum 28). Liège: Université de Liège, Histoire de l'art et archéologie de la Grèce antique, 225–229.

Pini, I. 1997. *Die Tonplomben aus dem Nestorpalast von Pylos*. Mainz: Verlag Philipp von Zabern.

Piteros, C., Olivier, J.-P. and Melena, J. L. 1990. Les Inscriptions en Linéaire B des Nodules de Thèbes (1982): La fouille, les documents, les possibilités d'interprétation. *Bulletin de Correspondance Hellénique* 114: 101–184. DOI: http://dx.doi.org/10.3406/bch.1990.1718

Poursat, J.-C. 1990. Hieroglyphic Documents and Sealings from Mallia, Quartier Mu: A functional analysis. In Palaima, T. G. (ed.), *Aegean Seals, Sealings and Administration: Proceedings of the NEH-Dickson Conference of the Program in Aegean Scripts and Prehistory of the Department of Classics, University of Texas at Austin, January 11–13, 1989* (Aegaeum 5). Liège: Université de Liège, Histoire de l'art et archéologie de la Grèce antique, 25–29.

Schoep, I. 1994. Ritual, Politics and Script on Minoan Crete. *Aegean Archaeology* 1: 7–25.

Schoep, I. 1995. Context and Chronology of Linear A Administrative Documents. *Aegean Archaeology* 2: 29–66.

Schoep, I. 1996. Towards an Interpretation of Different Levels of Administration in Late Minoan IB Crete. *Aegean Archaeology* 3: 75–85.

Schoep, I. 1996–1997. Sealed Documents and Data Processing in Minoan Administration: A review article. *Minos* 31–32: 401–415.

Schoep, I. 1999a. The Origins of Writing and Administration on Crete. *Oxford Journal of Archaeology* 18(3): 265–276. DOI: http://dx.doi.org/10.1111/1468-0092.00083

Schoep, I. 1999b. Tablets and Territories? Reconstructing Late Minoan IB political geography through undeciphered documents. *American Journal of Archaeology* 103(2): 201–221. DOI: http://dx.doi.org/10.2307/506745

Schoep, I. 2001a. Some Notes on the "Hieroglyphic" Deposit from Knossos. *Studi Micenei ed Egeo-Anatolici* 43: 143–158.

Schoep, I. 2001b. Managing the Hinterland: The rural concerns of urban administration. In Branigan, K. (ed.), *Urbanism in the Aegean Bronze Age* (Sheffield Studies in Aegean Archaeology 4). Sheffield: Sheffield Academic Press, 87–102.

Schoep, I. 2002a. *The Administration of Neopalatial Crete: A critical assessment of the Linear A tablets and their role in the administrative process* (Supplement 17). Salamanca: Ediciones Universidad de Salamanca.

Schoep, I. 2002b. The State of the Minoan Palaces or the Minoan Palace-State? In Driessen, J., Schoep, I. and Laffineur, R. (eds), *Monuments of Minos: Rethinking the Minoan palaces: Proceedings of the International Workshop "Crete of the hundred palaces?" held at the Université Catholique de Louvain, Louvain-la-Neuve, 14–15 December 2001* (Aegaeum 23). Liège: Université de Liège, Histoire de l'art et archéologie de la Grèce antique, 15–33.

Schoep, I. 2006. Looking Beyond the First Palaces: Elites and the agency of power in EM III–MM II Crete. *American Journal of Archaeology* 110(1): 37–64. DOI: http://dx.doi.org/10.3764/aja.110.1.37

Schoep, I. 2007. The Social and Political Context of Linear A Writing on Crete. In Lomas, K., Whitehouse, R. D. and Wilkins, J. B. (eds), *Literacy and the State in the Ancient Mediterranean*. London: Accordia Research Institute, 53–62.

Shelmerdine, C. W. and Bennet, J. 2008. Economy and Administration. In Shelmerdine, C. W. (ed.), *The Cambridge Companion to the Aegean Bronze Age*. Cambridge: Cambridge University Press, 289–309. DOI: http://dx.doi.org/10.1017/CCOL9780521814447.013

Steele, P. M. 2008. A Comparative Look at Mycenaean and Near Eastern Bureaucracies: 'Bilateral' documentation in the Linear B archives? *Kadmos* 47: 31–49.

Sullivan, L. 1896. The Tall Office Building Artistically Considered. *Lippincott's Monthly Magazine* 57: 403–409.

Tsipopoulou, M. and Hallager, E. 1996. A New Hieroglyphic Archive from Petras, Siteia. *Kadmos* 35: 164–167.

van Alfen, P. G. 1996–1997. The Linear B Inscribed Stirrup Jars as Links in an Administrative Chain. *Minos* 31–32: 251–274.

van Alfen, P. G. 2008. The Linear B Inscribed Vases. In Duhoux, Y. and Morpurgo Davies, A. (eds), *A Companion to Linear B: Mycenaean Greek texts and their world. Volume 1*. Leuven: Peeters, 235–242.

Ventris, M. and Chadwick, J. 1973. *Documents in Mycenaean Greek* (2nd edition). Cambridge: Cambridge University Press.

Weingarten, J. 1990a. More Unusual Minoan Clay Nodules: Addendum II. *Kadmos* 29(1): 16–23. DOI: http://dx.doi.org/10.1515/kadm.1990.29.1.16

Weingarten, J. 1986. Some Unusual Minoan Clay Nodules. *Kadmos* 25: 1–21.

Weingarten, J. 1990b. Three Upheavals in Minoan Sealing Administration: Evidence for radical change. In Palaima, T. G. (ed.), *Aegean Seals, Sealings and Administration: Proceedings of the NEH-Dickson Conference of the Program in Aegean Scripts and Prehistory of the Department of Classics, University of Texas at Austin, January 11–13, 1989* (Aegaeum 5). Liège: Université de Liège, Histoire de l'art et archéologie de la Grèce antique, 105–114.

Younger, J. G. 1996–1997. The Cretan Hieroglyphic Script: A review article. *Minos* 31–32: 379–400.

Younger, J. G. and Rehak, P. 2008. Minoan Culture: Religion, burial customs and administration. In Shelmerdine, C. W. (ed.), *The Cambridge Companion to the Aegean Bronze Age*. Cambridge: Cambridge University Press, 165–185. DOI: http://dx.doi.org/10.1017/CCOL9780521814447.008

Materiality of Minoan Writing: Modes of display and perception

Georgia Flouda

Heraklion Archaeological Museum

Introduction

Writing helps to objectify ideas and to mediate symbols by expressing and transmitting information and meaning through its visual form, which is also constituted by its materiality. Recent cross-disciplinary studies have demonstrated that considering writing not from a purely epigraphical stance but as material practice can transform research agendas by bridging archaeology, social anthropology and cognitive semiotics. A material practice approach specifically allows us to understand the following crucial questions: how the physical substance of the writing surface helps the inscribed objects transcend space and time (Zinna 2011: 635); also, how writing technologies embody our mental trajectories by shaping writing processes (Haas 1996). These technologies carry with them an embedded history of design, which tends to become more complex with each subsequent stage of development (Schmandt-Besserat 2007). Such a discourse is novel in Minoan epigraphy, which is either concerned mainly with attempts at script decipherment or is integrated into socioeconomic studies with a focus on administrative dynamics. In these narratives, the significance of visual display as well as other types of embodied perception of Minoan writing is usually overlooked. This chapter accordingly seeks to outline a framework for exploring modes of display and the perception of the two earliest Aegean scripts that were used on 2nd–millennium BC Crete. Since Cretan Hieroglyphic and Linear A are still undeciphered, their attestations will be studied as signs in the Peircean sense, "namely something which stands to somebody for something in some respect or capacity" (Peirce 1931: 2.228). Attention will be redirected from the written form of the relevant inscriptions, the signifier or representamen (Chandler 2007: 30), to the physical aspects of their material supports and to the symbolic messages projected by them. The premise underlying such a pursuit is that material,

---

How to cite this book chapter:
Flouda, G. 2013. Materiality of Minoan Writing: Modes of display and perception. In: Piquette, K. E. and Whitehouse, R. D. (eds.) *Writing as Material Practice: Substance, surface and medium.* Pp. 143-174. London: Ubiquity Press. DOI: http://dx.doi.org/10.5334/bai.h

size, shape and other functional aspects of the inscribed artefacts were also perceived by past actors as signifiers; these were employed and transmitted within various material and ideological contexts. For example, formal Egyptian hieroglyphic appearing on monuments may have implied a formal type of communication with the divine sphere, as opposed to the cursive hieratic version of the script (Wilson 2003: 22–23, 49–57).

In addressing the symbolic resources embodied by Minoan inscribed artefacts, I shall follow the notion that objects not only became invested with meaning through their association with people but also were themselves constitutive of meanings, behaviour and social relations (Dant 2005: 60–83; Gell 1998; Graves-Brown 2000; Knappett 2005). Meaning is formed from the individualised multi-sensorial experience of the objects and from discourse that includes performance, such as public display events, funerary ceremonies and periodically enacted rituals (Jones 2007: 42). Hence our examination of categories of artefact that bear Cretan Hieroglyphic and Linear A inscriptions will examine the symbolic connotations of these two scripts with particular attention directed the impact of the materiality of their supports on perception. Special emphasis will be given to emblematic artefacts, such as hieroglyphic sealstones — sphragistic devices inscribed with hieroglyphic signs. Moreover, the combination of script with images that may have constituted a visual code on these and on earlier seals will be discussed. In addition to hieroglyphic sealstones, metal, stone and clay objects carrying Linear A inscriptions of a non-administrative character will be considered. Semiotic relationships that are grounded in the material properties and the performative capacities of the objects themselves will also be explored, in order to detect aspects of artefactual meaning that may not be immediately obvious from a conventional perspective.

To this end, the following questions will be posed: how did the shape and size of the Cretan Hieroglyphic and Linear A inscription-carriers inform the creation of the relevant objects? Did the materials of the writing supports make possible different recording formats? Which physical and compositional parameters were pertinent to the experience of the inscriptions thereon by viewers, including elites, or by other segments of the population? In order to address the modes of perception of Minoan writing, the discussion will rely on integrational semiology, an approach that treats reading and writing as integrated and linked by "reciprocal presupposition" (Harris 1995: 6). From this perspective, the graphic symbols of the scripts are arranged in the "graphic space", namely the area where text is positioned and read (Harris 1995: 121), according to a visual logic that guides perception. This logic involves conventions whose structure can be understood as a "graphic rhetoric" (Drucker and McGann 2001: 96–98). In order to reconstruct the latter with regard to Minoan writing, I will treat directionality, alignment and scale of the Hieroglyphic and Linear A signs as indexes, and consider the ways in which these may have affected the experience of the inscribed artefacts by social actors, as well as the role of these objects in practices of remembrance.

Semiotic Associations and Visual Perception in Protopalatial Hieroglyphic Writing: The interface between images and text

Introducing the Writing Systems

The time of the earliest attestation of the two Cretan writing systems and the extent of literacy, during the period when these were established and used simultaneously (from the 18th until the early 17th century BC), remain open-ended questions. Through analogies with the latest of the three Aegean scripts, the deciphered Linear B, we know that both Cretan Hieroglyphic and Linear A represent logo-syllabic writing systems (Bennet 2008: 5). They are formed of logograms, i.e. signs representing a word or a 'morpheme'[1], and syllabograms, i.e. signs corresponding phonetically to syllables. The two scripts may stem from a common ancestor, which was most probably

Pottery Phase	Cultural Phase	Dates (BC)
Early Minoan (EM) I–III	Early Prepalatial	*c*.3100 / 3000–2100 / 2000
Middle Minoan (MM) IA	Late Prepalatial	2100 / 2000–1925 / 1900
Middle Minoan (MM) IB–II	Protopalatial	1925 / 1900–1750 / 1720
Middle Minoan (MM) III – Late Minoan (LM) IA–B	Neopalatial	1750 / 1720–1490 / 1470

Table 1: Chronological table.

introduced at the transition to the Protopalatial period (cf. **Table 1**), the 'Archanes script' (Godart 1999; Olivier and Godart 1996[2]: 31; Yule 1980: 209–210). The latter is documented by a few signs of pictorial character appearing exclusively on seals and arranged in isolation or in two standardised sign-groups. The possibility that these signs conveyed phonetic values is supported by their later occurrence within the Hieroglyphic and Linear A epigraphic corpus, as will be discussed in the following paragraphs.

The Cretan Hieroglyphic signary (Olivier and Godart 1996: 17) represents a fully developed stage of the writing system, as it was employed by Middle Minoan (hereafter MM) IIB, namely at the end of the Protopalatial period. The clay documents from the so-called Quartier Mu, a MM IIB residential and industrial complex of buildings at Malia (Olivier and Godart 1996: 27, #070–096), and from the MM IIB archive of the palace at Petras / Siteia (Tsipopoulou and Hallager 2010: 70–86) document the use of the script for administrative purposes in the north-central and eastern part of the island.[3] At the palace of Phaistos in the Mesara plain, Hieroglyphic was used sporadically at the end of MM IIB, alongside Linear A (Militello 2000: 235; 2002: 51–52, n. 1, n. 10). However, the earliest evidence for written administration at Knossos comes from high-profile buildings close to the first palace and includes a Linear A tablet that dates by context to the MM IIA period (Schoep 2006: 47, n. 82; Schoep 2007). Hieroglyphic appears well established in the bureaucracy of the Knossian palace's West Wing at the transition to and during the early Neopalatial period (MM IIB–IIIA; cf. Olivier and Godart 1996: 28, #001–069). At the aforementioned sites, transactions were recorded by means of various clay documents, including Hieroglyphic tablets, four-sided 'bars', 'crescents', 'medallions' and pierced labels conventionally called 'lames' (cf. Olivier and Godart 1996: *passim* on typology)[4] or Linear A tablets (Schoep 2002*a*: 16). The recording of income and expenditures was also implemented with clay sealings. These were formed by pressing the clay over knotted string attached to or hanging from goods, and then impressing it with sealstones; the sealings were often also incised with inscriptions (Tsipopoulou and Hallager 2010: 12–14, fig. 1). Furthermore, notational systems documenting specific types of transactions can be deduced from the occasional use of clay documents which were not attached to goods, namely 'noduli' (cf. MacDonald 2007: fig. 4.1, nos 8, 10; Weingarten 2007: 134–136, pl. 41) and clay 'proto-roundels' (Perna 1995: 104–122).

With regard to literacy, the readers of the Hieroglyphic inscriptions have been sought among the ranks of administrators or scribes (Karnava 2000: 236). However, recent studies emphasising power structures of a heterarchical nature, such as factions or corporate groups (Schoep 2002*c*: 117), prompt us to rethink the use of writing in the Protopalatial polities. In particular, a hieroglyphic tablet from a MM IIB context of the extra-urban regional sanctuary at Kato Syme records agricultural commodities and, consequently, supports the presence of a literate writer or, at least, reader, in the sanctuary (Karnava 2000: 225–226, 236; Lebessi et al. 1995). This, in turn, suggests the possibility of a wider use of the Hieroglyphic script outside the strict confines of the palatial centres. Moreover, the hypothesis that different social entities at Malia had access to power resources and may have been competing for power, is supported by the occurrence of stone prismatic seals in the residential part of the town (Schoep 2002*b*: 19–21). These prisms were produced locally at the Seal Cutter's Workshop of Quartier Mu (Poursat 1996: 7–22, 103–110,

149–153) and bear engraved hieroglyphic sign-groups, namely sequences of signs corresponding to 'morphemes'. These sign-groups have cross-links to the cursive ones, which were incised on various clay documents (inscribed clay 'cones', 'medallions', 'bars', pierced labels conventionally called 'lames') and on the clay sealings from the same complex (Olivier 1989a: 44). This attestation of the Hieroglyphic script on objects of two different materials forms the basis for reconstructing its use in an administrative framework.

Hieroglyphic seals were certainly being manufactured over a considerable length of time, and in different seal workshops (Poursat 1996: 103; Younger 1979: 266–267). At present, 155 examples are published (Hallager et al. 2011; Krzyszkowska 2012), dating from MM IB until MM IIB; their production seems to have ceased after the end of the Protopalatial period (Olivier and Godart 1996: 216–291; Hallager et al. 2011; Karnava 2000: 161; Krzyszkowska 2012). The development of different styles for rendering the script signs was certainly connected not only with the development of the carving techniques but also with the hardness of the materials used. For instance, by the end of MM IIB the Seal Cutter's Workshop at Malia specialised in the production of soft-stone prisms, which were engraved in the freehand technique (Anastasiadou 2011: 60–61). Therefore, in this case the material and the technique impacted the appearance of both the seal motifs and the hieroglyphic signs, which were rendered in a simplistic manner. In general, though, the way the hieroglyphic signs were reproduced on seals strengthens the notion that during the MM II period the seal engravers were aware of what the form of the script signs would be, when incised on clay (Younger 1990: 88–92). The coherence in the syntax of the seal inscriptions and the knowledge of certain scribal conventions also reinforces the case for the adoption of writing by the artisans of the Seal Cutter's Workshop (Boulotis 2008: 78; Karnava 2000: 229–231).

But who were the intended readers of the inscriptions on the MM II hieroglyphic seals? Was the form of the seals sufficient to indicate their purpose or was the existence of the inscriptions on them purely symbolic? Neither of these questions can be answered with certainty; the frequent attestation of specific hieroglyphic sign-groups both on seal faces and on administrative clay incised documents suggests that hieroglyphic seals served as administrative instruments and were not used to carry incantations or magic spells (Olivier 1990: 19). We can hypothesise that they were commissioned pieces, presumably from individuals who could also read them (Karnava 2000: 231). A particular pattern in the use of the hieroglyphic seals emerges when we examine the Knossian 'Hieroglyphic Deposit', a discard assemblage of sealed documents, whose dating remains controversial (Olivier and Godart 1996: 28; Younger 1999: 381; also Schoep 2006: 46, n. 81 arguing for a MM IIIA dating). Sets of different hieroglyphic seals had been used in conjunction in stamping and counter-stamping the relevant sealed documents found in the deposit. In this case, not only the shape of the resulting documents but also the number of the seal inscriptions stamped on them with inscribed seals may have corresponded to an established administrative hierarchy of seal owners (Weingarten 1995). Among the various seal devices used to stamp in the Knossian Hieroglyphic deposit and also at Malia, those inscribed with the standardised two-sign formulae 'trowel' – 'arrow' (Olivier and Godart 1996: signs 044–049) and 'trowel' – 'eye' (Olivier and Godart 1996: signs 044–005) were possibly institutional Hieroglyphic seals (Jasink 2009: 11; Olivier 1990: 17–18; Weingarten 1995: 303, 307). Nevertheless, the script remains undeciphered and therefore, we cannot confirm whether the seal inscriptions referred to social status or to the seal owners' office, titles, responsibilities or even professions (Boulotis 2008: 75; Weingarten 1994: 179–180).

An Alternative Interpretive Approach

An alternative is offered by following a holistic approach and studying hieroglyphic seals mainly as symbolic devices. From the perspective of Peircean semiotics a 'symbol' is based upon a habitual and, therefore, arbitrary or conventional connection between 'sign' and 'object' (Peirce 1931:

Figure 1: Examples of Cretan Hieroglyphic logograms (after Olivier and Godart 1996: 17).

369). With regard to symbols regulated by culture, this connection has to be perceived by a wider circle of people and not only by their owners. The semiotic significance of symbolic devices has to be renegotiated, each time they are transferred or inherited by the next generation. As a system of graphic notation "capable of transcribing linguistic statements" (Gelb 1952), writing also forms part of a symbolic behaviour, since textual signs call up their object by mediated habit (Robertson 2004: 18). The understanding of these signs presupposes the knowledge of the necessary code and, thus, necessitates initiation.

The hieroglyphic seal inscriptions share the same symbolic character with the standardised Hieroglyphic script, as attested on incised clay documents. Although most of the hieroglyphic signs are schematic depictions of human figures, animals or more or less recognisable objects, at a semantic level they do not identify with their visual form as pictographs do (Harris 1986: 32). In particular, some of the signs may have been logograms (**Figure 1**) representing a word or 'morpheme' and giving no indication of its phonetic value (Olivier and Godart 1996: 13, 17 table; Karnava 2000: 34). But most of the hieroglyphic signs probably functioned as syllabograms that corresponded phonetically to syllables. This applies also to the sign-groups that appear on the hieroglyphic seals, especially the ones that are attested on incised clay documents as well. Nonetheless, the linguistic function of the script signs on the hieroglyphic seals is blurred by the interspersed representational motifs that impinge upon the otherwise standardised inscriptions (Olivier and Godart 1996: 13–14, 17, 63). These motifs are sometimes decorative (e.g. spirals), but mainly pictorial in character (e.g. cat, wild boar, ibex, snake, U-sistrum, etc.). Depending on their size, they are either used as fillers of inscriptions (**Figure 2a–b**; also cf. CMS VI, 93, first sign on the left) or as solitary motifs on seal faces (e.g. Olivier and Godart 1996: #256.α–β, 257.α, 304.β, 309.α, 310.γ / CMS VI, 26.α.β; for photographs see Krzyszkowska 2005: 94, 97, nos 161a–c). So far, there is hardly any consensus on whether these motifs had a 'decorative' function or were perceived as script signs, even though in some cases they also belong to the script signary (Karnava 2000; Krzyszkowska 2005: 95–98; Olivier 2000; Poursat 2000). Although several of the solitary seal motifs could allegedly also convey linguistic meaning as ideograms (Jasink 2009: 11, n. 53), at least when combined with each other (Anastasiadou 2011: 67, n. 365), the issue has to be further explored.

Let us now examine how the Minoan seals were gradually established as emblems, namely badges used to represent individuals or social groups, by examining their iconography and their material features. From a social perspective, the principles underlying the use of Prepalatial seals as sphragistic instruments for laying claims to resources are still an issue under discussion (Relaki 2009). These seals most probably functioned as means of personal and collective identification, as inferred from their final use, namely funerary deposition in communal graves which were used

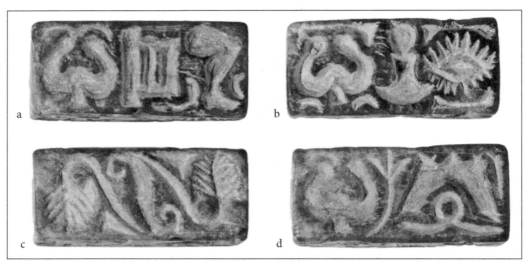

Figure 2: Four-sided steatite prism (Olivier and Godart 1996: #288), HM S-K2184 from Malia with horizontally aligned signs. a) side α; b) side β; c) side γ with seal motifs; d) side δ. Length: 1.54 cm.

for many generations (Relaki 2009: 369; Sbonias 1999: 27). In a few cases where the devices were kept with their owners even in the process of secondary burial, for example at the cemetery of Phourni near Archanes (Karytinos 1998: 85), they must have represented their owners or users by mediated habit. In terms of their iconography, the evolution of seals from the Prepalatial to the early Protopalatial period (Sbonias 1995: 74–121; Yule 1980: 229–230) suggests a gradual rise in symbolic awareness. The use of abstract linear or geometric motifs on the Early Minoan II–III soft stone and bone seals (**Figure 3a–c**), such as intersecting lines, cross-hatching, hatched triangles, lattice, meanders, etc., gave way to the production of ornamental compositions and the first iconic representations as exemplified by the EM III–MM IA hippopotamus ivory seal groups (**Figure 4a–e**; cf. Krzyszkowska 2005: 60–68). The larger circular seal faces and the fine-grained material of the hippopotamus ivory bifacial cylinders and conoids encouraged innovative syntheses of schematic floral, animal or human motifs and geometric ornaments, which covered the whole field (Krzyszkowska 2005: 63, 66). The 'Parading Lions / Spiral Group' of seals (**Figure 4b–d**; Krzyszkowska 2005: 66, nos 111a, 111c) especially demonstrates how lions, scorpions, goats and spiders were arranged in a rotating syntax with no privileged direction. These pictorial syntheses recall the preliterate Mesopotamian seal motifs (Schmandt-Besserat 2007: 30–33), which likewise appear before the development of writing in their own area, and they testify to the adoption of a new symbolic Cretan repertoire during the late Prepalatial period. Moreover, the study of the burial assemblages from which they originate supports the hypothesis that they may have signified emergent social groups (Sbonias 1995; 1999).

The First Definite Writing?

The transition to the Protopalatial period (MM IA–MM IB) signals the beginnings of the direct association of script entities with images on seal devices, a phenomenon that was to continue with the later hieroglyphic seals. By contrast with the aforementioned pictorial syntheses and a group of steatite, bone and 'white paste' seals decorated with spirals, floral and animal motifs (Krzyszkowska 2005: 68–69), the earliest seals of the 'Archanes Script Group' bear engraved script

Figure 3: Early Minoan II bone seals from the Ayia Triada tholos A with linear motifs. a) Height: 2.0 cm. CMS II.1, no. 17 / HM S-K444; b) Height: 1.8 cm. CMS II.1, no. 18 / HM S-K445; c) Height: 1.8 cm. CMS II.1, no. 24 / HM S-K452.

signs in isolation or in sign-groups (Sbonias 1995: 108–111, 166, table 3). Seals CMS II.1, no. 394, CMS II.1, no. 393 and CMS II.1, no. 391 (Olivier and Godart 1996: #202, #252, and #315, respectively) were recovered from secondary burial deposits in rooms I and II of Burial Building 6 at the Archanes / Phourni cemetery (**Figure 5b–d**). Although on the basis of associated pottery they have been dated to MM IA (Sakellarakis and Sapouna-Sakellaraki 1997: 326–330, 674, 680–681), their attribution to late MM IA–MM IB has been persuasively argued (Sbonias 1995: 108; Watrous 1994: 727, n. 241; Weingarten 2007: 137). Interestingly, the devices bear the earliest attested Minoan formulaic inscription, known as the 'Archanes formula'. This consists of two standardised sign-groups (Olivier and Godart 1996: signs 042–019 and 019–095–052), which also occur later on other 'Archanes Script Group' seals, on the hieroglyphic seals, as well as on Neopalatial stone libation tables carrying the Linear A 'libation formula' (Godart 1999: 299–302). Although the 'Archanes formula' signs have been called 'pictographic' (Brice 1997: 94; Grumach and Sakellarakis 1966: 113), we should recall that pictographs are signs bearing a pictorial resemblance to their referent. The 'Archanes formula' signs are rather "a graphic depiction of certain objects, people, or events that have significance within a particular culture" (Nuessel 2006: 592) and, thus, are not considered as true writing. However, due to their occurrence in the two later writing systems it seems likely that the standardised sign-groups of the 'Archanes formula' semantically conveyed phonetic values and thus should be considered candidates for 'true writing' (Schoep 2010: 71).

Furthermore, the signs 'sistrum', 'leg', 'hand', 'double-sickle'; and 'ship', which during the MM II period form part of hieroglyphic sign-groups, emerged for the first time isolated on the following bone multi-faced seals of the 'Archanes Script Group' (**Figure 6**): CMS II.1, no. 287 from Platanos tholos B, CMS II.1, nos. 391 and 392 from Archanes and CMS II.1, no. 126 from tholos K at Kalathiana (**Figure 7**). Among these, the Archanes seal CMS II.1, no. 391 (Olivier and Godart 1996: #315; **Figure 8**) demonstrates how its shape was chosen so as to provide the space for the display of signs with a probably different semantic function. A bone squared bar with a pierced cylindrical stalk is intersected at three points, thus, providing three cubes on which 14 seal faces with oval borders have been engraved. In a way which foreshadows the later hieroglyphic seals,

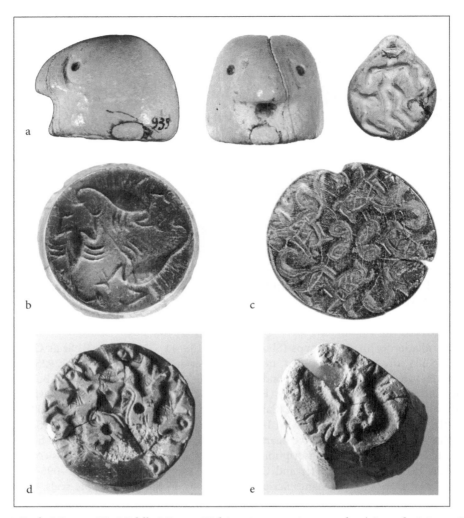

Figure 4: Early Minoan III–Middle Minoan IA hippopotamus ivory seals. a) Length: 2.3 cm. CMS II.1, no. 469 / HM S-K939 from Sphoungaras; b) Length: 3.5 cm; Width 3.5 cm; Thickness 3.2 cm. CMS II.1, no. 248 / HM S-K1039 from Platanos tholos A; c) Length: 1.97 cm; Width 1.9 cm; Thickness 2.97 cm. CMS II.1, no. 3 / HM S-K680 from Drakones tholos tomb D; d) Length: 3.33 cm; Width 3.32 cm; Thickness 2.97 cm. CMS II.1, no. 312a / HM S-K1104 from Platanos tholos B; e) Length 2.5 cm: Width 2.18 cm. CMS II.1, no. 442b / HM S-K1578 from the Trapeza cave.

the solitary signs 'sistrum', 'leg', 'hand' and 'double-sickle' are juxtaposed with the usual seal motifs of the period (floral motifs, humans and animals accompanied by C- or S-spirals) as well as with the two 'Archanes formula' sign-groups. The latter and possibly another, now elusive, sign-group notably occupy the same side of the seal (cf. CMS II.1, no. 391, faces G–I; Olivier and Godart 1996: 291). Thus, by impressing just this side on clay, one would get a seal impression of the formula. This hierarchical arrangement of the signs indicates how this new multi-faced seal type may have been handled and used in a tactile sense, integrating legibility and embodied performance.

Another instance, where the two sign-groups of the 'Archanes formula' are combined with pictorial motifs on the other seal faces is shown by the bone cube S35 / HM S-K2850, which was deposited in a late Prepalatial ossuary of the Moni Odigitria cemetery (Olivier and Godart 1996:

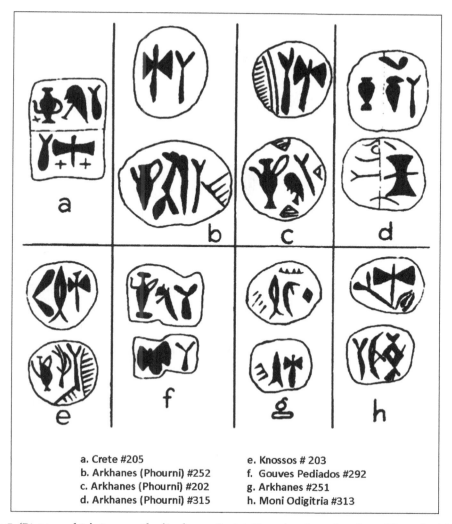

a. Crete #205

b. Arkhanes (Phourni) #252

c. Arkhanes (Phourni) #202

d. Arkhanes (Phourni) #315

e. Knossos # 203

f. Gouves Pediados #292

g. Arkhanes #251

h. Moni Odigitria #313

Figure 5: 'Pictographic' signs on the 'Archanes Script Group' seals and on later Hieroglyphic seals (after Sbonias 1995: table 3).

#313; Sbonias 2010: 204–205, 219–219). Two of its seal faces bear a schematic quadruped along with space-filling ornaments and what may possibly depict a standing human figure accompanied by a hieroglyphic sign. This 'Archanes formula' seal from central-south Crete may allude to social interaction with north-central Crete and specifically the Archanes area, although it is hard to follow the suggestion that the seal reached the south through exchange (Sbonias 2010: 204–205, 219). In any case, the institutional importance of the early 'Archanes formula' seals can only be inferred by analogy to the sphragistic use of later seals with the same content, as will be outlined below. The final deposition of the early inscribed seals in bone ossuaries makes it impossible to deduce whether they had initially functioned as personal attributes or as emblems of a corporate group. Yet still, the occurrence of the formula on three seal devices from Burial Building 6 could point to the special rights of a particular social group or institution (Sbonias 1999: 46).

Whether the solitary pictorial signs on the aforementioned seals from Archanes (**Figure 8**) and Kalathiana (**Figure** 7) were equivalent of writing when read in sequence, as suggested

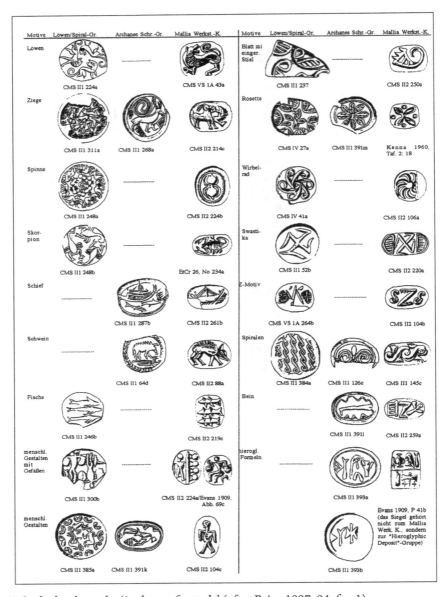

Figure 6: Seals that bear the 'Archanes formula' (after Brice 1997: 94, fig. 1).

(Sakellarakis and Sapouna-Sakellaraki 1997: 328, fig. 284; Sbonias 1995: 111), remains an open question. Arguably, they are not characterised by auto-indexicality (Coulmas 2003: 21), since they do not incorporate any information about the procedure of their own interpretation. Since they appear on symbolic devices which were used as markers of identity or status, it can be tentatively suggested that they were semasiographic codes without any phonetic value, but functioning as mnemonic aids; when impressed on early clay sealed documents, they would make a particular statement of ownership or responsibility.[5] These codes probably stemmed from the emblematic use of Minoan seal devices at least since the late Prepalatial period. I would like to suggest that the combination of signs with a pictorial character and pure script signs on the 'Archanes Script Group' of seals possibly reflects a successful emulation of the imported Egyptian scarabs. The

Figure 7: Seal, CMS II.1, no. 126 / HM S-K817 from Kalathiana tholos K. Length: 1.9 cm; Width 1.9 cm; Thickness 1.9 cm.

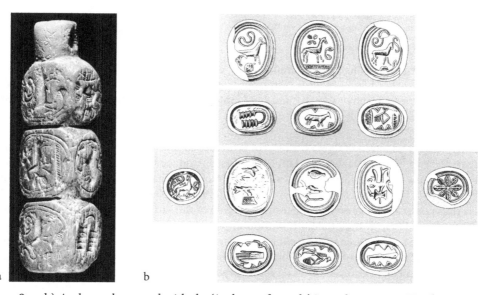

a   b

Figure 8: a–b) Archanes bone seal with the 'Archanes formula'. Length: 5.67 cm; Height: 1.28 cm. CMS II.1, no. 391 / HM S-K2260 (drawing after Sakellarakis and Sapouna-Sakellaraki 1997: fig. 284).

latter were deposited in MM IA Cretan tholos tombs and often incorporate C- or S-spirals and floral elements with Egyptian hieroglyphic signs (Aruz 2000: 2–3; Phillips 2010: 309, 313, fig. 3; see also Sparks, this volume). It may be relevant that the earliest imported scarab so far (CMS II.1, no. 395 / HM Y464), which probably dates to early MM IA, also comes from Burial Building 6, where the three 'Archanes formula' seals were found (Phillips 2008a: 123; Phillips 2008b: #50, 33,

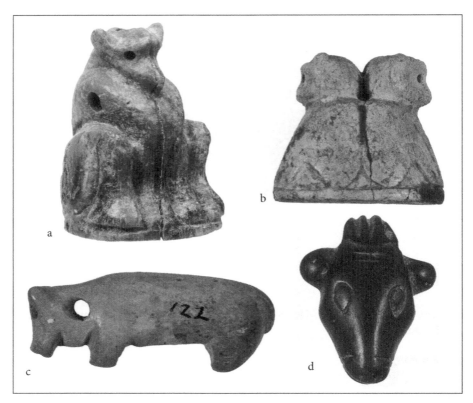

Figure 9: a) 'Egyptianising' stone amulet from Knossos. Height: c.1.5 cm. HM S-K631; b) Zoomorphic seal of hippopotamus tusk from Platanos tholos tomb A. Length: 2.5 cm; Width: 2.2 cm; Thickness: 3.5 cm. CMS II.1, no. 249 / HM S-K1040; c) Prepalatial bone amulet. Length: 3.0 cm. HM O-E122; d) Prepalatial stone amulet. Length: 2.0 cm. S-K1252.

302). An early interaction of Crete with Egypt is further supported by the 'Egyptianising' amulets and stamp seals (**Figure 9a–b**). The latter were first introduced into Crete in the EM III period and are carved with Egyptian imagery, such as the crouching baboon, a zoomorphic form of the god of writing (Thoth) and the lion (Aruz 2000: 3–4; Phillips 2008b: 227, 196; Phillips 2010: 314).

It is thus possible to suggest that the transformation of the early Minoan seal repertoire towards iconicity coincides with the gradual evolution of Minoan writing. Although the initial stages of the development of the 'Archanes formula' are elusive, it is tempting to see the appearance of the formula on seals with an emblematic function as meaningful. So, it may be possible that the formula's constituent signs evolved out of a gradual transformation from a representational to a symbolic function, as exemplified by the 'Parading Lions / Spiral Group' and 'Archanes Script Group' seals. The contention that emblematic devices, such as seals, may have been one of the sources of inspiration for symbolic visual imagery is reinforced by cross-cultural analogies relating to the earliest stages of other Near Eastern scripts.[6] Early iconic emblems drawn from the natural and ideal world and charged with a symbolic content are seen as connected with script invention in Predynastic Egypt, as shown by the finds from tomb j in cemetery U at Abydos (Baines 2004: 157–161, 164; Dreyer et al. 1998; Kahl 1994: 53–56, fig. 3; see also Piquette, this volume). A stronger analogy can be found between the 'Archanes formula' and the development of proto-cuneiform in Mesopotamia during the 4th millennium, a script which emerged from a long tradition of pictorial and symbolic representation found, in particular, in glyptic art (Cooper 2004: 77). In a similar vein, it has been recently suggested (Dahl 2009) that the marks of Proto-Elamite writing also support the relationship of this early script with seals.

On the other hand, the close connection of the Hieroglyphic script with material objects is supported by the fact that some of the MM II Hieroglyphic signs may recall earlier three-dimensional artefacts, such as amulets and specific types of seals. Minoan zoomorphic and anthropomorphic stamp seals were produced for the first time in the Prepalatial period. As suggested by a persistent conservatism in their shape (Sbonias 1995: 44–45), these seals probably had the same function as contemporary bone and stone amulets (**Figure 9c–d**) in the shape of whole animals, animal feet and everyday objects (Branigan 1970: 94–97, fig. 22). The shapes of two other Hieroglyphic signs are possibly derived from three-dimensional objects which had a symbolic meaning, namely the double axe and the Egyptian sistrum.[7] Both were initially employed on the 'Archanes Script Group' seals. Nevertheless, any possible link between these objects and the initial meaning of the relevant hieroglyphic signs at the stage of the invention of the latter is likely to have waned by the MM II period.

In the Protopalatial period, the two sign-groups of the 'Archanes formula' could be engraved either separately on different seal faces or together (**Figure 5**: examples **a, e–h**). This arrangement is also attested by the relevant seal impressions on clay sealed documents. For example, only the first sign-group of the formula 'axe' and 'fish' (Olivier and Godart 1996: signs 042–019) occurs on the clay documents CMS II.8, no. 56 (Olivier and Godart 1996: #134 and #135–137). Thus, using one or both parts of the 'Archanes formula' required pre-planning by the seal engraver, since it depended not only on choosing the appropriate seal shape, but sometimes also on the decision to place the two sign-groups on the same seal face or not. For instance, one of the two faces of the stamp seal CMS VII, no. 35 (Olivier and Godart 1996: #205; **Figure 10a**) shows both parts of the formula arranged together in two panels, while the other face depicts an ibex (Kenna 1967: 64). The arrangement of the full formula on a single prism face made it much easier to produce seal impressions on small clay documents, as shown by the partly preserved Knossian sealing CMS II.8, no. 40 (Olivier and Godart 1996: #179; **Figure 10b**). However, the three-sided steatite gable-shaped seal CMS VI, no. 14 shows that the formula could also be combined with a third sign-group. Interestingly, only the side with the second sign-group of the formula bears traces of intensive use (Olivier and Godart 1996: 253, #251). The same seems to hold true for the earlier bone 'Archanes formula' seal CMS II.1, no. 394, but not for CMS II.1, no. 393 (cf. Sakellarakis and Sapouna-Sakellaraki 1997: fig. 291).

Alignment and Directionality

The question of how MM II Hieroglyphic writing was perceived by the readers mainly relates to the parameters of alignment and directionality. Alignment refers to the relative position of the graphs with respect to each other, whereas directionality concerns the direction in which they were read. In the standardised incised Hieroglyphic documents, the signs are generally aligned horizontally and directed from right to left (CHIC: 62–63). The scribes usually prefixed an 'initial cross' or 'x' to the beginning of words and phrases, to let the reader know the direction in which these were to be read. The occasional absence of this 'initial cross' implies that the active script users were usually well trained and acquainted with the script (Karnava 2000: 230). By the late Protopalatial period, the same patterns of alignment were reinforced for the signs engraved on seals with the introduction of the 'frieze syntax' (Yule 1980: 65–68). The new popular shape of elongated prisms with three or four faces (**Figure 2a–d**) allowed the carving of motifs and signs in a clear horizontal alignment, so that the inscriptions were more easily read when impressed on clay. An added benefit was that this alignment corresponded to the organisation of the incised clay documents with the exception of the 'medallions', which due to their shape encouraged a circular arrangement of the inscriptions (MNAMON 2009–2012). More significantly, the material of the

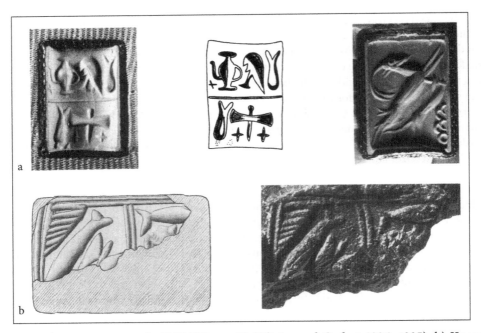

Figure 10: a) Agate stamp seal. CMS VII, no. 35 (Olivier and Godart 1996: #205); b) Knossian sealing. Length: 1.4 cm; Width 0.7 cm. CMS II.8, no. 29 / HM S-T372.

prisms, soft or hard stone, probably reflected different bureaucratic levels of responsibility, as stone type seems interrelated with the number of inscriptions. Soft stone prisms usually bore one face with an inscription, whereas the hard stone prisms — whether three- or four-sided — had most or all of their seal faces inscribed (Anastasiadou 2011: 66–67; Poursat 2000: 187–191). The fact that hard stones produced sharper clay impressions may explain this choice. At an iconographic level, the seal motifs used on prisms generally comprise human figures, goats, bucrania, schematically rendered quadrupeds, vases, ships, etc. An emphasis on depictions of human activities such as pot making, grape stamping, fishing and archery can be discerned. One possible interpretation of this development is the formation of new corporate groups within late Protopalatial society, which aimed to project their group identity in this manner.

Other Protopalatial seal devices of an elongated shape (e.g. amygdaloid or hemicylinder ones and seals with foliate backs) also produced a horizontal alignment (Karnava 2000: 165–173, table 32). An alternative to the horizontal layout of the inscription, such as division into four panels with groups of signs, is exemplified by the flattened cylinder CMS III.1, no. 149 (Olivier and Godart 1996: #206; **Figure 11a–b**). This variability in composition may indicate that seal engravers enjoyed a certain degree of freedom in how they chose to organise the seal imagery. Interestingly, the veined material of the cylinder reduces the legibility of the inscription, while readability from its clay impression would have been easier.

At this juncture, let us consider how the lack of alignment and directionality that characterises some Protopalatial Hieroglyphic seals with round or ellipsoidal faces (**Figure 12a–b**) can be explained. These shapes may have denoted a different sphere or level of administrative responsibility, although this cannot be demonstrated with certainty (Karnava 2000: 166–167). But even the signs that seem to move on these seal surfaces were probably meant to be read, as suggested by the 'initial cross' that appears on many of them (**Figure 13**). It can be posited that these signs employed two-dimensional space in an alternative way, like graphics often do (Hill-Boone 2004: 317–318). We can also draw a comparison with the lack of a horizontal alignment in many Greek

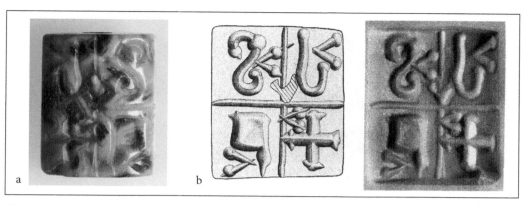

Figure 11: a) Flattened cylinder of agate, CMS III.1, no. 149 (Olivier and Godart 1996: #206); b) Drawing and cast.

inscriptions of the Archaic period. For example, all available flat surfaces of a bronze aryballos from Menelaion were exploited by an incised boustrophedon inscription, whose alternate lines run in opposite directions (Catling and Cavanagh 1976: 145–153, figs 1–2).

With regard to the content of the inscribed prisms, it has been argued that the number of the inscribed faces was related to the status of their owners and to the sign-groups they were allowed to use administratively (Poursat 2000: 189). In this case, the shape of the prism could have functioned as a signifier of the administrative authority of the social agents, as it provided the surface for engraving meaningful recurring sign-groups and their combinations (formulas). By examining the Hieroglyphic seals material, Karnava (2000: 200–201) has established that a standardised formula normally contained one to three of the common sign-groups, and one uncommon, probably intended to make each seal unique, perhaps personalising it. Nevertheless, the two most frequent sign-groups 044–049 and 044–005, which possibly stood for administrative entities, as discussed above, could have an autonomous meaning, since the first is more often associated with three-sided prisms bearing just one inscribed seal face (Karnava 2000: 200 ; Olivier 1990: 17).

However, it is difficult to assess how sign alignment and directionality influenced the understanding of the engraved inscriptions on the three- or four-sided prisms and of their negative impressions on clay. The alignment of the individual signs is characterised by a marked fluidity, making it difficult to define their 'standard' position (Olivier 1990: 15, n. 16). Additionally, there is no consistent orientation in which the sign-groups are engraved on the various faces of the same seal. Younger (1990: 88–92) has tentatively supported the hypothesis that the meaning of the inscriptions may rely on two or three impressed faces being read together. For this reason, the literate seal engravers possibly oriented the inscribed faces, either to form complementary meanings, or to facilitate separate impressions and readings. For example, on CMS XII, no. 112 (Olivier and Godart 1996: #287) the side with a horizontal layout is the one bearing the main hieroglyphic inscription. The other two inscriptions (044–049, 044–005) were arranged at right angles to the horizontal one, so that the seal user had to turn the seal 90° degrees in order to impress them on a clay sealing. However, this layout does not seem to support the view (Karnava 2000: 231) that the persons who used the seals as an impressing medium were illiterate.

Moreover, the seal engravers seem to have deliberately organised the figurally decorated and the inscribed seal faces to contrast with each other (Younger 1990: 92). As discussed above, the question of whether the 'decorative motifs' engraved on separate seal faces were really meant to be understood as script signs or as simple pictorial motifs, has not been satisfactorily answered yet. It has been suggested that this could be considered as a case of indirect representation, whereby the

Figure 12: Steatite petschaft seal, CMS III.1, no. 103 (Olivier and Godart 1996: #180). a) Seal face; b) Profile.

Figure 13: Quartier Mu steatite signet (Olivier and Godart 1996: #197). Length: 1.35 cm; Width 0.8 cm. HM S-K2390.

signs had not yet been transformed from 'icons' to symbols with phonetic value (Knappett 2008: 149–150). However, the different levels of arrangement of the so-called 'decorative motifs' and of their relationship with the script signs do not follow a linear chronological development (Karnava 2000: 174–189). So, when the script signs are transformed through the incorporation of decorative elements or, when they seem overtaken by the size of space-filling motifs, such as full-length human or animal figures or bucrania, they most possibly reveal the seal engraver's choice. Overall, however, due to the lack of conclusive contextual evidence which permits dating, it is difficult to detect any iconographic code that may have distinguished similar Hieroglyphic seals from each other and, by extension, their owners, as has been suggested (Weingarten 1995: 307).

Figure 14: Linear A clay tablet. Height: 1.8 cm. HT 7 / HM P-N10.

Linear A: The social and cultural construction of Neopalatial literacy

Administrative Uses

By the end of the MM III period, Linear A was the script used in most of the Cretan sites. The presence of many private Linear A clay archives and the circulation of inscribed documents outside Crete during the LM I period (Bennet 2008: 12) point to a widely distributed literacy, at least with regard to the ability to read. Persons actively involved in economic activities and merchants or traders would arguably have been literate or at least able to use logograms and numerical signs for basic notation (Boulotis 2008: 78). This hypothesis is corroborated by the fact that the standardised rules governing Linear A inscriptions on clay documents are practiced across different regions of the Aegean. The signs are always aligned horizontally and follow a left to right directionality (dextroverse inscriptions; **Figure 14**). But these rules, attested on clay objects, are not followed strictly on other materials, as discussed below.

Non-Administrative Uses

Linear A was also employed for purposes other than administration. Apart from some occasional painted inscriptions on pottery, carved or incised examples are found on a variety of durable material supports. These comprise architectural stone blocks, wall plaster, pottery, stone ritual and votive vessels, metal vessels, jewellery and a steatite seal from Knossos (CMS II.3, no. 23 / HM SK843). None of the inscriptions on these materials qualify as political statements (Schoep 2002b: 30), not even the two examples originally carved onto stone blocks, which were subsequently incorporated in a wall at the palace of Malia (Pelon 1980: 224, no. 301) and in the Kephala tholos grave near Knossos (Ze 16; cf. Godart and Olivier 1982: 138; Hood 1997: 116, pl. 1). Although

 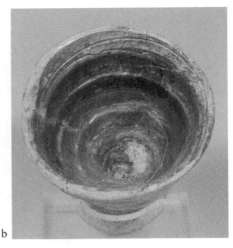

Figures 15: a) Ceramic conical cup. Diameter of rim: 8.4 cm. KN Zc 6 / HM P2630; b) Ceramic conical cup. Diameter of rim: 9.2 cm. KN Zc 7 / HM P2629.

the script remains undeciphered, it would not be unreasonable to assume that these architectural inscriptions were used to perpetuate the historical memory.

The compositional interaction of writing with image that had been characteristic of the Cretan Hieroglyphic script seems to have diminished in the Neopalatial period. Narrative scenes set in architectural contexts were never combined with writing (Cameron 1968: 59 presents a doubtful example). Moreover, no decorative pictorial elements were ever integrated into Linear A inscriptions. Following the evolutionary scheme of Arthur Evans (Evans 1909: 8–18, 134–148), researchers tried to explain the linear morphology of the signs themselves by suggesting that Linear A was a simplified script that evolved from the Hieroglyphic, but this argument is open to dispute (Bennet 2008: 5). Signs carved with chisels or even finer-tipped implements on steatite and serpentine objects and on small metal artefacts are distinguished by a more elaborate, 'archaic' character. A possible explanation for this may be the notion that their writers followed an 'inscriptional tradition' with close familiarity with the scripts (Schoep 2002*a*). But how was Linear A writing on artefacts that were produced outside the administrative sphere perceived? With regard to inscriptions rendered in materials other than clay, the type and size of the inscribed artefacts as well as the arrangement of the inscription thereon have to be considered in relation to the specific features of the artefactual context (Knappett 2004: 46). Differences in signs resulting from the inscribing techniques employed, as well as restrictions imposed by the materials used or by the shape of the inscription-carriers, are also considered below.

Alignment and Directionality

Linear A inscriptions on non-administrative objects are accentuated by variable alignment and directionality. The performative capacities of the materials and the shape of the artefacts seem to have been factors which influenced the use of the graphic space. The two clay handleless cups KN Zc 6–7 from a house basement at Knossos (**Figure 15a–b**) and the inscribed gold ring KN Zf 13 from Mavrospelio cemetery (**Figure 16a**) serve as examples whereby the available surface may have dictated a spiral arrangement (cf. Godart and Olivier 1982: 118–125 and 152–153, respectively). This arrangement makes sense in the context of the small circular bezel of the gold ring (diameter 1.0 cm × 0.85 cm). In comparison, placing the ink inscriptions on the interiors of the

a

b

Figure 16: a) Mavrospelio ring made of gold. Diameter: 1.0 cm × 0.85 cm. KN Zf 13 / HM X-A530;
b) Phaistos disc with stamped inscription, made of clay. Diameter: 15.8 × 16.5 cm.

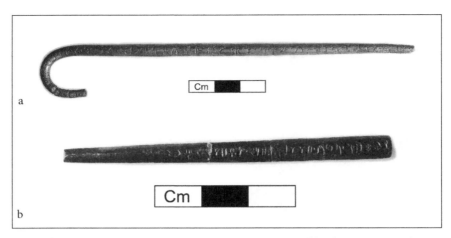

Figure 17: a) Silver pin. Length: 15 cm. KN Z 31 / HM X-A540; b) Silver pin. Length: 7 cm. PL Zf 1 / HM X-A498.

aforementioned cups, rather than the exteriors, may have related to visibility during their use as drinking vessels. As with archaic and classical kantharoi, holding the cups in order to fill them or to drink from them would have displayed the inscriptions. The readability of the inscriptions by the holder of the cup was facilitated by painting the cursive signs with their top towards the bottom of the cups, and also by directing the dextroverse spiral inscriptions from the centre of the base towards the rim. That the two painted inscriptions were meant to be read is also supported by visual reinforcement of the intended reading sequence: the beginning and the end of the second sign-group of cup KN Zc 6 (**Figure 15a**) were divided by a punctuation mark. The suggestion that the cups formed part of a foundation deposit for a new architectural phase of the building (end of the MM IIIB or early LM IA), because they bore magical spells and incantations (Banou 2001: 196), cannot be confirmed. Judging from the non-formulaic and non-consecrational nature of the inscriptions (Raison 1963: 25; Raison and Pope 1981: 223–224), the alternative hypothesis that they bore a dedicatory inscription seems more plausible (Evans 1921: 613–616).

By contrast, the inscription on the Mavrospelio ring KN Zf 13 can be compared to the stamped inscription on the Phaistos disc (**Figure 16b**). It is aligned along a spiral line and reads from the outer edge to the centre of the bezel. In contrast to the cups, however, the top of the signs face outwards. The comparison with the disc, which may convey a religious hymn (Boulotis 2008: 76; see also Whittaker, this volume), and the absence of separation marks between the sign-groups reinforce the probable magical underpinnings of the ring inscription. The final use of the ring as a burial gift deposited in the rich Mavrospelio tomb IX further supports the notion that it may bear a spell related to the ring's owner (Boulotis 2008: 75). Although it is unclear whether the ring was initially associated with the larnax found in the niche of chamber E1, its presence and the rest of the content of the chamber point to the high status of the burials (Forsdyke 1927: 266–267, 269). The inscribed silver pin KN Z 31 (Alexiou and Brice 1972: 113, n. 2, 116), which was recovered from another chamber of the same tomb offers further evidence in this respect (**Figure 17a**). A possible interpretation is that it may have been commissioned by another member of the same family or kin, who either had special ties with writing or was eager to legitimise his / her role through owning such a pin.

Inscriptions on this pin and also on three other LM I examples of precious metal associated with high-status burials at various sites have been interpreted as statements of a magical or religious character (Boulotis 2008: 75; **Figure 17b**; PL Zf 1; cf. Alexiou and Brice 1976: 18; ARKH Zf 9;

a   b

Figure 18: a) Stone libation table from Apodoulou with its two parts joined. Height: 6.5 cm. AP Za 1 / HM L2478; b) The two parts of the libation table separated.

cf. Sakellarakis and Sapouna-Sakellaraki 1997: 333, fig. 296; CR(?) Zf 1 / Ayios Nik.Mus. 9673; cf. Godart and Olivier 1982: 162). From a material point of view, the inscriptions were engraved after the silver or gold was cast and the material used affected the form of the signs to some extent. For example, the engraving of the signs using numerous small strokes onto the soft material of the gold pin CR(?) Zf 1 from eastern Crete accounts for their angular shape, as is also the case with the aforementioned gold ring KN Zf 13 (Schoep 2002a: 14). From an epigraphic perspective, the inscriptions on the pins are mostly hapaxes (one-offs) separated into numerous sign-groups by punctuation strokes (Olivier et al. 1981: 12, 14). Since these differ considerably from a palaeographic point of view and come from remote findspots, the pins could conceivably have been produced by different workshops (Schoep 2002a: 14).

In terms of the use of graphic space, the elongated shape of the hairpins dictated the horizontal alignment of the inscriptions. Nevertheless, this did not preclude a different orientation for individual signs, as attested on the silver pin KN Zf 31 from Mavrospelio (**Figure 17a**). The sign A310 that stands exactly at the end of the hook has been turned 90° clockwise (Godart and Olivier 1976: 313, pl. 2). With regard to directionality, only the inscription on the pin PL Zf 1 from Platanos (**Figure 17b**) reads from right to left (Alexiou and Brice 1976: 20–25). Overall, the material qualities of these hairpins were successfully manipulated for the addition of inscriptions. Due to their very small scale these inscriptions had to be held close to the eyes in order to be read. Although this quality does not seem to lend itself to a use of these objects for conspicuous display, writing must, in any case, have lent special symbolic properties to them. The final deposition of the pins as part of the burial assemblages indicates that they were personal items with emblematic value.

Two inscribed miniature double axes, one of gold and one of silver (AR Zf 1–2; cf. Godart and Olivier 1982: 162), which were deposited at the end of MM III in the Archalochori cave as part of a homogeneous hoard of metal objects, present a different social context from the burials (Marinatos 1962; Michailidou 2003: 302–303, 308–309). Although these two examples bear the same inscription, they differ palaeographically. The possibility that they came from the workshop, which produced the large bronze double axe with the unique inscription and the other large or miniaturised examples of the Arkalochori hoard (Boulotis 2008: 69, fig. 2), reinforces the contention that artisans working in metallurgy possessed some degree of literacy (Boulotis 2008: 78; Olivier et al. 1981: 22). The fact that metal objects of a functional character were also occasionally inscribed may also support this argument; examples include a lead weight from Mochlos (MO Zf 1; cf. Olivier 1989b) and a bronze axe at the British Museum (KA Zf 1 / BM 1954 10-20 1; Godart and Olivier 1982: 149).

Material aspects can be more explicitly studied as a symbolic index in the case of Neopalatial stone votive offerings with inscribed incantations reflecting the use of a common religious language

Figure 19: Stone libation table from Palaikastro. Height: 18.3 cm. PK Za 11 / HM L1341.

throughout large parts of Crete (Driessen 1994: 114). Although evidence for their production is scarce, the elaboration of the signs and their palaeography differ from site to site suggesting different places of manufacture (Schoep 2002a: 14). Inscribed stone 'libation tables' were mainly deposited at peak sanctuaries along with uninscribed examples. One of their uses is evidenced by their inclusion in deposits of carbonised remains mixed with pottery, animal bones and votive objects, such as the ones excavated at the extra-urban sanctuaries. The earliest securely-dated inscribed example comes from Building Ub in the Kato Syme sanctuary, where libation tables and MM IIIA cups were deposited around the remains of a series of fires (SY Za 6; cf. Muhly in Muhly and Olivier 2008: 198). On the whole, the data suggests that inscribed libation tables were intended for offerings; they were possibly used in performance rites that formed part of a popular cult involving food and drink consumption. Most seem to have followed a votive etiquette, as shown by the recurring variations of sequential sign-groups, including the standard Linear A 'libation formula' (Duhoux 2001: 182; Younger 2002). The exact meaning of the sign-groups is presently unknown, but they may have formed parts of prayers or expressions of thanks to the deities. The proposed phonetic transcription of the 'libation formula' [j]a-sa-sa-ra-me, has been interpreted as either being addressed to a presumed goddess (Grumach 1968: 15–17) or meaning 'sacred boon or homage' (Facchetti 1999: 130).

A few vessels inscribed with variations of the formula also occur in domestic contexts, such as Knossos, Prassas and Apodoulou (Schoep 2002a: 14). Among the numerous libation tables that were offered at sanctuaries, the inscribed examples represent a very small percentage of the total (Karetsou 1987: 86). At the sanctuary of Kato Syme, where at least 600 libation tables have been recovered, inscribed examples form less than 0.02% (Muhly in Muhly and Olivier 2008: 199–200). Their low incidence implies that the inscribed libation tables may have been offered by members of privileged or distinctive social groups (Schoep 1994: 20). Among the uninscribed examples of different shapes found at Syme, the most obvious distinguishing factor was size. In a half-dozen cases, which were probably set up on tall bases, the total height could be significantly larger,

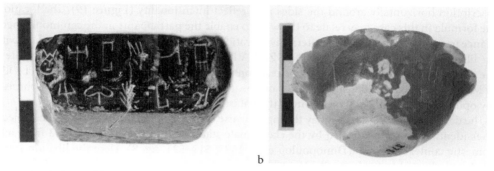

Figure 20: a) Stone libation table. Height: 1.9 cm: Width 4.3 cm. IO Za 2 / HM L3557 from Ioukhtas; b) Stone cup. Diameter 4.2 cm: Height: 2.5 cm. IO Za 6 / HM L3785 from Ioukhtas.

Figure 21: a) Alabaster ladle. Length: 6.5 cm. TL Za 1 / HM L1545 from Troullos; b) Stone ladle. Length: 10.3 cm. HM L2101 from the House of the Frescoes at Knossos.

reaching 31.8 cm (cf. Lebessi and Muhly 1990: 330–331, figs 19–20; Muhly in Muhly and Olivier 2008: 200, n. 15). Yet, the choice of adding an inscription to a libation table probably marked specific Syme votaries as "privileged individuals who could communicate directly with the divine" (Muhly in Muhly and Olivier 2008: 200–201). This suggestion could, in turn, corroborate the hypothesis that inscribed examples from this sanctuary and elsewhere contain personal names (Duhoux 1992: 81; Facchetti 1999: 130; Olivier in Muhly and Olivier 2008: 217).

Material qualities, such as shape and the proportions of the tops of the libation tables, may have influenced the placement of the inscriptions, given that the diameter of the cavity and the width of the raised collar and flat rim vary from piece to piece. For example, the inscription was placed on the vertical shoulder of libation table SY Za 9 due to its narrow rim (Olivier in Muhly and Olivier 2008: 213). In the case of the square example from Apodoulou AP Za 1 / HM L2478 (**Figure 18a–b**), which consisted of two separate pieces, the carving of the inscription around the sides of the top piece was the most obvious choice. But even the most common practice of aligning the inscription horizontally around the sides may reflect intentionality (**Figure 19**). The location of the formula in this case may relate to the wish to enable the participants in the ceremonial performance to see the inscription. The alternative location, on the top surface surrounding the cavity of the libation table (e.g. PK Za 8, 14–17, PS Za 1, VRY Za 1, IO Za 9, 15, SY Za 2), may indicate that the inscription was meant to be seen, or read, only by the person performing the rites (cf. Olivier in Muhly and Olivier 2008: 204). These patterns in the arrangement of the formula emphasise, in my opinion, the personal involvement of the votaries themselves in the offerings.

The desire for competitive display through the use of writing and, probably, through projecting one's identity is also manifested by the clay female statuette PO Zg 1 / HM P27663 from a later domestic context at Poros (Dimopoulou et al. 1993: 519–521, fig. 8). Here the libation formula has been adjusted to fit the available graphic space, being painted along the conical skirt of the statuette. A similar wish for competitive display may be evidenced through the offering of the miniaturised versions of stone votive vessels, which may have been used for the offering of precious liquids (Faure 1992: 95). As has been argued for similar examples from the peak sanctuary of Ioukhtas / Alonaki (Karetsou 1987: 86), the shape of these miniature vessels may evoke earlier forms. The inscriptions, positioned along the sides (e.g. IO Za 2 / HM L3557, IO Za 6 / HM L3785; cf. **Figure 20a–b**) or around the rim (e.g. TL Za 1 / HM L1545; cf. **Figure 21a**) appear to imitate the larger inscribed prototypes. The votaries claimed their right to address the divine element, but the inscription would only be visible on close inspection, such as when the vessel was held in the hand; alternatively, knowledge that writing was present and exclusive was probably all that mattered to the votaries. However, some of the inscriptions on the miniatures possibly included personal names (Facchetti 1999: 131; Monti 2005: 22), such as the stone cup IO Za 6 from Ioukhtas / Alonaki (**Figure 20b**) and the alabaster heart-shaped ladle TL Za 1 from Archanes / Troullos (**Figure 21a**). The signs on the latter were carved and also differentiated from the background with added colour.

It is also worth considering that the small size and weight of the miniaturised forms from Ioukhtas could be due to practical reasons, such as ease of transport along the long route to the peak of the Ioukhtas mountain. Nevertheless, ladles are also more commonly found in ritual contexts at settlements (Warren 1969: 49), as for example the aforementioned ladle from Archanes / Troullos (**Figure 21a**), the two similar stone ladles HM L2101 (**Figure 21b**) and HM L2102 from the House of the Frescoes at Knossos (Platon 1954: 444; Warren 1969: 49, fig. P289) as well as a small steatite vessel with two spoon-shaped hollows from Hogarth's House A at Gypsades (Hogarth 1899–1900: 73, fig. 13). Nonetheless, the marked concentration of inscribed and uninscribed miniature libation tables and cups in the wider region of Archanes (Ioukhtas and Troullos) and nearby Knossos probably reflects a local practice and the existence of a specialised workshop.

Conclusions

Symbolic behaviour is embodied in the regulation of social relationships through the use of Minoan writing on various material surfaces. This study has shown that the modes of display of the two Minoan scripts followed different paths. It is evident that captions, so popular in Near Eastern art, were probably never used in Minoan art. The display of the developed Hieroglyphic script of the MM IIB period was mostly dictated by a standardised administrative practice. The spatial organisation of script signs on the surface of the three- and four-sided prismatic seals enabled the latter to function as hierarchical devices, which could supplement or, even, substitute writing by making impressions on clay documents. Based on present evidence, we cannot assert whether the 'decorative' signs carved on Hieroglyphic seals represented writing that corresponded to spoken language. Non-verbal visualisations must have been more crucial to thought for the Minoans than we are able to understand presently, as shown particularly by the example of the 'Archanes Script Group' seals. I would like to suggest tentatively that the solitary pictorial signs first appearing on them were understood as semasiographic codes. These codes probably stemmed from the emblematic use of Minoan seal devices at least from the late Prepalatial period. During the transition to the Protopalatial period, the borrowed symbolism of the zoomorphic or anthropomorphic seals and those recalling amulets may derive from a sophisticated manipulation of related Egyptian forms of display and ideology (cf. e.g. Baines 2004).

The integration of the earliest script ('Archanes script') into three-dimensional seals and its interaction with image may have further fostered the pictorial character of the Hieroglyphic signs. The earliest seals that bear the standardised 'Archanes formula' were possibly aimed at projecting a message of restricted use and embodied new notions of ownership among the bearers of common uninscribed seals. Thus, they might have reflected a separate grouping within the Archanes community. Whether or not they symbolised the connection of specific elites with a supernatural element, as has been proposed by Sbonias (1995: 133), the management of a symbolic resource such as writing certainly was a key feature of social competition. Furthermore, the standardisation of the shape of the inscribed prismatic seals within the subsequent Protopalatial MM II glyptic tradition points to the establishment of social groupings and / or institutions with specific codes of communication during this period. The attestation of isolated impressions of MM II hieroglyphic seals in the Neopalatial Ayia Triada and Zakros administrative assemblages (CHIC: 30) supports the hypothesis that some of these seals may have functioned as hereditary symbolic devices, even after the Hieroglyphic script had ceased to be used.

During the Neopalatial period, individuals and groups of varying social status approached the production of Linear A and the use of the inscribed surfaces in different ways, allowing us to ascertain how the latter influenced the way knowledge was conveyed and perceived. Based on the evidence available, Linear A was not employed on monuments of public display, as was the case with Egyptian hieroglyphs. If it was felt necessary to communicate standardised narratives to multiple individuals simultaneously, other mechanisms must have been used. Portable objects inscribed in Linear A and made from different materials were commissioned for various reasons. An analytical focus on alignment and directionality has helped to make inferences about the "cultural biography" (Kopytoff 1986) of small-scale inscribed artefacts from costly materials, such as silver or gold hair pins and the gold Mavrospelio ring. These objects seem to have initially served an exclusive role for their owners in life, and were then buried with the deceased in order to serve him / her in the hereafter. If they were indeed produced by literate artisans, they could also reflect participation in a particular social group with access to symbolic resources, such as the secrets of metallurgy and writing. The removal of the pins from circulation through their deposition within elite burials possibly was a mechanism for maintaining their exclusive associations.

A ceremonial use of Linear A is documented beyond doubt by the formulaic inscriptions on Neopalatial stone libation vessels. The large inscribed libation tables from extra-urban sanctuaries were probably used for ritualised offering in the context of food and drink consumption. At the same time, they might have served as means of conspicuous display by the votaries. The possibility that some inscriptions contained personal names suggests that the votaries intended to show competitive generosity by declaring their association with the dedication. This intention is more evident in the case of the miniaturised versions of votives with inscriptions of a micrographic character. I suggest that these miniatures were produced with the aim of addressing an initiated group of participants in the rites, who adhered to a certain value code. Consequently, they may even legitimate claims of personal participation in the religious practice.

Last but not least, the role that the scale of writing played in imposing authority should be at the core of a material practice approach. On the basis of our analysis, it is possible to suggest that the micrographic character of the inscriptions multiplied the symbolic meaning of small ritual or prestige artefacts. In cases of display events, such as cult activities in the sanctuaries or burial deposition rituals, knowledge that writing was present, meaningful and exclusive would probably have mattered more for the social agents than the specific content of the inscription (cf. Baines 2004: 152). In another context, the sacred cave at Arkalochori, the hoarding of the two miniature, inscribed double axes could have been both a symbolic act and an ideal way to symbolically 'store' precious metals.

Acknowledgements

I am grateful to the organisers of the conference — Kathryn Piquette and Ruth Whitehouse — and also to the anonymous reviewers, as well as to Dr A. Karnava, Dr P. Muhly, Dr V. Petrakis, Dr G. Rethemiotakis and Dr J. Smith for their valuable suggestions on the first draft of this paper. Special thanks are due to Dr C. Stray who read the latter and corrected the English. The final draft was written in the fall of 2011 during my S. Seeger Research Fellowship at the Center for Hellenic Studies, Princeton University. Photographs 2–4 and 7–21 are reproduced courtesy of the Heraklion Museum – Archaeological Receipts Fund.

Abbreviations

BM = British Museum inventory number
CMS = *Corpus der Minoischen und Mykenischen Siegel*
CMS II.1 = Platon, N. 1969. *Corpus der Minoischen und Mykenischen Siegel. Iraklion Archäologisches Museum. Band II, Teil 1: Die Siegel der Vorpalastzeit*. Berlin: Gebr. Mann Verlag.
CMS II.3 = Platon, N. and Pini, I. 1984. *Corpus der Minoischen und Mykenischen Siegel. Iraklion Archäologisches Museum. Band II, Teil 3: Die Siegel der Neupalastzeit*. Berlin: Gebr. Mann Verlag.
CMS II.8 = Gill, M. A. V., Müller, W. and Pini, I. 2002. *Corpus der Minoischen und Mykenischen Siegel: Iraklion. Archäologisches Museum. Band II, Teil 8,1: Die Siegelabdrücke von Knossos*. Mainz am Rhein: Verlag Philipp von Zabern.
CMS III.1 = Müller, W. and Pini, I. 2007. *Corpus der Minoischen und Mykenischen Siegel: Iraklion. Archäologisches Museum*. Mainz am Rhein: Verlag Philipp von Zabern.
CMS VI = Hughes-Brock, H. and Boardman, J. 2009. *Corpus der Minoischen und Mykenischen Siegel: Oxford. The Ashmolean Museum*. Mainz am Rhein: Verlag Philipp von Zabern.
CMS VII = Kenna, V. E. G. 1967. *Corpus der Minoischen und Mykenischen Siegel. Die englischen Museen II. Band VII*. Berlin: Gebr. Mann Verlag.
HM = Heraklion Museum inventory number

Notes

[1] The term 'morpheme' denotes the smallest and most basic grammatical unit (Coulmas 2003: 33).
[2] Godart and Olivier (1996) numbers preceded by the symbol # refer to hieroglyphic documents. For the plain numbers that are conventionally used to denote the hieroglyphic signs, cf. Olivier and Godart 1996: 17, *tableau des signes standardisés de l'hiéroglyphique crétois* (MNA-MON 2009–2012). With regard to the directionality of the signs on hieroglyphic seals, the transcription in Olivier and Godart (1996) follows the way signs were engraved on the seals and not their positive impressions on clay.

[3] Hieroglyphic continued to be used at Malia during the beginning of the Neopalatial period (MM III), as shown by the documents of the 'Dépôt Hiéroglyphique' in the palace (Olivier and Godart 1996: 28, n. 11).

[4] 'Medallions' and 'crescents' were hanging documents inscribed in Cretan Hieroglyphic; they were used as primary documents from which data was transferred to four-sided clay bars, cf. Tsipopoulou and Hallager 2010: 74–79, 84–86, 258, and 12–14 (on types of hieroglyphic documents).

[5] This inference is supported by the three MM IB noduli of the Knossian Deposit A, which were stamped by an ivory / bone seal depicting an agrimi; Weingarten (2007: 135) interprets them as *laisser-passer* or private receipts.

[6] By MM IB, a transference of visual symbols from inscribed seals to pots may have taken place as suggested by Haggis (2007: 763–766) on the basis of the 'Lakkos deposit' from Petras.

[7] An early clay model of an Egyptian sistrum has been excavated in Archanes Burial Building 9 (Sakellarakis and Sapouna-Sakellaraki 1997: 329; Sapouna 2001: 267).

References

Alexiou, S. and Brice, W. C. 1972. A Silver Pin from Mavro Spelio with an Inscription in Linear A: Her. Mus. 540. *Kadmos* 11(2): 113–124. DOI: http://dx.doi.org/10.1515/kadm.1972.11.2.113

Alexiou, S. and Brice, W. C. 1976. A Silver Pin from Platanos with an Inscription in Linear A: Her. Mus. 498. *Kadmos* 15(1): 18–27. DOI: 10.1515/kadm.1976.15.1.18

Anastasiadou, M. 2011. *The Middle Minoan Three-Sided Soft Stone Prism: A study of style and iconography* (CMS Beiheft 9). Mainz: Verlag Philipp von Zabern.

Aruz, J. 2000. Artistic Change and Cultural Exchange: The glyptic evidence. In Pini, I. (ed.), *Minoisch-Mykenische Glyptik: Stil, Ikonographie, Funktion. V. Internationales Siegel-Symposium Marburg, 23.–25. September 1999* (CMS Beiheft 6). Berlin: Gebr. Mann Verlag, 1–13.

Baines, J. 2004. The Earliest Egyptian Writing: Development, context, purpose. In Houston, S. D. (ed.), *The First Writing: Script Invention as History and Process*. Cambridge: Cambridge University Press, 150–189.

Banou, E. 2001. 190a–b. Signed cups. In Karetsou, A., Andreadaki-Vlazaki, M. and Papadakis, N. (eds), *Crete – Egypt: Three thousand years of cultural links. Catalogue*. Herakleion: Hellenic Ministry of Culture, 196.

Bennet, J. 2008. Now You See It; Now You Don't! The disappearance of the Linear A script on Crete. In Baines, J., Bennet, J. and Houston, S. D. (eds), *The Disappearance of Writing Systems: Perspectives on literacy and communication*. London: Equinox, 1–29.

Boulotis, C. 2008. The Art of Cretan Writing. In Andreadaki-Vlazaki, M., Rethemiotakis, G. and Dimopoulou-Rethemiotaki, N. (eds), *From the Land of the Labyrinth: Minoan Crete, 3000–1100 B.C. Essays*. New York: Alexander S. Onassis Public Benefit Foundation (USA), 67–78.

Branigan, K. 1970. *The Tombs of Mesara: A study of funerary architecture and ritual in Southern Crete, 2800–1700 B.C.* London: Gerald Duckworth.

Brice, W. C. 1990. Notes on the Cretan Hieroglyphic Script. *Kadmos* 29(1): 1–10. DOI: http://dx.doi.org/10.1515/kadm.1990.29.1.1

Brice, W. C. 1997. Notes on the Cretan Hieroglyphic Script. *Kadmos* 36(2): 93–96. DOI: http://dx.doi.org/10.1515/kadm.1997.36.2.93

Cameron, S. A. 1968. The Painted Signs on Fresco Fragments from the "House of the Frescoes". *Kadmos* 7: 45–64.

Catling, H. W. and Cavanagh, C. 1976. Two Inscribed Bronzes from the Menelaion, Sparta. *Kadmos* 15: 145–157.

Chandler, D. 2007. *Semiotics: The basics* (2nd ed.). London and New York: Routledge.

Cooper, J. S. 2004. Babylonian Beginnings: The origin of the cuneiform writing system in comparative perspective. In Houston, S. D. (ed.), *The First Writing. Script invention as history and process*. Cambridge: Cambridge University Press, 71–99.

Coulmas, F. 2003. *Writing Systems: An introduction to their linguistic analysis*. Cambridge: Cambridge University Press.

Dahl, J. 2009. The Marks of Early Writing. Paper delivered at conference, "Writing as Material Practice: Substance, surface, and medium" held on 15–17 May 2009 at the Institute of Archaeology, University College London.

Dant, T. 2005. *Materiality and Society*. Maidenhead: Open University Press.

Dimopoulou, N., Olivier, J-P. and Rethemiotakis, G. 1993. Une statuette en argile avec inscription en Linéaire A de Poros/Irakliou. *Bulletin de Correspondance Hellénique* 117: 501–521. DOI: http://dx.doi.org/10.3406/bch.1993.4657

Dreyer, G. 1998. *Umm el-Qaab I: Das prädynastische Königsgrab U-j und seine frühen Schriftzeugnisse* (Archäologische Veröffentlichungen 86). Mainz am Rhein: Verlag Philipp von Zabern.

Driessen, J. 1994. A Fragmentary Linear A Inscription from Petsophas, Palaikastro (PK ZA 20). *Kadmos* 33(2): 149–152. DOI: http://dx.doi.org/10.1515/kadm.1994.33.2.149

Drucker, J. and McGann, J. 2001. Images as the Text: Pictographs and pictographic rhetoric. *Information Design Journal* 10(2): 95–106.

Duhoux, Y. 1992. Variations morphosyntaxiques dans les texts votifs Linéaires A. *Cretan Studies* 3: 65–88.

Duhoux, Y. 2001. Γραμμική Α. In Χρηστίδης, Α.-Φ. (ed.), *Ιστορία της Ελληνικής Γλώσσας. Από τις αρχές έως την ύστερη Αρχαιότητα*. Αθήνα: Ινστιτούτο Νεοελληνικών Σπουδών, 180–184.

Evans, A. 1909. *Scripta Minoa: The written documents of Minoan Crete with special reference to the archives of Knossos, Volume 1: The Hieroglyphic and Primitive Linear Classes*. Oxford: Clarendon Press.

Evans, A. 1921. *The Palace of Minos at Knossos: Volume 1. The Neolithic and Early and Middle Minoan Ages*. London: Macmillan and Co., Ltd.

Facchetti, G. M. 1999. Non-Onomastic Elements in Linear A. *Kadmos* 38: 121–136.

Faure, P. 1992. ATANU, ATANOWO, ATANUPI. *Cretan Studies* 3: 89–95.

Forsdyke, E. J. 1927. The Mavro Spelio Cemetery at Knossos. *Annual of the British School at Athens* 28: 243–296. DOI: http://dx.doi.org/10.1017/S0068245400011187

Gelb, I. 1952. *A Study of Writing*. Chicago: University of Chicago Press.

Gell, A. 1998. *Art and Agency: An anthropological theory*. Oxford: Clarendon Press.

Godart, L. 1999. L'écriture d'Arkhanès: Hiéroglyphique ou Linéaire A? In Betancourt, P. P., Karageorghis, V., Laffineur, R. and Niemeier, W.-D. (eds), *Meletemata: Studies in Aegean archaeology presented to Malcolm H. Wiener as he enters his 65th year*. Volume 1 (Aegaeum 20). Liège: Université de Liège, Histoire de l'art et archéologie de la Grèce antique and Austin, TX: University of Texas at Austin, Program in Aegean Scripts and Prehistory, 299–302.

Godart, L. and Olivier, J.-P. 1982. *Recueil des inscriptions en Linéaire A*. Volume 4. Paris: Geuthner dépositaire.

Godart, L. and Olivier, J.-P. 1976. Sur l'épingle de Mavro Spelio. *Bulletin de Correspondance Hellénique* 100: 309–314. DOI: http://dx.doi.org/10.3406/bch.1976.2047

Graves-Brown, P. M. (ed.) 2000. *Matter, Materiality and Modern Culture*. London: Routledge.

Grumach, E. 1968. The Minoan Libation Formula – Again. *Kadmos* 7: 7–26.

Grumach, E. and Sakellarakis, I. A. 1966. Die neuen Hieroglyphensiegel vom Phourni (Archanes) I. *Kadmos* 5(2): 109–114. DOI: http://dx.doi.org/10.1515/kadm.1966.5.2.109

Haas, C. 1996. *Writing Technology: Studies on the materiality of literacy*. Mahwah, NJ: Lawrence Earlbaum Associates.

Haggis, D. G. 2007. Stylistic Diversity and Diacritical Feasting at Protopalatial Petras: A preliminary analysis of the Lakkos deposit. *American Journal of Archaeology* 111(4): 715–775. DOI: http://dx.doi.org/10.3764/aja.111.4.715

Hallager, E., Papadopoulou, E. and Tzachili, I. 2011. VRY S (4/4) 01 – The first hieroglyphic inscription from western Crete. *Kadmos* 50: 63–174.

Harris, R. 1986. *The Origin of Writing*. La Salle, IL: Open Court Press.

Harris, R. 1995. *Signs of Writing*. London: Routledge.

Hill-Boone, E. 2004. Beyond Writing. In Houston, S. D. (ed.), *The First Writing: Script invention as history and process*. Cambridge: Cambridge University Press, 313–348.

Hogarth, D. G. 1899–1900. Knossos Summary Report of the Excavations in 1900: II. Early town and cemeteries. *Annual of the British School at Athens* 6: 70–85.

Hood, S. 1997. A Monumental Linear A Inscription from Knossos. *Annual of the British School at Athens* 36: 111–117.

Jasink, A. M. 2009. *Cretan Hieroglyphic Seals: A new classification of symbols and ornamental/filling motifs* (Biblioteca di "Pasiphae" 9). Pisa-Roma: Fabrizio Serra Ed.

Jones, A. 2007. *Memory and Material Culture*. Cambridge and New York: Cambridge University Press. DOI: http://dx.doi.org/10.1017/CBO9780511619229

Kahl, J. 1994. *Das System der ägyptischen Hieroglyphenschrift in der 0.–3. Dynastie*. Wiesbaden: Harrassowitz.

Karetsou, A. 1987. Duo nees epigrafes Grammikis Graphis A apo to iero koryfis Ioukhta. In Kastrinaki, L., Orphanou, G. and Giannadakis, N. (eds), *Eilapine: tomos timitikos yia ton kathiyiti Nikolao Platona. Volume 1*. Vikelea Dimotiki Vivliothiki, Heraklion, 85–91.

Karnava, A. 2000. *The Cretan Hieroglyphic Script of the Second Millennium* BC: *Description, analysis function and decipherment perspectives*. Unpublished PhD dissertation, Université Libre de Bruxelles.

Karytinos, A. 1998. Sealstones in Cemeteries: A display of social status? In Branigan, K. (ed.), *Cemetery and Society in the Aegean Bronze Age* (Sheffield Studies in Aegean Archaeology 1). Sheffield: Sheffield Academic Press, 78–86.

Kenna, V. E. G. 1967. *Corpus den Minoischen und Mykenischen Siegel Band 7: Die Englischen Museen 2*. Berlin: Verlag Gebr. Mann.

Knappett, C. 2004. The Affordances of Things: A post-Gibsonian perspective on the relationality of mind and matter. In DeMarrais, E., Gosden, C. and Renfrew, C. (eds), *Rethinking Materiality: The engagement of mind with the material world*. Cambridge: McDonald Institute Monographs, 43–51.

Knappett, C. 2005. *Thinking Through Material Culture: An interdisciplinary perspective*. Philadelphia, PA: University of Pennsylvania Press.

Knappett, C. 2008. The Neglected Networks of Material Agency: Artefacts, pictures and texts. In Knappett, C. and Malafouris, L. (eds), *Material Agency: Towards a non-anthropocentric approach*. New York, NY: Springer US, 139–156. DOI: http://dx.doi.org/10.1007/978-0-387-74711-8_8

Krzyszkowska, O. 2005. *Aegean Seals: An introduction* (BICS Supplement 85). London: Institute of Classical Studies.

Krzyszkowska, O. 2012. Seals from the Petras Cemetery: A preliminary overview. In Tsipopoulou, M. (ed.), *Petras: 25 years of excavations and studies. Acts of a two-day conference held at the Danish Institute at Athens, 9–10 October 2010* (Monographs of the Danish Institute at Athens Volume 16). Århus: Århus University Press, 145–156.

Lebessi, A. and Muhly, P. 1990. Aspects of Minoan Cult: Sacred enclosures: The evidence from the Syme Sanctuary (Crete). *Archäologischer Anzeiger* 1990: 315–336.

Lebessi, A., Muhly, P. and Olivier, J.-P. 1995. An Inscription in the Hieroglyphic Script from the Syme Sanctuary, Crete (SY Hf 01). *Kadmos* 34: 63–77. DOI: http://dx.doi.org/10.1515/kadm.1995.34.1.63

MacDonald, C. F. 2007. The Small Finds. In MacDonald, C. F. and Knappett, C. (eds), *Knossos Protopalatial Deposits in Early Magazine A and the South-west Houses* (The British School at Athens, Supplementary Volume 41). Oxford and Northampton: The British School at Athens, 121–131.

Marinatos, S. 1962. Zur Frage der Grotte von Arkalochori. *Kadmos* 1(2): 87–94. DOI: http://dx.doi.org/10.1515/kadm.1962.1.2.87

Michailidou, A. 2003. Measuring Weight and Value in Bronze Age Economies in the Aegean and the Near East: A discussion on metal axes of no practical use. In Foster, K. P. and Laffineur, R. (eds), *METRON: Measuring the Aegean Bronze Age: Proceedings of the 9th International Aegean Conference, New Haven, Yale University, 18–21 April 2002* (Aegaeum 24). Liège: Université de Liège, Histoire de l'art et archéologie de la Grèce antique and Austin, TX: University of Texas at Austin, Program in Aegean Scripts and Prehistory, 301–314.

Militello, P. 2000. "L'archivio di cretule" del vano 25 e un nuovo sigillo da Festòs. In Perna, M. (ed.), *Administrative Documents in the Aegean and Their Near Eastern Counterparts: Proceedings of the International Colloquium, Naples, February 29–March 2, 1996*. Torino: Paravia Scriptorium, 221–243.

Militello, P. 2002. Amministrazione e contabilità a Festòs, II: Il contesto archeologico dei documenti palatini. *Creta Antica* 3: 51–91.

MNAMON: Portal for Ancient Writing Systems in the Mediterranean: A critical guide to electronic resources 2009–2012. *Cretan Hieroglyphics: Examples of writing*. Laboratorio Informatico per le Lingue Antiche. http://lila.sns.it/mnamon/index.php?page=Esempi&id=35&lang=en&PHPSESSID=2a0a7e1b9d978d031dfa742731f1b9e7 [accessed 1 June 2012].

Monti, O. 2005. Considérations sur quelques termes des textes votifs linéaires A. *Kadmos* 44(1–2): 19–22. DOI: http://dx.doi.org/10.1515/KADM.2005.005

Muhly, P. and Olivier, J.-P. 2008. Linear A Inscriptions from the Syme Sanctuary, Crete. *Archaiologike Ephemeris* 2008: 197–223.

Nuessel, F. H. 2006. Pictography: Semiotic approaches. In Brown, K. (ed.) *Encyclopedia of Language and Linguistics* (2nd ed.). Oxford: Elsevier, 591–599.

Olivier, J.-P. 1989a. The Possible Methods in Deciphering the Pictographic Cretan Script. In Duhoux, Y., Palaima, T. G. and Bennet, J. (eds), Problems in Decipherment (Bibliothèque des cahiers de l'Institut de Linguistique de Louvain 9). Peeters: Louvain-La-Neuve, 39–58.

Olivier, J.-P. 1989b. Le "Disque de Mokhlos": une nouvelle inscription en linéaire A sur un poids de plomb, HM 83/MO Zf 1. *Kadmos* 28(1–2): 137–145. DOI: http://dx.doi.org/10.1515/kadm.1989.28.1-2.137

Olivier, J.-P. 1990. The Relationship Between Inscriptions on Hieroglyphic Seals and Those Written on Archival Documents. In Palaima, T. G. (ed.), *Aegean Seals, Sealings and Administration: Proceedings of the NEH-Dickson Conference of the Program in Aegean Scripts and Prehistory of the Department of Classics, University of Texas at Austin, January 11–13, 1989* (Aegaeum 5). Liège: Université de Liège, Histoire de l'art et archéologie de la Grèce antique and Austin, TX: University of Texas at Austin, Program in Aegean Scripts and Prehistory, 11–19.

Olivier, J.-P. 1995. Les sceaux avec des signes hiéroglyphiques: Que lire? Une question de bon sens. In Pini, I. and Poursat, J.-C. (eds), *Sceaux Minoens et Mycéniens* (CMS Beiheft 5). Berlin: Gebr. Mann Verlag, 169–181.

Olivier, J.-P. 2000. Les sceaux avec des inscriptions hiéroglyphiques. Comment comprendre? In Perna, M. (ed.), *Administrative Documents in the Aegean and Their Near Eastern Counterparts: Proceedings of the International Colloquium, Naples, February 29–March 2, 1996*. Torino: Paravia Scriptorium, 141–168.

Olivier, J.-P. and Godart, L. (eds) 1996. *Corpus Hieroglyphicarum Inscriptionum Cretae* (Études Crétoises 31). Paris: De Boccard.

Olivier, J.-P., Godart, L. and Laffineur, R. 1981. Une épingle minoenne en or avec inscription en Linéaire A. *Bulletin de Correspondance Hellénique* 105(1): 3–25. DOI: http://dx.doi.org/10.3406/bch.1981.1928

Peirce, C. S. 1931. *Collected Papers of Charles Sanders Peirce, Volume 1: Principles of philosophy* (Edited by C. Hartshorne, P. Weiss and A. W. Burks). Cambridge, MA: Harvard University Press.

Pelon, O. 1980. *Le palais de Malia V.2* (Études crétoises 25). Paris: P. Geuthner.

Perna, M. 1995. The Roundels of Phaistòs. *Kadmos* 34: 103–122. DOI: http://dx.doi.org/10.1515/kadm.1995.34.2.103

Phillips, J. 2008a. *Aegyptiaca on the Island of Crete in Their Chronological Context: A critical review.* Volume 1. Wien: Verlag der Österreichischen Akademie der Wissenschaften.

Phillips, J. 2008b. *Aegyptiaca on the Island of Crete in Their Chronological Context: A critical review.* Volume 2. Wien: Verlag der Österreichischen Akademie der Wissenschaften.

Phillips, J. 2010. Non-Administrative Glyptic Relations Between the Aegean and Egypt. In Müller, W. (ed.), *Die Bedeutung der minoischen und mykenischen Glyptik* (CMS Beiheft 8). Mainz am Rhein: Verlag Philipp von Zabern, 309–323.

Platon, N. 1954. Ta minoika oikiaka hiera. *Kretika Chronika* 8: 428–483.

Poursat, J.-C. 1996. *Fouilles exécutées à Malia: Le quartier Mu 3. Artisans minoens. Les maisons-ateliers du quartier Mu* (Études crétoises 32). Paris: P. Geuthner.

Poursat, J.-C. 2000. Les sceaux hiéroglyphiques dans l'administration minoenne: Usage et fonction. In Perna, M. (ed.), *Administrative Documents in the Aegean and Their Near Eastern Counterparts. Proceedings of the International Colloquium, Naples, February 29–March 2, 1996.* Torino: Paravia Scriptorium, 187–191.

Raison, J. 1963. Les coupes de Cnossos avec inscriptions en Linéaire A. *Kadmos* 2: 17–26.

Raison, J. and Pope, M. 1981. *Corpus transnuméré du linéaire A* (Bibliotheque des Cahiers de l'Institut de Linguistique de Louvain 18). Louvain-La-Neuve: Cabay.

Relaki, M. 2009. Rethinking Administration and Seal Use in Third Millennium Crete. *Creta Antica* 10(2): 353–372.

Robertson, J. S. 2004. The Possibility and Actuality of Writing. In Houston, S. D. (ed.), *The First Writing: Script invention as history and process.* Cambridge: Cambridge University Press, 16–38.

Sakellarakis, Y. and Sapouna-Sakellaraki, E. 1997. *Archanes: Minoan Crete in a new light*, 2 volumes. Athens: Ammos Publications.

Sapouna, P. 2001. 265. Sistrum. In Karetsou, A., Andreadaki-Vlazaki, M. and Papadakis, N. (eds), *Crete – Egypt: Three thousand years of cultural links: Catalogue.* Herakleion: Hellenic Ministry of Culture, 267.

Sbonias, K. 1995. *Frühkretische Siegel. Ansätze für eine Interpretation der sozial-politischen Entwicklung auf Kreta während der Frühbronzezeit* (British Archaeological Reports International Series 620). Oxford: Oxbow Books.

Sbonias, K. 1999. Social Development, Management of Production, and Symbolic Representation in Prepalatial Crete. In Chaniotis, A. (ed.), *From Minoan Farmers to Roman Traders: Sidelights on the economy of ancient Crete.* Stuttgart: Franz Steiner Verlag, 25–51.

Sbonias, K. 2010. Diversity and Transformation: Looking for meanings in the Prepalatial seal consumption and use. In Müller, W. (ed.), *Die Bedeutung der Minoischen und Mykenischen Glyptik. 6. Internationales Siegel-Symposium aus Anlass des 50 jährigen Bestehens des CMS Marburg, 9.–12. Oktober 2008.* Mainz am Rhein: Verlag Philipp von Zabern, 349–362.

Schmandt-Besserat, D. 2007. *When Writing Met Art: From symbol to story.* Austin: University of Texas Press.

Schoep, I. 1994. Ritual, Politics and Script on Minoan Crete. *Aegean Archaeology* 1: 7–25.

Schoep, I. 2002*a*. *The Administration of Neopalatial Crete: A critical assessment of the Linear A tablets and their role in the administrative process* (Minos Supplement 17). Salamanca: Ediciones Universidád de Salamanca.

Schoep, I. 2002*b*. The State of the Minoan Palaces or the Minoan Palace State? In Driessen, J, Schoep, I. and Laffineur, R. (eds), Monuments of Minos: Rethinking the Minoan palaces: Proceedings of the international workshop "Crete of the hundred Palaces?", held at the Université Catholique de Louvain, Louvain-la-Neuve, 14–15 December 2001 (Aegaeum 23). Liège: Université de Liège, Histoire de l'art et archéologie de la Grèce antique and Austin, TX: University of Texas at Austin, Program in Aegean Scripts and Prehistory, 15–33.

Schoep, I. 2002*c*. Social and Political Organisation on Crete in the Proto-palatial Period: The case of Malia in MM II. *Journal of Mediterranean Archaeology* 15(2): 102–125.

Schoep, I. 2006. Looking Beyond the First Palaces: Elites and the agency of power in EM III–MM II Crete. *American Journal of Archaeology* 110(1): 37–64. DOI: http://dx.doi.org/10.3764/aja.110.1.37

Schoep, I. 2007. The Inscribed Document. In MacDonald, C. F. and Knappett, C. (eds), *Knossos Protopalatial Deposits in Early Magazine A and the South-west Houses* (The British School at Athens, Supplementary Volume 41). Oxford and Northampton: The British School at Athens, 131–134.

Tsipopoulou, M. and Hallager, E. 2010. *The Hieroglyphic Archive at Petras, Siteia* (Monographs of the Danish Institute at Athens Volume 9). Århus: Aarhus University Press.

Warren, P. 1969. *Minoan Stone Vases*. Cambridge: Cambridge University Press.

Watrous, L. V. 1994. Review of Aegean Prehistory III: Crete from earliest Prehistory through the Protopalatial Period. *American Journal of Archaeology* 98(4): 695–753. DOI: http://dx.doi.org/10.2307/506551

Weingarten, J. 1994. Sealings and Sealed Documents at Bronze Age Knossos. In Evely, D., Hughes-Brock, H. and Momigliano, N. (eds), *Knossos: A labyrinth of history: Papers presented in honour of Sinclair Hood*. Oxford: British School at Athens and Oxbow Books, 171–188.

Weingarten, J. 1995. Sealing Studies in the Middle Bronze Age III: The Minoan Hieroglyphic Deposits at Mallia and Knossos. In Pini, I. and Poursat, J.-C. (eds), *Sceaux Minoens et Mycéniens* (CMS Beiheft 5). Berlin: Gebr. Mann Verlag, 285–311.

Weingarten, J. 2007. Noduli, Sealings and a Weight from Deposits A and E. In MacDonald, C. F. and Knappett, C. (eds), *Knossos Protopalatial Deposits in Early Magazine A and the South-west Houses* (The British School at Athens, Supplementary Volume 41). Oxford and Northampton: The British School at Athens, 134–139.

Wilson, P. 2003. *Hieroglyphs: A very short introduction*. Oxford: Oxford University Press.

Younger, J. G. 1979. The Lapidary's Workshop at Knossos. *Annual of the British School at Athens* 74: 258–268.

Younger, J. G. 1990. New Observations on Hieroglyphic Seals. *Studi Micenei ed Egeo-Anatolici* 28: 85–93.

Younger, J. G. 1999. The Cretan Hieroglyphic Script: A review article. *Minos* 31–32: 379–400.

Younger, J. G. 2002. *Linear A Texts in Phonetic Transcription. Texts employing the "libation" formula in full or in part*: http://www.people.ku.edu/~jyounger/LinearA/religioustexts.html#part1 [Accessed 25 November 2013].

Yule, P. 1980. *Early Cretan Seals: A study of chronology* (Marburger Studien zur Vor- und Frühgeschichte 4). Mainz: Philipp von Zabern.

Zinna, A. 2011. The Object of Writing. *Language Sciences* 33(4): 634–646. DOI: http://dx.doi.org/10.1016/j.langsci.2011.04.034

Saving on Clay: The Linear B practice of cutting tablets

Helena Tomas

University of Zagreb

Introduction

In this chapter I address the theme of writing as material practice through a case study on Aegean clay tablets and the procedure of cutting them into smaller tablets. Rather than setting the scene with a full overview of Aegean Bronze Age writing, a task that is ably accomplished in Helène Whittaker's contribution to this volume, I summarise the information most relevant to my topic. Helène informs us that Linear B was the oldest Greek script, and was preceded by another two major Aegean scripts, both mostly used in Minoan Crete and still undeciphered — Cretan Hieroglyphic Script and Linear A. The signaries of these three Aegean scripts, as well as the types of material surfaces on which they were inscribed, are more or less related. All three are syllabic scripts and employed mostly for writing down economic and other administrative matters of related societies (Shelmerdine and Bennet 2008; Tomas 2010; Younger and Rehak 2008: 173–177). Although many types of clay sealings were used for recording this administrative business, the clay tablet is the most prominent document type in Linear A and Linear B, whereas in Cretan Hieroglyphic it is present only in small quantities.

While the clay tablet is chosen as a focus of this chapter, it is important to stress at the outset that despite all being 'clay tablets', the three groups of documents — Cretan Hieroglyphic, Linear A and Linear B — display significant differences, as I have pointed out elsewhere (Tomas 2011). These differences concern physical features of the tablets (so-called pinacological features) and methods of organising text on them (epigraphical features), as well as semantic contents of the inscribed text. From all these a single pinacological feature has been selected for consideration here — the cut edges of clay tablets (with a special emphasis on Linear B tablets). The reason for such a narrow selection is motivated by the fact that some

How to cite this book chapter:

Tomas, H. 2013. Saving on Clay: The Linear B practice of cutting tablets. In: Piquette, K. E. and Whitehouse, R. D. (eds.) *Writing as Material Practice: Substance, surface and medium.* Pp. 175-191. London: Ubiquity Press. DOI: http://dx.doi.org/10.5334/bai.i

aspects of the practice of cutting clay tablets are among the most enigmatic of all pinacological features of Aegean clay tablets, yet they seem to reveal a very important administrative procedure, as will be elaborated below. Also this choice of topic fits particularly well the subject of this volume, since cutting of clay is a pre-eminently material practice, related to the specific material employed.

A Brief Outline of Aegean Clay Tablets

Chronology and Distribution

At present it remains unclear which of the two Minoan scripts is earlier. The answer to this question lies in the interpretation of the inscriptions from prepalatial seals of the so-called Archanes Script (Godart and Tzedakis 1992: 108, 121–122; Grumach and Sakellarakis 1966; see also Flouda, this volume; Whittaker, this volume): some interpret them as Cretan Hieroglyphic, some as Linear A (Godart 1999; Olivier and Godart 1996; Sakellarakis and Sapouna-Sakellaraki 1997: 326–330). For the present study, however, such a chronological intricacy has no crucial relevance, since the earliest preserved clay tablets postdate these Archanes seals. (I do not intend to get involved in a detailed discussion of the absolute chronology of the Aegean Bronze Age here. It suffices to say that Middle Minoan (MM) covers a period of c.2100 / 2000–1700 / 1600 BC and Late Minoan I (LM I) a period of c.1700 / 1600–1450 BC; for a detailed discussion, see Warren and Hankey 1989; see also Whittaker, this volume.)

I have already mentioned that Cretan Hieroglyphic tablets are rare: two have been discovered in the Hieroglyphic Deposit of the palace at Knossos, two in the palace of Malia, and one in the palace of Phaistos (Olivier and Godart 1996: 122–123, 172–175, 182–183). Whereas the Phaistos example is of an uncertain date, and the precise date of the Knossian Hieroglyphic Deposit is still a subject of debate (for the latter see the overview of different opinions in Schoep 2001: 147–148), the two tablets from Malia are securely dated to the MM III period (Chapouthier 1930).

A total of some 350 tablets has been discovered amongst Linear A documents, although many in a fragmentary state (Godart and Olivier 1976–1985). The earliest Linear A tablets are an MM IIA example from Knossos (del Freo 2007: 204–205; Schoep [2007] suggests that this may in fact be a Cretan Hieroglyphic tablet) and some 20 tablets from the MM IIB layers of the palace at Phaistos (Pugliese Carratelli 1958). Only a small number of Linear A tablets are of the MM III date while the majority are from the final phase of the administrative use of Linear A, that is, the end of the LM IB period (c.1450 BC), with the largest number, 147 tablets, coming from Haghia Triada (Ayia Triada) (Halbherr et al. 1977).

At least 5000 tablets with Linear B are known. The earliest are c.650 tablets from the Room of the Chariot Tablets at Knossos (hereafter RCT), dated to LM II or early LM IIIA1 (Driessen 1990: 117). The remainder of the approximately 2800 Knossian tablets are probably of LM IIIA2 date (the most recent overview of disputes concerning the date of the final destruction of Knossos and therefore of the majority of its Linear B tablets, is given in Driessen 2008: 70–72; the corpus of Knossian tablets is published by Chadwick et al. 1986–1998). Other Linear B tablets come from Chania on Crete and major Mycenaean centres on the Greek Mainland. Apart from a few odd examples from the LH IIIA period (Palaima 1983; Shelton 2002–2003), these are all of the LH IIIB date. The Pylos archive with approximately 1100 tablets is the largest in this group (Blegen and Rawson 1966: 92–101). It is followed by nearly 400 tablets from Thebes (Aravantinos et al. 2002; 2008), while there are smaller numbers of tablets from Mycenae, Tiryns and Chania (Andreadaki-Vlasaki and Hallager 2007; Godart 1988; Hallager and Vlasaki 1997; Melena and Olivier 1991; Sacconi 1974).

Shape

There are two principal shapes of Aegean clay tablets: the elongated (also called palm-leaf shaped tablets) and the page-shaped. Linear B makes use of both shapes (the former were used for simple entries, the latter for summarising records, cf. Driessen 1999: 207–208), whereas only page-shaped tablets were employed during the latest stages of Linear A. We do find several elongated tablets inscribed in Linear A, but they are dated to MM II or MM III; no elongated tablets with Linear A have been found amongst the latest surviving, LM IB documents. It should be noted that some LM IB Linear A tablets are far too fragmentary to make a definite decision about their shape, but, since not a single complete elongated tablet has been preserved in any LM IB deposit, we can assume that those tablets that are now fragmentary were also page-shaped when complete. As for Cretan Hieroglyphic tablets, the five preserved examples are all elongated, but thicker than most Linear A and Linear B elongated tablets.

Size

Linear A page-shaped tablets are generally smaller than Linear B ones, as is the average amount of information on them (on complete Linear A tablets the average number of signs per tablet is only 30). The overall proportion of the size of tablets and the 'crowdedness' of signs inscribed on them shows that Linear B page-shaped tablets hold a larger amount of information on the available space. As proposed elsewhere (Tomas 2011) there may be several reasons for this: the different nature of the two languages being recorded (Linear A sign-groups, i.e. words, are generally shorter than those of Linear B, see Duhoux 1978: 68), different methods of recording information (for example, Linear A may have used abbreviations more frequently), or different administrative practices (for example, Linear B page-shaped tablets may have been intended to contain more information than Linear A page-shaped tablets; perhaps in Linear A more extensive information was recorded on some other material, possibly perishable, cf. Driessen and Schoep 1999: 392; Olivier 1987: 230).

The small number of Cretan Hieroglyphic and Linear A elongated tablets precludes any sensible comparison to their numerous counterparts in Linear B, especially since the nature of elongated Linear B tablets changed drastically over time. Thus, elongated tablets tend to be smaller and with little text in the RCT, larger in the later Knossian deposits, and much larger and with more abundant text at Pylos. Driessen (1988: 132) notes that very small elongated tablets are frequent in the RCT and completely absent elsewhere: their dimensions are less than 0.6 cm thick, less than 0.2 cm high and less than 0.4 cm long. Their small size suggests that they were meant to be documents that could easily be carried around by individuals. Since it is precisely this type of tablet that in Linear B is most frequently the outcome of cutting (i.e. dividing of a larger tablet into smaller ones) they will be addressed below in more detail.

The Practice of Cutting Aegean Clay Tablets

The practice of cutting tablets is evident in both Linear A and Linear B administrative systems. The tablets were cut while still moist, probably with a knife, or other sharp tool. The few surviving Cretan Hieroglyphic tablets do not show traces of cutting, but this does not necessarily mean that this practice was unknown to the system.

The reasons for this practice seem to be clearer in Linear B than in Linear A. In Linear B, tablets were most probably cut after having been inscribed, when the residue of clay with no text was removed, possibly to be reused to form other tablets or to economise on space needed for their

Figure 1: Linear A tablet HT 1, 6.60 × 7.00 cm (Godart and Olivier 1976: 2).

transport and storage (see below). It is mostly elongated tablets that were cut (on their left or right side, or even both sides), whereas page-shaped tablets were cut only occasionally (usually at the bottom, exceptionally at the top). This habit of cutting tablets is especially apparent in the RCT, where about 20% of tablets were cut (whereas only 5% of the rest of the Knossian tablets were cut, cf. Driessen 1988: 134), and most of those are of an elongated shape. In addition to removing non-inscribed clay, another explanation has been proposed for the cutting of the RCT elongated tablets: the practice of dividing a set of information into separate records. By rejoining these small elongated tablets one can easily see that they initially belonged to one larger tablet. The name introduced to describe this kind of document is a '*simili*-join': larger tablets were probably divided into these smaller units for the purpose of rearranging the information (Driessen 1987), as is further elaborated below. *Simili*-joins are a feature almost unique to the RCT.

In comparison to Linear B, the practice of cutting tablets in Linear A is less well-understood. In Haghia Triada, the site with the largest number of Linear A tablets (147), only 10 tablets are cut, most of them at the bottom, some on their right or left sides (see also Schoep 1998–1999: 279). We cannot claim here that this was done, as in Linear B, after the text was inscribed and in order to remove a blank and therefore superfluous part of the tablet. In fact the scribes of the Haghia Triada tablets seem not to have been so preoccupied with saving space on tablets or neatness of filing. In most cases, when the tablets were cut, this was not done immediately below the end of the text, but further down or on the side, thus leaving plenty of unused space (e.g. HT 1, HT 2, HT 21, HT 92, HT 133, HT 154B, **Figure 1**). This suggests that the tablets at Haghia Triada were cut *before* they were inscribed and that the estimation of the space needed for the text was often incorrect, since many cut tablets are still too large for the inscribed text. By contrast, the tablet HT 10a was cut and then was too small for the required text, so the numbers at the end of the bottom line were crammed into the corner (**Figure 2**). (There is another possible explanation for the lack of space on this tablet: the tablet is a palimpsest, which means that it was probably cut to fit an erased text that was shorter than that which is preserved; cf. Piquette, this volume.)

Such a lack of coordination between the size of Haghia Triada tablets and the length of their inscriptions tells us something about the process of producing tablets. It is obvious that a tablet was conceived separately from the text, and at the time of its production the scribe did not yet have a clear idea of the amount of the text to be written thereon. Such a disparity furthermore suggests that the scribes of Haghia Triada did not produce their own tablets, but had assistants for

Figure 2: Linear A tablet HT 10, *recto* left (HT 10a) and *verso* right (HT 10b), 6.10 × 5.70 cm (Godart and Olivier 1976: 20).

that task, so called 'flatteners'. The opposite may be argued for the Linear A tablets from Chania. If we compare these to tablets from Haghia Triada, we notice that the former display a much better correlation between the size of a tablet and the length of its inscription. When Chania tablets were cut, this was in most cases done immediately beneath the last line (for example, KH 6, KH 8, KH 9, KH 10, KH 21, KH 58, etc.). This means that the collaboration between the scribe and the flattener was much closer in Chania than in Haghia Triada — or even that they were the same person (see also Schoep 2002: 76).

Whether a Linear A scribe and a flattener were the same person is an issue that requires a more thorough investigation, perhaps also a study of palm- and finger-prints which has helped to resolve similar questions in the case of Linear B tablets. Thus, Sjöquist and Åström's (1991) study of palm- and finger-prints in Knossos has shown that the tablets were usually made by assistants, only occasionally by the scribes themselves. The flatteners were sometimes children, perhaps apprentices, and sometimes adults whose hands saw hard work (visible from their rough and extended pores; Sjöquist and Åström 1991: 7, 20, 29–30). In contrast, for the case of Pylos, Palaima argues that scribes made their own tablets. His conclusion is not based on palm- and finger-prints, but on shapes of tablets that are characteristic of certain scribes (Palaima 1985: 102; 1988: 27; for a discussion of the correspondence between scribes and flatteners in the RCT, see Driessen 2000: 43–44, who concludes that they were never the same person; see also Firth 2012).

Until questions like this are answered for the Linear A tablets as well, we may provisionally conclude that Linear A scribes / flatteners had little foreknowledge of the amount of text that had to be fitted on a tablet. As for the cutting of tablets, it has been shown that this practice was less common in Linear A, and was also — Chania tablets excepted — inefficiently practised. If the purpose of this practice was to accommodate shorter texts, as in Linear B, why are most cut tablets still too large for the inscribed texts?

A More Detailed Discussion of Cutting Tablets in Linear B

In the above section two principal explanations are given for the practice of cutting Linear B tablets: saving on clay and rearranging the information. Let us now explore these two possibilities in more detail.

Saving on Clay

The easiest explanation for cutting Linear B tablets is saving on clay, since its surplus could be reused for producing further tablets. However, since clay is not a particularly scarce substance in Greece, saving was probably not the main motivation behind the practice of cutting tablets. A more likely aim appears to be a reduction of the size of tablets, and consequently of their weight, in order to economise on the space needed for their storage (for the maximum of one year, as numerous studies have shown). How were Linear B tablets stored?

In most cases Linear B tablets were found in such a state that it is impossible to say much about their initial storage. All over Knossos they were found in a secondary position, having fallen from the upper floor(s) during the destruction of the palace. The most we can say therefore is that Linear B archives in Knossos were stored above the ground floor: the upper rooms, with a good source of light, would have been an adequate setting for writing purposes (Begg 1987), but exactly what these archives looked like we do not know. The relatively small quantities of tablets from Mycenae, Tiryns and Chania make it difficult to discuss their archives. As for the fairly numerous Thebes tablets, their archaeological context is very much disturbed (Aravantinos et al. 2002: 8–15), which mostly precludes discussions about the organisation of the archive(s).

The only Linear B archive where a more precise method of storing tablets is known is the Archives Complex of Pylos, thanks to its placement on the ground floor. Here more than 1000 tablets were stored, probably on wooden shelves (Pluta 1996–1997: 240–241; for the meaning of the word 'archives' applied to Linear B administration see Olivier 1984: 15–18; Pluta 1996–1997: 240–241). The small size of the two archive-rooms and the construction of the shelves, possibly not fit for a heavy load, may have required strict removal of superfluous clay on tablets. However, until the corpus of Pylian tablets is published (with facsimile drawings and photographs), it is difficult to say if the storage method was in any way related to the practice of cutting the tablets; at this moment we cannot say what percentage of Pylian tablets was cut and what was the relationship between the amount of inscribed texts and cutting of the tablets.[1]

The transport of tablets within the palace may have also required removal of unused clay. It has been suggested that tablets were transported in wicker baskets on top of which clay labels were pressed. These labels had no string that would attach them to the baskets, but were simply pressed against them while the clay was still moist, so traces of wickerwork are visible on their backs. They had no seal-impression, but were incised (Wb series at Knossos: 35 examples, Wa series at Pylos: 19 examples). These labels labelled various sets of tablets as they were delivered to the archive, or as they were stored and filed (Blegen and Rawson 1966: 97; Chadwick 1958; Palaima 1988: 179; Palaima 1996: 380, n. 3; according to Palaima and Wright 1985: 260–261, labels were confined to transport only, and their small number in the Archives Complex suggests that they were probably not kept there for long after the baskets arrived; otherwise many more would have been found).

Rearranging the Information

This section takes us back to the RCT documents and already mentioned *simili*-joins. The practice of cutting the tablets is especially apparent in the RCT; here 124 tablets (nearly 20%) were cut, on their left or right side or even both sides. This group of documents consists of approximately 645 tablets (for a thorough study of these tablets see Driessen 2000). Only some 20 are page-shaped, and the rest are elongated. Nearly all tablets from the RCT that have been cut are elongated. Only a single page-shaped tablet from this deposit, KN Ap 5077, has traces of cutting (on the bottom). This tablet is a palimpsest. The text runs along its upper half, while the bottom half is not inscribed. Since the tablet is too large for the text that is preserved, it seems that it was cut after the tablet was inscribed for the first time (a similar explanation may, for example, be valid for cut KN Gm 840, not an RCT tablet, **Figure 3**).

Figure 3: Linear B tablet KN Gm 840, 10.70 × 11.10 cm (Chadwick et al. 1986: 333).

Elongated RCT tablets are typically cut on their right or left sides, immediately before the first sign or immediately after the last one, which suggests aiming to save on clay wherever possible. The RCT tablets generally give an impression of economy: the entire surface of the tablet is usually inscribed, without leaving any unused space, and when a tablet proved larger than needed, the unneeded parts seem to have been excised. The practice of cutting is especially frequent in the Vc and Sc series of the RCT tablets (lists of people and armour respectively), but also amongst scribes 115 and 141, who also worked in the south part of the West Wing of the Knossian palace (Driessen 1988: 135).

As mentioned above, another explanation has been proposed for the cutting of these RCT elongated tablets: the practice of dividing a set of information into separate records. This interpretation is suggested by some features of the Vc(1) set, in which the tablets consist of a personal name followed by the number one and a cut immediately after that (Chadwick 1968: 18). Driessen managed to join together a number of tablets of the Vc(1) series, and some of the tablets of the Xd series, proving that these small elongated tablets initially belonged to one larger tablet, and named them, as already said, *simili*-joins. *Simili*-joins are indicated by a plus sign inscribed in a circle in text editions.[2]

Apart from the actual cutting, another feature may be an indication of the practice of *simili*-joins. A certain number of elongated tablets from the RCT, of the Vc and Vd series, have vertical lines incised across them.[3] These lines are too long to be either word-dividers or numerals; they run practically from the top of a tablet to the bottom. It seems that their function was to divide certain sections of a tablet. The best example is Vd 7545+137 (**Figure 4**) where we can see three, possibly even four, such lines dividing the contents of the tablet into at least four sections (because the tablet is partly damaged, possible additional vertical lines are no longer visible). Perhaps vertical lines on this and other RCT tablets were incised to indicate where to cut them (Driessen 2000: 55). Evans (1935: 695) already entertained this possibility, suggesting that the purpose of these lines was to divide the tablet into six units but if so, the question is: why did they remain undivided? Although a significant number of such tablets were left undivided, I believe that it is correct to interpret incised vertical lines as indicators for cutting (note, however, that Duhoux [1999:

Figure 4: Linear B tablet KN Vd 7545+137, 15.6 × 3.35 cm (Chadwick et al. 1997: 252).

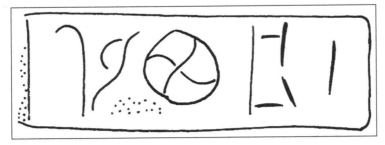

Figure 5: Linear B tablet KN Vc 64, 3.8 × 0.75 cm (Chadwick et al. 1986: 37).

228, n. 10] is not convinced about such an interpretation). Here is one example that supports this interpretation. On Vc 64 (**Figure 5**), a vertical line runs along the left edge of the tablet. We know that this tablet was cut at both ends, and has been identified as a *simili*-join. At least here we have evidence that the tablet was cut where indicated by an incised line.

As for the purpose of *simili*-joins, Driessen suggests that larger tablets were divided into smaller units for the purpose of rearranging the information: "…the men were booked for one reason, perhaps something they all had in common. This relationship was broken to create another one" (Driessen 1987: 161). I agree with Driessen on this matter, and here is a possible scenario of the purpose of such rearranging. The Vc series is composed of tablets with a personal name, often followed by the number one.[4] They may be individual records of people. Driessen has argued (1992: 202–203) that the Sc series represents the allocation of military equipment, the interpretation which is accepted by Oliver (1994: 54), whereas Vc tablets list individuals who were already equipped. As we have seen, some of these Vc tablets were initially parts of longer records that were divided into units — *simili*-joins. The initial record may have simply listed the names of people. By dividing this list into individual records, the information could have been rearranged as required, for example, according to the status of the people recorded, or according to their type of work (paid work or un-paid, slave work), or according to their particular duties, such as potters, textile workers, leather workers, etc. (a colleague once humorously reacted to this idea, describing my scenario as the earliest Excel system in Europe). Records of this type were probably written with the anticipation of a need to rearrange the data, meaning that the *simili*-joins may have been planned in advance. Hence the practice of marking tablets with vertical lines for cutting. These lines must have been incised when the tablet was still moist, i.e. either while inscribing the text, or not long afterwards.

Simili-joins are a feature almost unique to the RCT. We rarely find it anywhere else in Linear B and never in Linear A. The only other Linear B example, as detected by Olivier, is *simili*-joins B 7035 ⊕ B 808. The latter was found in the Long Corridor at Knossos, but the findspot of B 7035 is unknown (Driessen 1987: 161). *Simili*-joins from the RCT may be another reason for believing that this deposit is chronologically different from the rest of the Knossian documents. The practice of *simili*-joins may have been an early and experimental Linear B feature that ceased after the RCT period. A single later example (KN B 808 ⊕ B 7035) could be regarded as a short-lived legacy from the preceding RCT practice, which afterwards disappeared from the rest of the Linear B records, both on Crete and the Mainland. It must be noted, though, that lines possibly incised for the purpose of dividing a tablet have also been noticed at Mycenae. In this case, the lines are horizontal (e.g. at the bottom of the tablets MY Oe 117 and MY Oe 120, but are no longer easily visible since the tablets were snapped in two at this spot). Emmett Bennett noticed that these lines were incised more deeply than the ruling lines on these two tablets. He suggested that the purpose of these deeper incisions was precisely to facilitate the snapping of a tablet into two parts: "This would be equivalent to writing a line at the top of a sheet of paper and then folding it over and tearing off the top line" (Bennett 1958: 13).

Although the practice of incising lines for the purpose of dividing tablets is not recorded outside Linear B, there is a feature in Cretan Hieroglyphic that at least visually resembles it. Several Cretan Hieroglyphic tablets and bars are incised with vertical lines.[5] We saw that in the RCT these lines probably indicated where an elongated tablet was to be cut into separate, smaller tablets. The arrangement of vertical lines on Hieroglyphic documents, however, casts doubt on the idea that they had a similar purpose.

Most Cretan Hieroglyphic documents with vertical lines are inscribed on more than one side: four-sided bars are inscribed on all four sides, two-sided bars and one tablet are inscribed on both sides. RCT elongated tablets with vertical lines, on the other hand, are never inscribed on their *versos*. Moreover, vertical lines on Cretan Hieroglyphic documents rarely correspond in their position, so that if one were to cut the document following the vertical line on one side, the text would be severed on the other sides.

Some Cretan Hieroglyphic documents have two lines of text inscribed on one side and divided by a ruling line. The vertical lines on them are either not placed underneath each other, or appear in only one line and not in the other (for example, #063.a, #113.b, #120.a). It seems that in these cases the vertical lines are used to divide the information, i.e. separate entries into sections, rather than to divide the actual tablet.[6] Since in a few cases these vertical lines separate a sign-group from a number, they are used differently from the word-dividers known from Linear A and Linear B, which may separate sign-groups, logograms or transaction signs, but do not separate these categories of information from the following or preceding numbers. In Linear A it was usually the case that an entry ended with a number, and the next sign-group was therefore part of a new entry. This practice made it unnecessary to place a word divider between a number and the following sign-group in order to stress that they referred to separate entries, hence the small number of word-dividers in Linear A (Tomas 2003: chapter III, §5.7). However, it seems that Cretan Hieroglyphic needed to mark the separation of entries, and that vertical lines were employed for that purpose.

This brief study of the vertical lines on Hieroglyphic documents does not support a connection with the vertical lines on the RCT documents: the former appear to be used to separate entries, and the latter to guide the cutting of the tablet. That said, Olivier has noticed (1994–1995) that bars #057 and #058 (**Figures 6–7**) match nicely when placed against each other — they must have made up a single bar that was cut into two separate documents. Olivier consequently refers to them as 'simili-raccord', following Driessen's term (1987) '*simili*-joins'. Three sides of bar #057 have vertical lines. Although there is no line on the fourth side, Olivier argues that a line was initially there, but is no longer visible after the bar had been cut. Both parts have holes for suspension. Oliver claims that the two bars were inscribed by two different hands (1994–1995: 262), which was never the case with *simili*-joins in the RCT. All RCT *simili*-joins were inscribed by only two hands: 124r and 124s. Of these two, however, it was always the same hand that inscribed the matching *simili*-joins (Driessen 1987: 156–157, 162).

Let us now return to the topic of rearranging data on the RCT elongated tablets and examine another argument in favour of such an interpretation. Some of the RCT elongated tablets have a

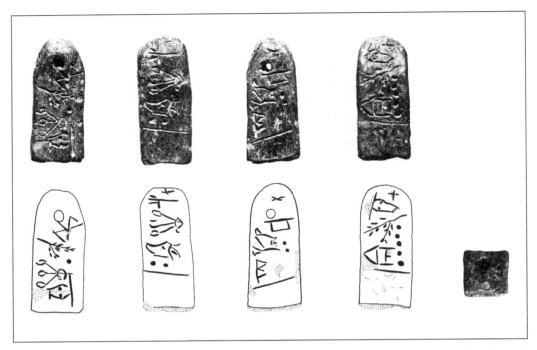

Figure 6: Cretan Hieroglyphic bar KN Hh (04) 02 / #057, 1.8 × 4.6 × 1.7 cm, circles on the first and third drawing are the holes for suspension (Olivier and Godart 1996: 110).

single sign inscribed on their *verso* (e.g. Xd 94+187, Vc173, Vc 177, Sc 7457, Xd 7813+7953, see **Figure 8**), or a single word, most commonly a complete or incomplete form of the ethnic *a-mi-ni-si-jo* (Sc 217, Sc 237, Sc 252, Sc 7476, Sc 7772, Sc 7782+8568, Sc 8471, see **Figure 9**). Since some of these tablets show traces of cutting, it is possible that the purpose of single signs / words on the *verso* was reclassification according to, say, the origin of the people registered: from *a-mi-ni-so* — the well-known site of Amnissos near Knossos (see Aura-Jorro 1985: 56). These tablets perhaps needed to be marked as different, since the other RCT elongated tablets seem to have dealt with only local business. Here follows the justification for the last statement.

Toponyms in the RCT records more commonly occur on page-shaped tablets. Out of 24 page-shaped tablets, 10 contain toponyms (42%). Out of 585 elongated tablets, only 23 contain toponyms (4%) (note that the shape of 36 RCT tablets cannot be determined due to their fragmentary state). Put in the context of the total of different words, 21% of the vocabulary from page-shaped tablets are toponyms, compared to only 6% in the case of elongated tablets (all counts are from Tomas 2003: chapters 2–3). One the one hand, this may indicate a difference in the function of the two types of documents in the RCT, namely that page-shaped tablets more often recorded transactions that involved the mention of toponyms, i.e. references to non-local business. Due to their low number of toponyms, on the other hand, it may be argued that the RCT elongated tablets were mainly involved in local transactions (cf. Bennet 1988: 21–22, n. 8, who pointed out that the majority of Linear B tablets do not contain place-names, in which case we assume that they refer to the storage of goods or activities conducted at the centre). If that is so, those elongated tablets with *a-mi-ni-si-jo* on their *verso* can be seen as an exception to this practice, and perhaps relate to individuals from *a-mi-ni-so*. This may be the reason why these tablets were differently marked, to distinguish them from the other elongated tablets that typically referred to transactions with individuals from Knossos. Driessen similarly uses two RCT examples of the ethnic *i-ja-wo-ne* (Xd

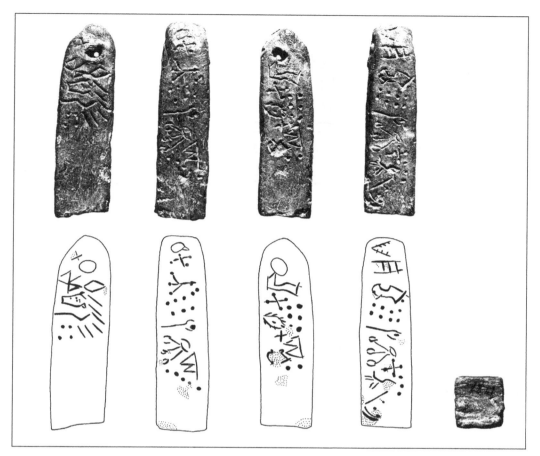

Figure 7: Cretan Hieroglyphic bar KN Hh (04) 03 / #058, 1.8 × 6.8 cm, circles on the first and third drawing are the holes for suspension (Olivier and Godart 1996: 111).

146.4, B 164.4) to argue that this group of people (Ionians) "must have been considered different from the groups the palace usually dealt with to deserve a specific ethnicon" (Driessen 1998–1999: 85).

If we accept that examples of *a-mi-ni-si-jo* on the *verso* mark out mentioned tablets as different from the rest, meaning that they may have dealt with non-local individuals, we can assume that these examples of *a-mi-ni-si-jo* were subsequently incised as classifying marks, according to which the elongated tablets may have been rearranged. Opisthographic tablets (i.e. those inscribed on both sides) are rare amongst the RCT elongated tablets — only 44 are opisthographic, 8%, (counts in Tomas 2003: chapter 3) — so inscribing *a-mi-ni-si-jo* on the *verso* was an exceptional epigraphic feature used to mark exceptional matters, that is, non-local transactions in the majority of tablets dealing with local ones.

It must be mentioned that *a-mi-ni-si-jo* is not the only ethnic mentioned on the RCT tablets. Altogether 10 ethnics have been recorded in the RCT: two on page-shaped tablets, and eight on elongated tablets (counts in Tomas 2003: chapter 2). Most occur elsewhere in Knossos, but *a-pu$_2$-ka* occurs only at Pylos apart from the RCT at Knossos. I am aware of the possibility that an ethnic can also refer to a place, like a toponym. In the RCT, however, it is also possible that ethnics denote people, i.e. an ethnic used instead of a personal name. This was already argued by Killen (1981:

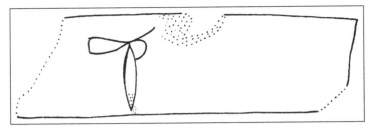

Figure 8: Linear B tablet KN Xd 7813+7953 *verso*, 5.9 × 1.85 cm (Chadwick et al. 1997: 299).

Figure 9: Linear B tablet KN Sc 237 *verso*, 7.3 × 2.35 cm (Chadwick et al. 1986: 103).

80): "…the use of ethnics as personal names is a widespread phenomenon on the tablets". In that sense it is significant that ethnics occur more frequently on elongated tablets since a great majority of them records personal names. They are here listed in the same way as other personal names, so they do not stand out as denoting different business. *A-mi-ni-si-jo* is the only ethnic marked on the *verso* of tablets.

Conclusion

It has been shown that the practice of cutting clay tablets, as far as present evidence tells us, was known to two of the total of three Aegean administrative systems. Cretan Hieroglyphic tablets, preserved in small numbers, do not show traces of cutting. Cretan Hieroglyphic bars, on the other hand, do have a single case of cutting. Inscribed vertical lines on such bars resemble similar lines which marked where the Linear B (RCT) elongated tablets should be cut, but it was concluded that the lines on Cretan Hieroglyphic documents did not have the same function.

Reasons behind Linear A cutting, especially in Haghia Triada, remain unclear, since cut tablets are too spacious for the inscribed text, so getting rid of superfluous parts of tablets is not a valid explanation.

In Linear B, at least in Knossos, cutting was practised on both types of tablets, the difference being that page-shaped tablets are less frequently cut than elongated tablets. In both cases, two alternative procedures of cutting are possible: 1) that a scribe had no clear preconception of the amount of the text for the particular tablet, so the tablet was cut after having been inscribed in order to remove the residue of clay with no text; 2) that even before writing, a scribe had a clear idea of the amount of the text, so that the tablet, if made too large, was cut even before it was inscribed. For the purpose of this study it does not particularly matter in which order this was done; we will probably never be able to reconstruct the order. For now it is more important to establish that page-shaped tablets were probably cut in order to remove unnecessary clay, whereas elongated tablets may also have been cut for the purpose of rearranging the information.

In connection to all this, I conclude with three points that remain unclear and therefore present areas for further research for the question of writing as material practice. The first point is that although Linear B had much firmer pinacological and epigraphical rules than Linear A (Tomas 2012), some uncut page-shaped tablets are too large for their text (for example, KN E 749+5532 or KN C 911), meaning that they were for some reason left uncut, even though the practice of cutting was familiar to Linear B scribes. We do not know why this is so.

Secondly, if we accept that Linear B tablets were cut to accommodate shorter texts, why are some *cut* tablets still too large for the text inscribed (for example, TH Av 104[+])191)? Cases like this are not plentiful, but they do recall similar cases of Linear A cut tablets from Haghia Triada, as previously discussed.

The final point may simply be a coincidence resulting from the poor state of preservation of Linear B tablets, but it is very interesting to note that in Knossos the left or the right side of many fully preserved elongated tablets has been produced by cutting (e.g. KN Fp 5, KN V 56 from other Knossian deposits, or KN Sc 103+5069+5145 and numerous examples from the RCT). Only a few fully preserved elongated tablets from Knossos have uncut edges! It is usually assumed that the Linear B flatteners formed smaller individual elongated tablets for an already targeted textual record, but this cutting evidence begs the question of whether this was really the case at Knossos. It is more likely that the flatteners would typically produce one long elongated tablet with no particular text in mind, and such a tablet was then written and cut into separate records as the information was forthcoming. Once the corpus is published, it will be interesting to see whether the Pylian elongated tablets support this suggestion and what other evidence may emerge to further clarify our understanding of these documents in relation to material practice.

Notes

1. Although in the National Archaeological Museum at Athens I had the opportunity to examine some Pylian tablets that appear to be cut deliberately (I thank Dr Lena Papazoglou-Manioudaki for granting me permission to examine the tablets), an understanding of the overall practice of cutting the Pylian tablets can be achieved only once this corpus is published.
2. Such tablets are: Vc(1) 64 ⊕ Xd 170 ⊕ Vc(1) 7540; Vc(1) 81 ⊕ Vc(1) 199; Vc(1) 108 ⊕ Vc(1) 184; Vc(1) 125 ⊕ Vc(1) 312; Xd 179 ⊕ Xd 191; Xd 216 ⊕ Xd 287; Xd 123 ⊕ Vc(1) 108 ⊕ Vc(1) 184; Vc(1) 181 ⊕ Xd 7838; Xd 7933 ⊕ I/3-28 (Driessen 1987: 156–157, 162, pls I–III).
3. These tablets are: Vd 62, Vc 64, Vd 136, Vd 137, Vd 138, Vd 7545 + 137 and possibly Vc 7529.
4. Vc 216 is a very interesting tablet from this point of view. It has an incomplete word since it is broken in the middle of the fourth sign. On the left edge the number one precedes the word. It has been suggested that this tablet was cut at the wrong place and that the number actually referred to the word inscribed before the preserved one (Chadwick 1968: 18).
5. Tablets: #120 (inscribed on both sides, but with a line on only one side); four-sided bars: #050 (a line on only one side), #057 (lines on three sides), #059 (two parallel lines on one side), #061 (on all four sides), #063 (on two sides), #095 (two pairs of two parallel lines on one side), #111 (still visible on one side, the rest of the document is badly damaged), #112 (on three sides), #113 (on three sides), #116 (on one side); two-sided bars: #089 (on both sides), #092 (on one side), #109 (on one side), and one line on the two-sided bar from Kato Syme. The numbering of the inscriptions follows the classification in Olivier and Godart 1996. For the Kato Syme document, not included in the corpus, see Lebessi et al. 1995.
6. Vertical lines are present on some Hieroglyphic seals as well, where they divide syllabic signs or sign-groups, for example #283.α, #297.δ and #298.δ (Olivier 1995: 176).

References

Andreadaki-Vlasaki, M. and Hallager, E. 2007. New and Unpublished Linear A and Linear B Inscriptions from Khania. *Proceedings of the Danish Institute at Athens* 5: 7–22.

Aravantinos, V. L., Godart, L. and Sacconi, A. 2002. *Thèbes: Fouilles de la Cadmée III. Corpus des documents d'archives en linéaire B de Thèbes (1–433)*. Pisa and Rome: Pasiphae.

Aravantinos, V. L., Godart, L. and Sacconi, A. 2008. La tavoletta TH Uq 434. In Sacconi, A., del Freo, M., Godart, L. and Negri, M. (eds), *Colloquium Romanum: Atti del XII Colloquio Internazionale de Micenologia. Roma, 20–25 febbraio 2006*. Pisa and Rome: Pasiphae, 23–33.

Aura-Jorro, F. 1985. *Diccionario Micénico*, Volume 1. Madrid: Instituto de Filología.

Begg, I. D. J. 1987. Continuity in the West Wing at Knossos. In Hägg, R. and Marinatos, N. (eds), *The Function of the Minoan Palaces: Proceedings of the Fourth International Symposium at the Swedish Institute in Athens, 10–16 June 1984*. Stockholm: Svenska Institutet i Athen, 179–184.

Bennet, J. 1988. 'Outside in the Distance': Problems in understanding the economic geography of Mycenaean palatial territories. In Olivier, J.-P. and Palaima, T. G. (eds), *Texts, Tablets and Scribes: Studies in Mycenaean epigraphy and economy offered to Emmett L. Bennett, Jr.* (Minos Supplement 10). Salamanca: Ediciones universidad de Salamanca, 19–41.

Bennett, E. L. 1958. *The Mycenae Tablets II* (Transactions of the American Philosophical Society 48/1). Philadelphia: The American Philosophical Society.

Blegen, C. W. and Rawson, M. 1966. *The Palace of Nestor at Pylos in Western Messenia*, Volume 1. Princeton: Princeton University Press.

Chadwick, J. 1958. The Mycenaean Filing System. *Bulletin of the Institute of Classical Studies* 5(1): 1–5. DOI: http://dx.doi.org/10.1111/j.2041-5370.1958.tb00606.x

Chadwick, J. 1968. The Organization of the Mycenaean Archives. In Bartoněk, A. (ed.), *Studia Mycenaea: Proceedings of the Mycenaean Symposium, Brno, April 1966*. Brno: Universita J. E. Purkyně, 11–21.

Chadwick, J., Godart, L., Killen, J. T., Olivier, J.-P., Sacconi, A. and Sakellarakis, Y. A. 1986 (I), 1990 (II), 1997 (III), 1998 (IV). *Corpus of Mycenaean Inscriptions from Knossos* (Incunabula Graeca 88). Cambridge and Rome: Cambridge University Press – Edizioni dell'Ateneo.

Chapouthier, F. 1930. *Les écritures minoennes au palais de Mallia* (Études Crétoises 2). Paris: Geuthner.

del Freo, M. 2007. Rapport 2001–2005 sur les textes en écriture hiéroglyphique crétoise, en linéaire A et en linéaire B. In Sacconi A., del Freo, M., Godart, L. and Negri, M. (eds), *Colloquium Romanum: Atti del XII Colloquio Internazionale de Micenologia. Roma, 20–25 febbraio 2006*. Pisa and Rome: Pasiphae, 199–222.

Driessen, J. 1987. Observations on 'Simili-joins' in the Room of the Chariot Tablets at Knossos. In Killen, T., Melena J. L. and Olivier, J.-P. (eds), *Studies in Mycenaean and Classical Greek Presented to John Chadwick* (*Minos* 20–22). Salamanca: Universidad de Salamanca, 151–162.

Driessen, J. 1988. The Scribes of 'The Room of the Chariot Tablet'. In Olivier, J.-P. and Palaima, T. G. (eds), *Texts, Tablets and Scribes: Studies in Mycenaean epigraphy and economy offered to Emmett L. Bennett, Jr.* (Minos Supplement 10). Salamanca: Universidad de Salamanca, 123–165.

Driessen, J. 1990. *An Early Destruction in the Mycenaean Palace at Knossos: A new interpretation of the excavation field-notes of the South-East area of the west wing* (Acta Archaeologica Lovaniensia – Monographiae 2). Leuven: Katholieke Universiteit Leuven.

Driessen, J. 1992. Collector's Items: Observations sur l'élite mycénienne de Cnossos. In Olivier, J.-P. (ed.), *Mykenaïka. Actes du IXᵉ Colloque international sur les textes mycéniens et égéens organisé par le Centre de l'Antiquité Grecque et Romaine de la Fondation Hellénique des Recherches*

Scientifiques et l'École française d'Athènes, Athènes, 2–6 Octobre 1990 (Supplement to *Bulletin de Correspondance Hellénique*, no. 25). Paris: de Boccard, 197–214.

Driessen, J. 1998–1999. *Kretes* and *Iawones*: Some observations on the identity of Late Bronze Age Knossians. In Bennet, J. and Driessen, J. (eds), *A-na-qo-ta. Studies Presented to J. T. Killen* (*Minos* 33–34). Salamanca: Universidad de Salamanca, 83–105.

Driessen, J. 1999. The Northern Entrance Passage at Knossos: Some preliminary observations on its potential role as 'Central Archive'. In Deger-Jalkotzy, S., Hiller, S. and Panagl, O. (eds), *Floreant Studia Mycenaea: Akten des X. Internationalen Mykenologischen Colloquiums in Salzburg vom 1.–5. Mai 1995*. Vienna: Österreichischen Akademie der Wissenschaften, 205–226.

Driessen, J. 2000. *The Scribes of the Room of the Chariot Tablets at Knossos: Interdisciplinary approach to the study of a Linear B deposit* (Minos Supplement 15). Salamanca: Universidad de Salamanca.

Driessen, J. 2008. Chronology of the Linear B Texts. In Duhoux, Y. and Morpurgo Davies, A. (eds), *A Companion to Linear B: Mycenaean Greek texts and their world*. Louvain-la-Neuve: Peeters, 69–79.

Driessen, J. and Schoep, I. 1999. The Stylus and the Sword: The role of scribes and warriors in the conquest of Crete. In Laffineur, R. (ed.), *Polemos: Le Contexte Guerrier en Égée à l'Âge du Bronze. Actes de la 7e Recontre égéene internationale, Université de Liège, 14–17 Avril 1998* (Aegaeum 19). Liège and Austin: Université de Liège and University of Texas at Austin, 389–401.

Duhoux, Y. 1978. Une analyse linguistique du linéaire A. In Duhoux, Y. (ed.), *Études Minoennes, I. Le linéaire A*. Louvain: Institut de Linguistique de Louvain, 65–129.

Duhoux, Y. 1999. La séparation des mots en linéaire B. In Deger-Jalkotzy, S., Hiller, S. and Panagl, O. (eds), *Floreant Studia Mycenaea, Akten des X. Internationalen Mykenologischen Colloquiums in Salzburg vom 1.–5. Mai 1995*. Vienna: Österreichische Akademie der Wissenschaften, 227–236.

Evans, A. 1935. *The Palace of Minos at Knossos*, Volume 4. London: Macmillan.

Firth, R. 2012. Re-visiting the Tablet-makers of Knossos. In Kyriakidis, E. (ed.), *Proceedings of the International Colloquium "The Inner Workings of Mycenaean Bureaucracy", University of Kent, Canterbury, 19–21 September 2008* (Pasiphae, Rivista di filologia e antichità egee V). Rome and Pisa: Fabrizio Serra Editore, 81–94.

Godart, L. 1988. Autour des textes en linéaire B de Tirynthe: Ausgrabungen in Tiryns 1982/83. *Archäologischer Anzeiger* 1988: 245–251.

Godart, L. 1999. L'écriture d'Arkhanès: hiéroglyphique ou linéaire A? In Betancourt, P. P., Karageorghis, V., Laffineur, R. and Niemeier, W.-D. (eds), *Meletemata: Studies in Aegean archaeology presented to Malcolm H. Wiener as he enters his 65th year* (Aegaeum 20). Liège and Austin: Université de Liège and University of Texas at Austin, 299–302.

Godart, L. and Olivier, J.-P. 1976 (I), 1979 (II), 1976 (III), 1982 (IV), 1985 (V). *Recueil des inscriptions en linéaire A*. Paris: École française d'Athènes.

Godart, L. and Tzedakis, Y. 1992. *Témoignages archéologiques et épigraphiques en Crète occidentale du Néolithique au Minoen récent III B* (Incunabula Graeca 93). Rome: Istituto per gli Studi Micenei ed Egeo-Anatolici.

Grumach, E. and Sakellarakis, Y. 1966. Die neuen Hieroglyphensiegel vom Phourni (Archanes) I. *Kadmos* 5(2): 109–114. DOI: http://dx.doi.org/10.1515/kadm.1966.5.2.109

Halbherr, F., Stefani, E. and Banti, L. 1977. Haghia Triada nel periodo tardo palaziale. *Annuario della Scuola Archeologica di Atene* 55: 9–296.

Hallager, E. and Vlasaki, M. 1997. New Linear B Tablets from Khania. In Driessen, J. and Farnoux, A. (eds), *La Crète mycénienne* (Supplement to *Bulletin de Correspondance Hellénique*, no. 30). Athens: Centre national de la Recherche scientifique, 169–174.

Killen, J. T. 1981. Mycenaean Possessive Adjectives in -e-jo. *Transactions of the Philological Society* 1981: 66–99.

Lebessi, A., Muhly, P. and Olivier, J.-P. 1995. An Inscription in the Hieroglyphic Script from the Syme Sanctuary, Crete (SY Hf 01). *Kadmos* 34(1): 63–77. DOI: http://dx.doi.org/10.1515/kadm.1995.34.1.63

Melena, J. and Olivier, J.-P. 1991. *Tithemy: The tablets and nodules in Linear B from Tiryns, Thebes and Mycenae* (Minos Supplement 12). Salamanca: Universidad de Salamanca.

Olivier, J.-P. 1984. Administrations at Knossos and Pylos: What differences. In Shelmerdine, C. W. and Palaima, T. G., *Pylos Comes Alive: Industry + administration in a Mycenaean palace*. New York: Fordham University, 11–18.

Olivier, J.-P. 1987. Structure des archives palatiales en linéaire A et en linéaire B. In Lévy, E. (ed.), *Le système palatial en Orient, en Grèce et à Rome. Actes du Colloque de Strasbourg 19–22 juin 1985*. Leiden: Université des sciences humaines de Strasbourg, 227–235.

Olivier, J.-P. 1994. L'économie des royaumes mycéniens d'après les tablettes en linéaire B. *Les Dossiers d'Archéologie* 195: 50–65.

Olivier, J.-P. 1994–1995. Un *simili*-raccord dans les barres en hiéroglyphique de Knossos (*CHIC* #057 ⊕ #058). *Minos* 29–30: 257–269.

Olivier, J.-P. 1995. Les sceaux avec des signes hiéroglyphiques: Que lire? Une question de bon sens. In Müller, W. (ed.), *Sceaux minoens and mycéniens, IVe symposium international 10–12 Septembre 1992, Clermont-Ferrand* (Corpus der Minoischen und Mykenischen Siegel, Beiheft 5). Mainz: Akademie der Wissenschaften und der Literatur, 169–181.

Olivier, J.-P. and Godart, L. 1996. *Corpus Hieroglyphicarum Inscriptionum Cretae* (Études Crétoises 31). Paris: École française d'Athènes and École française de Rome.

Palaima, T. G. 1983. Evidence for the Influence of the Knossian Graphic Tradition at Pylos. *Concilium Eirene* 16: 80–84.

Palaima, T. G. 1985. Appendix. In Åström, P. and Sjöquist, K.-E. *Pylos: Palmprints and palmleaves* (Studies in Mediterranean Archaeology, Pocket Book, no. 31). Göteburg: Paul Åströms Förlag, 99–107.

Palaima, T. G. 1988. *The Scribes of Pylos* (Incunabula Graeca 87). Rome: Edizioni Dell'Ateneo.

Palaima, T. G. 1996. 'Contiguities' in the Linear B Tablets from Pylos. In de Miro, E., Godart, L. and Sacconi, A. (eds), *Atti e Memorie del Secondo Congresso Internazionale di Micenologia* (Incunabula Graeca 98). Rome: Istituto per gli studi micenei, 379–396.

Palaima, T. G. and Wright, J. C. 1985. Ins and Outs of the Archives Rooms at Pylos: Form and function in a Mycenaean Palace. *American Journal of Archaeology* 89: 251–262. DOI: http://dx.doi.org/10.2307/504328

Pluta, K. M. 1996–1997. A Reconstruction of the Archives Complex at Pylos: A preliminary report. *Minos* 31–32: 231–250.

Pugliese Carratelli, G. 1958. Nuove epigrafi minoiche di Festo. *Annuario della Scuola Archeologica di Atene* 35–36: 363–388.

Sacconi, A. 1974. *Corpus delle iscrizioni vascolari in lineare B* (Incunabula Graeca 58). Rome: Edizioni dell'Ateneo.

Sakellarakis, Y. and Sapouna-Sakellaraki, E. 1997. *Archanes: Minoan Crete in a new light*. Athens: Ammos Publications.

Schoep, I. 1998–1999. Minoan Administration at Haghia Triada: A multi-disciplinary comparison of the Linear A tablets from the Villa and the Casa del Lebete. In Bennet, J. and Driessen, J. (eds), *A-na-qo-ta: Studies presented to J. T. Killen* (Minos 33–34). Salamanca: Universidad de Salamanca, 273–294.

Schoep, I. 2001. Some Notes on the 'Hieroglyphic' Deposit from Knossos. *Studi Micenei ed Egeo-Anatolici* 43(1): 143–158.

Schoep, I. 2002. *The Administration of Neopalatial Crete: A critical assessment of the Linear A tablets and their role in the administrative process* (Minos Supplement 17). Salamanca: Universidad de Salamanca.

Schoep, I. 2007. The Inscribed Document. In Macdonald, C. F. and Knappett, C. (eds), *Knossos: Protopalatial deposits in early magazine A and the south-west houses* (British School of Athens Supplementary Volume 41). London: British School of Archaeology at Athens, 131–134.

Shelmerdine, C. W. and Bennet, J. 2008. Mycenaean States: Economy and administration. In Shelmerdine, C. W. (ed.), *The Cambridge Companion to the Aegean Bronze Age*. Cambridge: Cambridge University Press, 289–309. DOI: http://dx.doi.org/10.1017/CCOL9780521814447.013

Shelton, K. 2002–2003. A New Linear B Tablet from Petsas House, Mycenae. *Minos* 37–38: 387–396.

Sjöquist, K.-E. and Åström, P. 1991. *Knossos: Keepers and kneaders* (Studies in Mediterranean Archaeology, Pocket book, no. 82). Gothenburg: Paul Åströms Förlag.

Tomas, H. 2003. *Understanding the Transition between Linear A and Linear B Scripts*. Unpublished D.Phil. dissertation, University of Oxford.

Tomas, H. 2010. Cretan Hieroglyphic and Linear A. In Cline, E. H. (ed.), *The Oxford Handbook of the Bronze Age Aegean*. Oxford: Oxford University Press, 340–355.

Tomas, H. 2011. Linear A tablet ≠ Linear B tablet. In Andreadaki-Vlazaki, M. and Papadopoulou, E. (eds), *Pepragmena tou I' Diethnous Kritologikou Synedriou / Proceedings of the 10th Cretological Conference, Hania, 1–8 October 2006, Volume A1*. Chania: Filologikos Syllogos "O Hrysostomos", 331–343.

Tomas, H. 2012. Linear A Scribes and Their Writing Styles. In Kyriakidis, E. (ed.), *Proceedings of the International Colloquium "The Inner Workings of Mycenaean Bureaucracy", University of Kent, Canterbury, 19–21 September 2008* (Pasiphae, Rivista di filologia e antichità egee V). Rome and Pisa: Fabrizio Serra Editore, 35–58.

Warren, P. and Hankey, V. 1989. *Aegean Bronze Age Chronology*. Bristol: Bristol Classical Press.

Younger, J. G. and Rehak, P. 2008. Minoan Culture: Religion, burial customs, and administration. In Shelmerdine, C. W. (ed.), *The Cambridge Companion to the Aegean Bronze Age*. Cambridge: Cambridge University Press, 165–185. http://dx.doi.org/10.1017/CCOL9780521814447.008

Straight, Crooked and Joined-up Writing: An early Mediterranean view

Alan Johnston

University College London

Background

In this chapter my intention is to consider the extent to which writing surfaces, rather than other considerations, may be seen to have influenced the appearance of text in the early centuries of alphabetic writing in the Mediterranean world, with special emphasis on Greek-speaking and -writing areas, thus addressing the question of materiality that is the focus of this volume. My title may suggest a teleological approach — we use, or should I say used to use, joined-up writing, and therefore how did people in the 7th to 4th centuries BC square up to this inevitability? But the very fact that I feel obliged to say "used to use" demonstrates a procedural weakness of that approach. Yet it is patently obvious that by the time of the destruction of Pompeii there was widespread popular use of 'literary', hasty writing, and it is of interest to see in what ways this development was generated, and especially where its roots lie.

Here there arises a basic modern division between scholars, which revolves around the use of the word 'cursive'; it is as good a starting point as any. Papyrologists and palaeographers reserve the word for a complete system of writing in which the straight line is largely replaced by the flowing curve; epigraphists on the other hand are happy to use the word for individual letter forms — 'this inscription has cursive tendencies', be it the nearly, but never completely, joined-up, 'scrawl' of imperial Latin, or the occasional letter form which adopts a rounded not angular shape.

The variation of use of the term is easy enough to comprehend and take into proper account, but should be kept in mind (for a thorough review of the mechanics and effect of such writing in the Roman period, see Parkes 2008).

'Joined-up' writing in fact need not bother us much. I merely note that the only form of truly joined writing which appears in the period concerned is the ligature, which is a constant enough

How to cite this book chapter:

Johnston, A. 2013. Straight, Crooked and Joined-up Writing: An early Mediterranean view. In: Piquette, K. E. and Whitehouse, R. D. (eds.) *Writing as Material Practice: Substance, surface and medium.* Pp. 193-212. London: Ubiquity Press. DOI: http://dx.doi.org/10.5334/bai.j

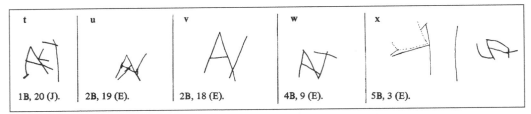

t	u	v	w	x
1B, 20 (J).	2B, 19 (E).	2B, 18 (E).	4B, 9 (E).	5B, 3 (E).

Figure 1: Ligatures among underfoot graffiti on Attic vases (after Johnston 1980: fig. 3).

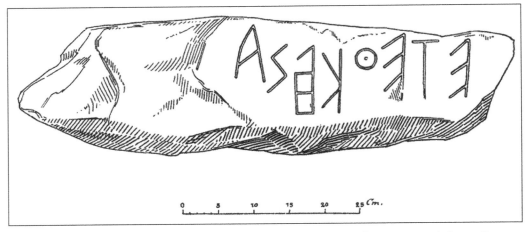

Figure 2: Ligature within a word, stone tomb-marker on Thera, 7th century BC (after Hiller von Gaertringen 1898: no. 781).

feature of very largely non-cursive, in whatever sense, writing from around 550 BC onwards (see **Figure 1**, on Attic vase bases). It starts, and in most cases continues, as a personal, occasionally corporate, identificatory symbol, a continuation of one of the most prominent early uses of the alphabet, and before that of non-alphabetic signs, to mark personal property. Some regional preferences are apparent here, especially on the island of Thera (**Figure 2**), where two letters *within* words can be so linked (Inglese 2008: 56–57); we will have cause to consider regionality of writing practices consistently, a factor to be set beside any more generalised aspects of writing technique.

Papyrus and its Echoes in the Classical Period

These are not well-trodden paths — and when we push through the undergrowth we will see why. I begin with a text from near the end of the period under consideration, an unique post-firing graffito cut on the floor of an Athenian black-painted shallow bowl of *c*.350 BC from the Kerameikos excavations, though without a precise find location (**Figure 3**). It is perhaps the longest such graffito text known, apart from a set of modern forgeries, interesting in themselves (Corbett and Woodhead 1955), and certainly unique in other respects. I abbreviate the arguments I proposed (Johnston 1985: especially 297) that this is a record of some kind of reckoning of a month's work by a group of slaves or metics during a year, the name of whose archon is unfortunately only partly preserved in the first line. I refuse to believe this is a one-off, yet it has no substantial parallel in the very considerable corpus of Athenian inscriptions on stone of the period; therefore it is probably an occasional notation of what otherwise would have been committed in ink to an organic surface,

Figure 3: Graffito under the foot of a plate, from the Kerameikos, Athens (Johnston 1985: pl. 58). Kerameikos Museum 2242.

whether wood or papyrus. Yet there is minimal reflection of the use of the brush or pen — i.e. the cursive letter — here, just one apparent simplified *sigma*. It would be useful to set beside it the only papyrus record which I know from Athens of roughly contemporary date (probably a generation or two earlier). Regrettably however it is a blank; what was soon after its discovery described to me (Nikolaos Yalouris pers. comm.) as a "pudding" does not seem to have survived in any legible way. Some tiny uninscribed scraps are on display in the Peiraeus Archaeological Museum; yet I have the word of the workman who excavated the tomb that the lettering that was visible on the document look like "this" (pointing to the smaller texts on the back of a common or garden cigarette packet), i.e. what in modern Greek or Roman script we call small capitals.[1]

This is not the only evidence one can bring to bear, but it is *direct* evidence of what we can glean from other secondary sources to be the norm for the written texts of all the great classical authors' 'first folios'. I mention here in particular the book-rolls appearing in scenes painted on 5th-century red-figure vases (**Figure 4**), sometimes with legible texts (Avronidaki 2008: 17–18; Immerwahr 1990: 99), and then the description of lettering given in a play by Euripides, as preserved in a quotation in Athenaeus' *Deipnosophistae* (book x, 454b–d): a *sigma* is likened to the composite Scythian bow. Athenaeus goes on to cite a passage from the later poet Aischrion, perhaps of *c*.350–325, where the words used to describe the same letter *sigma* change from the angled composite bow to the plain arc (Bergk 1878–1882: ii 516, fragment 1; Lloyd-Jones and Parsons 1983, under the heading "Aischrion").

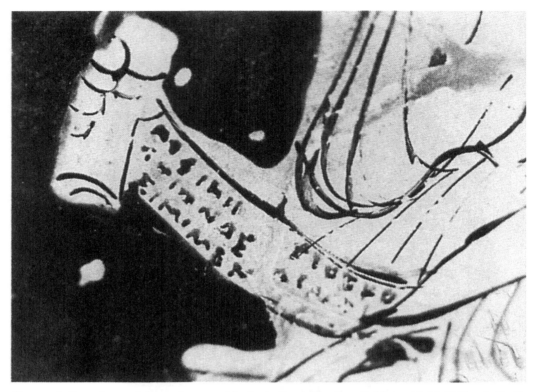

Figure 4: Boeotian red-figured vase with depiction of book-roll (Avronidaki 2008: pl. 7, 4). Whereabouts unknown.

This is precisely the general change that we see in our earliest preserved papyrus text, but it appears a little later, since in the earliest such texts, datable to around 350–325 BC the crooked 'Scythian bow' is written (e.g. Johnston 1997: 108, fig. 18, published more fully by Turner 1975; **Figure 5**)[2], and only towards the end of the century does the simple rounded arc begin to predominate, together with other slight signs of literary cursivity — that is to say, in Greek texts. The nearest, perhaps only, parallel in the non-Greek world is the Zagreb mummy (**Figure 6**) with its extensive Etruscan text (most recently van der Meer 2007). While the date is disputed, probably of the mid-Hellenistic period, we see here little sign of the trends towards cursive writing visible in the Greek record.

Earlier Forays

Here we have an awkward chronological clash regarding the subject of cursivity between the literary references and preserved texts, involving the period *c.*350 to 300 BC. There are though some even earlier, if sporadic, stirrings. One learns a lot from writers who have made, or think they have made 'errors' — and this is not the place to enter on the thorny question of defining orthography; there is room for a doctoral thesis on the topic if only any classical archaeologist-cum-epigrapher would take on such a banal task. First, I repeat a point I have made regarding a much earlier text (Johnston and Jones 1978: 104–105), on an Athenian or Attic amphora of 625–600 BC on display in the British Museum (**Figure 7**) — where the cutter of an owner's graffito started incising, correctly, an *omicron*, but finished it off as a *sigma*, which should in fact have been the following letter;

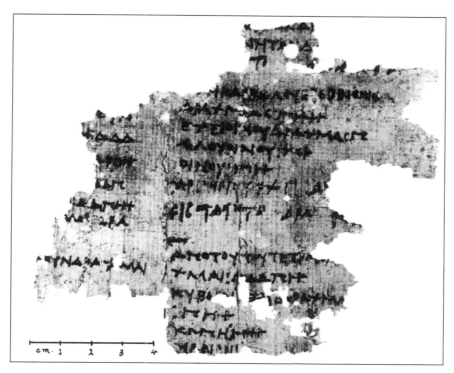

Figure 5: Papyrus from Saqqara, Egypt, excavation no. Sak 71/2 GP9, no. 5676 (after Johnston 1997: fig. 18). Photograph courtesy of the Egypt Exploration Society.

Figure 6: Detail of Etruscan mummy binding with part of the painted text (van der Meer 2007: 201). Zagreb Museum.

Figure 7: Graffiti on shoulder of Attic oil jar, from Vulci (Johnston and Jones 1978: fig. 1). British Museum GR 1848.0619.9.

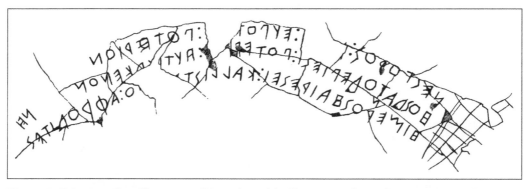

Figure 8: Drawing of graffito text on 'Nestor's cup' (Jeffery 1990: pl. 47, 1). Lacco Ameno Museum, Ischia.

he confused himself, but only because he could mistake a rounded arc as the top of a *sigma*. One could have wished for some such happenstance in the earliest long text from the Mediterranean Iron Age, the much discussed ceramic 'Nestor's cup' from Pithekoussai of *c.*720 BC (Jeffery 1990: pl. 47, 1; **Figure 8**); but it does not quite happen — an *omicron* in the first line is corrected to an *epsilon* in a somewhat ugly manner, and in the second line an omitted *nu* is rather more deftly inserted just below its proper place and an *epsilon* was half cut before the inscriber realised the letter should be *alpha*; but at least it all demonstrates a concern for what was perceived as accuracy.

Here we are getting back to near the origins of Greek alphabetic writing; for whatever reason and at whatever precise period around 900–800 BC, some Greek-speakers geometricised the Semitic alphabet, fitting the somewhat casual angles of the Semitic signs to the visual human-made representations on artefacts prevailing in the contemporary Greek world — patterns involving straight lines, regularly at 90° or 45°, and circles — the Geometric *style*. Where that particular style was weakest, on Crete, where far more luxuriant and inventive pictorial designs were common enough, we find the weakest such adaptations of the Semitic letter forms. For example, Crete is one of the areas that retains some of the complexity of the Semitic *yod* in its *iota* — unlike

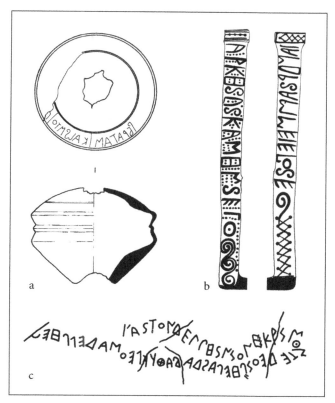

Figure 9: a) Graffito on jug, from Knossos (Johnston 1996: fig. 107, 84); b) House model, door jambs, with painted texts (Jeffery 1990: pl. 79, 4–5). Thera Museum; c) Rock-cut text, from Thera (Jeffery 1990: pl. 91, 1a).

the majority of the rest who boldly adopt a simple vertical stroke. Such a curly *iota* is found in a 7th-century graffito on a pot from Knossos (Johnston 1996), for example. In contrast, on the island of Thera, which is clearly dependent on Crete for its alphabet, the *iota* appears not only in painted texts — most strikingly a 'doll's-house' (Jeffery 1990: 470, A and pl. 79) and the unpublished example of the deceased's name painted on the foot of a similar Athenian oil amphora used as a grave marker, both *c.*600 BC. It is also important to note examples occuring in rock-cut graffiti. Occasionally on these we find the same letters made of either curving or straight strokes, or indeed single letters employing both, in the same text (e.g. Inglese 2008: 469, 473; **Figure 9**).

This form of mixed usage continues. Curving lines are cut on stone, and on pots, straight lines are used in painted texts, with little particular pattern of usage that I can observe. The overall framework, however, always remains the geometricised set of signs of the period of origin, as noted at the beginning of the previous paragraph.

Surfaces

We should also recognise that writing is deployed on a vast range of preserved materials, with no exceptions known to me, except obsidian and amber; even one lead architectural clamp from the Agora excavations has a text, albeit very difficult to read, cut on it (David Jordan pers. comm.). The full extent of painted texts will never be known to us; it would be a nice pipe-dream to think

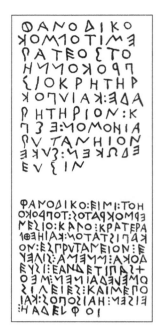

Figure 10: Marble stele of Phanodikos, from Sigeion (Jeffery 1990: pl. 71, 43–44). British Museum GR 1816.0610.107.

that in, say, 2030, somebody will write "people made the claim only two decades ago that we would never read such texts". In the British Museum is a remarkable early marble monument, of *c.*600 BC (**Figure 10**), where both angular and curvy *sigmas* are still discernible — Phanodikos' stele, an epigraphic colossus to place beside contemporary sculptural *tours de force* up to four times life size (Jeffery 1990: 371, no. 43, pl. 71). It was removed by Elgin from near the site of ancient Sigeion in the Troad. The cutting on it of a similar text in two different Greek dialects and scripts, Attic and Ionic, says much about the independence of the small Greek states of the period and their local pride, but also something about locally-driven writing habits. Ann Jeffery noted that in the area of Ionia there is much scruffy looking writing on stone dated to the 6th century, and she wondered whether this may have been the result of the reported flowering here of many branches of written literature, presumably produced in ink, at this time (Jeffery 1990: 57). It is certainly a tendency far different from that of Athens later, in the 5th century, where we see a new 'aesthetic', I use the word deliberately, of formally patterned chessboards of letters. Ironically, however, that *stoichedon* system may have been initiated in Ionia, an early example being the scruffy lettering, but also patterned, text on the side of the throne dedicated on Samos by Aiakes (**Figure 11**), a piece, whether sculpture or text, of much disputed date — 540 or 500? BC — (see Immerwahr 1990: 96–97 for an assessment, even if he tends towards an Athenian origin for the system).

Unfortunately we have little substantial evidence to support Jeffery's suggestion; while we can now point to an expanding series of personal letters written mostly on lead from the broad Ionian world, which are of high interest in other respects — especially for the fact that financial problems seem to be the sole topic of epistolary intercourse — they add little regarding the written word. The grammar sometimes fails to reach A-level standards but that again is by the way. More useful is the reference in one such text (**Figure 12**) to documents written on skins (see Avram 2007: 239 for general bibliography; *diphtheria* are mentioned in the text from Olbia, Dana 2007: 75–76, with n. 16).

A recent suggestion that this part of the world did see wide use of cursive writing in the period under consideration has been put forward by Adiego (1998: especially 57–79; 2007: 230–233),

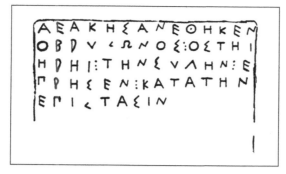

Figure 11: Engraved dedication of Aiakes, found on a marble seated figure (Jeffery 1990: pl. 63, 13). Samos Museum.

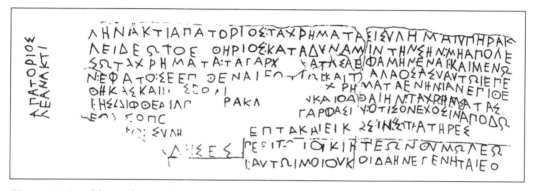

Figure 12: Lead letter from Olbia, Black Sea (Dana 2007: 75). Whereabouts unknown.

who finds the oddities of letter shapes in Carian texts best explained by positing that the forms we have in inscriptions from the later 7th century onward are petrifications of unattested cursive forms used in the area in an earlier period. Much as one would like to see a rational explanation of the Carian alphabet, on all analogy this one seems highly improbable.

The Reader

Concern for any readership is a further aspect worth considering. It is something that is scarcely apparent in the *stoichedon* system, which had a broad vogue in the 5th and 4th centuries BC. I note an intriguing exception which suggests that Athenian public documents could be deliberately inscribed in a slightly less severe manner: there is a tendency in financial texts to break the line not after the required *x* letters, but at the end of a syllable closest to the *x*[th] letter. More generally, however, in the course of time lettering tends to get smaller and in official texts administrative jargon more profuse. The *stoichedon* system also seems to have sounded the death knell of the use of interpuncts in formal texts. Greek and Latin texts are notorious for not having word division (not totally true, but a safe general statement).

Interpuncts were used in the Near East and in the Bronze Age Greek syllabic script. They do occur in alphabetic texts, but with no great regularity (Morpurgo-Davies 1987: especially 270–271, for an overview). Nestor's cup (**Figure 8**) in fact is one of the more striking examples where punctuation is used on a generous scale. I have noted that interpuncts, usually two or three dots, appear in roughly one in 50 informal texts of the 6th to 5th centuries at Greek sites where our corpus

Figure 13: 'Hekatompedon' inscription, reused marble metope (after Kirchner 1948: fig. 20). Epigraphical Museum of Athens 6794.

is large enough to bear such statistical analysis. Its most consistent use is in texts of the archaic period in Athens (Lang 1976; 1990; Threatte 1980: 73–84; and my own counts), though figures vary substantially from one type of text to another: perhaps one in 15 for painted texts on pots, one in 60 for graffiti on pots, including the political ostraka, mostly from the 480s, some one in five for sepulchral stone texts, but two in three for dedicatory texts inscribed in stone. An overall explanation is hard to find, though there may be a hint that interpuncts were fairly widely used in the early period in brush and ink writing on perishable materials. The most striking example is in the highly ornate and early *stoichedon* text, also of the 480s, known as the Hekatompedon decree (**Figure 13**), where the difficulties of adapting punctuation to *stoichedon* are clearly demonstrated

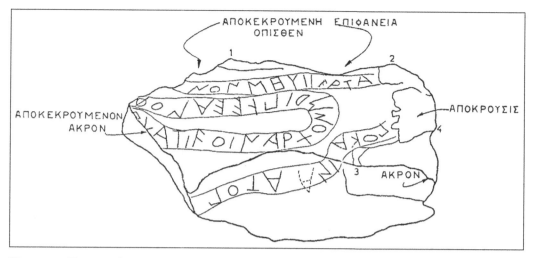

Figure 14: Tiryns cult text, *c*.600–550 BC (after Verdelis et al. 1975: 159). In situ.

— squeezed in or taking up a complete letter space (*stoichos*). In later Greek stone texts its use is very largely confined to hiving off numerals or limiting abbreviations. Outside the Greek world variety in its usage is apparent. In Etruscan about one in 25 of the 317 early texts in the corpus united by Bagnasco Gianni (1996) have (a variety of) interpuncts, although usage is more considerable in the classical period and after. On the other hand no interpunct appears in the 400 or so mainly late archaic and classical texts from Elymian Segesta (Agostiniani 1977).

One underlying factor that may explain lack of punctuation may lie in the habit of tracing texts physically letter by letter in the reading process (a word used for reading, *ananemo*, has the root meaning "to pick up"); the boustrophedon form of writing facilitated this process by not requiring the reader to go back to start a new line. The fact that the two earliest Greek texts preserved which have more than one line, the Nestor cup and its twin from Eretria (Johnston and Andreiomenou 1989), are not written boustrophedon but in lines running right to left may demonstrate a preoccupation with marking the separate lines, a preference not shown in other more or less contemporary verse texts. I also have a need to apologise for wrongly introducing into the literature a further aid to the reader, in the form of guidelines between which the letters were cut, meandering over the stones covering the late Mycenaean underground gallery at Tiryns (Jeffery 1990: 429; **Figure 14**); the cultic texts are randomly distributed, but the guidelines given in the original drawings in the publication of the material (Verdelis et al. 1975) were the responsibility not of the inscribers, but of the editors, who wished to facilitate the task of the modern reader.

Round the Angles

There are, however, some cases where the nature of the surface surely did lead to particular usages, over and above the matter of rounded pen / brush strokes already tackled above. A number of letters in various Greek and Etruscan scripts have rounded elements; in some they are in a sense secondary, *beta* and *rho* (B, P) can have rounded loops, and in some scripts *gamma* and *delta* (Γ and Δ) also can have substantial rounded sections. But in all these we find angled alternatives in regular use, and to date I have detected no patterns emerging, either locally or in various media, but would wish to conduct a fuller review. Under the same heading, however, we can note a vogue to the use of squared-off circular parts of letters where more than half a circle is involved — *theta, omicron,*

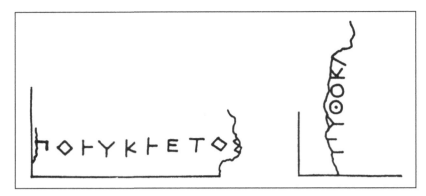

Figure 15: Signature of the sculptor Polykleitos, from Olympia, 450–425 BC (Jeffery 1990: pl. 30, 45). Olympia Museum 675.

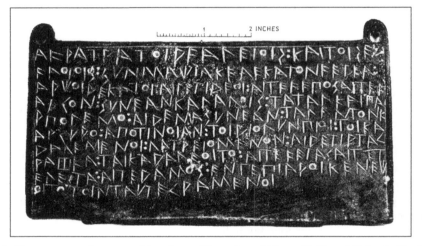

Figure 16: Treaty cut on bronze tablet, from Olympia, *c.*500 BC (Jeffery 1990: pl. 42, 6). British Museum GR 1824.0499.17.

phi, omega — on bronze and stone, particularly in some areas of the Peloponnese. Polykleitos uses such forms in his signatures on statue bases (**Figure 15**; but this is probably not the reason why Varro (in Pliny, *Natural History*, xxxiv 56) describes his statues as "four-square"!). On such hard surfaces the inscribing of circular letters took three main forms, beyond that of doing one's best with driving a chisel: turning the curve into straight lines, using individual points to make up the curve, or using some form of punch or compass, the latter often leaving a central point (**Figure 16**).[3] Here we can at least make the observation that such usages are at best extremely rare in the *painted* letters of Greek vase inscriptions; I know of none, but stand to be corrected.

Let us turn back to *sigma* — or the three- or four-stroke sign which does duty for the main sibilant in many Greek poleis or *iota* in a minority. We have already noted that it can have a curving profile, whatever the medium. I just mention a few more cases, where in fact it is the sibilant that is so shown and is of three strokes. It is quite regularly used in texts inscribed into stone and metal of Rhegion in South Italy (**Figure 17**), but rarer elsewhere — here a most peculiar case (British Museum GR 1888.6-1.421; **Figure 18**), an exception that proves the rule if there ever was one — among the 2500 graffiti from Naukratis. What I discussed earlier with respect to later developments in the 4th century BC is of a different character: the so-called lunate *sigma*, and its

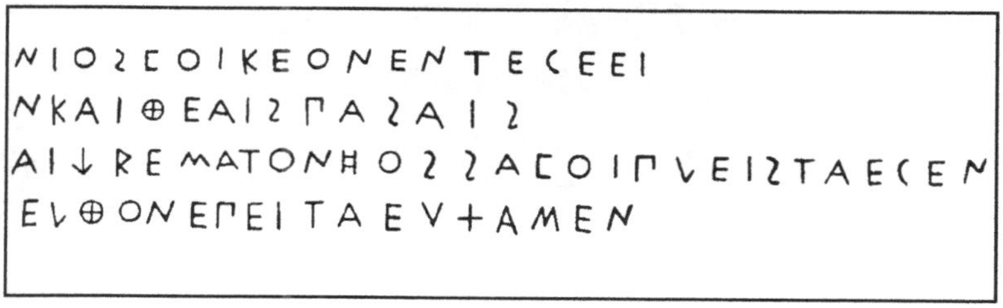

NIO?COIKEONENTECEEI
NKAI⊕EAI?ΓA?AI?
AI↓REᴹATONHO??ACOIΓVEI?TAECEN
EV⊕ONEΓEITAEV+AMEN

Figure 17: Dedication by Mikythos of Rhegion, on stone base at Olympia, 470–50 BC (Jeffery 1990: pl. 49, 8). Olympia Museum.

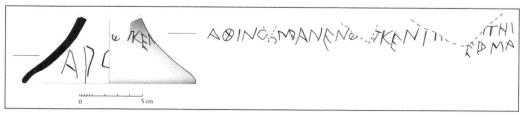

Figure 18: Graffito under foot of Chian cup, from Naukratis, *c*.600–575 BC. British Museum GR 1888.6-1.421. Drawing by Denitsa Nenova.

cousin the lunate *epsilon*, quite clearly results from the rapid brush writing of the four-stroke *sigma* that became the major simple sibilant sign in the Greek alphabet by the late 5th century. We can see some hints of this change in a few painted inscriptions on Attic white-ground lekythoi of the middle of that century, with a minimising of the 'heart' of the letter (Immerwahr 1990: 158, S14; **Figure 19**). Here it is of relevance to note that there is no clear, immediate successor to that set, and just one possible predecessor, a truly unusual text: among the cache of baked clay tablets found in the ruins of Persepolis in ancient Media termed the Fortification tablets, there is one written in Greek (**Figure 20**) and the date must be somewhere around 500 BC — we have no need to debate the closer issue here (Lewis 1977: 12–13, n. 55). It is a short note of the disbursement of an amount of wine, and the *sigma* appears in both forms, four-bar and, on a fairly sharply curving surface, in a clear lunate form. It is indeed an oddity that is not readily explained, as Lewis notes; can it be a single surviving example of what may have been a form in widespread use on perishable media, in Media?

By way of concluding remarks, we can discern in general a very slow adoption of 'cursive' shapes in informal writing in the classical period, with occasional but very scattered examples of such lettering in its broadest sense in earlier periods. It seems reasonable to argue that the formal scripts of the Greek poleis in the 5th and 4th centuries BC may have acted as a brake on such change, the *stoichedon* system being perhaps the most effective of such devices. At the same time it is proper to look at other aspects of contemporary material culture to see whether similar forms of what we may call conservatism are apparent there. It is such a large topic that one must be selective and so cautious in drawing conclusions that are too sweeping. Modern students of the ancient world perhaps look too closely for change and innovation, overlooking such conservatism. It is mentioned most frequently, I would suggest, in the context of dating; 'such a type is long-lasting and we should not press the evidence' is not an uncommon sentence, though perhaps not so much used of the period we have under scrutiny, when certainly *artistic* change continued apace.

Two areas where conservatism can be seen however are religion and trade. While it is clear that the major polis cults did enjoy new developments, especially in monumentality of the architectural environment, at a more humble level it has been argued that the increase in quantities of

Figure 19: 'Abbreviated' *sigma* on Attic white-ground lekythos, *c.*450 BC. British Museum D49 (GR 1893.1115.7). Courtesy Trustees of the British Museum.

Figure 20: Clay ball, from Persepolis. Courtesy of Persepolis Fortification Archive Project, Oriental Institute, University of Chicago.

small mould-made terracottas in many sanctuaries in the classical period reflects a concern for stability, not change, in cult and its attendant rituals (von Hesberg 2007). On what would appear to be a completely different level we may note the relationship, or lack of relationship, between vase shapes and their suitability for stacking on board ship, i.e. 'progressive' cooperation between potter and trader. It is a topic that needs greater attention than can be given here, but I just note two aspects that one might consider counter-intuitive. The shapes of storage or transport amphoras respond little to the requirements for easy packing until, in crude terms, the 3rd century BC (Johnston 1984). One type, from Mende (**Figure 21**), oddly enough one that is mentioned by

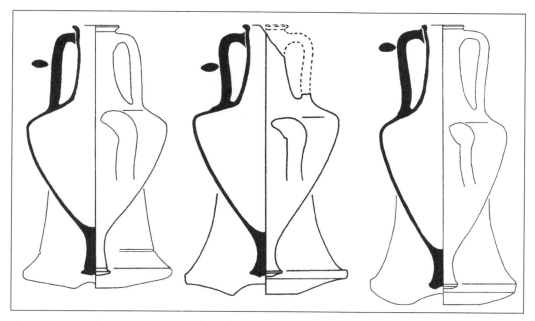

Figure 21: Mendean amphoras of 5th to 4th century BC (after Monakhov 2003: fig. 62).

Figure 22: Athenian cup, Aberdeen University, Marischal College, inv. no. 9648. Courtesy of Aberdeen University Collections.

Demosthenes in a court speech involving shipments, takes on even more 'aesthetic' shapes in the 4th century. Here it could be said to reflect the trend in shape development in Attic red-figured ware, to what one might fairly call Victorian values, with ever slimmer stems and flowering, fragile rims; yet the late red-figured krater is exported very widely, from Spain to the Black Sea. One might argue exceptions, for example the solid Castulo cup of the 5th century BC, but also remember the elegant stemmed kylix, in near mass production from *c.*550 until the 4th century BC (Shefton 1996; **Figure 22**). Not only transport, but kiln furniture is affected (see the highly intricate kiln supports required, and made, for the better firing of South Italian equivalents of later Attic red-figured pots at Metaponto [Cracolici 2003]).

In writing there are similar tensions between aesthetic concerns and practicality, and they receive similarly mixed solutions. An informal scribble on a sherd, of *c.*475–450 BC from the Agora at Athens demonstrates this wonderfully (Lang 1976: C21; **Figure 23**), with its scratched sketch

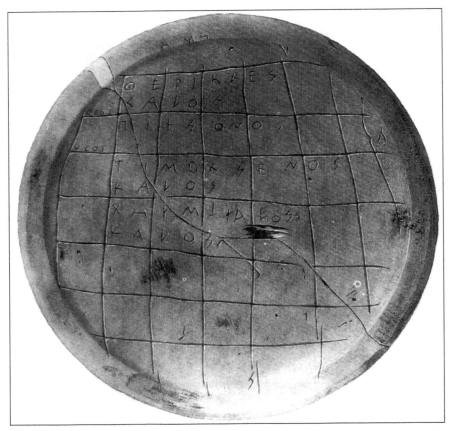

Figure 23: Graffito under foot of Attic vase, from Athens (Immerwahr 1990: fig. 165; Lang 1976: C21). Agora Museum P5164.

of an official stone text, complete with grid for the lettering and the heading invoking the gods, albeit the rest of the text is far more in keeping with contemporary painted names on pots. Or one can cite (**Figure 24**) the use of truly monumental lettering, of a lapidary kind, in some ceramic texts, where smaller size and normally hastier script are otherwise found, all I think dedications to deities (Johnston 1997: 109–111; we can add to my list published there splendid unpublished examples on Panathenaic amphora(s) dedicated in the Athena sanctuary at Kamiros on Rhodes).

I finish with a stone text to demonstrate a final aspect that has consequences for our topic. It is a 'speaking object', though in fact a counter-example but an interesting one. A tombstone of c.540 BC, with a text inscribed such that it rises up from the ground, as if the dead were speaking (Jeffery 1990: pl. 73, 1); very often indeed the epitaphs do treat the stele in the first person, and we find the usage very widely spread in the Greek and Etruscan world from the 7th century. Here however, rather perversely it is the unknown reader of the text who is in the first person "I am in pain looking on the tombstone of young Autokleides" (**Figure 25**). The material effect of the words rising from the ground is inexplicably lost.

A broad range of related texts that offer names, but of a more casual nature are the identificatory labels that painters and sometimes gem-cutters and the like put on their figured scenes. From the beginning, around 700 BC on present evidence, painters tried whenever possible to begin the label as near to the head of the relevant figure as possible, as if he or she were speaking their name. I noted earlier that something approaching the cursive *sigma* can be found on painted inscriptions on mid

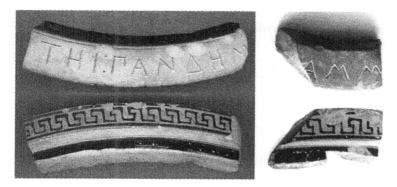

Figure 24: Dedication to Aphrodite Pandemos, from Naukratis, *c.*500 BC (Höckmann and Möller 2006: 16, fig. 11). British Museum GR 1900.0214.6 and Bonn, Akademisches Kunstmuseum 697.90.

Figure 25: Grave stele of Autokleides, *c.*550–525 BC, from Athens (Jeffery 1990: pl. 73, 1). Epigraphical Museum of Athens 13474.

5th-century pots, but they are rare and isolated occurrences within a group which is noteworthy however for another aspect most of them share, in that they reflect the new aesthetic of the squared off *stoichedon* style, with labels very often related more to the surface than the figures, and there are hints that such usage may have been derived from large-scale wall or panel painting (**Figure 19**).

In sum we may see in the development of script in the classical period a similar neglect of 'pure' technology as in other areas of everyday life, as against the remarkable intellectual input into epistemology and the arts, as we would call them, not least in the words written in the seemingly still conservative scripts. The fact that many of those words were publicly uttered in somewhat basic theatrical surroundings, before the rise of the monumental theatre in the 4th century, is a further example of such social attitudes.

Concluding Remarks

With respect to the closer theme of this volume, I have considered a number of the issues arising from the use of different surfaces and their possible reflection in the script of the broad period, c.800 to 300 BC. Direct connections seem few and are sporadic; the Greek-speaking world adapted a Semitic 'alphabet' into its contemporary decorative tradition and the resulting letters in general terms changed but slowly thenceforth. Use of 'brush and ink' cursive forms, on whatever surface, is highly sporadic in that world until the 4th century BC. Some aids to reading, or 'picking up' the letters, are used; in the earlier part of the period these include the boustrophedon system and interpuncts, but both disappear by c.500 BC, when stoichedon writing would seem to have a blocking effect on more 'fluid' approaches. Cursive lettering does become more frequent in our preserved record in the later 4th century BC, largely, we must assume, through the influence of papyrus-written texts, even though these would by then have been in general use for at least 200 years.

Notes

[1] The tomb, in a plot beside Leoforos Vouliagmeni, southeast of the Akropolis, is essentially unpublished; apparently it contained no pottery, only a wide range of musical and writing instruments, but is stratigraphically connected with a 5th-century BC burial. I learned in 2010 that some inscribed parts do survive (Martin West pers. comm.; and see now Pöhlmann and West 2012).

[2] The present whereabouts of the piece are uncertain (John Tait pers. comm.), but we may note that Eric Turner saw two hands at work, one using a brush, the other a reed.

[3] I note here an example of surface being of importance to *modern* scholarship: those who advocate an early date for the transfer of the alphabet from the Levant to the Greek world (see Jeffery 1990: 426–427 for an overview) have argued that the Greek *omicron* with a central dot is a clear echo of the Semitic *ayin*, 'eye', which had lost that dotted iris by the 1st millennium BC. They are of course no such thing; all early *omicrons*, to my knowledge, do without it also.

References

Adiego Lajara, I. 1998. Die neue Bilingue von Kaunos und das Problem des karischen Alphabets. *Kadmos* 37: 57–79.

Adiego Lajara, I. 2007. *The Carian Language*. Leiden: Brill.

Agostiniani, L. 1977. *Iscrizioni anelleniche di Sicilia: le iscrizioni elime*. Florence: Olschki.

Avram, A. 2007. Some Thoughts About the Black Sea and the Slave Trade Before the Roman Domination (6th–1st centuries BC). In Gabrielson, V. and Lund, J. (eds), *The Black Sea in Antiquity: Regional and interregional economic exchanges*. Aarhus: University Press, 239–251.

Avronidaki, Ch. 2008. Boeotian Red-figure Imagery on Two New Vases by the Painter of the Dancing Pan. *Antike Kunst* 51: 8–22.

Bagnasco Gianni, G. 1996. *Oggetti iscritti di epoca orientalizzante in Etruria*. Florence: Olschki.

Bergk, T. 1878–1882. *Poetae Lyrici Graeci* (4th edition). Leipzig: Teubner.

Corbett, P. E. and Woodhead, A. G. 1955. A Forger of Graffiti. *Annual of the British School at Athens* 50: 251–265. DOI: http://dx.doi.org/10.1017/S0068245400018670

Cracolici, V. 2003. *I sostegni di fornace dal kerameikos di Metaponto*. Bari: Edipuglia.

Dana, M. 2007. Lettres grecques dialectales nord-pontiques. *Revue des ÉtudesAnciennes* 109: 67–97.

Hiller von Gaertringen, F. 1898. *Inscriptiones Graecae XII, 3, Part vii, Thera et Therasia*. Berlin: Reimer.

Höckmann, U. and Möller, A. 2006. The Hellenion at Naukratis: Questions and observations. In Villing, A. and Schlotzhauer, U. (eds), *Naukratis: Greek diversity in Egypt*. London: British Museum Press, 11–22.

Immerwahr, H. 1990. *Attic Script*. Oxford: Oxford University Press.

Inglese, A. 2008. *Thera arcaica: le iscrizioni rupestri dell'agora degli dei*. Tivoli: Tored.

Jeffery, L. H. 1990. *The Local Scripts of Archaic Greece* (revised edition with supplement by A. W. Johnston). Oxford: Oxford University Press.

Johnston, A. W. 1980. *Trademarks on Greek Vases*. Warminster: Aris and Phillips.

Johnston, A. W. 1984. The Development of Amphora Shapes: Symposium and shipping. In Brijder, H. (ed.), *Ancient Greek and Related Pottery (Proceedings of the International Vase Symposium Amsterdam 1984)*. Amsterdam: Allard Pierson Museum, 208–211.

Johnston, A. W. 1985. A Fourth Century Graffito from the Kerameikos. *Athenische Mitteilungen* 100: 283–307.

Johnston, A. W. 1996. Note on the Graffito. In Coldstream, J. N. and Catling, H. W. (eds), *Knossos North Cemetery: Early Greek tombs* (British School at Athens, supplementary volume 28). London: British School at Athens, 463.

Johnston, A. W. 1997. All Runes to Me. In Nyström, S. (ed.), *Runor och ABC*. Stockholm: Sällskapet Runica et Mediaevalia, 93–112.

Johnston, A. W. and Andreiomenou, A. K. 1989. A Geometric Graffito from Eretria. *Annual of the British School at Athens* 84: 217–220. DOI: http://dx.doi.org/10.1017/S0068245400020955

Johnston, A. W. and Jones, R. E. 1978. The 'SOS' Amphora. *Annual of the British School at Athens* 73: 103–141. DOI: http://dx.doi.org/10.1017/S0068245400006195

Kirchner, J. 1948. *Imagines Inscriptionum Atticarum*. Berlin: Mann

Lang, M. 1976. *Graffiti and Dipinti* (The Athenian Agora 21). Princeton: American School of Classical Studies at Athens.

Lang, M. 1990. *Ostraka* (The Athenian Agora 25). Princeton: American School of Classical Studies at Athens.

Lewis, D. M. 1977. *Sparta and Persia: Lectures delivered at the University of Cincinnati, Autumn 1976 in memory of Donald W. Bradeen*. Leiden: Brill.

Lloyd-Jones, H. and Parsons, P. (eds) 1983. *Supplementum Hellenisticum*. Berlin: de Gruyter.

Monakhov, S. Yu. 2003. *Greceskie Amfori v Prichernomore*. Moscow: Kimmerida.

Morpurgo-Davies, A. 1987. Folk-linguistics and the Greek Word. In Cardona, G. and Zide, N. (eds), *Festschift for Henry Hoenigswald*. Tübingen: Narr, 263–280.

Parkes, M. B. 2008. *Their Hands Before Our Eyes: A closer look at scribes*. Aldershot: Ashgate.

Pöhlmann, E. and West, M. L. 2012. *The Oldest Greek Papyrus and Writing Tablets. Zeitschrift für Papyrologie und Epigraphik* 180: 1–16.

Shefton, B. 1996. The Castulo Cup: An Attic shape in black glaze of special significance in Sicily. In Palermo, D., Gigli, R., and Caruso, F. (eds), *I vasi attici ed altre ceramiche coeve in Sicilia: atti del convegno internazionale: Catania, Camarina, Gela, Vittoria, 28 marzo–1 aprile 1990* (*Cronachedi Archeologia* 29–30). Palermo: Nuova Graphicadue, 85–98.

Threatte, L. 1980. *The Grammar of Attic Inscriptions*, 1. Berlin: de Gruyter.

Turner, E. 1975. Four Obols a Day Men at Saqqara. In Bingen, J., Cambier, G. and Nachtergael, G. (eds), *Le Mondegrec: pensée, littérature, histoire, documents: hommages à Claire Préaux*. Brussels: Editions de l'Université de Bruxelles, 573–538.

van der Meer, L. 2007. *Liber linteus Zagrabiensis: The linen book of Zagreb: A comment on the longest Etruscan text*. Louvain: Peeters.

Verdelis, N., Jameson, M. and Papachristodoulou, I. 1975. Επιγραφαὶ Τίρυνθος. *Αρχαιολογικὴ Εφημερίς*, 150–205.

von Hesberg, H. 2007. Votivenseriationem. In Frevel, Chr. and von Hesberg, H. (eds), *Kult und Kommunikation: Medien in Heiligtumem der Antike*. Wiesbaden: Reichert, 279–310.

"It Is Written"?: Making, remaking and unmaking early 'writing' in the lower Nile Valley

Kathryn E. Piquette

Freie Universität Berlin

Introduction

Analysis and interpretation of inscribed objects often focus on their written meanings and thus their status as products of completed action. Attention is less commonly directed to the ways in which past actors intermingled and transformed material substances via particular tools and embodied behaviours — the material practices which give rise to graphical expression and anchor subsequent acts of symbolic meaning (re-)construction. Building on research into the materiality of early writing and related image making (see Piquette 2007; 2008), this chapter focusses on one aspect of written object 'life histories' — the processes of remaking and unmaking. I explore below the dynamic unfolding and reformulation of 'writing' and related imagery as artefact within the context of a selection of early inscribed objects from the lower Nile Valley (**Figure 1**). The more portable writing surfaces include over 4000 objects, including small labels, ceramic and stone vessels, stelae, seals and seal impressions, implements, and personal items (Regulski 2010: 6, 242). The geographically- and temporally-related marks on fixed stone surfaces (variously referred to as 'petroglyphs', 'rock art', 'rock inscriptions' or 'graffiti', e.g. Redford and Redford 1989; Storemyr 2009) also constitute a crucial dataset for questions of early writing and image-making practices in north-east Africa, but fall outside the scope of this chapter. For its basis, this inquiry examines comparatively three inscribed find types: small perforated plaques or 'labels' of bone, ivory and wood; stone vessels; and stone stelae. Archaeologically, most are associated with large richly-equipped tomb complexes. I briefly touch on finds dating to the Late Predynastic (c.3300 / c.3200–3100 BCE),

How to cite this book chapter:

Piquette, K. E. 2013. "It Is Written"?: Making, remaking and unmaking early 'writing' in the lower Nile Valley. In: Piquette, K. E. and Whitehouse, R. D. (eds.) *Writing as Material Practice: Substance, surface and medium.* Pp. 213-238. London: Ubiquity Press. DOI: http://dx.doi.org/10.5334/bai.k

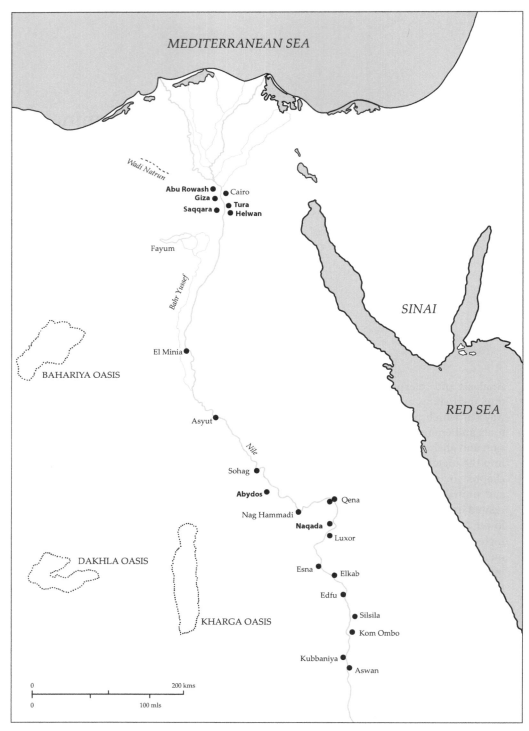

Figure 1: Map of Egypt with main find sites for inscribed labels, vessels and stelae in bold (after Spencer 1993: 19, fig. 6).

Cultural Phase	Calibrated Dates BCE	Dynasty	Period	Rulers
		2		Hetepsekhemwy
Naqada IIID	from c.2900 onwards			Qa'a Semerkhet
Naqada IIIC2	c.3000–2900			Adjib Den
Naqada IIIC1	c.3100–3000	1	Early Dynastic	Merneith Djet Djer Neithotep (?) Aha Narmer
Naqada IIIA1–IIIB	c.3300 / 3200–3100	'0'	Proto-Dynastic	Irj-Hor / Ka (?) Owner of Tomb U-j
Naqada IIC–IID2	c.3650–3300 / 3200			
Naqada IA–IIB	c.3900–3650		Predynastic	

Table 1: Chronological chart (after Hendrickx 1996: 64; Wilkinson 2001 [1999]: 27).

before turning to examples of written culture from the first half of the Early Dynastic Period (c.3100–2800 / 2770 BCE; **Table 1**).

Social Historical Context

The social history of this early period is reconstructed mainly on the basis of evidence found in funerary contexts. It is thought that members of a small number of polities rose to prominence in Upper Egypt, gradually accumulating political power at local, and eventually regional, levels. The main geographical areas of Upper and Lower Egypt, and outlying desert areas, were brought under the control of a single ruler who administered the so-called 'territorial state' through various political-religious institutions run by groups of officials (Baines 1995; Kohler 2010; Trigger et al. 2001 [1983]; Wengrow 2006; Wilkinson 2001 [1999]). Among the array of cultural developments associated with processes of Egyptian 'state' formation were marking systems including early hieroglyphic and hieratic scripts (Kahl 2001; Regulski 2009), which developed in conjunction with related marking practices (e.g. Baines 2004; Bard 1992; van den Brink 1992). The earliest widely-accepted evidence for 'writing' appears in Upper Egypt during the Late Predynastic period (c.3300 / 3200 BCE), although there is limited direct support for deciphering phonetic values and grammatical function (see Regulski 2008: 992). Much of the early scriptorial evidence is pictorial; given its depictive attempting to distinguish too strictly 'art' from 'writing' can be unhelpful. One wonders whether the term 'writing' is best avoided for this earliest evidence given the endless and often inconclusive debates and teleology that has characterised attempts at decipherment (e.g. cf. Baines 2004: 161–167 and Breyer 2002 with Dreyer 1998: 139-145). Palaeographic, art historical, and other approaches demonstrate that increasingly standardised sets of intermingled script – image motifs variously construct, communicate and display relationships of social and divine power, with particular emphasis on the ideology of rulership (Baines 2004). Numerical marks, names and titles or other 'personal identifiers' (hereafter 'PI', see Piquette 2010: 56), and indicators of social status and affiliation point to developing administrative structures and the importance of marking goods as well personal and collective identities (Piquette 2007; Wengrow 2006: 200–207).

Other archaeological evidence from cemetery, ceremonial and limited settlement sites provides parallel evidence for increasingly complex social stratification, and centralisation of bureaucratic, political and religious institutions. It is from this general social historical context that the case studies presented below derive, but with the recognition that for the theme of writing as a material practice, these objects were probably part of the activities and experiences of a very restricted segment of early Egyptian society.

About the Past, Constituting the Past

In contrast to notions of the inscribed object as something that 'is written' or constitutes a 'written source' which tell us *about* the past, early graphical expression is seen here as meaningfully constituted through the material actions of past individuals and as products of those actions. A mark or sign is thus seen as having efficacy in the past rather than just providing evidence about it (see Moreland 2006). For its theoretical and methodological bases, this study is informed by structuration, a practice theory which situates the agency of the knowledgeable individual in a mutually constituting relationship with social structures (e.g. Giddens 1984). According to this duality, the focus on choice requires consideration of the individual actor or technician, but always in terms of the ways in which individual choice was informed by, and re-informed, related social structures (cf. Meskell 2004: 53). Criticism has been levelled at what has been perceived, on the one hand, as structuration's over-individualising view on past actors, or on the other hand, as offering a grand unitary account where action overemphasises collectives and institutions, although these critiques have been challenged (Gardner 2007; 2008). Collective representations consist of the results of individual decisions to participate in the reproduction of certain past choices. Thus, the personal is necessarily social, the individual body forever part of the body politic, and the operational gestures of a single technician's hands, in making an inscribed label for example, are therefore tied to — though not totally determined by — collective representations (see Dobres 2000: 216). Whether episodes of action relate to a single and / or multiple individuals is not always archaeologically visible. Nevertheless, I hope the analysis of material patterning among the object types examined here gives some idea of the social structures reproduced or renegotiated across time-space through technological choice and related scribal and semantic intention, thus contributing to a more holistic and synchronically-derived understanding of written meanings (cf. Baines 2008: 842; see also Piquette 2013).

Signs of Production

As mentioned, it is difficult to locate many aspects of inscribed object production and use in time-space prior to deposition in the cemetery. However, some episodes of activity involved in the transformation of artefact materials and their inscription can be inferred from manufacture marks and other surface modifications. Through first-hand inspection or high resolution photographs or other documentation techniques of artefact surfaces (see Piquette forthcoming), it is possible to infer many behaviours involved in acts of marking. Moreover, when grounded in theories of social practice, the notion of *chaîne opératoire* research affords a great deal of empirical observation regarding the sequential activities of ancient materials processing. In conceptualising graphical practices it is also important to populate accounts with past people and embodied actions rather than focusing alone on tools and the results of their use (see Dobres 2000: 21–22, fig. 1.2, 166–169).

As I have discussed elsewhere, an artefactual emphasis in the study of early Egyptian graphical evidence reveals the impact of materiality on image expression and appearance, including the restricted choice of certain material resources, methods for conversion and shaping, techniques for rendering imagery (e.g. the subtraction or addition of materials), and changes and continuities in conventions for image organisation (Piquette 2007; 2008). For example, the sequence in which inscription and the cutting and shaping of Late Predynastic bone labels occurred can be inferred from incised images which appear to have been cropped when the plaque was separated from its parent bone plate (Dreyer 1998: 137; Kahl 2001: 111; see also Wengrow 2008: 1027). Images cut through by the perforation, also indicate that incision took place prior to the drilling / carving of the perforation (e.g. Dreyer 1998: [T] 123, [D] 125, no. 90, [P] pl. 31, no. 90). Patterning among some inscribed labels dating to the reign of Qa'a, the last ruler of the 1st Dynasty (Piquette 2008: 103–104), exemplifies the theoretical point concerning the unfolding of inscribed meaning as both process and outcome of that process, and as manifold in its meaningful construction (roughly expressed: material + tool + embodied engagement + technique + compositional choice + time + social space = image) and consumption (image(s) + embodied engagement and perception by knowledgeable agent of constructive act and / or result + time + social space = meaning construction).

Inscribed Labels

More than 430 inscribed whole and fragmentary perforated plaques form one of the largest surviving corpora of script-bearing material from the Nile Valley from the period of *c.*3300 / 3200 BCE to *c.*2800 BCE (**Table 1**). These dockets or labels range in size from about 1.0–9.5 cm in height and width, with most tending towards the smaller dimensions (e.g. **Figures 2–3**). Largely on the basis of later written evidence the label inscriptions are understood as communicating the date, quantity and quality of funerary goods or other associated commodities, as well as place names, personal names, and titles. It is generally assumed that labels were affixed to items deposited in the tomb, such as containers of oil, clothing, jewellery, implements and other items the deceased required for a successful afterlife. Overall, labels and label fragments are encountered at seven cemetery sites in the lower Nile Valley (**Figure 1**), although the vast majority derive from the upper Egyptian cemetery site of Abydos. The labels can be divided chronologically into two main phases. Of some 370 published examples from Abydos, almost 200 come from a Predynastic / Later Predynastic cemetery (U) at this site, most being found in and around the large multi-chambered tomb U-j (Dreyer 1998). These have been dated to the Naqada IIIA1 cultural phase (*c.*3300 / 3100 BCE; Boehmer et al. 1993; Görsdorf et al. 1998). The remainder date from the Naqada IIIC–early D cultural phases (*c.*3100–2770 BCE), or the entire 1st Dynasty.

These plaques are marked using four main techniques involving incision and / or the application of pigment (Piquette 2008). At least five different kinds of graphical episode can be discerned:

1. inscription
2. inscription > further inscription
3. inscription > partial erasure
4. inscription > full erasure
5. inscription > erasure > possible re-inscription

A selection of these is detailed below.

Inscription > (Partial and Full) Erasure

At least 12 inscribed labels bear marks indicating that after initial inscription surface material was subsequently removed with the apparent intention of partially or fully eliminating the original

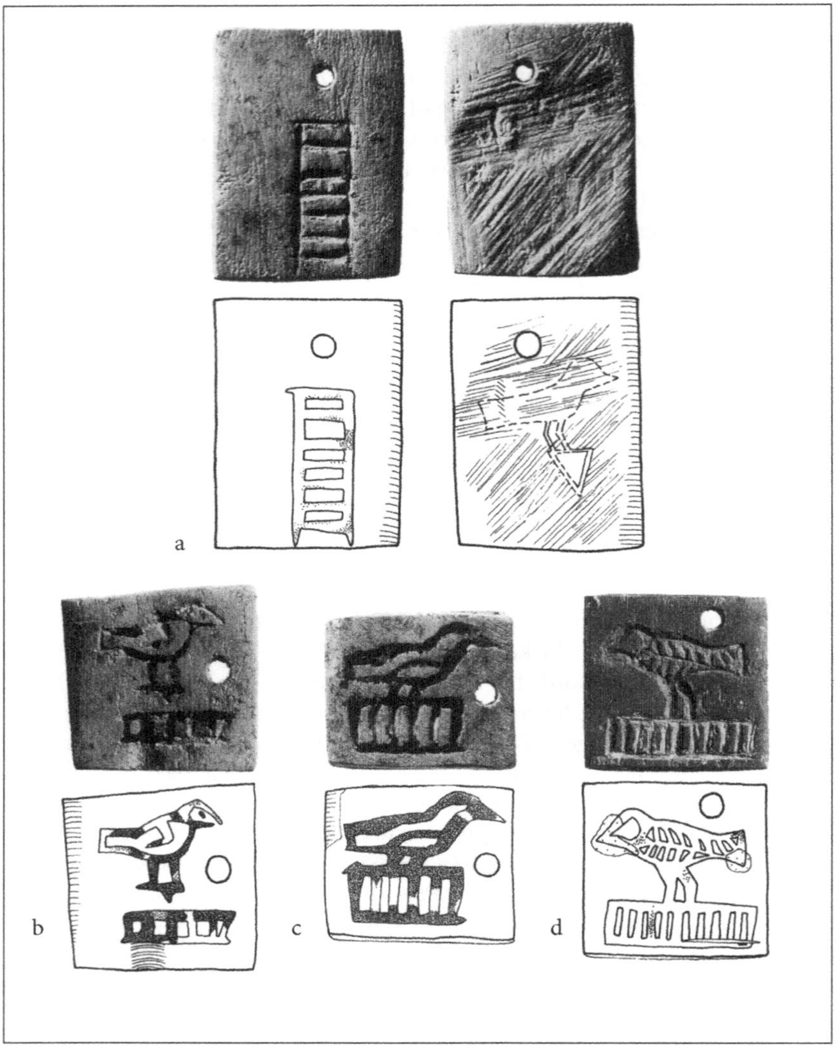

Figure 2: Inscribed bone labels from Cemetery U, Abydos dated to the Naqada IIIA1 phase. a) Label with 'rectangular shape' or possible 'N39' / 'pool' incised on one face and an erasure on the opposite face, the shape of 'G5-s33(?)' / 'bird perched on triangular support' still being discernible. H 1.25 cm; W 1.7 cm; TH 0.15–0.2 cm. Provenance: Tomb U-j S. Ab K 834. Source No. 4396; b) Label bearing an abutting combination of 'rectangular shape' and 'bird'. H 1.3 / 1.35 cm; W 1.5 cm; TH 0.25–0.3 cm. Provenance: U-j 11. Ab K 654. Source No. 4348; c) Label bearing the non-abutting combination of 'rectangular shape' and 'G5-s33(?)' / 'bird perched on triangular support'. H 1.5 / 1.6 cm; W 1.7 / 1.5 cm; TH 0.1–0.2 cm. Provenance: U-j 11. Ab K 655. Source No. 4364; d) Label bearing an abutting combination of 'rectangular shape' and 'bird'. H 1.5 cm; W 1.5 cm; TH 0.25–0.2 cm. Provenance: U-j 11. Ab K 658. Source No. 4349. All Dreyer 1998. 2a: [T] 131, no. 156, [D] 133, fig. 81, no. 156, [P] pl. 34. no. 156; 2b: [T] 126, no. 108, [D] 127, fig. 79, no. 108, [P] pl. 32, no. 108; 2c: [T] 128, no. 124, [D] 127, fig. 79, no. 124, [P] pl. 32, no. 124; 2d: [T] 126, no. 109, [D] 127, fig. 79, no. 109, [P] pl. 32, no. 109). Courtesy Günter Dreyer and the Deutsches Archäologisches Institut Kairo.

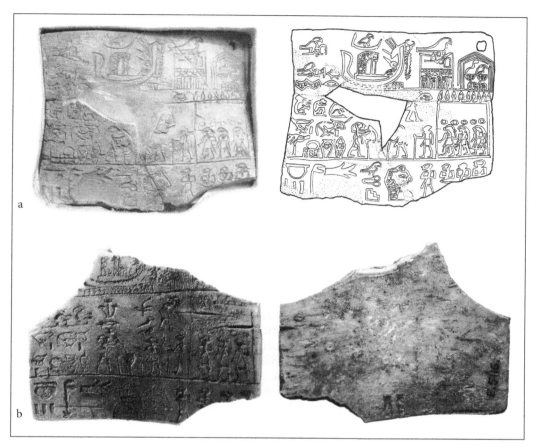

Figure 3: Two ivory labels showing an erasure in the lower left of the bottom register. Warping and colour due in part to exposure to high heat, probably during the firing of the tomb. a) Photograph and drawing of recto. H 4.8 cm; W 5.6 cm; TH 0.2 cm. Provenance: Naqada, mastaba tomb attributed to Neith, chamber 'γ' (de Morgan 1897: [T] 161, 165, 167, 234, [D] 167, fig. 549). Source No. 0240. JE 31773. Author's photograph, courtesy the Egyptian Museum, Cairo, drawing from Spencer 1993: 63, with permission Richard Parkinson); b) Photograph of recto and verso. H 3.5+ cm; W 4.5 cm; TH 0.17–0.26 cm. Provenance: Naqada, near mastaba tomb attributed to Neith (Garstang 1905: 61, figs 2–3). Source No. 0241. E.5116. Author's photographs, courtesy the Garstang Museum of Archaeology, University of Liverpool.

inscription. In the following sub-sections I present those labels which evidence this sequence of graphical acts and consider the possible implications.

Begin Again?

A small Naqada IIIA1 bone label (Ab K 834) from Cemetery U, Abydos, is one of the earliest surviving labels showing evidence for graphical content adjustment and seems to be unique among this early group. It was incised on one face with 'G5-s33(?)' / 'bird perched on triangular support' which was then vigorously scraped away, although not completely (**Figure 2a**). The opposite face bears an entirely different image, a 'rectangular shape' in a vertical orientation.[1] It is unclear whether the acts of incision + erasure occurred before or after the incision on the opposite face. A possible clue to the relationship between the two motifs is the co-occurrence on other contemporary labels of the 'bird perched on triangular support' motif with instances of a morphologically similar 'architectural element (?)' (**Figure 2b**). However, these are paired on the same face with the latter oriented horizontally with, and in at least two further instances, the 'bird' perches directly on this rectangular feature (**Figure 2c–d**). One might venture various explanations for the erasure, from error correction during the label production phase to re-purposing or re-cycling at a later stage of use, but if this was ever a common part of early labelling practices it seems to have been restricted to functions that preceded the funerary ritual or the activities that led to deposition in the tomb.

(Co)modification

I now turn to the early 1st Dynasty when more elaborate labels come into use. Two labels of elephant ivory, found in / around a tomb dated to the reign of Aha and located at the Upper Egyptian site of Naqada (de Morgan 1897; Garstang 1905: 61, fig. 1; **Figure 3a–b**), bear virtually-identical incised imagery organised in three horizontal registers. Each exhibits an area on the left in the lower-most register that has been scraped away. These are the only examples from the reign of Aha preserving the lower register on this label type, but comparison with similar examples dated to the preceding and following reign (Narmer and Djer, respectively), suggests that the erased area on these Naqada labels may have contained numerical or other information related to an offering or other commodity with which the label was associated (Newberry 1912: 288).

Their parallel treatment suggests that both labels were subject to the same general set of original circumstances of creation, but also subsequent changes to those circumstances. If numerical or related item information had been present but was then erased, perhaps this was due to changes in quantities or other features of items involved in the equipping of the tomb or the funeral. The obliteration of product and / or numerical information raises a range of questions about the function of such labels and the intentions behind their use. Did original and subsequent circumstances arise prior to or after the arrival of the labels, and presumably associated goods, to the tomb? Why was this new information not updated on the label? The absence of quantitative or qualitative information would seem to contradict the function often posited for the labels, that of the administration of goods exchange (e.g. Ciałowicz 2001: 134, 138–139) — a function which also seems to have been secondary if the amount of compositional space dedicated to elaborate narrative imagery is any indication of priority. In contrast to the more comprehensive and vigorous removal of the entire, albeit less complex, composition of Ab K 834 discussed above, the act of 'erasure' here involves the relatively careful removal of marks from a larger composition. We might conjecture that the person who made these tidy erasures intended the space to be re-inscribed with new or updated information, or perhaps the labels had ceased to play a strictly administrative role by the time of deposition. Could this adjustment relate to label de-activation and / or re-deployment in the context of the deceased's transition from life to afterlife? While firm conclusions cannot be drawn at this juncture this example highlights the potential importance of, in addition to the creation of writing, studying its obliteration.

Renegotiating Events

A small fragment of an incised wooden label from Abydos (**Figure 4**), also dated to the reign of Aha, depicts what appears to be the preparation of oil or wine (see James 1995), or some other product involving crushing or pressing. A very similar scene appears in the middle register of each of the two ivory labels discussed above (**Figure 3a–b**); on each side of a large mortar and pestle

Figure 4: Fragment of an incised wooden label showing what appears to be an oil or wine pressing scene. The detail (right) shows that an image to the right of the 'mortar and pestle', possibly a 'human figure', has been erased (cf. **Figure 3**). H 1.78+ cm; W 2.31+ cm; TH 0.41 cm. Provenance: Abydos, tomb complex Z attributed to Djer, subsidiary grave Z3 (Petrie 1900: 21). Source No. 0943. E.0078. Photograph and detail with permission © Royal Museums of Art and History, Brussels. Drawing from Petrie 1900: pl. 13, no. 5, courtesy of the Egypt Exploration Society.

stands a human figure, the left figure holding / manipulating the pestle. Another figure on the far right leans on a staff and appears to oversee the activity. On the wooden label fragment (**Figure 4**), however, we find that the space between the vessel and the figure on the right (who, rather than holding a staff, holds an arm up toward the body) is in fact empty. First-hand inspection reveals that the surface of this apparently empty area has been reworked. Rather than the type of scraping consistent with surface preparation, a slight concave depression attests to the removal of surface material. That something was there previously, perhaps a human figure, is also suggested by comparison with a similar scene in both labels in **Figure 3a–b**.

This erasure, previously unremarked to my knowledge, is particularly intriguing for several reasons. As noted, this scene is paralleled on the two ivory labels from Naqada, each of which also bears an erasure albeit in the lower-most register on the left. In contrast to the removal of what seems to be quantitative or qualitative product information, the erasure on the wooden fragment occurs in the context of narrative imagery in what appears to be a middle register and thus seems to relate to a different semantic category. Some scenes on labels have been interpreted as year names, understood to have been named according to festivals, cultic or other scheduled events, or perhaps assigned retrospectively after important campaigns or expeditions (Kahl 2006: 99–100). If we assume label production and pre-depositional use occurred in the context of centralised administrative activities, as suggested by the presence of similar iconography at the two different but contemporary cemetery sites (Naqada and Abydos), one would expect product dating conventions to be fixed at the time of label creation. Even if this scene was not related to goods dating, but to commissioning, production, packaging, dispatch, or delivery — whether directly to the tomb complex or to officials, family or friends involved in tomb preparation who then brought the label and associated item(s) to the tomb as part of the funeral or subsequent mortuary activities — the presence of this erasure in one of three surviving examples suggests that despite any centralisation of labelling activities, label meaning and use was subject to re-negotiation at a more local level, in this case at Abydos.

Changing Identities

The practice of erasure persists at least into the mid-1st Dynasty as attested on several other label fragments from Abydos. Ab K 2602 and Ab K 2536 are two virtually-identical labels found in debris to the north of tomb complex T during re-excavation of this area (Dreyer et al. 1998: 162–163, pl. 12a; 2003: 93–94; **Figure 5a–b**). In the upper-most register each bears a 'niched frame' motif containing the PI of a ruler conventionally rendered 'Djet'. To the left of the 'niched frame', a vertical swath of the surface traversing Registers 1 and 2 has been vigorously scraped away.

From a compositional perspective the practioner's disregard for the register line is noteworthy. Surface removal episodes identified on other labels conform to compositional divisions of graphical space established at the time of initial drafting, units of semantic or narrative meaning being organised within a single register, column or other circumscribed space. It is unusual though not impossible that a semantic link was present between image clusters that traversed registers, or perhaps the individual undertaking the erasure took advantage of a coincidence whereby separate images requiring removal happened to be aligned one above the other.

Making sense of the erased area to the left of a 'niched frame' motif in Register 1 is aided by comparison with two surviving labels also bearing the 'niched frame' of Djet (Vikentiev 1959: 4, 6, fig. 1, pls 1, 3). As exemplified by **Figure 5c**, both show a PI incised to the left, perhaps the name of an official 'Sekhem-ka-sedj' (cf. Emery 1954: 102–103, fig. 105; Wilkinson 2001 [1999]: 124). Tantalising clues on the surface of the label detail in **Figure 5a** show the faint remains of what may be a 'D28' / 'pair of arms', as well as the remnants of an incised trough from another sign above and to the right.[2] If 'Sekhem-ka-sedj' or another PI was originally present on Ab K 2602 or Ab K 2536, these would provide precedents for the three later labels also bearing PI similarly located erasures (below).

While this erased area in Register 1 was not re-inscribed in either case, one wonders whether the 'architectural feature?' in the midst of the heavily-scratched area in Register 2 of Ab K 2536 (**Figure 5b**) was added after the erasure episode. First-hand study is necessary to confirm the sequence of surface transformations although slight stylistic differences may be discernible, including narrower and apparently shallower incisions.

Among the preserved / available labels datable to the subsequent reign of Den, three incised examples exhibit erasures with a key similarity to those just discussed. To the left of the 'niched frame' motif there is a blank area with abrasions also consistent with the removal of surface material (**Figures 6–8**). Above each is a cluster comprised of 'S20' / 'seal on lanyard' and 'L2' / 'bee', traditionally interpreted as 'seal bearer of the ruler of Upper Egypt'. Comparison with 4–5 similarly-composed, contemporary labels and fragments (all from Abydos: Source Nos 1253, 1254, 1390, 4087, and possibly 1312, see also 1252), shows a cluster or PI conventionally rendered as 'Hemaka'. No other PI is attested below the 'S20' / 'seal on lanyard' and 'L2' / 'bee' cluster on contemporary surviving labels, presenting the possibility that 'Hemaka' was originally inscribed in this location. But what was the reason for the obliteration of an aspect of the seal bearer's identity?

Despite the presence of 'S20' / 'seal on lanyard' and 'L2' / 'bee' cluster on these labels, the parallels they exhibit with Ab K 2536 and Ab K 2602 datable to the reign of Djet (above) are notable.

Figure 5: Incised labels bearing the PIs of Djet. a) Label (probably of elephant ivory, pers. comm. Günter Dreyer), showing erasure. H 2.95–3.05 cm; W 3.1 cm; TH 0.33-0.38 cm. Provenance: Abydos, near tomb complex T in area T-NOOO (Dreyer et al. 2003: [T] 94). Source No. 4807. Ab K 2602. Photograph courtesy Günter Dreyer and the Deutsches Archäologisches Institut Kairo; b) Ivory label with an erasure in a location similar to 5a. Provenance: Abydos, fragments found during two seasons in areas T-NW + T-NOOO, northwest and northeast, respectively, of tomb complex T attributed to Den (Dreyer et al. 1998: [T] 162–163, [P] pl. 12a; 2003: [T] 93–94, [P] pl. 18f). H 3.15 cm; W 3.9 cm; TH 0.35 cm. Source No. 4084. Ab K 2536. Photograph courtesy Günter Dreyer and the Deutsches Archäologisches Institut Kairo; c) Recto and verso of an incised and colour-infilled elephant ivory label. Provenance: Saqqara, tomb S3504, dated to the reign of Djet (Emery 1954: 3, 102–103, fig. 105). Source No. 986. JE 16830. Author's photograph, courtesy the Egyptian Museum, Cairo.

Figure 6: Incised label fragment (upper half) of wood bearing the PI of Den, a mid-1ˢᵗ Dynasty ruler. The imagery below the 'S20' / 'seal on lanyard' and 'L2' / 'bee' has been erased (cf. **Figure 7–8**). Provenance: Abydos, tomb complex T attributed to Den, Chamber S1 (Dreyer et al. 1990: [T] 80–81, [P] pl. 26a). H 2.7+ cm; W 6.9 cm; TH 0.6 cm. Source No. 1372. Ab K 381. Photograph courtesy Günter Dreyer and the Deutsches Archäologisches Institut Kairo.

Figure 7: Incised label fragment of elephant ivory bearing the PI of Den. Imagery below the 'S20' / 'seal on lanyard' and 'L2' / 'bee' has been erased (cf. **Figures 6** and **8**). Provenance: Abydos, tomb complex T attributed to Den (Petrie 1900: [T] 21, [P] pl. 11, no. 5). Source No. 1249a–b. E.1122. Author's photographs, courtesy the Ashmolean Museum. Drawings from Petrie 1900: [D] pl. 14, nos 12–12 A, courtesy of the Egypt Exploration Society.

If we assume that, based on complete examples, the space to the left of the niched frame was reserved for the PI of an official, seal bearer or otherwise, it is possible in each case of erasure that the individual retired, died or otherwise ceased to hold that post. It is tempting to conjecture a degree of continuity between reigns (see **Table 1**) whereby the same individual served Djet and Den rulers (and presumably the intervening ruler/regent Merneith), but who then fell out of favour or whose identity was otherwise deemed necessary to remove.

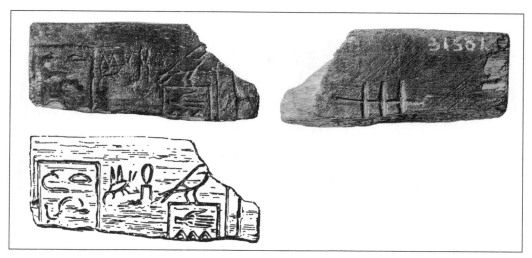

Figure 8: Incised label fragment of wood bearing the PI of Den. Imagery below the 'S20' / 'seal on lanyard' and 'L2' / 'bee' has been erased (cf. Figures 6–7). Provenance: Abydos, surface find. H 2.6+ cm; W 5.5 cm; TH 0.3–0.7 cm. Source No. 1366. JE 31581. Author's photograph, courtesy the Egyptian Museum, Cairo. Drawing from de Morgan 1897: 234, fig. 782.

The presence of both erased and un-erased labels in the same cemetery at Abydos raises essential questions about processes of label creation and function(s). It is curious that the identity markers for one of the highest positions in the two lands at that time — seemingly key information for a label to carry, not least judging by its juxtaposition with the PI of the Egyptian ruler — could be omitted. That partially complete (or more accurately, 'partially unmade') labels were nevertheless 'valid' for use in the Egyptian ruler's burial or associated rituals or ceremonies questions the understanding of these objects as administrative documents. These omissions may also point to a role for (some) labels where function took on a more symbolic aspect, such as deposition in the tomb to ensure the continuing efficacy of events and goods depicted and described on their surfaces. A more mundane explanation is that erasures were part of preparation for re-use that ultimately never took place. An abundance of later evidence attests to the re-use of scribal / artistic materials and products (Caminos 1986), but evidence among the labels for re-use, such as palimpsest in areas related to quantitative and qualitative product details, or PI information seems to be unattested.

Postscript?

In addition to erasure episodes, the labels bear other evidence for scribal acts that possibly took place after their initial making. More than 60 are inscribed on both faces, raising the question of production sequence and the passage of time between them. In those cases where the same technique for both sides occurs in a similar style and sign density, and organisation is similar (e.g. de Morgan 1897: 167, fig. 550–551, 553–555 A–B), the relationship between faces and episodes can be understood to be temporally and semantically more immediate. For labels which lack symmetry across these variables, it seems reasonable to assume that the most densely inscribed face was intended to be the primary side. From this point of departure then, differences in image density, organisation, and style may indicate two phases of inscription, and where technique is different the relationship between graphic episodes is probably even less direct.

On back in red pigment

Figure 9: Wooden label inscribed using incision and red colour infill on the primary face, with applied red colour on the secondary face. Provenance: Abydos, tomb B 18 (Narmer) / B 19 (Aha) (Petrie 1901: [T] 21, 51, [P] pl. 3A, no. 5). H 6.79 cm; W 9.45 cm; TH 0.71 cm. Source No. 0284a–b. E 9396. Author's photographs, courtesy University of Pennsylvania Museum of Archaeology and Anthropology. Drawings after Petrie 1901: pl. 10, nos 2–3, courtesy of the Egypt Exploration Society.

For example, stepping back in time to label evidence from the earlier reign of Aha, two double-sided wooden labels bear densely incised imagery on their primary sides (**Figures 9–10**). In contrast, the opposite faces are not only sparsely inscribed, but this has been accomplished using red and black colour, probably applied with a rush pen. The secondary side of **Figure 9** bears a 'U34ᵛ#' / 'mace / drill?' in red colour and other possible imagery too faded to identify. The similar but more fragmentary wooden label in **Figure 10** bears on its secondary face alternating images of a 'vessel' and 'semi-circular shape', also in red colour located 'on', or 'protruding from', a black 'rectangle', which may depict a 'Y5#' / 'gaming board' or container and its contents.

Both labels present an interesting parallel with the pair of elephant ivory labels from Naqada presented above, in that they also constitute a pair with material, technical, inscriptional, spatial, and temporal similarities. Both wooden labels appear to be made of the same type of wood (based on weight and visual inspection only), and were cut to the same general size, with similar narrative imagery and signs incised and formatted in four horizontal registers. Both were excavated from Cemetery B at Abydos (tombs B18 and B19; Petrie 1901: 21, 51), and date to around the time of Aha based on this find context and the presence of this ruler's PI on each label.

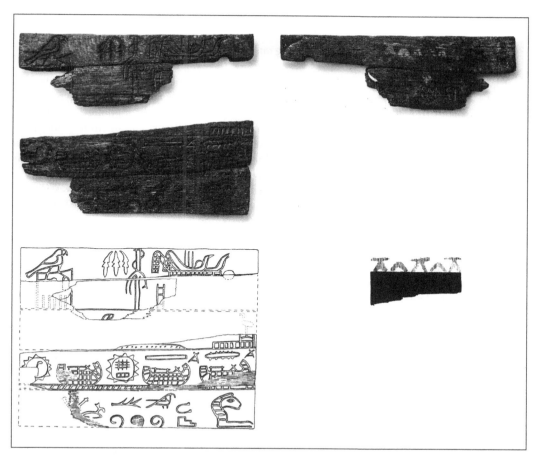

Figure 10: Fragmentary wooden label inscribed using incision on the primary face, with applied pigment on the secondary face (photography of full recto not permitted due to fragile condition). Provenance: Abydos, tomb B 18 (Narmer?) / B 19 (Aha?) (Petrie 1901: [T] 21, [P] pl. 3A, no. 6). H 5+ cm; W 9.6 cm; TH 0.23–0.4 cm. Source No. 0283a–b. EA 35518. Author's photograph, courtesy Trustees of the British Museum. Drawings from Petrie 1901: pl. 11, nos. 2–3, courtesy of the Egypt Exploration Society.

These and other examples of mixed image-making methods raise the possibility that the use of different techniques and styles for the two faces reflects greater temporal separation between production episodes. Perhaps incision of the primary side was the result of the immediate concerns of the (commissioner and) label-maker, while the addendum (?) was undertaken by a (different?) individual using different materials and writing implement, at a different time (and place?). Like the pairs of Naqada and Abydos labels, the life histories of these two examples, also from Abydos, seem to have been closely related, based on their temporal and spatial affiliations and the materiality of their inscriptions — an intersection of variables which can perhaps be understood as an indicator of the close proximity in which commissioners, label-makers and users sometimes operated.

To contextualise these graphical practices attested on label evidence, I would now like to turn briefly to contemporary examples of erasure, addendum and non-completion on Early Dynastic stone vessels and stelae.

Inscribed Stone Vessels and Stelae

Constructing, Deconstructing and Curating Personal Identity

Inscription on stone is sometimes characterised as intending permanency and immutability (e.g. Hiebert et al. 2000: 8; Kreamer et al. 2007: 110), yet many examples from ancient Egypt exhibit evidence for adjustment, addendum, palimpsest and erasure. Attested throughout the Pharaonic period (e.g. Der Manuelian 1999; Gozzoli 2000; Yoyotte 1951), erasure can be understood as an act of *damnatio memoriae* or the result of other changes in social status and relationships between individuals or between people and inscribed things, such as 'ownership'. Evidence of similar changing relationships is also evidenced on Early Dynastic stone objects including vessels.

Over half of all known early inscribed objects (more than 4500) are inscribed on vessels, the majority being made of hard stone, although most survive as fragments (Regulski 2010: 6, 26; see also El-Khouli 1978). Among these are a variety of rock and mineral types (e.g. basalt, diorite, granite, yellow limestone, quartz crystal, etc., see Aston 1994: 11–73), shaped into a range of forms (Aston 1994: 106–128). They are typically found in high status funerary contexts (e.g. Petrie 1901: pl. 46–53), and to a lesser extent ceremonial contexts (e.g. Quibell 1989 [1900]: pls 31 (2), 36). Vessel imagery contrasts somewhat with that of the labels. The former floats and clusters together with few narratival relationships between images in a compositional field with undefined boundaries beyond the surface area provided by the vessel. On the labels, narrative scenes are attested more often, particularly in the first-half of the 1st Dynasty, and compositional space is organised by register and column lines as well as the rectangular shape of the plaque itself (Piquette 2007). It therefore seems evident that images on the vessels, while depictive, are intended to serve a more scriptorial than pictorial function. The use of image categories such as 'sign', 'writing' or 'inscription' seems appropriate for the stone vessel imagery, but assumptions concerning a communicative function and a relationships to spoken language, such as the pronunciation of 'readings' from this early period, should be considered provisional (Trigger et al. 2001 [1983]: 56; see also Engel 1997: 434–435)

A survey of vessel inscriptions shows that they were made by removing surface material through incisions and less commonly, low relief carving. Many incisions are infilled with pigment / paste, as also attested on the inscribed labels (above). This would have aided visibility but colour also could also serve a symbolic purpose (Griffith in Petrie 1901: 51). Incised inscription usually occurs on the exterior of the vessel. Red or black colour applied directly to the vessel surface, attested more commonly during the 2nd Dynasty, was often located on the interior vessel surface (Regulski 2004: 955). Among the vessels and vessel fragments at least four types of scribal practice can be distinguished:

1. inscription
2. inscription > inscription
3. inscription > partial erasure / complete erasure
4. inscription > erasure > re-inscription

Subsequent to initial inscription (1), at least a dozen vessels bear inscriptions of type (2). These consist of a series of PIs laid out horizontally and understood as 'royal' titles (conventionally rendered *nsw.t-bi.t* and *nbty*) associated with Den, Adjib, Semerkhet and Qa'a (see Helck 1987: 101; see also Raffaele 2001 / 2002). It is suggested that after initial inscription, presumably commencing during the reign of the first ruler's PI in the list, the successor appropriated or otherwise acquired a vessel. The PI of the successor was then inscribed beside the predecessor's PI (see Kahl 2006: 96–99 for ideological influences on sequence for cylinder seals). Such examples highlight another way in which time is bound up in mark making. In comparison with the use of different

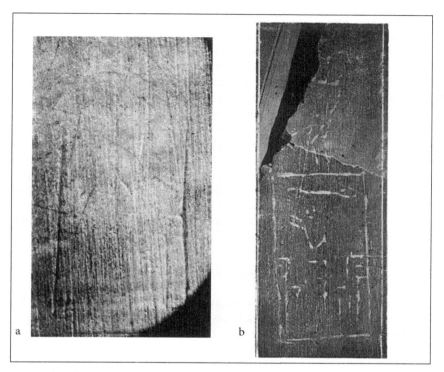

Figure 11: Details of stone vessels bearing erasures of the PI of Adjib. Provenance: Abydos, tomb complex U, attributed to Semerkhet, Adjib's successor (Petrie 1900: [T] 20). Not to scale. Photographs from Petrie 1900: [P] pl. 6, nos 9 and 11, courtesy of the Egypt Exploration Society.

techniques on different faces of a label and implications for the passage of time (above), here a temporal aspect that spans lifetimes is foregrounded in the sequence of graphical expressions of individual identity and social position.

One of the earliest occurrences of sign erasure (3) on stone vessels derives from Abydos tomb complex X attributed to Adjib. These had apparently been inscribed during the previous reigns of Merneith and Den based on traces of their PIs. Excavation of Abydos tomb complex U ascribed to Semerkhet also yielded a number of stone vessels bearing erasures (Petrie 1900: 19–20). Just visible beneath two examples are the faint remains of signs identified by Flinders Petrie as the name of Adjib, Semerkhet's predecessor (**Figure 11**), while others bore erasures of the PI of Merneith (Petrie 1900: 19, pl. 5, no. 5, see also 20, pl. 7, no. 6). This practice of erasing (though not completely enough to prevent the PI from being reconstructed) continued into the Old Kingdom. In the Valley Temple complex of Menkaure, a 4th Dynasty ruler, a cache of Early Dynastic vessels contained examples bearing both erasures and re-incision. These included an erased and re-inscribed vessel with the PI of Hetepsekhemwy and the erased PI of his successor, Nebra, on another (Reisner 1931).

These various episodes of scribal unmaking and remaking provide the modern investigator with valuable evidence for charting succession and lengths of reign (e.g. Kahl 2006). They also raise the question of whether these activities should be understood as *damnatio memoriae*, theft or usurpation, or seen as economically motivated. The notion of 'heirlooms' (see Jeffreys 2003) and seeing these activities as maintenance or curation may be more appropriate for some vessels, particularly those which bear accumulations of PI inscriptions rather than erasure. The proposal that an inscription was carved by an individual who was not fully literate and made an error in the copying process thus leading to erasure (Dusinberre 2005: 52), is probably not relevant here. Unlike the majority of labels for which making, use and deposition appear to be relatively restricted in time-space (e.g. spanning one, two or three reigns at most), the inscribed stone vessels exhibit more diverse and extended life histories. This may have involved greater opportunities for changes in function and meaning over the generations, as the vessels took on different kinds of significance for those who engaged with and experienced them — presumably rulers, scribes / artisans and individuals working in the funerary domain, if not the great beyond.

A potentially important link might be observed in the relationship between inscribed vessels and changes in high status funerary practices. During the 1st Dynasty, inscribed stone vessels turned up in close association with the burial chamber and the ruler's body. By the mid-Old Kingdom, inscribed vessels were still deployed within the funerary domain, but deposited some distance from the pyramid (where the body was presumably entombed), within the Valley Temple where the cult of the ruler was perpetuated. Further study of burial chamber deposition versus placement elsewhere may elucidate the nature and significance of vessel curation where inscriptions undergo replacement versus accumulation.

Partially Incomplete, Partially Complete

The final inscribed find type briefly treated in this chapter is a funerary stele. The vast majority of early stelae derive from the large mudbrick tomb complexes built for many Early Dynastic rulers at Abydos. The entrance to the main structure, the burial chamber and series of side chambers (Reisner 1936), was probably flanked by two large 'royal' stone stelae each adorned with the ruler's PI (e.g. Amélineau 1899: pls 34–37; 1904: pl. 18; Petrie 1900: pl. 1). Surrounding the burial chamber and magazines were rows of male and female human (and some faunal) subsidiary graves. Based on general archaeological association it seems that more than 300 graves were marked with small 'private' limestone stelae (e.g. Martin 2011: 2–3; Petrie 1900: pl. 33; see also Martin 2003 on 'royal: private' distinction). Small numbers of signs and often a seated or standing human figure were painted, carved, hammered, pecked or scratched onto / into the upper part of often roughly shaped slabs.

A small number of stelae show evidence for multiple or incomplete graphical episodes (e.g. Martin 2011: Stelae 96, 122, 131, 132, 142, 193, 201). A relatively large and exceptionally elaborate example of the so-called private stelae (No. 48) was found in a small chamber (unlikely its original context) to the west of the burial chamber of Qa'a (**Figure 12**; Petrie 1900: 26–27, 44–45, pls 30–31, 36). Based on Petrie's (1900: 26–27) written description and Geoffrey Thorndike Martin's (2011: 44) more recent study, this medium-sized rectangular limestone slab is smoothly dressed on the front from the top to the bottom of the panel. Below this the surface is roughly dressed and the back carefully worked. The edges were rounded off rather than squared. The inscription was sketched onto the surface in a red-brown pigment and finalised in black. Work was then begun to roughly hammer the matrix from around the drafted images, but intriguingly, the task was never completed. This is particularly apparent on the right in the second row where the height of the surface around the sign has not been reduced completely. Consequently, some images are unclear save for traces in red and black colour.

If we assume a right to left 'reading' direction (into the faces of the images), it is interesting to note that the process of surface transformation appears to have been undertaken in a different sequence from reading, leaving the right-most images in the second and third rows incompletely defined, including the upright staff held by the stele-owner. From the perspective of the presumed right-left reading direction and importance of this object as a vehicle for expressing the owner's identity, it seems unusual that the image of the owner, and the beginning of the row just above, were not prioritised in the production process. Perhaps the act of inscription in certain media may

Figure 12: Limestone stele No. 48 with incomplete carving along the right side. Dated to the end of the 1st Dynasty. Provenance: Abydos, "[t]his lay in a chamber on the west of Qa'a" (Petrie 1900: [T] 26 and pl. 60, [P] pl. 36, no. 48, [D] pl. 30 [with red-brown drafting lines indicated] and pl. 31, no. 48; also Martin 2011: [T] 44, [D] 45, Stela 48, [P] pl. 14, Stela 48). H 84.2 cm; W 37.5 cm; D 8.5 cm. Source No. 1865. JE 34416. Egyptian Museum, Cairo. Photograph and drawing courtesy Geoffrey Thorndike Martin and Harrassowitz.

have been undertaken according to the combined intentions and technological requirements of the scribe and / or other craftsperson(s) involved.

This evidence for the process of drafting, redrafting and partial carving, as well as erasure, raises a whole host of questions about why objects were not completed prior to being brought to the cemetery. It may be the case that in some circumstances aspects of production took place at or near the grave side (see also Martin 2011: 1). Alternatively, rather than seeing this stele as 'unfinished', perhaps its status within its past context of practice was constructed in a more contingent way. As long as a sufficient proportion of the imagery was present and / or discernible by the viewer (where intended), then perhaps the stele was considered to be sufficiently complete to serve its intended purpose. For this and the numerous other smaller stelae found in the same cemetery, the focus of material-graphical action appears to have been marking the personal identity

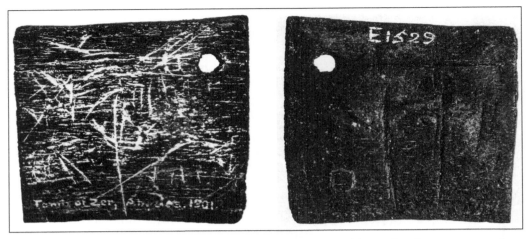

Figure 13: A wooden label showing what appears to be a roughly rendered inscription, subsequently scratched out (modern writing on the lower primary face in white ink reads, "Tomb of Zer, Abydos. 1901."). And on secondary face marked 'O' in pencil. Provenance: Abydos, tomb complex O, attributed to Djer (Petrie 1901: [T] 24, [P] pl. 6A, no. 5). H 3.6–3.8 cm; w 3.8–4.1 cm; TH 0.2–0.3 cm. Source No. 0643. E.1529. Author's photograph, courtesy Ashmolean Museum.

of the deceased. In addition to the inscription, this function may have also been accomplished via the spatial location of the stel(a)e adjacent to (or inside?) the tomb or grave of the individual concerned. If meaning was situated in and constructed through a network of spatial and material, as well as iconographic and semantic relationships, perhaps that an element was not 'fully' expressed would not have been perceived as problematic.

Discussion

In the preceding sections, I have examined three find types bearing graphical imagery, labels, stone vessels and stelae, with emphasis on their materiality in terms of surface transformation and evidence for practices of making, remaking, unmaking as well as partial making. If matter was removed from a surface rather than added to it, an image could not be easily changed or erased and work accumulated an internal 'stratigraphy' (Davis 1989: 184). At the same time, as part of different object types with different material properties, these surfaces were not simply passive foundations to support graphical imagery, but actively constituted and influenced expression and practice. By thinking through the *chaîne opératoire* of image-making we come to understand the ways in which imagery simultaneously embodied material processes and their outcomes.

Whether in making images fully or partially, or subsequently undertaking their adjustment, the particular contexts of those acts revealed different sets of choices and outcomes. For the wooden label in **Figure 13**, rather than a more comprehensive erasure, crossing out was used. This may have been a way of effectively decommissioning or cancelling potential use for ritual (?) or administrative (?) purposes. Perhaps the depositional context of the cemetery was nevertheless one of discard. The perforated bone plaque from the northern Egyptian cemetery site of Saqqara in **Figure 14** reveals a similar scribal act but on a smaller scale, indicative of intentions and choices bound up in a different set of circumstances. Here the marks of crossing out appear to be the correction of a perceived error, that the upper part of this large central sign or depiction was deemed to protrude too much. Such an adjustment seemingly resulted in the

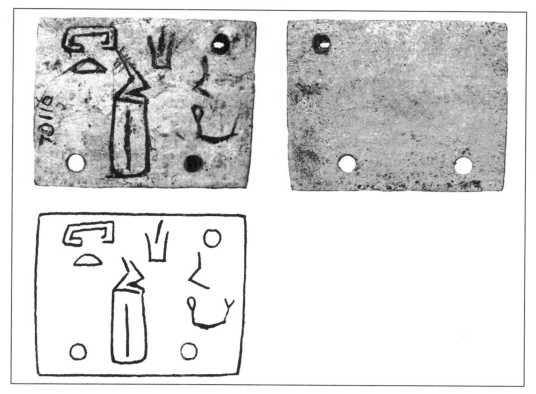

Figure 14: Incised ivory plaque showing the upper tip of the large central sign ('s25' / 'bag' [following Weill 1940: 222–223]) that has been scratched out. Provenance: North Saqqara, Tomb 3035. Dated to the 1st Dynasty reign of Djer? / Den (Emery and Sa'ad 1938: [T] 39, [P] pl. 17C (Cat. No. 413), [D] pl. 18C [Cat. No. 413]). H 2.6–2.61 cm; W 3.15–3.24 cm; TH 0.15–0.29 cm. Source No. 1422. JE 70116. Author's photograph, courtesy the Egyptian Museum, Cairo. Drawing from Emery and Sa'ad 1938: pl. 18B.

continuation of the object's intended use based on its well-preserved find context in Tomb 3035 at North Saqqara, which included, in addition to the leather bag and other finds, another almost identically perforated and inscribed plaque bearing a similar 'container' with a more truncated top (see Emery and Sa'ad 1938: [T] 39, [P] pl. 17B, [D] pl. 18B (412); Source No. 1422; Egyptian Museum JE 70115).[3]

To sum up, overall the majority of evidence for graphical adjustment consists of surface removal following original incision. Addendum is more difficult to distinguish, apart from cases such as the wooden labels marked using different in techniques (**Figures 9–10**) or inscriptions including sequences of ruler PIs. The erasure of applied pigment through 'washing' or a similar removal method is likely, but microscopy and multi-spectral analysis are needed for detection.

Because the investigator encounters only the material outcomes of action, it is easy to be seduced by the apparent fixity of the material evidence. Similarities in general archaeological context, repertoire and style, both palaeographic and compositional, point toward much of this graphical evidence being a realisation of the same emerging system (although this must remain an open question for the NIIIA1 survivals). On the basis of the high status find contexts, perceived values of materials (particularly ivory and stone), the elaborate nature of much initial inscription, this early written evidence is often infused with an air of regal or courtly precision, formality, monumentality, and fixity if not permanence. Scribal and iconographic practice is often seen as on a par with the might and power of early rulers, the administration of the early Egyptian 'state', recording and commemorating activities undertaken during their reigns, and conveying some definitive message about royal prerogative and control over people and goods in life and the afterlife.

Detailed consideration of the relationship between the material substances and surfaces, technological action, and the temporal and spatial conditions of making, use and reception shows that the ways in which that 'system' was practised was nevertheless variable and contingent. Indeed, 'writing' may be conceptualised as a relatively discrete category and concept in many cultural contexts. When examined in detail through the lens of practice theories (e.g. Dobres 2000), we find that individuals reproduced / renegotiated developing conventions and social structures in particularistic and complex ways. The majority of the evidence supports a firm social relationship between graphical / scribal activities and 'royal' and elite power and the maintenance of political authority, but these small details provide important insight into the nuance of individual and local experience. The multi-layered processes for image making, unmaking and re-making, the interactions between scribes / artisan, materials, tools, images and meaning, lends weight to Dobres' (2000: 130–132) notion of the 'becoming' of material culture — a concept which I argue must also form a cornerstone of research on written evidence.

Inasmuch as writing is understood to have been developed by elite members of early Egyptian society in order to consolidate and maintain authority, to formulate ideologies of rulership and cosmic stability, and otherwise 'fix' symbolic meaning, perhaps the devil is in the detail when we consider that writing simultaneously embeds material messages of mutability and transformation.

Acknowledgements

For permissions and assistance with images I would like to thank Marwa Abd elRazek, Ashley Cooke, Chris Eyre, Dirk Huyge, Barbara Krauss, Steven Snape, Cordula Werschkun, the Egypt Exploration Society, and The Griffith Institute. My thanks are also due to Richard Parkinson, Jeffrey Spencer and other staff of the British Museum Department of Ancient Egypt and Sudan for research access to objects. I am particularly grateful to Günter Dreyer and the Deutsche Archäologisches Institut Kairo for permitting the publication of the label Ab K 2602 in **Figure 5a**. My gratitude is also owed to Andrew Gardner, Ruth Whitehouse and the reviewers for comments on earlier drafts.

Notes

[1] Here the artefact assumes the same orientation as when the erased 'bird' motif is viewed in an upright position. The conventional publication for NIIA1 labels prioritises the upright position of clearly identifiable figural images with the effect that perforations are rarely located on the side (cf. Piquette 2010: 59). However, the intended orientation of the preserved image on the label in **Figure 2a** may be questioned when we consider that the other instances of this rectangular shape co-occur as part of a 'bird' / 'bird on perch' combination. Based on morphological similarities with later examples, this rectangular shape may be classed as 'N39' / 'pool' (Regulski 2010: 532) — a designation that inherently requires horizontal orientation and also complements the upright orientation of the accompanying 'bird'. Thus, together with the schematic nature of the preserved image on **Figure 2a**, which makes its iconic significance difficult to discern, and the precedent for the variable location of the perforation, intended orientation must remain an open question, whether in the past context of production or use (e.g. label attachment, grasping, viewing, turning).

[2] Faint depressions in the shape of 'D28' / 'pair of arms' suggest the same sign, if not cluster, was also originally inscribed in the label in **Figure 5b**. In both cases, the sequence of surface transformations and the underlying marks could be clarified with the application of a computational photographic technique, such as Reflectance Transformation Imaging (e.g. Piquette 2011; see also Earl et al. 2011).

[3] Compared with other NIIIA1 or NIIIC–early D 'labels', the number of perforations (3) and graphical content of this pair are unique, raising the question of whether either should be considered a 'label' in the same sense as single-perforated examples.

References

Amélineau, E. 1899. *Les Nouvelles Fouilles d'Abydos: 1895–1896 – Part I*. Paris: Ernest Leroux.

Amélineau, E. 1904. *Les Nouvelles Fouilles d'Abydos: 1897–1898*. Paris: Ernest Leroux.

Aston, B. G. 1994. *Ancient Egyptian Stone Vessels: Materials and forms* (Studien Zur Archäologie und Geschichte Altägyptens 5). Heidelberg: Heidelberger Orientverlag.

Baines, J. 1995. Origins of Egyptian Kingship. In O'Connor, D. and Silverman, D. P. (eds), *Ancient Egyptian Kingship*. New York: E. J. Brill, 95–156.

Baines, J. 2004. The Earliest Egyptian Writing: Development, context, purpose. In Houston, S. D. (ed.), *The First Writing: Script invention as history and process*. Cambridge: Cambridge University Press, 150-189.

Baines, J. 2008. Birth of Writing and Kingship: Introduction. In Midant-Reynes, B., Tristant, Y., Rowland, J. and Hendrickx, S. (eds), *Egypt at Its Origins 2: Proceedings of the international conference "Origin of the State: Predynastic and Early Dynastic Egypt", Toulouse (France), 5th–8th September 2005* (Orientalia Lovaniensia Analecta 172). Leuven: Peeters, 839–847.

Bard, K. A. 1992. Origins of Egyptian Writing. In Friedman, R. and Adams, B. (eds), *The Followers of Horus: Studies dedicated to Michael Allen Hoffman 1944–1990*. Oxford: Oxbow Books, 297–306.

Boehmer, R. M., Dreyer, G. and Kromer, B. 1993. Einige frühzeitliche 14C-Datierungenaus Abydos and Uruk. *Mitteilungen des Deutschen Archäologischen Instituts, Abteilung Kairo* 49: 63–68.

Breyer, F. A. K. 2002. Die Schriftzeugnisse des Prädynastischen Königsgrabes U-j in Umm el-Qaab: Versuch einer Neuinterpretation. *Journal of Egyptian Archaeology* 88: 53–65.

Caminos, R. 1986 Some Comments on the Re-use of Papyrus. In Bierbrier, M. (ed.), *Papyrus: Structure and usage* (British Museum Occasional Paper 60). London: British Museum Press, 43–61.

Ciałowicz, K. M. 2001. *La naissance d'un royaume: l'Égypte dès la période prédynastique à fin de la Ier dynastie*. Krakòw: Ksiegarnia Akademicka.

Davis, W. 1989. Find Symbols in History. In Morphy, H. (ed.), *Animal into Art*. London: Unwin Hyman, 179–189.

de Morgan, J. 1897. *Recherches sur les Origines de l'Égypte: Ethnographie préhistorique et tombeau royal de Négadah*. Paris: Ernest Leroux.

Der Manuelian, P. 1999. Semi-Literacy in Egypt: Some erasures from the Amarna Period. In Teeter, E. and Larson, J. A. (eds), *Gold of Praise: Studies on ancient Egypt in honor of Edward F. Wente* (Studies in Ancient Oriental Civilization 58). Chicago: Oriental Institute, University of Chicago, 285–289.

Dobres, M.-A. 2000. *Technology and Social Agency: Outlining a practice framework for archaeology*. Oxford: Blackwell.

Dreyer, G. 1998. *Umm el-Qaab I: Das prädynastische Königsgrab U-j und seine frühen Schriftzeugnisse*. Mainz am Rhein: Philipp von Zabern.

Dreyer, G., Boessneck, J., von den Driech, A. and Klug, S. 1990. Umm el-Qaab: Nachuntersuchungen im frühzeitlichen Königsfriedhof 3./4. Vorbericht. *Mitteilungen des Deutschen Archäologischen Instituts, Abteilung Kairo* 46: 53–89.

Dreyer, G., Hartmann, R., Hartung, U., Hikade, T., Köpp, H., Lacher, C., Müller, V., Nerlich, A. and Zink, A. 2003. Umm el-Qaab: Nachuntersuchungen im frühzeitlichen Königsfriedhof 13./14./15. Vorbericht. *Mitteilungen des Deutschen Archäologischen Instituts, Abteilung Kairo* 59: 69–138.

Dreyer, G., Hartung, U., Hikade, T. and Müller, V. 1998. Umm el-Qaab: Nachuntersuchungen im frühzeitlichen Königsfriedhof 9./10. Vorbericht. *Mitteilungen des Deutschen Archäologischen Instituts, Abteilung Kairo* 54: 78–167.

Dusinberre, E. R. M. 2005. *Gordion Seals and Sealings: Individuals and society*. Philadelphia: University of Pennsylvania Museum.

Earl, G., Basford, P. J., Bischoff, A. S., Bowman, A., Crowther, C., Hodgson, M., Martinez, K., Isaksen, L., Pagi, H., Piquette, K. E. and Kotoula, E. 2011. Reflectance Transformation Imaging Systems for Ancient Documentary Artefacts. In Dunn, S., Bowen, J. and Ng, K. (eds), *EVA London 2011: Electronic Visualisation and the Arts. Proceedings of a conference held in London, 6–8 July 2011*. Bristol: BCS, The Chartered Institute for IT, 147–154. http://eprints.soton.ac.uk/id/eprint/204531 [accessed 01 September 2013].

El-Khouli, A. 1978. *Egyptian Stone Vessels Predynastic Period to Dynasty III: Typology and analysis*. 3 volumes. Mainz am Rhein: von Zabern.

Emery, W. B. 1954. *Excavations at Saqqara: Great tombs of the First Dynasty II*. London: Egypt Exploration Society.

Emery, W. B. and Sa'ad, Z. Y. 1938. *Excavations at Saqqara: The tomb of Hemaka*. Cairo: Government Press.

Engel, E.-M. 1997. *Das Grab des Qa'a in Umm el-Qa'ab: Architektur und Inventar, I–III*. Unpublished PhD dissertation, Göttingen University.

Gardner, A. 2007. *An Archaeology of Identity: Soldiers & society in late Roman Britain*. Walnut Creek: Left Coast Press.

Gardner, A. 2008. Agency. Chapter 7 in Bentley, R. A., Maschner, H. D. G., Chippindale, C. (eds), *Handbook of Archaeological Theories*. Walnut Creek, CA: AltaMira Press, 95–108.

Garstang, J. 1905. The Tablet of Mena. *Zeitschrift für ägyptische Sprache und Altertumskunde* 42: 61–64.

Görsdorf, J., Dreyer, G. and Hartung, U. 1998. New 14C Dating of the Archaic Royal Necropolis Umm El-Qaab at Abydos (Egypt). *Radiocarbon* 40(1–2): 641–647.

Giddens, A. 1984. *The Constitution of Society: Outline of the theory of structuration*. Berkeley: University of California Press.

Gozzoli, R. B. 2000. The Statue BM EA 37891 and the Erasure of Necho II's Names. *Journal of Egyptian Archaeology* 86: 67–80. DOI: http://dx.doi.org/10.2307/3822308

Helck, W. 1987. *Untersuchungen zur Thinitenzeit*. Wiesbaden: Harrassowitz.

Hendrickx, S. 1996. The Relative Chronology of the Naqada Culture: Problems and possibilities. In Spencer, A. J. (ed.), *Aspects of Early Egypt*. London: British Museum Press, 36–69.

Hiebert, R. E., Gibbons, S. J. and Silver, S. 2000. *Exploring Mass Media for a Changing World*. Mahwah, NJ: Lawrence Erlbaum Associates.

James, T. G. H. 1995. The Earliest History of Wine and Its Importance in Ancient Egypt. In McGovern, P., Fleming, S. and Katz, S. (eds), *The Origins and Ancient History of Wine*. Luxembourg: Gordon and Breach, 197–213.

Jeffreys, D. 2003. All in the Family?: Heirlooms in ancient Egypt. In Tait, J. (ed.), *'Never Had the Like Occurred': Egypt's view of its past*. London: UCL Press, 197–211.

Kahl, J. 2001. Hieroglyphic Writing During the Fourth Millennium BC: An analysis of systems. *Archéo-Nil* 11: 102–134.

Kahl, J. 2006. Inscriptional Evidence for the Relative Chronology of Dyns. 0–2. In Hornung, E., Krauss, R. and Warburton, D. A. (eds), *Ancient Egyptian Chronology* (Handbook of Oriental Studies: Section One: The Near and Middle East). Leiden: Brill, 94–115.

Kohler, E. C. 2010. Theories of State Formation. In Wendrich, W. (ed.), *Egyptian Archaeology*. Oxford: Blackwell Publishing, 36–54.

Kreamer, C. M., Roberts, M. N., Harney, E. and Purpura, A. 2007. *Inscribing Meaning: Writing and graphic systems in African art*. National Museum of African Art (U.S.). New York: Smithsonian, National Museum of African Art.

Martin, G. T. 2003. An Early Dynastic Stela from Abydos: Private or royal? In Quirke, S. (ed.), *Discovering Egypt from the Neva: The Egyptological legacy of Oleg D. Berlev*. Berlin: Achet, 79–84.

Martin, G. T. 2011. *Umm el-Qaab VII: Private stelae of the Early Dynastic Period from the Royal Cemetery at Abydos* (Archäologische Veröffentlichungen 123). Wiesbaden: Harrassowitz.

Meskell, L. 2004. *Object Worlds in Ancient Egypt: Material biographies past and present*. Oxford: Berg.

Moreland, J. 2006. Archaeology and Texts: Subservience or enlightenment. *Annual Review of Anthropology* 35: 135–151. DOI: http://dx.doi.org/10.1146/annurev.anthro.35.081705.123132

Newberry, P. E. 1912. The Wooden and Ivory Labels of the First Dynasty. *Proceedings of the Society of Biblical Archaeology* 34: 279–289.

Petrie, W. M. F. 1900. *The Royal Tombs of the Earliest Dynasties, Part I*. London: Egypt Exploration Fund.

Petrie, W. M. F. 1901. *The Royal Tombs of the Earliest Dynasties, Part II*. London: Egypt Exploration Fund.

Piquette, K. E. 2007. *Writing, 'Art' and Society: A contextual archaeology of the inscribed labels of Late Predynastic–Early Dynastic Egypt*. Unpublished PhD dissertation, University of London.

Piquette, K. E. 2008. Re-Materialising Script and Image. In Gashe, V. and Finch, J. (eds), *Current Research in Egyptology 2008: Proceedings of the ninth annual symposium, which took place at the KNH Centre for Biomedical Egyptology, University of Manchester, January 2008*. Bolton: Rutherford Press, 89–107.

Piquette, K. E. 2010. A Compositional Approach to a First Dynasty Inscribed Label Fragment from the Abydos Tomb Complex Ascribed to Qa'a. *Zeitschrift für Ägyptische Sprache und Altertumskunde* 137(1): 54–65. DOI: http://dx.doi.org/10.1524/zaes.2010.0005

Piquette, K. E. 2011. Reflectance Transformation Imaging and Ancient Egyptian Material Culture. *Damqatum: The CEHAO newsletter – El boletín de noticias del CEHAO* 7: 16–20. http://bibliotecadigital.uca.edu.ar/repositorio/revistas/damqatum7-eng.pdf [accessed 15 August 2013].

Piquette, K. E. 2013. Structuration and the Graphical in Early Dynastic Culture. In Dann, R. J. and Exell, K. (eds), *Egypt: Ancient histories, modern archaeologies*. Amherst, NY: Cambria Press, 51–99.

Piquette, K. E. forthcoming. Scribal Practice and an Early Dynastic Stone Vessel Inscription: Material and aesthetic implications. In Dodson, A. Johnston, J. J. and Monkhouse, W. (eds), *Festschrift in Honour of John Tait*. London: Golden House Publications.

Quibell, J. E. 1989 [1900]. *Hierakonpolis, Part I*. London: Histories and Mysteries of Man Ltd.

Raffaele, F. 2000 / 2001. *Stone Vessels inscriptions of Egyptian Early Dynastic Kings*. http://xoomer.virgilio.it/francescoraf/hesyra/aufgefasse.htm [accessed 25 April 2009].

Redford, S. and Redford, D. B. 1989. Graffiti and Petroglyphs Old and New from the Eastern Desert. *Journal of the American Research Center in Egypt* 26: 3–49. DOI: http://dx.doi.org/10.2307/40000700

Regulski, I. 2004. 2nd Dynasty Ink Inscriptions from Saqqara Paralleled in the Royal Museums of Art and History, Brussels. In Hendrickx, S., Friedman, R. F., Cialowicz, K. M. and Chlodnicki, M. (eds), *Egypt at its Origins: Studies in memory of Barbara Adams. Proceedings of the international conference "Origin of the State: Predynastic and Early Dynastic Egypt", Krakow, 28th August – 1st September 2002* (Orientalia Lovaniensia Analecta 138). Leuven: Peeters, 949–970.

Regulski, I. 2008. The Origin of Writing in Relation to the Emergence of the Egyptian State. In Midant-Reynes, B., Tristant, Y., Rowland, J. and Hendrickx, S. (eds), *Egypt at Its Origins 2: Proceedings of the international conference "Origin of the State: Predynastic and Early Dynastic Egypt", Toulouse (France), 5th–8th September 2005* (Orientalia Lovaniensia Analecta 172). Leuven: Peeters, 985–1009.

Regulski, I. 2009. The beginning of Hieratic Writing in Egypt. *Studien zur Altägyptischen Kultur* 38: 259–274.

Regulski, I. 2010. *A Palaeographic Study of Early Writing in Egypt* (Orientalia Lovaniensia Analecta 195). Leuven: Peeters.

Reisner, G. A. 1931. *Mycerinus: The temples of the third pyramid at Giza.* Cambridge: Cambridge University Press.

Reisner, G. A. 1936. *The Development of the Egyptian Tomb Down to the Accession of Cheops.* Cambridge, MA: Harvard University Press.

Spencer, A. J. 1993. *Early Egypt: The rise of civilisation in the Nile Valley.* London: British Museum Press.

Storemyr, P. 2009. A Prehistoric Geometric Rock Art Landscape by the First Nile Cataract. *Archéo-Nil* 19: 121–150.

Trigger, B. T., Kemp, B. J., O'Connor, D. and Lloyd, A. B. 2001 [1983]. *Ancient Egypt: A social history.* Cambridge: Cambridge University Press.

van den Brink, E. C. M. 1992. Corpus and Numerical Evaluation of the "Thinite" Potmarks. In Friedman, R. and Adams, B. (eds), *The Followers of Horus: Studies dedicated to Michael Allen Hoffman, 1949–1990.* Oxford: Oxbow, 265–296.

Vikentiev, V. 1959. Études d'Épigraphie protodynastique. II: Deux tablettes en ivoire (I dyn.) et les linteaux de Medamoud (XII–XIIIe dyn.). *Annales du Service des Antiquités de l'Égypte* 56: 1–30.

Weill, R., 1940. Deux mots de la Ire dynastie, aux inscriptions du tombeau de "Hemaka" à Saqqarah. *Revue d'Égyptologie* 4: 222–223.

Wengrow, D. 2006. *The Archaeology of Early Egypt: Social transformations in North East Africa, 10,000–2650 BC.* Cambridge: Cambridge University Press.

Wengrow, D. 2008. Limits of Decipherment: Object biographies and the invention of writing. In Midant-Reynes, B., Tristant, Y., Rowland, J. and Hendrickx, S. (eds), *Egypt at Its Origins 2: Proceedings of the international conference "Origin of the State: Predynastic and Early Dynastic Egypt", Toulouse (France), 5th–8th September 2005* (Orientalia Lovaniensia Analecta 172). Leuven: Peeters, 1021–1032.

Wilkinson, T. A. H. 2001 [1999]. *Early Dynastic Egypt.* London: Routledge.

Yoyotte, J. 1951. Le martelage des nom royaux éthiopiens par Psammétique II. *Revue de Égyptologie* 8: 215–239.

Written Greek but Drawn Egyptian: Script changes in a bilingual dream papyrus

Stephen Kidd

Brown University

In a 3rd-century BCE Greco-Egyptian letter inscribed on papyrus, a man writes to his friend about a recent dream. He is writing in Greek, but in order to describe his dream accurately, he says, he must write the dream itself in Egyptian; after saying his Greek farewell, he recounts the dream and begins writing in a Demotic hand. This shift in languages entails a number of transitions: a new vocabulary, a wildly different grammar, but also one very important change — a change of script. In this chapter, I will explore the conceptual background between shifting from Greek to Demotic in this letter — not in linguistic or socio-political terms, but in terms of the actual practice of writing and the ideological trappings that accompany each writing-system. I will argue that the two scripts (not just the two languages) inform the letter-writer's decision to choose and elevate Demotic as the proper vehicle for recounting his dream.

I will make this argument in three parts: first, by examining the different ways that these two languages were physically written; second, by 'getting inside' the process of writing an alphabetic (Greek) versus a logographic (Demotic) script; and third, by recreating the subjective experience of the alphabetic – logographic shift through comparative evidence (English and Chinese). Although I do not argue that there is something objectively more lofty or mystical in a logographic script, I do argue that when two cultures come into contact (Greek and Egyptian, English and Chinese) the opportunity is available to compare scripts and to create a hierarchy of uses for them.

This papyrus — a product of Greco-Egyptian cultural contact in 3rd-century Egypt — exhibits such a hierarchy in that these different scripts, Greek and Egyptian, appropriate their own registers and purposes. It is possible to see (after examining a) the materiality, b) the writing process and c) the subjective experience) an entire matrix of scriptorial ideology behind this language shift — an ideology which helps to explain why this Greco-Egyptian man, Ptolemaios, chooses Egyptian for his dream content. After all, he is making the transition from every-day affairs to

How to cite this book chapter:
Kidd, S. 2013. Written Greek but Drawn Egyptian: Script changes in a bilingual dream papyrus.
In: Piquette, K. E. and Whitehouse, R. D. (eds.) *Writing as Material Practice: Substance, surface and medium.* Pp. 239-252. London: Ubiquity Press. DOI: http://dx.doi.org/10.5334/bai.l

the religious visions of the night, and as much as cultural and religious reasons might help to explain this shift, the actual, physical writing does as well. The difference between these two scripts is that of the mundane real world and that of the symbolic dream world — the Greek written, but the Egyptian drawn.

The Papyrus

Here are the translations of the central fragments of the 3rd-century BCE papyrus letter (translation with minor changes from Renberg and Naether 2010):
[In Greek]

P.Cairo 10328, *recto*

…it also (?) seemed good to me that I should fully inform you about my dream, so that you will know in what ways the gods know you. I have written below in Egyptian so that you will know precisely (*aigyptisti de hypegrapsa, hopôs akribôs eidêis*). When I was about to go to sleep, I wrote two short letters, the one concerning Taunchis the daughter of Thermouthis and the other concerning Tetimouthis the daughter of Taues, who is the daughter of Ptolemaios, and yet one more…

P.Cairo 30961, *recto*

…pour a drink for (or anoint) yourself, in which manner I too celebrated a fine (*kalên*) day. Farewell. Year 2, Phaophi 26.

[*At this point in P.Cairo 30961 recto, Ptolemaios starts to write in Demotic*] I saw myself in a dream in the following way: I am standing at the doorway of the sanctuary. A priest is sitting there, and many people (*~remetch*) are standing beside him. The priest spoke to the people who were standing there: "…"

P.Cairo 30961, *verso*

…I spoke [to the] aforementioned [prie]st: "The man of Pamoun – who is it?" He said: "It is Nebwotis". See, the answer which they gave me: the man of Pamoun whom he named: "He is /That's life". He says: "Taunchis", (and) she said to me: "The man of Pamoun, who is it?" He said, "Nebwotis is it, who has said it". The one who is there says: "A woman is it outside giving to me…"

This letter has been dated to the 3rd century BCE, and has been conjectured to be from the Fayum region, although the most recent editors have cast doubt on this provenance (Bagnall and Derow 2004; Goodspeed 1902; Renberg and Naether 2010; Spiegelberg 1908; Wilcken and von Mitteis 1912; Witkowski 1911). If it is indeed of a 3rd-century date, it must be late, due to the use of the reed pen for writing the Egyptian, which suggests a date after 230 BCE (Depauw 1997: 83). The question of interest for this papyrus is why Ptolemaios switches from Greek to Egyptian in order to describe his dream. He writes "I have written below in Egyptian, so that you may accurately understand". But does this mean that Akhilles' Greek was not proficient? As Wilcken and von Mitteis suggested a century ago, such a conclusion would be absurd, since if Ptolemaios had thought Akhilles' knowledge of Greek was inadequate, he would not have written him a Greek letter in the first place (Wilcken and von Mitteis 1912: 74). It seems that the reason for the language shift must be due to something other than language competence. One could identify cultural reasons for the shift

Figure 1: P.Cairo 30961 *recto*. Photograph Ahmed Amin, Egyptian Museum, Cairo.

(e.g. that when bilinguals discuss religious topics in Ptolemaic Egypt, either in spoken or written form, they might tend toward using Egyptian rather than Greek). Or one might identify linguistic reasons (e.g. that in order to interpret a dream properly one must look to the words themselves — a style of dream interpretation found in both Greek and Egyptian dream-interpretation manuals). I consider such possibilities elsewhere (Kidd 2011). Here, however, rather than pursuing linguistic or religious reasons, I would like to consider the physical influences that were present when Ptolemaios made this language shift, especially regarding the scripts themselves and the material practice of writing these two scripts. Arguably, the material of the writing surface, the pens, and the ink were just as entangled in Ptolemaios' experience of writing as the immaterial, conceptualized words and sounds, so it is worth considering the materials more closely in their own right. If Greek and Egyptian were generally written with different tools via different embodied practices, could these physical differences inform the language shift? Although language-shifts are generally conceived of as cerebral events, the motions of the hand, the materiality of the pens, and the application of ink on papyrus may also drive the transitions of language, not as passive accompaniments, but active agents. It is to these materials I now turn.

The Materiality of Writing Greek and Egyptian

When Ptolemaios wrote this letter he used a pen made of reed, both for the Greek and the Egyptian parts (**Figure 1**). But this was not usually the case in the 3rd century. Rather, there seems to have been a strict division between the tools that were used to write Greek and the tools that were used to write Demotic. A Greek writing Greek would generally use a pen made of reed while an Egyptian writing Egyptian would use a pen made of rush. Although the differences between these two pens have been described already in detail by Tait (1998) and Clarysse (1993), it is worth giving a quick overview again here.

When a Greek wrote Greek in 3rd-century BCE Egypt, the process of writing his or her language was quite different from an Egyptian writing Egyptian. The pen that a Greek used was made from Egyptian reed (**Figure 2**), to be exact the stem of the *Phragmites communis* (Tait 1988: 477). These reed stems could be cut as long as 26.5 cm, and after drying, would be sharpened to a broad

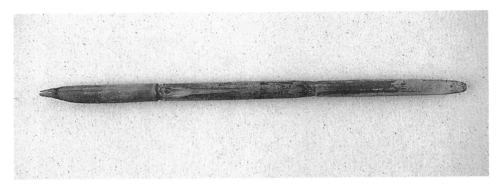

Figure 2: Reed pen, Roman period, Karanis. KM 3820, Kelsey Museum of Archaeology, University of Michigan.

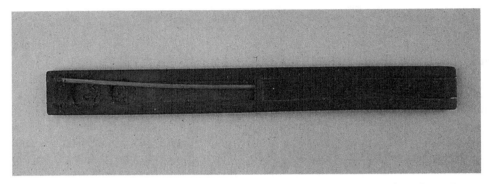

Figure 3: Rush pen inserted into holder built into palette. KM 1971.2.184 a–b, Kelsey Museum of Archaeology, University of Michigan.

point, and split at the nib in the same way that quills were later used. When the reed would lose its point it would have to be sharpened again in order to function properly (in a papyrus containing verses from the Greek playwright Menander, this reed sharpening occurred roughly every 50 lines, Turner 1971: 8). In this process, the originally long pen would eventually be whittled down pencil-like to a stump of some 6.0 cm long. One such reed-stump was even found lengthened with a bit of wood (Lucas 1934: 133).

The Egyptian pen (**Figure 3**), on the other hand, was really not a pen at all, but rather a brush. Not made from thick reed (the diameter of which was about 1.0 cm) but from the much thinner Egyptian rush (about 0.15 cm in diameter, or ~1/5 the thickness of the reed). The rush, or to be exact, the *Juncus acutus* (Tait 1988: 477), grew generally in Egyptian salt marshes, and its stem was cut to a similar length as the reed (specimens found from 16–23 cm, Lucas 1934: 133). But rather than being sharpened like the reed, it was cut diagonally at the end, bruised and frayed (some say by chewing, but others note that chewing is both unnecessary and, considering the ink, messy) in order to work the naturally-occurring fibers into brush-like form.

These different pens required different accoutrements. The Greek scribe used the reed with a metallic-based ink and an inkwell (**Figure 4**): once the ink was absorbed in the nib, the writer held the pen at an angle, and wrote (from left to right) until the ink dried up, at which point the pen was dipped back into the inkwell and the process started anew. The image of this writer is not far off from modern writing (before the invention of the fountain pen which required the hand to rest on the writing-surface in order to produce a sharper pen angle) — the dipping in the inkpot, the holding of the pen at the angle, etc. For the Egyptian scribe, however, the process of writing

Figure 4: Faience inkwell, Ptolemaic-Roman period, Fayoum. KM 4969, Kelsey Museum of Archaeology, University of Michigan.

is closer to our associations not of writing, but of painting — especially watercolour painting. For one, the brush-like rush was not used with an inkwell, but a palette (**Figure 3**), which held a cake of black, carbon-based 'watercolour' in one oval (a mixture of black pigment from charred organic materials and a gum arabic binding) and a cake of red 'watercolour' in the other (red pigment from iron oxide; see Nicholson and Shaw 2000: 238, and Clarysse 1993: 189 for the differences between Greek metallic based ink versus Egyptian carbon-based ink). The writer then applied water with the brush to the 'watercolour', and then proceeded to apply this ink to the surface (papyrus, ostracon, etc.), not holding the pen at an angle as one did with the reed, but holding the brush vertically, with the hand floating freely over the papyrus ("about 5 cm from its writing end" [Clarysse 1993: 189]), writing right to left.

The differences in these two types of pens may have even affected how the scribe sat when he or she wrote. From an early Egyptian sculpture known as 'The Seated Scribe' (Louvre E3023), it can be seen that writing (c.2500 BCE) was practiced sitting on the floor in a cross-legged position — the scribe stretching his kilt tautly across his knees in order to provide support for the papyrus. Although it has been supposed that this posture of writing continued not just for later Egyptian scribes but for Greek ones as well, Turner makes the important observation that the Greek reed pen, unlike the Egyptian rush, was hard, sharp, and, due to the pressure it sometimes required, could easily have punctured the papyrus if it were not supported by some harder surface. He suggests that some hard material such as a writing-board might have been needed to support the reed's pressure: and indeed, there have been finds of small writing desks (**Figure 5**), as well as depictions of Greek scribes writing while seated on chairs (see Turner 1971: 7–8 for references).

Thus, there are a number of differences between the material practices of writing for an Egyptian and a Greek — not just regarding the pens used (rush, reed), but also the accoutrements (inkwells, palettes), the holding positions, and possibly even the sitting positions for the writing as well. With such striking physical differences between these two practices of writing, one wonders whether there were also conceptual differences between Egyptian rush-writing and Greek reed-writing.

Figure 5: Wooden writing table, Karanis. KM 2.4802, Kelsey Museum of Archaeology, University of Michigan.

That is, would Ptolemaios, for example, in writing the Egyptian of this letter with a reed and not a rush, have considered himself to be writing in a 'Greek' way? Would such practice have seemed strange to him? During this same period when Ptolemaios was writing this letter with a reed pen, Egyptian scribes elsewhere were just beginning to abandon the rush pen and adopt the reed for writing Greek, the language of the new ruling class (although Egyptian documents still were written with the rush); gradually, the reed pen came to dominate more generally (by the 2nd century CE, both Greek and Egyptian were written with the reed pen; Clarysse 1993; Depauw 1997: 83; Tait 1988: 481). But in Ptolemaios' day, there was still a fairly strict division between writing Egyptian with a rush and Greek with a reed.

One would expect that if there were truly a different conception of 'Greek' and 'Egyptian' writing — i.e. that Greek is a language to be written with a reed, and Egyptian a language to be 'painted' with a rush — Ptolemaios would have switched pens for the Egyptian portion of the letter. But this would have been extraordinarily inexpedient: understandably, when Ptolemaios switched to Egyptian for his dream, he did not put away the reed, clean the inkpot, locate an Egyptian rush, cake some watercolour onto a palette, fill up a clean pot with water, and begin writing again. Instead he continued on with the reed pen — and the same thing seems to have happened in P.Duk.Inv. 675 (cf. Sosin and Manning 2003). Yet that expediency, I think, ought not erase those two images of Greek 'writing' and Egyptian 'painting'. Even at the moment when transition between the two practices seems most effortless (i.e. when the Egyptian language is written with a Greek reed), this does not mean that the images and cognitive associations of 'Egyptian' and 'Greek' writing disappeared. One might think, for example, of melodies associated with certain instruments, or sculptures associated with certain materials. The ease of transference for the immaterial aspect of those melodies or forms does not abrogate the memories of the materials associated with those forms, or the performances associated with those melodies. Although now lost behind the remaining object, when Ptolemaios shifted from Greek to Egyptian, it seems likely that there was a vast network of different images and physical memories flooding his mind, not just those less material aspects of communication (e.g. meanings, sentences and sounds).

The reason why raising such questions is important, is that it helps one to begin to think of language in more material terms, and language-shifts not as purely cerebral events, but as events interconnected with physical practices and the memories of such practices. For the Greco-Egyptian of Ptolemaios' day, the processes of writing Greek and Egyptian were highly different — while Greek was 'written', Egyptian was 'painted' — and so Ptolemaios, in his language shift, was not just choosing between two different languages, but between what were usually two very different practices of writing. Of course, there is more to this notion of 'painting' Demotic than just its material practice: there is also the script itself. Like Egyptian trilingual inscriptions where a hierarchy of scripts is on display — a relief picture at the top, hieroglyphs at the second tier, Demotic on the third and Greek on the fourth — certain scripts claim a higher level of visuality than others (i.e. certain scripts are logographic rather than alphabetic, creating images rather than spellings). It might be claimed that there are two aspects to 'painting', then: not just the painting materials used to 'paint' Demotic, but the Demotic script itself which demands a higher level of visuality than an alphabetic script like Greek. This difference in scripts is the subject of the next section.

Alphabetic Versus Logographic Scripts

In Chapter 6 of his *Interpretation of Dreams*, Sigmund Freud imagines dreams as languages containing both alphabetic scripts and pictographic ones. Discussing "the Dream-Work", he writes:

> The dream-thoughts and the dream-content are presented to us like two versions of the same subject-matter in two different languages. Or, more properly, the dream-content seems like a transcript of the dream-thoughts into another mode of expression... The dream-thoughts are immediately comprehensible, as soon as we have learnt them. The dream-content, on the other hand, is expressed as it were in a pictographic script, the characters of which have to be transposed individually into the language of the dream-thoughts... (Freud 1954: 277).

Freud's metaphor of two different dream-languages rides not on how the language of dreams is spoken, but how it is written: the same subject matter is being described first in an everyday script, second in a pictographic one. Ptolemaios' bilingual letter is in some ways a bizarre realization of Freud's dream-script: in order to describe his dream, Ptolemaios shifts from an alphabetic script (Greek), to another, non-alphabetic form of writing (Demotic Egyptian). Although Demotic is a not a pictographic script, it is derived from one (early hieroglyphs), and the way in which it was written was fundamentally different from Greek. In this section of this chapter, I will consider Ptolemaios' language-shift *vis-à-vis* the actual movements of writing. After analyzing two words from the papyrus (one Greek, one Demotic), I will consider the alphabetic and logographic scripts in terms of the painting-versus-writing spectrum discussed above, only now in terms of picture-versus-script. If there is a sliding scale between word and picture (as some Egyptian trilingual decrees suggest), Greek and Demotic may have been perceived at different points on that scale.

Greek is an alphabetic script while Demotic was derived from earlier hieroglyphs and thus was something rather different. From original pictograms, hieroglyphs evolved into a much more complex script which was able to represent sounds as well as ideas. The script even developed an alphabet of sorts which could clarify the meaning of certain words and supplement the Egyptian vocabulary with loan words and foreign names. But one must be clear about this 'alphabet': Demotic's alphabetic elements never formed an alphabet in the Greek sense, learned front-to-back at the beginning of school. It was never an alphabet which — like the Periodic Table — could break down any word of the known world into its natural elements. Indeed, an Egyptian person (before the invention of Coptic) could never have constructed a sublime alphabetic concept like

'I am the Alpha and the Omega'. Thus, although there was something of an alphabet in Demotic, it was used as more of an auxiliary tool than the fundamental basis of the written language. What makes Demotic interesting for this dream letter is its logographic aspect — so the distinction between alphabetic and logographic is worth outlining in closer detail here.

On the fragment of papyrus where the shift between Greek and Egyptian scripts can actually be seen (**Figure 1**), the first three lines are written in Greek. To take an example from these lines is the Greek word '*kalên*' which means 'fine, beautiful': in order to write '*kalên*' Ptolemaios needed to write a *kappa* which he smoothly linked to an *alpha*, and then to a *lambda*; after a new break with the *eta*, he finished with the *nu*. In '*kalên*' each of the five letters is its own self-standing element — that is, when Ptolemaios finished the strokes required to write the *kappa*, he proceeded on to the *alpha*, and so forth (cf. Johnston, this volume). In Demotic it is quite different: to take an example from the letter one can see the word '*~remetch*' which means 'man'. In Demotic it is written as 'ϼ ', The word is two syllables, but 'ϼ' is all that needs to be written: it simply means 'man', and there are no smaller elements into which it can be divided. To write this logographic word in the Greek alphabet would require nine letters (*anthrôpos*). Of course, 'ϼ' is an unusually simple word for Demotic as far as writing is concerned and usually many more strokes are required, but a simple example is useful here. When Ptolemaios dragged the reed pen across the page to write Greek, the telos of his writing can be placed not at the level of the word but that of the letter (or perhaps the syllable, cf. Cribiore 1996: 40–42): here he pulls the stroke downward to make the spine of a *kappa*, and here he has finished the *kappa* and moved onto the *alpha*. Each motion of the pen is teleologically driven not by the word but by the alphabetic letter. But with the Demotic word 'ϼ', where is the telos? Here Ptolemaios drags the line downwards to create the spine of what? At what point has he reached some sort of half-way point, like a '*rem*' or a '*metch*'? At no point. Not until the whole word, the whole *image* is complete is there any sense of resolution or finality.

One might envision a spectrum between image and alphabet, drawing and writing. Although neither of these scripts, Greek nor Egyptian, provide actual pictures, if one considers such scripts on a sliding scale (from writing to drawing) would the two scripts be located at different points? For the former, the motions of the pen find their telos in an alphabetic letter, for the latter the motions can find no other telos than the 'man' himself standing before the writer's eyes 'ϼ'. It may seem like a minor point but it is an important one: the script mediates the relationship between (literate) persons and their language. Certain ideas, anxieties, and creative possibilities are simply not available to a Greek writer but available to an Egyptian (and vice versa) for no reason other than their scripts. When one turns to Demotic's predecessor script, Hieroglyphs, some of these script-based thoughts can be inferred. Penelope Wilson writes of the Pyramid Texts of Dynasty 5 inside the burial chambers of kings Teti and Pepi I where animal hieroglyphs were individually mutilated (Wilson 2003: 71): "The animal signs were written without legs, birds had their heads cut off, knives were inserted into the bodies of snakes or crocodiles, human figures were drawn incomplete, etc.", in the fear that these hieroglyphic images would come to life and threaten the dead person in his or her eternity. Is such a fear possible for a Greek, or for anyone with an alphabetic script? Alphabetic scripts have their own use of *damnatio memoriae*, but the fear of the word can never be realized in such a way that the words *qua* images become the animals they appear to be. Egyptian, at least in hieroglyphic form (which again is the ancestor of the Demotic script), is rooted in a visuality which an alphabetic script cannot attain. Furthermore, this visuality is both conscious and manipulated in that sliding scale between words and art. For example, in Egyptian there are a number of so-called 'determinatives' — pictures which clarify visually a word's meaning (note the ϲ determinative to the left of the central tear in **Figure 6**). If one can imagine English being written not with an alphabet but 'Egyptianly', determinatives would make it easier to differentiate between two homophonic words such as the verb 'to bear' and the animal 'a bear'. By adding a determinative — a little picture of a bear next to one word and a picture of a person carrying something next to the other — the homophones can be distinguished. These

Figure 6: P.Cairo 30961 *recto* (detail): the 'eye-determinative' at the end of the Egyptian word for 'dream'.

are clearly visual elements of writing. But what is interesting is that these elements were not just passively received as a natural part of writing and reading but were often actively played with in 'art' (used in a non-westernizing general sense; cf. Baines 1989). For example, there are a number of Egyptian pictures and sculptures with inscriptions bearing words without determinatives — a grammatically unusual feature. Why is this so? Because the picture or the sculpture itself also functions as one giant determinative for the inscription's 'ungrammatical' word. Rather than writing a determinative of a man or woman, the composer of the inscription used the sculpture as script, as the determinative (cf. Wilson 2003: 68–83). This is an entirely different 'art of writing', in that the boundaries between art and writing — much stricter in alphabetic scripts — become permeable to the extent that it is difficult to locate exactly where the writing stops and the mimetic visual art begins (cf. Baines 1985; 1989; 1994).

In contrast, alphabets, although less amenable to certain kinds of visual play, allow for possibilities that logographic scripts cannot have. Not just expressions like 'I am the Alpha and Omega' or a feeling for the divisibility of the written world into its constituent elements (in Greek, *stoikhea* can mean both 'letters' and 'physical elements'), but alphabetic scripts give rise to their own sorts of games or delusions. The 2nd-century CE Greek writer Athenaeus (10.453c) reports an 'Alphabetic Tragedy' written by the comic playwright Callias in 5th-century BCE Athens — probably produced shortly after Athens' alphabet reform in 403 BCE (Slater 2002). In the play, the members of the Chorus are individual letters and the songs they sing consist of letters combining into syllables: a familiar school exercise for literate Greeks (for early alphabet education, cf. Cribiore 1996: 37–40). It seems like it would be dreadful to listen through every single syllabic combination (e.g. '*beta alpha ba*' or '*gamma alpha ga*', etc.) but since it was set to tragic music and probably a tragic parody, it must have been at least mildly amusing. But what is important here is that this Greek fixation on sound and elemental combinations could not have had the same force for an Egyptian — for even though Egyptians, too, could 'spell out' sounds, much of the logographic aspect of their script stood beyond alphabetic elements in a realm of pure visuality.

It may be argued that graphical boundaries ought not be so starkly drawn, since if one only reads a little further in Athenaeus (10.454a–f) visual aspects of the Greek alphabet can be found. Athenaeus quotes three scenes (from Euripides' *Theseus*, Agathon's *Telephus*, and a play of Theodektos) where an illiterate man (*agrammatos*) describes an inscription to someone else (inscriptions of the name 'Theseus'). Since the man is illiterate he can only describe what the letters look like — e.g. a 'Scythian bow' or a 'lock of hair' which would represent a *sigma*. But it must be emphasized that this is a playfully staged experience of illiteracy, not reading. The letter *sigma* has nothing to do with these objects, and this is part of the dramatist's game. But logograms, although they, too, are not pictograms, still function on that plane of visuality that alphabets do not: the image is the word. To read Greek in the way that these illiterate characters do is to misread and to misunderstand the basics of letters forming syllables. This foreign way of reading is what is being staged in these three plays as an emphasis on how unusual it is to locate such a visual dimension in Greek.

Regarding the particular case study of this chapter, when Ptolemaios wrote the line "*aigyptisti de hypegrapsa, hopôs akribôs eidêis*", what precisely did he mean? There are two points of pressure in translating this Greek sentence in this particular context, two points where a reader might play with translation. The first is this verb '*hypegrapsa*' a compound of the verb '*graphein*': on the one hand, it can mean 'to write', on the other it can mean 'to paint, draw'. The second is this verb '*eidêis*': on the one hand it means 'to know', on the other it can mean 'to see'. In other words, if one wanted to be perverse, one could translate the sentence as "I have *sketched out* below in Egyptian, in order that you *see* accurately". This is, of course, not what Ptolemaios had in mind but it raises the question: where exactly does Egyptian lie on that spectrum of meanings for *graphein*, where between writing and painting? When Akhilles read the Demotic part of the letter, did he change positions on this hypothetical scale of reading versus seeing? When compared to Greek, one can perceive a heightened visuality between Egyptian logograms and alphabetic permutations.

But it may be questioned 'perceivable to whom'? Who would consider one script more 'visual' than another, and who would consider 'visuality' as a criterion for scriptural hierarchy? Ancient testimony is scarce for Greek views of Demotic or vice versa. Although a number of Greeks discuss Egyptian scripts — Herodotus (2.36), Diodorus Siculus (3.3), Chairemon (fragment 12), Clement of Alexandria (*Strom.* 5.4), Horapollo, etc. — their understanding is far from the bilingualism suggested by this letter. Furthermore, it is one thing to consider hieroglyphs' relationship to an alphabetic script, and quite another to consider a much later cursive descendant of those hieroglyphs (i.e. Demotic). For that reason, in the next section, I would like to turn briefly to comparative evidence: another alphabetic script (English) coming into contact with another hieroglyphic descendant (Chinese). This comparandum will be helpful for observing the ways in which scriptural hierarchies construct themselves and how such hierarchies of visuality become articulated (especially when the original hieroglyph is no longer recognizable, as in Demotic and Chinese.) Possibilities emerge of how Ptolemaios might have subjectively experienced these two scripts, Greek and Egyptian, whether he experienced them as fundamentally different, and whether he allotted primacy to one or the other.

Subjective Experiences of Chinese Versus English

Hieroglyphs are one thing, Demotic Egyptian another. The first bears units of language that actually look like pictures (even if they are not pictograms), the second, as a hieroglyphic descendant bears only traces of those pictures. Demotic is a simplified cursive script, and unless one was trained by looking at Demotic and Egyptian side-by-side (perhaps looking, e.g. at trilingual inscriptions), and taught the relationships between words, it is doubtful that the common scribe would actively be able to see the original hieroglyph behind the Demotic scrawl. But even if the original 'pictures' have become so simplified that they disappear, does some element of visuality remain? I would like to argue that it does, and to do so, I will turn to the 'abstract art' of Chinese writing.

Although Chinese writing — which first appears around the 14th century BCE in what is now Anyang, Henan Province (Shizheng 2008) — evolved far from its original hieroglyphs (like

Demotic), its signs are still often considered representations as though these signs were 'capturing' an original image and expressing that image in an abstract form. So write the curators of the recent 2006 Metropolitan Museum exhibition on Chinese writing titled 'Brush and Ink':

> In China, calligraphy, 'the art of writing', is regarded as the quintessential visual art, ranking above painting as the most important vehicle for individual expression. As such, calligraphy may be appreciated in much the same way as some abstract art — by following the artist's every gesture, re-experiencing the kinesthetic action of creation as preserved in the inked lines. This installation will trace the 1,600-year history of brush writing from its genesis as a fine art in the 4th century A.D….to its recent transformation…into a form of abstract art (Metropolitan Museum of Art 2006).

To what extent can alphabetic writing be considered an 'abstract art'? I do not mean to what extent can alphabetic writing be used *within* abstract art, as for example, American artist Cy Twombly does. I mean the writing itself being viewed not as a 'spelling out' of the word but somehow an abstract representation of the word. One would be hard-pressed to find testimony of alphabetic 'representation', but it is precisely this idea of abstract representation versus 'spelling out' which frequently occurs in the Chinese-English testimonia.

Whether it is a native Chinese speaker who learned English or vice versa, the Chinese language assumes a certain artistic, aesthetic or even spiritual primacy over English — not for how the language sounds, but for how it is written. What is most interesting is that this primacy is rarely articulated in any objective way, i.e. "Chinese script is a more aesthetic / spiritual style of writing because of x, y, and z" but rather the testimonia often take recourse to metaphor as though the writer cannot quite grasp why one language / script is loftier than the other. There is good reason for this: quite simply one language / script is not loftier than the other. Both languages (English and Chinese, or Greek and Egyptian), when isolated from each other carry out the same mundane functions of daily transaction. But once in contact with each other, (creative) comparisons arise of how it 'feels' to write or read the script of one language rather than the other.

Take, for example, the English poet Ezra Pound. Learning an alphabetic script first and only later learning a logographic one, Pound describes the logographic language in almost mystical terms — not for how it sounds, not for its spoken grammar, but for how it is written. For Pound, in the *ABC of Reading*, the Chinese language consists of pictures based on sight, not sound (Pound 1951: 20), which certain people do not need to learn but can immediately recognize: "the Chinese ideogram is based on something everyone knows" (Pound 1951: 22). It is the ultimate language of poetry, because instead of defining, e.g. the term 'red' through increasing logical abstractions (e.g. 'color', 'hue', 'spectrum'), it "puts together abbreviated pictures of a rose, a cherry, iron rust, a flamingo". Pound's ideas in this book are largely derived from Ernest Fenollosa's *Essay on the Chinese Written Character* to which Pound ascribes a profound importance. Fenollosa also soars to lofty heights in describing the potential of the Chinese character's visuality: "…Chinese notation is something very much more than…arbitrary symbols. It is based upon a vivid short-hand picture of the operations of nature" (Fenollosa and Pound 2008: 80). While the spoken word depends on "sheer convention", the Chinese method proceeds upon "natural suggestion". The objectivity of Pound's and Fenollosa's discussions of Chinese — as though it were a language beyond grammar and derived from nature itself — naturally comes under fierce criticism from those with a better understanding of the language (cf. Kennedy 1958). But the point I want to highlight here is the extent to which the written aspect of the language — which Pound and Fenollosa consider visual due to its non-alphabetic nature — is exalted, to even mystical, spiritual heights.

This spirituality of written Chinese is found in many books on the Chinese character. Rose Quong for example, writes "Chinese written characters reveal the thought process of the Chinese mind and of the universal mind, as well… They have universal appeal because most of these characters were originally pictures" (Quong 1973: 9). The causal reason here for the "universality" of the Chinese character is its connection to originally pictographic hieroglyphs (which is something it shares with Demotic). Quong's discussion of the "life-movement" (1973: 9) of the Chinese brush, again, I would argue is nothing objective, but a very particularly articulated subjective experience of comparing two forms of writing — alphabetic and logographic. Diane Wolff (1974: 9) describes the script similarly: "If one understands how Chinese characters are constructed, he can see them better, and see, too, the unceasing poetry of the language to its very roots" and "a Chinese word is really a piece of visual architecture, like a painting, a photomontage, or a collage" (Wolff 1974: 18). If we consider these attitudes from the converse perspective — that is, rather than a native practitioner of an alphabetic language learning logographic script, but vice versa — similar sentiments can be found. Chiang Yee, in his book on *Chinese Calligraphy* writes that "a Chinese man examining Western calligraphy from the Magna Carta to Bacchylides [will see that it is] elegant but lacking in *variety* because of the restricted nature of alphabetic forms" (Chiang 1954: 3). To the Chinese or logographic eye, European or alphabetic languages are just "a collection of lifeless letters" (1954: 4) while "a good Chinese character is an artistic thought" (1954: 14) with "each ideogram throwing on the mind an isolated picture…while European words contain no visual ideas". And finally "Chinese is in nature and origin entirely different from any other language. It is perhaps the only pure language in the world". Whether it is West describing East or East describing West, similar sentiments are attested: an exaltation of the logographic over the alphabetic.

Although the grammars of Egyptian and Chinese are very different, there is little need to discuss these differences here since my aim is to explore but one aspect of writing practice as experience — that of the alphabetic script versus the logographic one. The question that remains is whether a Greco-Egyptian could have held similar perceptions. Although there is no firm evidence for Demotic 'calligraphy' as is attested for the earlier Egyptian hieratic script, trilingual Greco-Egyptian inscriptions — which bear a relief at the top, hieroglyphs at the second tier, Demotic on the third, and Greek on the fourth — suggest a certain hierarchy as well as a sliding scale of visuality. Perhaps, Greek too, in comparison with Demotic was perceived to be 'just a collection of lifeless letters'. The contact of logographic and alphabetic scripts forces comparison and hierarchy: the varied perceptions of scripts, as well as that sliding scale of visuality, seem just as applicable to Greek and Egyptian as English and Chinese.

Conclusion

In this chapter, in order to appreciate the mental processes of a 3rd-century Greco-Egyptian bilingual writer, I have focused on the change of this writer's script as well as the material practice of his script. Although this physical practice (and the perceptions of such practice) are not, I would argue, the driving factor behind this code-shift (for it would suggest that if the two were in conversation, Ptolemaios would have not taken recourse to using Egyptian for his dream), it is perfectly plausible to add the script-change as an influence upon the language-shift itself. Ptolemaios' conception of these two languages was not just in their sound, and in their literature, their semantics, syntax and networks of meaning — but his conception of these languages also involved certain material aspects of writing, both visual and experiential. I argued this via three main points: a) that the scripts of each language were bound up in very different material practices (Egyptian rush, Greek reed) even if in this particular instance only the reed was deployed; b) that a logographic language is fundamentally different from an alphabetic language (the former pushing the Greek term '*graphein*' into more artistic, visual terrain); and c) that when two cultures collide (as here Greece and Egypt) each language takes on certain subjective experiences which would not exist were the cultures to remain separate. As with English and Chinese, the logographic script can assume a certain spiritual or natural primacy over the typically more mundane alphabetic script. Taking these three points together then, I suggest that Ptolemaios' shift was informed not only by the (audible) languages as they were processed in his brain, but very much by the scripts themselves as they were experienced in the motions of his hands, the movement of his eyes, and the material objects he used to interact with these scripts. This case study suggests that code-shifts, although probably not caused by, can at least be informed by the materiality of writing — the way writing is experienced physically, the way it appears on the page, and the images of 'writing' that appear in the mind of someone engaged in such practice.

References

Bagnall, R. S. and Derow, P. 2004. *The Hellenistic Period: Historical sources in translation.* Malden, MA: Blackwell. DOI: http://dx.doi.org/10.1002/9780470752760

Baines, J. 1985. *Fecundity Figures: Egyptian personification and the iconology of a genre.* Warminster: Aris and Phillips.

Baines, J. 1989. Communication and Display: The integration of early Egyptian art and writing. *Antiquity* 63: 471–482.

Baines, J. 1994. On the Status and Purpose of Ancient Egyptian Art. *Cambridge Archaeology Journal* 4(1): 67–94. DOI: http://dx.doi.org/10.1017/S0959774300000974

Chiang, Y. 1954. *Chinese Calligraphy: An introduction to its aesthetic and technique.* London: Methuen and Co.

Clarysse, W. 1993. Egyptian Scribes Writing Greek. *Chronique d'Égypte* 68: 186–201.

Cribiore, R. 1996. *Writing, Teachers, and Students in Graeco-Roman Egypt.* Atlanta: Scholars Press.

Depauw, M. 1997. *Companion to Demotic Studies.* Brussels: Fondation égyptologique reine Elisabeth.

Fenollosa, E. and Pound, E. 2008. *The Chinese Written Character as Medium for Poetry.* New York: Fordham University Press.

Freud, S. 1954. *Interpretation of Dreams.* London: G. Allen and Unwin.

Goodspeed, E. J. 1902. *Greek Papyri from the Cairo Museum.* Chicago: The University of Chicago Press.

Kennedy, A. G. 1958. Fenollosa, Pound, and the Chinese Character. *Yale Literary Magazine* 126(5): 24–36.

Kidd, S. 2011. Dreams in Bilingual Ptolemaic Papyri. *The Bulletin of the American Society of Papyrologists* 48: 113–133.

Lucas, A. 1934. *Ancient Egyptian Materials and Industries.* London: E. Arnold and Co.

Metropolitan Museum of Art 2006. *Brush and Ink: The Chinese art of writing, September 2, 2006–January 21, 2007.* http://www.metmuseum.org/en/exhibitions/listings/2006/brush-and-ink [accessed on 13 August 2011].

Nicholson, P. T. and Shaw, I. (eds) 2000. *Ancient Egyptian Materials and Technology.* Cambridge: Cambridge University Press.

Pound, E. 1951. *ABC of Reading.* London: Faber.

Quong, R. 1973. *Chinese Written Characters.* Boston: Beacon Press.

Renberg, G. and Naether, F. 2010. "I Celebrated a Fine Day": An overlooked Egyptian phrase in a bilingual letter preserving a dream narrative. *Zeitschrift für Papyrologie und Epigraphik* 175: 49–71.

Shizheng, W. 2008. The Evolution and Artistry of Chinese Characters. In Youfen, W. (ed. and trans.), *Chinese Calligraphy.* New Haven: Yale University Press, 47–65.

Slater, N. W. 2002. Dancing the Alphabet: Performative literacy on the Attic stage. In Worthington, I. and Foley J. M. (eds), *Epea and Grammata: Oral and written communication in Ancient Greece*. Leiden: Brill, 117–129.

Sosin, J. and Manning, J. 2003. Palaeography and Bilingualism: P.Duk.inv. 320 and 675. *Chronique d'Égypte* 78: 202–210.

Spiegelberg, W. 1908. *Die demotischen Denkmäler*. Leipzig: W. Drugulin.

Tait, W. J. 1988. Rush and Reed: The pens of Egyptian and Greek scribes. In B. G. Mandilaras (eds), *Proceedings of the XVIII International Conference of Papyrology, Athens 25–31 May 1986, Volume 2*. Athens: Greek Papyrology Society, 477-481.

Turner, E. 1971. *Greek Manuscripts of the Ancient World*. Oxford: Clarendon Press.

Wilcken, U. and von Mitteis, L. 1912. *Grundzüge und Chrestomathie der Papyruskunde*. Leipzig: B. G. Teubner.

Wilson, P. 2003. *Sacred Signs: Hieroglyphics in ancient Egypt*. Oxford: Oxford University Press.

Witkowski, S. 1911. *Epistulae Privatae Graecae*. Leipzig: B. G. Teubner.

Wolff, D. 1974. *An Easy Guide to Everyday Chinese*. New York: Harper and Row.

The Other Writing: Iconic literacy and Situla Art in pre-Roman Veneto (Italy)

Elisa Perego

The British School at Rome and University College London

Introduction

In this chapter I discuss the relationship between 'Situla Art' and alphabetic writing in the Italian region of Veneto, *c.*650–275 BC. 'Situla Art' refers to a metalworking tradition, with realistic images embossed and engraved on a range of bronze items, especially the bucket-shaped vessels known as 'situlae', which have come to designate the entire situla art phenomenon. By taking further the approach of Luca Zaghetto (2002; 2006; 2007), who has suggested interpreting the iconographic motifs of this complex decorative technique as a real language, I adopt the concept of iconic literacy — the skill of producing and interpreting images — to compare the elaboration of situla art and traditional literacy in a crucial phase of development for Iron Age North-east Italy.

Importantly, the aim of the study is neither to demonstrate that situla art was structurally equivalent to alphabetic writing nor to delineate general differences and similarities in the logic of iconic and verbal literacy. Rather, following (a) recent developments in sociolinguistics that proposed breaking down the dichotomy between verbal and iconic literacies and (b) Brian Street's insights into literacy's social and ideological value (Street 1984), my analysis explores the socio-ritual similarities and differences existing between these two modes of communication by tackling the socio-cultural milieu that produced them.

Background

Situla Art: Definition, diffusion and interpretation

Situla art is a conventional phrase indicating an artistic and craft movement which spread between the 7th and 3rd centuries BC in the North Adriatic basin (*Arte Situle* 1961; Capuis 2001;

How to cite this book chapter:

Perego, E. 2013. The Other Writing: Iconic literacy and Situla Art in pre-Roman Veneto (Italy).
In: Piquette, K. E. and Whitehouse, R. D. (eds.) *Writing as Material Practice: Substance, surface and medium.* Pp. 253-270. London: Ubiquity Press. DOI: http://dx.doi.org/10.5334/bai.m

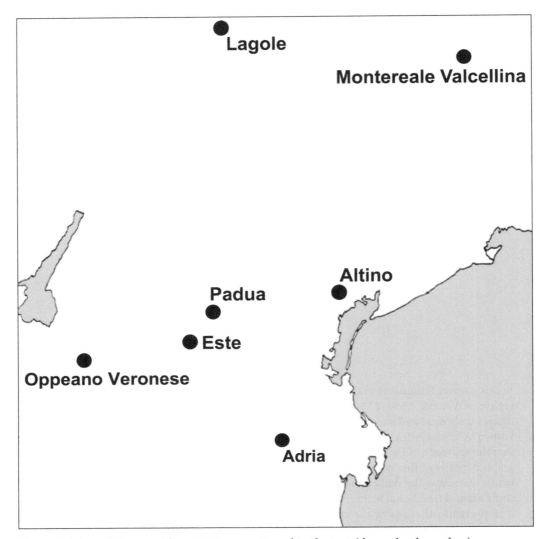

Figure 1: Map of Veneto with main sites mentioned in the text (drawn by the author).

Frey 1969; Lucke and Frey 1962; Zaghetto 2002; 2006; 2007; **Figure 1**). The artistic techniques of situla art entailed embossing and engraving realistic images on bronze items as diverse as lids, helmets, knife scabbards, belt plates, mirrors and vases. Approximately 150 decorated items have been recovered from the area located between the Po Valley and the Danube plain, including the central Alpine region, Slovenia and Lombardy. All these items have been generally recovered from graves, although the funerary context may have not been their primary destination. Other finds come from Bologna and the Ombrone Valley. In Veneto, situla art objects have been found in graves from both the main centres of Este and Padua and minor locations in the Veronese and the Piave Valley (Capuis 2001; **Figure 1**). The earliest Venetic examples of situla art come from Este and date to 650–625 BC.

The situla art imagery is usually naturalistic and includes anthropomorphic motifs, everyday objects, animals and plants. Humans are involved in several different activities, including feasts, processions, warfare, hunting, farming, textile production, childbirth and intercourse (e.g. Capuis

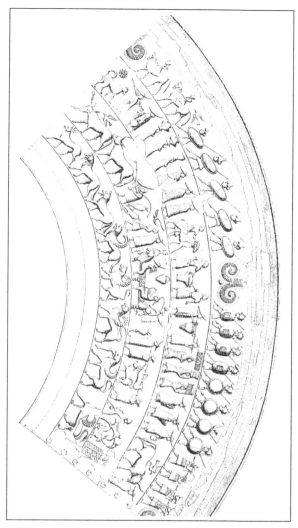

Figure 2: Reproduction of situla art motifs from the Certosa situla, Bologna (Lucke and Frey 1962).

2001; Gangemi 2008: 141; Zaghetto 2007). Objects include weapons, drinking implements, clothes and furniture. The faunal repertoire comprises both real animals and imaginary creatures such as winged lions. Each iconic element (human, animal, plant and objects) was arranged with others either in long bands of extreme complexity or in single scenes of limited extension — the former generally appearing on situlae (**Figures 2–3**), the latter on smaller items. While the complexity of the scene was probably influenced by the surface available, it remains possible that some motifs were chosen to appear on selected items for ideological reasons not always identifiable.

A major example of Venetic situla art is the situla recovered from Este Benvenuti tomb 126, *c.*600 BC. On the Benvenuti situla, the narrative frame is arranged in three horizontal friezes running round the vessel's body on different levels (Capuis and Chieco Bianchi 1992: 74, 76–77). The first frieze features two drinking scenes with elite male drinkers, a man attending a horse, a boxing game and a procession of imaginary animals. The central frieze displays both fantastic and realistic animals accompanied by another man. The third frieze, just above the vessel's foot, features a

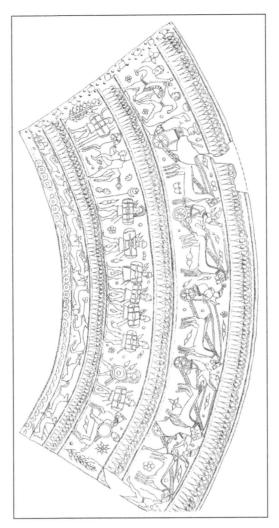

Figure 3: Reproduction of situla art motifs from the Arnoaldi situla, Bologna (Lucke and Frey 1962).

procession of both fully armed men and captives led by a charioteer; in a smaller scene, a warrior attacks a horn player. A minor example of Venetic situla art is the small symposium scene on the belt plaque from Este Carceri tomb 48, which I discuss below.

A repertoire of motifs similar to those of situla art is occasionally found on ceramic containers from Veneto (Capuis and Chieco Bianchi 1992: 81) and on some carved wooden chairs found in elite tombs of Central Italy, including the famous Tomba del Trono of Verucchio (von Eles 2002). The relation between situla art and these occurrences remains poorly understood. In Veneto, the production of decorated bronze items also included small votive laminas embossed and engraved with human or animal figures. These artefacts, however, are considered a different form of cultural manifestation in respect to situla art, especially because they have been found only in sanctuary contexts (Capuis 2001).

The origins and meaning of situla art are much debated (*Arte Situle* 1961; Capuis 2001; Frey 1969). Given the widespread adoption of iconographic motifs initially developed in the eastern

Mediterranean, some scholars have advocated an 'oriental' origin for this artistic language (Di Filippo Balestrazzi 1967; 1980). Although this hypothesis is now outdated, an influence from the East is evident and may have spread in Italy through commercial contacts and the presence of foreign artisans (Capuis 2001: 201). The birth of situla art is now ascribed to 7th-century Etruria: local and / or foreign artisans would have then moved from Etruria to Bologna, and from there to Este and Slovenia (Capuis 2001: 200–201; Colonna 1980). Despite evidence for the development of this artistic tradition in time-space, the meaning of situla art remains unclear. The decorative motifs have been variously interpreted as:

- Generic reproductions of the mid-1st millennium aristocratic lifestyle;
- Representations of the afterlife;
- Evocations of myths connected with death, marriage and rebirth.

Nonetheless, several broader problems undermine these explanations, including the fact that no interpretation has provided a comprehensive explanation of the entire figurative system.

Recent research by Zaghetto (2002; 2006; 2007) has suggested interpreting the iconographic motifs of situla art as a real language, with its own rules which can be decoded on the basis of structural linguistics and semiotic approaches to reconstruct the whole meaning of the 'text'. From this perspective each iconic element (e.g. a hat) is considered as a word, while groups of related images (e.g. a procession) are equivalent to sentences, and the entire decorated object expresses the full meaning of a complete text, or a discourse, in which the individual elements are combined together to convey a message far more complex than the mere sum of its basic components. Another innovation of Zaghetto's analysis is the attention paid to the geographical and chronological distribution of the artefacts. Following a scrutiny of all the minor iconic elements (i.e. 'words' such as clothes) displayed on items from different locations and chronological periods, Zaghetto has suggested that each representation was probably deeply related to the cultural context in which the object was produced, if not a faithful depiction of real — or realistic — episodes of local life. In the case of the Benvenuti situla, for example, the drinking vessels on the first frieze clearly depict implements in use in 7th-century Veneto, including the situla itself. By contrast, the analysis of the 'sentences' has highlighted the existence of a recurring repertoire of scenes (e.g. 'the procession' and 'the lovemaking') probably referring to situations which held shared meaning for all 'consumers' of situla art, regardless of their language and ethnic origin. Situla art, therefore, has been interpreted as a means of communication developed to facilitate interaction between members of widely distributed elites unable to communicate verbally because they spoke different languages. This interpretation is strengthened by the adoption of some situla art items in international gift-exchange. An example is the Providence situla, originally produced in the Alpine region but found at Bologna and depicting a possible meeting between Etruscan and Alpine elite individuals (Zaghetto 2007: 180). The inscription found on the vessel, composed of Raetic or Alpine characters and written in a poor Etruscan language, clarifies that a 'community' donated the situla to a man.

In the case of the Castelvetro mirror, a detailed examination of each iconographic motif has allowed Zaghetto (2002: 40–41) to propose a convincing interpretation of the entire 'text'. The mirror includes three iconic panels. In panel one, a man sitting on a 'throne' is conversing with a veiled woman. This man indicates the number 'two' with his fingers. Nearby, a second woman is talking to another man. This woman indicates the number 'three' with her fingers. The second man wears a cap which is different in its shape and size from the larger hat worn by the 'enthroned' man. A careful analysis of the repertoire of clothing worn by figures in situla art has suggested that the adoption of different kinds of headgear probably indicated significant differences in social standing. The man with the large hat seated on the chair or throne, also a symbol of power, is probably an aristocrat, while the second man may have been a subordinate or the member of a lower social group. Panel two depicts a procession of three horses accompanied by three men, two of whom wear caps similar to that used by the 'low-class' man in panel one. On other situla art objects, similar processions of men and animals are generally associated with representations of sacrifice. According to Zaghetto, however, the Castelvetro procession is different, as it does not include the two characteristic images always associated with the ritual procession, namely the 'man who walks alone' and the 'sacrificial axe'. The meaning of the Castelvetro procession is clarified by panel three, which includes a couple making love on a couch. A second man wearing a large hat similar to that used by the enthroned individual observes the lovemaking. The scenes have been interpreted by Zaghetto as depicting the nuptial process. Panel one shows a discussion about the dowry, which is represented by the three horses in panel two. These are alluded to by the gesture of the woman in panel one, who indicates the number 'three', and are clearly led towards the lovemaking. The man with the large hat in panel three is possibly the same depicted enthroned in panel one, now attending the lovemaking as a witness of the nuptial agreement.

Iron Age Veneto

The following paragraphs offer a brief overview of Venetic social organisation, historical development and funerary ritual in order to introduce the context under study. This chapter focuses on selected evidence from the main Venetic settlement of Este, a choice motivated by the quality of the material available here, which surpasses that from any other Venetic centre excavated to date. A particular emphasis is given to the funerary evidence from the well-published Benvenuti-Ricovero cemetery (c.850–25 BC), a nucleus of around 300 tombs located in the Este Northern burial area (Bianchin Citton et al. 1998; Chieco Bianchi 1987; Chieco Bianchi and Calzavara Capuis 1985; 2006). This cemetery is notable for a concentration of exceptional written artefacts and situla art products and yielded some of the wealthiest graves ever unearthed in Veneto, proving that it was a privileged burial site for the Este elites over the entire Iron Age.

According to conventional Italian scholarship, during the Iron Age, Veneto was inhabited by a population of Indo-European origin — the Veneti of the Graeco-Roman tradition — which developed an increasingly complex and hierarchical society over the 1st millennium (Capuis 2009; Capuis and Chieco Bianchi 1992; Prosdocimi 2002). The appearance of exceptionally wealthy graves during the 8th century probably indicates the rise of local elites who reinforced their status through the acquisition, interment and probable pre-funerary display of exotica, bronze weaponry, precious ornaments and luxurious dining sets. Between the 7th and 6th centuries, Veneto's stronger involvement in the dense network of cultural exchanges between Italy, Continental Europe and the Mediterranean is revealed by larger imports of luxury goods and the adoption of situla art. The interaction with neighbouring populations, as well as internal growth, were among the factors which led to urbanisation, the adoption of writing and more structured rituals practised in sanctuaries. The significant involvement of Venetic elites in formalised cult practices is suggested by the abundance of bronze votive offerings at the main sanctuary sites (e.g. Ruta Serafini 2002). The development of Venetic society from the 5th century remains partially obscure due to a lack of intact grave assemblages, although socio-political change might partially relate to the presumed penetration of large 'Celtic' groups in the Po Valley from c.400 BC (Gambacurta 2003). An increasing intervention of Rome in Veneto took place from the 2nd century BC, and led in approximately two centuries to the loss of Venetic language and material culture, as well as to the end of the local people's political independence (e.g. Cuscito 2009).

Evidence for Iron Age Venetic socio-political organisation remains scanty. Some information can be inferred from the Venetic inscriptions and funerary evidence (Capuis 2009; Perego 2012a). Already in the 9th century Venetic society was probably structured around membership in kin groups, but over the following centuries it may have evolved toward a more articulated organisation of extended elite families and their subordinates. The erection of multiple family tombs in use for several generations is attested from the 3rd century BC to the early Roman period (Balista and Ruta Serafini 1992; Capuis 2009).

Cremation is the main funerary ritual attested (e.g. Capuis 2009). Inhumation was also practised, but possibly for individuals belonging to marginal or non-elite social groups (Perego 2012a). As situla art products and funerary inscriptions come exclusively or almost exclusively from cremation graves, the latter are the focus of my analysis. Cremated remains were typically placed in cinerary vessels covered by a lid. It was not unusual to mingle the bones of multiple individuals in the same urn or to bury several urns in the same grave (Bianchin Citton et al. 1998; Perego 2012a; 2012b). At Este, urns were usually placed in stone containers, especially for rich burials. Grave goods such as ornaments and tools often accompanied the dead. Vessels and food were also placed in tombs, but generally outside the urn. The graves dramatically differed from each other in terms of wealth and ritual complexity. Non-elite tombs contained limited funerary equipment and were generally lacking in foreign goods. Conversely, elite graves contained up to hundreds of items and were characterised by exotica, lavish ornaments, bronze banqueting services, situlae, bronze belts, weaving implements, and, more rarely, situla art products, axes, inscribed objects and weapons (Bianchin Citton et al. 1998; Capuis 2009; Capuis and Chieco Bianchi 1992; Chieco Bianchi 1987; Chieco Bianchi and Calzavara Capuis 1985; 2006). Despite the evolution in shape / type of grave goods and the social changes occurring over time, 8th–3rd century BC Este elite tombs show the persistence of specific burial rites and grave-goods associations, suggesting the existence of a shared ritual language preserved until the late Iron Age.

Literacy in Iron Age Veneto

The extent of literacy in Iron Age Veneto is unknown. The number of inscriptions recovered so far amount to less than 1000 over a period of six centuries, but this may be a product of preservation if texts were also written on perishable items now vanished. Writing was possibly adopted from the Etruscans between the late 7th and the first half of the 6th century. The spread of alphabetic writing in Veneto, therefore, may be a few decades later than the introduction of situla art in the same region; the modalities of its introduction in Veneto, however, remain uncertain. A Greek-modified alphabet was used to write the local language, known as Venetic, an Indo-European idiom with similarities to Latin (Gamba et al. 2013; Marinetti 1992; 1999; 2004; 2008; Pellegrini and Prosdocimi 1967; Prosdocimi 1988; Whitehouse and Wilkins 2006).

Approximately 600 inscriptions have been published from different Venetic localities. The bulk of this documentation comes from Este (Marinetti 1992). Here, 250+ texts and pseudo-texts were unearthed in a single location, the sanctuary of Baratella, suggesting that writing was relevant to the cult. Other significant groups of inscriptions come the sanctuaries of Lagole in northern Veneto (c.100 inscriptions) and Altino Fornace near Venice (c.35–40) (Fogolari and Gambacurta 2001; Cresci Marrone and Tirelli 2009). Inscribed objects in smaller quantities derive from Padua (c.20) and many minor Venetic centres, which have generally produced no more than one to 10 inscriptions each (e.g. Marinetti 1999; 2004; Pellegrini and Prosdocimi 1967; Prosdocimi 1988). Several new inscriptions, however, have been recently recovered from settlements such as Oppeano and Montereale Valcellina (e.g. Marinetti 2008): the publication of this evidence, therefore, might modify the scenario outlined here.

The Venetic texts presently known are found on a wide range of stone, ceramic and metal artefacts, including gravestones, urns, drinking vessels, votive pedestals, laminas and metal reproductions of real writing implements. The bulk of the Venetic corpus comprises hundred poorly preserved texts or inscriptions consisting of single or repeated letters. The remaining dataset includes about 250 items bearing texts consisting of an average of 6–10 words. These texts usually carry female and male onomastic formulas. Verbs and nouns are rare. Votive texts may mention a divine name and a limited range of verbs probably meaning 'to give' or 'to offer', while epitaphs often include only the name of the deceased. A longer inscription (c.100 words) has recently emerged at Este, proving that Venetic writing was put to more complex uses than previously supposed. The meaning of the inscription remains obscure although current scholarship interprets it as a ritual text or an inscription dealing with land and pasture management (Marinetti 1999; Whitehouse and Wilkins 2006).

Based on the evidence currently known, the context of use for writing in Iron Age Veneto may have mainly been limited to the ritual sphere. According to Whitehouse and Wilkins (2006: 533), most of the inscriptions dating to the 6th–3rd centuries BC (351 out of 466, 75.3%) are votive in subject matter and come from sanctuary sites. Of the remaining 115, 72 (15.4%) are from funerary contexts and have been found either on tombstones erected outside the grave or on small objects buried within the tomb. Another 25 (5.3%) are probably funerary inscriptions as well, although their context of discovery is uncertain. Only rare texts are possible marks of ownership and an absolute minority (1%) may have been public inscriptions. The bulk of the inscriptions dating between the late 3rd century BC and the early Roman period (c.1st century BC) is still from sanctuary and funerary contexts, although the use of literacy partially changed, possibly in connection to Rome's expansion and the spread of Latin. Today, therefore, there is no clear evidence that Venetic writing was widely devoted to secular and daily uses or related to the practical functioning of the state (Whitehouse and Wilkins 2006: 534). Overall, the typology and contexts of deposition for 6th–3rd centuries BC inscriptions suggest that early literacy might have been mainly restricted to high-ranking individuals who adopted writing as a means of display in the ritual context (Lomas 2007). This seems confirmed by the relative scarcity of texts scratched on humble pottery vis-à-vis the relative abundance of inscriptions on more luxurious materials such as bronze and stone (for a similar discussion of Etruscan literacy, see Stoddart and Whitley 1988). Cornell (1991) offered an alternative account of the spread of literacy in ancient Italy by arguing for a more widespread competence even in non-elite contexts: the probable loss of most inscriptions on fragile materials may have prevented us from identifying non-elite forms of literacy. This latter possibility of poor preservation and the existence of biases towards elite and ritual writing cannot be discounted for Veneto as well: this is indeed suggested by the increasingly common discovery of brief inscriptions on pottery in settlement contexts (Marinetti 2008).

Theory

Literacy and Communication

In a narrow sense, literacy is often defined as the ability to read and write. This definition is usually applied to the Venetic context as well and has been adopted to frame my previous discussion of Venetic writing. Especially following recent technological developments, however, innovative research in anthropology, psycholinguistics and semiotics has promoted a wider adoption of the term 'literacy' to include the ability to use a wider array of media and modes of communication ranging from the internet to special systems of notation such as mathematical and musical notation systems (e.g. Buckingham 1993; Coiro et al. 2008; Gee 2008; Kress 2003; Selber 2004). In a broader sense, therefore, literacy can be defined as the recipient's awareness of the conventions which regulate the production, transmission and interpretation of any message, including for example emoticons, numeric codes, the mechanisms of video gaming, and the texts produced through microblogging and social networking. Verbal literacy implies the understanding and use of verbal messages (referring here to both speech and written texts) while iconic literacy entails the creation and comprehension of visual images (Kress 2003; Messaris and Moriarty 2005:

481–482). Numerous visual communication studies have investigated the differences and similarities between writing, spoken language and the language of images, with divergent conclusions (e.g. Messaris 1994; 1997; Messaris and Moriarty 2005). A pitfall sometimes identifiable in these studies is that verbal and iconic modes of communication have been described and compared mainly in terms of their semantic and syntactic properties (Messaris 1997: viii), without fully exploring how the social context and the transposition of a message on a material support may influence people's understanding of the relation between images and words.

The Materiality of Writing: Situla art and the Venetic script as social practices

In this chapter I adopt the broader definition of literacy outlined above to compare the parallel development of Venetic writing and situla art at Iron Age Este. The relation between writing and iconography is explored by casting light on the social milieu in which people's engagement with situla art and written texts was constructed. Following Street's seminal volume on the social functioning and ideological value of literacy (Street 1984), research has suggested that literacy cannot be considered just as a set of technical skills, but as a historically situated social practice deeply embedded in socio-political dynamics. Literacy practices are meaningful and embedded in broader social goals and cultural practices; they are also patterned by power relations and social institutions and can be inferred from events mediated by literacy productions (in our case, for example, the rituals in which situla art objects were used). Literacy practices evolve over time and new ones are often acquired through processes of informal learning and sense making; furthermore, different literacies exist in associations with different domains of life: hence, some literacies are more dominant and visible than others (Barton and Hamilton 1998: 8).

From this perspective, both situla art and Venetic writing were entangled within the wider social background to which the entire Venetic communication system belonged. Issues of power negotiation and selected consumption according to the recipient's social standing pertain to all means of communication and become visible through the transposition of literacy practices into material form. Having taken material form, literacy practices may deeply impact even on people's embodiment and sensory perception, as I argue below. In this sense, both iconography and writing — as social and material products — share deep similarities of fundamental importance for this work.

Notably, the social milieu in which both situla art and writing were introduced probably consisted of various elite contexts. Ongoing contact with neighbouring populations offered Venetic dominant groups the opportunity to acquire novel techniques and materials to promote their prominence over commoners and competing peers. In this socio-political setting, it was not only writing and iconography that became means of status construction: this function must have been extended to all means of communication developing in the elite context, from the adoption of specific clothes to bodily gestures, which can be sometimes recovered through a scrutiny of the available material evidence. An example is offered by ritual drinking. The consumption and display of rare beverages and vessels by the Este elite was surely intended to convey a message (e.g. expression of wealth) which was also deeply entangled with high-ranking people's use of writing and situla art, as discussed below.

The creation of a sophisticated 'visual' language which implied the display of rare and often exotic implements such as luxurious ornaments, bronze banqueting sets, situla art products and inscriptions contributed to the construction of elite identities. When first introduced in Veneto, writing itself was possibly perceived and adopted in a similar way to iconography. As many were unable to read, the script may have essentially been a means of visual display, especially on monumental gravestones (Lomas 2007: 149–150). The exhibition of powerful status symbols was also accompanied by the elaboration of ritual practices including the consumption of sophisticated beverages at elite banquets and funerary ceremonies. People's awareness of the conventions governing the use and display of exotica and luxurious items, including situla art and early written objects (c.550–275 BC), was a form of literacy, in a broader sense. Being literate in this mainly visual language meant that the elites possessed adequate cultural knowledge to make sense not only of Venetic inscriptions and situla art motifs, but also of the messages encoded in the ritual gestures such as formal drinking both represented on situla art and practised in salient moments of their lives.

It is worth emphasising the strong corporeal overtones of this elite language, from the visual stimulation promoted by the brightness of polished bronze items to the tactile and visual engagements with the smoothness and luminescence of the rare colourful materials (e.g. glass and amber) used for lavish ornaments. Also rooted in bodily experience were eating practices such as meat consumption and the ingestion of alcohol, at the time presumably a rare and precious intoxicant, at least in its more sophisticated forms. The introduction and development in Veneto of these bodily practices and their representation in material forms must have promoted new elite forms of self-perception deeply rooted in high-ranking people's engagement with rituals, objects and foodstuffs probably not available to lower social strata.

Analysis

Situla Art and Writing at Iron Age Este: Use, ritual, and display

At Este, material supports for situla art included elaborate bronze belt plaques and lozenge-shaped belts, knife scabbards, large drinking and / or high-handled cups and situlae (Capuis and Chieco Bianchi 1992). Sympotic (i.e. related to the ritual consumption of sophisticated beverages, presumably including alcohol) implements such as situlae and drinking cups were also occasionally inscribed, although never when decorated with situla art, as discussed below. All the artefact types listed above acted as status symbols highly appreciated by the local elites, as their widespread deposition in prominent graves testifies. Moreover, the most luxurious drinking vessels, weaponry and belts were often exotic products, either as directly imported items or local reproductions of foreign models, a characteristic which probably increased their worth. The high symbolic value of these artefacts is further attested by the fact that they were not only used to carry the decoration but were also portrayed among the decorative motifs of situla art, thus constituting part of the situla art 'language' itself.

For example, situlae are commonly depicted on Venetic and non-Venetic situla art products as key components of highly ritualised elite activities such as processions and libations (*Arte Situle* 1961; Frey 1969). Although soon integrated into Venetic material culture, they were originally vessels of exotic origin with a widespread geographical distribution, from Continental Europe to Central Italy. Their employment at elite banquets highlights the 'international' rituality of alcohol consumption, whose role in promoting commensality, hospitality and power dynamics in late prehistory is well-acknowledged (e.g. Dietler 1990; Iaia 2005: 207–219; 2006; for Veneto see Perego 2010; 2012a). Not surprisingly, therefore, practices of ritual drinking are often represented on situla art objects, which allow us to glimpse the lost language of the ritualised gestures constituting the ritual banquet.

The diffusion of situlae in Veneto relates to the adoption by the local elites of sophisticated practices of consumption which often featured exotic components and were integrated into a larger spectrum of ritual technologies of status construction and expression. The same must have been true of other practices represented on situla art, and bearing strong elite overtones, such as hunting, weaving, sacrificing animals, playing games and conducting warfare. Notably, many artefacts usually appearing in Veneto in wealthy graves (e.g. axes, weaponry, weaving tools, and arrows) relate closely to these practices. Within the tomb, these items were also often accompanied by bronze banqueting equipment, situla art products and, more rarely and mainly from the late Iron Age, inscribed artefacts. As Riva (2010) argues for Orientalising Etruria, the introduction of new food technologies in the elite context is not only to be related to the creation of new modes of political negotiation via the ritual banquet, but also to the promotion of novel practices of embodiment which altered the construction and perception of the elite individual's self. As such, the specialised equipment for ritual food preparation and consumption may have acted as a metaphorical extension of the elite person him / herself while signalling group belonging (Perego 2012a). In Veneto, for example, the intimate relationship between the situla and the self was reinforced by the occasional adoption of the situla vessel shape for elite funerary urns. This close association of situlae with the elite body was taken even further through the practice of the anthopomorphisation of the urn, which has been identified so far only in the case of wealthy graves. This was achieved by wrapping the situla-urn in a cloth or dress and / or by embellishing it with ornaments and belts employed to re-create the lost integrity of the cremated body. Interestingly, this practice is also well-known from Etruscan and Centro-Italian funerary contexts (e.g. von Eles 2002), and may have been adopted by the Veneto elite alongside the other foreign practices described in this chapter.

The Early Iron Age

One of the earliest Este graves signalling the elaboration by prominent local groups of a shared ritual language in use until the 3rd century is Ricovero tomb 236, a multiple grave of exceptional wealth and ritual complexity dating to the 8th century (Iaia 2006; Chieco Bianchi and Calzavara Capuis 1985: 300–312). The most prestigious urn in the grave was a bronze situla either imported from Continental Europe or produced locally by imitating an exotic vessel shape. While the bones of the deceased have been lost, the weaponry possibly imported from the eastern Alpine region and the pins usually associated with male depositions indicate a male burial. The latter may have been accompanied by a female individual, as suggested by the presence inside the situla of ornaments generally associated with women. The second urn in the grave, a ceramic vessel, yielded rich female ornaments. Apart from weaponry, ornaments and pins, the bronze situla-urn contained a sympotic service for the preparation and distribution of an indeterminate beverage, possibly wine or beer. This sympotic equipment included two different handled containers probably employed to carry the main beverage (e.g. alcohol) and any additional components (e.g. water), while the three strainers might have been used to filter the residuals generally found in ancient fermented beverages. Finally, the high-handled cups were probably used to remove the liquid from the 'krater' — the larger vessel in which alcohol was mixed with water. The 'krater' was possibly represented in this case by the situla-urn itself. These sympotic implements bear evidence of burning and may have burnt with the dead. The deposition of a sympotic set on the pyre and later in the urn was an extremely rare practice at Este, where banqueting vessels were usually placed unburned in the grave outside the urn. The close connection between the sympotic set from tomb 236 and the dead buried in the bronze situla seems intended to reinforce the vessels' pertinence to the elite individual(s) buried here, who may have been in charge of the intoxicating beverage's preparation. The grave assemblage also included an exceptionally sophisticated ceramic drinking and dining set. Part of this service was found in the tomb container and part was placed intentionally broken on the tomb's covering slab. The ceramic drinking set included numerous high-handled cups possibly used by the deceased's fellow diners, either in their everyday life or during the funeral (Iaia 2006). The latter may have been allowed to drink, but not to manipulate the precious intoxicant — a prerogative possibly belonging to the person(s) buried in the situla-urn with the bronze set for beverage preparation and consumption. Two other implements interpreted as incense burners seem to recall practices of purification common at the Graeco-Etruscan banquet / symposium: their presence reinforces the idea that the Venetic elite were constructing their social identity in part through the adoption of foreign rituals.

Although pre-dating the spread of both situla art and writing in Veneto, Ricovero tomb 236 proves that the channels of cultural transmission were already established at this stage. The Venetic elites exhibited their openness towards non-local practices of consumption and their ability to adapt diverse cultural influences to their needs. The emphasis granted to the ingestion of sophisticated beverages, presumably alcohol, demonstrates that the ritual techniques of formal drinking later associated with situla art and writing were already a medium adopted to advertise the elites' status. Significantly, many of the ritual practices adopted in this grave remained in use at Este until the 3rd century BC, often in tombs containing situla art and inscribed objects, as exemplified by the graves described below.

Benvenuti tombs 122, 124, and 126 were erected near each other between c.625 and 550 BC. These yielded grave goods bearing some of the most ancient and most sophisticated — in terms of compositional complexity — situla art objects from the Ricovero-Benvenuti cemetery. The exceptional wealth and close proximity of the tombs suggest they belonged to an elite group. The rare and exotic grave goods found within indicate that the tomb owners, or their living kin or associates, might have been able to monopolise the production and / or acquisition of prestigious bronze status symbols (Chieco Bianchi and Calzavara Capuis 2006: 46). The most ancient grave, Benvenuti 122, contained two urns dating to c.625–600 BC and probably belonging to women (Chieco Bianchi and Calzavara Capuis 2006: 267–276). The most ancient urn consisted of a bronze situla embellished with a complex decoration of dots, studs and stylised birds of Central European inspiration. This vessel was covered by a bronze drinking cup whose Central European geometric ornamentation is accompanied by vegetal and animal motifs in the manner of the earliest Bolognese situla art style. An influence from Etruria and Bologna is also visible in the luxurious ornaments from the urns. In the case of Benvenuti tomb 126, the famous Benvenuti situla was re-used as a container for a small ceramic urn containing the remains of a 1- to 3-year old child (Chieco Bianchi and Calzavara Capuis 2006: 320–331). The urn was adorned with luxurious ornaments and wrapped in a cloth giving the cinerary human-like qualities. The theme of drinking was evoked not only by the situla itself, but also by the scenes of ritual drinking embossed on the vase and described above. The presence of three high-handled cups in the tomb further emphasised this possible reference to alcohol consumption.

The third tomb of the group, Benvenuti 124, dates to c.550 BC (Chieco Bianchi and Calzavara Capuis 2006: 294–301) and yielded three ceramic urns with the remains of three adults and two children. One of the urns was placed inside a bronze situla, whose lid bore a situla art motif of animals and geometric dots. The grave also yielded a sophisticated bronze drinking set, two bone and bronze distaffs, rich ornaments, a knife from the Adriatic *koinè* and an axe. A bronze belt plaque and two *fibulae* were from Lombardy.

As for the earlier Ricovero tomb 236, these graves reveal a clear intersection of diverse cultural influences incorporated into the material culture and lifestyle of the Este elite. Drinking still features as a fundamental means of social promotion and self-expression, while situla art is adopted as a novel status symbol promoting new ways of elite self-representation. In the case of the Benvenuti situla, which featured images of aristocrats involved in socially distinctive activities, the impact of the new technology over the elite individual's self-perception must have been considerable. In a cultural context in which representations of human beings were possibly rare or absent at this early stage, the Benvenuti situla's owners, perhaps for the very first time, were able to ideally project themselves and their world on the new medium, like in a mirror.

From the 6ᵗʰ Century to the Late Iron Age

The production of elaborate situla art motifs on large bronze containers seems to vanish at Este during the 6ᵗʰ century. This has been related to the social changes brought about by the incipient urbanisation, which may have altered the consumption habits of previous situla art commissioners or even wiped out the previous elite groups (Capuis 2001). At Este, this time-span was also characterised by the development of the first local sanctuaries as new loci of public display and political negotiation (Ruta Serafini 2002). It was at that moment that writing presumably appeared in Veneto as a novel technique of status expression, possibly favoured by the new proto-urban elites. The latter, however, also maintained older practices of status construction, including ritual drinking. Significantly, one of the most ancient Venetic inscriptions presently known was inscribed on a bronze cup of Etruscan form, the *kantharos* from Lozzo near Este (Locatelli and Marinetti 2002). *Kantharoi* were widely employed at the Etruscan elite banquet and exported. The Lozzo cup dates between *c.*625–575 BC although the inscription may have been added later. The area of discovery was occupied in Roman times by a sanctuary. The Venetic inscription is probably votive in nature, suggesting that a cult was already established at Lozzo during the Iron Age. The *kantharos* must have been a valuable item in many respects. Apart from the exceptional value attributed by the Este elite to bronze containers, its exoticism due to its Etruscan shape and its reference to privileged drinking practices relate it to prominent individuals. The emphasis granted to the donors through the inscription of their personal names on the vessel testifies of new forms of expressing the elite individuals' self and social role in a novel context of display — the sanctuary — via the novel technology of writing.

The Lozzo *kantharos* embodied a close relationship between three of the main aspects of the elite 'language' which I have sketched out so far, namely writing, drinking and the acquisition of exotica. A similar relationship between drinking, the adoption of foreign rituals and, in this case, situla art is evidenced by a belt plaque from Este Carceri tomb 48 (500–450 BC). This belt plaque features a single situla art scene which appears to reproduce the reclined symposium of Graeco-Etruscan inspiration (Capuis and Chieco Bianchi 1992: 95): a woman wrapped in a veil is represented about to serve a man reclining on a couch. The ideology of the reclined symposium may have spread into Veneto from the 6ᵗʰ–5ᵗʰ century BC alongside the importation of Greek drinking vessel shapes and possibly wine. It is unclear, however, when and to what extent the Venetic elites came to imitate the complex ritual practices of the reclined Graeco-Etruscan symposium. This uncertainty is compounded by the extreme selectivity exhibited by the inhabitants of Veneto in the choice of imported vessel types, as they adopted only a restricted number of the whole range of sympotic vessels available in Greece and Etruria. The widespread deposition of local ware even within the wealthiest Venetic graves further suggests the persistence of localised modes of consumption. The ambivalent reaction of Venetic elites towards the new sympotic practice is revealed by the Carceri plaque itself, where the woman holds a jug clearly resembling an Etruscan *schnabelkanne*. This beaked jug shape — albeit widely attested in regions such as Etruria, Lombardy and Continental Europe — was extremely rare in Veneto. Jugs of any type remained uncommon here until the 3ʳᵈ century. Their rarity, set against the still widespread use of high-handled cups to serve beverages, further suggests the persistence of traditional drinking practices. It is significant, therefore, that in the case of the Carceri belt plaque a new and possibly uncommon ritual practice — the reclined symposium featuring the employment of a rare vessel shape, the *schnabelkanne* — was related to a medium, situla art, whose distinctive social value has been already emphasised. These associations reinforce the special nature of both the practice and the medium and emphasise the sophistication of these privileged modes of self-expression.

It is also worth emphasising again the exceptional value attributed in Veneto to elaborate bronze belts and belt plaques, as both status symbols and ceremonial artefacts. Due to their social value and proximity to the body, belts probably constituted important vehicles for communicating an individual's elevated status, as testified by both their deposition in wealthy graves and their display in sanctuaries as prestigious miniature offerings or depictions on laminas (Capuis and Chieco Bianchi 1992: 84, 97). The importance of belts and belt-elements in the funerary context is emphasised by the wide range of ritual manipulations undergone by these artefacts, including deliberate fragmentation, burning, and deposition around the urn to promote the latter's identification with the elite body. Este Nazari tomb 161 (400–350 BC) provides an example of this kind of ritual (Tirelli 1981). In this wealthy grave, two bronze situlae contained a ceramic urn each. The largest situla was wrapped in cloth. A lozenge-shaped belt decorated with situla art motifs was fastened around this vessel, apparently to give human-like qualities to the urn-container. This deposition emphasises again the symbolic link elaborated over the centuries between situla art itself, sophisticated practices of 'humanisation' of the urn and the employment of situlae as urns in elite graves. The grave also yielded a rich service for drinking and for food preparation, including meat roasting. This emphasis on the preparation of solid foodstuff via the deposition of roasting spits, firedogs, knives and slices is characteristic of wealthy graves from the 4th century and suggests the spread of new elite habits of display and consumption. Not surprisingly, the interment of these implements was often accompanied by the deposition of situla art objects and inscribed vessels (e.g. Capuis and Chieco Bianchi 1992: 86–87).

Evidence enabling the clearest synthesis of the ritual practices described above is offered by finds unearthed in Ricovero tomb 23/1984, 300–250 BC (Chieco Bianchi 1987). This grave of exceptional wealth displays both an intentional ritual conservatism going back to the 8th century and an extraordinary openness towards contemporaneous cultural influences especially from Etruria and the international port-of-trade of Adria, located on the Adriatic Sea slightly south of the main Venetic area. The urn found in the grave was a *skyphos* containing the remains of an unsexed individual. The *skyphos* was placed within a bronze situla incised with the name of the deceased, a woman called *Nerka Trostiaia*. The situla was also wrapped in cloth embellished with rich ornaments probably pinned or sewn on it, again intended to evoke the human body. The importance of alcohol consumption was also emphasised via the deposition of an extremely rich banqueting set at the bottom of the grave, which included several imported items. An Attic redfigure krater was found broken on the tomb's covering slab, possibly indicating the continuation of a ritual practice that is already attested 500 years earlier in Ricovero tomb 236. Importantly, this grave featured the latest example of situla art presently known at Este, the bronze model of a piece of furniture decorated with animal images.

Mutually Exclusive Spheres?

It is noteworthy that in Veneto, despite the adoption of writing and situla art within the same social milieu and often in connection with exotica, foreign ritual practices and sympotic rituals, inscriptions have never been found to date on objects bearing situla art. This is true for the vast majority of the entire situla art corpus presently known, with only a couple of exceptions (Zaghetto 2007: 180). An obvious explanation for this pattern is that situla art and writing were different communicative systems. The former was a non-linguistic symbol-based system spread over a vast area inhabited by different ethnic groups and possibly developed to facilitate interaction between people unable to speak the same language. The latter was the written form of languages (e.g. Venetic) presumably spoken in the more restricted area where the related inscriptions have emerged. This important observation, however, does not explain why the receivers / owners of situla art items, who may have been exposed to, or even taken control of, writing as well, decided not to inscribe their possessions (or have them inscribed), for example in giftexchange with people speaking the same language or at the funeral, by putting the deceased's name on a decorated situla-urn. For the Veneto, this 'otherness' between the two 'languages' seems compounded by the fact that the interment of both written items and situla art objects in the same grave seems to have been uncommon, with some exceptions such as *Nerka*'s tomb. As suggested by Whitehouse (pers. comm.), a possible explanation is that few Venetic inhabitants were 'bilingual' in the two 'languages'. It is worth noting, however, that this pattern may partially relate to the limited number of intact wealthy graves dating between the 5th and 3rd centuries BC. It is also possible that inscriptions were written on perishable materials now vanished. Another possible explanation for this pattern, however, may reside in the uses to which writing was put after its introduction in Veneto. Although writing may have spread in Veneto as early as the late 7th or 6th century BC, at Este the presence of inscriptions inside the grave (i.e. the context in which situla art items are found) is extremely rare before the late 4th – early 3rd century BC. One possible exception is a male name inscribed on a bronze tripod or cup buried in a grave dating to the 5th or 4th century BC (Marinetti 1992: 138). The practice of inscribing the deceased's name on urns started in the 3rd century and became more common in the following centuries, especially from *c.*75–25 BC. The epitaph inscribed on *Nerka*'s situla is one of the earliest examples of this practice. A similar epitaph is incised on a contemporary situla-urn buried in a wealthy multiple grave, namely Benvenuti tomb 123 (Chieco Bianchi and Calzavara Capuis 2006: 276–294). This tomb yielded several items comparable with *Nerka*'s grave goods, including lavish ornaments, a bronze model of a loom, three axes and a *skyphos*. Again, the inscribed situla-urn was possibly wrapped in a cloth. Interestingly, no situla art product comes from this grave, although this may relate to the several re-openings the tomb underwent.

Before 325–300 BC writing was generally adopted in cemetery contexts to mark the gravestones ascribing the ownership of tombs and / or burial plots to prestigious individuals and families. The individuals mentioned on tombstones were 75% male. In the mortuary context, therefore, writing was mainly associated with the male individual and the monumentality, visibility and durability of funerary monuments erected outside the grave. A possible shift in the function and values accorded to writing may have taken place around 300 BC with the spread of 'hidden' and more intimate dedications on small, portable items buried in the grave, such as urns and vessels which bore male and female names in a similar proportion. Inscriptions on small objects were not unknown at Este before, but mainly appeared on votive offerings dedicated in sanctuaries, entailing different ways of constructing and expressing personal and social identities. This shift towards a 'hidden' funerary literacy took place when situla art seems to disappear. The deposition of situla art products and written objects in the same grave was therefore limited to *c.*325–250 BC, when the two 'languages' were briefly in use in the same context at the same time. Later, the progressive erosion of the previous prominent groups' social identity in favour of novel forms of display and consumption probably led to the disappearance of situla art — a language which had lost its significance in the new social setting. Before *c.*325, I cannot exclude the possibility that writing and situla art were used contemporaneously in the same context outside the grave. However, it seems that, despite their common pertinence to the elite 'language' outlined above, their final destination was different, and entailed a diverse conceptualisation of the two media, due to complex social motivations which are not presently identifiable.

Conclusion

By drawing on (a) Zaghetto's interpretation of situla art as a sophisticated communication system, (b) recent developments in sociolinguists breaking down the division between iconic and verbal literacies and (c) Street's understanding of literacy as an ideological practice whose nature is context-dependent and power-laden, this chapter discussed the reciprocal interplay between Venetic writing and iconography at Iron Age Este, with an emphasis on their material dimension and their role in elite consumption practices. Both writing and situla art were most likely adopted from non-local contexts by Venetic privileged groups in order to enhance their social prominence and advertise their access to exotic goods and knowledge of rituals and ideas attested in foreign regions. Hence, I outlined a preliminary account of the intricate relationship between writing, situla art and other means of status expression adopted by the Este elite, such as formal drinking. This relationship suggests that — when considered in the perspective adopted in this chapter — the conventional scholarly habit of studying situla art and writing as unrelated phenomena taken outside their similar social milieu of development is less persuasive. By contrast, the Este elites were able to elaborate a complex hybrid language, flexible but partially stable over time, which was probably adopted to advertise the social prominence and affiliation of its recipients and creators. The adoption of foreign modes of status enhancement and consumption as well as the continuous re-elaboration and transmission of the entire 'package' may have promoted changes in bodily practices and forms of self-perception and self-representation of the elite person him / herself. Both situla art and writing were part of the 'package' and their importance in 'creating' Este elite individuals cannot be underestimated.

Acknowledgements

I want to warmly thank Ruth Whitehouse, Kathryn Piquette and the anonymous reviewers for their comments upon earlier versions of this paper.

References

Arte Situle 1961. *Arte delle Situle dal Po al Danubio: Exhibition Catalogue*. Firenze: Sansoni.

Balista, C. and Ruta Serafini, A. 1992. Este Preromana: Nuovi dati sulle necropoli. In Tosi, G. (ed.), *Este Antica dalla Preistoria all'Età Romana*. Este: Zielo, 109–123.

Barton, D. and Hamilton, M. 1998. *Local Literacies: A study of reading and writing in one community*. London: Routledge.

Bianchin Citton, E., Gambacurta, G. and Ruta Serafini, A. (eds) 1998. *…Presso l'Adige Ridente… Recenti Rivenimenti Archeologici da Este a Montagnana*. Padova: ADLE.

Buckingham, D. 1993. Towards New Literacies: Information technology, English and media education. *The English and Media Magazine* Summer: 20–25.

Capuis, L. 2001. L'Arte delle Situle Quarant'anni Dopo. *Arheološki Vestnik* 52: 199–205.

Capuis, L. 2009. *I Veneti: Civiltà e cultura di un popolo dell'Italia Preromana* (3rd edition revised). Milano: Longanesi.

Capuis, L. and Chieco Bianchi, A. M. 1992. Este Preromana: Vita e cultura. In Tosi, G. (ed.), *Este Antica dalla Preistoria all'Età Romana*. Este: Zielo, 41–108.

Chieco Bianchi, A. M. 1987. Dati Preliminari su Alcune Tombe di III Secolo da Este. In Vitali, D. (ed.), *Celti ed Etruschi nell'Italia Centro-Settentrionale dal V Secolo a.C alla Romanizzazione: Atti del Colloquio Internazionale. Bologna 12–14 Aprile 1985*. Imola: Bologna University Press, 191–236.

Chieco Bianchi, A. M. and Calzavara Capuis, L. 1985. *Le Necropoli di Casa di Ricovero, Casa Muletti Prosdocimi, Casa Alfonsi*. Roma: Giorgio Bretschneider Editore.

Chieco Bianchi, A. M. and Calzavara Capuis, L. (eds) 2006. *La Necropoli di Villa Benvenuti*. Roma: Giorgio Bretschneider Editore.

Coiro, J., Knobel, M., Lankshear, C. and Leu, D. J. (eds) 2008. *Handbook of New Literacies Research*. New York: Lawrence Erlbaum Associates.

Colonna, G. 1980. Rapporti Artistici tra il Mondo Paleoveneto e il Mondo Etrusco. In *Este e la Civiltà Paleoveneta a Cento Anni dalle Prime Scoperte: Atti dell'XI Convegno di Studi Etruschi e Italici, Este, Padova, 27 Giugno–1 Luglio 1976*. Firenze: L. S. Olschki, 177–190.

Cornell, T. J. 1991. The Tyranny of the Evidence: A discussion of the possible uses of writing in Etruria and Latium in the Archaic Age. In *Literacy in the Roman World* (Journal of Roman

Archaeology Supplementary Series 3). Ann Arbor, MI: Department of Classical Studies, University of Michigan, 7–343.

Cresci Marrone, G. and Tirelli, T. (eds) 2009. *Altnoi. Il Santuario Altinate: Strutture del Sacro a Confronto e i Luoghi di Culto lungo la Via Annia. Atti del Convegno. Venezia 4–6 Dicembre 2006.* Rome: Quasar.

Cuscito, G. (ed.) 2009. *Aspetti e Problemi della Romanizzazione: Venetia, Histria e Arco Alpino Orientale.* Trieste: Editreg Sass.

Dietler, M. 1990. Driven by Drink: The role of drinking in the political economy and the case of Iron Age France. *Journal of Anthropological Archaeology* 9(4): 352–406. http://dx.doi.org/10.1016/0278-4165(90)90011-2

Di Filippo Balestrazzi, E. 1967. Rapporti iconografici di alcuni monumenti dell'arte delle situle: Materiali per uno studio delle trasmissioni figurative. *Venetia* 1: 97–200.

Di Filippo Balestrazzi, E. 1980. Nuovi confronti iconografici e un'ipotesi sui rapporti tra l'area delle situle e il mondo orientale. In *Este e la Civiltà Paleoveneta a Cento Anni dalle Prime Scoperte: Atti dell'XI Convegno di Studi Etruschi e Italici, Este, Padova, 27 Giugno–1 Luglio 1976.* Firenze: L. S. Olschki, 153–170.

Fogolari, G. and Gambacurta, G. (eds) 2001. *Materiali Veneti e Romani del Santuario di Lagole di Calalzo al Museo di Pieve di Cadore.* Rome: Giorgio Bretschneider Editore.

Frey, O-H. 1969. *Die Entstehung der Situlenkunst: Studien zur Figurlich Verzieten Toreutik von Este* (Romisch-Germanische 31). Berlin: De Gruyter.

Gamba, M., Gambacurta, G., Ruta Serafini, A., Tiné, V. and Veronese, F. (eds) 2013. *Venetkens: Viaggio nella terra dei veneti antichi.* Venezia: Marsilio.

Gambacurta, G. 2003. Il *Venetorum Angulus* e la Pressione Celtica (IV–III Secolo a.C.). In Malnati, L. and Gamba, M. (eds), *I Veneti dai Bei Cavalli.* Treviso: Canova, 81–92.

Gangemi, G. 2008. Dinamiche Insediative nel Bellunese. Età Preromana: Aggiornamenti. In *I Veneti Antichi. Novità e Aggiornamenti. Atti del Convegno di Studio. Isola della Scala, 15 Ottobre 2005.* Sommacampagna: Cierre Edizioni, 139–153.

Gee, J. P. 2008. *What Video Games Have to Teach Us About Learning and Literacy* (revised and updated). Basingstoke: Palgrave Macmillan.

Iaia, C. 2005. *Produzioni Toreutiche della Prima Età del Ferro in Italia Centro-Settentrionale: Stili decorativi, circolazione, significato.* Pisa: Editoriali e Poligrafici Internazionali.

Iaia, C. 2006. Servizi Cerimoniali da 'Simposio' in Bronzo del Primo Ferro in Italia Centro-Settentrionale. In von Eles, P. (ed.), *La Ritualità Funeraria tra Età del Ferro e Orientalizzante in Italia. Atti del Convegno. Verrucchio, 26–27 Giugno 2002.* Pisa: Istituti Editoriali e Poligrafici Internazionali, 103–110.

Kress, G. 2003. *Literacy in the New Media Age.* London: Routledge. http://dx.doi.org/10.4324/9780203164754

Locatelli, D. and Marinetti, A. 2002. La Coppa dello Scolo di Lozzo. In Ruta Serafini, A. (ed.), *Este Preromana: Una città e i suoi santuari.* Este: Zielo, 201–202.

Lomas, K. 2007. Writing Boundaries: Literacy and identity in the ancient Veneto. In Lomas, K., Whitehouse, R. and Wilkins, J. (eds), *Literacy and the State in the Ancient Mediterranean.* London: Accordia Research Institute, 149–169.

Lucke, W. and Frey, O-H. 1962. *Die Situla in Providence (Rhode Island).* Berlin: De Gruyter.

Marinetti, A. 1992. Epigrafia e Lingua di Este Preromana. In Tosi, G. (ed.), *Este Antica dalla Preistoria all'Età Romana.* Este: Zielo, 125–172.

Marinetti, A. 1999. Venetico 1976–1996. Acquisizioni e Prospettive. In Paoletti, O. (ed.), *Protostoria e Storia del 'Venetorum Angulus': Atti del XX Convegno Internazionale di Studi Etruschi e Italici. Portogruaro (Ve), Quarto d'Altino (Ve), Este (Pd), Adria (Ro). 16–19 Ottobre 1996.* Firenze: L. S. Olschki, 391–436.

Marinetti, A. 2004. Venetico: Rassegna di Nuove Iscrizioni (Este, Altino, Auronzo, S. Vito, Asolo). *Studi Etruschi* 70: 389–408.

Marinetti, A. 2008. Lo Stato Attuale dell'Epigrafia Venetica. *Quaderni di Archeologia del Veneto* 25: 189–193.

Messaris, P. 1994. *Visual Literacy: Image, mind and reality*. Boulder: Westview Press.

Messaris, P. 1997. *Visual Persuasion: The role of images in advertising*. Thousand Oaks: Sage Publications.

Messaris, P. and Moriarty, S. 2005. Visual Literacy Theory. In Smith, K., Moriarty, S., Barbatsis, G. and Kenney, K. (eds), *Handbook of Visual Communication*. Mahwah: Lawrence Erlbaum Associates, Publishers, 481–502.

Pellegrini, G. B. and Prosdocimi, A. 1967. *La Lingua Venetica*. Padova: Zielo.

Perego, E. 2010. Osservazioni Preliminari sul Banchetto Funerario Rituale nel Veneto Preromano: Acquisizione, Innovazione e Resistenza Culturale. In Mata Parreño, C., Pérez Jordà, G. and Vives-Ferrándiz Sánchez, J. (eds), *De la Cuina a la Taula: IV Reunió d'Economia en el Primer Millenni a.C.* Saguntum (Papeles del Laboratorio de Arqueología de València, Extra 9). València: Universitat de València, 287–294.

Perego, E. 2012a. *The Construction of Personhood in Veneto (Italy) Between the Late Bronze Age and the Early Roman Period*. Unpublished PhD dissertation, University College London.

Perego, E. 2012b. Family Relationships in Late Bronze Age, Iron Age and Early Roman Veneto (Italy): Preliminary considerations on the basis of osteological analysis and epigraphy. In Lawrence, R. and Stromberg, A. (eds), *Families in the Greco-Roman World*. London: Continuum, 121–142.

Prosdocimi, A. L. 1988. La Lingua. In Fogolari, G. and Prosdocimi, A. L. (eds), *Este Preromana. Lingua e Cultura*. Padova: Programma, 225–420.

Prosdocimi, A. L. 2002. Veneti, Eneti, Euganei, Ateste: I nomi. In Ruta Serafini, A. (ed.), *Este Preromana: Una Città e i Suoi Santuari*. Treviso: Canova, 45–76.

Riva, C. 2010. *The Urbanisation of Etruria: Funerary practices and social change, c.700–600 BC*. Cambridge: Cambridge University Press.

Ruta Serafini, A. (ed.) 2002. *Este Preromana. Una città e i suoi santuari*. Treviso: Canova.

Selber, S. 2004. *Multiliteracies for a Digital Age*. Carbondale: Southern Illinois University Press.

Stoddart, S. and Whitley, J. 1988. The Social Context of Literacy in Archaic Greek and Etruria. *Antiquity* 62: 761–772.

Street, B. V. 1984. *Literacy in Theory and Practice*. Cambridge: Cambridge University Press.

Tirelli, M. 1981. Una Nuova Lettura della Tomba Nazari 161 di Este (Padova). *Archeologia Veneta* 4: 7–28.

von Eles, P. (ed.) 2002. *Guerriero e Sacerdote: Autorità e comunità nell'Età del Ferro a Verucchio. La Tomba del Trono*. Firenze: All'Insegna del Giglio.

Whitehouse, R. and Wilkins, J. 2006. Veneti and Etruscans: Issues of language, literacy and learning. In Herring E., Lemos, I., Lo Schiavo F., Vagnetti, L., Whitehouse, R. and Wilkins, J. (eds), *Across Frontiers: Papers in honour of David Ridgeway and Francesca R. Serra Ridgeway*. London: Accordia Research Institute, 531–548.

Zaghetto, L. 2002. Dalla 'Parola' alle 'Frasi': Unità semplici e unità strutturate nel linguaggio delle immagini. Il caso dell'arte delle situle. In Colpo, I., Favaretto, I. and Ghedini, F. (eds), *Iconografia 2001: Studi sull'immagine*. Rome: Quasar, 31–43.

Zaghetto, L. 2006. La Ritualità nella Prima Arte delle Situle. In von Eles, P. (ed.), *La Ritualità Funeraria tra Età del Ferro e Orientalizzante in Italia: Atti del Convegno. Verrucchio 26–27 Giugno 2002*. Pisa: Istituti Editoriali e Poligrafici Internazionali, 41–45.

Zaghetto, L. 2007. Iconography and Language: The missing link. In Lomas, K., Whitehouse, R. and Wilkins, J. (eds), *Literacy and the State in the Ancient Mediterranean*. London: Accordia Research Institute, 171–181.

'Tombstones' in the North Italian Iron Age: Careless writers or athletic readers?

Ruth D. Whitehouse

University College London

Introduction

Several different types of inscribed stone monument of the North Italian Iron Age are interpreted as funerary markers and so could be described as 'tombstones'. In the traditional classification of these monuments, the primary criterion used is the language of the inscription — Etruscan or Venetic — and the monuments assigned to the two different language groups are almost never discussed together. In this traditional scholarship, language boundaries are considered to constitute very hard edges and to correlate precisely with distinctions between archaeological cultures. A second criterion is the typology of the monuments, variously described as *stelae, cippi* or *ciottoloni*.[1] What is never included in the classification process, and is rarely discussed in any detail, is the arrangement of the writing on the surface of the stone and its relationship to the iconography, where present.

This chapter examines the tombstones from a different perspective, that places the form and arrangement of the writing (rather than the language or content of the inscription) at the centre of the analysis. However, I shall begin by providing a brief description of the monuments, in order to make it easier to relate my discussion to the published literature (though, while I shall cite the most important works on the various monuments, I shall make no attempt to present a comprehensive bibliography, which is unnecessary in the present context). The map (**Figure 1**) shows the location of the sites mentioned in the text.

The Monuments

Monuments Inscribed in Etruscan

This section includes only those monuments found in northern Italy, in the northern extension of Etruscan territory, in the Po Valley. Stelae inscribed in Etruscan, of different types from

How to cite this book chapter:

Whitehouse, R. D. 2013. 'Tombstones' in the North Italian Iron Age: Careless writers or athletic readers? In: Piquette, K. E. and Whitehouse, R. D. (eds.) *Writing as Material Practice: Substance, surface and medium.* Pp. 271-288. London: Ubiquity Press. DOI: http://dx.doi.org/10.5334/bai.n

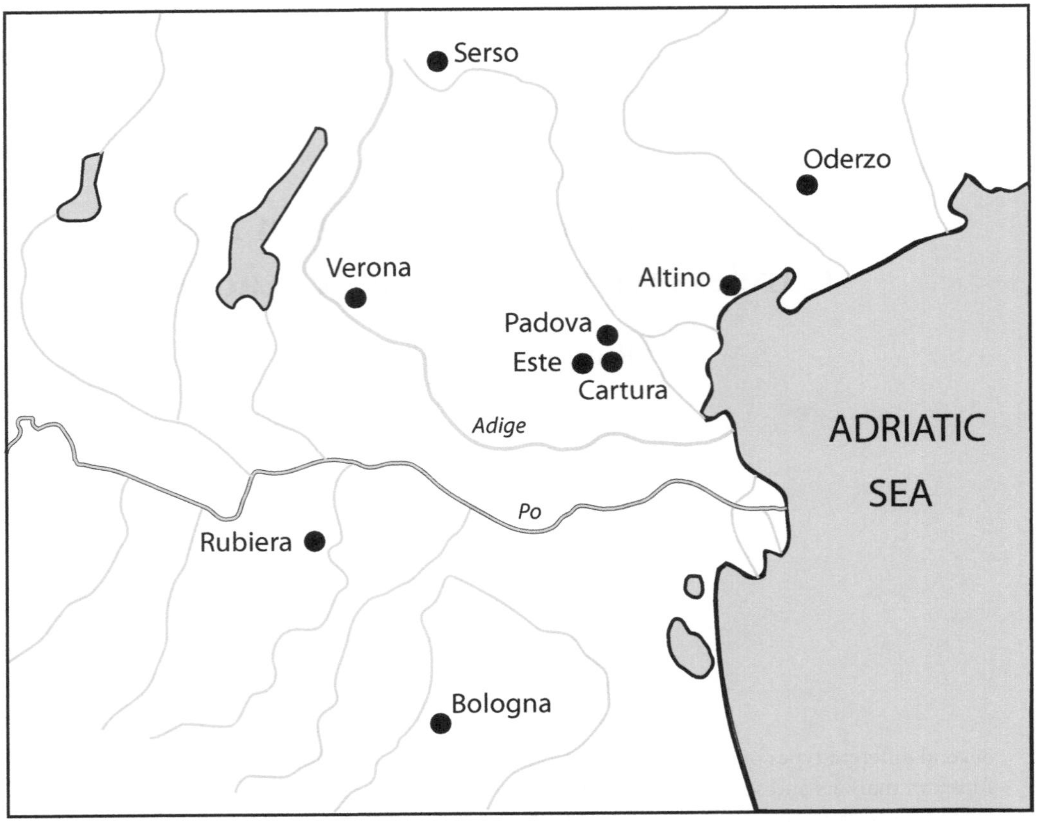

Figure 1: Map of northeast Italy showing location of main sites mentioned in the text.

those found in the north, occur on many sites throughout Etruria proper (equivalent to modern Tuscany, northern Lazio and parts of Umbria).

Stelae from Bologna (**Figures 2–3**)

More than 230 funerary stelae, complete or fragmentary, are known from the Villanovan and Etruscan cemeteries of Bologna (Etruscan *Felsina*), dating from the 8th or 7th century BC to the 4th century BC (Ducati 1911; 1943; Meller Padovani 1977; Stary-Rimpau 1988). They are made of sandstone and vary in shape from generically anthropomorphic early examples to mostly horse-shoe-shaped forms in the full Etruscan period. They are all decorated, carved in low relief and often originally painted, in a variety of different styles, often with figured scenes. Only 14 have inscriptions (and one of these is unreadable) and only these are included in this discussion. These inscribed stelae are dated to the 5th (or possibly late 6th) and the 4th centuries BC. Few of the monuments are complete, so it is difficult to ascertain their size range. The smallest of the complete monuments (stele 211) is 109 cm high while the largest (stele 10) is estimated to have been at least 270 cm high. The widths range from *c.*60 cm to *c.*160 cm and the thicknesses from *c.*20 to 44 cm. The monuments combine iconography and inscriptions; the carved decoration occurs not only on the main surface but often continues round the sides and onto the reverse. The inscriptions are normally on the main surface, but one large stele has three inscriptions, one of which is on the back. The inscriptions are mostly horizontal and written from right to left but one rectangular

Figure 2: Bologna stele 42. Sandstone. Height: 191 cm. The incised inscription, in Etruscan, reads from right to left. It is transliterated as mi vetus [k[athles suthi and translated as 'I am the grave of Vetu Kathle'. Bologna, Museo Civico Archeologico, inv. no. Ducati 42. © Bologna, Museo Civico Bologna.

stele with rounded corners has an inscription round the upper edge extending round both corners. A common position for the inscriptions is in bands located between the decorative friezes.

Of all the monuments discussed in this chapter, the Bologna stelae are the most certain 'tombstones' since some have been excavated in cemeteries, including the Certosa cemetery, well known for its richly equipped tombs of the 6th and 5th centuries BC. The stelae were found in association with specific tombs, where they had been used as markers. The inscriptions refer to the deceased individuals and include both male and female names.

Cippi from Rubiera (**Figure 4a–b**)

The only other inscribed Etruscan 'tombstones' from northern Italy are two cippi found close to the Secchia river near Rubiera, on the southern edge of the Po Valley, c.50 km northwest of Bologna (De Simone 1992). The cippi were not found in an archaeological excavation and their precise context is unknown. However, the area has yielded ancient burials and it is plausible to interpret them as funerary markers. They are cylindrical in shape with rounded tops. The smaller monument (*cippo* 1) is 141 cm high and has a circumference of 115 cm, while the larger one (*cippo* 2) is 170 cm high with a circumference of 100 cm. Like many of the Bologna stelae, they

Figure 3: Bologna stele 15. Sandstone. Height: 100 cm. The incised inscription, in Etruscan, reads from right to left. It is transliterated as velus kaiknas arnthrusla and translated as '(grave) of Vel Kaikna (son) of Arnthur'. Bologna, Museo Civico Archeologico: inv. no. Ducati 15. © Bologna, Museo Civico Bologna.

are decorated in low relief with orientalising motifs, but they are very different in form, with their cylindrical shape and both the decorative friezes and the inscriptions running continuously round the monument. The inscriptions are located between the decorative friezes and run horizontally, from right to left. They are dated on stylistic grounds (of both decoration and inscription) to the later 7th century BC.

Monuments Inscribed in Venetic

Most of the funerary monuments inscribed in Venetic come from the two southern Venetic cities of Padua and Este and there are marked differences in the funerary practices of the two cities. A small number of related monuments come from other Venetic centres; here they are discussed under the headings of those from Padua and Este.

Stelae from Padua (**Figures 5–6**)

The characteristic form is a rectangular stone stele decorated and inscribed on one side only, made of limestone or trachyte. 15 examples are known of 6th to 4th (or early 3rd century) BC date, from different locations in the city of Padua (Padova), of which eight bear legible inscriptions in Venetic (Fogolari 1988; Prosdocimi 1988; Zampieri 1994), while a further example of the 1st century BC is inscribed in Latin (Lomas 2006; Zampieri 1994). Two others of a related type are known: one from Monselice and one from Altino (**Figure 7**; Martini Chieci Bianchi and Prosdocimi 1969; Scarfi

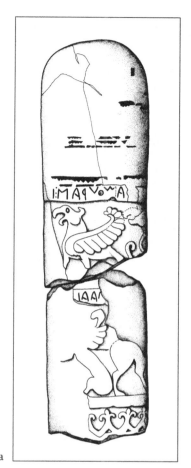

a   b

Figure 4: Rubiera stelae, Et Pa 1.1 and Et Pa 1.2. a) Sandstone. Height: 141 cm. The incised inscription, in Etruscan, reads from right to left and runs round the circumference of the stone. It is transliterated as mi aviles amthuras ima ame [---]eius lqr b) [---]ma al[---] and translated as 'I am of Avle Amthura ????'; b) Sandstone. Height: 177 cm. The incised inscription, in Etruscan, reads from right to left and runs round the circumference of the stone. It is transliterated as kuvei puleisnai mi isive [---] mise [---] mulvlenke zilath mi salalati amake; the translation is disputed but seems to involve two people, one female (Kuvei Puleisnai) and a second, assumed to be male, who was zilath at a place called either Misala or Sala. Reggio Emilia, Musei Civici (after De Simone 1992: Tav. 1).

1969–1970; Zampieri 1994). None have been found in situ but they are assumed to have been set into the ground as tomb markers; this assumption is supported by the fact that in many cases the bottom of the stone was left rough and was presumably not intended to be visible. The monuments are quite small: only one is more than a metre high, the one from Altino, which has a height of 115 cm. The others range in height from 54 to 95 cm, while widths range from 45 to 69 cm. They have a central reserved panel on the upper part of the stone containing a scene incised or carved in low relief. The inscription runs round the panel taking up one, two, three or four sides; each is written from right to left, except for the 1st-century example in Latin, which is written from left to right.

Figure 5: Padua stele, Pa2. Trachyte. Height: 86 cm. The incised inscription, in Venetic, reads from right to left, starting in the bottom right corner and running round three sides of the relief carved figured panel. It is transliterated as mi aletei veignoi karamniioi ekupetaris ego and translated as 'I am to Aletes Veignos Karamniios the ekupetaris' or 'I am the ekupetaris to Aletes Veignos Karamniios'. Verona, Museo Lapidario Maffeiano: inv. 28741.

Cippi from Este (**Figures 8–9**)

These cippi are small obelisk-shaped (pyramidal) stones, mostly made of trachyte, some of which bear inscriptions but no iconography. Cippi, of which there are also many uninscribed examples, may have been set up outside a group of tombs or a tumulus covering several tombs and are thought to mark a kinship group rather than individual burials (Balista and Ruta Serafini 1992; Fogolari 1988: 99–105; Marinetti 1988: 136–137, 147–149; Prosdocimi 1988: 247–259). They are mostly dated to the 5th and 4th centuries BC, though their use could begin as early as the late 6th century and go on as late as the 3rd century. Twenty-four typical inscribed examples are known while there are also three stelae of other forms. Like the Paduan stelae, the stones often have rough bases presumably intended to be set in the ground and therefore not visible. They average 50–60 cm in height, while the largest is 150 cm tall and the smallest only c.30 cm. They are normally rectangular rather than square in section, measuring from c.14 × 20 cm to 31 × 40 cm above the rough base, reducing in dimensions towards the top. The inscriptions run vertically in one, two or three lines, in boustrophedon form when there is more than one line. Most cippi have inscriptions on one face only, but three have two adjacent sides inscribed.

Ciottoloni from Padua (**Figures 10–11**)

The ciottoloni are natural pebbles of glacially smoothed Alpine porphyry, with maximum dimensions ranging from 16 to 46 cm. They were probably used as funerary markers, although few have been found in any meaningful context. There are 18 examples incised in Venetic, of which 17 come from the territory of Padua or close by, while one comes from Oderzo; a further example

Figure 6: Padua stele, Pa3bis. Trachyte. Height: 90 cm. The incised inscription, in Venetic, reads from right to left, starting in the bottom right corner and running round four sides of the incised figured panel. It is transliterated as enogenei enetiioi eppetaris albarenioi and translated as 'to Enogenes Enetios Albarenios the ekupetaris' or '(I am) the ekupetaris to Enogenes Enetios Albarenios'. Padova, Museo Civico. © Assessorato alla Cultura, Comune di Padova.

comes from Serso and is inscribed not in Venetic but Raetic (found in the area northwest of the Venetic region). The inscriptions are mostly short but a few are longer; they tend to run round the longer circumference of the stone although more complicated arrangements also occur, including one figure-of-eight design. They lack any iconography except for one example of a stylised key design, which appears on the example with the inscription in the form of a figure-of-eight (**Figure 11**). They are often attributed dates from the 6th to the 1st centuries BC on a mixture of linguistic and general associational criteria, although none very secure. Calzavara Capuis et al. (1978: 188–190) have argued for an early date (mid–5th century BC or earlier) for all the *ciottoloni* on the basis of name-forms, palaeography and the archaeological context of one example from Piovego.

The Cartura Stone (**Figure 12**)

A unique monument found near Cartura, on the border between the territories of Este and Padua, is sometimes considered a variant of the *ciottolone* class, but is in fact quite distinctive. Unlike the *ciottoloni*, it is made of limestone and is not a natural pebble but has been worked into shape. It is oval in form but has a flat top and bottom and straight sides with bevelled edges at top and bottom (it is sometimes colloquially known as 'the cheese' because of its shape). It measures 27 × 17

Figure 7: Altino stele, Tr7. Trachyte. Height: 115 cm. The incised inscription, in Venetic, reads from right to left; although the top part is badly damaged it is possible to see that it originally had 6 lines, starting in the bottom right corner and arranged in a spiral pattern, with line 5 inside line 1 and line 6 inside line 2. It is transliterated as ostialai A[---- | ----| ---]nai-kve ekvopetars | fremaist[---- | ----ia]bos and translated as 'to Ostiala a[-------] and [-------] na Freimast[-----] the ekupetaris' or 'Funerary monument to Ostiala a[-------] and for [------] na, Fremaist[----]'. Altino, Museo Archeologico Nazionale: inv. AL 11732. Published with the permission of Ministero dei beni e delle attività culturali e del turismo; reproduction prohibited.

cm and has a height of 100 cm. This stone bears one of the longest and most complicated of all the Venetic funerary inscriptions, with eight words, running right to left round the upper edge of the circumference of the stone. It is dated to the 6th century BC, among the earliest of the Venetic inscriptions. However, the stone was found without archaeological context and the dating is based on letter form and the absence of punctuation — an inherently weak basis, as John Wilkins and I have argued elsewhere (Whitehouse and Wilkins 2006: 542–543).

Other Monuments

There are a few other stone monuments that appear to have been used as funerary markers in the Venetic centres; these are stelae or cippi of various shapes, some quite irregular, and do not fall into any clear class. They are excluded from the present discussion.

Figure 8: Este stele, Es2. Trachyte. Height: 64.5 cm. The incised inscription, in Venetic, reads from right to left, starting in the top left corner and running first down, then up, then down again. It is transliterated as ego fukssiai voltiommninai and translated as 'I am (the tomb) to Fukssia Voltiomnina'. Este, Museo Nazionale di Atestino. Published with the permission of Ministero dei beni e delle attività culturali e del turismo; reproduction prohibited.

The Inscriptions

The Content of the Inscriptions

I do not propose to discuss the content of the inscriptions in any detail here, since they are not the focus of my study. However, it is worth noting that they represent the aspect of the tomb-stones that demonstrates the greatest similarity, transcending the major differences of language (Etruscan or Venetic) and of form of monument (stele, cippus or ciottolone). Because they are formulaic in nature and characteristically short, often two or three words only and very rarely more than six, they are frequently translated with confidence. However, in fact neither language is fully understood and there is much debate among linguists about both syntax and lexicon. Nonetheless we can see that most inscriptions include a one- or two-part name, assumed to be that of the owner of the tomb being marked; in the Etruscan inscriptions the name appears in what is taken to be the genitive case, while the Venetic ones are in what is taken to be the dative. Both male and female names appear. While many of the inscriptions consist of the name alone, others take the form of so-called 'talking inscriptions', beginning in the Etruscan examples with 'mi', in the Venetic with 'ego'. In a small number of cases, in both Etruscan and Venetic, a term is used that is interpreted as relating to either an office held by the deceased, or to a status or class. In Etruscan the term is 'zilath', usually interpreted as a magistracy; in Venetic the term is 'ekupetaris' (and variants), sometimes interpreted as referring to membership of an equestrian class or, more

Figure 9: Este stele, Es13. Trachyte. Height: 29 cm. The incised inscription, in Venetic, reads from left to right, starting in the bottom left corner and running first up, then down. It is transliterated as fougonte[i urk]leoi (ego may be missing) and translated as '(I am the tomb) to Fugontes Urkleos'. Este, Museo Nazionale di Atestino. Published with the permission of Ministero dei beni e delle attività culturali e del turismo; reproduction prohibited.

specifically, as meaning a charioteer. In some of the Etruscan examples the term 'suthi' appears and is interpreted as meaning 'grave'.

Examples of Etruscan inscriptions (transcribed and translated) are:

- pesnas kathles salchis   of Pesna Kathle (Bologna stele 47)
- mi suth i thanchvilus titlalus   I (am) the grave of Thanchvil, (daughter) of Titlalu (Bologna stele 105)
- [------]as' levels zilacnuk[e]   [I am the grave of ????? ????]as', son of Leve, who was zilath (Bologna stele 25, inscription a)

Examples of Venetic inscriptions (transcribed and translated) are:

- hostihavos toupeio   to Tihavos Toupeio (Padua ciottolone Pa7)
- ego voltiomnoi iuvantioi   I am to Voltiomnos Iuvantios (Este cippus Es4)
- aletei veignoi karamniioi ekupetaris ego   I am to Aletes Veignos Karamniios, the ekupetaris (Padua stele Pa2)

Arrangement of the Inscriptions

In contrast to the content of the inscriptions, which are repetitively similar, their arrangement on the tombstones demonstrates marked differences. In this section I shall describe the main variants

Figure 10: Padua ciottolone Pa25. Porphyry. Dimensions: 23 × 17 × 14 cm. Photographs taken from different sides of ciottolone with transcription of complete inscription. The incised inscription, in Venetic, reads from right to left and runs round the circumference of the stone. It is transliterated as tivalei bellenei and translated as 'to Tivales Bellenios'. Museo di Scienze Archeologiche e d'Arte dell'Università di Padova. Published with the permission of Ministero dei beni e delle attività culturali e del turismo; reproduction prohibited.

and indicate the implications for the reader (I shall turn to the writer later). I assume here that the reader would have encountered the stone in its fixed position on or by the tomb and would have had to move his or her eyes, head, or body, to read the inscription.

Inscriptions in Horizontal Lines on a Flat Surface

Inscriptions in horizontal lines occur on the majority of the Bologna stelae, inscribed in Etruscan, where they are characteristically placed in bands running between the zones of decoration (**Figures 2–3**). This is the variant that most resembles modern tombstones, in that it requires the reader to stand in front of the monument, involving movement only of the eyes, or perhaps slight movements of the head (though from right to left, in contrast to the direction of modern western writing). What is different from most modern tombstones, however, is the subservient relationship of the writing to the decoration: in most of the Bologna stelae the inscriptions are not very large, with a maximum letter height of *c*.8.0 or 9.0 cm, and the figured scenes dominate the visual impression.

Inscriptions in Horizontal Lines Around the Circumference of the Stone

Different versions of horizontal inscriptions occur on the two Rubiera cippi, written in Etruscan (**Figure 4a-b**). They resemble the Bologna stelae in that the inscriptions are located in horizontal

Figure 11: Padua ciottolone Pa26. Porphyry. Dimensions: 25.7 × 23 × 17 cm. Photographs taken from different sides of the ciottolone and transcription of complete inscription. The incised inscription, in Venetic, reads from left to right and runs round the circumference of the stone in a figure-of-eight configuration. It is transliterated as fugioi tivalioi andetioi ekupetaris ego and translated as 'I am to Fugios Tivalios Andetios the ekupetraris' or 'I am the monument to Fugios Tivalios Andetios'. Este, Museo Nazionale di Atestine: inv. IG 145813. Published with the permission of Ministero dei beni e delle attività culturali e del turismo; reproduction prohibited.

Figure 12: The Cartura stone Es122. Limestone. Dimensions: 27 × 17 × 10 cm. The incised inscription, in Venetic, reads from right to left and runs round the circumference of the stone. It is transliterated as ego fontei ersiniioi vinetikaris vivoi oliialekve murtuvioi atisteit and translated as 'I am to Fontis Ersinios; the vinetikaris set this up (to him) whether living or dead'. Este, Museo Nazionale Atestino: inv. IG 41528. Published with the permission of Ministero dei beni e delle attività culturali e del turismo; reproduction prohibited.

bands separating zones decorated with figured scenes. However, unlike the Bologna stelae, the monuments are cylindrical in shape and both the decorative friezes and the inscriptions run right round the stones. To read the inscriptions fully, the reader would have to walk round the stones in a clockwise direction (since the direction of writing is again right to left).

Very different in form from these cippi are the ciottoloni from Padua, inscribed in Venetic (**Figures 10–11**), but they also, in most cases, have inscriptions running round the circumference of the stone, as does the unique Cartura stone (**Figure 12**). They are mostly written from right to left, but a few run left to right. Although these stones are not large (none exceeds 50 cm in their longest dimension), they would nonetheless have required the reader to walk round them to read the full inscription. Moreover, if they were placed directly on the ground surface — and we have no evidence on this one way or the other — an adult reader would also have had to bend or kneel to read them.

Inscriptions written around the circumference of a stone can pose an additional problem for the reader, in those cases where there is no gap in the text — which is to identify where the beginning is. The formulaic nature of the inscriptions means that this can usually be assessed plausibly — possibly more easily by the original reader than the modern linguist — but it would nonetheless have to be sought and would not have been obvious at first sight.

Inscriptions in Straight Lines Around the Sides of a Figured Panel

Inscriptions around the sides of a figured panel occur on the stelae from Padua, Monselice and Altino (**Figures 5–7**), all but one inscribed in Venetic, one in Latin. The Venetic examples run right to left, the Latin one left to right. Of those where the inscription can be read or reconstructed reasonably completely, two run along the top only, three run around two sides, two along three sides, two along four sides, while one — the example from Altino with an empty panel where the figured scene normally occurs — consists of six lines arranged in a spiral fashion (**Figure 7**). The one- and two-line inscriptions begin at the top, in the Venetic examples starting in the top right-hand corner, in the Latin example in the left-hand corner; the three- and four-line inscriptions all begin on the right side starting in the bottom right-hand corner. The six-line inscription also begins in the bottom right-hand corner and is arranged in a spiral fashion, with line 5 wrapping round inside line 1 and line 6 wrapping around inside line 2 along the top of the stone. All the inscriptions are written as if inscribed on a continuous baseline, with the letters aligned with their tops towards the edge of the stone and the bottoms facing inwards. In the case of the four- and six-line inscriptions, this means that the bottom (fourth) line is upside down in comparison to the top (second) line.

For the reader, these inscriptions require considerably more movement of the head than horizontal inscriptions do. (S)he must first lean to the right to read line 1, straighten up to read line 2 across the top, then lean to the left to read line 3. To read line 4, where present, the reader must be able to read upside down writing (or stand on his or her head).

A single example of the Bologna stelae, inscribed in Etruscan, presents a variant of this type. The fragmentary stele 137 seems to have had a three-sided inscription around the top of the stone, running right to left as usual, but in this case the corners are rounded, so the inscription is curved at both ends.

Inscriptions in Vertical Lines

Inscriptions in vertical lines occur on the cippi from Este, inscribed in Venetic (**Figures 8–9**). The necessity to place the inscriptions vertically is created by the choice of small obelisk-shaped monuments as tombstones: the narrow widths would not accommodate more than three or four letters on a line, which would be impractical for the length of inscriptions required. Even exploited lengthways, the inscriptions mostly require two lines and in two cases, three. In two further cases, the inscription occupies two adjacent faces of the stone, creating one further three-line (Es137) and one four-line inscription (Es8). One other stone (Es9), with inscriptions on two faces is normally treated as bearing two separate two-line inscriptions. The multi-line inscriptions are all written boustrophedon, usually but not always starting at the top of the stone in the left-hand top corner, with the second line running upwards and the third, where present, down again. Two different arrangements occur. Some inscriptions are written as sitting on separate baselines, so that the letters are all the same way up and the first line reads right to left and the second left to right. Others, however, are written as on a continuous baseline, so that the letters of the second line are upside down in relation to those on the first. These two different arrangements impose different movements on the reader: for the first type (s)he has to alternate movements of the head to the left, then right, while for the second type the whole body has to be repositioned to read the second line and then again for the third line, where present. It is worth pointing out that reading inscriptions arranged vertically, while perfectly possible, is never particularly easy. In the case of the Este cippi, which rarely stand more than half a metre high above ground level, adult readers would have had to bend down, or even kneel, as well as move their heads from left to right. In the case of the three cippi that are inscribed on two adjacent sides, the reader would also have to move bodily to read the second side.

Inscriptions in Elaborate Arrangements

Two of the ciottoloni have inscriptions in more elaborate arrangements. One (**Figure 11**) has an inscription written left to right in a figure-of-eight configuration. This is also the only ciottolone to have any decoration: an abstract key symbol on what was presumably the upper surface of the stone. The other (Pa27) which was found in the same area, has a three-line inscription arranged right to left in an overall horseshoe shape; it starts with the middle line, then moves on to the bottom line and then on to the top line. It is written as on a continuous baseline, which in this case results in the letters of the bottom line (line 2) being upside down in relation to those of the upper two lines (lines 1 and 3). Reading these inscriptions would involve walking round the stone, bending and head and eye movements.

Discussion

What emerges most obviously from this survey is the variety found both in the types of monument and in the arrangement of the inscriptions. As we have seen, the inscriptions are not presented in a 'user-friendly' manner, at least from a modern perspective, often requiring the reader to walk, bend and move the head and eyes in ways unfamiliar to us today. The arrangement of the inscription seems to be constrained by the nature of the monument: the size and shape of the stone and the placing of the decoration, where present. It seems reasonable to deduce that the primary choice made was of the *stone*, with the inscription being a secondary consideration. This argument is supported by the fact that uninscribed versions of all the main monument types are attested and, except in the case of the Paduan stelae, the uninscribed versions dominate numerically. While the inscription may have offered 'added value', to use another contemporary term, it was clearly not an essential component of the tombstone.

Having concentrated on the role of the reader so far, it is time to consider that of the writer, a term I use here to refer to the stone mason who carved the inscription (leaving aside the issue of who commissioned it or who composed it, whether the same person or a third party). We have no archaeological information about the production of the stones, but I make the assumption that they were produced in workshops, which would have had equipment that allowed the stones (few of which are outstandingly large or heavy) to be moved to facilitate the writing process, i.e. to be turned round or over. Thus the writer would have been able to write horizontally at all times, whatever the position or direction of the line in the final monument. Whether this was in fact the case could perhaps be elucidated by detailed study of the surfaces of the stones using a technique such as RTI (Reflection Transformation Imaging: see Earl et al. 2011; Piquette forthcoming; see also Piquette and Whitehouse, **Figure 1**, this volume), which could show up tool marks, and indicate direction, angle and depth of carving; however, no such work has been undertaken on the Italian monuments and this remains a project for the future. Most of the stones used for the monuments — limestone, sandstone and trachyte — are relatively soft and easy to carve, the exception being the porphyry of the ciottoloni, which is a hard volcanic rock. The inscriptions are generally carved competently, with well-formed letters of more or less equal size, constrained by bands designed to contain them. These bands are created between zones of decoration (in the Bologna and Rubiera stelae) or around the edge of a figured panel (in the Paduan stelae), or by the incision of straight lines (in the case of the Este cippi); even the more elaborate ciottoloni have such incised lines. There are no obvious mistakes of composition and the inscriptions in Venetic include punctuation marks, in the elaborate system developed for that script. None of the inscriptions mark word divisions (Venetic punctuation separates syllables) and no attempt is made to make word divisions coincide with edges or corners of stones: the continuous text carries on regardless.

Whether the stone masons composed the inscriptions themselves or copied from templates composed by others, it seems likely that they would have become competent at reading these short and simple texts. Whether this was also true of the readers is far less clear. To explore further what reading entailed at this time, we may try to outline the 'visitor experience' in an Iron Age cemetery in northern Italy. 'Visitor experience' is another contemporary concept, but I mean it here not in the sense in which it is used by museum and cultural heritage specialists, but in terms of the *original* visitor experience of those who encountered the monuments at the time they were erected or not long after. This inherently hypothetical exercise is made even more tentative by the lack of detailed archaeological contextual information available; nonetheless it is worth undertaking as it serves to focus on one key concern of the current volume – that is the material practices involved in the consumption of writing. The only assumptions I make are that the monuments were standing in the open on or near the tombs, which were usually arranged in cemeteries, and that visibility was not impeded by the presence of buildings or, for that matter, shrubs or trees (which, of course, we do not know).

The monuments are relatively small. While the largest of the Bologna stelae may have been 207 cm tall when complete, this was exceptional: most of the stones were under 150 cm tall, many less than 100 cm, and some no more than 50 cm — a range not unlike that to be found in a traditional English churchyard. When standing, particularly in groups in a cemetery, they would probably have been visible from a few hundred metres away, but would not have appeared very impressive at this distance. As one approached, the stones would have appeared larger and the presence of decoration would have become apparent, though details of scenes would not have been clear until one was quite close to the monument. What about the inscriptions themselves? The heights of the letters ranges from c.3 to 8 or 9 cm. To help us visualise this, it is worth noting that the larger size is close to that of UK car number plates, which the British driving test requires drivers to be able to read at a distance of 20.5 m (Driving Standards Agency 2013) — and quite a lot larger than found on most tombstones today. Script with letters 3 cm high, much more comparable to that of modern tombstones, can be read at about half that distance in average daylight. Whether these distances would have applied in the case of the Iron Age tombstones is unclear. It is one thing to read black letters standing out against a white or yellow background, quite another to make out letters inscribed in stone. There is some evidence that some of the inscriptions may have been painted or infilled with coloured matter, but we do not know how widespread this practice was or how long such colour would have survived on stone surfaces or in incisions or carved depressions in stones left out in the open. In practice the inscriptions would probably have been read from a position quite close to the stone, much as we read tombstones in a churchyard today, a quite intimate experience. Where the Iron Age experience would have differed from the modern one is in the bodily engagement involved. Whereas we would tend to stand, or perhaps sit or kneel, in a stationary position in front of the gravestone, the Iron Age visitor would have been prepared to walk round the monument, to bend and to twist their head from side to side and back again, or perhaps to undertake more difficult bodily contortions, if they wished to read the inscription in its entirety. Since bodies vary in size and agility, these movements would have been easier for some than others. The young and able-bodied could have accomplished them reasonably easily, whereas the old, arthritic or pregnant would have encountered greater difficulty. Interestingly, the people who would have been able to read them most easily (from a corporeal point of view) were children: not only would they have been more agile generally, but they would not have had to stoop to read them.

The question that arises is whether Iron Age people did indeed undertake this bodily engagement, or whether it sufficed to know that the inscription was present, that the tombstone had been completed in this way. This leads onto the question of who the expected reader was. Calculations of the proportion of literate people in ancient cultures are difficult to make (see Harris 1989 for classic discussion of this subject, while Stoddart and Whitley 1988 and Cornell 1991 offer divergent opinions on ancient Italy), but it is always assumed that the figures were very low and there is no reason to believe that northern Italy in the Iron Age was any exception. So, the number of people who *could* have read the inscriptions was probably small, although they would presumably have been concentrated in the elite families that erected the more elaborate tombstones and had greater access to education. We need to ask also whether the inscriptions were intended exclusively for the time they were erected and for the people who commissioned them, presumably the family of the deceased, or whether they were also intended for posterity and for viewing by strangers, as we know was the case with many Roman funerary inscriptions (see, for example Carroll 2009). In the absence of explicit references in the inscriptions themselves, which sometimes occur in the Roman examples, there is no way we can answer this question, but it does affect our conclusion about the intended readability of the inscriptions. For the family and friends of the deceased, and anybody else present at the funeral, the identity of the deceased was known and would not have had to be read from the stone, as would be the case for passing strangers or future visitors. While it is reasonable to imagine that the erection of a tombstone would always have had connotations of long-term survival and preservation of the memory of the deceased, this may not have involved any specific attempt to produce readable inscriptions for the future. The overall impression we gain is that the writers were concerned with producing texts containing the correct information and had little concern for their readability, either short- or long-term.

On the other hand, this impression may arise from unwarranted presentist assumptions about the nature of reading. In an examination of the materiality of writing in 1st-millennium BC Italy (Whitehouse 2008), I have looked at examples from a wide range of monuments and smaller artefacts found in several different areas of Italy. I have found that the characteristics described here in connection with the north Italian tombstones occur in many other cases too, not only on stelae, but also on portable artefacts such as pottery vessels, clay loomweights, bronze vessels, plaques and figurines, and jewellery items such as rings and fibulae made of precious metals (see also Perego, this volume). We find inscriptions running in many ways other than in straight lines: in loops, circles or spirals, for instance, or, three-dimensionally, continuously round the neck, body or base of a pottery or metal vessel or up the side of a figurine and across its shoulders (see Cessford, this volume, who also describes artefacts with writing arranged in several different ways, albeit from more recent contexts in the UK). To read such inscriptions requires a bodily engagement that is unfamiliar to us as modern readers, though in the case of the portable artefacts it would probably have involved turning the object in the hands rather than more dynamic movement of the eyes, head or body, as it would in the case of the stelae and other fixed monuments. In any case reading in the Iron Age would have been not just a cerebral but also a physical experience, in a way that is unfamiliar to us today.

So — what can we conclude in relation to the Iron Age tombstones? On the one hand, the writers seem not to have been concerned primarily with producing readable texts, but with including the necessary information (mainly the name, and sometimes the status, of the deceased) in the available space. This information may have been perceived as necessary as much for the world of the dead (the deceased individual, familial ancestors and divine beings) as for the world of the living. On the other hand, in the world of the living, among visitors to the cemetery, though not many people would have been able to read the inscriptions, those that could would have expected to engage with the monuments in a corporeal way and would not have found it strange to bend, twist and walk round them in order to read what was written on them. By taking a material practice approach, we can understand better both the production and the consumption of the written texts in terms of the human body, the capacities and limitations of its motor skills and the functioning of its senses. We can appreciate the effects that the differences between human bodies might have — whether arising from size, age, condition or specific ability / infirmity — and understand how they might have affected the processes of 'reading' and 'writing'. We have already noted how 'reading', in the corporeal sense described here, might have been easier for children with their more agile movements, better eyesight and viewpoints closer to the ground; by contrast 'writing' in the same sense might have required the more developed motor skills and physical strength of healthy adults. These corporeal abilities might have had little connection to the cerebral skills required to understand the linguistic content of inscriptions ('reading' and 'writing' as these terms are more usually understood); however they were certainly relevant to the ways in which the tombstones were produced and consumed and therefore to the way they functioned in society.

Notes

[1] The terms *stele* (Greek; the Italian version is either *stela* or *stele*) and *cippus* (Latin; the Italian version is *cippo*) are both used to describe standing stones. I have been unable to find definitions that separate them consistently, although there is a tendency to use *stele* for rectangular stones with flat faces and *cippus* for other shapes, such as cylinders or obelisk shapes. In this chapter I use the terms traditionally employed for the particular monuments in question. The Italian term *ciottolone* means literally 'big pebble', which is an accurate description of this type of monument.

References

Balista, C. and Ruta Serafini, A. 1992. Este preromana: Nuovi dati sulle necropolis. In Tosi, G. (ed.), *Este Antica: dalla preistoria all'età romana*. Padua: Zielo, 111–123.

Calzavara Capuis, L., Martini Chieco Bianchi, A. M. and Prosdocimi, A. L. 1978. Due nuovi ciottoloni con iscrizione venetica. *Studi Etruschi* 46: 179–203.

Carroll, M. 2009. 'Vox tua nempe mea est': Dialogues with the dead in Roman funerary commemoration. *Accordia Research Papers* 11 (2007–2008): 37–76.

Cornell, T. J. 1991. The Tyranny of the Evidence: A discussion of the possible uses of literacy in Etruria and Latium in the archaic age. In *Literacy in the Roman World* (Journal of Roman Archaeology Supplementary Series Number 3). Ann Arbor, RI: Department of Classical Studies, University of Michigan, 7–33.

De Simone, C. 1992. *Le iscrizioni etrusche dei cippi di Rubiera* (Archaeologica Regiensia 6). Reggio Emilia: Comune di Reggio Emilia.

Driving Standards Agency 2013. *The Official Highway Code*. London: HMSO (Her Majesty's Stationery Office).

Ducati, P. 1911. Le pietre funerarie felsinee. *Monumenti antichi dei Lincei* 20: 360–724.

Ducati, P. 1943. Nuove stele funerarie felsinee. *Monumenti antichi dei Lincei* 39: 374–446.

Earl, G., Basford, P. J., Bischoff, A. S., Bowman, A., Crowther, C., Hodgson, M., Martinez, K., Isaksen, L., Pagi, H., Piquette, K. E. and Kotoula, E. 2011. Reflectance Transformation Imaging Systems for Ancient Documentary Artefacts. *Electronic Visualisation and the Arts*, July, London. http://ewic.bcs.org/upload/pdf/ewic_ev11_s8paper3.pdf [accessed 21 October 2013].

Fogolari, G. 1988. La cultura. In Fogolari, G. and Prosdocimi, A. L. (eds), *I Veneti Antichi: Lingua e cultura*. Padua: Editoriale Programma, 1–225.

Harris, W. V. 1989. *Ancient Literacy*. Cambridge, MA: Harvard University Press.

Lomas, K. 2006. The Stele of Ostiala Gallenia: Funerary commemoration and cultural identity in northeast Italy. In Herring, E., Lemos, I., Lo Schiavo, F., Vagnetti, L., Whitehouse, R. and Wilkins, J. (eds), *Across Frontiers: Etruscans, Greeks, Phoenicians and Cypriots: Studies in honour of David Ridgway and Francesca Romana Serra Ridgway*. London: Accordia Research Institute, 451–462.

Marinetti, A. 1992. Este preromana: Epigrafia e lingua. In Tosi, G. (ed.), *Este Antica: dalla preistoria all'età romana*. Padua: Zielo, 127–172.

Martini Chieco Bianchi, A. M. and Prosdocimi, A. L. 1969. Una nuova stele paleoveneta iscritta. *Studi Etruschi* 37: 511–514.

Meller Padovani, P. 1977. *Le stele villanoviane di Bologna*. Capo di Ponte: Edizioni del Centro.

Piquette, K. E. forthcoming. Reflectance Transformation Imaging: A new method for the digitisation and study of early Egyptian graphical culture. In Graff, G., Jiménez-Serrano, A. and Bailly, M. (eds), *Préhistoires de l'écriture: iconographie, pratiques graphiques et émergence de l'écrit dans l'Egypte prédynastique / Prehistories of writing: Iconography, graphic practices and the forming process of writing in Predynastic Egypt*. Actes de la table-ronde de décembre 2010. Aix-en-Provence: Préhistoires méditerranéennes.

Prosdocimi, A. L. 1988. La lingua. In Fogolari, G. and Prosdocimi, A. L. (eds), *I Veneti Antichi: Lingua e cultura*. Padua: Editoriale Programma, 225–422.

Scarfi, B. M. 1969–1970. Altino (Venezia): Le iscrizioni funerary romane provenienti dagli scavi 1965–1968 e da rinvenimenti sporadici. *Atti dell'Istituto Veneto di Scienze, Lettere ed Arti* 128: 207–89.

Stary-Rimpau, J. S. 1988. *Die Bologneser Stelen des 7. bis 4. Jh. v. Chr.* Marburg: Phillipps-Universität.

Stoddart, S. and Whitley, J. 1988. The Social Context of Literacy in Archaic Greece and Etruria. *Antiquity* 62: 761–772.

Whitehouse, R. 2008. The Materiality of Writing: Case studies from 1st millennium BC Italy. McDonald Lecture, 19 November 2008, Cambridge (being prepared for publication).

Whitehouse, R. and Wilkins, J. 2006. Veneti and Etruscans: Issues of language, literacy and learning. In Herring, E., Lemos, I., Lo Schiavo, F., Vagnetti, L., Whitehouse, R. and Wilkins, J. (eds), *Across Frontiers: Etruscans, Greeks, Phoenicians and Cypriots: Studies in honour of David Ridgway and Francecsa Romana Serra Ridgway*. London: Accordia Research Institute, 531–548.

Zampieri, G. 1994. *Il Museo Archeologico di Padova*. Milan: Electa.

Different Times, Different Materials and Different Purposes: Writing on objects at the Grand Arcade site in Cambridge

Craig Cessford

Cambridge Archaeological Unit

Introduction

Like many other topics the subject of the materiality of writing in 18th–20th century Britain has received relatively little attention, principally because it has been conceived of as part of an unproblematic "familiar past" (Tarlow and West 1999) that is perceived as similar to the present or sufficiently well understood through other sources that archaeology does not have a significant contribution to make. There are also other major issues that differentiate the 18th–20th centuries from earlier periods, most notably that the material culture is predominantly mass-produced in a way that few earlier examples of writing are; additionally many types of material culture of the period are truly global in extent. In contrast with earlier periods in Britain where there is relatively limited archaeological evidence for writing, the problem here is that the amount of data is often too large. One way to approach this richness of data is to eschew the more broad brush quasi 'culture-historical' approaches often adopted for earlier periods, where material spanning several centuries and large geographical areas is studied in order to generate a large enough 'corpus' of material to make meaningful comments. Instead the evidence from 18th–20th century Britain allows us to work on a much more intimate scale of individual households at particular points in time as represented by 'feature groups'.

Any such attempt to consider 18th–20th century writing must recognise that the dominant material upon which writing was produced was paper, which is rarely preserved archaeologically even in 18th–20th century contexts, although there are exceptions (Crook and Murray 2006:

How to cite this book chapter:

Cessford, C. 2013. Different Times, Different Materials and Different Purposes: Writing on objects at the Grand Arcade site in Cambridge. In: Piquette, K. E. and Whitehouse, R. D. (eds.) *Writing as Material Practice: Substance, surface and medium.* Pp. 289-317. London: Ubiquity Press. DOI: http://dx.doi.org/10.5334/bai.o

66–69, 80–85; Dickens 2001: 117, 124). This is true of many periods, where post-depositional processes and environmental conditions have often largely destroyed all traces of the dominant writing material. In the case of the 18th–20th centuries much of the material has been recovered from material dumped in below ground features where conditions have destroyed all paper, although in contrast to earlier periods we have a much better understanding of 18th–20th century writing on paper since vast corpora are preserved in libraries and archives. Despite the poor preservation of paper in 18th–20th century archaeological contexts, many forms of writing that do survive archaeologically on more durable mediums are related in some way to the dominant paper medium. That the relationship between writing on paper and other mediums is often complex and ambiguous is perhaps best illustrated by an example found on a stone at the Nine Ladies stone circle in Derbyshire, where a graffito of the name "Bill Stumps" is incised onto an outlying orthostat of a Bronze Age stone circle (**Figure 1**). The incising of this name mirrors a fictional incident in Charles Dickens's *The Posthumous Papers of the Pickwick Club* published in 1836–1837, raising the question of whether the writing on the stone was inspired by Dickens writing on paper or whether Dickens was inspired by the inscription. Dickens does not appear to have visited the area until after he wrote the book so it is concluded that his writing published and circulated in a paper-based form inspired the graffito (Guilbert 2001).

Although paper rarely survives archaeologically in 18th–20th century contexts, it has recently begun to be viewed from a more archaeological, or at least material culture standpoint. Particular attention is being paid to the materiality of paper-based writing, of the 19th century (Hack 2005; Hall 2000; Marsden 2006; von Mucke 1999), as part of a general 'material turn' (Pykett 2005) in Victorian studies inspired largely by the work of Asa Briggs (1988) who asked historians to contemplate Victorian materialities, not least because the Victorians themselves were fascinated with objects and things.

While English is, unsurprisingly, the dominant language encountered in inscribed material culture from British sites of this period, a range of other European languages is occasionally attested, particularly French, but the next most common language is Chinese (see below). The majority of, but not all, examples of written objects during this period were mass produced. In theory this resulted in the production of virtually identical examples, and this has implications for many of the themes relevant to the materiality of writing. Prior to the 18th century many, perhaps most, examples of writing that individuals encountered were effectively unique. This constitutes a markedly different type of encounter and it is notable that the earlier types of writing that were mass produced, most obviously coins, are largely absent from considerations of the materiality of writing. 18th–20th century mass production is, however, counteracted to a certain extent by the fact that some of the 'mass production' was relatively small-scale with localised distributions where products travelled at most a few dozen miles, whilst some types are truly global in their reach with examples found distributed around the world (see below). Additionally the great expansion of choice in some types of material at this time, such as ceramics, meant that, although produced on a massive scale, they might well be locally unique and restricted to a single household in an area. Such considerations must underpin the nature of the particular engagements with writing that will be presented subsequently.

Feature Groups

Archaeologically, material remains of writing are with a few exceptions relatively rare in Britain prior to the 18th century. As a result, in bringing together enough material to enable meaningful comment most considerations of topics such as this generally have a relatively broad temporal and geographical scope. These tend to be 'culture-historical' in their approach, emphasising similarities and broad patterns (e.g. Evans 1987; Okasha 1995). A rather different approach is possible for

Figure 1: The Nine Ladies Bronze Age embanked stone circle, Stanton Moor, Derbyshire, with the "Bill Stumps" graffito on the broken King Stone. Photograph courtesy of Chris Collyer.

18th–20th century Britain, and indeed much of the rest of the world. Around the middle of the 18th century a significant change occurs in the nature of the archaeological record in Britain. Increasing numbers of short-term deliberate depositional events survive, frequently containing hundreds of 'items' that can broadly be interpreted as 'feature groups', closed assemblages of domestic artefacts discarded as a single deposit (Barker and Majewski 2006: 207; Fryer and Shelley 1998; Pearce

2000). These are interpreted as 'household clearance' events, such as those described in 19th-century fiction in which they are characterised as profoundly brutal and disturbing (Trotter 2008). Objects that had been viewed by the Victorians as 'household gods' (Cohen 2006) imbued with personal meaning and social memory became simply commodities with an exchange value, and in the case of the material in the archaeological record simply 'stuff' that is just waste matter (Trotter 2008) except in the contexts of deposition and potentially subsequent archaeological recovery.

The phenomenon of feature groups presents investigators studying writing from a material cultural perspective with various interpretive possibilities and challenges. The contextual richness of such deposits means that they can become the primary analytical unit, rather than more spatially and temporally diffuse entities such as sites or cultures. These feature groups lend themselves to consideration through a form of "thick description", which does not look at material in isolation but takes account of context so that the things become more meaningful to an outsider (Geertz 1973), and the preservation of detailed archaeological associations provides a wealth of information about the meaning(s) of objects when situated in their various contexts.

Deposits of this type are attested in earlier periods in Britain but prior to the 16th century they do not occur with any frequency. Only in the mid-18th century do they become a more common occurrence. The increase in levels of discard in 'feature groups' at this time is probably linked to a consumer revolution, where in contrast to earlier periods dominated by scarcity and frugality there was a marked increase in consumption of a wide range goods and products by individuals from different social and economic backgrounds (Bermingham and Brewer 1995; Brewer and Porter 1993; Fairchilds 1993). This consumer revolution was fuelled by competitive emulation whereby individuals and groups lower down the social scale sought to imitate those higher up (McKendrick et al. 1982) or the restructuring of social relations particularly with regard to the changing nature of the *bourgeoisie* who owned the means of capitalist production, and to a growing and more assertive middle class (McCracken 1990). However, discussions of such assemblages often employ, albeit implicitly, the "Pompeii Premise" (Binford 1981; Schiffer 1985), assuming that the deposit represents a single moment frozen in time and that whoever made the deposit was also the original owner and/or user of the material. Once quantified these assemblages are used as the raw material for discussions of a host of themes, including social status and gender relations. Minimal consideration is usually given to the fact that the dumped material has probably been carefully selected. Still fashionable or valuable material was probably saved for further use, either on the same site or elsewhere (Johnson 1996: 182–183). This becomes apparent when the material from large assemblages is compared to that derived from other types of context, such as those related to middening and night soiling. The relative proportions of different material types and wares in the different types of deposit vary markedly, demonstrating that discard in 'feature groups' was carefully organised.

The nature of the assemblages, where objects are often complete or substantially complete and where broken typically consist of large unabraded fragments that can readily be refitted, means that material from these features can be quantified in terms of a count of 'minimum number of items' (MNI). This method is relatively straightforward, although not entirely unproblematic, for certain types of material such as ceramics (Brooks 2005), glass (Willmott 2002), clay pipes and worked bone objects. Based upon these MNI counts and the number of items with writing on them it is possible to calculate the percentage of writing-bearing items from the overall assemblage (**Table 1**). There are a number of complicating factors such as incomplete items and items that bear more than one form of writing, which affect the quantification. The quantification used in this study specifically excludes categories of material that never or rarely bear any writing and focus principally upon ceramics, vessel glass and clay tobacco pipes.

The general availability of well surveyed cartographic evidence from the mid-18th century onwards means that such assemblages can almost always be linked to particular plots or properties, while documentary sources mean that in many, but by no means all, instances land can be linked to known households. While there are occasional instances where some or all of the material deposited may originate from outside the particular plot in which it was recovered, the composition of most of the assemblages strongly indicates that they relate to a single household and originated on the plot where they were recovered. Such 'household archaeology' which developed in the 1970s (Wilk and Rathje 1982) has been extensively applied to archaeological remains of the post-1800 period (Allison 2003; Barile and Brandon 2004; Beaudry 1999; King 2006). The 'household' commonly consists of a nuclear family plus other elements, such as extended family members, household servants, employees and lodgers but can also encompass larger entities such as large businesses that included dozens of staff members. Nonetheless, it is clear from contemporary documentary sources that such large business 'households' were still viewed in familial and paternalistic terms (Roberts 1979). These feature groups can therefore be understood as representing assemblages of artefacts that relate to a single household and were discarded at a particular point in time, although the individual artefacts and assemblages also possess longer term 'biographies' (see below), and as such are an admittedly biased sample of the material culture of a given household.

By undertaking a detailed study of inscribed objects in a series of feature groups in what follows below, it is possible to arrive at a more nuanced understanding of writing materials and associated practices, in contrast to accounts produced by considering written evidence from a much wider geographical and temporal distribution. The material in this chapter derives from the large-scale excavations covering 1.5 hectares undertaken at the Grand Arcade site in Cambridge (**Figure 2**), by the Cambridge Archaeological Unit in 2005–2006 (Cessford and Dickens, in preparation). This site is located on the edge of historic Cambridge, lying mainly in a suburb outside the town boundary known as the King's Ditch. The assemblages discussed here relate to a single 'street block' or group of plots bounded by street lines (Conzen 1960: 5), bounded by St. Andrew's Street, Downing Street, and the King's Ditch and its successor St. Tibb's Row.

While the writing on objects can be categorised in many different ways, two particular distinctions appear to be particularly significant. These are:

- Writing that is primarily visual or primarily tactile
- Writing that was apparent during normal usage of the item and writing that was concealed during normal usage of the item

Of more than 40 feature groups investigated eight are considered here, although two of the feature groups are related, so this study effectively comprises six groups (**Table 1**). The features have been selected to provide a chronological range covering the longest possible period and also to include those with the more informative examples of writing.

The Features

Francis Tunwell's Planting Bed, F.6425

The first feature group to be considered is a planting bed dug in a large garden c.1760–1790, probably when it was being leased by a local merchant Francis Tunwell (**Figure 3**). A quantity of glass and pottery vessels and fragments was deliberately deposited in the base of the planting bed to act as a 'percolation fill' (Cotter et al. 1992: 161, 307–309, 450) to aid drainage. Among the glass vessels, only one was marked, having a rounded oval bottle seal with the text "PYRMONT WATER" around a crowned shield with the coat of arms of the principality of Waldeck-Pyrmont in Germany. Pyrmont mineral water became popular in Britain in the early 18th century and by

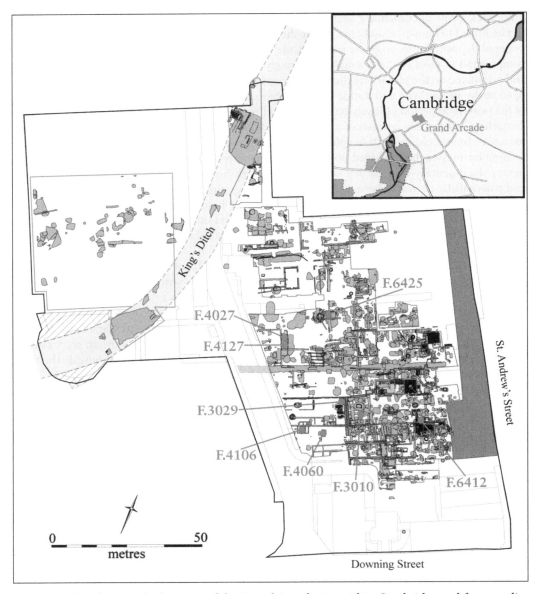

Figure 2: Plan showing the location of the Grand Arcade site within Cambridge and features discussed. Contains Ordnance Survey data © crown copyright and database right 2012.

1730 over 70,000 bottles a year were being imported into London (Hembry 1990: 176). The use of the English term "WATER" rather than the German "*WASSER*" indicates that they were produced primarily for export rather than local consumption in Germany, and they are relatively common finds in both Britain and North America in the period *c*.1720–1770 (Noël-Hume 1971: 61–62). Mineral water from different springs supposedly had their own distinctive medicinal properties and consumers selected the water that matched their needs. To guarantee its authenticity Pyrmont water was exported in distinctively-shaped bottles with seals embossed with a crest and the name of the water put on at the time of manufacture. This particular bottle seal is poorly executed, being

Feature No.	Date	Pottery MNI	Pottery writing MNI	Pottery writing %	Glass MNI	Glass writing MNI	Glass writing %	Clay pipe MNI	Clay pipe writing MNI	Clay pipe writing %	Total objects MNI	Total objects writing MNI	Total objects writing %
3010	Mid 19th	54	15	27.8	23	0	0.0	3	0	0.0	80	15	18.8
3029	Early 19th	205	20	9.8	13	0	0.0	10	1	10.0	228	21	9.2
4027	1913–1925	121	25	20.7	115	43	37.4	1	0	0.0	237	68	28.7
4060	1882–1885	178	10	5.6	121	9	7.4	5	2	40.0	304	21	6.9
4106	1882–1885	236	31	13.1	11	5	45.5	0	0	0.0	247	36	14.6
4127	1913–1925	379	63	16.6	45	5	11.1	0	0	0.0	424	68	16.0
6412	Early 19th	179	28	15.6	69	1	1.4	17	9	52.9	265	38	14.3
6425	1760–1790	11	0	0	34	1	2.9	6	6	100.0	51	7	13.7
Totals and overall %		1363	192	14.1	431	64	14.8	42	18	42.9	1836	274	14.9

Table 1: Quantities and percentages of objects bearing writing from selected feature groups at Grand Arcade, Cambridge. *MNI = Minimal Number of Items.

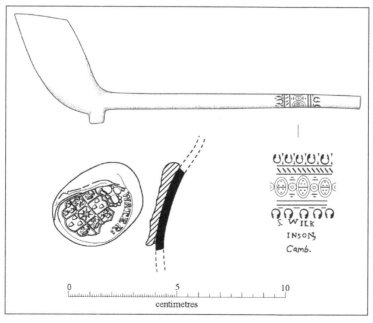

Figure 3: Material from Francis Tunwell's planting bed, F.6425. Marked clay tobacco pipe of Samuel Wilkinson and seal from a Pyrmont water. Drawings by Vicki Herring.

badly aligned and the word "PYRMONT" is almost completely indecipherable. Related to an inherent problem with the technology of glass seals, illegibility and misalignment was not uncommon. Seals begin to be applied to glass bottles around 1650. A warm blob of glass would be applied to the body of the bottle and then impressed with an engraved metal die. As the body of the bottle was rounded there were often problems with the edges of the seal not being fully impressed, as seen in our case. Similarly, if the die was applied whilst glass blob was too runny the impression would be blurred. If the glass was too solid the impression would also be unclear. Given that sealed bottles required the creation of a metal die and the seals were rather time-consuming to apply, such bottles were considerably more expensive than unmarked examples and were always a small minority of those produced and in use, and this is reflected in their archaeological frequency in assemblages. Accounts from 1676 indicate that sealed bottles cost 4½d apiece, whereas plain examples were only 3½d (Thorpe 1938). By the time this particular bottle was exported to Cambridge, Pyrmont Water was a well-established international brand; the writing was only one element in a package of distinctive bottle shape, coat of arms and text, so it was not necessary for the writing to be legible. Although technically tactile the glass seal must be viewed as visual writing, as it would not have been touched during normal use. The seals were placed low down on the body or high up on the shoulder of the bottle in locations that would have been awkward to hold the bottle by; additionally the writing and designs on seals were not sufficiently large or pronounced enough for their detail to be 'read' tactilely. Indeed their positioning appears deliberate to ensure that they did not impinge upon the grip of the individual holding the bottle, ensuring that they remained visible. The seals are not legible at distance and it is likely that only the pourer could have read them.

Also found in the Francis Tunwell deposit were six clay tobacco pipe stems. These bore the relatively ornate 'Wyer' style decoration (Walker and Wells 1979) and the name and location of the manufacture, "S.WILK / INSON, / Camb." or "S.WILK- / INSON, / Cambg.". Samuel Wilkinson was active in Cambridge from at least 1762 until his death in 1787. His practice of marking his pipe-stems was an innovation locally, as most 18th-century Cambridge pipemakers did not mark their pipes or only used simple initials on the side of the spur, a small projection at the base of the bowl. Wilkinson's stem marks were much more visible than spur marks, but are frequently quite poorly executed. Given this and the fact that the mark was placed 80–100 mm from the bowl in the area where the smoker would commonly grip the stem, engagement with writing here would have been primarily a tactile experience. The relatively poor execution of the words was a result of the fact that they were applied by roller stamps which produced variable results. Nevertheless, the mark was arranged so that the text could be read by the smoker holding the pipe, so the visual aspect was still clearly of some importance. This visual importance is also confirmed by a few pipes from other contexts that do not bear Wilkinson's name but some other slogan, such as one marked "PARKER / for ever, / Huzzah", probably produced during the parliamentary election campaign of William Parker Hammond in 1783. It is impossible to be certain why Wilkinson marked his pipes when most of his local competitors did not, but the most likely reason is that they constituted a form of branding for a finer product, since Wilkinson's pipes were of better quality and finish than other contemporary local pipes. Wilkinson's stem mark is a form of branding similar to Pyrmont Water, but much more localised. From production to distribution, these particular pipes had travelled only about 200m, whereas the Pyrmont Water had travelled over 600 kilometres to reach Cambridge. The distribution of Wilkinson's pipes appears to extend not more than 25 kilometres from Cambridge. Wilkinson's marks were also more short-lived, spanning 25–35 years, whereas Pyrmont Water was common in Britain for almost a century. The longer temporal span and greater geographical spread meant that there was likely to be much greater brand awareness, recall and recognition of the Pyrmont Water. This is significant in terms of writing as material practice as it meant that the text of the Pyrmont Water could be recognised and in a sense 'read' without being legible.

Although this is the earliest feature group to contain examples of writing it was already present on two markedly different types of artefact that were used by the same household. The different types of writing function in markedly different ways, which were linked to the physical and technological nature of the items and to the different spatial and temporal spheres that the products operated within.

The Cock Inn Cellar, F.3029

The next group comes from the backfilling of a cellar in c.1828–1845, when an inn on this site was owned by John Purchas (1788–1848) and the proprietor was John Pike or William Bacon (**Figure 4**). The majority of the writing on ceramics relates to vessels marked "R Hopkins" on their underside (MNI 10), identifiable as Richard Hopkins, the cook for Gonville and Caius College (1805–1810) and Trinity Hall (1810). On some vessels of this kind this name is hand-painted (MNI 5) while on others it is transfer-printed (MNI 5), but all have similar moulding and blue hand-painted feather edge decoration. These vessels also have the impressed mark "TURNER", indicating they were manufactured by Turner's of Longton, Stoke on Trent (Hillier 1965).

Transfer-printing was invented in the mid-1750s and involved engraving a flat copper plate with the desired pattern; the plate was inked and pressed or transferred to a fine sheet of tissue paper. This was then applied to the pottery, which was fired at a low temperature fusing the ink onto the body; a protective clear glaze was then applied and the item was fired again at a higher temperature. The copper plates were time-consuming to produce initially but could be reused a large number of times, indicating that Hopkins must have commissioned a considerable number of vessels from Turner's. It would appear that all these transfer-printed names were produced from the same copper plate. Although the transfer-printing can be viewed as a technological advance as compared with impression, it is inferior in terms of legibility and aesthetic appearance in this instance. By contrast, the Turner vessels are of noticeably better quality fabric and finish than the other plates in the assemblage made from the same general fabric and the maker's marks can be viewed as a form of quality related branding, similar to Samuel Wilkinson's pipes. This may also explain why Turner's used their full name for the mark whilst other manufacturers just used initials, as by the time these plates were produced Turner's had gained a significant reputation (Hillier 1965) and the name may well have had noticeably positive associations in the minds of consumers. At this time college cooks were semi-independent contractors, responsible for the internal management of the kitchens and the provision of food. They had to supply the ceramics used and it is likely that the cooks and college names on plates were placed there either in an attempt to prevent theft or as a mechanism related to compensation for breakages. As such they can be viewed as part of an 'institutional' archaeology (Evans 1990; Evans and Pollard 1999); the writing must have operated at both personal and institutional levels and the meanings and associations conveyed at the different levels may well have varied. Both the impressed maker's marks and the hand-painted or transfer-printed cook's name were positioned so as to be invisible during use but are visual in nature: even though the impressed marks avail themselves to tactile engagement via the raised and depressed surfaces which form the letters, they are positioned so they would not be felt easily during use. The visual : tactile dichotomy is somewhat simplistic with some types of writing operating in both spheres; it is also worth noting that although the plates were used for serving food the writing may also have served functions at other times such as when the plates were being stored, selected for use, washed, etc.

There were a number of other creamware vessels with the names of College and College cooks, including "Trinity Hall" and "TRINETY H...", "CAI..." for Gonville and Caius College and "B F Tunw...", which can be linked to Bates Francis Tunwell, the Emmanuel College cook (1794–1806). There were also impressed makers' marks "IH" (J. Heath of Hanley c.1770–1800) and "CB" (Charles Bourne of Fenton c.1807–1830). Whilst documentary sources suggest several routes

Figure 4: Material from The Cock Inn cellar, F.3029. Pottery with "for my dear", ale mark, transfer printed and hand-painted "R. Hopkins" and "The Sailor's Return and Farewell" jug. Drawing by Vicki Herring and photographs by Dave Webb and author.

through which various cooks' plates may have ended up at the Cock Inn, the presence of pieces marked with college names is difficult to explain. The wares may have been purloined, but this is difficult to prove. Some of the marked plates probably ceased to be used for their original college function 10 to 20 years prior to their deposition, indicating that individual pieces and the assemblage as a whole have a 'biography' that must be taken into account in our interpretations of the function and meaning of writing (see below).

Very different is a creamware cup decorated with the hand-painted text that probably read "For my dear", as this would have been visible during normal use. Also visible during normal use was an ale measure mark comprised of a crown over the initials "WR" on a stoneware tankard-shaped ale measure jug. The jug was marked in compliance with the act of 1700 for ascertaining the measures used for retailing ale and beer which covered vessels of up to a quart capacity used in inns and other commercial establishments and was in force until 1876 (Binson 1970). This mark can be viewed as part of an "archaeology of regulation" (Egan 2009: 281), as it was mandated by a higher authority. This writing was both a material expression of institutionalised structures concerning regulation and associated practices, as well as actively constituting the physical execution of those practices (e.g. decanting certain types of liquids).

A pearlware jug also found in the Cock Inn cellar shows "The Sailor's Farewell and Return" motif, a common design c.1790–1800 (Lewis and Lewis 2006: 2, 15, 156). Consisting of two scenes, the first depicts the departing sailor and his lass waving goodbye with his ship in the background. The second shows the returning sailor consoling his girl who has wed another in his absence. While there is no writing on this jug, numerous other contemporary vessels decorated with this design do bear writing. The design relates to a traditional folk song and the jug would have brought to mind the words of the song to those knowledgeable viewers who saw it. Essentially when texts become well known they can be evoked on material objects with the text itself being immaterial.

This is paralleled by 'literary ceramics' deposited in the 1840s at High Wycombe, Buckinghamshire. These were decorated with scenes from a number Walter Scott's novels, Miguel de Cervantes' *Don Quixote* and James Thompson's *The Seasons* (Lucas 2003; Lucas and Regan 2003). These 'literary ceramics' lack text altogether and indeed the selection of images, "suggests, ironically…that the production and consumption of literary images on transfer-printed earthenwares was only successful in so far as such images were relatively independent of their literary reference, or that the literary reference was at least almost universally known" (Lucas 2003: 140).

Within the wider cultural context, this jug and similar 'literary ceramics' with imagery calling to mind certain phrases or verses, can be seen as a kind of material reification of writing, despite its physical absence. Likewise, since not all viewers, whether children or adults, would have been literate, even where writing is present imagery could have also served mnemonic purposes. Depending on the knowledge of the viewer then, writing and image could have served as two different means to the same end, or could have been seen as complementary or overlapping in their purpose. These examples highlight the complexity of the relationships between writing, literacy and oral traditions that should be borne in mind when considering both the physical expression of written meanings and their invisible counterparts.

Sarah Dobson's Planting Pit, F.3010

The third group is from a planting bed dug c.1822–1840 in a garden used by a school run by Sarah Dobson (**Figure 5**). The dating and composition of the assemblage makes it clear that it relates to the school, whose premises were occupied by Sarah Dobson along with her nieces, a number of pupils who lived at the premises and two servants. Here, writing is only found on pottery, the majority of which consists of manufacturer and pattern names transfer-printed on the underside of the vessels. As the writing would have been invisible when the plates and cups were being used for dining and drinking, this suggests it was not intended to be read frequently. Engagement would have been much more restricted, perhaps only being read during washing up or occasionally when an individual wished to purchase more items of the same pattern. The writing from this assemblage that would have been visible during use includes two children's cups with pink transfer-printed 'moralising' decoration (Cessford 2009: 313–317; Crook et al. 2005: 148; Jeffries et al.

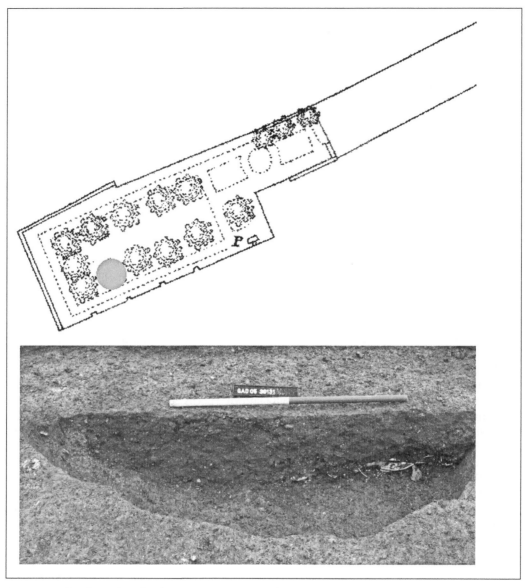

Figure 5: Sarah Dobson's planting pit, F.3010, showing its location in the garden. Author's photograph.

2009: 336–340; Karskens 2001: 74–76). This also included the text "For I have food while others starve or beg from door to door" (**Figure 6**), part of the song "Whene'er I take my walks abroad". Comprising the second half of one verse from a six-verse song, the text on the cup represents less than 10% of the original poem which appears in the collection "Divine and Moral Songs for Children" by Isaac Watts (1674–1748), a leading early 18th-century non-conformist hymn-writer, theologian and logician (Argent 1999).

Despite his nonconformist beliefs Watts's work with its straightforward and relatively gentle Christian ideas plus its lilting metre became extremely popular and was frequently reproduced on children's ceramics of the period (Riley 1991: 228–232). The relationship between writing and the

Whene'er I take my walks abroad,
How many poor I see?
What shall I render to my God
For all his gifts to me?

Not more than others I deserve,
Yet God hath given me more;
For I have food, while others starve,
Or beg from door to door.

How many children in the street
Half naked I behold?
While I am clothed from head to feet,
And cover'd from the cold.

While some poor wretches scarce can tell
Where they may lay their head,
I have a home wherein to dwell,
And rest upon my bed.

While others early learn to swear,
And curse, and lie, and steal,
Lord, I am taught thy name to fear,
And do thy holy will.

Are these thy favours, day by day
To me above the rest?
Then let me love thee more than they,
And try to serve thee best.

Figure 6: Children's cup with decoration and text from Isaac Watts's song "Whene'er I take my walks abroad" from F.3010. Photographs by Dave Webb.

material context of its expression is illustrated particularly well among these finds, especially the impact of the materiality on the content of the writing. The physical form of the cups, with their rounded smaller surfaces, means that they generally have just one or two lines of verse in contrast to the plates with their large flat surfaces which usually bore a whole verse, if not two. There are also differences in the ratio of text and image between plates and cups, the plates tending to be dominated by text, while the cups were often dominated by associated imagery. However, in a planting hole near to the planting bed a fragment of another child's cup was found with part of the text of another work by Isaac Watts entitled *Innocent Play*. In this case the text seemed to be the dominant decorative feature as there was no evidence of any accompanying image. The text probably therefore included the entire first verse of this three-verse poem.

As well as differences in the ratio of decoration types, an interesting difference between artefact types emerges when we consider embodied practice. The image and / or text on a cup is arranged so that it wraps around the exterior. It is therefore never visible to the user in its entirety and requires rotation for full viewing. Likewise, for non-user viewers the decoration would only be revealed episodically as the cup was filled, drunk from, and otherwise manipulated during the course of use. In contrast, the text on the plate would be wholly visible when the plate was empty, whether on display in a cupboard or as part of a freshly laid table. Yet similar to the cup, its decoration, too, would be partially concealed when filled with food and a process of revelation would ensue as the plate was emptied of its contents. Thinking about these finds and their textual and pictorial decoration in terms of daily practice reveals a complex network of meanings that extends beyond, and therefore require consideration alongside, purely semantic functions.

Returning to the planting bed, found along with the cups and plates just discussed were seven vessels with "Sicilian" pattern decoration (**Figure 7**), including four plates, two large serving dishes and a cup. Together these can be understood as forming a 'service', the presence of which can be linked to developing 19th-century ideas and practices of domesticity and gentility (Fitts 1999). One of these actually bore on its underside the label "Sicilian", which appears to be a pattern name inspired by the gothic novel *A Sicilian Romance* by Ann Radcliffe (1764–1823) published in 1790 (Coysh and Heywood 1982: 338; 1986: 183). In this respect these vessels, too, may be understood as a form of 'literary ceramic', connected to changing perceptions of fiction and its accompanying illustrations. Their use may be understood as mediating ideals of the picturesque and suitable subjects for transfer-print patterns (Lucas 1993). In the case of the Sicilian pattern the image of the Mediterranean scene could have functioned independently of the novel, simply as a picturesque view. However, Radcliffe's books assert traditional moral values such as honour and integrity while making strong political statements concerning the oppression of women in patriarchal society. Given the composition and nature of the 'household' living at the premises, it is likely that Sarah Dobson was responsible for purchasing most, if not all, the ceramics and the ideas expressed by Radcliffe may well have appealed to her.

The cups associated with Isaac Watts bear only a small portion of the original songs that they derive from, whilst the Sicilian pattern vessels have no text from Radcliffe's book. This again reinforces the point that the translation between paper and other mediums was successful when the text and / or images were relatively independent of their literary reference or the literary reference was almost universally known.

The writing associated with Sarah Dobson's school is particularly significant as it relates to an institution where the process of writing itself was central to the establishment, as demonstrated by the fact that 17 of the 18 slate pencils recovered during the excavations can be associated with this school. The pencils also suggest that many members of the household who used the vessels discussed would have been able to read the writing present on them, something that is crucial to consider when the materiality of writing is being discussed. Although the cups with texts were used by children, it was Sarah Dobson who controlled their selection and it is in the light of her world view that they must primarily be interpreted, although it should be recognised that other members of the household may have read very different meanings into the texts. Any such interpretation must hinge upon whether the texts present in the assemblage functioned independently, or whether they derived their significance from the larger works that they referenced.

0   5   10
centimetres

Figure 7: "Sicilian" pattern vessels from F.3010. Photographs by Dave Webb.

Thomas Wicks's Soakaway, F.6412

The fourth group of writing-bearing objects comes from the backfilling of a brick-lined soaka-way dating to the early 19th century which yielded finds relating to the occupancy of Thomas Wicks, a cook at nearby Emmanuel College (1807–1852; **Figure 8**). One of the most common forms of writing in this context was the impressed maker's marks on creamware pottery, including

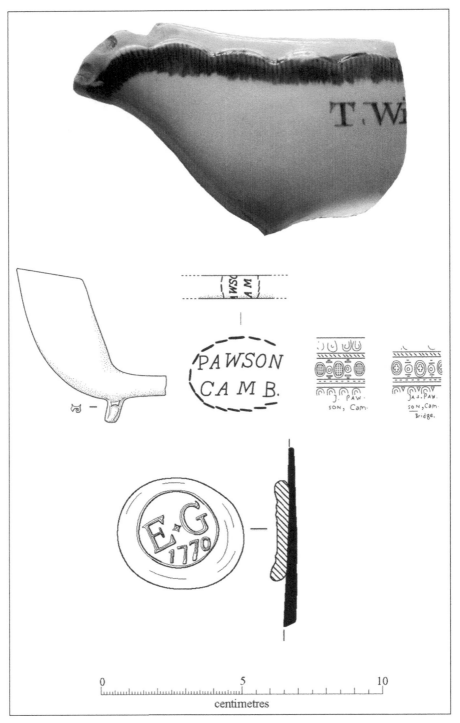

Figure 8: Material from Thomas Wicks's soakaway, F.6412. Sauceboat belonging to Wicks, clay tobacco pipes manufactured by James and Ann Pawson and bottle seal stamped "EG 1770". Author's photograph, drawings by Vicki Herring.

Wedgwood (MNI 12) and Turner (MNI 9). As with the earlier Turner marks, these also appear to be a form of quality-related branding. A number of 'services' of related vessels were identifiable, one of these included a sauceboat with "T.Wi…" hand-painted in gilt indicating that this must have belonged to Thomas Wicks. While some of the vessels in this service are incomplete, others are whole enough to ascertain that they were not marked with Wicks name. This raises the question of why some vessels in a service were marked and others were not. One possibility is that the sauceboat was a relatively expensive item, which made it worth marking. Alternatively it may have been linked to the rather different role of the sauceboat, which would have been used by all the diners at the table, rather than just one individual as a plate would.

Among the soakaway finds there was also a wine bottle with a glass seal marked "E G 1770" relating to the individual for whom the bottle was manufactured and the year in which this occurred. No one with these initials can be linked to the property and as Thomas Wicks was only baptised in 1774, four years after the bottle was manufactured, it is unlikely that the writing had any special meaning for him personally. This seal is better executed than the Pyrmont bottle discussed previously, although it is slightly misaligned. The initials "E G" are clearly legible, unlike those on the Pyrmont Water bottle; indeed if such a personal seal had been so poorly executed during manufacture as the Pyrmont Water one, it is likely that the bottle would have been rejected as the seal would have been rendered pointless.

Additional finds included nine used clay tobacco pipes bearing the mark of Cambridge-based pipe makers James and / or Ann Pawson. James inherited the pipe-making premises and business of his uncle-in-law Samuel Wilkinson, who has already been mentioned, in 1786. In 1813 James's wife, Ann, succeeded him, remaining active until 1823. Initially James Pawson marked the pipes in a similar manner to Wilkinson, with ornate curvilinear decoration and the writing "J·PAW- / SON, Cam-, Bridge" or "JAS.PAW. / SON, Cam·/ Bridge", which was impressed using a roller stamp before the pipe was fired. At some point either James or Ann Pawson switched to the stem mark "PAWSON CAMB" enclosed in a circle. All these marks were similar in terms of location and size to those on the pipes produced by Wilkinson that have already been discussed. They were relatively small and would have been obscured by the smoker's hand whilst they were being used, so engagement during use would have been primarily tactile rather than visual and it would only have been possible to read the text by deliberately examining the pipe. By continuing with the same style of stem marks as his predecessor, James Pawson was perpetuating a branding tradition and with it the business 'goodwill' or reputation built up by Wilkinson. The transition to the different style of mark was probably prompted by the roller stamps that the Pawsons used becoming so worn that they were un-useable, by which time that style had gone out of use and such roller stamps were no longer being produced.

The instances of writing from Thomas Wicks's soakaway are of themselves generally unremarkable, indeed they were similar to examples deposited decades earlier. In some respects this is key to their functioning as these are essentially repetitive forms of writing where similar texts in similar forms had been occurring in similar locations on similar types of artefacts for periods that often exceed the lifetime of a typical individual who read them. Although the texts themselves are often relatively novel, giving the name of a particular maker or owner, the act of reading is one embedded in daily social practice and memory (cf. Hodder and Cessford 2004).

Barrett's Ceramic Retailers, F.4060 and F.4106

The next assemblages are rather different as they relate, in part at least, not to items owned by a particular household but to the stock of a business that sold a range of material including items with writing on them. Between 1882 and 1885 the Barrett family, retailers in china, earthenware and glass, reorganised the rear area of their premises at No. 25 St. Andrew's Street. Two separate features were backfilled during this period, a rectangular sunken structure (F.4060; **Figure 9**) and a cellar (F.4106; **Figure 10**). The finds in these features appear to represent a mixture of contemporary finds related to the Barrett family business, plus some older items linked to the clearance of the garden. These latter artefacts include the remarkable find of a large and nearly complete Martaban storage jar. The vessel, originally from Southeast Asia, was stamped with the Chinese symbol for the Boar (*inoshishi*), one of the 12 years of the '*Sheng xiao*' commonly known as the Chinese Zodiac. The symbol is relatively small in relation to the overall size of the vessels and quite discrete due to the 'textured' nature of jar. There does not ever appear to have been an active trade in these jars with Europe, instead they seem to have been used occasionally as containers for water, oil and other substances on board vessels and thus made their way to Europe. Occasional pieces of Martaban have been found in 17th–19th century contexts in Britain before, but usually only as single or small numbers of sherds. The much more complete example from Cambridge probably arrived in Britain in the same manner as the others, but it may have acquired a kind of curio status subsequently, perhaps by a member of Emmanuel College given its find location on property occupied (*c.*1833–1847) by the college butler Charles Burbage. He seems to have put the jar to use in the garden, perhaps as a water container judging by the pattern of limescale on the vessel. The boar symbol relates to the year that the jar was manufactured. Its small size relative to the large object and given the probability that it rapidly became unintelligible once it moved away from its area of production make it likely that many of the individuals who came into contact with the jar were probably unaware of its presence, could not have understood the symbol, and may not even have recognised it as a form of writing.

After the alphabetic script used to write the English language, Chinese characters are the most common form of writing found at this site. They occur on both Chinese imports and local imitations. The majority of instances appear on local British ceramics and include blue and white transfer-printed designs of a Chinese style, yet the 'texts', and indeed even individual characters, are frequently gibberish. This is part of a much wider phenomenon, whereby from the 17th century onwards Chinese artistic influences had a huge influence on British culture leading to the development of the '*Chinoiserie*' style (Honour 1961; Impey 1977).

An approach that is increasingly being applied to 18th–20th century archaeological material (e.g. Dellino-Musgrave 2005; Mytum 2003) is the concept of artefact 'biographies' (Lucas 2005). This is particularly apposite for the Martaban jar boar symbol, a symbol that would have been intelligible to many in its production context, but probably not to most sailors, merchants or others on board the European vessel that transported the jar to Britain, or those otherwise involved in its transport to Cambridge. Unlike in many parts of the world, there is no evidence for a Chinese community in Cambridge and only limited evidence that anyone could have read the symbol. Cambridge University Library obtained its first Chinese book in 1632, but there was no official academic interest in Chinese until Sir Thomas Francis Wade (1818–1895) was appointed the first holder of the Chair of Chinese (1888–1895), some three years after the Martaban jar was deposited. A nearby department store, Robert Sayle, had strong links with Shanghai and Hong Kong possibly as early as *c.*1860 and certainly by *c.*1870–1872, continuing until the early 20th century (Sieveking 2004: 32–33). It is likely that some members of the Robert Sayle business, including members of the Sayle family itself, would have been able to read Chinese characters.

Based on present evidence, the ability of most viewers / users of the jar to read the writing was limited. Nevertheless, many would have been able to recognise the type of script which may have served as a reminder of its biography and led to it being kept, gifted and reused for a time, especially when it remained in a collegiate context. Its role in Burbage's garden is less clear, although it is possible that this was a place of social display where the jar signalled Burbage's role as a relatively powerful college servant with access to unusual objects from rare lands and, perhaps more significant from the point of view of those viewing it, the ability to appropriate material that was usually restricted to the local social elite.

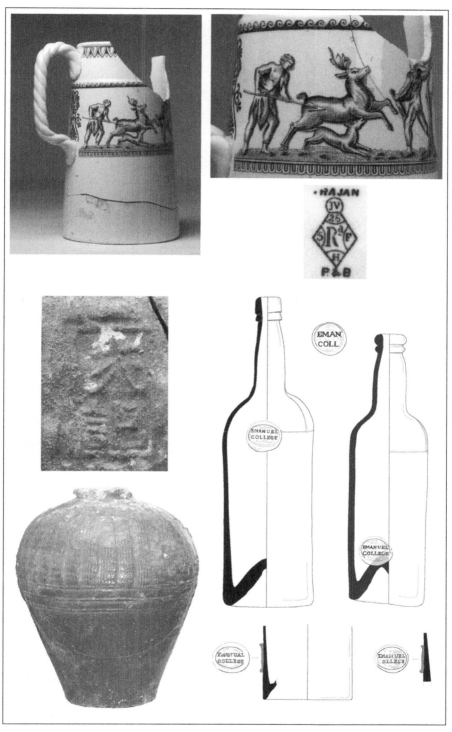

Figure 9: Material from Barrett's sunken rectangular garden structure, F.4060. Trajan pattern jug, Martaban jar with boar stamp and bottles with Emmanuel College seals. Photographs by Dave Webb, drawings by Vicki Herring.

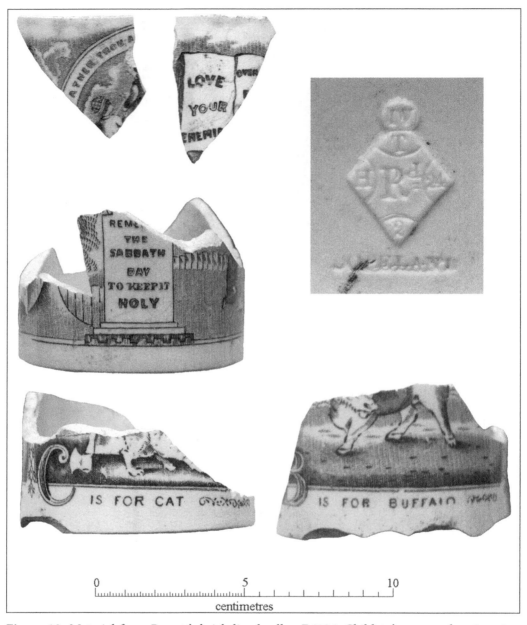

Figure 10: Material from Barrett's brick-lined cellar, F.4106. Children's cups and registration mark from Copeland teapot (not to scale). Author's photographs.

Several glass bottles including two with seals marked "EMANUEL / COLLEGE" and "EMANUAL / COLLEGE" dated c.1820–1860 were also probably brought to the site by Burbage, the college butler, and re-used as building material as several have traces of mortar on them. There are seven known wordings of Emmanuel College seals ("EMANUAL COLLEGE", "EMANUEL COLLEGE", "EMMAN. COLL", "EMAN. COLL", "COLL. EMAN", "EMM. COLL" and "EMANUEL COLL" [Morgan 1977: 70]), and it is likely that each distinct seal represents a separate order from a glassmaker (Banks 1997; 2002). The Emmanuel College seals are all relatively well executed and carefully aligned, contrasting with the earlier glass seals discussed. There are no technological reasons for this improvement and the most likely reason is simply that the college was a demanding client and the high social status of its members meant that they required, and were in a position to enforce, high standards.

Archaeological finds linked to the Barrett family business date largely to the 1870s. There are two ceramic water jugs, decorated in black and green respectively, with geometric bands and classical hunting scenes and transfer-printed marks on the base consisting of a diamond-shaped registration mark containing a mixture of letters and numbers, the pattern name "TRAJAN", and the maker's mark "P&B". Between 1842 and 1883 some pottery was marked with a diamond shape printed or impressed on the base, a symbol relating to the British Patent Office Registry of Designs. In the case of the Trajan jugs, this indicates the class or type of material (IV, clay ware), the bundle or number of items included in the registration (5), and the day (28th), month (H, April) and year (F, 1873) of the registration. Important for the 'archaeology of regulation', the information conveyed in the diamond registration mark was so highly codified that it was likely that only a small percentage of the vessel users would have understood it. Moreover, it would have been largely invisible during normal use. Similarly the maker's mark "P&B", Powell and Bishop, who were in partnership in Hanley Stoke on Trent (1876–1878), was probably equally cryptic. The pattern name "TRAJAN", the impression of which was incompletely executed, may evoke the Roman emperor Marcus Ulpius Trajanus (52–117 AD), perhaps via a literary allusion inspired by Pliny the Younger's Panegyric *Panegyricus Trajani* of 100 AD where Trajan is praised for his interest in hunting (81.1–3; Bennett 1997: 66).

At some level the decoration on the Trajan pattern jug was designed to appeal to individuals who considered themselves cognisant and appreciative of the aesthetics of classical art, yet by this date such influences were no longer restricted to the social elite and the jug is by no means an exclusive product. The name Trajan encodes meaning based upon knowledge of a relatively exclusive text, which members of the educated elite would be aware of but which probably escaped members of the lower classes who emulated them.

The Barrett's brick-lined cellar (F.4106) included at least four identical white stoneware teapots, each bearing the maker's name "COPELAND" and diamond registration mark impressed into the base manually using a stamp before firing. This diamond mark is similar to the codified information on the Trajan jugs just discussed, indicating that this was a clay ware (class IV), the bundle or number of items included in the registration (2), and the day (24th), month (H, April) and year (T, 1867). The layout here is slightly different from the later Trajan jugs as the organisation of diamond registration marks changed in 1868. In contrast to the transfer-printed Trajan pattern, the diamond mark and maker's name are embossed and therefore three-dimensional. However, rather than this reflecting a specific choice related to the writing, the technique used for the registration mark in both cases relates to the technique used for the overall decoration of the item. Embossing and transfer-printing both have their strengths as techniques when used for writing, transfer-printing with its greater colour contrast is generally easier to read whilst embossing is more durable. Material expressions of writing need consideration in relation to the context of manufacture since their appearance is linked to wider technological practices.

The same cellar assemblage included four highly fragmentary children's mugs also bearing writing. A purple transfer-printed alphabet cup has the text "B IS FOR BUFFALO, C IS FOR CAT" running around the bottom of the side of the cup, although the vagaries of production mean that "BUFFALO" is partly missing. Another purple transfer-printed cup fragment has the text "LOVE YOUR ENEMIE…OVER…", the first part of which derives from Matthew 5:44 "But I tell you: Love your enemies and pray for those who persecute you". Rather appropriately given its Biblical origin, this text is made to appear as if it is in a book. A third purple transfer-printed scene of children playing has the text "...ATHER THOU A...", the whole cup would have shown "MY FATHER THOU ART THE GUIDE OF MY YOUTH" (Jeremiah 3:4) and "THY WORK IS A LAMP UNTO MY FEET" (Psalm 119:105) (Riley 1991: 248–249). A black transfer-printed example has the text "REME[MBER] / THE SABBATH / DAY / TO KEEP IT / HOLY" from the fourth commandment (Exodus 20:8). This text is shown carved on a stone object, alluding to the 10 commandments Moses received on two stone tablets from his god. Children's ceramics promoting piety and virtue were common in Britain in the 19th century (Riley 1991: 226–259) and these types were frequently given as Sunday School prizes for good attendance and achievement (Riley 1991: 248). The selection and extraction of texts on these cups from a longer paper-based piece of writing mirrors the practice already discussed of only including a small proportion of an original text, and implies that either the audience was familiar enough with the original text to understand the meaning of the fragment used or that its meaning was clear enough to function independently.

What is particularly interesting here is that, although the cups from this cellar on which the writing occurs are virtually identical in size, form and material, the way the writing is presented in terms of its location, font used and integration with images varies considerably, effectively relating it to its Biblical origins. This writing is also strongly linked to children, a phenomenon present in several other features discussed here. Items of material culture linked specifically to children are relatively rare in terms of the overall assemblages from the site, but writing occurs on a much higher proportion of these than on items associated with adults. Also significant is that the location, scale, and other features of its material expression indicate that writing that is intended to be visible, read, and its meaning well understood. The wider social context of this is that the concept of childhood changed markedly during the 19th century and the middle class in particular came to view it as much more separate and distinct from the adult world. This involved numerous changes, particularly with regard to education — something which is relevant to explaining in part the significance of the materiality of this particular writing, especially its clear visibility.

The Robert Sayle Cellar, F.4027 and F.4127

The final assemblages I examine in this chapter date to 1913-1925 when a double-roomed cellar (F.4027 and F.4127) used by the department store Robert Sayle was backfilled (Cessford 2012; **Figure 11**). This is the latest feature discussed and by this time writing had become even more common, appearing on a wider range of materials and object types. The majority of the items with writing on them appear to be the possessions of members of staff who lived at a dormitory on the premises, so in some sense they are a 'household' group albeit one much larger and very different from most of the others that have been considered here. There is relatively little that relates directly to the business itself, although some plastic oval-shaped furniture fittings, probably for drawers, were embossed with "R.SAYLE & CO. / CAMBRIDGE" representing a form of corporate labelling.

A range of ceramics, whole and fragmentary, was also found here, many of which bore writing of one type or another. The majority of these were manufacturer and pattern names rendered using the transfer-print method and many of which were poorly executed and are illegible or only semi-legible. Registration marks continue to be used, but from 1884 onwards the diamond shaped marks ceased and were replaced with a consecutive numbering system, such as "Rd.No.510607" which designated The Pompadour pattern. Whilst the earlier diamond system had been heavily codified it potentially conveyed some information to those with an understanding of the system such as pottery retailers, whereas now the consecutive numbering system was an abstract number that in isolation meant virtually nothing. Many of the ceramics from this feature are also marked "ENGLAND"; the McKinley Tariff Act of 1890 meant that all imports to the USA needed to carry

Figure 11: Material from Robert Sayle cellar, F.4027 and F.4127. Queens' College eggcups, R. Sayle & Co label and sign language plate. Photographs by Dave Webb and author, drawings by Vicki Herring.

the name of the country of manufacture and in practice this meant that much material for domestic use was also marked.

Another item from the department store cellar was an alphabet plate with raised moulded letters on the rim running from A to Z around the rim. Within this was a blue transfer-printed central scene of a group of dolls surrounded by the symbols of the manual sign language alphabet. On the back is a transfer-printed mark "R^D.N°.426673 / H. AYNSLEY & Co / LONGTON / ENGLAND". The moulded letters on the rim are essentially an 'off the peg' element, used for a wide variety of children's plates. It is apparent in this case, as in most instances, that when the transfer-printed design was added during a later stage of the manufacturing process, no attempt was made to orient the two designs so the layout of the letters corresponded. Sign language is a visual-gestural language and British Sign Language as it exists today probably originated in the 18th century. From the 1860s sign language fell out of official favour and oralism, which uses spoken language consisting of lip reading, speech, the process of watching mouth movements and mastering breathing technique, was strongly promoted. This became official policy after 1889 and the late 1890s and the early 1900s were the heyday of the oralist approach and sign language was heavily discouraged. It is unclear if items such as this plate, whose design was registered in 1904, were produced for deaf children specifically, or if they were part of a campaign and were used by other children (Riley 1991: 120–121). In any case given the dominance of oralism at the time, such plates can in some respects be viewed as artefacts of 'resistance' (Frazer 1999), with members of the deaf community resisting the perceived wisdom of those exercising control over social and education policy. In some sense resistance is the opposite of regulation, although as this plate bears both sign language, which was disapproved of by the authorities, and also a Government imposed registration mark, the writing is comprised of elements from both on a single item. Evidence of 'resistance' is much rarer than that of 'regulation', although this may be due in part to the former often being more subtly expressed. One example of this is at a property where the name of the owner, Emmanuel College, is prominently displayed on the frontage whilst the tenants' initials were placed in a more discrete location in a manner that suggests illicit behaviour **(Figure 12)**.

By the early 20th century the presence of writing on artefacts had become much more common — a trend that is apparent throughout the 19th century. With increasing frequency it appears that in this text-saturated world most instances of writing were expressed in a way that suggests they were not meant to be read. Increasingly writing was placed and designed to be as unobtrusive as possible when the item was being used for its primary purpose. Such texts were either mandated by the authorities or were intended to be read infrequently and for often rather abstruse purposes. Running counter to this in a few instances, such as the sign language plate, the text maintains its visibility and remains central to the use and social meaning of the item on which it appears. In such cases the writing often becomes increasingly prominent, to counteract the effects of its text-saturated world.

Conclusion

The aim of this study has been to demonstrate the importance of accounting for writing as material and as part of individual and social practice. The 'feature group' approach has an important contribution to make to the study of the materiality of writing of 18th–20th century Britain. Whilst each feature contains its own narrative, the aim of analysis at the scale of the 'feature group' was not solely to consider the individual assemblage in isolation but as a starting point for discovering larger patterns. The 'elephant in the room' is the fact that what survives archaeologically is only a subset of past writing materialities. The most common medium for writing in 18th–20th century Britain, probably by several orders of magnitude, was undoubtedly paper. This did not survive in any of the feature groups discussed, but in those rare archaeological instances where paper does survive from this period it vastly outnumbers writing on other materials (e.g. Crook and Murray 2006). Archaeologically, this scenario where the dominant medium for writing is the least likely to survive is paralleled in other cultures (e.g. Waal 2011). It is clear that in 18th–20th century Britain writing on paper was regarded as the norm, with all other materials viewed as secondary. Indeed many of the examples discussed are derived either directly or indirectly from writing on paper. Examples of this include the cup with text from a published poem **(Figure 6)**, the Sicilian pattern vessels which rely upon a novel for much of their meaning **(Figure 7)**, the Trajan pattern jug whose imagery relates to the *Panegyricus Trajani* **(Figure 9)** and children's mugs which derive from and in one case actually depict the bible **(Figure 10)**, the book *par excellence* of Britain during this period. In other cases the writing makes no sense without the existence of writing on paper; for example registration marks are meaningless without both the enabling Act of Parliament and the supporting 'paper trail' of the individual registration process **(Figures 9–11)**. The archaeological

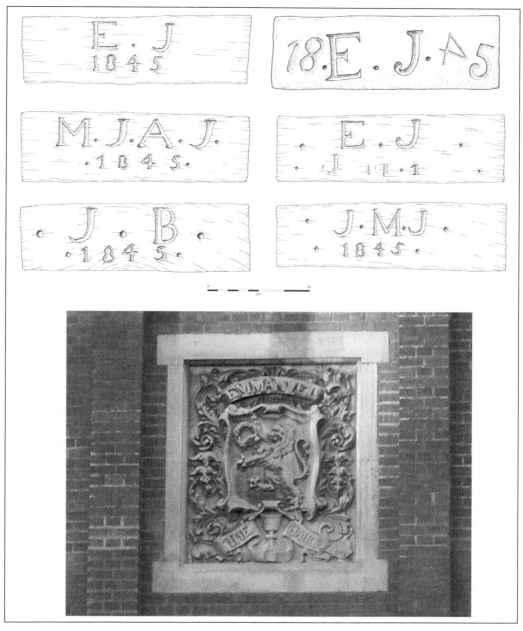

Figure 12: Blocks and brick from the 1845 warehouse marked with the initials of the tenant at the time Edward Jay, plus his wife Jane Maria Jay, assistant James Baker, eldest daughter Maria Jane Anne Jay and son Edward Jay their son. Plus view of the frontage sign of Emmanuel College. Photograph by Dave Webb, drawings by Vicki Herring.

preponderance of writing on what might be viewed as secondary expression raises significant questions about what studying its materiality can tell us.

The use of writing, both on paper and other materials, becomes increasing prevalent over the period in question. As a counterpoint to this phenomenon the texts and their meanings on materials other than paper in many cases becomes less visible — apparently not meant to be read by those who are otherwise consumers of the objects. Furthermore, much of the writing relates to regulation and there are also repeated links to the education of children and both commercial and institutional branding. All of these phenomena, as well as the crucial underpinning factor of increasing literacy rates at this time, must therefore be situated in the context of major historical processes of the period such as modernity, capitalism and consumerism. The archaeological study of writing as material practice at the scale of feature groups sheds light on how particular households in specific temporal, spatial and social *milieux* interacted with those forms of writing that survive. At a broader level these specific examples attest to the development and spread of a text-saturated culture, a phenomenon which is inextricably intertwined with the major historical processes affecting 18th–20th century Britain.

Acknowledgements

This chapter builds upon the dedicated work of the entire team involved in the excavation, post-excavation and publication phases of work at Grand Arcade. This work has been funded by the Grand Arcade Partnership, which consists of the Universities Superannuation Scheme and Grosvenor Developments Ltd. In particular I would like to thank my project manager Alison Dickens for her support. Specific aspects of this chapter draw upon the specialist work of Richard Darrah (timber), Andy Hall (pottery) and Vicki Herring (glass).

References

Allison, P. M. 2003. The Old Kinchega Homestead: Household archaeology in outback New South Wales Australia. *International Journal for Historical Archaeology* 7(2): 161–194. DOI: http://dx.doi.org/10.1023/A:1027417332638

Argent, A. 1999. *Isaac Watts: Poet, thinker, pastor*. London: Congregational Memorial Hall Trust.

Banks, F. 1997. *Wine Drinking at Oxford* (British Archaeological Report Series No. 257). Oxford: British Archaeological Reports.

Banks, F. 2002. *The Wine Bottles of All Souls College, Oxford, 1750–1850*. Denton: Vidonia Press.

Barile, K. S. and Brandon, J. C. (eds) 2004. *Household Chores and Household Choices: Theorizing the domestic sphere in historical archaeology*. Tuscaloosa: University of Alabama Press.

Barker, D. and Majewski, T. 2006. Ceramic Studies in Historical Archaeology. In Hicks, D. and Beaudry, M. (eds), *The Cambridge Companion to Historical Archaeology*. Cambridge: Cambridge University Press, 205–231.

Beaudry, M. C. 1999. House and Household: The archaeology of domestic life in early America. In Egan, G. and Michael, R. (eds), *Old and New Worlds*. Oxford: Oxbow Books, 117–126.

Bennett, J. 1997. *Trajan: Optimus princeps*. London: Routledge.

Bermingham, A. and Brewer, J. (eds) 1995. *The Consumption of Culture 1600–1800*. London: Routledge.

Binford, L. R. 1981. Behavioural Archaeology and the "Pompeii Premise". *Journal of Anthropological Research* 37: 195–208.

Binson, M. 1970. The Significance of Ale-measure Marks. *Post–Medieval Archaeology* 4: 165–166.

Brewer, J. and Porter, R. 1993. *Consumption and the World of Goods*. London: Routledge.

Briggs, A. 1988. *Victorian Things*. London: Batsford.

Brooks, A. 2005. *An Archaeological Guide to British Ceramics in Australia, 1788–1901*. Sydney: Australasian Society for Historical Archaeology.

Cessford, C. 2009. Post-1550 Urban Archaeology in a Developer-funded Context: An example from Grand Arcade, Cambridge. In Horning, A. and Palmer, M. (eds), *Crossing Paths or Sharing Tracks? Future Directions in the Archaeological Study of post-1550 Britain and Ireland*. Woodbridge: Boydell and Brewer, 301–321.

Cessford, C. 2012. Life in a "Cathedral of Consumption": Corporate and personal material culture recovered from a cellar at the Robert Sayle Department Store in Cambridge, England, ca. 1913–21. *International Journal of Historical Archaeology* 16(4): 784–808. DOI: http://dx.doi.org/10.1007/s10761-012-0200-3

Cessford, C. and Dickens, A. in preparation. *From King's Ditch to Department Store: Investigations of an 11ᵗʰ–20ᵗʰ century suburb and the town ditch of Cambridge.*

Cohen, D. (ed.) 2006. *Household Gods: The British and their possessions*. New Haven: Yale University Press.

Conzen, M. R. G. 1960. *Alnwick, Northumberland: A study in town plan analysis* (Publication No. 27). London: Institute of British Geographers.

Cotter, J. L. Roberts, D. G. and Parrington, M. 1992. *The Buried Past: An archaeological history of Philadelphia*. Philadelphia: University of Pennsylvania Museum Press.

Coysh, A. W. and Heywood, R. K. 1982. *The Dictionary of Blue and White Printed Pottery 1780–1880. Volume 1*. Woodbridge: Antique Collectors' Club.

Coysh, A. W. and Heywood, R. K. 1986. *The Dictionary of Blue and White Printed Pottery 1780–1880. Volume 2*. Woodbridge: Antique Collectors' Club.

Crook, P., Ellmoos, P. and Murray, T. 2005. *Keeping up with the McNamaras: A historical archaeology of the Cumberland and Gloucester Streets site, The Rocks, Sydney* (Archaeology of the Modern City Series Volume 8). Sydney: Historic Houses Trust of New South Wales.

Crook, P. and Murray, T. 2006. *An Historical Archaeology of Institutional Refuge: Life at the Hyde Park Barracks, Sydney* (Archaeology of the Modern City Series Volume 12). Sydney: Historic Houses Trust of New South Wales.

Dellino-Musgrave, V. 2005. British Identities through Pottery in Praxis: The case study of a Royal Navy ship in the South Atlantic. *Journal of Material Culture* 10(3): 219–243. DOI: http://dx.doi.org/10.1177/1359183505057145

Dickens, A. 2001. King's College Chapel, Cambridge: A study of artefacts recovered from beneath the choir stalls. *Proceedings of the Cambridge Antiquarian Society* 90: 115–126.

Egan, G. 2009. Material Concerns: The state of post-Medieval finds studies. In Horning, A. and Palmer, M. (eds), *Crossing Paths or Sharing Tracks? Future directions in the archaeological study of post-1550 Britain and Ireland*. Woodbridge: Boydell and Brewer, 273–286.

Evans, C. 1990. 'Power on silt': Towards an archaeology of the East India Company. *Antiquity* 64: 643–661.

Evans, C. and Pollard, J. 1999. The Institutional Façade: Architectural recording at the Old Schools, University of Cambridge. *Antiquaries Journal* 79(1): 213–243. DOI: http://dx.doi.org/10.1017/S0003581500044528

Evans, J. 1987. Graffiti and the Evidence of Literacy and Pottery use in Roman Britain. *Archaeological Journal* 144: 191-204.

Fairchilds, C. 1993. Consumption in Early Modern Europe: A review article. *Comparative Studies in Society and History* 35(4): 850–858. DOI: http://dx.doi.org/10.1017/S0010417500018740

Fitts, R. K. 1999. The Archaeology of Middle-Class Domesticity and Gentility in Victorian Brooklyn. *Historical Archaeology* 33: 39–62.

Frazer, B. 1999. Reconceptualizing Resistance in the Historical Archaeology of the British Isles: An editorial. *International Journal of Historical Archaeology* 3(1): 1–10. DOI: http://dx.doi.org/10.1023/A:1022017630718

Fryer, K. and Shelley, A. 1998. Excavation of a Pit at 16 Tunsgate, Guildford, Surrey, 1991. *Post-Medieval Archaeology* 31: 139–230.

Geertz, C. 1973. Thick Description: Towards an interpretive theory of culture. In Geertz, C. (ed.), *The Interpretation of Cultures*. New York: Basic Books, 3–30.

Guilbert, G. 2001. 'Foolishly Inscribed' but Well Connected: Graffiti on the King, Stanton Moor. *Derbyshire Archaeological Journal* 121: 190–195.

Hack, D. 2005. *The Material Interests of the Victorian Novel*. London: University of Virginia Press.

Hall, N. 2000. The Materiality of Letter Writing: A nineteenth century perspective. In Barton, D. and Hall, N. (eds), *Letter Writing as a Social Practice* (Studies in Written Language and Literacy 9). Amsterdam: John Benjamins, 83–108.

Hembry, P. 1990. *The English Spa, 1560–1815: A social history*. London: Athlone.

Hillier, B. 1965. *Master Potters of the Industrial Revolution: The Turners of Lane End*. London: Cory, Adams and McKay.

Hodder, I. and Cessford, C. 2004. Daily Practice and Social Memory at Çatalhöyük. *American Antiquity* 69(1): 17–40. DOI: http://dx.doi.org/10.2307/4128346

Honour, H. 1961. *Chinoiserie: The vision of Cathay*. London: John Murray.

Impey, O. R. 1977. *Chinoiserie: The impact of oriental styles on Western art and decoration*. London: Oxford University Press.

Jeffries, N., Owens, A., Hicks, D., Featherby, R. and Wehner, K. 2009. Rematerialising Metropolitan Histories? People, places and things in modern London. In Horning, A. and Palmer, M. (eds), *Crossing Paths or Sharing Tracks? Future directions in the archaeological study of post-1550 Britain and Ireland*. Woodbridge: Boydell and Brewer, 323–349.

Johnson, M. 1996. *An Archaeology of Capitalism*. Oxford: Blackwell.

Karskens, G. 2001. Small Things, Big Pictures: New perspectives from the archaeology of Sydney's Rocks neighbourhood. In Mayne, A. and Murray, T. (eds), *The Archaeology of Urban Landscapes: Explorations in slumland*. Cambridge: Cambridge University Press, 69–85.

King, J. A. 2006. Household Archaeology, Identities, and Biographies. In Hicks, D. and Beaudry, M. (eds), *The Cambridge Companion to Historical Archaeology*. Cambridge: Cambridge University Press, 293–313.

Lewis, J. N. C. and Lewis, G. 2006. *Pratt Ware: English and Scottish relief decorated and underglaze coloured earthenware, 1780–1840* (2nd second edition). Woodbridge: Antique Collectors' Club.

Lucas, G. 2003. Reading Pottery: Literature and transfer-printed pottery in the early nineteenth century. *International Journal of Historical Archaeology* 7(2): 127–143. DOI: http://dx.doi.org/10.1023/A:1025032201278

Lucas, G. 2005. *The Archaeology of Time*. London: Routledge.

Lucas, G. and Regan, R. 2003. The Changing Vernacular: Archaeological excavations at Temple End, High Wycombe, Buckinghamshire. *Post-Medieval Archaeology* 37: 165–206.

Marsden, S. J. 2006. Imagination, Materiality and the Act of Writing in Emily Brontë's Diary Papers. *Nineteenth-Century Contexts: An interdisciplinary journal* 28(1): 35–47. DOI: http://dx.doi.org/10.1080/08905490600691499

McCracken, G. 1990. *Culture and Consumption*. Bloomington: Indiana University Press.

McKendrick, N. Brewer, J. and Plumb, J. H. 1982. *The Birth of a Consumer Society: The commercialisation of Eighteenth Century England*. Bloomington: Indiana University Press.

Morgan, R. 1977. *Sealed Bottles: Their history and evolution (1630–1930)*. Burton-on-Trent: Midlands Antique Bottle Publishing.

Mytum, H. 2003. Artefact Biography as an Approach to Material Culture: Irish gravestones as a material form of genealogy. *Journal of Irish Archaeology* 12/13: 111–127.

Noël-Hume, I. 1971. *A Guide to Artifacts of Colonial America*. New York: Alfred A. Knopf.

Okasha, E. 1995. Literacy in Anglo-Saxon England: The evidence from inscriptions. *Anglo-Saxon Studies in Archaeology and History* 8: 69–74.

Pearce, J. I. 2000. A Late 18th-century Inn Clearance Assemblage from Uxbridge, Middlesex. *Post-Medieval Archaeology* 34: 144–86.

Pykett, L. 2005. The Material Turn in Victorian Studies. *Literature Compass* 1: 1–5.

Riley, N. 1991. *Gifts for Good Children: The history of children's china, 1790–1890, Part 1*. Ilminster: Richard Dennis.

Roberts, D. 1979. *Paternalism in Early Victorian England*. London: Croom Helm.

Schiffer, M. B. 1985. Is There a "Pompeii Premise" in Archaeology? *Journal of Anthropological Research* 41: 18–41.

Sieveking, L. M. 2004. A History of Robert Sayle, Part 1, 1840–1969. In Sayle, R. (ed.), *A History of Robert Sayle*. Cambridge: Robert Sayle, 7–130.

Tarlow, S. and West, S. (eds), 1999. *The Familiar Past?: Archaeologies of later historical Britain*. London: Routledge. DOI: http://dx.doi.org/10.4324/9780203019092

Thorpe, W. A. 1938. The Glass Sellers' Bills at Woburn Abbey. *Journal of the Society of Glass Technology* 22: 165–205.

Trotter, D. 2008. Household Clearances in Victorian Fiction. *19: Interdisciplinary Studies in the Long Nineteenth Century* 6: 1–19. http://www.19.bbk.ac.uk/index.php/19/issue/view/69 [accessed 1 September 2010].

von Mucke, D. E. 1999. The Imaginary Materiality of Writing in Poe's "Ligeia". *Differences: A journal of feminist cultural studies* 11(2): 53–75. DOI: http://dx.doi.org/10.1215/10407391-11-2-53

Waal, W. 2011. They Wrote on Wood: The case for a hieroglyphic scribal tradition on wooden writing boards in Hittite Anatolia. *Anatolian Studies* 61: 21–34. DOI http://dx.doi.org/10.1017/S0066154600008760

Walker, I. C. and Wells, P. K. 1979. Regional Varieties of Clay Tobacco Pipe Markings in Eastern England. In Davey, P. (ed.), *The Archaeology of the Clay Tobacco Pipe, 1* (British Archaeological Reports British Series No. 63). Oxford: British Archaeological Reports, 3–66.

Wilk, R. R. and Rathje, W. L. 1982. Household Archaeology. *American Behavioral Scientist* 25: 617–639. DOI http://dx.doi.org/10.1177/000276482025006003

Willmott, H. 2002. *Early Post-Medieval Vessel Glass in England, c.1500–1670* (Council for British Archaeology Research Report No. 132). York: Council for British Archaeology.

Writing Conservation: The impact of text on conservation decisions and practice

Elizabeth Pye
University College London

Introduction

The purpose of conservation is to investigate and preserve objects, and the information they hold, and to make both accessible for study and enjoyment now and in the future. This paper focuses on conservation as a means of interpreting meaning, in that decisions on conservation procedures depend on assessing the material, the significance and the intended future use of an object. The presence of writing frequently adds significance and possible uses which must be taken into account. It also has a considerable influence on conservation decisions; in extreme cases conservators may be faced with a choice between long-term preservation without investigation of written text, or material alteration (and possible loss of some other potentially valuable evidence) in order to retrieve text. This chapter also discusses the advent of digital imaging which has introduced exciting new possibilities for elucidation and preservation of, and access to, written text.

Conservation as a Method of Study

Conservation is usually seen as straightforward process of treating objects to remedy existing damage and to prevent further deterioration. But there are layers of investigation and assessment of each object which support conservation, and are essential to achieving a satisfactory outcome (and which, at the same time, provide information of wider interest). Also essential for a satisfactory outcome is to establish the aims of conservation and these depend largely on the future use of the object. Thus, if there is visible writing, or the potential to reveal writing, on an object, and

How to cite this book chapter:
Pye, E. 2013. Writing Conservation: The impact of text on conservation decisions and practice. In: Piquette, K. E. and Whitehouse, R. D. (eds.) *Writing as Material Practice: Substance, surface and medium.* Pp. 319-333. London: Ubiquity Press. DOI: http://dx.doi.org/10.5334/bai.p

the future use focuses on studying and displaying this writing, conservation will normally focus on making sure the text is rendered legible and durable, as far as this is possible.

Objects and Documents

Most conservators see objects as documents, and the investigative processes we use as a way of 'reading' objects. Ironically, books and documents are not often seen as multidimensional objects, thus the concept of the book as an object encompasses *all* the material aspects such as paper, inks, binding, etc. This has become the focus of specialist studies (see, for example, Centre for the History of the Book, University of Edinburgh, or Centre for the Study of the Book, Bodleian Library Oxford). This situation is partly shaped by the way objects and documents are used. Libraries preserve their holdings for their continued original use (reading) and for relatively ready access by the public, whereas museums limit the use (and particularly the original use) of their collections and tend to focus on long-term preservation. Thus, in some ways the approach to care of library material is akin to regular repair and maintenance aimed at keeping books and documents in working order, whereas the approach in museums is to conserve objects through restricting direct access, except for specific educational and research purposes. Of course, major libraries also hold historically valuable written material which is treated much like museum objects, with an emphasis on conservation, and on research aimed at adding to the sum of information about the individual item, as well as about writings in general.

Principles Governing Conservation Practice

Behind much conservation thinking lies the concept of the biography of an object (Appadurai 1986; Gosden and Marshall 1999). Each object may have gone through many changes in its so-called 'life', each of which may have left some kind of trace. These traces may be the results of material changes, such as corrosion of metals, or caused through human agency, such as the wear marks induced by use. Thus objects contain a range of material and conceptual evidence and can be seen as embodied technical and social history, or documents waiting to be read. Much of this information remains latent until elucidated during conservation.

A key conservation principle is that understanding objects is an essential first step in reaching conservation decisions. Conservators examine ('read') objects in great detail. Their assessment and diagnosis of the objects' conservation needs depends on: investigation of material(s) (thus of technologies); condition (thus of deterioration, signs of use, modification, repair or recycling); significance (thus of history, and of meaning assigned to these objects by different past and present individuals and groups); and future use (thus of potential to make new or further meanings). This assessment must involve communication and collaboration with other scholars and interest groups, particularly when developing an understanding of significance. It will also involve laboratory investigation such as microscopic examination and materials testing which may reveal a range of information not accessible through normal visual examination.

Another of the principles of conservation is that procedures should not affect the identity — the materials or the various possible meanings — of the object. In the past this was coupled with the principle of reversibility: that any changes induced by conservation could be reversed if necessary, thus supporting the aim of minimising change to the object. However, the principle of reversibility now remains only as an attractive idea, since it is widely acknowledged to be impossible to put into practice effectively (Appelbaum 1987; Muñoz Viñas 2005: 183–188).

The principle of minimum intervention (which to some extent replaces reversibility) acknowledges that conservation inevitably changes either the material (e.g. through cleaning) or the perception of an object (e.g. through analysis or restoration processes) or possibly both (Muñoz Viñas 2009). So the aim is to minimise change by doing as little as possible to the object *provided* it is enough to achieve a satisfactory conservation result. The intention is that this approach will not only limit change to the materials and/or distortion of the meaning(s), but that it should allow for further investigation in the future, and if necessary, future retreatment. To apply this principle effectively it is essential to understand the object well enough to be confident about where (and where not) to intervene with conservation treatment.

Values Assigned to Objects

The identity which conservation aims to safeguard can be seen as the sum of the values assigned to the object. Values are accumulated (and lost) throughout the life of the object. Value may change when an object is studied and reinterpreted, and it is quite possible for apparently insignificant, mass-produced objects to be assigned new value, perhaps because of changes in fashion or because of a link with a significant person or event.

One set of values is related to the material character of an object. A wide range of organic and inorganic materials has been used to provide surfaces for writing, some of them more durable than others; the character and working properties (e.g. hardness, ductility) provide insight into the eventual form of the writing (Brown 1998). The *Babylon* exhibition, held at the British Museum in 2008 (Finkle and Seymour 2008), included the display of large numbers of clay writing tablets which demonstrated very clearly not only the technique of impressing a writing tool into soft clay, but the remarkable survival of the tablets themselves (though some or many of these may have been made more durable by baking as part of conservation treatment — see below). In the case of books, the form of the book and the style of the binding may have technological, historical and aesthetic value, and may carry important information about previous ownership (Foot 1984). Although the wording of a text may be highly significant on its own, preserving the material original means that there remains the potential to learn more from it in the future. In addition to text, documents may carry other important material evidence, such as seal impressions or signatures, which indicates the text's authenticity and legal standing.

Complementing the material values assigned to an object are the meanings which may be attached to it. Obliterated text on a coin or medal may be frustrating if the aim is to identify it, but it may add other values by indicating how long the coin may have been in circulation, or how lovingly a medal may have been polished. Here, loss of material may mean gain in another aspect of meaning. The material and form of writing has meaning, e.g. for early printed text, both the uneven layout and the heavy impressions left in the page indicate the difficulties of regulating early hand printing, especially if cheaply produced (**Figure 1**). Handwriting provides an insight into the person: the skill of a medieval scribe seen in the Domesday book (National Archives 2009); the apparent energy and confidence of John Stewart Mill's handwriting, as seen in the documents displayed in the exhibition entitled *Taking Liberties* held at the British Library in 2009 (Ashley 2008).

The Presence of Text and its Effect on the Perceived Values of Objects

How does the presence of writing on an object affect the balance of the material and conceptual values, and consequent conservation choices? The role of the text in relation to the material and function of the object has an important impact on its relative value. There are perhaps three levels at which the relationship of text and material can be considered. The first is where the function of the object is purely to provide written information, and the material feature is regarded mainly as a carrier for the text (e.g. newspaper). The second involves text which is a significant feature of

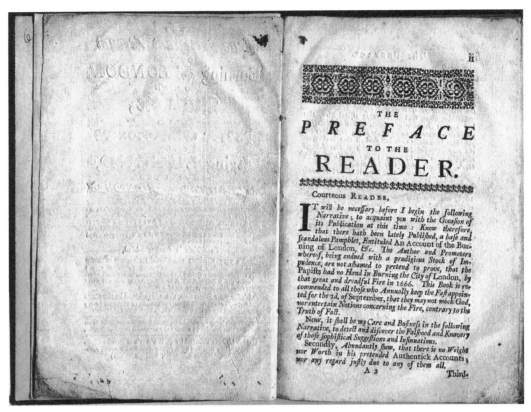

Figure 1: Book of tracts, dated 1720, about the causes of the Fire of London (1666). The uneven layout and the heavy impressions left in the page indicate the unregulated nature of some early (and probably cheap) printing. Photograph by Nick Balaam.

the function of the object, but where the material, too, is important, e.g. the denomination and other details on a coin as well as the metal or alloy from which the coin is made (Oddy 1980: 31), or cups awarded as prizes where the dedicatory inscriptions are an important feature, but so are the material and form of the cup. **Figure 2** shows two pewter tankards awarded as prizes during the 19th century; the form and material indicate a comparatively modest status, and so do the inscriptions (one was awarded as a consolation prize in an athletics event!). The third type of relationship of text with material involves writing which indicates quality or source but does not affect the function of the object, e.g. makers' marks on tools or ceramics, shelf marks on books. In this case the text is only one feature of the object as a whole, and normally will not affect the way the object is used, though it may impart historical information to the understanding of that object (Caple 2006: 56–59).

In practice, because of its evidential value, the presence (or assumed presence), of any form of writing will almost always take priority over other factors during preliminary investigation, and when making conservation decisions. It will be considered important to investigate the surface of any kind of object which would be expected to carry writing (e.g. a coin), to elucidate obscured lettering or to preserve text that is already visible. **Figure 3** shows three superficially similar copper alloy coins excavated in the author's garden. Although corroded, it is the visible text which identifies them as a Russian two kopek piece (1840), a South African penny (1898), and a British penny (1907). Once the coins are read it is possible to speculate that the first might have been

Figure 2: Two pewter tankards awarded as prizes during the 19th century. These were more or less standard-pattern tankards exported throughout the British Empire, then 'personalised' with a suitable inscription. One was awarded in 1865 as a consolation prize in an athletics event in Oxford, and the other in 1872 after a racquets tournament in Hong Kong. Photograph by Nick Balaam.

Figure 3: Reverse of three superficially similar copper alloy coins excavated in the author's garden. Although corroded, it is the visible text which identifies them (from left to right) as a Russian two kopek piece (1840), a South African penny (1898), and a British penny (1907). Photograph by Nick Balaam.

brought back to rural Norfolk by a soldier returning after the Crimean War (1853–1856) and the second after the Boer War (1899–1902)!

The investigation may establish not just the letters or words, but how the text was written, e.g. impressed into damp clay, scratched into plaster, formed in the die for a coin, cast or engraved into metal, printed onto paper; it will help to indicate whether the intention was for the text to be long-lasting or transitory. It will contribute to understanding the extent to which the text affects the significance of the object as a whole.

Dilemmas in Conservation Practice: Approaches to dealing with text

Conservation practice ranges from preliminary investigation, through preventive measures, to remedial techniques, and to restoration; it may involve removing a vulnerable object from circulation and replacing it with a replica or surrogate. The conservator is faced with several dilemmas: if an object demonstrates several values, and has clearly gone through a number of changes to condition and meaning, should it be conserved in its current state, or should an attempt be made to regain something of an earlier state (Brooks et al. 1996)? Should a musical instrument, or clock, be conserved so that it can demonstrate its original function of producing sound, or keeping time (this may involve repairing or replacing worn parts), or should it be cleaned of later accretions and stabilised as a static example in a typological sequence, or conserved complete with all the damage resulting from association with a notable event (a bugle used in a famous battle, a clock which went down with the *RMS Titanic*)?

Should a book be conserved so that the pages can once more be turned safely, or should it be kept in its well-thumbed and disintegrating state to demonstrate prolonged use? **Figure 4** depicts an early 18th-century Greek and Latin lexicon showing evidence of early 19th-century schoolboy use. The structure of the book and the binding are not exceptional and the text is now probably of little practical use, although its age and consequent idiosyncrasies may be of interest. It is the object as a whole including the signs of use and wear, and the annotations (no longer seen, at least by some, as defacement but as adding charm) which provides interesting social evidence. This has been conserved as is, with no attempt to repair (despite its relatively poor condition), in order to demonstrate its history of use and to avoid prioritising any particular aspect. It is simply given good general care to prevent further damage.

The treatment of the lexicon is an example of preventive conservation. This form of conservation is considered the most ethical approach since it involves as little change to an object as possible (Pye 2001: 130; Williams 1997). It aims to conserve both material and meaning, but will not necessarily elucidate concealed text. If the obscuring corrosion on a coin or Roman military diploma is considered stable, these objects could simply be given good storage conditions (preventive conservation), but the text would remain illegible to the naked eye (although it may be possible to detect detail using X-radiography). In practice the perceived significance of the lettering on the coin or the text of the diploma would almost certainly lead to the decision to remove the corrosion. This would enhance legibility but not necessarily improve long-term stability of the metal without further conservation treatment, since a stable corrosion layer will have been disrupted. Thus, the materiality of the writing governs conservation choices, often regardless of the material condition of the object as a whole.

The Drive to Reveal Text

The requirement to clarify or reveal lettering brings the problem of balancing the benefit of elucidating text with the risk of damage or loss. The discovery, in the mid-18th century, of a mass of papyrus scrolls at Herculaneum (the Roman town buried by volcanic ash during the eruption of Mount Vesuvius in AD 79) provides a historical example. Ever since their discovery, classical scholars have been understandably eager to read the contents of the scrolls, and extensive efforts had been made to unroll them. The scrolls are partially carbonised and extremely fragile. A successful, but excessively slow, method for unrolling was perfected in the mid-18th century by

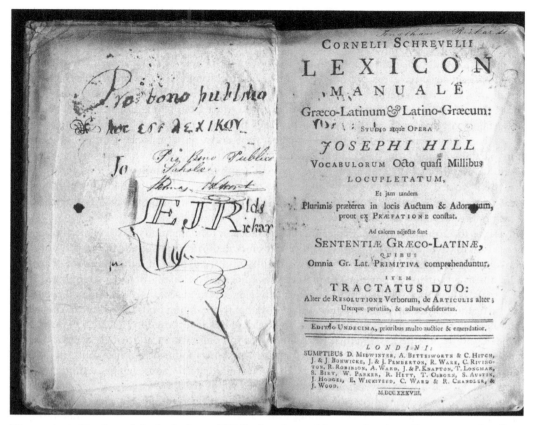

Figure 4: A Greek and Latin lexicon (1738) showing evidence of early 19th-century schoolboy annotations. On the covers there are more graffiti and on the end papers there are caricatures (possibly of the teachers?). Photograph by Nick Balaam.

Piaggio, but scholars and scientists (including Sir Humphry Davy — the eminent 19th-century chemist) continued to experiment in the hope of finding a better approach (Gilberg 1988). Almost all attempts resulted in failure and apparently very large numbers of the scrolls were lost. However exciting new imaging techniques have now made it possible to elucidate the text on similar scrolls (Baumann et al. 2008; Chabries et al. 2003).

Conservation cleaning is a current example of risking loss of material of an object in order to reveal the materiality of text. This technique is used to remove superficial accretions which may be masking the significance of an object where this is demonstrated by surface detail (e.g. tool marks, decoration, and text). But cleaning is a complex procedure since it may be difficult to distinguish where the informative surface lies (on corroded metals it may lie not beneath, but *within* the layers of corrosion, Pye 2001: 135). Cleaning may also damage other significant evidence such as remaining traces of paint. Inscriptions cut in stone were frequently coloured but if the traces of pigment are masked by, or mingled with, dirt or deterioration products of the stone they may be removed by ill-judged cleaning. This situation calls for both careful preliminary investigation, and for collaboration with specialists familiar with the inscriptions. Other important technological features may be as difficult to detect and equally vulnerable to cleaning, such as minutely thin layers of silver on Roman debased 'silver' coinage (Vlachou et al. 2003). Thus cleaning (that apparently innocuous, even beneficial, process) is potentially destructive and often controversial.

Conservation documentation goes some way to preserving evidence through recording, but even meticulous documentation of the stages and effects of cleaning cannot compensate for the removal of evidence and loss of material relationships.

To balance the information gained with the potential for loss of other information, cleaning may focus on selective areas only, or may not be taken through to completion. Excavated coins are cleaned to reveal lettering, mint marks and other detail because of their importance in dating the coin (and, on an archaeological excavation, the context from which it came). This is usually undertaken mechanically as this method provides the most control and the ability to monitor carefully what is being revealed; however, it is a time-consuming process. Thus coins are often only partially cleaned, the process being taken just far enough to gain adequate information for identification (Seeley 1980: 6). Coin hoards present another conservation problem since the coins are often 'welded' together by corrosion. In this case the drive to identify the number, range and date(s) of the coins usually leads to the use of (less controllable but potentially rapid) chemical treatments to separate the coins.

Despite the conservation principles discussed above, a fundamentally irreversible process has been used for over a century to preserve the text on cuneiform tablets made of (usually) unfired, sun-dried clay. Because of the problems of fragility and frequently of damaging and obscuring salts absorbed during deposition, the tablets have been traditionally fired to strengthen them. This makes them more easily handleable for reading and more resistant to salt removal processes, but turns the clay tablets into ceramics, thus permanently changing both the colour of the tablets and the material evidence of manufacture. The treatment was recorded in the late 19th century by Friedrich Rathgen (the first chemist to be employed in conservation and widely accepted as the 'father' of modern scientific conservation) and, with some modification, has continued in use (Gilberg 1987; Rathgen 1905; Thickett et al. 2002). It is still used for some tablets, although a more cautious, and less interventive, approach may be used where feasible.

The drive to preserve or protect the text, even possibly at the cost of other aspects of an object, can also be seen in the ways in which books were cared for traditionally. It was considered important to keep books in use (i.e. readable) and to do this the removal of old, worn and damaged bindings and their replacement with new ones, was a widespread and accepted practice. This kept the body of the book well protected and the text accessible; however not only was the earlier binding lost but the process of rebinding might involve other losses through practices such as trimming of pages. Recently a much more conservative approach has been adopted with existing bindings being retained and conserved wherever possible. Historically significant early bindings were not affected by this practice but many more ordinary bindings were lost, and there continues to be a potential conflict over the views of where the value lies — in the text or in the binding (Foot 1984). With similar emphasis on preserving text, in 1999 Karen Pavelka gave a paper at a conference on 'reversibility' in which she discussed the difficulties she faced as an archive conservator with responsibility for keeping archives accessible to readers. She acknowledged that she sometimes used irreversible practices such as trimming the edges of damaged and 'fraying' documents. By sacrificing some of the material (the edges) she aimed to minimise the further, and worse, damage likely to be incurred during continued handling (Pavelka 1999).

A different dilemma was posed by the discovery in 1973 of a mass of wooden writing tablets in a waterlogged context at Vindolanda Roman fort in Northumberland (Bowman 1983). Traces of writing in ink were visible but clearly fugitive, and without conservation treatment the wooden tablets would have collapsed and disintegrated (resulting, of course, in the loss of text). The normal treatment for waterlogged wood at that time involved immersion in a synthetic wax which would have darkened the wood and obscured the writing. An alternative treatment was used which involved the potentially dangerous process of heating ether (a highly flammable solvent) in order to dissolve the resin used to strengthen the wood tablets. It was possible to do this safely because the tablets are small and the work could be carried out under carefully controlled conditions (Blackshaw 1974). Had they been larger this treatment might not have been used. Today we would probably prefer to use a freeze-drying technique, after testing carefully to assess the effect on the text (this technique was not widely available in the 1970s). Another option open to us now would be to digitally record and disseminate the visible text before attempting conservation of the physical tablets. Thus, we might display (and preserve) the text in virtual form rather than risk affecting the materiality of the tablets themselves. Indeed, the digital documentation of visible text prior to conservation is a viable option for most, if not all, types of written document.

Digital Conservation and Restoration

For centuries, replicas or surrogates have been made of important objects, e.g. casts of famous sculptures. The aim was to provide access to people who could not see the 'real' thing. **Figure 5** shows a silver decadrachm of Syracuse (5th century BC) in the British Museum (**Figure 5a**) together with two forms of 19th-century surrogate — a silver electrotype (**Figure 5b**) and a moulded paper 'squeeze' (**Figure 5c**). For the same reasons, copies of texts have been made either as transcripts or in print. The advent of photography meant that the appearance of the text could be captured, so original texts could be conserved by limiting access and providing a photographic copy. Today, digital imaging has enormously expanded the possibilities of viewing and studying damaged and fragmentary text (MacDonald 2006).

This expanded use of digital imaging and of surrogates, has led to the use of the phrase 'digital preservation' or 'informational preservation' (Keene 2005: 138; Muñoz Viñas 2005: 23). It has changed the balance of risk and benefit since the original material is exposed to fewer risks (perhaps only the one-off manipulation needed to make a clear image) and the text becomes readily accessible. This form of conservation is now in common use for newspapers (which, being printed on low-grade paper, deteriorate very readily; British Library 2009*a*). Today's newspaper is replaced with tomorrow's surrogate, and only selected examples of the original newspaper are kept for evidence and legal reasons (put into permanent, controlled and, effectively, inaccessible storage).

Perhaps the most remarkable example of a major document now digitally imaged, virtually reunited, and accessible on a dedicated website is the *Codex Sinaiticus*. This is the earliest surviving copy of the Christian Bible and one of the earliest known bound books, different parts of which are held in different institutions (in Egypt, Germany, Russia, and the UK). On the website there is information about the conservation needed to prepare for imaging, and it is possible to view the pages in both normal and raking light, displaying a realistic impression of their condition (raking light throws surface topography into visible relief thus giving an indication of the materiality of both text and substrate; Codex 2009).

Furthermore, digital imaging, particularly 3D imaging, has introduced the possibilities of digital investigation and digital restoration. Details of text can be digitally enhanced and the image, or the 3D virtual model, can be moved or rotated to achieve a better view — all without manipulation or damage to the material original. This is particularly useful with cuneiform tablets as they are cushion-shaped with the text often running over the edge and onto the rounded sides making it impossible to view all the text in the same plane (Hahn et al. 2006; Kumar et al. 2003). Whereas hitherto the only way to enhance text was to modify the original object (e.g. white paint applied to the lettering on the Rosetta Stone as recently as 1981, see British Museum 2009), digital imaging can be used to enhance lettering without touching the original. This has been used on fragmentary papyri, and has the potential to aid matching up and repositioning separated fragments (Sparavigna 2009). Reflectance Transformation Imaging (RTI) is also being used to flesh out the

Figure 5: a) A silver decadrachm of Syracuse (5th century BC) in the British Museum. CM BMC Syracuse 63. © Trustees of the British Museum; b) A 19th-century full-size silver electrotype (surrogate) of the same coin, subsequently made into a brooch. Photograph by Nick Balaam; c) Full-size moulded paper 'squeezes' (surrogates) taken from electrotypes of coins in the British Museum (plates accompanying Leake 1850). The same decadrachm is shown at the top of the 'page'. Photograph by Nick Balaam.

faint inscriptions (Earl et al. 2011) and details of ductus, and tool and technique types used by past scribes (Piquette forthcoming). Furthermore, Stephen Quirke (2011) discusses the potential of using digital images for computer aided palaeography. Digital enhancement can also be used both to 'clean' stained or foxed paper and to increase definition of the written text without intervention on the material original, thus avoiding the use of washing or bleaching processes which may have limited visual success and be potentially damaging (Ramponi et al. 2005).

Detecting the Presence of Text

X-radiography and examination under infrared or ultraviolet light have all been in use by conservators for some time to detect obscured surface detail, such as writing. Perhaps the most exciting example of detecting text, while minimising risk to the material, is represented by the work of the EDUCE project (Enhanced Digital Unwrapping for Conservation and Exploration). This uses micro CT (computerised tomography) to detect carbon ink, and thus text, obscured by folds in documents or by overlying pages, and was first used to 'virtually flatten' distorted manuscripts at the British Library. The technique shows considerable promise in detecting text within multi-layered documents and may prove to be a successful means for virtually unrolling and reading the ancient scrolls from Herculaneum — but this is more difficult since many of these are, themselves, at least partially carbonised (Baumann et al. 2008; International Institute for Conservation 2009b).

The Power and Potential of the 'Real Thing'

Despite the possibilities offered by digital and other techniques for capturing, studying and reading virtual texts, the real thing is still valued and conserved. Significant examples of writing such as Dickens' novels are normally considered important for their content, and are available in recent or current print so most of us may never see the original handwritten or printed book 'in the flesh' (though it is now possible to see many texts on-line). However, the originals are conserved as the primary evidence of the author's work, and for the information they provide about *how* they were written, such as how the story evolved, and how often the text was revised (e.g. the first draft of Dickens' *Nicholas Nickleby* — see British Library 2009b).

The impact of the real thing was amply demonstrated by the exhibition held at the British Library in 2009, entitled *Taking Liberties: The struggle for Britain's freedoms and rights*. Almost all of the documents displayed have been widely distributed in later print but libraries and archives have conserved the originals. Displayed together, their materiality (parchment, papers of all kinds and sizes, inks, varied handwriting, and early printing) told an evocative story of attempts to secure and retain British liberties. The exhibition earned enthusiastic reviews from people moved by seeing the original documents (Ashley 2008; Taking Liberties 2009). The value attached to the 'real thing' gives particularly poignant emphasis to the tragedy of the collapse of the Cologne archive building in 2009 and the feared loss of many early documents (Icon 2009a; International Institute for Conservation 2009a).

An often quoted example of the reverence shown for the 'real thing' is the extraordinary conservation protection given to the American Declaration of Independence which is on view in the US National Archives. Since 1951 it had been protected from the damaging effects of oxygen by being sealed in an atmosphere of helium; more recently its casing has been redesigned and it is now housed in a highly sophisticated protective frame containing humidified argon (American Declaration of Independence 2009). Similar reverence is shown for the *Magna Carta*. In 2009 the four remaining copies of the first version (dated to 1215) were inscribed into the UNESCO Memory of the World Register. Lincoln Cathedral's copy is the only one of the four which is allowed to travel, and almost as much protection is given to it as to the Declaration of Independence (Icon 2009*b*). Of course this is a level of preservation and protection that can be accorded to only very few documents.

Conclusion

Until recently the presence of writing on an object has been given priority over other features when making conservation decisions, even if it may mean sacrifice of other material evidence. The advent of digital imaging means that both the general public and researchers may now interact with a virtual object rather than the original, and it has led to the widespread availability of virtual texts, as well as to the concept of digital preservation. However digital texts are primarily useful in deciphering written words, thus it is normally the text that is the focus of the imaging rather than other features such as margins and page edges, or bindings. Furthermore, imaging is not yet able to transmit satisfactory information about the materiality of the writing itself and of the substrate (clay, papyrus, parchment, paper, etc.). Thus digital imaging largely provides an immaterial and relatively flat view of the book or document. 3D and 2D+ imaging, such as Reflectance Transformation Imaging (RTI; e.g. Graeme et al. 2011; Piquette forthcoming;) and virtual handling of objects are rapidly developing, but even these cannot yet provide the subtle sensory information about materiality provided when we touch the real thing with our own hands (for example appreciation of surface texture, apparent temperature, weight, and so on; Prytherch and Jefsioutine 2007).

Moreover, the widespread use of digital images brings a new conservation dilemma — how to conserve the storage devices (e.g. CDs and DVDs) and the hardware and software needed to run them (e.g. Keene 2002). These are already presenting major conservation problems since the technology is developing so fast that earlier versions become rapidly obsolete and unusable, also because plastics are involved in the manufacture of hardware and disks, and many plastics are unstable. Even virtual objects and texts are vulnerable, thus the materiality of both writing and substrate continues to be of primary importance (particularly when interpreting meaning) and remains the focus of conservation practice.

Acknowledgements

I am very grateful to Claire Freer who, at my encouragement, explored aspects of this topic in an excellent Masters dissertation (Freer 2008); I am also grateful to the editors of this volume for inviting me to contribute, and to Nick Balaam who took the photographs, and read and criticised this text.

References

American Declaration of Independence 2009. *Saving the National Treasures*. http://www.pbs.org/wgbh/nova/charters/case.html [accessed 30 April 2009].

Appadurai, A. (ed.) 1986. *The Social Life of Things: Commodities in cultural perspective*. Cambridge: Cambridge University Press.

Appelbaum, B. 1987. Criteria for Treatment: Reversibility. *Journal of the American Institute for Conservation*, 26(2): 65–73. DOI: http://dx.doi.org/10.2307/3179456

Ashley, M. 2008. *Taking Liberties: The struggle for Britain's freedoms and rights*. London: The British Library.

Baumann, R., Porter, D. C. and Seales, W. 2008. The Use of Micro-CT in the Study of Archaeological Artifacts. In *Art 2008: Proceedings of the 9th International Conference on NDT of Art, Jerusalem, 2008*, 1–9. http://212.8.206.21/article/art2008/papers/244Seales.pdf [accessed 26 February 2011].

Blackshaw, S. M. 1974. The Conservation of the Wooden Writing-Tablets from Vindolanda Roman Fort, Northumberland. *Studies in Conservation* 19(4): 244–246. DOI: http://dx.doi.org/10.2307/1505731

Bowman, A. 1983. *The Roman Writing Tablets from Vindolanda*. London: British Museum Publications.

British Library 2009a. *Newspapers Digitisation Project*. http://www.bl.uk/reshelp/findhelprestype/news/newspdigproj/index.html [accessed 27 November 2013].

British Library 2009b. *Charles Dickens' 'Nicholas Nickleby'*. http://www.bl.uk/onlinegallery/onlineex/englit/nickleby/ [accessed 27 November 2009].

British Museum 2009. *History Uncovered in Conserving the Rosetta Stone*. http://www.british-museum.org/explore/highlights/article_index/h/history_uncovered_in_conservin.aspx [accessed 27 November 2009].

Brooks, M., Lister, A., Eastop, D. and Bennett, T. 1996. Artifact or Information? Articulating the conflicts in conserving archaeological textiles. In Roy, A. and Smith, P. (eds), *Preprints of the contributions to the Copenhagen Congress, 26–30 August 1996: Archaeological conservation and its consequences*. London: International Institute for Conservation, 16–21.

Brown, M. 1998. *Writing and Scripts*. London: The British Library.

Caple, C. 2006. *Objects: Reluctant witnesses to the past*. Oxford: Routledge.

Casey, P. and Cronyn, J. 1980. *Numismatics and Conservation*. Durham: University of Durham, Department of Archaeology.

Centre for the History of the Book, University of Edinburgh. http://www.chb.hss.ed.ac.uk/ [accessed 26 November 2013].

Centre for the Study of the Book, Bodleian Library Oxford. http://www.bodley.ox.ac.uk/csb/ [accessed 26 February 2011].

Chabries, D., Booras, S. and Bearman, G. 2003. Imaging the Past: Recent applications of multispectral imaging technology to deciphering manuscripts. *Antiquity* 77: 359–373.

Codex 2009. *Codex Sinaiticus: Experience the oldest Bible*. www.codexsinaiticus.org [accessed 12 November 2009].

Earl, G., Basford, P. J., Bischoff, A. S., Bowman, A., Crowther, C., Hodgson, M., Martinez, K., Isaksen, L., Pagi, H., Piquette, K. E. and Kotoula, E. 2011. Reflectance Transformation Imaging Systems for Ancient Documentary Artefacts. In Dunn, S., Bowen, J. and Ng, K. (eds), *EVA London 2011: Electronic Visualisation and the Arts. Proceedings of a conference held in London, 6–8 July 2011*. Bristol: BCS, The Chartered Institute for IT, 147–154. http://ewic.bcs.org/category/15376 [accessed 14 March 2013].

Finkel, I. L. and Seymour, M. J. (eds) 2008. *Babylon: Myth and reality*. London: British Museum.

Foot, M. 1984. The Binding Historian and the Book Conservator. *The Paper Conservator* 8: 77–83.

Freer, C. 2008. *Conserving Artefacts with Text*. Unpublished MA dissertation, University College London.

Gilberg, M. 1987. Friedrich Rathgen: The father of modern archaeological conservation. *Journal of the American Institute of Conservation* 26(2): 105–120. DOI: http://dx.doi.org/10.2307/3179459

Gilberg, M. 1988. Antonio Piaggio and the Conservation of the Herculaneum Papyri. In Daniels, V. (ed.), *Early Advances in Conservation*. London: British Museum Publications, 1–6.

Gosden, C. and Marshall, Y. 1999. The Cultural Biography of Objects. *World Archaeology* 31(2): 169–178. DOI: http://dx.doi.org/10.1080/00438243.1999.9980439

Hahn, D. V., Duncana, D. D., Baldwina, K. C., Cohen, J. D. and Purnomob, B. 2006. Digital Hammurabi: Design and development of a 3D scanner for cuneiform tablets. In Corner, B., Li, P. and Tocheri, M. (eds), *Three-Dimensional Image Capture and Applications VII: Proceedings of the SPIE* 6056: 130–141. DOI: http://dx.doi.org/10.1117/12.641219

Icon 2009*a*. Cologne Disaster Report. In *Icon News* September 2009. London: Institute for Conservation, 17–19.

Icon 2009*b*. Looking after Lincoln's Magna Carta. In *Icon News* September 2009. London: Institute for Conservation, 15–16.

International Institute for Conservation 2009*a*. Cologne Archive Collapses. *News in Conservation* 11, April 2009. London: International Institute for Conservation, 1.

International Institute for Conservation 2009*b*. Unwrapping the Hidden Past. *News in Conservation* 12, June 2009. London: International Institute for Conservation, 4–5.

Keene, S. 2002. Preserving Digital Materials: Confronting tomorrow's problems today. *The Conservator* 26(1): 93–99. DOI: http://dx.doi.org/10.1080/01410096.2002.9995181

Keene, S. 2005. *Fragments of the World: Uses of museum collections*. Oxford: Elsevier Butterworth-Heinemann.

Kumar, S., Snyder, D., Duncan, D., Cohen, J. and Cooper, J. 2003. Digital Preservation of Ancient Cuneiform Tablets Using 3D-scanning. In *Proceedings of the Fourth International Conference on 3-D Digital Imaging and Modeling 2003*. Banff, Canada: IEEE Computer Society, 326–333. DOI: http://dx.doi.org/10.1109/IM.2003.1240266

Leake, W. M. 1850. Plates of Coins to Accompany Topographical and Historical Notes on Syracuse. *Transactions of the Royal Society of Literature of the United Kingdom*. Second series, volume 3: 237–376.

MacDonald, L. (ed.) 2006 *Digital Heritage: Applying digital imaging to cultural heritage*. Oxford: Butterworth-Heinemann.

Muñoz Viñas, S. 2005. *Contemporary Theory of Conservation*. Oxford: Butterworth Heinemann.

Muñoz Viñas, S. 2009. Minimal Intervention Revisited. In Richmond, A. and Bracker, A. (eds), *Conservation Principles, Dilemmas and Uncomfortable Truths*. London: Butterworth-Heinemann in association with the Victoria and Albert Museum, 47–59.

National Archives, 2009. *Domesday: Britain's finest treasure*. http://www.nationalarchives.gov.uk/domesday/ [accessed 15 November 2009].

Oddy, W. A. 1980. Conservation and the Requirements of the Scientist in Numismatics. In Casey, P. and Cronyn, J. (eds), *Numismatics and Conservation*. Durham: University of Durham, Department of Archaeology, 31–37.

Pavelka, K. L. 1999. Access as a Factor Contributing to Compromise in Conservation-treatment Decisions. In Oddy, A. and Carroll, S. (eds), *Reversibility: Does it exist?* (British Museum Occasional Paper 135). London: British Museum, 105–110.

Piquette, K. E. forthcoming. Reflectance Transformation Imaging: A new method for the digitisation and study of early Egyptian graphical culture. In Graff, G., Jiménez-Serrano, A. and Bailly, M. (eds), *Préhistoires de l'écriture: iconographie, pratiques graphiques et émergence de l'écrit dans l'Egypte prédynastique/Prehistories of writing: Iconography, graphic practices and the forming process of writing in Predynastic Egypt. Actes de la table-ronde de décembre 2010*. Aix-en-Provence: Préhistoires méditerranéennes.

Prytherch, D. and Jefsioutine, M. 2007. Touching Ghosts: Haptic technologies in museums. In Pye, E. (ed.), *The Power of Touch: Handling objects in museum and heritage contexts*. Walnut Creek: Left Coast Press, 223–240.

Pye, E. 2001. *Caring for the Past: Issues in conservation for archaeology and museums*. London: James and James.

Quirke, S. 2011. Agendas for Digital Palaeography in an Archaeological Context: Egypt 1800 BC. In Fischer, F., Fritze, C. and Vogeler, G. (eds), *Kodikologie und Paläographie im digitalen*

Zeitalter 2 / Codicology and Palaeography in the Digital Age 2 (Schriften des Instituts für Dokumentologie und Editorik 3). Norderstedt: Books on Demand, 279–294.

Ramponi, G., Stanco, F., Dello Russo, W., Pelusi, S. and Mauro, P. 2005. Digital Automated Restoration of Manuscripts and Antique Printed Books. *Proceedings of EVA 2005: Electronic Imaging and the Visual Arts, Florence, Italy, 14–18 March 2005.* http://iplab.dmi.unict.it/download/Elenco%20Pubblicazioni%20(PDF)/International%20Conferences/EVA05.pdf   [accessed 26 February 2011].

Rathgen, F. 1905. *The Preservation of Antiquities* (translated by G. A. Auden and H. A. Auden). Cambridge: Cambridge University Press.

Seeley, N. J. 1980. Aims and Limitations in the Conservation of Coins. In Casey, P. and Cronyn, J. (eds), *Numismatics and Conservation.* Durham: University of Durham, Department of Archaeology, 5–9.

Sparavigna, A. 2009. *Digital Restoration of Ancient Papyri.* http://arxiv.org/ftp/arxiv/papers/0903/0903.5045.pdf [accessed 28 April 2009].

Taking Liberties 2009. *Taking Liberties: The struggle for Britain's freedoms and rights.* http://www.bl.uk/onlinegallery/takingliberties [accessed 30 April 2009].

Thickett, D., Odlyha, M. and Ling, D. 2002. An Improved Firing Treatment for Cuneiform Tablets. *Studies in Conservation* 47(1): 1–11. DOI: http://dx.doi.org/10.2307/1506830

Vlachou, C., McDonnell, J. and Janaway, R. 2003. The Investigation of Degradation Effects in Silvered Copper Alloy Roman Coins. In Townsend, J., Eremin, K. and Adriaens, A. (eds), *Conservation Science 2002.* London: Archetype, 236–241.

Williams, S. L. 1997. Preventive Conservation: The evolution of a museum ethic. In Edson, G. (ed.), *Museum Ethics.* London and New York: Routledge, 198–206.

Epilogue

John Bennet
University of Sheffield

I am writing these words on a sheet of white paper, with a (cheap, disposable) fountain pen. By the time you read what I am writing, however, it will have been transformed. First, I will transfer it by a different set of bodily actions (typing on a keyboard) and through the software on my computer to convert it in to a string of 1s and 0s. I will then send it through the ether to the editors who will, in turn, submit it in a similar digital form to the publisher. The publisher will use the digital file to produce a paper version, in essentially the same way that books have been produced for over 500 years, since the development of the printing press (in Europe) by Johannes Gutenberg. The chances are that you are now reading this in a form familiar for half a millennium, although you might well be viewing it on a digital device, again translated by that device's software into an arrangement of black and white pixels that mimics the printed page. Such are the processes of writing and reading in the second decade of the 21st century...

What *is* writing?

The term 'writing' embodies *two* meanings — a *process*, involving the interaction of human bodies with materials normally mediated through various tools (pen, keyboard, etc.), and *substance* (cf. Piquette and Whitehouse, this volume), the material residues of those bodily actions on, or in, the surface of media of many kinds, permanent to varying degrees, even virtual, but visually legible, often tangible, at any time after writing has happened subject to preservation of the medium itself (cf. Cessford, this volume, on the range of media and their preservation in 18th- to 20th-century Cambridge). For those of us who study writing in the past, the former is rarely visible (although writing or writers are sometimes represented visually and we occasionally recover writing tools; cf. e.g. Coe and Kerr 1997) and has to be deduced from the latter. In this respect, writing is like many other material products of the past: we have to reconstruct, or 'reverse-engineer', the process of production, the *chaîne opératoire*, from the artefacts themselves.

Writing, of course, implies a complementary, but distinct and sequential process of engagement with the product, a process that is visual and/or tactile and embodied and requires the

How to cite this book chapter:
Bennet, J. 2013. Epilogue. In: Piquette, K. E. and Whitehouse, R. D. (eds.) *Writing as Material Practice: Substance, surface and medium.* Pp. 335-342. London: Ubiquity Press. DOI: http://dx.doi.org/10.5334/bai.q

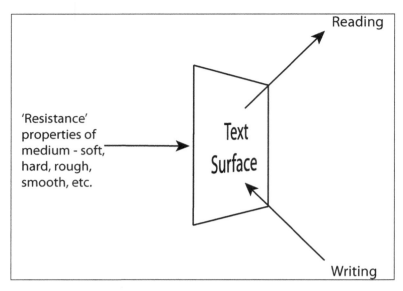

Figure 1: Diagram encapsulating concisely the processes associated with 'writing' and 'reading'.

presence of the material residues of writing. For the purposes of this epilogue, I loosely use the term 'reading' for this process, but suggest that 'reading' can potentially encapsulate a broader set of engagements than merely making sense of and absorbing a representation of language. Although this is perhaps clearest in contributions to this volume that explicitly deal with non-language-based 'writing' (e.g. Salomon, on *khipu*; or Perego on 'iconic literacy'), it underpins the material-based approach that pervades the whole collection. The diagram in **Figure 1** seeks to encapsulate concisely the processes associated with writing and reading. Because it is a material practice, writing requires a physical surface, on or into which it is applied, and requires bodily movements particular to different techniques for its production, the techniques dependent on the nature of the interaction between tool and medium. The process of writing might involve a single action — in the case, for example, of stamping or application of a transfer print ('indirect' forms of writing) — or multiple actions: flowing strokes (cf. Ingold 2007), where a brush or pen is used; staccato incisions or impressions, where a stylus is used on clay; repeated staccato actions, where a chisel is used on stone ('direct' forms of writing). The 'choreography' of writing — how the implement (brush, stylus) was held; how the surface was rotated, or not, to facilitate marking — was brought vividly home to those attending the original UCL Institute of Archaeology conference in demonstrations of Egyptian scripts written with a brush by professional scribe and calligrapher, Paul Antonio, and of cuneiform impressed into clay by British Museum Assistant Keeper of Cuneiform Collections, Jonathan Taylor. It also lies at the heart of Kidd's (this volume) exploration of the bilingual, bi-scriptural world of Ptolemaios, a late 3rd-century BCE 'Egyptian'.

Although it occupies a period of time, we can think of the 'moment of writing' (cf. Piquette, this volume) in contrast to the potentially *multiple* 'moments of reading' that might take place many times, minutes, days, even centuries or millennia afterwards, including the 'special case' of reading involving decipherment because knowledge of the original system has been lost. Depending on the portability of the material written upon, 'reading' may take place in the same location or at a distance; it may be achieved by the same actor, or a different one, or even be only an 'implied' reading aimed at supernatural beings. 'Reading', too, requires bodily movement: at a minimum, relatively small head, eye (e.g. Dehaene 2009: 12–18) and hand movements, but potentially quite extensive movements to appreciate writing laid out in (for us) unusual formats — an 'athletics of reading' (cf. Johnston; Whitehouse, both this volume).

But this material process is not unique to writing. Because writing as a product is a visual medium (cf. Robertson 2004), the scheme sketched above could be applied to other forms of representation applied to surfaces and loosely termed 'art' (cf. Perego, this volume); indeed, in many ways, writing is a particular form of representation. Like all forms of representation, its appreciation is not limited to the visual dimension: it may involve, even require (as in Braille) touch, or movement, and may, directly or by association (e.g. the text applied to consumption vessels in 18th-century Cambridge [Cessford, this volume], or classical Greece [Johnston, this volume]), instil bodily experiences of taste or smell. Denise Schmandt-Besserat (2007) has also suggested that writing and art in early Mesopotamia 'co-evolved', with the formatting and layout of writing affecting that of other visual media. It is no accident that theorists of writing from antiquity to the 20th century saw its origin in pictures (e.g. Evans 1908; Gelb 1963; Tylor 1865: 83–106; Warburton 1765, Book IV). The same idea drove the interpretations of Egyptian hieroglyphs by Horapollo (e.g. Cory 1840) and arguably delayed the decipherment of Maya writing by over a century after Abbé Brasseur de Bourbourg's publication of Bishop Diego de Landa's account of the Maya 'alphabet' (Brasseur de Bourbourg 1864; cf. Coe 1992: 99–106).

The above considerations are appropriate to a volume on writing as 'material practice', but definitions of writing as a technology often emphasise the *content* of writing systems: *how* they work as systems, rather than their material manifestations. Powell (2009: 13), for example, defines writing — simply and concisely — as "a system of markings with a conventional reference that communicates information". We might add at the end of this definition "through time and (potentially) space"; writing removes the need for a reader to 'be there'. For Powell there is no necessary link between writing and the representation of speech, a point also made by Boone (2004: 313), who defines it as "conventional, permanent, visual marks to communicate relatively specific ideas", also illustrating other "semasiographic representation systems", such as music notation, dance notation, algebra, and chemical formulae (Boone 2004: 317–335; cf. also Boone and Mignolo 1994).

Others insist on a systematic link to spoken language for a representational system to qualify as 'writing'. Robertson, for example, maintains that "writing is truly writing when it systematically represents speech" (Robertson 2004: 20). This is slightly ironic, since Robertson invokes Peircean semiotics to explain how writing can work as a representational system and Peirce was attempting to develop a much broader, inclusive understanding of how signs work (Robertson 2004: 18–19). As Powell (2009: 18) points out, such definitions echo de Saussure (1983 [1992]: 24): "[a] language and its written form constitute two separate systems of signs. The sole reason for the existence of the latter is to represent the former". Definitions that insist on writing's systematic relationship with speech break down at the *khipu* (Salomon, this volume), Mixtec pictorial codices (e.g. Boone 2004) or even early Sumerian 'numerical' and 'numerico-ideographic' tablets (e.g. Cooper 2004: 75–76, figs 4.4–4.5). Systems that are deeply implicated with images, like the Egyptian (cf. Baines 1989), Mayan (cf. Jackson, this volume), or Cretan Hieroglyphic (cf. Flouda; Whittaker, both this volume), also challenge definitions that limit writing to the representation of spoken language. Equally, not all writing is for reading by human eyes (e.g. certain inscriptions in Egyptian tombs or Greco-Roman curse tablets), nor strictly representative of human language (e.g. magic spells of the 'abracadabra' type).

Although we might not wish to limit a definition of writing to that of notating speech, most of the papers in this collection treat writing systems with precisely this limitation. At the other extreme, we might wish to constrain a broader definition, so as to avoid the possibility that *any* visual marks can constitute a writing system. There is a risk in doing so, however, because it presumably sets writing systems, however broadly defined, apart from other representational or mnemonic practices (cf. Gosden 2008, for example), equally material in basis. We may wish to keep in mind the possibility that writing, in some cultures, was one of a number of elite material practices that demanded a broader cultural, rather than a narrow linguistic literacy (cf. Perego, this volume).

In the case of writing, the term 'conventional' is critical. Even *khipu* had conventions, as does musical notation, for example, and texting, as used on mobile phones (cf. Crystal 2008). Among other factors, it is convention that constrains the spread of a particular script beyond its use community (cf. Kidd, this volume, for an example of the strong link between script and language in Ptolemaic Egypt); for it to do so, the 'convention' must change (as it did, for example, when Greek-speakers adapted the Phoenician system to record their language). Extensions of script use across linguistic boundaries are much easier in the case of a script with a limited number of signs (especially an alphabet), although they are possible where prestigious and/or specialised literacy existed, as in the cultural inertia that kept Sumero-Akkadian cuneiform in use into the 1st century BC (e.g. Black 2008; Brown 2008) to record structurally different languages (Sumerian versus Akkadian, Babylonian, Assyrian versus Hittite versus Old Persian) through both time and space (from Mesopotamia to both east and west, where it ran into the even more tenacious Egyptian tradition [e.g. Stadler 2008]). It is perhaps significant that both were replaced by alphabetic scripts: Aramaic, Greek, and Coptic.

Resistance to destabilisation through changing the 'convention' represents one reason why, in a multi-ethnic, multi-lingual, multi-scriptural area like the Levantine coastal region (cf. Sparks, this volume), at the interface between Egyptian and cuneiform systems, new 'simplified' written notations (proto-Canaanite; alphabetic Ugaritic cuneiform) emerged in response to, rather than as an adaptation of any one system; something similar might be implied by the Aegean syllabic scripts that arose on the margins of literate communities of the eastern Mediterranean (cf. Finlayson; Flouda; Tomas; Whittaker, all this volume).

Before Writing

Studies of writing as a social practice often emphasise its social *context* rather than *content*, especially in relation to its origins. For Goody, Ong, Havelock and others, writing (especially alphabetic writing) transformed society (e.g. Goody and Watt 1968; Havelock 1986; Ong 1982). In contrast to early accounts of the origins of writing that emphasised form (pictures to signs), contextual studies into the origins of writing emphasise the function that early writing fulfilled within a given society. Such studies are often 'teleological' in their conclusions — writing arose as an 'imperfect' form, 'incomplete' in relation to its later manifestations. Perhaps most familiar here is the Egyptian hieroglyphic system, whose origins are often sought in late Predynastic funerary contexts, notably that of Tomb U-j at Abydos (e.g. Dreyer 1998; see also Baines 2004). Rather than seeing the tiny labels or pots with large painted signs as the first intimations of greater 'things to come' in the fully-fledged hieroglyphic system, Piquette (2007) and others prefer to see these as part of a late 4th-millennium BC context of material practice (see also Piquette, this volume; 2008). A similar argument can be made for the earliest clay 'documents' in Sumer and, perhaps, for the earliest Aegean script use as part of a set of elite practices of display, rather than the first, imperfect steps towards a means of administrative control (cf. Bennet 2008: 5–6; Flouda, this volume; Schoep 2006: 44–48). In most cases, so the argument goes, the basic need was to deal with the amount and complexity of data to be recorded. Postgate, Wang and Wilkinson (1995), for example, argued that writing always occurs because of a need to record economic data and that the different forms it took are products of taphonomic processes that differentially preserve certain materials (cf. also Pye, this volume). Houston perceptively points out, however, that the "*materiality* of script differed by cultural setting" (Houston 2004: 350, his emphasis). It is difficult to imagine, for example, that we are missing extensive collections of clay documents from late Pre-Dynastic Egypt or masses of perishable papyrus texts from later 4th-millennium BC Mesopotamia.

Denise Schmandt-Besserat (1996) famously derived writing from accounting practices already millennia old by the time the first numerical tablets were produced in Southern Iraq and Iran, the system only subsequently being enriched by the development of signs with phonetic values (cf. also Cooper 2004). Her argument emphasises that *function* and *content* are not necessarily co-extensive. A system (like the *khipu*, or her early tokens, for example) responded to a need to record and organise information, one of a number of material practices, while a phonetic element was introduced to make clear elements that could more effectively be realised through language, such as the names of institutions, divinities or individuals. Postgate (1994: 51–70) points out that cuneiform writing took centuries to acquire the range of uses that we now regard as *de rigueur* for any self-respecting writing system. Here a distinction between mechanics and content is important: the late 4th-millennium BC recording system elucidated by Schmandt-Besserat and others did not contain within it the germs of the Epic of Gilgamesh. More recently, the printing press, derived from the technologies of wine production (the screw press) and sealing / stamping in the 16th century, defines the way we view text on screen using radically different technologies.

Emphasis on origins is important in another sense, in that writing — in the narrow sense — was not 'invented' each time it appeared; there were a limited number of original 'inventions': Egypt and Mesopotamia, although many see them as linked (e.g. Postgate 1994: 56), China and Central America. From these origins, it then spread, in the case of the Old World both to east and west, although not always as fully-formed systems (given the inertia of convention), but sometimes as the 'idea' of writing. The latter point implies a knowledge of the principles of a system and its social role. Is the invention of writing a one-way process, like the adoption of agriculture or urbanism? Systems can be lost (cf. Baines et al. 2008), but more often through replacement (most spectacularly evident in the spread of systems based ultimately on the Phoenician alphabet through much of the Old World). A particularly striking example is the replacement in the early 1920s of the Ottoman script by its western cousin, the Roman alphabet, as part of Kemal Atatürk's westernisation programme for the newly-formed Republic of Turkey (e.g. Lewis 1999: 27–39). A counter example to replacement is, of course, the loss of the syllabic Linear B script in the Aegean, unlike in Cyprus, where a syllabic script lived on alongside the novel alphabet. This example is a salutary reminder that social forces can outweigh material practices; in the Aegean it is most likely that oral practices lived on, while written died out.

After Writing?

If the invention or adoption of writing is a 'point of no return', like agriculture or urbanism, is a time 'after writing' conceivable? The *chaîne opératoire* for the production of this particular text sketched at its beginning worked until the late 19th century, when sound recording became possible in a recognisable form for the first time (Gelatt 1977: 17–82; Milner 2009: 29–49); in the early 21st century it is now possible to make sound permanent. Just as the introduction of the alphabet has been implicated in the transformation of 'Homeric' oral poetry (e.g. Powell 1991), so has the introduction of recording machinery to record not just the words, but the very sound of Yugoslav bards (even their visual performance: see the CD insert to Lord 2000). The 'permanence' of the modern world, however, is digital permanence (as Pye, this volume, reminds us), because all data — visual (including writing *and* image) and aural — are encoded in the same manner, using 0s and 1s, the only limitations being the amount of physical storage available and the resolution at which sound and image can be sampled at 'recording' and later (dis)played. Convergence is the key word: not only are all these media encoded in the same raw material, but our devices for recording and playing back are identical too: it is possible to use your digital tablet to write, capture images and sounds, even to paint (e.g. Grant 2010). This does seem to represent a Gutenberg moment, although it will take some time for future generations to appreciate it — just as it has taken us millennia to be in a position to appreciate writing in some of the many diverse material manifestations, themselves implicated in particular historical circumstances, explored in

a

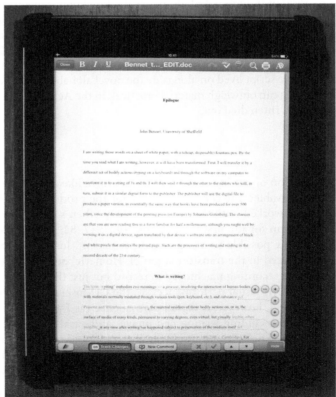

b

Figure 2: a) Stylus impressed clay tablet from Jemdet Nasr, dated to the Uruk III period (*c.*3200–3000 BC). 8.1 cm × 7.7 cm. BM 116730. © Trustees of the British Museum; b) John Bennet's Apple iPad. Author's photograph.

this stimulating volume. It is perhaps ironic that modern terminology gives us the appearance of coming full-circle (**Figure 2a–b**): from early cuneiform tablets to 21st-century 'tablets'?

Acknowledgements

I am most grateful to the editors not only for the invitation to participate in the conference where these papers were originally presented, but also for their input to this contribution. John Moreland also provided characteristically perceptive and valuable comments at a late stage, despite having many other things to do.

References

Baines, J. 1989. Communication and Display: The integration of early Egyptian art and writing. *Antiquity* 63: 471–482.

Baines, J. 2004. The Earliest Egyptian Writing: Development, context, purpose. In Houston, S. D. (ed.), *The First Writing: Script invention as history and process*. Cambridge: Cambridge University Press, 150–189.

Baines, J., Bennet, J. and Houston, S. D. (eds) 2008. *The Disappearance of Writing Systems: Perspectives on literacy and communication*. London: Equinox.

Bennet, J. 2008. Now You See It; Now You Don't! The disappearance of the Linear A script on Crete. In Baines, J., Bennet, J. and Houston, S. D. (eds), *The Disappearance of Writing Systems: Perspectives on literacy and communication*. London: Equinox, 1–29.

Black, J. 2008. The Obsolescence and Demise of Cuneiform Writing in Elam. In Baines, J., Bennet, J. and Houston, S. D. (eds), *The Disappearance of Writing Systems: Perspectives on literacy and communication*. London: Equinox, 45–72.

Boone, E. H. 2004. Beyond Writing. In Houston, S. D. (ed.), *The First Writing: Script invention as history and process*. Cambridge: Cambridge University Press, 313–348.

Boone, E. H. and Mignolo, W. D. (eds) 1994. *Writing Without Words: Alternative literacies in Mesoamerica and the Andes*. Durham, NC: Duke University Press.

Brasseur de Bourbourg, É.-C. 1864. *Relation des choses de Yucatan de Diego de Landa*. Paris: Arthus Bertrand.

Brown, D. 2008. Increasingly Redundant: The growing obsolescence of the cuneiform script in Babylonia from 539 BC. In Baines, J., Bennet, J., and Houston, S. D. (eds), *The Disappearance of Writing Systems: Perspectives on literacy and communication*. London: Equinox, 73–101.

Coe, M. D. 1992. *Breaking the Maya Code*. London: Thames and Hudson.

Coe, M. D. and Kerr, J. 1997. *The Art of the Maya Scribe*. London: Thames and Hudson.

Cooper, J. S. 2004. Babylonian Beginnings: The origin of the cuneiform writing system in comparative perspective. In Houston, S. D. (ed.), *The First Writing: Script invention as history and process*. Cambridge: Cambridge University Press, 71–99.

Cory, A. T. 1840. *The Hieroglyphics of Horapollo Nilous*. London: William Pickering.

Crystal, D. 2008. *Txtng: The Gr8 Db8*. Oxford: Oxford University Press.

Dehaene, S. 2009. *Reading in the Brain: The new science of how we read*. London: Penguin.

Dreyer, G. 1998. *Umm el-Qaab I: Das prädynastische Königsgrab U-j und seine frühen Schriftzeugnisse*. Mainz am Rhein: Philipp von Zabern.

Evans, A. J. 1908. The European Diffusion of Primitive Pictography and its Bearing on the Origin of Script. In Marett, R. R. (ed.), *Anthropology and the Classics: Six lectures delivered before the University of Oxford*. Oxford: Clarendon Press, 9–43.

Gelatt, R. 1977. *The Fabulous Phonograph, 1877–1977*. London: Cassell.

Gelb, I. J. 1963. *A Study of Writing*. Chicago: University of Chicago Press.

Goody, J. and Watt, I. 1968. The Consequences of Literacy. In Goody, J. (ed.), *Literacy in Traditional Societies*. Cambridge: Cambridge University Press, 27–68.

Gosden, C. 2008. History Without Text. In Baines, J., Bennet, J. and Houston, S. D. (eds), *The Disappearance of Writing Systems: Perspectives on literacy and communication*. London: Equinox, 335–346.

Grant, C. 2010. David Hockney's Instant iPad Art. http://www.bbc.co.uk/news/technology-11666162 [accessed 17 October 2013].

Havelock, E. A. 1986. *The Muse Learns to Write: Reflections on orality and literacy from antiquity to the present*. London: Yale University Press.

Houston, S. D. (ed.) 2004. *The First Writing: Script invention as history and process*. Cambridge: Cambridge University Press.

Ingold, T. 2007. *Lines: A brief history*. London: Routledge.

Lewis, G. 1999. *The Turkish Language Reform: A catastrophic success*. Oxford: Oxford University Press.

Lord, A. B. 2000. *The Singer of Tales*. Cambridge, MA: Harvard University Press.

Milner, G. 2009. *Perfecting Sound Forever: The story of recorded music*. London: Granta.

Ong, W. J. 1982. *Orality and Literacy: The technologizing of the word*. London: Methuen. DOI: http://dx.doi.org/10.4324/9780203328064

Piquette, K. E. 2007. *Writing, 'Art' and Society: A contextual archaeology of the inscribed labels of Late Predynastic–Early Dynastic Egypt*. Unpublished PhD dissertation, University College London.

Piquette, K. E. 2008. Re-materialising Script and Image. In Gashe, V. and Finch, J. (eds), *Current Research in Egyptology 2008: Proceedings of the ninth annual symposium, which took place at the KNH Centre for Biomedical Egyptology, University of Manchester, January 2008*. Bolton: Rutherford Press, 89–107.

Postgate, J. N. 1994. *Early Mesopotamia: Society and economy at the dawn of history*. London: Routledge.

Postgate, J. N., Wang, T. and Wilkinson, T. 1995. The Evidence for Early Writing: Utilitarian or ceremonial? *Antiquity* 69: 459–480.

Powell, B. B. 1991. *Homer and the Origin of the Greek Alphabet*. Cambridge: Cambridge University Press. DOI: http://dx.doi.org/10.1017/CBO9780511552700

Powell, B. B. 2009. *Writing: Theory and history of the technology of civilization*. Oxford: Wiley-Blackwell.

Robertson, J. S. 2004. The Possibility and Actuality of Writing. In Houston, S. D. (ed.), *The First Writing: Script invention as history and process*. Cambridge: Cambridge University Press, 16–38.

Saussure, F. de 1983 [1922]. *Course in General Linguistics* (trans. R. Harris). London: Duckworth.

Schmandt-Besserat, D. 1996. *How Writing Came About*. Austin, TX: University of Texas Press.

Schmandt-Besserat, D. 2007. *When Writing Met Art: From symbol to story*. Austin, TX: University of Texas Press.

Schoep, I. 2006. Looking Beyond the First Palaces: Elites and the agency of power in EM III–MM II Crete. *American Journal of Archaeology* 110(1): 37–64. DOI: http://dx.doi.org/10.3764/aja.110.1.37

Stadler, M. A. 2008. On the Demise of Egyptian Writing: Working with a problematic source basis. In Baines, J., Bennet, J. and Houston, S. D. (eds), *The Disappearance of Writing Systems: Perspectives on literacy and communication*. London: Equinox, 157–181.

Tylor, E. B. 1865. *Researches into the Early History of Mankind and the Development of Civilization*. London: John Murray.

Warburton, W. 1765. *The Divine Legation of Moses Demonstrated, in Nine Books*, Volume III (4th edition, corrected and enlarged). London: A. Millar and J. and R. Tonson.

Lightning Source UK Ltd.
Milton Keynes UK
UKOW07n2113200316

270512UK00003B/12/P